MARX AND ENGELS ON ECONOMICS, POLITICS, AND SOCIETY

Essential Readings with Editorial Commentary

MARX AND ENGELS ON ECONOMICS, POLITICS, AND SOCIETY

Essential Readings with Editorial Commentary

John E. Elliott

Professor of Economics
University of Southern California
Los Angeles, California

Goodyear Publishing Company / Santa Monica, California

Library of Congress Cataloging in Publication Data

Marx, Karl, 1818–1883.
Marx and Engels on economics, politics, society.

Includes bibliographical references.
1. Marxian economics. 2. Capitalism.
3. Communism. 4. Alienation (Philosophy)
I. Engels, Friedrich, 1820–1895. Selections.
II. Elliott, John E. III. Title.
HB97.5.M32513 1980 335.4'12 80-10202
ISBN 0-87620-608-9

Current printing (last digit):
10 9 8 7 6 5 4 3 2 1

Y-6089-0

Printed in the United States of America

Design: Linda M. Robertson

To Rosie, my life's companion
and own true love
and
To Karl Marx and Frederick Engels

Acknowledgments

Excerpts from *The First International and After: Political Writings,* Volume III, by Karl Marx, translated by David Fernbach. Copyright © 1974 by *New Left Review.* Reprinted by permission of Random House, Inc.

Excerpts from *Grundrisse: Foundations of the Critique of Political Economy,* by Karl Marx, translated by Martin Nicolaus. Copyright © 1973 by Martin Nicolaus. Reprinted by permission of Random House.

Excerpts from Karl Marx: *Early Writings,* translated and edited by T.B. Bottomore. Copyright © 1963 by T.B. Bottomore. Used with permission of McGraw-Hill Book Company.

Excerpts from *Karl Marx, On Revolution,* edited and translated by Saul K. Padover. Copyright © 1971 by Saul K. Padover. Used with permission of McGraw-Hill Book Company.

Excerpts from Karl Marx, *Selected Writings in Sociology and Social Philosophy,* translated by T.B. Bottomore; edited, with an introduction and notes, by Mr. Bottomore and Maximilien Rubel. Copyright © 1964 by Mr. Bottomore and Maximilien Rubel. Used with permission of McGraw-Hill Book Company.

Excerpt from *The Thought of Karl Marx: An Introduction,* pp. 136–37. Copyright © 1971 by David McLellan. Reprinted by permission of Literistic, Ltd.

Excerpts from *Writings of the Young Marx On Philosophy and Society,* edited by Lloyd D. Easton and translated by Karl H. Guddat. Copyright © 1967 by Lloyd D. Easton and Karl Guddat. Reprinted by permission of Doubleday and Company, Inc.

Excerpt from letter to Hyndman, Cambridge University Press.

Excerpts from *Capital,* Volumes 2 and 3, Charles Kerr, Publishers.

Excerpts from *Capital,* Volume 1, Modern Library.

Excerpts from International Publishers: *Letters to Dr. Kugelmann,* © 1934; *Karl Marx and Frederick Engels Correspondence 1846–1895,* © 1936; *Anti-Duhring,* © 1939; *The German Ideology,* © 1947; *Theories of Surplus Value,* © 1952; *Marx Engels Selected Works,* © 1968; *A Contribution to the Critique of Political Economy,* © 1970; *Anarchism and Anarcho-Syndicalism,* © 1972; *Marx Engels Collected Works,* © 1975, 1976; *Marx Engels Selected Works,* Volumes 1, 2, n.d.

Abbreviations

AAS: *Anarchism and Anarcho-Syndicalism* (International Publishers, 1972).

AB: *Articles on Britain*

EW: *Karl Marx: Early Writings* (McGraw-Hill, 1964), edited by Tom Bottomore.

IP: International Publishers

K: Charles Kerr Publishers

KM: Shlomo Avineri, *Social and Political Thought of Karl Marx* (Cambridge University Press, 1968).

KMPW, III: *Karl Marx Political Writings,* Vol. III (Random House, 1974).

LK: Letters to Dr. Kugelmann (International Publishers, 1934).

ME: *Marx on Economics* (Harcourt Brace, 1961), edited by Robert Freedman.

MECW: *Marx Engels Collected Works* (International Publishers, 1975, 1976).

MESW: *Marx Engels Selected Works,* one volume edition (International Publishers, 1968).

MESW I, II: *Marx Engels Selected Works,* Vols. I, II (International Publishers, N.D.).

ML: Modern Library

MR: *Marx on Revolution* (McGraw-Hill, 1971), edited by Saul K. Padover.

RH: Random House

SC: *Karl Marx and Frederick Engels Correspondence 1846–1895* (International Publishers, 1936).

SSP: *Selected Writings in Sociology and Social Philosophy* (McGraw-Hill, 1956), edited by Tom Bottomore and Maximilien Rubel.

TKM: David McLellan, *The Thought of Karl Marx* (Harper & Row, 1971).

YM: *Writings of the Young Marx on Philosophy and Society* (Doubleday, 1967), edited by Lloyd D. Easton and Kurt H. Guddat.

Preface

This book provides a comprehensive and representative selection of the writings of Marx and Engels on economics, politics, and society, organized around leading topical themes. Editorial essays and commentary interspersed throughout the book provide background to the readings, put them in context, and connect them with one another. These commentaries may be read at the outset in lieu of an introductory essay since, when taken together, they provide an overview and summary of the thought of Marx and Engels on the main topical themes of the book.

Many anthologies on the thought of Marx and Engels are organized in a chronological or quasi-chronological mode. While this approach has certain advantages for biography and general intellectual history, from the perspectives of economic theory and of social and political thought and philosophy, a topical approach seems better suited to most classroom situations. Selections are drawn from Marx's and Engels' life works, ranging from the writings of the early 1840's, through the "middle" writings of the 1850's, on to the mature writings of the 1860's and beyond. Included are generous selections from the 1844 *Economic and Philosophical Manuscripts, The German Ideology, Grundrisse,* and *Capital,* as well as shorter selections from other major works and numerous excerpts from speeches, articles and letters. For convenience in reading, selections—which have in most instances been edited—are presented without ellipses (. . .) to indicate omitted material, except where publishers have asked for them. Readers are encouraged to consult the original sources for further study. A full chronological bibliography of works cited, together with a brief supplementary reading list, is provided.

I am grateful to many people for their help in the preparation of this book. Janet Merritt and the highly capable staff at the Modelling Research Group in the Department of Economics at the University of Southern California exercised both patience and skill in typing and retyping drafts of the manuscript. Jim Boyd, Al Goodyear, Jean Varven, Stacey Maxwell, and Jayne Cox, of Goodyear Publishing Company, guided the project through production and on to publication. Daniel Fusfeld, E. K. Hunt, Stewart Long, and Murray Wolfson read the manuscript at various stages and offered insightful suggestions for improvement. Students in my courses in Marxian Political Economy over the last several years served both as inspiration and as a means of testing the content and organization of the book in a classroom setting. My wife, Rosie, companionably worked with me in the physical preparation of the book, tolerantly accepted my inordinate attachments to both the Marx-Engels literature and our typewriter, and helpfully listened to and commented on the readability of the editorial sections. Most of all, of course, I am indebted to Karl Marx and Frederick Engels whose writings constitute the main content of this book.

March 1981

Contents

Introduction

The joint consideration of economic, social and political dimensions of classical Marxian thought reflects the fact that, for Marx and Engels, economic and sociopolitical categories essentially coalesce. The economy is a system of power and social relations, as well as a set of social processes for production and distribution. Politics reflects underlying class relations in society which, in turn, are rooted in differing circumstances concerning the ownership and control of the physical means of production. Consequently, exclusive focus upon either economic or sociopolitical aspects of Marxian thought, however useful for certain limited purposes, is bound to be misleading.

The focus of this collection is on modern industrial capitalism. Chapter 1 begins with capitalism's origins and predecessors. This places the discussion of capitalism in historical context and introduces the idea that, for Marx and Engels, capitalism itself is a process of social change toward a prospective, post-capitalist future. Chapter 2 considers capitalism's institutional structure and social relations. Although capitalism is a market economy, characterized by market exchange relations, market exchange alone is not sufficient to clearly differentiate capitalism from other systems of economy and society. Basic to capitalism's institutional structure are: (1) a class division of society into a small group of capitalists who own and control the physical means of production, and a much larger group of workers, who own their own labor power but lack ownership of the physical means of production; (2) a social process of production wherein the capital-labor relation becomes a master-servant relationship in which the capitalist controls both the production process and the organization and division of labor.

Chapters 3 through 6 examine capitalism's creative and progressive properties, especially its revolutionizing, universalizing, and industrializing proclivities (chapter 3), and its contradictory and destructive properties (chapters 4–6), notably alienation, exploitation, crisis, depression, and unemployment. These chapters demonstrate vividly the basic duality in the Marxian heritage of social theory. As Ernest Mandel has aptly put it, Marx and Engels "sang a veritable hymn of praise to the glory of capitalism in their *Communist Manifesto,* which nevertheless sounded its knell. . . . (Their) poetic description of the achievements of the capitalist mode of production serves only to underline still more strikingly the contradictions which it at the same time engenders. . . . Marx sees no contradiction between acknowledging and emphasizing this 'historically necessary mission' of capitalism and constantly pillorying whatever is exploitative, inhuman, and oppressive in it. Marx keeps in view all the time the(se) two *contradictory aspects* of capitalist historical reality. . ."[1]

The next two chapters consider capitalism's social change and transformation in the course of its own development (chapter 7) and prospective transition to the post-capitalist order (chapter 8). For Marx and Engels, the first of these two themes is a complex, interactive blend of capitalism's economic contradictions, social tensions and conflicts, and institutional transformation. The second theme is embedded in the revolutionary theory and strategy of original Marxism which (notably, for the case of Marx) should be distinguished, as Joseph Schumpeter insightfully put it years ago, from both democratic revolution and conspiratorial communist revolution.[2]

The final chapter brings together the scattered views of Marx and Engels on the communist future. It is true that Marx, perhaps prudently, refused to write "recipes for the cookshops of the future." Still, he (and Engels) wrote far more extensively on this subject than is popularly supposed, focusing in particular on broad aspects of the character, organization, and structure of the prospective future society, in contrast to analytic models of its prospective behavior. Chapter 9 considers the evolution of the view of communism in the Marx-Engels writings and examines Marx's—and especially Engels'—commentary on communism's organization and behavior.

It is possible to detect elements of both change and continuity in the evolution of the economic, political, and social thought of Marx and Engels, as well as differences in the perspectives of the two thinkers. Some of the more prominent changes and differences will be apparent in the readings (and are noted in the editorial commentary), but for the most part, I agree with such writers as Ollman[3] and Tucker[4] in emphasizing the essential, underlying unity in Marxian thought, at least from 1844 on. Although the primary attention here is upon Marx, especially in the economics writings, the similarities and overlappings between the social theories of Marx and Engels, as well as their jointly authored works, reinforce the common practice of treating the two together. In addition, some of the later writings of Engels serve as a complement to (or rough proxy for) Marx's views.

---

[1]Ernest Mandel, *The Formation of the Economic Thought of Karl Marx* (New York: Monthly Review, 1971), pp. 56–57, 110.

[2]Joseph A. Schumpeter, *Capitalism, Socialism and Democracy* (New York: Harper, 1950), p. 58.

[3]Bertel Ollman, *Alienation: Marx's Conception of Man in Capitalist Society* (Cambridge: Cambridge University Press, 1976).

[4]Robert Tucker, *Philosophy and Myth in Karl Marx* (Cambridge: Cambridge University Press, 1972).

MARX AND ENGELS ON ECONOMICS, POLITICS, AND SOCIETY

Essential Readings with Editorial Commentary

1 Capitalism's Origins and Predecessors

For Marx, capitalism in particular, like economic systems generally, was perceived as a historical phenomenon. Marx was interested not merely in the functioning or dysfunctioning of capitalism, but in such questions as these: How did capitalism emerge? How does it develop and mature? Where is it going? How is it preparing the conditions for the form of economic society that will follow it?

The central factor pertinent to answering questions such as these, Marx believed, was the social relations among people in the process of production, notably the division of societies into owners and nonowners of the means of production (factories, machinery, mines, land). These socioeconomic production relations fundamentally reflect the stage of development of conditions of society's productive forces (technology, resources) and, in turn, profoundly affect surrounding political, legal, and religious institutions, and ideas generally.

In the interest of brevity and simplicity, we may summarize these complex historical connections by saying, as Marx occasionally did (selection 1.1), that changes in society's productive forces condition social and class relations in production and that changes in the economic structure—comprised of productive forces *and* social relations—in turn condition the political and ideological "superstructure." This kind of summary, though useful for quickly identifying some key elements in social change, oversimplifies both history and Marx's view of it. Although he clearly regarded socioeconomic relations as fundamental in history and dominant in capitalism, Marx's more sophisticated presentations typically recognized mutual interconnections among technology, markets, property, and politics. For example, the invention of the compass (a technological change) facilitated an age of exploration and thereby increased trade and exchange in modern times; but expanded markets (an economic change) stimulated greater combination and division of labor. The emergence of a new capitalist economic structure eventually resulted in shifts in political power from a landholding aristocracy to merchants, manufacturers, and industrialists; but the political system, once rearranged on more liberal and democratic lines, was used to pass laws, such as factory legislation, which promoted the interests of workers.

Marx early identified capitalist property relations, market exchange, and division of labor as major elements in capitalism's economic structure. In Chapter 1 we will consider the Marxian analysis of the historical evolution and early development of these institutions, first presented in outline form in *The*

German Ideology, written by Marx and Engels in 1845–46. In this early collaborative work, one of several, the young authors give a systematic account of their conception of what came to be called "historical materialism." Roughly translated, this rather forbidding expression turns out to be essentially methodological, rather than deeply philosophical, in intent and character. Marx and Engels are here not so much debating the ultimate nature of reality as they are presenting and illustrating their own intellectual commitment to (1) the study of people as members of social classes or groups (landowners, capitalists, workers, etc.) rather than as undifferentiated human kind; (2) an emphasis upon the socioeconomic structure of production and property relations as a central topic for investigation; (3) the placement of these first two topics in a historical context or setting. Selection 1.2, taken from *The German Ideology,* describes the origins and mutually interwoven development of capitalism's major socioeconomic institutions.

The transformation from feudalism into capitalism was perceived by Marx and Engels as an evolutionary development of a profoundly revolutionary character and with dramatic revolutionary consequences. Capitalism emerged and developed by degrees out of feudal society. No dramatic single event marked the transition, but eventually it became apparent that in the citadels of both economic and political power, industrial capital and the capitalist had triumphed over landed capital and the landholding aristocracy, a virtually worldwide system of market exchange had replaced the paroachial and localized socioeconomic relations of an earlier epoch, and division of labor prevailed in manufacturing industry as well as in society at large. Selection 1.3 identifies some of the leading elements in this revolutionary transition of socioeconomic systems, with excerpts ranging from the writings of the early Marx to the later Engels.

For Marx, capitalism is characterized not merely by the private ownership of industrial capital, but by the division of society into a relatively large number of propertyless workers who, because they do not own capital, must work for those few who do. Now, once this fundamental capital-labor relationship is established, it is not difficult to envision how it can be perpetuated through the processes of production and investment, that is, through the normal functioning of the capitalist economic system. But how was the capital-labor relation established in the first place? How did serfs or artisans (or their descendants) become transformed into workers? How did others become capitalists? One possible and popular interpretation is that at one point, people (other than emperors, the nobility, and clergy) were essentially equal. Some, however—the provident ones—worked long and hard, saved their money, accumulated savings and invested in little businesses, and, bit by bit, expanded, adding employees as they did so. Others—the prodigal ones—less industrious or skilled, worked and saved less, and gradually went to work for the provident ones. Whatever truth there is to this view, Marx regarded it as essentially a *kinderfibel* (a nursery fable). For Marx, the capital-labor relation is not a "natural" form of production, but is instead the result of a complex process in capitalism's "prehistory." On the side of labor, two key "historic presuppositions" must be established: one, the exchange of free labor capacity for money, and two, the separation of labor from its means of production and reproduction. These presuppositions required, on the one hand, dissolution of the peasantry's relation to the soil as a "natural condition of production," accomplished by the dismissal and eviction, often forcibly, of retainers and small cottagers from the land. By coercive government policies, they were then drawn onto the "narrow path" of the labor market. On the other hand, the establishment of a modern labor force rested on the separation of the craftsman and artisan from his instruments of production as a small proprietor. This separation was accomplished in the early days of mercantile and manufacturing capitalism by the gradual extension of control by merchants over the production process, illustrated notably by spinning and weaving, and by the gradual development of manufacturing especially in rural areas, outside the control of urban guilds.

At the same time, the process that placed workers in juxtaposition with capital placed capitalists in juxtaposition with workers. With the dissolution of the old mode of production and the beginnings of the modern proletariat through the dispossession of peasantry and artisans, budding merchants and manufacturers, were enabled by mobile wealth based on usury and merchantile profits to buy tools and implements of production and to purchase the labor power of the workers who had been "set free." The forces unleashed by the emerging capitalist mode of production not only dissolved the feudal order, but also led on to the establishment of the modern capital-labor relation

These comments reflect a summary of Marx's analysis as found in the *Grundrisse* of 1857–58, a series of notebooks unpublished in Marx's lifetime and intended as preparatory studies for *Capital.*[1] In *Capital* itself, (Selection 1.4), Marx develops his argument more fully and focuses upon a variety of heroic and "primitive" means of capital accumulation, ranging from the enclosure of lands, through private and public theft, to the slave trade. Marx's central idea here is a distinction between being and becoming a capitalist. Once established, a capitalist class functions essentially in terms of the rules and institutions of capitalist economy (see chapters 4 and 5 below.) But the establishment of the capital-labor relation required methods of "primitive capital accumulation" preceding, both logically and chronologically, the capitalist economy itself.[2]

1.1 OVERVIEW: MARX'S INTERPRETATION OF HISTORY

SUMMARY: THE 1859 STATEMENT

In the social production which men carry on they enter into definite relations that are indispensable and independent of their will; these relations of production correspond to a definite stage of development of their material powers of production. The sum total of these relations of production constitutes the economic structure of society—the real foundation, on which rise legal and political superstructures and to which correspond definite forms of social consciousness. The mode of production in material life determines the general character of the social, political and spiritual processes of life. It is not the consciousness of men that determines their existence, but, on the contrary,

[1]Karl Marx, *Grundrisse (Introduction to the Critique of Political Economy)* (New York: Harper, 1973), pp. 460–65, 497–507 and passim. John E. Elliott, 'The *Grundrisse* as Social Theory: Link Between Young Marx and Mature Marx," *Social Science Quarterly*, September 1978, pp. 245–46.

[2]These two processes of capital accumulation may overlap. For example, Marx observed that the rapid growth of the textile industry in early nineteenth century England rested in part upon imported cotton produced by slave labor in the southern states of America.

their social existence determines their consciousness. At a certain stage of their development, the material forces of production in society come in conflict with the existing relations of production, or—what is but a legal expression for the same thing—with the property relations within which they had been at work before. From forms of development of the forces of production these relations turn into their fetters. Then comes the period of social revolution. With the change of the economic foundation the entire immense superstructure is more or less rapidly transformed. In considering such transformations the distinction should always be made between the material transformation of the economic conditions of production which can be determined with the precision of natural science, and the legal, political, religious, aesthetic or philosophic—in short ideological forms in which men become conscious of this conflict and fight it out. Just as our opinion of an individual is not based on what he thinks of himself, so can we not judge of such a period of transformation by its own consciousness; on the contrary, this consciousness must rather be explained from the contradictions of material life, from the existing conflict between the social forces of production and the relations of production. No social order ever disappears before all the productive forces, for which there is room in it, have been developed; and new higher relations of production never appear before the material conditions of their existence have matured in the womb of the old society. Therefore, mankind always takes up only such problems as it can solve; since, looking at the matter more closely, we will always find that the problem itself arises only when the material conditions necessary for its solution already exist or are at least in the process of formation. In broad outlines we can designate the Asiatic, the ancient, the feudal, and the modern bourgeois methods of production as so many epochs in the progress of the economic formation of society. The bourgeois relations of production are the last antagonistic form of the social process of production—antagonistic not in the sense of individual antagonism, but of one arising from conditions surrounding the life of individuals in society; at the same time the productive forces developing in the womb of bourgeois society create the material conditions for the solution of that antagonism. This social formation constitutes, therefore, the closing chapter of the prehistoric stage of human society.

Marx, A Contribution to the Critique of Political Economy (1859), pp. 11–13

THE GERMAN IDEOLOGY

Premises of the Materialist Interpretation of History

The premises from which we begin are not arbitrary ones, not dogmas, but real premises from which abstraction can only be made in the imagination. They are the real individuals, their activity and the material conditions under which they live, both those which they find already existing and those produced by their activity. These premises can thus be verified in a purely empirical way.

The first premise of all human history is, of course, the existence of living human individuals. Thus the first fact to be established is the physical organisation of these individuals and their consequent relation to the rest of nature. Of course, we cannot here go either into the actual physical nature of man, or into the natural conditions in which man finds himself—geological, oreohydrographical, climatic and so on. The writing of history must always set out from these natural bases and their modification in the course of history through the action of men.

Men can be distinguished from animals by consciousness, by religion or anything else you like. They themselves begin to distinguish themselves from animals as soon as they begin to *produce* their means of subsistence, a step which is conditioned by their physical organisation. By producing their means of subsistence men are indirectly producing their actual material life.

The way in which men produce their means of subsistence depends first of all on the nature of the actual means of subsistence they find in existence and have to reproduce. This mode of production must not be considered simply as being the production of the physical existence of the individuals. Rather it is a definite form of activity of these individuals, a definite form of expressing their life, a definite *mode of life* on their part. As individuals express their life, so they are. What they are, therefore, coincides with their production, both with *what* they produce and with *how* they produce. The nature of individuals thus depends on the material conditions determining their production. . . .

This production only makes its appearance with the *increase of population.* In its turn this presupposes the *intercourse* of individuals with one another. The form of this intercourse is again determined by production.

The fact is, therefore, that definite individuals who are productively active in a definite way enter into these definite social and political relations. Empirical observation must in each separate instance bring out empirically, and without any mystification and speculation, the connection of the social and political structure with production. The social structure and the State are continually evolving out of the life-process of definite individuals, but of individuals, not as they may appear in their own or other people's imagination, but as they *really* are; i.e. as they operate, produce materially, and hence as they work under definite material limits, presuppositions and conditions independent of their will.

The production of ideas, of conceptions, of consciousness, is at first directly interwoven with the material activity and the material intercourse of men, the language of real life. Conceiving, thinking, the mental intercourse of men, appear at this stage as the direct efflux of their material behaviour. The same applies to mental production as expressed in the language of politics, laws, morality, religion, metaphysics, etc. of a people. Men are the producers of their conceptions, ideas, etc.—real, active men, as they are conditioned by a definite development of their productive forces and of the intercourse corresponding to these, up to its furthest forms. Consciousness can never be anything else than conscious existence, and the existence of men is their actual life-process. If in all ideology men and their circumstances appear upside-down as in a *camera obscura,* this phenomenon arises just as much from their historical life-process as the inversion of objects on the retina does from their physical life-process.

In direct contrast to German philosophy which descends from heaven to earth, here we ascend from earth to heaven. That is to say, we do not set out from what men say, imagine, conceive, nor from men as narrated, thought of, imagined, conceived, in order to arrive at men in the flesh. We set out from real, active men, and on the basis of their real life-process we demonstrate the development of the ideological reflexes and echoes of this life-process. The phantoms formed in the human brain are also, necessarily, sublimates of their material life-process, which is empirically verifiable and bound to material premises. Morality, religion, metaphysics, all the rest of ideology and their corresponding forms of consciousness, thus no longer retain the semblance of independence. They have no history, no development; but men, developing their material production and their material intercourse, alter, along with this their real existence, their thinking and the products of their thinking. Life is not determined by consciousness, but consciousness by life. In the first method of approach the starting-point is consciousness taken as the living individual; in the second method, which conforms to real life, it is the real living individuals themselves, and consciousness is considered solely as *their* consciousness.

This method of approach is not devoid of premises. It starts out from the real premises and does not abandon them for a moment. Its premises are men, not in any fantastic isolation and rigidity, but in their actual, empirically perceptible process of development under definite conditions. As soon as this active life-process is described, history ceases to be a collection of dead facts as it is with the empiricists (themselves still abstract), or an imagined activity of imagined subjects, as with the idealists.

Where speculation ends—in real life—there real, positive science begins: the representation of the practical activity, of the practical process of development of men. Empty talk about consciousness ceases, and real knowledge has to take its place. . . .

History: Fundamental Conditions

We must begin by stating the first premise of all human existence and, therefore, of all history, the premise, namely, that men must be in a position to live in order to be able to "make history". But life involves before everything else eating and drinking, a habitation, clothing and many other things. The first historical act is thus the production of the means to satisfy these needs, the production of material life itself. And indeed this is an historical act, a fundamental condition of all history, which today, as thousands of years ago, must daily and hourly be fulfilled merely in order to sustain human life. . . . Therefore in any interpretation of history one has first of all to observe this fundamental fact in all its significance and all its implications and to accord it its due importance. . . .

The second point is that the satisfaction of the first need (the action of satisfying, and the instrument of satisfaction which has been acquired) leads to new needs; and this production of new needs is the first historical act. . . .

The third circumstance which, from the very outset, enters into historical development, is that men, who daily remake their own life, begin to make other men, to propagate their kind: the relation between man and woman, parents and children, the *family*. The family, which to begin with is the only social relationship, becomes later, when increased needs create a new social relations and the increased population new needs, a subordinate one, and must then be treated and analysed according to the existing empirical data, not according to "the concept of the family". These three aspects of social activity are not of course to be taken as three different stages, but just as three aspects or three "moments", which have existed simultaneously since the dawn of history and the first men, and which still assert themselves in history today.

The production of life, both of one's own in labour and of fresh life in procreation, now appears as a double relationship: on the one hand as a natural, on the other as a social relationship. By social we understand the co-operation of several individuals, no matter under what conditions, in what manner and to what end. It follows from this that a certain mode of production, or industrial stage, is always combined with a certain mode of co-operation, or social stage, and this mode of co-operation is itself a "productive force". Further, that the multitude of productive forces accessible to men determines the nature of society, hence, that the "history of humanity" must always be studied and treated in relation to the history of industry and exchange. . . . Thus it is quite obvious from the start that there exists a materialistic connection of men with one another, which is determined by their needs and their mode of production, and which is as old as men themselves. This connection is ever taking on new forms, and thus presents a "history" independently of the existence of any political or religious nonsense which in addition may hold men together.

Marx-Engels, *The German Ideology* (1845–46), excerpts from Part 1.

"True" Socialism

The relation between German socialism and the proletarian movement in France and England is the same as that between German liberalism, as it has hitherto existed, and the movement of the French and English bourgeoisie. Alongside the German communists, a number of writers have appeared who have absorbed a few French and English communist ideas and amalgamated them with their own German philosophical premises. These "socialists" or "true socialists", as they call themselves, consider foreign communist literature not as the expression and the product of a real movement but as purely theoretical writings which have been evolved—in the same way as they imagine the German philosophical systems to have been evolved—by a process of "pure thought". It never occurs to them that, even when these writings do preach a system, they spring from the practical needs, the whole conditions of life of a particular class in particular countries. They innocently take on trust the illusion, cherished by some of these literary party representatives, that they are concerned with the "most reasonable" social order instead of with the needs of a particular class and time. . . . And what is the *"truth"* which they impart to socialism and communism? Since they find the ideas contained in socialist and communist literature quite unintelligible—partly by reason of their ignorance even of the literary connections, partly on account of their above-mentioned misunderstanding of socialist and communist literature—they attempt to clarify them by invoking the German ideology and notably that of Hegel and Feuerbach. They detach the communist systems, critical and polemical writings from the real movement, of which they are but the expression, and force them into an arbitrary connection with German philosophy. They detach the consciousness of certain historically conditioned spheres of life from these spheres and evaluate it in terms of true, absolute, i.e. German philosophical consciousness. With perfect consistency they transform the relations of these particular individuals into relations of "Man"; they interpret the thoughts of these particular individuals concerning their own relations as thoughts about "Man". In so doing, they have abandoned the realm of real history and returned to the realm of ideology, and since they are ignorant of the real connection, they can without difficulty fabricate some fantastic relationship with the help of the "absolute" or some other ideological method. This translation of French ideas into the language of the German ideologists and this arbitrarily constructed relationship between communism and German ideology, then, constitute so-called "true socialism"...true socialism, concerned no longer with real human beings but with "Man", has lost all revolutionary enthusiasm and proclaims instead the universal love of mankind. It turns as a result not to the proletarians but to the two most numerous classes of men in Germany, to the petty bourgeoisie with its philanthropic illusions and to the ideologists of this very same petty bourgeoisie. ... The lack of any *real,* passionate, practical party conflict in Germany meant that even the social movement was at first a *merely* literary one. True socialism is a perfect example of a social literary movement that has come into being without any real party interests and now, after the formation of the communist party, it intends to persist in its [literary mode].

Marx-Engels, *The German Ideology* (1845–46), excerpts from Parts 2 and 3.

THESES ON FEUERBACH

I

The chief defect of all hitherto existing materialism—that of Feuerbach included—is that the thing, reality, sensuousness, is conceived only in the form of the object or of *contemplation,* but not as *human sensuous activity, practice,* not subjectively. Hence it happened that the *active* side, in contradistinction to materialism, was developed by idealism—but only abstractly, since, of course, idealism does not know real, sensuous activity as such. Feuerbach wants sensuous objects, really distinct from the thought objects, but he does not conceive human activity itself as *objective* activity. Hence, in *Das Wesen des Christentums,* he regards the theoretical attitude as the only genuinely human attitude, while practice is conceived and fixed only in its dirty-judaical manifestation. Hence he does not grasp the significance of "revolutionary," of practical-critical, activity.

II

The question whether objective truth can be attributed to human thinking is not a question of theory but is a *practical* question. Man must prove the truth, that is, the reality and power, the this-sidedness of his thinking in practice. The dispute over the reality or non-reality of thinking which is isolated from practice is a purely *scholastic* question.

III

The materialist doctrine that men are products of circumstances and upbringing, and that, therefore, changed men are products of other circumstances and changed upbringing, forgets that it is men who change circumstances and that it is essential to educate the educator himself. Hence, this doctrine necessarily arrives at dividing society into two parts, one of which is superior to society.

The coincidence of the changing of circumstances and of human activity can be conceived and rationally understood only as revolutionising practice.

IV

Feuerbach starts out from the fact of religious self-alienation, of the duplication of the world into a religious, imaginary world and a real one. His work consists in resolving the religious world into its secular basis. He overlooks the fact that after completing this work, the chief thing still remains to be done. For the fact that the secular basis detaches itself from itself and establishes itself in the clouds as an independent realm can only be explained by the cleavage and self-contradictions within this secular basis. The latter must itself, therefore, first be understood in its contradiction and then, by the removal of the contradiction, revolutionised in practice. Thus, for instance, after the earthly family is discovered to be the secret of the holy family, the former must then itself be criticised in theory and revolutionised in practice.

V

Feuerbach, not satisfied with *abstract thinking,* appeals to *sensuous contemplation;* but he does not conceive sensuousness as practical, human-senuous activity.

VI

Feuerbach resolves the religious essence into the human essence. But the human essence is no abstraction inherent in each single individual. In its reality it is the ensemble of the social relations.

Feuerbach, who does not enter upon a criticism of this real essence, is consequently compelled:

(1) To abstract from the historical process and to fix the religious sentiment as something by itself and to presuppose an abstract—*isolated*—human individual.

(2) The human essence, therefore, can with him be comprehended only as "genus," as an internal, dumb generality which merely *naturally* unites the many individuals.

VII

Feuerbach, consequently, does not see that the "religious sentiment" is itself a social product, and that the abstract individual whom he analyses belongs in reality to a particular form of society.

VIII

Social life is essentially *practical.* All mysteries which mislead theory into mysticism find their rational solution in human practice and in the comprehension of this practice.

IX

The highest point attained by contemplative materialism, that is, materialism which does not comprehend sensuousness as practical activity, is the contemplation of single individuals in civil society.

X

The standpoint of the old materialism is *"civil"* society; the standpoint of the new is *human* society, or socialised humanity.

XI

The philosophers have only *interpreted* the world, in various ways; the point, however, is to *change* it.

Marx, *Theses on Feuerbach* (1845).

1.2 DEVELOPMENT OF PROPERTY, MARKETS AND DIVISION OF LABOR

Division of Labor and Forms of Property

The relations of different nations among themselves depend upon the extent to which each has developed its productive forces, the division of labour and internal intercourse. This statement is generally recognised. But not only the relation of one nation to others, but also the whole internal structure of the nation itself depends on the stage of development reached by its production and its internal and external intercourse. How far the productive forces of a nation are developed is shown most manifestly by the degree to which the division of labour has been carried. Each new productive force, insofar as it is not merely a quantitative extension of productive forces already known (for instance the bringing into cultivation of fresh land), causes a further development of the division of labour.

The division of labour inside a nation leads at first to the separation of industrial and commercial from agricultural labour, and hence to the separation of *town* and *country* and to the conflict of their interests. Its further development leads to the separation of commercial from industrial labour. At the same time through the division of labour inside these various branches there develop various divisions among the individuals co-operating in definite kinds of labour. The relative position of these individual groups is determined by the methods employed in agriculture, industry and commerce (patriarchalism, slavery, estates, classes). These same conditions are to be seen (given a more developed intercourse) in the relations of different nations to one another.

The various stages of development in the division of labour are just so many different forms of ownership, i.e. the existing stage in the division of labour determines also the relations of individuals to one another with reference to the material, instrument, and product of labour.

The first form of ownership is tribal ownership. It corresponds to the undeveloped stage of production, at which a people lives by hunting and fishing, by the rearing of beasts or, in the highest stage, agriculture. In the latter case it presupposes a great mass of uncultivated stretches of land. The division of labour is at this stage still very elementary and is confined to a further extension of the natural division of labour existing in the family. The social structure is, therefore, limited to an extension of the family; patriarchal family chieftains, below them the members of the tribe, finally slaves. The slavery latent in the family only develops gradually with the increase of population, the growth of wants, and with the extension of external relations, both of war and of barter.

The second form is the ancient communal and State ownership which proceeds especially from the union of several tribes into a *city* by agreement or by conquest, and which is still accompanied by slavery. Beside communal ownership we already find movable, and later also immovable, private property developing, but as an abnormal form subordinate to communal ownership. The citizens hold power over their labouring slaves only in their community, and on this account alone, therefore, they are bound to the form of communal ownership. It is the communal private property which compels the active citizens to remain in this spontaneously derived form of association over against their slaves. For this reason the whole structure of society based on this communal ownership, and with it the power of the people, decays in the same measure as, in particular, immovable private property evolves. The division of labour is already more developed. We already find the antagonism of town and country; later the antagonism between those states which represent town interests and those which represent country interests, and inside the towns themselves the antagonism between industry and maritime commerce. The class relation between citizens and slaves is now completely developed.

With the development of private property, we find here for the first time the same conditions which we shall find again, only on a more extensive scale, with modern private property. On the one hand, the concentration of private property, which began very early in Rome. . . and proceeded very rapidly from the time of the civil wars and especially under the Emperors; on the other hand, coupled with this, the transformation of the plebeian small peasantry into a proletariat, which, however, owing to its intermediate position between propertied citizens and slaves, never achieved an independent development.

The third form of ownership is feudal or estate property. If antiquity started out from the *town* and its little territory, the Middle Ages started out from the *country*. This different starting-point was determined by the sparseness of the population at that time, which was scattered over a large area and which received no large increase from the conquerors. In contrast to Greece and Rome, feudal development at the outset, therefore, extends over a much wider territory, prepared by the Roman conquests and the spread of agriculture at first associated with it. The last centuries of the declining Roman Empire and its conquest by the barbarians destroyed a number of productive forces; agriculture had declined, industry had decayed for want of a market, trade had died out or been violently suspended, the rural and urban population had decreased. From these conditions and the mode of organisation of the conquest determined by them, feudal property developed under the influence of the Germanic military constitution. Like tribal and communal ownership, it is based again on a community; but the directly producing class standing over against it is not, as in the case of the ancient community, the slaves, but the enserfed small peasantry. As soon as feudalism is fully developed, there also arises antagonism to the towns. The hierarchical structure of landownership, and the armed bodies of retainers associated with it, gave the nobility power over the serfs. This feudal organisation was, just as much as the ancient communal ownership, an association against a subjected producing class; but the form of association and the relation to the direct producers were different because of the different conditions of production.

This feudal system of landownership had its counterpart in the *towns* in the shape of corporative property, the feudal organisation of trades. Here property consisted chiefly in the labour of each individual person. The necessity for association against the organised robber-nobility, the need for communal covered markets in an age when the industrialist was at the same time a merchant, the growing competition of the escaped serfs swarming into the rising towns, the feudal structure of the whole country: these combined to bring about the *guilds*. The gradually accumulated small capital of individual craftsmen and their stable numbers, as against the growing population, evolved the relation of journeyman and apprentice, which brought into being in the towns a hierarchy similar to that in the country.

Thus the chief form of property during the feudal epoch consisted on the one hand of landed property with serf labour chained to it, and on the other of the labour of the individual with small capital commanding the labour of journeymen. The organisation of both was determined by the restricted conditions of production—the small-scale and primitive cultivation of the land, and the craft type of industry. There was little division of labour in the heyday of feudalism. Each country bore in itself the antithesis of town and country; the division into estates was certainly strongly marked; but apart from the differentiation of princes, nobility, clergy and peasants in the country, and masters, journeymen, apprentices and soon also the rabble of casual labourers in the towns, no division of importance took place. In agriculture it was rendered difficult by the strip-system, beside which the cottage industry of the peasants themselves emerged. In industry there was no division of labour at all in the individual trades themselves, and very little between them. The separation of industry and commerce was found already in existence in older towns; in the newer it only developed later, when the towns entered into mutual relations.

The grouping of larger territories into feudal kingdoms was a necessity for the landed nobility as for the towns. The organisation of the ruling class, the nobility, had, therefore, everywhere a monarch at its head. . . .

Division of Labor and Consciousness

. . . . Language, like consciousness, only arises from the need, the necessity, of intercourse with other men. Where there exists a relationship, it exists for me: the animal does not enter into *"relations"* with anything, it does not enter into any relation at all. For the animal, its relation to others does not exist as a relation. Consciousness is, therefore, from the very beginning a social product, and remains so as long as men exist at all. . . . Man's consciousness of the necessity of associating with the individuals around him is the beginning of the consciousness that he is living in society at all. . . . This consciousness receives its further development and extension through increased productivity, the increase of needs, and, what is fundamental to both of these, the increase of population. With these there develops the division of labour, which was originally nothing but the division of labour in the sexual act, then that division of labour which develops spontaneously or "naturally" by virtue of natural predisposition (e.g. physical strength), needs, accidents, etc. etc. Division of labour only becomes truly such from the moment when a division of material and mental labour appears. . . .

Moreover, it is quite immaterial what consciousness starts to do on its own: out of all such muck we get only the one inference that these three moments, the forces of production, the state of society, and consciousness, can and must come into contradiction with one another, because the *division of labour* implies the possibility, nay the fact that intellectual and material activity—enjoyment and labour, production and consumption—devolve on different individuals, and that the only possibility of their not coming into contradiction lies in the negation in its turn of the division of labour. . . .

Division of Labor, Property, and Society

With the division of labour, in which all these contradictions are implicit, and which in its turn is based on the natural division of labour in the family and the separation of society into individual families opposed to one another, is given simultaneously the *distribution,* and indeed the *unequal* distribution, both quantitative and qualitative, of labour and its products, hence property: the nucleus, the first form, of which lies in the family, where wife and children are the slaves of the husband. This latent slavery in the family, though still very crude, is the first property, but even at this early stage it corresponds perfectly to the definition of modern economists who call it the power of disposing of the labour-power of others. Division of labour and private property are, moreover, identical expressions: in the one the same thing is affirmed with reference to activity as is affirmed in the other with reference to the product of the activity.

Further, the division of labour implies the contradiction between the interest of the separate individual or the individual family and the communal interest of all individuals who have intercourse with one another. And indeed, this communal interest does not exist merely in the imagination, as the "general interest", but first of all in reality, as the mutual interdependence of the individuals among whom the labour is divided. And finally, the division of labour offers us the first example of how, as long as man remains in natural society, that is, as long as a cleavage exists between the particular and the common interest, as long, therefore, as activity is not voluntarily, but naturally, divided, man's own deed becomes an alien power opposed to him, which enslaves him instead of being controlled by him. For as soon as the distribution of labour comes into being, each man has a particular, exclusive sphere of activity, which is forced upon him and from which he cannot escape. He is a hunter, a fisherman, a shepherd, or a critical critic, and must remain so if he does not want to lose his means of livelihood; while in communist society, where nobody has one exclusive sphere of activity but each can become accomplished in any branch he wishes, society regulates the general production and thus makes it possible for me to do one thing today and another tomorrow, to hunt in the morning, fish in the afternoon, rear cattle in the evening, criticise after dinner, just as I have a mind, without ever becoming hunter, fisherman, shepherd or critic. This fixation of social activity, this consolidation of what we ourselves produce into an objective power above us, growing out of our control, thwarting our expectations, bringing to naught our calculations, is one of the chief factors in historical development up till now.

And out of this very contradiction between the interest of the individual and that of the community the latter takes an independent form as the *State*, divorced from the real interests of individual and community, and at the same time as an illusory communal life, always based, however, on the real ties existing in every family and tribal conglomeration—such as flesh and blood, language, division of labour on a larger scale, and other interests—and especially, as we shall enlarge upon later, on the classes, already determined by the division of labour, which in every such mass of men separate out, and of which one dominates all the others. . . . The form of intercourse determined by the existing productive forces at all previous historical stages, and in its turn determining these, is *civil society*. The latter, as is clear from what we have said above, has as its premises and basis the simple family and the multiple, the so-called tribe, the more precise determinants of this society are enumerated in our remarks above. Already here we see how this civil society is the true source and theatre of all history, and how absurd is the conception of history held hitherto, which neglects the real relationships and confines itself to high-sounding dramas of princes and states.

Civil society embraces the whole material intercourse of individuals within a definite stage of the development of productive forces. It embraces the whole commercial and industrial life of a given stage and, insofar, transcends the State and the nation, though, on the other hand again, it must assert itself in its foreign relations as nationality, and inwardly must organise itself as State. The word "civil" society emerged in the eighteenth century, when property relationships had already extricated themselves from the ancient and medieval communal society. Civil society as such only develops with the bourgeoisie; the social organisation evolving directly out of production and commerce, which in all ages forms the basis of the State and of the rest of the idealistic superstructure, has, however, always been designated by the same name.

Division of Labor: Town and Country

The greatest division of material and mental labour is the separation of town and country. The antagonism between town and country begins with the transition from barbarism to civilisation, from tribe to State, from locality to nation, and runs through the whole history of civilisation to the present day (the Anti-Corn Law League).

The existence of the town implies, at the same time, the necessity of administration, police, taxes, etc.; in short, of the municipality, and thus of politics in general. Here first became manifest the division of the population into two great classes, which is directly based on the division of labour and on the instruments of production. The town already is in actual fact the concentration of the population, of the intruments of production, of capital, of pleasures, of needs, while the country demonstrates just the opposite fact, isolation and separation. The antagonism between town and country can only exist within the framework of private property. It is the most crass expression of the subjection of the individual under the division of labour, under a definite activity forced upon him—a subjection which makes one man into a restricted town-animal, the other into a restricted country-animal, and daily creates anew the conflict between their interests. Labour is here again the chief thing, power *over* individuals, and as long as the latter exists, private property must exist. The abolition of the antagonism between town and country is one of the first conditions of communal life, a condition which again depends on a mass of material premises and which cannot be fulfilled by the mere will, as anyone can see at the first glance. (These conditions have still to be enumerated.) The separation of town and country can also be understood as the separation of capital and landed property, as the beginning of the existence and development of capital independent of landed property—the beginning of property having its basis only in labour and exchange.

In the towns which, in the Middle Ages, did not derive ready-made from an earlier period but were formed anew by the serfs who had become free, each man's own particular labour was his only property apart from the small capital he brought with him, consisting almost solely of the most necessary tools of his craft. The competition of serfs constantly escaping into the town, the constant war of the country against the towns and thus the necessity of an organised municipal military force, the bond of common ownership in a particular kind of labour, the necessity of common buildings for the sale of their wares at a time when craftsmen were also traders, and the consequent exclusion of the unauthorised from these buildings, the conflict among the interests of the various crafts, the necessity of protecting their laboriously acquired skill, and the feudal organisation of the whole of the country: these were the causes of the union of the workers of each craft in guilds. We have not at this point to go further into the manifold modifications of the guild-system, which arise through later historical developments. The flight of the serfs into the towns went on without interruption right through the Middle Ages. These serfs, persecuted by their lords in the country, came separately into the towns, where they found an organised community, against which they were powerless and in which they had to subject themselves to the station assigned to them by the demand for their labour and the interest of their organised urban competitors. These workers, entering separately, were never able to attain to any power, since, if their labour was of the guild type which had to be learned, the guild-masters bent them to their will and organised them according to their interest; or if their labour was not such as had to be learned, and therefore not of the guild type, they became day-labourers and never managed to organise, remaining an unorganised rabble. The need for day-labourers in the towns created the rabble.

These towns were true "associations", called forth by the direct need, the care of providing for the protection of property, and of multiplying the means of production and defence of the separate members. The rabble of these towns was devoid of any power, composed as it was of individuals strange to one another who had entered separately, and who stood unorganised over against an organised power, armed for war, and jealously watching over them. The journeymen and apprentices were organised in each craft as it best suited the interest of the masters. The patriarchal relationship existing between them and their masters gave the latter a double power—on the one hand because of their influence on the whole life of the journeymen, and on the other because, for the journeymen who worked with the same master, it was a real bond which held them together against the journeymen of other masters and separated them from these. And finally, the journeymen were bound to the existing order by their simple interest in becoming masters themselves. While, therefore, the rabble at least carried out revolts which remained completely ineffective because of their powerlessness, the journeymen never got further than small acts of insubordination within separate guilds, such as belong to the very nature of the guild-system. The great risings of the Middle Ages all radiated from the country, but equally remained totally ineffective because of the isolation and consequent crudity of the peasants.

In the towns, the division of labour between the individual guilds was as yet [quite naturally derived] and, in the guilds themselves, not at all developed between the individual workers. Every workman had to be versed in a whole round of tasks, had to be able to make everything that was to be made with his tools. The limited commerce and the scanty communication between the individual towns, the lack of population and the narrow needs did not allow of a higher division of labour, and therefore every man who wished to become a master had to be proficient in the whole of his craft. Thus there is found with medieval craftsmen an interest in their special work and in proficiency in it, which was capable of rising to a narrow artistic sense. For this very reason, however, every medieval craftsman was completely absorbed in his work, to which he had a contented, slavish relationship, and to which he was subjected to a far greater extent than the modern worker, whose work is a matter of indifference to him.

Capital in these towns was a naturally derived capital, consisting of a house, the tools of the craft, and the natural, hereditary customers; and not being realisable, on account of the backwardness of commerce and the lack of circulation, it descended from father to son. Unlike modern capital, which can be assessed in money and which may be indifferently invested in this thing or that, this capital was directly connected with the particular work of the owner, inseparable from it and to this extent *estate* capital.

Separation of Commerce and Industry

The next extension of the division of labour was the separation of production and commerce, the formation of a special class of merchants; a separation which, in the towns bequeathed by a former period, had been handed down (among other things with the Jews) and which very soon appeared in the newly formed ones. With this there was given the possibility of commercial communications, transcending the immediate neighbourhood, a possibility, the realisation of which depended on the existing means of communication, the state of public safety in the countryside, which was determined by political conditions (during the whole of the Middle Ages, as is well known, the merchants travelled in armed caravans), and on the cruder or more advanced needs (determined by the stage of culture attained) of the region accessible to intercourse.

With commerce the prerogative of a particular class, with the extension of trade through the merchants beyond the immediate surroundings of the town, there immediately appears a reciprocal action between production and commerce. The towns enter into relations *with one another*, new tools are brought from one town into the other, and the separation between production and commerce soon calls forth a new division of production between the individual towns, each of which is soon exploiting a predominant branch of industry. The local restrictions of earlier times begin gradually to be broken down.

It depends purely on the extension of commerce whether the productive forces achieved in a locality, especially inventions, are lost for later development or not. As long as there exists no commerce transcending the immediate neighbourhood, every invention must be made separately in each locality, and mere chances such as irruptions of barbaric peoples, even ordinary wars, are sufficient to cause a country with advanced productive forces and needs to have to start right over again from the beginning. In primitive history every invention had to be made daily anew and in each locality independently. How little highly developed productive forces are safe from complete destruction, given even a relatively very extensive commerce, is proved by the Phoenicians, whose inventions were for the most part lost for a long time to come through the ousting of this nation from commerce, its conquest by Alexander and its consequent decline. Likewise, for instance, glass-painting in the Middle Ages. Only when commerce has become world commerce and has as its basis large-scale industry, when all nations are drawn into the competitive struggle, is the permanence of the acquired productive forces assured.

The Rise of Manufacturing

The immediate consequence of the division of labour between the various towns was the rise of manufactures, branches of production which had outgrown the guild-system. Manufactures first flourished, in Italy and later in Flanders, under the historical premise of commerce with foreign nations. In other countries, England and France for example, manufactures were at first confined to the home market. Besides the premises already mentioned manufactures depend on an already advanced concentration of population, particularly in the countryside, and of capital, which began to accumulate in the hands of individuals, partly in the guilds in spite of the guild regulations, partly among the merchants.

That labour which from the first presupposed a machine, even of the crudest sort, soon showed itself the most capable of development. Weaving, earlier carried on in the country by the peasants as a secondary occupation to procure their clothing, was the first labour to receive an impetus and a further development through the extension of commerce. Weaving was the first and remained the principal manufacture. The rising demand for clothing materials, consequent on the growth of population, the growing accumulation and mobilisation of natural capital through accelerated circulation, the demand for luxuries called forth by the latter and favoured generally by the gradual extension of commerce, gave weaving a quantitative and qualitative stimulus, which wrenched it out of the form of production hitherto existing. Alongside the peasants weaving for their own use, who continued, and still continue, with this sort of work, there emerged a new class of weavers in the towns, whose fabrics were destined for the whole home market and usually for foreign markets too.

Weaving, an occupation demanding in most cases little skill and soon splitting up into countless branches, by its whole nature resisted the trammels of the guild. Weaving was, therefore, carried on mostly in villages and market-centres without guild organisation, which gradually became towns, and indeed the most flourishing towns in each land.

With guild-free manufacture, property relations also quickly changed. The first advance beyond naturally derived estate capital was provided by the rise of merchants whose capital was from the beginning movable, capital in the modern sense as far as one can speak of it, given the circumstances of those times. The second advance came with manufacture, which again made mobile a mass of natural capital, and altogether increased the mass of movable capital as against that of natural capital.

At the same time, manufacture became a refuge of the peasants from the guilds which excluded them or paid them badly, just as earlier the guild-towns had [served] as a refuge for the peasants from [the oppressive landed nobility].

Simultaneously with the beginning of manufactures there was a period of vagabondage caused by the abolition of the feudal bodies of retainers, the disbanding of the swollen armies which had flocked to serve the kings against their vassals, the improvement of agriculture, and the transformation of great strips of tillage into pasture land. From this alone it is clear how this vagabondage is strictly connected with the disintegration of the feudal system. As early as the thirteenth century we find isolated epochs of this kind, but only at the end of the fifteenth and beginning of the sixteenth does this vagabondage make a general and permanent appearance. These vagabonds, who were so numerous that, for instance, Henry VIII of England had 72,000 of them hanged, were only prevailed upon to work with the greatest difficulty and through the most extreme necessity, and then only after long resistance. The rapid rise of manufactures, particularly in England, absorbed them gradually.

With the advent of manufactures, the various nations entered into a competitive relationship, the struggle for trade, which was fought out in wars, protective duties and prohibitions, whereas earlier the nations, insofar as they were connected at all, had carried on an inoffensive exchange with each other. Trade had from now on a political significance.

With the advent of manufacture the relationship between worker and employer changed. In the guilds the patriarchal relationship between journeyman and master continued to exist; in manufacture its place was taken by the monetary relation between worker and capitalist—a relationship which in the countryside and in small towns retained a patriarchal tinge, but in the larger, the real manufacturing towns, quite early lost almost all patriarchal complexion.

Manufacture and the movement of production in general received an enormous impetus through the extension of commerce which came with the discovery of America and the sea-route to the East Indies. The new products imported thence, particularly the masses of gold and silver which came into circulation and totally changed the position of the classes towards one another, dealing a hard blow to feudal landed property and to the workers; the expeditions of adventurers, colonisation; and above all the extension of markets into a world market, which had now become possible and was daily becoming more and more a fact, called forth a new phase of historical development, into which in general we cannot here enter further. Through the colonisation of the newly discovered countries the commercial struggle of the nations amongst one another was given new fuel and accordingly greater extension and animosity.

The expansion of trade and manufacture accelerated the accumulation of movable capital, while in the guilds, which were not stimulated to extend their production, natural capital remained stationary or even declined. Trade and manufacture created the big bourgeoisie; in the guilds was concentrated the petty bourgeoisie, which no longer was dominant in the towns as formerly, but had to bow to the might of the great merchants and manufacturers. Hence the decline of the guilds, as soon as they came into contact with manufacture.

The intercourse of nations took on, in the epoch of which we have been speaking, two different forms. At first the small quantity of gold and silver in circulation involved the ban on the export of these metals; and industry, for the most part imported from abroad and made necessary by the need for employing the growing urban population, could not do without those privileges which could be granted not only, of course, against home competition, but chiefly against foreign. The local guild privilege was in these original prohibitions extended over the whole nation. Customs duties originated from the tributes which the feudal lords exacted as protective levies against robbery from merchants passing through their territories, tributes later imposed likewise by the towns, and which, with the rise of the modern states, were the Treasury's most obvious means of raising money.

The appearance of American gold and silver on the European markets, the gradual development of industry, the rapid expansion of trade and the consequent rise of the non-guild bourgeoisie and of money, gave these measures another significance. The State, which was daily less and less able to do without money, now retained the ban on the export of gold and silver out of fiscal considerations; the bourgeois, for whom these masses of money which were hurled onto the market became the chief object of speculative buying, were thoroughly content with this; privileges established earlier became a source of income for the government and were sold for money; in the customs legislation there appeared the export duty, which, since it only [placed] a hindrance in the way of industry, had a purely fiscal aim.

The second period began in the middle of the seventeenth century and lasted almost to the end of the eighteenth. Commerce and navigation had expanded more rapidly than manufacture, which played a secondary role; the colonies were becoming considerable consumers; and after long struggles the separate nations shared out the opening world market among themselves. This period begins with the Navigation Laws[1] and colonial monopolies. The competition of the nations among themselves was excluded as far as possible by tariffs, prohibitions and treaties; and in the last resort the competitive struggle was carried on and decided by wars (especially naval wars). The mightiest maritime nation, the English, retained preponderance in trade and manufacture. Here, already, we find concentration in one country.

Manufacture was all the time sheltered by protective duties in the home market, by monopolies in the colonial market, and abroad as much as possible by differential duties. The working-up of home-produced material was encouraged (wool and linen in England, silk in France), the export of home-produced raw material forbidden (wool in England), and the [working up] of imported material neglected or suppressed (cotton in England). The nation dominant in sea trade and colonial power naturally secured for itself also the greatest quantitative and qualitative expansion of manufacture. Manufacture could not be carried on without protection, since, if the slightest change takes place in other countries, it can lose its market and be ruined; under reasonably favourable conditions it may easily be introduced into a country, but for this very reason can easily be destroyed. At the same time through the mode in which it is carried on, particularly in the eighteenth century, in the countryside, it is to such an extent interwoven with the vital relationships of a great mass of individuals, that no country dare jeopardise its existence by permitting free competition. Insofar as it manages to export, it therefore depends entirely on

[1]*Navigation Laws*—a series of Acts passed in England from 1381 onwards to protect English shipping against foreign competition.

the extension or restriction of commerce, and exercises a relatively very small reaction [on the latter]. Hence its secondary [importance] and the influence of [the merchants] in the eighteenth century. It was the merchants and especially the shippers who more than anybody else pressed for State protection and monopolies; the manufacturers also demanded and indeed received protection, but all the time were inferior in political importance to the merchants. The commercial towns, particularly the maritime towns, became to some extent civilised and acquired the outlook of the big bourgeoisie, but in the factory towns an extreme petty-bourgeois outlook persisted. The eighteenth century was the century of trade.[2]

This period is also characterised by the cessation of the bans on the export of gold and silver and the beginning of the trade in money; by banks, national debts, paper money; by speculation in stocks and shares and stockjobbing in all articles; by the development of finance in general. Again capital lost a great part of the natural character which had still clung to it.

The Rise Of Large-Scale Industry

The concentration of trade and manufacture in one country, England, developing irresistibly in the seventeenth century, gradually created for this country a relative world market, and thus a demand for the manufactured products of this country, which could no longer be met by the industrial productive forces hitherto existing. This demand, outgrowing the productive forces, was the motive power which, by producing big industry—the application of elemental forces to industrial ends, machinery and the most complex division of labour—called into existence the third period of private ownership since the Middle Ages. There already existed in England the other pre-conditions of this new phase: freedom of competition inside the nation, the development of theoretical mechanics, etc. (Indeed, the science of mechanics perfected by Newton was altogether the most popular science in France and England in the eighteenth century.) (Free competition inside the nation itself had everywhere to be conquered by a revolution—1640 and 1688 in England, 1789 in France.) Competition soon compelled every country that wished to retain its historical role to protect its manufactures by renewed customs regulations (the old duties were no longer any good against big industry) and soon after to introduce big industry under protective duties. Big industry universalised competition in spite of these protective measures (it is practical free trade; the protective duty is only a palliative, a measure of defence *within* free trade), established means of communication and the modern world market, subordinated trade to itself, transformed all capital into industrial capital, and thus produced the rapid circulation (development of the financial system) and the centralisation of capital. By universal competition it forced all individuals to strain their energy to

[2]The movement of capital, although considerably accelerated, still remained, however, relatively slow. The splitting-up of the world market into separate parts, each of which was exploited by a particular nation, the exclusion of competition among themselves on the part of the nations, the clumsiness of production itself and the fact that finance was only evolving from its early stages, greatly impeded circulation. The consequence of this was a haggling, mean and niggardly spirit which still clung to all merchants and to the whole mode of carrying on trade. Compared with the manufacturers, and above all with the craftsmen, they were certainly big bourgeois; compared with the merchants and industrialists of the next period they remain petty bourgeois. Cf. Adam Smith.

the utmost. It destroyed as far as possible ideology, religion, morality, etc. and where it could not do this, made them into a palpable lie. It produced world history for the first time, insofar as it made all civilised nations and every individual member of them dependent for the satisfaction of their wants on the whole world, thus destroying the former natural exclusiveness of separate nations. It made natural science subservient to capital and took from the division of labour the last semblance of its natural character. It destroyed natural growth in general, as far as this is possible while labour exists, and resolved all natural relationships into money relationships. In the place of naturally grown towns it created the modern, large industrial cities which have sprung up overnight. Wherever it penetrated, it destroyed the crafts and all earlier stages of industry. It completed the victory of the commercial town over the countryside. [Its first premise] was the automatic system. [Its development] produced a mass of productive forces, for which private [property] became just as much a fetter as the guild had been for manufacture and the small, rural workshop for the developing craft. These productive forces received under the system of private property a one-sided development only, and became for the majority destructive forces; moreover, a great multitude of such forces could find no application at all within this system. Generally speaking, big industry created everywhere the same relations between the classes of society, and thus destroyed the peculiar individuality of the various nationalities. And finally, while the bourgeoisie of each nation still retained separate national interests, big industry created a class, which in all nations has the same interest and with which nationality is already dead; a class which is really rid of all the old world and at the same time stands pitted against it. Big industry makes for the worker not only the relation to the capitalist, but labour itself, unbearable.

It is evident that big industry does not reach the same level of development in all districts of a country. This does not, however, retard the class movement of the proletariat, because the proletarians created by big industry assume leadership of this movement and carry the whole mass along with them, and because the workers excluded from big industry are placed by it in a still worse situation than the workers in big industry itself. The countries in which big industry is developed act in a similar manner upon the more or less non-industrial countries, insofar as the latter are swept by universal commerce into the universal competitive struggle.[1]

These different forms are just so many forms of the organisation of labour, and hence of property. In each period a unification of the existing productive forces takes place, insofar as this has been rendered necessary by needs.

Marx-Engels, *The German Ideology* (1845–46), excerpts from Part 1.

[1]Competition separates individuals from one another, not only the bourgeois but still more the workers, in spite of the fact that it brings them together. Hence it is a long time before these individuals can unite, apart from the fact that for the purposes of this union—if it is not to be merely local—the necessary means, the great industrial cities and cheap and quick communications, have first to be produced by big industry. Hence every organised power standing over against these isolated individuals, who live in relationships, daily reproducing this isolation, can only be overcome after long struggles. To demand the opposite would be tantamount to demanding that competition should not exist in this definite epoch of history, or that the individuals should banish from their minds relationships over which in their isolation they have no control.

1.3 FROM FEUDALISM TO CAPITALISM

VICTORY OF THE CAPITALIST

The small landowner who works on his own account stands...in the same relation to the large landowner as does the artisan who possesses his *own* tools to the factory owner. The small estate has become merely a tool. For the small landowner rent of land disappears entirely, and there remains at most the interest on his capital and the wages of his labour, since rent can be depressed to such an extent by competition that it becomes no more than the interest on capital which is not invested by the owner himself.

Furthermore,...given equal fertility and equally efficient exploitation of lands, mines and fisheries, the produce is proportionate to the amount of capital employed. Thus, the victory of the large landowner. ...

Finally, only the wealthiest people can live on rent. Hence the competition between landowners who do not lease their land to tenants increases. Some of the landowners are ruined and there is further accumulation of large landed property.

This competition has the further consequence that a large part of landed property falls into the hands of capitalists, who then become landed proprietors; while the smaller landowners, generally speaking, are already nothing but capitalists. Thus a part of large landed property becomes industrial property.

The final result is, therefore, the abolition of the distinction between capitalist and landowner, so that broadly speaking there remain only two classes in the population, the working class and the capitalist class. This disposal of landed property and transformation of the land into a commodity is the final ruin of the old aristocracy and the complete triumph of the aristocracy of money.

Romanticism sheds many sentimental tears over this event, but we shall not do so. Romanticism always confuses the infamy involved in this *disposal of land* with the wholly reasonable and, within the system of private property, necessary and desirable consequences of the *disposal of landed property*. In the first place, feudal landed property is already essentially land which has been disposed of, alienated from men and now confronting them in the shape of a few great lords.

Already in feudal landownership the ownership of the soil appears as an alien power ruling over men. The serf is the product of the land. In the same way, the heir, the first-born son, belongs to the land. It inherits him. The rule of private property begins with the ownership of land, which is its basis. But in feudal landownership the lord *appears* at least as king of the land. Likewise, there is the appearance of a more intimate connexion between the owner and the land than is the case in the possession of mere *wealth*. Landed property assumes an individual character with its lord, has its own status, is knightly or baronial with him, has its privileges, its jurisdiction, its political rights, etc. It appears as the inorganic body of its lord. Hence the adage, *nulle terre sans maitre,* in which the joint growth of lordship and landed property is expressed. The rule of the landed property does not, therefore, appear as the direct rule of capital. Its dependants stand to it more in the relation in which they stand to their fatherland. It is a narrow kind of nationality.

Feudal landed property gives its name to its lord, as a kingdom gives its name to a king. His family history, the history of his house, etc., all this makes the landed property individual to him, makes it formally belong to a house, to a person. Similarly, the workers on the estate are not in the condition of *day-labourers,* but are partly the property of the lord, as in the case of serfs, and partly stand to him in relations of respect, subordination and duty. His relation to them is therefore directly political and has even an *agreeable* side. Customs and character differ from one estate to another and seem to be in harmony with the type of land, whereas later only a man's pocket, not his own character or individuality, attracts him to an estate. Finally, the lord does not try to extract the maximum profit from his estate. He rather consumes what is there, and tranquilly leaves the care of producing it to the serfs and tenant farmers. That is the *aristocratic* condition of landownership which reflects a romantic *glory* upon its lords.

It is inevitable that this appearance should be abolished, that landed property, the *root* of private property, should be drawn completely into the movement of private property and *become a commodity;* that the rule of the property owner should appear as the naked rule of private property, of capital, dissociated from all political colouring; that the relation between property owner and worker should be confined to the economic relationship of exploiter and exploited; that all personal relationships between the property owner and his property should cease, and the latter become purely *material* wealth; that in place of the honourable marriage with the land there should be a marriage of interest, and the land as well as man himself be reduced to the level of an object of speculation. It is inevitable that the root of landed property, sordid self-interest, should also appear in a cynical form. It is inevitable that immovable monopoly should turn into mobile and restless monopoly—into competition; and that the idle enjoyment of the products of other people's blood and toil should turn into a bustling trade in the same commodity. Finally, it is inevitable that in this competition, landed property, in the form of capital, should manifest its domination over both the working class and the property owners themselves, who are being ruined or advanced by the laws governing the movement of captial. So the medieval adage, *nulle terre sans seigneur,* is replaced with a new adage, *l'argent n'a pas de maitre,* which expresses the complete domination of living men by dead matter.

As regards the controversy over the division or non-division of landed property, the following is to be observed.

The *division of landed property* negates the *large-scale monopoly* of landed property, i.e abolishes it, but only by *generalizing* it. It does not abolish the basis of monopoly, private property. It attacks the existence, but not the real essence, of monopoly, and in consequence it falls victim to the laws of private property. For the division of landed property corresponds to the movement of competition in the industrial sphere. This division of the implements of production and separation of labour (which must be carefully distinguished from the division of labour: the work is not divided among many individuals, but the same work is carried out by each individual; it is a multiplication of the same kind of work) does not only bring economic disadvantages; like all competition it leads to further accumulation.

When the division of landed property takes place, therefore, the only alternatives are to return to an even more hateful form of monopoly, or to negate and abolish the division of landed property itself. This latter course is not, however, a return to feudal property, but the abolition of private property in land altogether. The first supersession of monopoly is always an extension and generalization of it. The supersession of monopoly which has attained its widest and most inclusive existence is its complete destruction. Association, applied to the land, has the advantage from an economic point of view of large-scale ownership, while at the same time it realizes the original tendency of the division of land, namely equality. Moreover, association restores the intimate relationships between man and the land in a rational way, instead of through serfdom, overlordship and a foolish mystique of property. The land ceases to be an object of sordid speculation, and through the freedom of work and enjoyment becomes once more man's real personal property. One great advantage of the division of landed property is that the property of the masses is destroyed in a different way from that of industry, and they are no longer willing to accept serfdom.

As for the large estates, their defenders have always sophistically identified the economic advantages of large-scale agricultural production with the existence of large landed property, as if these advantages would not reach their greatest extent, and bring social benefits for the first time, with the abolition of private property. Similarly, they have attacked the commercial spirit of the small landowners, as though the large estates did not contain this petty trading in germ, even in their feudal form—not to speak of the modern English form in which the feudalism of landlords, and the trading and industry of tenant farmers, are combined.

Just as large landed property can return the reproach of monopoly made from the standpoint of small landholdings, since the division of land is also based upon the monopoly of private property, so can the small holdings reject the reproach of having divided the land, for the division of land exists also in the case of large estates, but in an inflexible, crystallized form. Private property, indeed, is everywhere based upon division. Moreover, since the division of landed property leads again to large landed property as capital wealth, feudal property is bound to be divided, or at least to fall into the hands of capitalists, however it may twist and turn.

For large landed property, as in England, drives the greater part of the industrial population into poverty and reduces its own workers to utter misery. It thus creates and augments the power of its enemies, capital and industry, so far as it thrusts the poor and a whole sphere of activity into the other camp. It makes the majority of the country industrial, and thus the enemy of large landed property. Where industry has attained considerable power, as at present in England, it opposes foreign monopolies to that of large landed property and forces the latter into competition with foreign landed property. Under the rule of industry, landed property could only maintain its feudal dimensions with the help of a monopoly against foreign countries, in order to protect itself against the universal laws of trade which contradict its feudal nature. Once thrown into competition it must conform with the laws of competition like any other commodity which is subject to them. But it becomes thereby so fluctuating, growing and diminishing, passing from hand to hand, that no law can keep it any longer in a few predestined hands. The direct consequence is its fragmentation in many hands, a prey to the power of industrial capital.

In the end, large landed property which has been kept in existence by force and has created alongside itself a formidable industry, leads more rapidly to crisis than does the division of landed property alongside which the power of industry remains in second place.

As we can see in England, large landed property has cast off its feudal character and has taken on an industrial character to the extent that it wants to make as much money as possible. It gives the owner the highest possible rent, and the tenant farmer the highest possible profit on his capital. Consequently the agricultural workers are soon reduced to the minimum level of subsistence, and the farmer class establishes the power of industry and capital within landed property. Through competition with foreign countries the rent of land ceases, in the main, to constitute an independent source of income. A large section of the landowners is obliged to take the place of the tenant farmers who sink in this way into the proletariat. On the other hand, many tenant farmers will acquire landed property, for the large landowners, who have abandoned themselves to the enjoyment of their comfortable revenues and are usually unfitted for large-scale agricultural management, have very often neither the capital nor the experience to exploit the land. Consequently, a section of them is completely ruined. Ultimately, the wages which have already been reduced to a minimum must be further reduced, in the face of new competition; and that leads necessarily to revolution.

Landed property had to develop in both these ways, in order to experience in both of them its inevitable decline. So also industry had to ruin itself both in the form of monopoly and in the form of competition, in order to arrive at faith in man. . . .

The *distinction* between capital and land, profit and ground rent, and the distinction of both from wages, *industry, agriculture, immovable* and *movable* private property, is a *historical* distinction, not one inscribed in the nature of things. It is a *fixed* stage in the formation and development of the antithesis between capital and labour. In industry, etc., as opposed to immovable landed property, only the mode of origin and the antithesis to agriculture through which industry has developed, is expressed. As a *particular* kind of labour, as a more *significant, important* and *comprehensive* distinction, it exists only so long as industry (town life) is established *in opposition to* landed property (aristocratic feudal life) and still bears the characteristics of this contradiction in itself in the form of monopolies, crafts, guilds, corporations, etc. In such a situation, labour still appears to have a *social* meaning, still has the significance of *genuine* communal life, and has not yet progressed to *neutrality* in relation to its content, to full self-sufficient being, i.e. to abstraction from all other existence and thus to *liberated* capital.

But the necessary *development* of labour is liberated *industry,* constituted for itself alone, and *liberated capital.* The power of industry over its opponent is shown by the rise of *agriculture* as a real industry, whereas formerly most of the work was left to the soil itself and to the *slave* of the soil through whom the land cultivated itself. With the transformation of the slave into a *free* worker, i.e. into a *hireling,* the landowner himself is transformed into a lord of industry, a capitalist.

This transformation takes place at first through the medium of tenant farmer. But the tenant is the representative, the revealed *secret,* of the landowner. Only through him does the landowner have an *economic* existence, existence as a property owner; for the ground rent of his land only exists as a result of the competition between tenants. Thus the landowner *has* already become to a large extent, in the person of the tenant farmer, a *common* capitalist. And this must be fulfilled in reality; the capitalist directing agriculture (the tenant) must become a landowner, or vice versa. The *industrial trade* of the tenant is that of the landowner, for the existence of the former establishes that of the latter.

Recollecting their contrasting origins and descent the landowner recognizes the capitalist as his insubordinate, liberated and enriched slave of yesterday, and sees himself as a *capitalist* who is threatened by him. The capitalist sees the landowner as the idle, cruel and egoistical lord of yesterday; he knows that as a capitalist he injures the landowner, and yet that industry is responsible for the latter's present social significance, for his possessions and pleasures. He regards the landowner as the antithesis of *free* enterprise and of *free* capital which is independent of every natural limitation. This opposition is extremely bitter and each side expresses the truth about the other. It is only necessary to read the attacks upon immovable property by representatives of movable property, and vice versa, in order to obtain a clear picture of their respective worthlessness. The landowner emphasizes the noble lineage of his property, feudal souvenirs, reminiscences, the poetry of remembrance, his openhearted character, his political importance, etc., and when he talks in economic terms asserts that agriculture *alone* is productive. At the same time he portrays his opponent as a sly, bargaining, deceitful, mercenary, rebellious, heartless and soulless individual, an extortionate, pimping, servile, smooth, flattering, desiccated rogue, without honour, principles, poetry or anything else, who is alienated from the community which he freely trades away, and who breeds, nourishes and cherishes competition and along with it poverty, crime and the dissolution of all social bonds. . . .

Movable property, for its part, points to the miracle of modern industry and development. It is the child, the legitimate, native-born son, of the modern age. It pities its opponent as a simpleton, *ignorant* of his own nature (and this is entirely true) who wishes to replace moral capital and free labour by crude, immoral coercion and serfdom. It depicts him as a Don Quixote who, beneath the appearance of *directness, decency,* the *general interest* and stability, conceals his incapacity for development, greedy self-indulgence, selfishness, sectional interest and evil intention. It exposes him as a cunning *monopolist*; it pours cold water upon his reminiscences, his poetry and his romanticism, by a historical and satirical recital of the baseness, cruelty, degradation, prostitution, infamy, anarchy and revolt, of which the romantic castles were the workshops.

It (movable property) claims to have won political freedom for the people, to have removed the chains which bound civil society, to have linked together different worlds, to have established commerce which promotes friendship between peoples, to have created a pure morality and an agreeable culture. It has given the people, in place of their crude wants, civilized needs and the means of satisfying them. But the landowner—this idle spectator in grain—raises the price of the people's basic necessities of life and thereby forces the capitalist to raise wages without being able to increase productivity, thus hindering and ultimately arresting the growth of national income and the accumulation of capital upon which depends the creation of work for the people and of wealth for the country. He brings about a general decline, and parasitically exploits *all* the advantages of modern civilization without making the least contribution to it, and without abandoning any of his feudal prejudices. Finally, let him—for whom cultivation and the land itself exist only as a heaven-sent source of money—regard the *tenant farmer* and say whether he himself is not a *straightforward, fantastic, cunning* scoundrel, who in his heart and in reality has long been captivated by *free* industry and by the *delights* of trade, however much he may resist them and prattle about historical reminiscences or moral and political aims. Everything which he can really bring forward in justification is true only of the *cultivator of the land* (the capitalist and the labourers) of whom the landowner is rather the *enemy*; thus he testifies against himself. *Without* capital, landed property is lifeless and worthless matter. It is indeed the civilized victory of movable property to have discovered and created human labour as the source of wealth, in place of the lifeless things. . . .

From the *real* course of development . . . there follows the necessary victory of the capitalist, i.e. of developed private property, over undeveloped, immature private property, the landowner. In general, movement must triumph over immobility, overt self-conscious baseness over concealed, unconscious baseness, *avarice* over *self-indulgence*, the avowedly restless and able self-interest of *enlightenment* over the local, worldly-wise, simple, idle and fantastic *self-interest of superstition*, and *money* over the other forms of private property.

The states which have a presentiment of the danger represented by fully developed free industry, pure morality, and trade which promotes the amity of peoples, attempt, but quite in vain, to arrest the capitalization of landed property.

Landed property, as distinct from capital, is private property, capital, which is still afflicted by local and political prejudices; it is capital which has not yet emerged from its involvement with the world, *undeveloped* capital. In the course of its *formation on a world scale* it must achieve its abstract, i.e. *pure* expression.

Marx, *Manuscripts* (1844), EW, pp. 112–19, 140–44.

BOURGEOIS AND PROLETARIANS

The history of all hitherto existing society is the history of class struggles.

Freeman and slave, patrician and plebeian, lord and serf, guild master and journeyman—in a word, oppressor and oppressed—stood in constant opposition to one another, carried on an uninterrupted, now hidden, now open fight that each time ended in a revolutionary reconstitution of society at large, or in the common ruin of the contending classes.

In the early epochs of history, we find almost everywhere a complicated arrangement of society into various orders, a manifold graduation of social rank. In ancient Rome we have patricians, knights, plebeians, slaves; in the Middle Ages, feudal lords, vassals, guild masters, journeymen, apprentices, serfs; in almost all of these classes, again, subordinate graduations.

The modern bourgeois society that has sprouted from the ruins of feudal society has not done away with class antagonisms. It has but established new classes, new conditions of oppression, new forms of struggle in place of the old ones.

Our epoch, the epoch of the bourgeoisie, possesses, however, this distinctive feature: it has simplified the class antagonisms. Society as a whole is more and more splitting up into two great hostile camps, into two great classes directly facing each other: Bourgeoisie and Proletariat.

From the serfs of the Middle Ages sprang the chartered burghers of the earliest towns. From these burgesses the first elements of the bourgeoisie were developed.

The discovery of America, the rounding of the Cape, opened up fresh ground for the rising bourgeoisie. The East Indian and Chinese markets, the colonization of America, trade with the colonies, the increase in the means of exchange and in commodities generally, gave to commerce, to navigation, to industry, an impulse never before known, and thereby, to the revolutionary element in the tottering feudal society, a rapid development.

The feudal system of industry, under which industrial production was monopolized by closed guilds, now no longer sufficed for the growing wants of the new markets. The manufacturing system took its place. The guild masters were pushed to one side by the manufacturing middle class; division of labour between the different corporate guilds vanished in the face of division of labour in each single workshop.

Meantime the market kept ever growing, the demand ever rising. Even manufacturing no longer sufficed. Thereupon steam and machinery revolutionized industrial production. The place of manufacture was taken by the giant, Modern Industry, the place of the industrial middle class by industrial millionaires, the leaders of whole industrial armies, the modern bourgeoisie.

Modern industry has established the world market for which the discovery of America paved the way. This market has given an immense development to commerce, to navigation, to communication by land. This development has, in its turn, reacted on the extension of industry; and in proportion as industry, commerce, navigation, railways extended, in the same proportion the bourgeoisie developed, increased its capital, and pushed into the background every class handed down from the Middle Ages.

We see, therefore, how the modern bourgeoisie is itself the product of a long course of development, of a series of revolutions in the modes of production and of exchange.

Each step in the development of the bourgeoisie was accompanied by a corresponding political advance of that class. An oppressed class under the sway of the feudal nobility, an armed and self-governing association in the medieval commune, here independent urban republic (as in Italy and Germany), there taxable "third estate" of the monarchy (as in France), afterwards, in the period of manufacturing proper, serving either the semi-feudal or the absolute monarchy as a counterpoise against the nobility, and in fact a cornerstone of the great monarchies in general, the bourgeoisie has at last, since the establishment of Modern Industry and of the world market, conquered for itself, in the modern representative state, exclusive political sway. The executive of the modern state is but a committee for managing the common affairs of the whole bourgeoisie.

Marx-Engels, *Communist Manifesto* (1848), excerpt from Part I.

ENGELS ON SCIENTIFIC SOCIALISM AND THE MATERIALIST INTERPRETATION OF HISTORY

Modern socialism is, in its essence, the direct product of the recognition, on the one hand, of the class antagonisms existing in the society of today between properietors and non-proprietors, between capitalists and wage-workers; on the other hand, of the anarchy existing in production. . . .

A materialistic treatment of history was propounded, and a method found of explaining man's "knowing" by his "being," instead of, as heretofore, his "being" by his "knowing."

From that time forward socialism was no longer an accidental discovery of this or that ingenious brain, but the necessary outcome of the struggle between two historically developed classes—the proletariat and the bourgeoisie. Its task was no longer to manufacture a system of society as perfect as possible, but to examine the historico-economic succession of events from which these classes, and their antagonism had of necessity sprung, and to discover in the economic conditions thus created the means of ending the conflict. . . . The socialism of earlier days certianly criticised the existing capitalistic mode of production and its consequences. But it could not explain them, and, therefore, could not get the mastery of them. It could only simple reject them as bad. The more strongly this earlier socialism denounced the exploitation of the working class, inevitable under capitalism, the less able was it clearly to show in what this exploitation consisted and how it arose. But for this it was necessary—(1) to present the capitalistic method of production in its historical connection and its inevitableness during a particular historical period, and therefore, also, to present its inevitable downfall; and (2) to lay bare its essential character, which was still a secret. This was done by the discovery of *surplus value.* It was shown that the appropriation of unpaid labour is the basis of the capitalist mode of production and of the exploitation of the worker that occurs under it; that even if the capitalist buys the labour power of his labourer at its full value as a commodity on the market, he yet extracts more value from it than he paid for; and that in the ultimate analysis this surplus value forms those sums of value from which are heaped up the constantly increasing masses of capital in the hands of the possessing classes. The genesis of capitalist production and the production of capital were both explained.

These two great discoveries, the materialistic conception of history and the revelation of the secret of capitalistic production through surplus value, we owe to Marx. With these discoveries socialism became a science. The next thing was to work out all its details and relations.

The materialist conception of history starts from the proposition that the production of the means to support human life and, next to production, the exchange of things produced, is the basis of all social structure; that in every society that has appeared in history, the manner in which wealth is distributed and society divided into classes or orders is dependent upon what is produced, how it is produced, and how the products are exchanged. From this point of view the final causes of all social changes and political revolutions are to be sought, not in men's brains, not in men's better insight into eternal truth and justice, but in changes in the modes of production and exchange. They are to be sought not in the *philosophy*, but in the *economics* of each particular epoch. The growing perception that existing social institutions are unreasonable and unjust, that reason has become unreason and right wrong, is only proof that in the modes of production and exchange changes have silently taken place with which the social order, adapted to earlier economic conditions, is no longer in keeping. From this it also follows that the means of getting rid of the incongruities that have been brought to light must also be present, in a more or less developed condition, within the changed modes of production themselves. These means are not to be invented by deduction from fundamental principles, but are to be discovered in the stubborn facts of the existing system of production.

What is, then, the position of modern socialism in this connection?

The present structure of society—this is now pretty generally conceded—is the creation of the ruling class of today, of the bourgeoisie. The mode of production peculiar to the bourgeoisie, known, since Marx, as the capitalist mode of production, was incompatible with the feudal system, with the privileges it conferred upon individuals, entire social ranks and local corporations, as well as with the hereditary ties of subordination which constituted the framework of its social organisation. The bourgeoisie broke up the feudal system and built upon its ruins the capitalist order of society, the kingdom of free competition, of personal liberty, of the equality, before the law, of all commodity owners, of all the rest of the capitalist blessings. Thenceforward the capitalist mode of production could develop in freedom. Since steam, machinery, and the making of machines by machinery transformed the older manufacture into modern industry, the productive forces evolved under the guidance of the bourgeoisie developed with a rapidity and in a degree unheard of before. But just as the older manufacture, in its time, and handicraft, becoming more developed under its influence, had come into collision with the feudal trammels of the guilds, so now modern industry, in its more complete development, comes into collision with the bounds within which the capitalistic mode of production holds it confined. The new productive forces have already outgrown the capitalistic mode of using them. And this conflict between productive forces and modes of production is not a conflict engendered in the mind of man, like that between original sin and divine justice. It exists, in fact, objectively, outside us, independently of the will and actions even of the men that have brought it on. Modern socialism is nothing but the reflex, in thought, of this conflict in fact; its ideal reflection in the minds, first, of the class directly suffering under it, the working class.

Now, in what does this conflict consist?

Before capitalistic production, i.e., in the Middle Ages, the system of petty industry obtained generally, based upon the private property of the labourers in their means of production; in the country, the agriculture of the small peasant, freeman or serf; in the towns, the handicrafts organised in guilds. The instruments of labour—land, agricultural implements, the workshop, the tool—were the instruments of labour of single individuals, adapted for the use of one worker, and, therefore, of necessity, small, dwarfish, circumscribed. But, for this very reason they belonged, as a rule, to the producer himself. To concentrate these scattered, limited means of production, to enlarge them, to turn them into the powerful levers of production of the present day—this was precisely the historic role of capitalist production and of its upholder, the bourgeoisie. In the fourth section of *Capital* Marx has explained in detail, how since the fifteenth century this has been historically worked out through the three phases of simple cooperation, manufacture and modern industry. But the bourgeoisie, as is also shown there, could not transform these puny means of production into mighty productive forces without transforming them, at the same time, from means of production of the individual into *social* means of production only workable by a collectivity of men. The spinning-wheel, the hand-loom, the blacksmith's hammer, were replaced by the spinning-machine, the power-loom the steam-hammer; the individual workshop, by the factory implying the cooperation of hundreds and thousands of workmen. In like manner, production itself changed from a series of individual into a series of social acts, and the products from individual to social products. The yarn, the cloth, the metal articles that now came out of the factory, were the joint product of many workers, through whose hands they had successively to pass before they were ready. No one person could say of them: "I made that; this is *my* product."

But where, in a given society, the fundamental form of production is that spontaneous division of labour which creeps in gradually and not upon any preconceived plan, there the products take on the form of *commodities*, whose mutual exchange, buying and selling, enable the individual producers to satisfy their manifold wants. And this was the case in the Middle Ages. The peasant, e.g., sold to the artisan agricultural products and bought from him the products of handicraft. Into this society of individual producers, of commodity producers, the new mode of production thrust itself. In the midst of the old division of labour, grown up spontaneously and upon *no definite plan*, which had governed the whole society, now arose division of labour upon a *definite plan*, as organised in the factory; side by side with *individual* production appeared *social* production. The products of both were sold in the same market, and, therefore, at prices at least approximately equal. But organisation upon a definite plan was stronger than spontaneous division of labour. The factories working with the combined social forces of a collectivity of individuals produced their commodities far more cheaply than the individual small producers. Individual production revolutionised all the old methods of production. But its revolutionary character was, at the same time, so little recognised that it was, on the contrary, introduced as a means of increasing and developing the production of commodities. When it arose, it found ready-made, and made liberal use of, certain machinery for the production and exchange of commodities: merchants' capital, handicraft, wage-labour. Socialised production thus introducing itself as a new form of the production of commodities, it was a matter of course that under it the old forms of appropriation remained in full swing, and were applied to its products as well.

In the medieval stage of evolution of the production of commodities, the question as to the owner of the product of labour could not arise. The individual producer, as a rule, had, from raw material belonging to himself, and generally his own handiwork, produced it with his own tools, by the labour of his own hands or of his family. There was no need for him to appropriate the new product. It belonged wholly to him, as a matter of course. His property in the product was, therefore, based *upon his own labour*. Even where external help was used, this was, as a rule, of little importance, and very generally was compensated by something other than wages. The apprentices and journeymen of the guilds worked less for board and wages than for education, in order that they might become master craftsmen themselves.

Then came the concentration of the means of production and of the producers in large workshops and manufactories, their transformation into actual socialised means of production and socialised producers. But the socialised producers and means of production and their products were still treated, after this change, just as they had been before, i.e., as the means of production and the products of individuals. Hitherto, the owner of the instruments of labour had himself appropriated the product, because, as a rule, it was his own product and the assistance of others was the exception. Now the owner of the instruments of labour always appropriated to himself the product, although it was no longer *his* product but exclusively the product of the *labour of others*. Thus, the products now produced socially were not appropriated by those who had actually set in motion the means of production and actually produced the commodities, but by the *capitalists*. The means of production, and production itself, had become in essence socialised. But they were subjected to a form of appropriation which presupposes the private production of individuals, under which, therefore, everyone owns his own product and brings it to market. The mode of production is subjected to this form of appropriation, although it abolishes the conditions upon which the latter rests.*

This contradiction, which gives to the new mode of production its capitalistic character, *contains the germ of the whole of the social antagonisms of today*. The greater the mastery obtained by the new mode of production over all important fields of production and in all manufacturing countries, the more it reduced individual production to an insignificant residuum, *the more clearly was brought out the incompatibility of socialised production with capitalistic appropriation.*

The first capitalists found, as we have said, alongside of other forms of labour, wage-labour ready-made for them on the market. But it was exceptional, complementary, accessory, transitory wage-labour. The agricultural labourer, though, upon occasion, he hired himself out by the day, had a few acres of his own land on which he could at all events live at a pinch. The guilds were so organised that the journeyman of today became the master of tomorrow. But all this changed, as soon as the means of production became socialised and concentrated in the hands of capitalists. The means of production, as well as the product, of the individual producer became more and more worthless; there was nothing left for him but to turn wage-worker under the capitalist. Wage-labour, aforetime the exception and accessory, now became the rule and basis of all produciton; aforetime complementary, it now became the sole remaining function of the worker. The wage-worker for a time became a wage-worker for life. The number of these permanent wage-workers was further enormously increased by the breaking-up of the feudal system that occurred at the same time, by the disbanding of the retainers of the feudal lords, the eviction of the peasants from their homesteads, etc. The separation was made complete between the means of production concentrated in the hands of the capitalists, on the one side, and the producers, possessing nothing but their labour-power, on the other. *The contradiction between socialised production and capitalistic appropriation manifested itself as the antagonism of proletariat and bourgeoisie.*

We have seen that the capitalistic mode of production thrust its way into a society of commodity-producers, of individual producers, whose social bond was the exchange of their products. But every society based upon the production of commodities has this peculiarity: that the producers have lost control over their own social interrelations. Each man produces for himself with such means of production as he may happen to have, and for such exchange as he

*It is hardly necessary in this connection to point out that, even if the *form* of appropriation remains the same, the *character* of the appropriation is just as much revolutionised as production is by the changes described above. It is, of course, a very different matter whether I appropriate to myself my own product or that of another. Note in passing that wage-labour, which contains the whole capitalistic mode of production in embryo, is very ancient; in a sporadic, scattered form it existed for centuries alongside of slave-labour. But the embryo could duly develop into the capitalistic mode of production only when the necessary historical preconditions had been furnished. [*Note by Engels.*]

may require to satisfy his remaining wants. No one knows how much of his particular article is coming on the market, nor how much of it will be wanted. No one knows whether his individual product will meet an actual demand, whether he will be able to make good his costs of production or even to sell his commodity at all. Anarchy reigns in socialised production.

But the production of commodities, like every other form of production, has its peculiar, inherent laws inseparable from it; and these laws work, despite anarchy, in and through anarchy. They reveal themselves in the only persistent form of social interrelations, i.e., in exchange, and here they affect the individual producers as compulsory laws of competition. They are, at first, unknown to these producers themselves, and have to be discovered by them gradually and as the result of experience. They work themselves out, therefore, independently of the producers, and in antagonism to them, as inexorable natural laws of their particular form of production. The product governs the producers.

In medieval society, especially in the earlier centuries, production was essentially directed toward satisfying the wants of the individual. It satisfied, in the main, only the wants of producer and his family. Where relations of personal dependence existed, as in the country, it also helped to satisfy the wants of the feudal lord. In all this there was, therefore, no exchange; the products, consequently, did not assume the character of commodities. The family of the peasant produced almost everything they wanted: clothes and furniture, as well as means of subsistence. Only when it began to produce more than was sufficient to supply its own wants and the payments in kind to the feudal lord, only then did it also produce commodities. This surplus, thrown into socialised exchange and offered for sale, became commodities.

The artisans of the towns, it is true, had from the first to produce for exchange. But they, also, themselves supplied the greatest part of their own individual wants. They had gardens and plots of land. They turned their cattle out into the communal forest, which, also, yielded them timber and firing. The women spun flax, wool, and so forth. Production for the purpose of exchange, production of commodities, was only in its infancy. Hence, exchange was restricted, the market narrow, the methods of production stable; there was local exclusiveness without, local unity within; the Mark in the country, in the town, the guild.

But with the extension of the production of commodities, and especially with the introduction of the capitalist mode of production, the laws of commodity production, hitherto latent, came into action more openly and with greater force. The old bonds were loosened, the old exclusive limits broken through, the producers were more and more turned into independent, isolated producers of commodities. It became apparent that the production of society at large was ruled by absence of plan, by accident, by anarchy; and this anarchy grew to greater and greater height. . . .

Engels, *Socialism* (1880), MESW, pp. 399, 416–22.

BOURGEOIS REVOLUTIONS

The long fight of the bourgeoisie against feudalism culminated in three great, decisive battles.

The first was what is called the Protestant Reformation in Germany. The war cry raised against the Church by Luther was responded to by two insurrections of a political nature: first, that of the lower nobility under Franz von Sickingen, 1523, then the great Peasants' War, 1525. Both were defeated, chiefly in consequence of the indecision of the parties most interested, the burghers of the town—on indecision into the causes of which we cannot here enter. From that moment the struggle degenerated into a fight between the local princes and the central power, and ended by blotting out Germany, for two hundred years, from the politically active nations of Europe. The Lutheran Reformation produced a new creed indeed, a religion adapted to absolute monarchy. No sooner were the peasants of North-East Germany converted to Lutheranism than they were from freemen reduced to serfs.

But where Luther failed, Calvin won the day. Calvin's creed was one fit for the boldest of the bourgeoisie of his time. His predestination doctrine was the religious expression of the fact that in the commerical world of competition success or failure does not depend upon a man's activity or cleverness, but upon circumstances uncontrollable by him. It is not of him that willeth or of him that runneth, but of the mercy of unknown superior economic powers; and this was especially true at a period of economic revolution, when all old commercial routes and centres were replaced by new ones, when India and America were opened to the world, and when even the most sacred economic articles of faith—the value of gold and silver—began to totter and to break down. Calvin's church constitution was thoroughly democratic and republican; and where the kingdom of God was republicanised, could the kingdoms of this world remain subject to monarchs, bishops and lords? While German Lutheranism became a willing tool in the hands of princes, Calvinism founded a republic in Holland, and active republican parties in England, and, above all, Scotland.

In Calvinism, the second great bourgeois upheaval found its doctrine ready cut and dried. This upheaval took place in England. The middle class of the towns brought it on, and the yeomanry of the country districts fought it out. Curiously enough, in all the three great bourgeois risings, the peasantry furnishes the army that has to do the fighting; and the peasantry is just the class that, the victory once gained, is most surely ruined by the economic consequences of that victory. A hundred years after Cromwell, the yeomanry of England had almost disappeared. Anyhow, had it not been for that yeomanry and for the *plebeian* element in the towns, the bourgeoisie alone would never have fought the matter out to the bitter end, and would never have brought Charles I to the scaffold. In order to secure even those conquests of the bourgeoisie that were ripe for gathering at the time, the revolution had to be carried considerably further—exactly as in 1793 in France and 1848 in Germany. This seems, in fact, to be one of the laws of evolution of bourgeois society.

Well, upon this excess of revolutionary activity there necessarily followed the inevitable reaction which in its turn went beyond the point where it might have maintained itself. After a series of oscillations, the new centre of gravity was at last attained and became a new starting-point. The grand period of English history, known to respectablity under the name of "the Great Rebellion," and the struggles succeeding it, were brought to a close by the comparatively puny event entitled by Liberal historians "the Glorious Revolution."

The new starting-point was a compromise between the rising middle class and the ex-feudal landowners. The latter, though called, as now, the aristocracy, had been long since on the way which led them to become what Louis Phillippe in France became at a much later period, "the first bourgeois of the kingdom." Fortunately for England, the old feudal barons had killed one another during the Wars of the Roses. Their successors, though, mostly scions of the old families, had been so much out of the direct line of descent that they constituted quite a new body, with habits and tendencies far more bourgeois than feudal. They fully understood the value of money, and at once began to increase their rents by turning hundreds of small farmers out and replacing them by sheep. Henry VIII, while squandering the Church lands, created fresh bourgeois landlords by wholesale; the innumerable confiscations of estates regranted to absolute or relative upstarts, and continued during the whole of the seventeenth century, had the same result. Consequently, ever since development of industrial production, had, on the contrary, sought to indirectly profit thereby; and there had always been a section of the great landowners willing, from economical or political reasons, to cooperate with the leading men of the financial and industrial bourgeoisie. The compromise of 1689 was, therefore, easily accomplished. The political spoils of "pelf and place" were left to the great landowning families, provided the economic interests of the financial, manufacturing and commercial middle class were sufficiently attended to. And these economic interests were at that time powerful enough to determine the general policy of the nation. There might be squabbles about matters of detail, but, on the whole, the aristocratic oligarchy knew too well that its own economic prosperity was irretrievably bound up with that of the industrial and commercial middle class.

From that time, the bourgeoisie was a humble, but still a recognised component of the ruling classes of England. With the rest of them, it had a common interest in keeping in subjection the great working mass of the nation. . . .

The Great French Revolution was the third uprising of the bourgeoisie, but the first that had entirely cast off the religious cloak, and was fought out on undisguised political lines; it was the first, too, that was really fought out up to the destruction of one of the combatants, the aristocracy, and the complete triumph of the other, the bourgeoisie. In England the continuity of pre-revolutionary and post-revolutionary institutions, and the compromise between landlords and capitalists, found its expression in the continuity of judicial precedents and in the religious preservation of the feudal forms of the law. In France the Revolution constituted a complete breach with the traditions of the past; it cleared out the very last vestiges of feudalism, and created in the *Code Civil* a masterly adaption of the old Roman law—that almost perfect expression of the juridical relations corresponding to the economic stage called by Marx the production of commodities—to modern capitalistic conditions; so masterly that this French revolutionary code still serves as a model for reforms of the law of property in all other countries, not excepting England. . . .

To return to our British bourgeois. The French Revolution gave him a splendid opportunity, with the help of the Continental monarchies, to destroy French maritime commerce, to annex French colonies, and to crush the last French pretensions to maritime rivalry. That was one reason why he fought it. Another was that the ways of this revolution went very much against his grain. Not only its "execrable" terrorism, but the very attempt to carry bourgeois rule to extremes. What should the British bourgeois do without his aristocracy, that taught him manners, such as they were, and invented fashions for him—that furnished officers of the army, which kept order at home, and the navy, which conquered colonial possessions and new markets abroad? There was indeed a progressive minority of the bourgeoisie, that minority whose interests were not so well attended to under the compromise; this section, composed chiefly of the less wealthy middle class, did sympathise with the Revolution, but it was powerless in Parliament. . . .

While the Revolution ensured the political triumph of the bourgeoisie in France, in England Watt, Arkwright, Cartwright, and others initiated an industrial revolution, which completely shifted the centre of gravity of economic power. The wealth of the bourgeoisie increased considerably faster than that of the landed aristocracy. Within the bourgeoisie itself, the financial aristocracy, the bankers, etc., were more and more pushed into the background by the manufacturers. The compromise of 1689, even after gradual changes it had undergone in favour of the bourgeoisie, no longer corresponded to the relative position of the parties to it. The character of these parties, too, had changed; the bourgeoisie of 1830 was very different from that of the preceding century. The political power still left to the aristocracy, and used by them to resist the pretensions of the new industrial bourgeoisie, became incompatible with the new economic interests. A fresh struggle with the aristocracy was necessary; it could end only in a victory of the new economic power. First, the Reform Act was pushed through, in spite of all resistance, under the impulse of the French Revolution of 1830. It gave to the bourgeoisie a recognised and powerful place in Parliament. Then the repeal of the Corn Laws, which settled, once for all, the supremacy of the bourgeoisie, and especially of its most active portion, the manufacturers, over the landed aristocracy. This was the greatest victory of the bourgeoisie; it was, however, also the last it obtained in its own exclusive interest. Whatever triumphs it obtained later on, it had to share with a new social power, first its ally, but soon its rival.

The industrial revolution had created a class of large manufacturing capitalists, but also a class—and a far more numerous one—of manufacturing workpeople. This class gradually increased in numbers, in proportion as the industrial revolution seized upon one branch of manufacture after another, and in the same proportion it increased in power. This power it proved as early as 1824, by forcing a reluctant Parliament to repeal the acts forbidding combinations of workmen. During the Reform agitation, the working men constituted the Radical wing of the Reform party; the Act of 1832 having excluded them from the suffrage, they formulated their demands in the People's Charter, and constituted themselves, in opposition to the great bourgeois Anti-Corn Law party, into an independent party, the Chartists, the first working men's party of modern times.

Then came the Continental revolutions of February and March 1848, in which the working people played such a prominent part, and, at least in Paris, put forward demands which were certainly inadmissible from the point of view of capitalist society. And then came the general reaction. First the defeat of the Chartists on the 10th April, 1848, then the crushing of the Paris working men's insurrection in June of the same year, then the disasters of 1849 in Italy, Hungary, South Germany, and at last the victory of Louis Bonaparte over Paris, 2nd December, 1851. For a time, at least, the bugbear of working-class pretensions was put down. . . .

It seems a law of historical development that the bourgeoisie can in no European country get hold of political power—at least for any length of time—in the same exclusive way in which the feudal aristocracy kept hold of it during the Middle Ages. Even in France, where feudalism was completely extinguished, the bourgeoisie, as a whole, has held full possession of the Government for very short periods only. During Louis Philippe's reign, 1830-48, a very small portion of the bourgeoisie ruled the kingdom; by far the larger part were excluded from the suffrage by the high qualification. Under the Second Republic, 1848-51, the whole bourgeoisie ruled, but for three years only; their incapacity brought on the Second Empire. It is only now, in the Third Republic, that the bourgeoisie as a whole have kept possession of the helm for more than twenty years; and they are already showing lively signs of decadence. A durable reign of the bourgeoisie has been possible only in countries like America, where feudalism was unknown, and society at the very beginning started from a bourgeois basis. And even in France and America, the successors of the bourgeoisie, the working people, are already knocking at the door.

In England, the bourgeoisie never held undivided sway. Even the victory of 1832 left the landed aristocracy in almost exclusive possession of all the leading Government offices. . . . The fact was, the English middle class of that time were, as a rule, quite uneducated upstarts, and could not help leaving to the aristocracy those superior Government places where other qualifications were required than mere insular narrowness and insular conceit, seasoned by business sharpness. Even now the endless newspaper debates about middle-class education show that the English middle class does not yet consider itself good enough for the best education, and looks to something more modest. Thus, even after the repeal of the Corn Laws, it appeared a matter of course that the men who had carried the day, the Cobdens, Brights, Forsters, etc., should remain excluded from a share in the official government of the country, until twenty years afterwards a new Reform Act opened to them the door of the Cabinet. The English bourgeoisie are, up to the present day, so deeply penetrated by a sense of their social inferiority that they keep up, at their own expense and that of the nation, an ornamental caste of drones to represent the nation worthily at all state functions; and they consider themselves highly honoured whenever one of themselves is found worthy of admission into this select and privileged body, manufactured, after all, by themselves.

The industrial and commerical middle class had, therefore, not yet succeeded in driving the landed aristocracy completely from political power when another competitor, the working class, appeared on the stage. The reaction after the Chartist movement and the Continental revolutions, as well as the unparalleled extension of English trade from 1848-66 (ascribed vulgarly to Free Trade alone, but due far more to the colossal development of railways, ocean steamers and means of intercourse generally), had again driven the working class into the dependency of the Liberal Party, of which they formed, as in pre-Chartist times, the Radical wing. Their claims to the franchise, however, gradually became irresistible; while the Whig leaders of the Liberals "funked," Disraeli showed his superiority by making the Tories seize the favourable moment and introduce household suffrage in the boroughs, along with a redistribution of seats. Then followed the ballot; then in 1884 the extension of household suffrage to the counties and a fresh redistribution of seats, by which electoral districts were to some extent equalised. All these measures considerably increased the electoral power of the working class, so much so that in at least 150 to 200 constituencies that class now furnishes the majority of voters. But parliamentary government is a capital school for teaching respect for tradition; if the middle class look with awe and veneration upon what Lord John Manners playfully called "our old nobility," the mass of the working people then looked up with respect and deference to what used to be designated as "their betters," the middle class. Indeed, the British workman, some fifteen years ago, was the model workman, whose respectful regard for the position of his master, and whose self-restraining modesty in claiming rights for himself, consoled our German economists of the *Katheder-Socialist* school for the incurable communistic and revolutionary tendencies of their own working-men at home.

But the English middle class—good men of business as they are—saw farther than the German professors. They had shared their power but reluctantly with the working class. They had learnt, during the Chartist years, what that *puer robustus sed militiosus*, the people, is capable of. And since that time, they had been compelled to incorporate the better part of the People's Charter in the Statutes of the United Kingdom. . . .

In fact, in England . . . the working people have begun to move again. They are, no doubt, shackled by traditions of various kinds. Bourgeois traditions, such as the widespread belief that there can be but two parties, Conservatives and Liberals, and that the working class must work out its salvation by and through the great Liberal Party. Working-men's traditions, inherited from their first tentative efforts at independent action, such as the exclusion, from ever so many old Trade Unions, of all applicants who have not gone through a regular apprenticeship; which means the breeding, by every such union, of its own blacklegs. But for all that the English working class is moving; . . . It moves, like all things in England, with a slow and measured step, with hesitation here, with more or less unfruitful, tentative attempts there; it moves now and then with an overcautious mistrust of the name of socialism, while it gradually absorbs the substance; and the movement spreads and seizes one layer of the workers after another. . . . And if the pace of the movement is not up to the impatience of some people, let them not forget that it is the working class which keeps alive the finest qualities of the English character, and that, if a step in advance is once gained in England, it is, as a rule, never lost afterwards. . . .

But the triumph of the European working class does not depend upon England alone. It can only be secured by the cooperation of, at least, England, France, and Germany. In both the latter countries the working-class movement is well ahead of England. In Germany it is even within measurable distance of success. The progress it has there made during the last twenty-five years is unparalleled. It advances with ever-increasing velocity. If the German middle class have shown themselves lamentably deficient in political capacity, discipline, courage, energy, and perseverance, the German working class have given ample proof of all these qualities. Four hundred years ago, Germany was the starting-point of the first upheaval of the European middle class; as things are now, is it outside the limits of possibility that Germany will be the scene, too, of the first great victory of the European proletariat?

Engels, *Introduction to "Socialism: Utopian and Scientific"* (1892), MESW, pp. 388–98.

SOCIAL CLASSES IN THE TRANSITION TO CAPITALISM

The British Constitution

But what is the British Constitution? Does its essence lie in a representative system and a limitation of the power of the executive? These features distinguish it neither from the Constitution of the United States of North America nor from the constitutions of the numerous British joint-stock companies which know "their business." The British Constitution is, in fact, merely an out-of-date, superannuated, obsolete compromise between the bourgeoisie, who are *not officially* but actually *ruling* in all decisive spheres of bourgeois society, and the landed aristocracy, who are *governing officially*. Originally, after the "glorious" revolution of 1688, only a section of the bourgeoisie, the *financial aristocracy,* was included in the compromise. The Reform Bill of 1831 admitted another section, the *millocracy*, as the English call them, that is, the high dignitaries of the *industrial* bourgeoisie. The history of legislation since 1831 is the history of concessions made to the industrial bourgeoisie, ranging from the Poor Law to the repeal of the Corn Laws, and from the repeal of the Corn Laws to the death-duties on real estate.

If the bourgeoisie—even only the top layer of the middle classes—has been generally recognised as the *ruling class* in *political respects*, this has been done only on the condition that the entire administration in all details, even the executive functions of legislative power, that is, the actual legislation in both

Houses of Parliament, should remain in the hands of the landed aristocracy. In the 1830s the bourgeoisie preferred the renewal of the compromise with the mass of the English people. The aristocracy, subjected to certain principles laid down by the bourgeoisie, now ruled exclusively in the Cabinet, in Parliament, in the Administration, in the Army and the Navy—one half, and relatively the most important half, of the British nation. . . .

Marx, *The British Constitution* (1855) AB, pp. 221–22.

Tories and Whigs

The political parties of Great Britain are sufficiently known in the United States. It will be sufficient to bring to mind, in a few strokes of the pen, the distinctive characteristics of each of them.

Up to 1846 the Tories passed as the guardians of the traditions of Old England. They were suspected of admiring in the British Constitution the eighth wonder of the world; to be *laudatores temporis acti*, enthusiasts for the throne, the High Church, the privileges and liberties of the British subject. The fatal year, 1846, with its repeal of the Corn Laws, and the shot of distress which this repeal forced from the Tories, proved that they were enthusiasts for nothing but rent of land, and at the same time disclosed the secret of their attachment to the political and religious institutions of Old England. These institutions are the very best institutions, with the help of which *large landed property*—the landed interest—has hitherto ruled England, and even now seeks to maintain its rule. The year 1846 brought to light in its nakedness the *substantial class interest* which forms the *real base* of the Tory party. The year 1846 tore down the traditionally venerable lion's hide, under which Tory class interest had hitherto hidden itself. The year 1846 transformed the Tories into *Protectionists.* Tory was the sacred name, Protectionist is the profane one; Tory was the political battle-cry, Protectionist is the economical shout of distress; Tory seemed an idea, a principle, Protectionist is an interest. Protectionists of what? Of their own revenues, of the rent of their own land. Then the Tories, in the end, are bourgeois as much as the remainder, for where is the bourgeois who is not a protectionist of his own purse? They are distinguished from the other bourgeois in the same way as rent of land is distinguished from commercial and industrial profit. Rent of land is conservative, profit is progressive; rent of land is national, profit is cosmopolitical; rent of land believes in the State Church, profit is a dissenter by birth. The repeal of the Corn Laws in 1846 merely recognized an already accomplished fact, a change long since enacted in the elements of British civil society, viz., the subordination of the landed interest to the moneyed interest, of property to commerce, of agriculture to manufacturing industry, of the country to the city. Could this fact be doubted since the country population stands, in England, to the towns' population in the proportion of one to three? The substantial foundation of the power of the Tories was the rent of land. The rent of land is regulated by the price of food. The price of food, then, was artificially maintained at a high rate by the Corn Laws. The repeal of the Corn Laws brought down the price of food, which in its turn brought down the rent of the land, and with sinking rent broke down the real strength upon which the political power of the Tories reposed.

What, then, are they trying to do now? To maintain a political power, the social foundation of which has ceased to exist. And how can this be attained? By nothing short of a *counter-revolution*, that is to say, by a reaction of the state against society. They strive to retain forcibly institutions and a political power which were condemned from the very moment at which the rural population found itself outnumbered three times by the population of the towns. And such an attempt must necessarily end with their destruction; it must accelerate and make more acute the social development of England; it must bring on a crisis.

The Tories recruit their army from the farmers, who have either not yet lost the habit of following their landlords as their natural superiors, or who are economically dependent upon them, or who do not yet see that the interest of the farmer and the interest of the landlord are no more identical than the respective interests of the borrower and of the usurer. They are followed and supported by the Colonial Interest, the Shipping Interest, the State Church party, in short, by all those elements which consider it necessary to safeguard their interests against the necessary results of modern manufacturing industry, and against the social revolution prepared by it.

Opposed to the Tories, as their herditary enemies, stand the Whigs, a party with whom the American Whigs have nothing in common but the name.

The British Whig, in the natural history of politics, forms a species which, like all those of the amphibious class, exists very easily, but is difficult to describe. Shall we call them, with their opponents, Tories out of office, or, as continental writers love it, take them for the representatives of certain *popular* principles? In the latter case we should get embarrassed in the same difficulty as the historian of the Whigs, Mr. Cooke, who, with great naiveté, confesses in his *History of Parties* that it is indeed a certain number of 'liberal, moral and enlightened principles' which constitutes the Whig party, but that it was greatly to be regretted that during the more than a century and a half that the Whigs have existed, they have been, when in office, always prevented from carrying out these principles. So that in reality, according to the confession of their own historian, the Whigs represent something quite different from their professed 'liberal and enlightened principles'. Thus they are in the same position as the drunkard brought up before the Lord Mayor who declared that he represented the temperance principle but from some accident or other always got drunk on Sundays.

But never mind their principles; we can better make out what they are in historical fact; what they carry out, not what they once believed, and what they now want other people to believe with respect to their character.

The Whigs, as well as the Tories, form a fraction of the large landed proprietors of Great Britain. Nay, the oldest, richest and most arrogant portion of English landed property is the very nucleus of the Whig party.

What, then, distinguishes them from the Tories? The Whigs are the *aristocratic representatives* of the bourgeoisie, of the industrial and commercial middle class. Under the condition that the bourgeoisie should abandon to them, to an oligarchy of aristocratic families, the monopoly of government and the exclusive possession of office, they make to the middle class, and assist it in conquering, all those concessions which in the course of social and political development have shown themselves to have become *unavoidable* and *undelayable*. Neither more nor less. And as often as such an unavoidable measure has been passed, they declare loudly that herewith the end of historical progress has been obtained; that the whole social movement has carried its ultimate purpose, and they then 'cling to finality.' They can support more easily than the Tories a decrease of their rental revenues, because they consider themselves as the heaven-born farmers of the revenues of the British Empire. They can renounce the monopoly of the Corn Laws, as long as they maintain the monopoly of government as their family property. Ever since the 'Glorious Revolution' of 1688 the Whigs, with short intervals, caused principally by the the first French revolution and the consequent reaction, have found themselves in the enjoyment of the public offices. Whoever recalls to his mind this period of English history will find no other distinctive mark of Whigdom but the maintenance of their family oligarchy. The interests and principles which they represent besides, from time to time, do not belong to the Whigs; they are forced upon them by the development of the industrial and commercial class, the bourgeoisie. After 1688 we find them united with the Bankocracy, just then rising into importance, as we find them in 1846 united with the Millocracy. The Whigs as little carried the Reform Bill of 1831 as they carried the Free Trade Bill of 1846. Both reform movements, the political as well as the commercial, were movements of the bourgeoisie. As soon as either of these movements had ripened into irresistibility, as soon as, at the same time, it had become the safest means of turning the Tories out of office, the Whigs stepped forward, took up the direction of the government, and secured to themselves the governmental part of the victory. In 1831 they extended the political portion of reform as far as was necessary in order not to leave the middle class entirely dissatisfied; after 1846 they confined their free-trade measures so far as was necessary in order to save to the landed aristocracy the greatest possible amount of privileges. Each time they took the movement in hand in order to prevent its forward march, and to recover their own posts at the same time.

It is clear that from the moment when the landed aristocracy is no longer able to maintain its position as an independent power, to fight, as an independent party, for the government position, in short, that from the moment when the Tories are definitively overthrown, British history has no longer any room for the Whigs. The aristocracy once destroyed, what is the use of an aristocratic representation of the bourgeoisie against this aristocracy?

It is well known that in the Middle Ages the German emperors put the just then arising towns under imperial governors, *'advocati,'* to protest these towns against the surrounding nobility. As soon as growing population and wealth gave them sufficient strength and independence to resist, and even to attack the nobility, the towns also drove out the noble governors, the *advocati*.

The Whigs have been these *advocati* of the British middle class, and their government monopoly must break down as soon as the landed monopoly of the Tories is broken down. In the same measure as the middle class has developed its independent strength, they have shrunk down from a party to a coterie. . . .

Marx, *Tories and Whigs* (1852), AB, pp. 109–14.

Free Traders and Chartists

While the Tories, the Whigs, the Peelites—in fact, all the parties we have hitherto commented upon—belong more or less to the past, the Free Traders (the men of the Manchester School, the Parliamentary and Financial Reformers) are the *official representatives of modern English society*, the representatives of that England which rules the market of the world. They represent the party of the self-conscious bourgeoisie, of industrial captial striving to make available its social power as a political power as well, and to eradicate the last arrogant remnants of feudal society. This party is led on by the most active and most energetic portion of the English bourgeoisie—the *manufacturers.* What they demand is the complete and undisguised ascendancy of the bourgeoisie, the open, official subjection of society at large to the laws of modern, bourgeois production, and to the rule of those men who are the directors of that production. By free trade they mean the unfettered movement of capital; freed from all political, national and religious shackles. The soil is to be a marketable commodity, and the exploitation of the soil is to be carried on according to the common commercial laws. There are to be manufacturers of food as well as manufacturers of twist and cottons, but no longer any lords of the land. There are, in short, not to be tolerated any political or social restrictions, regulations or monopolies, unless they proceed from 'the eternal laws of political economy', that is, from the conditions under which capital produces and distributes. The struggle of this party against the old English institutions, products of a superannuated, an evanescent stage of social development, is resumed in the watchword: *Produce as cheap as you can, and do away with all the* faux frais *of production* (with all superfluous, unnecessary expenses in production). And this watchword is addressed not only to the private individual, but the the *nation at large* principally.

Royalty, with its 'barbarous splendors,' its court, its civil list and its flunkeys—what else does it belong to but to the *faux frais* of production? The nation can produce and exchange without royalty; away with the crown. The sinecures of the nobility, the House of Lords? *Faux frais* of production. The large standing army? *Faux frais* of production. The colonies? *Faux frais* of production. The State Church, with its riches, the spoils of plunder or of mendicity? *Faux frais* of production. Let parsons compete freely with each other, and everyone pay them according to his own wants. The whole circumstantial routine of English law, with its Court of Chancery? *Faux frais* of production. National wars? *Faux frais* of production. England can exploit foreign nations more cheaply while at peace with them.

You see, to these champions of the British bourgeoisie, to the men of the Manchester School, every institution of Old England appears in the light of a piece of machinery as costly as it is useless, and which fulfils no other purpose but to prevent the nation from producing the greatest possible quantity at the least possible expense, and to exchange its products in freedom. Necessarily, their last word is the bourgeois republic, in which free competition rules supreme in all spheres of life; in which there remains altogether that *minimum* only of government which is indispensable for the administration, internally and externally, of the common class interest and business of the bourgeoisie; and where this minimum of government is as soberly, as economically organized as possible. Such a party, in other countries, would be called *democratic*. But it is necessarily revolutionary, and the complete annihilation of Old England as an aristocratic country is the end which it follows up with more or less consciousness. Its nearest object, however, is the attainment of a parliamentary reform which should transfer to its hands the legislative power necessary for such a revolution.

But the British bourgeois are not excitable Frenchmen. When they intend to carry a parliamentary reform they will not make a February revolution. On the contrary. Having obtained, in 1846, a grand victory over the landed aristocracy by the repeal of the Corn Laws, they were satisfied with following up the material advantages of this victory, while they neglected to draw the necessary political and economic conclusions from it, and thus enabled the Whigs to reinstate themselves into their hereditary monopoly of government. During all the time from 1846 to 1852, they exposed themselves to ridicule by their battle-cry: Broad principles and practical (read *small*) measures. And why all this? Because in every violent movement they are obliged to appeal to the *working class*. And if the aristocracy is their vanishing opponent, the working class is their arising enemy. They prefer to compromise with the vanishing opponent rather than to strengthen the arising enemy, to whom the future belongs, by concessions of a more than apparent importance. Therefore, they strive to avoid every forcible collision with the aristocracy; but historical necessity and the Tories press them onwards. They cannot avoid fulfilling their mission, battering to pieces Old England, the England of the past; and the very moment when they will have conquered exclusive political dominion, when political dominion and economic supremacy will be united in the same hands, when, therefore, the struggle against capital will no longer be distinct from the struggle against the existing government—from that very moment will date the *social revolution of England*.

We now come to the Chartists, the politically active portion of the British *working class*. The six points of the Charter which they contend for contain nothing but the demand of universal suffrage, and of the conditions without which universal suffrage would be illusory for the working class, such as the ballot, payment of members, annual general elections. But universal suffrage is the equivalent for political power for the working class of England, where the proletariat forms the large majority of the population, where, in a long, though underground, civil war, it has gained a clear consciousness of its position as a class, and where even the rural districts know no longer any peasants, but only landlords, industrial capitalists (farmers) and hired labourers. The carrying of universal suffrage in England would, therefore, be a far more socialistic measure than anything which has been honoured with that name on the Continent.

Its inevitable result, here, is *the political supremacy of the working class.*

Marx, *The Chartists* (1852), AB, pp. 116–19.

1.4 PRIMITIVE ACCUMULATION

The Secret of Primitive Accumulation

The accumulation of capital presupposes surplus-value; surplus-value presupposes capitalistic production; capitalistic production presupposes the pre-existence of considerable masses of capital and of labour-power in the hands of producers of commodities. The whole movement, therefore, seems to turn in a vicious circle, out of which we can only get by supposing a primitive accumulation (previous accumulation of Adam Smith) preceding capitalistic accumulation; an accumulation not the result of the capitalist mode of production, but its starting point. . . .

In actual history it is notorious that conquest, enslavement, robbery, murder, briefly force, play the great part [in primitive accumulation]. As a matter of fact, the methods of primitive accumulation are anything but idyllic.

In themselves, money and commodities are no more capital than are the means of production and of subsistence. They want transforming into capital. But this transformation itself can only take place under certain circumstances that centre in this, viz., that two very different kinds of commodity-possessors must come face to face and into contact; on the one hand, the owners of money, means of production, means of subsistence, who are eager to increase the sum of values they possess, by buying other people's labour-power; on the other hand, free labourers, the sellers of their own labour-power, and therefore the sellers of labour. Free labourers, in the double sense that neither they themselves form part and parcel of the means of production, as in the case of slaves, bondsmen, etc., nor do the means of production belong to them, as in the case of peasant-proprietors; they are, therefore, free from, unencumbered by, any means of production of their own. With this polarisation of the market for commodities, the fundamental conditions of capitalist production are given. The capitalist system presupposes the complete separation of the labourers from all property in the means by which they can realise their labour. As soon as capitalist production is once on its own legs, it not only maintains this separation, but reproduces it on a continually extending scale. The process, therefore, that clears the way for the capitalist system, can be none other than the process which takes away from the labourer the possession of his means of production; a process that transforms, on the one hand, the social means of subsistence and of production into capital, on the other, the immediate producers into wage-labourers. The so-called primitive accumulation, therefore, is nothing else than the historical process of divorcing the producer from the means of production. It appears as primitive, because it forms the pre-historic stage of capital and of the mode of production corresponding with it.

The economic structure of capitalistic society has grown out of the economic structure of feudal society. The dissolution of the latter set free the elements of the former.

The immediate producer, the labourer, could only dispose of his own person after he had ceased to be attached to the soil and ceased to be the slave, serf, or bondman of another. To become a free seller or labour-power, who carries his commodity wherever he finds a market, he must further have escaped from the regime of the guilds, their rules for apprentices and journeymen, and the impediments of their labour regulations. Hence, the historical movement which changes the producers into wage-workers, appears, on the one hand, as their emancipation from serfdom and from the fetters of the guilds, and this side alone exists for our bourgeois historians. But, on the other hand, these new freedmen became sellers of themselves only after they had been robbed of all their own means of production, and of all the guarantees of existence afforded by the old feudal arrangements. And the history of this, their expropriation, is written in the annals of mankind in letters of blood and fire.

The industrial capitalists, these new potentates, had on their part not only to displace the guild masters of handicrafts, but also the feudal lords, the possessors of the sources of wealth. In this respect their conquest of social power appears as the fruit of a victorious struggle both against feudal lordship and its revolting prerogatives, and against the guilds and the fetters they laid on the free development of production and the free exploitation of man by man. The chevaliers d'industrie, however, only succeed in supplanting the chevaliers of the sword by making use of events of which they themselves were wholly innocent. They have risen by means as vile as those by which the Roman freed-man once on a time made himself the master of his *patronus*.

The starting-point of the development that gave rise to the wage-labourer as well as to the capitalist, was the servitude of the labourer. The advance consisted in a change of form of this servitude, in the transformation of feudal exploitation into capitalist exploitation. To understand its march, we need not go back very far. Although we come across the first beginnings of capitalist production as early as the fourteenth or fifteenth century, sporadically, in certain towns of the Mediterranean, the capitalistic era dates from the sixteenth century. Wherever it appears, the abolition of serfdom has been long effected, and the highest development of the middle ages, the existence of sovereign towns, has been long on the wane.

In the history of primitive accumulation, all revolutions are epoch-making that act as levers for the capitalist class in course of formation; but, above all, those moments when great masses of men are suddenly and forcibly torn from their means of subsistence, and hurled as free and "unattached" proletarians on the labour market. The expropriation of the agricultural producer, of the peasant, from the soil, is the basis of the whole process. The history of this expropriation, in different countries, assumes different aspects, and runs through its various phases in different orders of succession, and at different periods. In England alone, which we take as our example, has it the classic form.

Expropriation of the Agricultural Population from the Land

In England, serfdom had practically disappeared in the last part of the fourteenth century. The immense majority of the population consisted then, and to a still larger extent, in the fifteenth century, of free peasant proprietors, whatever was the feudal title under which their right of property was hidden. In the larger seignorial domains, the old bailiff, himself a serf, was displaced by the free farmer. The wage-labourers of agriculture consisted partly of peasants, who utilised their leisure time by working on the large estates, partly of an independent special class of wage-labourers, relatively and absolutely few in numbers. The latter also were practically at the same time peasant farmers, since, besides their wages, they had allotted to them arable land to the extent of four or more acres, together with their cottages. Besides they, with the rest of the peasants, enjoyed the usufruct of the common land, which gave pasture to their cattle, furnished them with timber, fire-wood, turf, etc.[1] . . .

The prelude of the revolution that laid the foundation of the capitalist mode of production, was played in the last third of the fifteenth, and the first decade of the sixteenth century. A mass of free proletarians was hurled on the labour-market by the breaking-up of the bands of feudal retainers. . . . Although the royal power, itself a product of bourgeois development, in its strife after absolute sovereignty forcibly hastened on the dissolution of these bands of retainers, it was by no means the sole cause of it. In insolent conflict with king and parliament, the great feudal lords created an incomparably larger proletariat by the forcible driving of the peasantry from the land, to which the latter had the same feudal right as the lord himself, and by the usurpation of the common lands. The rapid rise of the Flemish wool manufactures, and the corresponding rise in the price of wool in England, gave the direct impulse to these evictions. The old nobility had been devoured by the great feudal wars. The new nobility was the child of its time, for which money was the power of all powers. Transformation of arable land into sheep-walks was, therefore, its cry. . . .

The process of forcible expropriation of the people received in the sixteenth century a new and frightful impulse from the Reformation, and from the consequent colossal spoliation of the church property. The Catholic church was, at the time of the Reformation, feudal proprietor of a great part of the English land. The suppression of the monasteries, etc., hurled their inmates into the proletariat. The estates of the church were to a large extent given away to rapacious royal favourites, or sold at a nominal price to speculating farmers and citizens, who drove out, *en masse,* the hereditary sub-

[1]We must never forget that even the serf was not only the owner, of the piece of land attached to his house, but also a co-possessor of the common land.

tenants and threw their holdings into one. The legally guaranteed property of the poorer folk in a part of the church's tithes was tactily confiscated. . . .

Even in the last decade of the seventeenth century, the yeomanry, the class of independent peasants, were more numerous than the class of farmers. . . . About 1750, the yeomanry had disappeared, and so had, in the last decade of the eighteenth century, the last trace of the common land of the agricultural labourer. We leave on one side here the purely economic causes of the agricultural revolution. We deal only with the forcible means employed.

After the restoration of the Stuarts, the landed proprietors carried, by legal means, an act of usurpation, effected everywhere on the Continent without any legal formality. They abolished the feudal tenure of land, i.e., they got rid of all its obligations to the State, "indemnified" the State by taxes on the peasantry and the rest of the mass of the people, vindicated for themselves the rights of modern private property in estates to which they had only a feudal title, and, finally, passed those laws of settlement, which, *mutatis mutandis,* had the same effect on the English agricultural labourer, as the edict of the Tartar Boris Godunof on the Russian peasantry.

The "glorious Revolution" brought into power, along with William of Orange, the landlord and capitalist appropriators of surplus-value. They inaugurated the new era by practising on a colossal scale thefts of state lands, thefts that had been hitherto managed more modestly. These estates were given away, sold at a ridiculous figure, or even annexed to private estates by direct seizure. All this happened without the slightest observation of legal etiquette. The crown lands thus fraudulently appropriated, together with the robbery of the Church estates, as far as these had not been lost again during the republican revolution, form the basis of the today princely domains of the English oligarchy. The bourgeois capitalists favoured the operation with the view, among others, to promoting free trade in land, to extending the domain of modern agriculture on the large farm-system, and to increasing their supply of the free agricultural proletarians ready to hand. Besides, the new landed aristocracy was the natural ally of the new bankocracy, of the newly-hatched *haute finance,* and of the large manufacturers, then depending on protective duties. . . .

Communal property—always distinct from the State property just dealt with—was an old Teutonic institution which lived on under cover of feudalism. We have seen how the forcible usurpation of this, generally accompanied by the turning of arable into pasture land, begins at the end of the fifteenth and extends into the sixteenth century. But, at that time, the process was carried on by means of individual acts of violence against which legislation, for a hundred and fifty years, fought in vain. The advance made by the eighteenth century shows itself in this, that the law itself becomes now the instrument of the theft of the people's land, although the large farmers make use of their little independent methods as well. The parliamentary form of the robbery is that of Acts for enclosures of Commons, in other words, decrees by which the landlords grant themselves the people's land as private property, decrees of expropriation of the people. . . .

Whilst the place of the independent yeoman was taken by tenants at will, small farmers on yearly leases, a servile rabble dependent on the pleasure of the landlords, the systematic robbery of the Communal lands helped especially, next to the theft of the State domains, to swell those large farms, that were called in the eighteenth century capital farms or merchant farms, and to "set free" the agricultural populations as proletarians for manufacturing industry.

In the nineteenth century, the very memory of the connexion between the agricultural labourer and the communal property had, of course, vanished. To say nothing of more recent times, have the agricultural population received a farthing of compensation for the 3,511,770 acres of common land which between 1801 and 1831 were stolen from them and by parliamentary devices presented to the landlords by the landlords?

The last process of wholesale expropriation of the agricultural population from the soil is, finally, the so-called clearing of estates, i.e., the sweeping men off them. All the English methods hitherto considered culminated in "clearing." . . . But what "clearing of estates" really and properly signifies, we learn only in the promised land of modern romance, the Highlands of Scotland. . . .

In the eighteenth century the hunted-out Gaels were forbidden to emigrate from the country, with a view of driving them by force to Glasgow and other manufacturing towns. As an example of the method obtaining in the nineteenth century, the "clearing" made by the Duchess of Sutherland will suffice here. This person, well instructed in economy, resolved, on entering upon her government, to effect a radical cure, and to turn the whole country, whose population had already been, by earlier processes of the like kind, reduced to 15,000, into a sheep-walk. From 1814 to 1820 these 15,000 inhabitants, about 3000 families, were systematically hunted and rooted out. All their villages were destroyed and burnt, all their fields turned into pasturage. . . . Thus this fine lady appropriated 794,000 acres of land that had from time immemorial belonged to the clan. . . . The whole of the stolen clan-land she divided into 29 great sheep farms, each inhabited by a single family, for the most part imported English farm-servants. In the year 1835 the 15,000 Gaels were already replaced by 131,000 sheep. . . .

The spoliation of the church's property, the fraudulent alienation of the State domains, the robbery of the common lands, the usurpation of feudal and clan property, and its transformation into modern private property under circumstances of reckless terrorism, were just so many idyllic methods of primitive accumulation. They conquered the field for capitalistic agriculture, made the soil part and parcel of capital, and created for the town industries the necessary supply of a "free" and outlawed proletariat.

Bloody Legislation against the Expropriated, from the End of the Fifteenth Century. Forcing Down of Wages by Acts of Parliament.

The proletariat created by the breaking up of the bands of feudal retainers and by the forcible expropriation of the people from the soil, this "free" proletariat could not possibly be absorbed by the nascent manufactures as fast as it was thrown upon the world. On the other hand, these men, suddenly dragged from their wanted mode of life, could not as suddenly adapt themselves to the discipline of their new condition. They were turned *en masse* into beggars, robbers, vagabonds, partly from inclination, in most cases from stress of circumstances. Hence at the end of the fifteenth and during the whole of the sixteenth century, throughout Western Europe a bloody legislation against vagabondage. The fathers of the present working-class were chastised for their enforced transformation into vagabonds and paupers. Legislation treated them as "voluntary" criminals, and assumed that it depended on their own goodwill to go on working under the old conditions that no longer existed. . . .

Thus were the agricultural people, first forcibly expropriated from the soil, driven from their homes, turned into vagabonds, and then whipped, branded, tortured by laws grotesquely terrible, into the discipline necessary for the wage system.

It is not enough that the conditions of labour are concentrated in a mass, in the shape of capital, at the one pole of society, while at the other are grouped masses of men, who have nothing to sell but their labour-power. Neither is it enough that they are compelled to sell it voluntarily. The advance of capitalist production develops a working-class, which by education, tradition, habit, looks upon the conditions of that mode of production as self-evident laws of nature. The organization of the capitalist process of production, once fully developed, breaks down all resistance. The constant generation of a relative surplus-population keeps the law of supply and demand of labour, and therefore keeps wages, in a rut that corresponds with the wants of capital. The dull compulsion of economic relations completes the subjection of the labourer to the capitalist. Direct force, outside economic conditions, is of course still used, but only exceptionally. In the ordinary run of things, the labourer can be left to the "natural laws of production," i.e., to his dependence on capital, a dependence springing from, and guaranteed in perpetuity by, the conditions of production themselves. It is otherwise during the historic genesis of capitalist production. The bourgeoisie, at its rise, wants and uses the power of the state to "regulate" wages, i.e., to force them within the limits suitable for surplus-value making, to lengthen the working-day and to keep the labourer himself in the normal degree of dependence. This is an essential element of the so-called primitive accumulation.

The class of wage-labourers, which arose in the latter half of the fourteenth century, formed then and in the following century only a very small part of the population, well protected in its position by the independent peasant proprietary in the country and the guild-organization in the town. In country and town master and workman stood close together socially. The subordination of labour to capital was only formaly—i.e., the mode of production itself had as yet no specific capitalistic character. Variable capital preponderated greatly over constant. The demand for wage-labour grew, therefore, rapidly with every accumulation of capital, whilst the supply of wage-labour followed but slowly. A large part of the national product, changed later into a fund of capitalist accumulation, then still entered into the consumption fund of the labourer.

Legislation of wage-labour, (from the first, aimed at the exploitation of the labourer and, as it advanced, always equally hostile to him), is started in England by the Statute of Labourers, of Edward III., 1349. . . . Coalition of the labourers is treated as a heinous crime from the fourteenth century to 1825, the year of the repeal of the laws against Trades' Unions. The spirit of the Statute of Labourers of 1349 and of its offshoots, comes out clearly in the fact, that indeed a maximum of wages is dictated by the State, but on no account a minimum.

In the sixteenth century, the condition of the labourers had . . . become much worse. The money wage rose, but not in proportion to the depreciation of money and the corresponding rise in the prices of commodities. Wages, therefore, in reality fell. Nevertheless, the laws for keeping them down remained in force, together with the ear-clipping and branding of those "whom no one was willing to take into service." . . .

Genesis of the Capitalist Farmer

Now that we have considered the forcible creation of a class of outlawed proletarians, the bloody discipline that turned them into wage-labourers, the disgraceful action of the state which employed the police to accelerate the accumulation of capital by increasing the degree of exploitation of labour, the question remains: whence came the capitalists originally? For the expropriation of the agricultural population creates, directly, none by great landed proprietors. As far, however, as concerns the genesis of the farmer, we can, so to say, put our hand on it, because it is a slow process evolving through many centuries. The serfs, as well as the free small proprietors, held land under very different tenures, and were therefore emancipated under very different economic conditions. In England the first form of the farmer is the bailiff, himself a serf. . . . During the second half of the fourteenth century he is replaced by a farmer, whom the landlord provides with seed, cattle and implements. His condition is not very different from that of the peasant. Only he exploits more wage-labour. Soon he becomes a métayer, a half-farmer. He advances one part of the agricultural stock, the landlord the other. The two divide the total product in proportions determined by contract. This form quickly disappears in England, to give place to the farmer proper, who makes his own capital breed by employing wage-labourers, and pays a part of the surplus product, in money or in kind, to the landlord as rent. So long, during the fifteenth century, as the independent peasant and the farm-labourer working for himself as well as for wages, enriched themselves by their own labour, the circumstances of the farmer, and his field of production, were equally mediocre. The agricultural revolution which commenced in the last third of the fifteenth century, and continued during almost the whole of the sixteenth (excepting, however, its last decade), enriched him just as speedily as it impoverished the mass of the agricultural people.

The usurpation of the common lands allowed him to augment greatly his stock of cattle, almost without cost, whilst they yielded him a richer supply of manure for the tillage of the soil. To this, was added in the sixteenth century, a very important element. At that time the contracts for farms ran for a long time, often for 99 years. The progressive fall in the value of the precious metals, and therefore of money, brought the farmers golden fruit. Apart from all the other circumstances discussed above, it lowered wages. A portion of the latter was now added to the profits of the farm. The continuous rise in the price of corn, wool, meat, in a word of all agricultural produce, swelled the money capital of the farmer without any action on his part, whilst the rent he paid, (being calculated on the old value of money) diminished in reality. Thus they grew rich at the expense both of their labourers and their landlords. No wonder therefore, that England, at the end of the sixteenth century, had a class of capitalist farmers, rich, considering the circumstances of the time.

Reaction of the Agricultural Revolution on Industry. Creation of the Home Market for Industrial Capital.

The thinning-out of the independent, self-supporting peasants not only brought about the crowding together of the industrial proletariat. . . . In spite of the smaller numbers of its cultivators, the soil brought forth as much or more produce, after as before, because the revolution in the conditions of landed property was accompanied by improved methods of culture, greater cooperation, concentration of the means of production, etc., and because not only were the agricultural wage-labourers put on the strain more intensely, but the field of production on which they worked for themselves, became more and more contracted. With the setting free of a part of the agricultural population, therefore, their former means of nourishment were also set free. They were now transformed into material elements of variable capital. The peasant, expropriated and cast adrift, must buy their value in the form of wages, from his new master, the industrial capitalist. That which holds good of the means of subsistence holds with the raw materials of industry dependent upon home agriculture. They were transformed into an element of constant capital. . . . The expropriation and eviction of a part of the agricultural population not only set free for industrial capital, the labourers, their means of subsistence, and material for labour; it also created the home market.

In fact, the events that transformed the small peasants into wage-labourers, and their means of subsistence and of labour into material elements of capital, created, at the same time, a home-market for the latter. Formerly, the peasant family produced the means of subsistence and the raw materials, which they themselves, for the most part, consumed. These raw materials and means of subsistence have now become commodities; the large farmer sells them, he finds his market in manufactures. Yarn, linen, coarse woollen stuffs—things whose raw materials had been within the reach of every peasant family, had been spun and woven by it for its own use—were now transformed into articles of manufacture, to which the country districts at once served for markets. The many scattered customers, whom stray artisans until now had found in the numerous small producers working on their own account, concentrate themselves now into one great market provided for by industrial capital. Thus, hand in hand with the expropriation of the self-supporting peasants, with their separation from their means of production, goes the destruction of rural domestic industry, the process of separation between manufacture and agriculture. And only the destruction of rural domestic industry can give the internal market of a country that extension and consistence which the capitalist mode of production requires. ... Modern Industry alone, and finally, supplies, in machinery, the lasting basis of capitalistic agriculture, expropriates radically the enormous majority of the agricultural population, and completes the separation between agriculture and rural domestic industry, whose roots—spinning and weaving—it tears up. It therefore also, for the first time, conquers for industrial capital the entire home market.

Genesis of the Industrial Capitalist

The genesis of the industrial[1] capitalist did not proceed in such a gradual way as that of the farmer. Doubtless many small guild-masters, and yet more independent small artisans, or even wage-labourers, transformed themselves into small capitalists, and (by gradually extending exploitation of wage-labour and corresponding accumulation) into full-blown capitalists. ... The snail's-pace of this method corresponded in no wise with the commercial requirements of the new world-market that the great discoveries of the end of the fifteenth century created. But the middle age had handed down two distinct forms of capital, which mature in the most different economic social formations, and which, before the circumflex era of the capitalist mode of production, are considered as capital quand même—usurer's capital and merchant's capital. ...

The money capital formed by means of usury and commerce was prevented from turning into industrial capital, in the country by the feudal constitution, in the towns by the guild organization. These fetters vanished with the dissolution of feudal society, with the expropriation and partial eviction of the country population. The new manufacturers were established at sea-ports, or in inland points beyond the control of the old municipalities and their guilds. Hence in England an embittered struggle of the corporate towns against these new industrial nurseries.

The discovery of gold and silver in America, the extirpation, enslavement and entombment in mines of the aboriginal population, the beginning of the conquest and looting of the East Indies, the turning of Africa into a warren for the commercial hunting of black-skins, signalised the rosy dawn of the era of capitalist production. These idyllic proceedings are the chief momenta of primitive accumulation. On their heels treads the commercial war of the European nations, with the globe for a theatre. It begins with the revolt of the Netherlands from Spain, assumes giant dimensions in England's anti-jacobin war, and is still going on in the opium wars against China, etc.

The different momenta of primitive accumulation distribute themselves now, more or less in chronological order, particularly over Spain, Portugal, Holland, France, and England. In England at the end of the seventeenth century, they arrive at a systematical combination, embracing the colonies, the

[1]Industrial here in contradistinction to agricultural. In the "categoric" sense the farmer is an industrial capitalist as much as the manufacturer.

national debt, the modern mode of taxation, and the protectionist system. These methods depend in part on brute force, e.g., the colonial system. But they all employ the power of the State, the concentrated and organised force of society, to hasten, hothouse fashion, the process of transformation of the feudal mode of production into the capitalist mode, and to shorten the transition. Force is the midwife of every old society pregnant with a new one. It is itself an economic power. . . .

The system of protection was an artificial means of manufacturing manufacturers, of expropriating independent labourers, of capitalising the national means of production and subsistence, of forcibly abbreviating the transition from the medieval to the modern mode of production. The European states tore one another to pieces about the patent of this invention, and, once entered into the service of the surplus-value makers, did not merely lay under contribution in the pursuit of this purpose their own people, indirectly through protective duties, directly through export premiums. They also forcibly rooted out, in their dependent countries, all industry, as, e.g., England did with the Irish woollen manufacture. . . .

Colonial system, public debts, heavy taxes, protection, commercial wars, etc., these children of the true manufacturing period, increase gigantically during the infancy of Modern Industry. The birth of the latter is heralded by a great slaughter of the innocents. Like the royal navy, the factories were recruited by means of the press-gang. . . . Child-stealing and child-slavery [were necessary] for the transformation of manufacturing exploitation into factory exploitation, and the establishment of the "true relation" between capital and labour-power. . . .

Whilst the cotton industry introduced child-slavery in England, it gave in the United States a stimulus to the transformation of the earlier, more or less patriarchal slavery, into a system of commercial exploitation. In fact, the veiled slavery of the wage-earners in Europe needed, for its pedestal, slavery pure and simple in the new world. . . .

To establish the "eternal laws of Nature" of the capitalist mode of production, [it was necessary to] complete the process of separation between labourers and conditions of labour, to transform, at one pole, the social means of production and subsistence into capital, at the opposite pole, the mass of the population into wage-labourers, into "free labouring poor," that artificial product of modern society. If money, according to Augier, "comes into the world with a congenital blood-stain on one cheek," capital comes dripping from head to foot, from every pore, with blood and dirt.

Marx, *Capital,* I (1867), chaps. 26–31 (excerpted).

2 Capitalism's Institutional Structure and Social Relations

What are the basic, identifying characteristics of capitalist economy? In the popular view, illustrated by most American dictionaries, capitalism is associated with private, rather than governmental, ownership of the means of production. But this immediately raises a number of questions, quite apart from those connected with the separation of legal titular ownership from actual managerial control, as, for example, in large-scale corporations. First, if the privateness of ownership is the distinguishing characteristic of capitalism, then feudalism—the dominant form of economic organization in medieval Europe—is simply a subspecies of capitalism. Feudalism, after all, was characterized by the private control of land by the feudal lord and the private cultivation of land by the serf-peasant, who typically owned his own simple tools and animals. And what about the mom and pop grocery store or family farm, run entirely by the owner and his family? Are they "capitalists" merely by virtue of their ownership? Second, is ownership the *exclusive* criterion for identifying systems of economy? Are there no others? Third, can capitalism be properly understood, even in brief definition, apart from social relations among people? Was Robinson Crusoe, for example, a capitalist simply because he used "capital goods"?

Marx's approach to these complex issues was to focus sharply upon the social relations among men in the process of production. Capitalism, indeed "capital" itself, is, for Marx, a social relation. (This immediately eliminates the Robinson Crusoe economy from the running, because at least prior to Friday's arrival, social relations were nonexistent.) The central characteristic of capitalism, then, is a social relation between a relatively small number of capitalists and a relatively and absolutely large number of workers. Both are private owners, the capitalists of the physical means of production, the workers of their capacity to labor. But it is the division of society into the two groups of private owners, rather than the privateness of the ownership per se, that is the crucial point.

Because workers do not own physical means of production, they must, to earn a living, work for the capitalists, who do own the factories, mines, farms, and other places of production and employment. But because the workers own their own labor power and are free to move about at will, capitalists must use economic means to attract workers to work for them rather than the physical coercion and other forms of noneconomic control found in systems of slave or serf labor. In short, capitalism is characterized by market exchange. On the one hand, workers sell their labor power, for a certain period of time during the workday or workweek, in exchange for wages. On the other hand, capitalists sell their outputs of commodities, produced for market exchange, notably, though not exclusively, to workers in exchange for money.

Once inside the factory and at work in the process of production, however, the social connection between capitalists and worker reverts from that of respective private owners to that of a master-servant relationship. The capitalist is the employer and thereby the "boss." He, or his delegate, decides what to produce and how to produce it, organizes, combines, divides, and coordinates labor, determines investment and technology policies, and markets the products of the enterprise. The sole ownership claim of the worker, leaving aside such contemporary refinements as profit sharing and the like, is his wage.

In brief, Marx's definition of capitalism's institutional structure focuses upon social relations, and has three main properties: (1) the social process of market exchange, both on labor markets and markets for final products, wherein workers and capitalists interact as free and equal private owners and exchangers; (2) the division of society's (typically private) owners of economic resources into a small group of capitalists owning physical means of production, and a much larger group of workers owning their own labor power but lacking ownership of physical means of production; (3) the social process of production, wherein the capital-labor relation becomes a master-servant relationship, and the capitalist is in control of the production process and the organization and division of labor. Each of these elements of capitalism will now be considered in turn.

A. COMMODITIES AND MARKET EXCHANGE

Capitalism is a market exchange economy; indeed, it universalized market exchange throughout the entire world and spread the exchange process and monetary calculation from markets for consumption goods to markets for labor power, machinery, factories, and land as well. But not all exchange economies are capitalist. Failure to understand this point can be a source of considerable confusion, as in the common tendency to extend the principles of a simple exchange economy to the more complicated phenomena of a modern industrial capitalist exchange economy.

Marx's method of dealing with this confusion, as implied by the preceding sentence, is to distinguish between "simple commodity production," or a simple exchange economy, and the more complex capitalist exchange economy. The distinction is partly historical, for Marx perceives simple exchange economy as a kind of transition stage between feudalism and capitalism. But the distinction is largely a methodological device to sharpen and clarify the conception and analysis of capitalism by perceiving an exchange economy, but abstracting from its uniquely capitalist features. Both simple commodity production and capitalism are exchange economies; that is, in both, products are produced as "commodities" for market exchange. But in simple commodity production, exchange is restricted to the goods market, because the small peasant and artisan proprietors are private owners of both their own farms or shops *and* of their own labor power. There are no separate classes of capitalists and workers because work and individual ownership coalesce. In capitalism, exchange is extended to the labor market as well as to the goods market, because work and ownership of the physical means of production have become separated, with a consequent separation of worker and capitalist. In effect, the simple exchange economy is

Marx's version of Adam Smith's "early and rude state of society" prior to the accumulation of capital and private appropriation of land. In Ronald Meek's apt phrase, it is a useful kind of "mythodology."[1]

Marx uses this distinction between types of exchange economy, and the corollary distinction between the exchange process and the production process within capitalist economy, in several ways. First, as is described in selection 2.A.1, the exchange economy is characterized by or at least gives a very strong impression of freedom and equality of market participants. In the "depths," however, beneath this "surface process," "entirely different processes go on, in which this apparent individual equality and liberty disappear." Second, as is discussed in selection 2.A.2, the distinction between the two types of exchange economy (and between exchange and production) is paralleled by a distinction between market power and property power. Under free competition, market power is negligible. But competition, although the basis for freedom from the restrictions of guild and government regulation, is at the same time the institutional form most suitable for the development and dominion of capital, that is, of property power. Thus, competition is not the "final" or "absolute" form of individual freedom. Third, the exchange process under capitalism is extended to the labor market, a "very Eden of the innate rights of man." This exchange process, however, differs radically from that under simple commodity production, because the exchange of labor power rests on the worker's propertylessness (Selection 2.A.3). Next, Marx explains that money and exchange are connected with capital and production (selection 2.A.4). In an economy where products are produced for direct use, market exchange is nonexistent or negligible. In a barter economy, commodities (C) are directly exchanged for one another: C-C. In a simple money exchange economy, commodities are exchanged for money (M) which in turn is used to purchase other commodities: C-M-C. Under capitalism, the circulation of commodities and money is reversed: M-C-M. This is connected with capital because "the first form of appearance of capital is money."

Finally, in selection 2.A.5, Marx relates market exchange to the phenomenon of "value." This topic has undoubtedly elicited greater controversy and discussion than any other single element in Marx's economic analysis of capitalism. Selection 5.C.10 examines how Marx's theory of value relates to such topics as exploitation, surplus value, competition, and prices. This selection is at a much higher level of abstraction and focuses on the relations of value to society's institutional structure and social relations. On the one hand, Marx argues, in a market exchange economy, "labour is represented by the value of its product and labour time by the magnitude of that value" (see selection 4.A.1, below). On the other hand, abstracting from use value, i.e., the relationship between people and commodities whereby commodities yield utility and satisfy human wants, the "common property" of commodities, qualitatively, is that they are "products of labour." Indeed, because market exchange is indifferent to the various specific forms of labour, we may speak of "human labour in the abstract," and, quantitatively, may differentiate commodities in accord with the relative magnitudes of general abstract labor required to produce them, that is, with the respective portions of society's labor power allocated to their production. In general, Marx concludes, the "value of one commodity is to the value of any other, as the labour-time necessary for the production of the one is to that necessary for the production of the other."

[1] "Karl Marx's Economic Method," in *Economics and Ideology* (London: Chapman and Hall, 1967), p. 98.

The quantitative aspects of this analysis can be most easily seen in a simple exchange economy, or in Adam Smith's "early and rude state of society." There, profit and wages would have no meaning, and it would seem intuitively evident that the relative equilibrium exchange values or relative prices of any pair of commodities (deer and beavers, in Smith's example) would be determined primarily if not exclusively by the relative amounts of labor time required to produce the commodities. Marx extends this argument to capitalist exchange through the use of a series of simplifying assumptions.[2] At this point in the analysis, the most important of these assumptions may be derived by noting Marx's distinction between the early stage of manufacturing capitalism and the later stage of "modern industry." Under manufacturing capitalism, the competitive exchange process has proceeded to the point of equalizing profit rates *within* industries, but resources are *not yet fully*, competitively mobile *between* industries. Later, under industrial capitalism, competition extends to relations between as well as within industries. The point of the distinction, for our purposes here, is that in the earlier stage of manufacturing capitalism, technological conditions, and thus the ratio of capital to labor, will be essentially the same among the different enterprises within a given industry. Consequently, relative exchange values will not be shifted about in one direction or another because of different amounts of capital per worker. And when competition has done its work—that is, has equalized profit rates among enterprises and equalized wage rates for workers of any given skill—relative exchange values will once again equal or at least approximate the relative amounts of labor time required for the production of the various commodities.

All of this, it should be emphasized, rests upon a number of simplifying assumptions, the specification of which we have omitted in the interest of brevity. And none of this should be taken to imply that Marx denies a strategic role for other forces in the determination of "use value" or wealth, as distinguished from "value" in his sense of the term, perceived as the "common substance" of "exchange values." Generally speaking, Marx explains, value varies directly with the quantity of labor and inversely with labor's productivity. Consequently, labor skills, science, technology, machinery, and social organization all affect value indirectly, through labor productivity.

2.A.1 SIMPLE EXCHANGE ECONOMY AND CAPITALIST EXCHANGE ECONOMY

As we have seen, in simple circulation as such (exchange value in its movement), the action of the individuals on one another is, in its content, only a reciprocal, self-interested satisfaction of their needs; in its form, [it is] exchange among equals (equivalents). Property, too, is still posited here only as the appropriation of the product of labour by labour, and of the product of alien labour by one's own labour, in so far as the product of one's own labour is bought by alien labour. Property in alien labour is mediated by the equivalent of one's own labour. This form of property—quite like freedom and

[2] See, e.g., John E. Elliott, *Comparative Economic Systems* (Englewood Cliffs: Prentice-Hall, 1973), Chap. 5.

equality—is posited in this simple relation. In the further development of exchange value this will be transformed, and it will ultimately be shown that private property is the product of one's own labour is identical with the separation of labour and property, so that labour will create alien property and property will command alien labour. ...

The special difficulty in grasping money in its fully developed character as money...is that a social relation, a definite relation between individuals, here appears as a metal, a stone, as a purely physical external thing which can be found, as such, in nature, and which is indistinguishable in form from its natural existence. Gold and silver, in and of themselves, are not money. Nature does not produce money, any more than it produces a rate of exchange or a banker. In Peru and Mexico gold and silver did not serve as money, although it does appear here as jewellery, and there is a developed system of production. To be money is not a natural attribute of gold and silver, and is therefore quite unknown to the physicist, chemist etc. as such. But money is directly gold and silver. ... To the degree to which opposition against the ruling relations of production grows, and these latter themselves push ever more forcibly to cast off their old skin—to that degree, polemics are directed against metallic money or money in general, as the most striking, most contradictory and hardest phenomenon which is presented by the system in a palpable form. One or another kind of artful tinkering with money is then supposed to overcome the contradictions of which money is merely the perceptible appearance. Equally clear that some revolutionary operations can be performed with money, in so far as an attack on it seems to leave everything else as it was, and only to rectify it. ... As long as these operations are directed against money as such, they are merely an attack on consequences whose causes remain unaffected, i.e. disturbance of the productive process, whose solid basis then also has the power, by means of a more or less violent reaction, to define and to dominate these as mere passing *disturbances*.

On the other hand, it is in the character of the money relation—as far as it is developed in its purity to this point, and without regard to more highly developed relations of production—that all inherent contradictions of bourgeois society appear extinguished in money relations as conceived in a simple form; and bourgeois democracy even more than the bourgeois economists takes refuge in this aspect (the latter are at least consistent enough to regress to even simpler aspects of exchange value and exchange) in order to construct apologetics for the existing economic relations. Indeed, in so far as the commodity or labour is conceived of only as exchange value, and the relation in which the various commodities are brought into connection with one another is conceived as the exchange of these exchange values with one another, as their equation, then the individuals, the subjects between whom this process goes on, are simply and only conceived of as exchangers. As far as the formal character is concerned, there is absolutely no distinction between them and this is the economic character, the aspect in which they stand towards one another in the exchange relation; it is the indicator of their social function or social relation towards one another. Each of the subjects is an exchanger, i.e. each has the same social relation towards the other that the other has towards him. As subjects of exchange, their relation is therefore that of *equality*. It is impossible to find any trace of distinction, not to speak of contradiction, between them; not even a difference. Furthermore, the commodities which they exchange are, as exchange values, equivalent, or at least count as such (the most that could happen would be a subjective error in the reciprocal appraisal of values, and if one individual, say, cheated the other, this would *happen not because of the nature of the social function in which they confront one another,* for this is *the same*, in this they are *equal*; but only because of natural cleverness, persuasiveness etc., in short only the purely individual superiority of one individual over another. The difference would be one of natural origin, irrelevant to the nature of the relation as such, and it may be said in anticipation of further development, the difference is even lessened and robbed of its original force by competition etc.). As regards the pure form, the economic side of this relation—the content, outside this form, here still falls entirely outside economics, or is posited as a natural content distinct from the economic, a content about which it may be said that it is still entirely separated from the economic relation because it still directly coincides with it—then only three moments emerge as formally distinct: the subjects of the relation, *the exchangers* (posited in the same character); the objects of their exchange, exchange values, *equivalents*, which not only are equal but are expressly supposed to be equal, and are posited as equal; and finally the act of exchange itself, the mediation by which the subjects are posited as exchangers, equals, and their objects as equivalents, equals. The equivalents are the objectification of one subject for another, i.e. they themselves are of equal worth, and assert themselves in the act of exchange as equally worthy, and at the same time as mutually indifferent. The subjects in exchange exist for one another only through these equivalents, as of equal worth, and prove themselves to be such through the exchange of the objectivity in which the one exists for the other. Since they only exist for one another in exchange in this way, as equally worthy persons, possessors of equivalent things, who thereby prove their equivalence, they are, as equals, at the same time also indifferent to one another; whatever other individual distinction there may be does not concern them; they are indifferent to all their other individual peculiarities. . . . Only the differences between their needs and between their production gives rise to exchange and to their social equation in exchange; these natural differences are therefore the precondition of their social equality in the act of exchange, and of this relation in general, in which they relate to one another as productive. . . . Further. In so far as these natural differences among individuals and among their commodities (products, labour etc. are not as yet indifferent here, but exist only in the form of commodities) . . . form the motive for the integration of these individuals, for their social interrelation as exchangers, in which they are *stipulated* for each other as, and *prove* themselves to be, equals, there enters, in addition to the quality of equality, that of *freedom*. Although individual A feels a need for the commodity of individual B, he does not appropriate it by force, nor vice versa, but rather they recognize one another reciprocally as proprietors, as persons whose will penetrates their commodities. Accordingly, the juridical moment of the Person enters here, as well as that of freedom, in so far as it is contained in the former. No one seizes hold of another's property by force. Each divests himself of his property voluntarily. But this is not all: individual A serves the need of individual B by means of the commodity *a* only in so far as and because individual B serves the need of individual A by means of the commodity *b*, and vice versa. Each serves the other in order to serve himself; each makes use of the other, reciprocally, as his means. Now both things are contained in the consciousness of the two individuals: (1) ... each arrives at his end only in so far as he serves the other as means; (2) ... each becomes means for the other (being for another) only as end in himself (being for self); ...(3) this reciprocity is a necessary fact, presupposed as natural precondition of exchange, but, ... as such, it is irrelevant to each of the two subjects in exchange. That is, the common interest which appears as the motive of the act as a whole is recognized as a fact by both sides; but, as such, it is not the motive, but rather proceeds, as it were, behind the back of these self-reflected particular interests, behind the back of one individual's interest in opposition to that of the other. In this last respect, the individual can at most have the consoling awareness that the satisfaction of his antithetical individual interest is precisely the realization of the suspended antithesis, of the social, general interest. Out of the act of exchange itself, the individual, each one of them, is reflected in himself as its exclusive and dominant (determinant) subject. With that, then, the complete freedom of the individual is posited: voluntary transaction; no force on either side; positing of the self as means, or as serving, only as means, in order to posit the self as end in itself, as dominant and primary; finally, the self-seeking interest which brings nothing of a higher order to realization; the other is also recognized and acknowledged as one who likewise realizes his self-seeking interest, so that both know that the common interest exists only in the duality, many-sidedness, and autonomous development of the exchanges between self-seeking interests. The general interest is precisely the generality of self-seeking interests. Therefore, when the economic form, exchange, posits the all-sided equality of its subjects, then the content, the individual as well as the objective material which drives towards the exchange, is *freedom*. Equality and freedom are thus not only respected in exchange based on exchange values but, also, the exchange of exchange values is the productive, real basis of all *equality* and *freedom*. As pure ideas they are merely the idealized expressions of this basis; as developed in juridical, political, social relations, they are merely this basis to a higher power. And so it has been in history. Equality and freedom as developed to this extent are exactly the opposite of the freedom and equality in the world of antiquity, where developed exchange value was not their basis, but where, rather, the development of that basis destroyed them. Equality and freedom presuppose relations of production as yet unrealized in the ancient world and in the Middle Ages. Direct forced labour is the foundation of the ancient world; the community rests on this as its foundation; labour itself as a 'privilege,' as still particularized, not yet generally producing exchange values, is the basis of the world of the Middle Ages. Labour is neither forced labour; nor, as in the second case, does it take place with respect to a common, higher unit (the guild).

Now, it is admittedly correct that the [relation between those] engaged in exchange, in so far as their motives are concerned, i.e. as regards natural motives falling outside the economic process, does also rest on a certain compulsion; but this is, on one side, itself only the other's indifference to my need as such, to my natural individuality, hence his equality with me and his freedom, which are at the same time the precondition of my own; on the other side, if I am determined, forced, by my needs, it is only my nature, this totality of needs and drives, which exerts a force upon me; it is nothing alien (or, my *interest* posited in a general, reflected form). But it is, after all, precisely in this way that I exercise compulsion over the other and drive him into the exchange system. . . .

Since money is only the realization of exchange value, and since the system of exchange values has realized itself only in a developed money system, or inversely, the money system can indeed only be the realization of this system of freedom and equality. . . . Finally, even equality now posits itself tangibly, in money as medium of circulation, where it appears now in one hand, now in another, and is indifferent to this appearance. Each appears towards the other as an owner of money, and, as regards the process of exchange, as money itself. . . . A worker who buys commodities for 3s. appears to the seller in the same function, in the same equality—in the form of 3s.—as the king who does the same. All distinction between them is extinguished. . . . In so far as money here appears as the material, as the general commodity of contracts, all distinction between the contracting parties is, rather, extinguished. In so far as money, the general form of wealth, becomes the object of accumulation, the subject here appears to withdraw it from circulation only to the extent that he does not withdraw commodities of an equal price from circulation. Thus, if one individual accumulates and the other does not, then none does it at the expense of the other. One enjoys real wealth, the other takes possession of wealth in its general form. If one grows impoverished and the other grows wealthier, then this is of their own free will and does not in any way arise from economic relation, the economic connection as such, in which they are placed in relation to one another. Even inheritance and similar legal relations, which perpetuate such inequalities, do not prejudice this natural freedom and equality. If individual A's relation is not in contradiction to this system originally, then such a contradiction can surely not arise from the fact that individual B steps into the place of individual A, thus perpetuating him. This is, rather, the perpetuation of the social relation beyond one man's natural lifespan: its reinforcement against the chance influences of nature, whose effects as such would in fact be a suspension of individual freedom. Moreover, since the individual in this relation is merely the individuation of money, therefore he is, as such, just as immortal as money, and his representation by heirs is the logical extension of this role.

If this way of conceiving the matter is not advanced in its historic context, but is instead raised as a refutation of the more developed economic relations in which individuals relate to one another no longer merely as exchangers or as buyers and sellers, but in specific relations, no longer all of the same character; then it is the same as if it were asserted that there is no difference, to say nothing of antithesis and contradiction, between natural bodies, because all of them, when looked at from, e.g. the point of view of their weight, have weight, and are therefore equal; or are equal because all of them occupy three dimensions. Exchange value itself is here similarly seized upon in its simple character, as the antithesis to its more developed, contradictory forms. In the course of science, it is just these abstract attributes which appear as the earliest and sparsest; they appear in part historically in this fashion, too; the more developed as the more recent. In present bourgeois society as a whole, this positing of prices and their circulation etc. appears as the surface process, beneath which, however, in the depths, entirely different processes go on, in which this apparent individual equality and liberty disappear. It is forgotten, on one side, that the *presupposition* of exchange value, as the objective basis of the whole of the system of production, already in itself implies compulsion over the individual, since his immediate product is not a product for him, but only *becomes* such in the social process, and since it *must* take on this general but nevertheless external form; and that the individual has an existence only as a producer of exchange value, hence that the whole negation of his natural existence is already implied; that he is therefore entirely determined by society; that this further presupposes a division of labour etc., in which the individual is already posited in relations other than that of mere *exchanger,* etc. That therefore this presupposition by no means arises either out of the individual's will or out of the immediate nature of the individual, but that is, rather, *historical,* and posits the individual as already *determined* by society. It is forgotten, on the other side, that these higher forms, in which exchange, or the relations of production which realize themselves in it, are now posited, do not by any means stand still in this simple form where the highest distinction which occurs is a formal and hence irrelevant one. What is overlooked, finally, is that already the simple forms of exchange value and of money latently contain the opposition between labour and capital etc. Thus, what all this wisdom comes down to is the attempt to stick fast at the simplest economic relations, which conceived by themselves, are pure abstractions; but these relations are, in reality, mediated by the deepest antithesis, and represent only one side, in which the full expression of the antitheses is obscured.

What this reveals, on the other side, is the foolishness of those socialists (namely the French, who want to depict socialism as the realization of the ideals of *bourgeois* society articulated by the French revolution) who demonstrate that exchange and exchange value etc. are *originally* (in time) or *essentially* (in their adequate form) a system of universal freedom and equality, but that they have been perverted by money, capital etc. Or, also, that history has so far failed in every attempt to implement them in their true manner, but that they have now, like Proudhon, discovered, e.g. the real Jacob, and intend now to supply the genuine history of these relations in place of the fake. The proper reply to them is: that exchange value or, more precisely, the money system is in fact the system of equality and freedom, and that the disturbances which they encounter in the further development of the system are disturbances inherent in it, are merely the realization of *equality and freedom,* which prove to be inequality and unfreedom. It is just as pious as it is stupid to wish that exchange value would not develop into capital, nor labour which produces exchange value into wage labour. What divides these gentlemen from the bourgeois apologists is, on one side, their sensitivity to the contradictions included in the system; on the other, the utopian inability to grasp the necessary difference between the real and the ideal form of bourgeois society, which is the cause of their desire to undertake the superfluous business of realizing the ideal expression again, which is in fact only the inverted projection of this reality. And now, indeed, in opposition to these socialists there is the stale argumentation of the degenerate economics of most recent times . . . *which demonstrates* that economic relations everywhere express *the same* simple determinants, and hence that they everywhere express the equality and freedom of the simple exchange of exchange values; this point entirely reduces itself to an infantile abstraction. For example, the relation between capital and interest is reduced to the exchange of exchange values. Thus, after first taking from the empirical world the fact that exchange value exists not only in this simple form but also in the essentially different form of capital, capital is then in turn reduced again to the simple concept of exchange value; and interest, which, to crown all, expresses a specific relation of capital as such, is similarly torn out of this specificity and equated with exchange value; the whole relation in its specific character is reduced to an abstraction and everything reduced to the undeveloped relation of commodity exchange. In so far as I abstract from what distinguishes a concrete from its abstract, it is of course the abstract, and does not differ from it at all. *According to this, all economic categories are only so many names for what is always the same relation, and this crude inability to grasp the real distinctions is then supposed to represent pure common sense as such. . . .*

Marx, *GRUNDRISSE* (1857–58), pp. 238–49.

2.A.2. COMPETITION AND EXCHANGE

Because competition appears historically as the dissolution of compulsory guild membership, government regulation, internal tariffs and the like within a country, as the lifting of blockades, prohibitions, protection on the world market—because it appears historically, in short, as the negation of the limits and barriers peculiar to the stages of production preceding capital; because it was quite correctly, from the historical standpoint, designated and promoted by the Physiocrats as *laissez faire, laissez passer;* it has [therefore] never been examined even for this merely negative side, this, its merely historical side, and this has led at the same time to the even greater absurdity of regarding it as the collision of unfettered individuals who are determined only by their own interests—as the mutual repulsion and attraction of free individuals, and hence as the absolute mode of existence of free individuality in the sphere of consumption and of exchange. Nothing can be more mistaken. While free competition has dissolved the barriers of earlier relations and modes of production, it is necessary to observe first of all that the things which were a barrier to it were the inherent limits of earlier modes of production, within which they spontaneously developed and moved. These limits became barriers only after the forces of production and the relations of intercourse had developed sufficiently to enable capital as such to emerge as the dominant principle of production. The limits which it tore down were barriers to its motion, its development and realization. It is by no means the case that it thereby suspended all limits, nor all barriers, but rather only the limits not corresponding to it, which were barriers to it. Within its own limits—however much they may appear as barriers from a higher standpoint, and are posited as such by its own historic development—it feels free, and free of barriers, i.e. as limited only by itself, only by its own conditions of life. Exactly as guild industry, in its heyday, found in the guild organization all the fullness of freedom it required, i.e. the relations of production corresponding to it. After all, it posited these out of itself, and developed them as *its* inherent conditions, and hence in no way as external and constricting barriers. The historical side of the negation of the guild system etc. by capital through free competition signifies nothing more than that capital, having become sufficiently strong, by means of the mode of intercourse adequate to itself, tore down the historic barriers which hindered and blocked the movement adequate to it. But competition is very far from having only this historic significance, or merely being *this negative* force. *Free competition* is the relation of capital to itself as another capital, i.e. the conduct of capital as capital. The inner laws of capital—which appear merely as tendencies in the preliminary historic stages of its development—are for the first time posited as laws; production founded on capital for the first time posits itself in the forms adequate to it only in so far as and to the extent that free competition develops, for it is the free development of the mode of production founded on capital; the free development of its conditions and of itself as the process which constantly reproduces these conditions. It is not individuals who are set free by free competition; it is, rather, capital which is set free. As long as production resting on capital is the necessary, hence the fittest form for the development of the force of social production, the movement of individuals within the pure conditions of capital appears as their freedom; which is then also again dogmatically propounded as such through constant reflection back on the barriers torn down by free competition. Free competition is the real development of capital. By its means, what corresponds to the nature of capital is posited as external necessity for the individual capital; what corresponds to the concept of capital, is posited as external necessity for the mode of production founded on capital. The reciprocal compulsion which the capitals within it practise upon one another, on labour etc. (the competition among workers is only another form of the competition among capitals), is the *free,* at the same time the *real* development of wealth as capital. So much is this the case that the most profound economic thinkers, such as e.g. Ricardo, *presuppose* the absolute predominance of free competition in order to be able to study and to formulate the adequate laws of capital—which appear at the same time as the vital tendencies governing over it. But free competition is the adequate form of the productive process of capital. The further it is developed, the purer the forms in which its motion appear. What Ricardo has thereby admitted, despite himself, is the *historic nature* of capital, and the limited character of free competition, which is just the free movement of capitals and nothing else. i.e. their movement within conditions which belong to no previous, dissolved stages, but are its own conditions. The predominance of capital is the presupposition of free competition, just as the despotism of the Roman Caesars was the presupposition of the free Roman 'private law.' As long as capital is weak, it still itself relies on the crutches of past modes of production, or of those which will pass with its rise. As soon as it feel strong, it throws away the crutches, and moves in accordance with its own laws. As soon as it begins to sense itself and become conscious of itself as a barrier to development, it seeks refuge in forms which, by restricting free competition, seem to make the rule of capital more perfect, but are at the same time the heralds of its dissolution and of the dissolution of the mode of production resting on it. Competition merely *expresses* as real, posits as an external necessity, that which lies within the nature of capital; competition is nothing more than the way in which the many capitals force the inherent determinants of capital upon one another and upon themselves. Hence not a single category of the bourgeois economy, not even the most basic, e.g. the determination of value, becomes real through free competition alone; i.e. through the real process of capital, which appears as the interaction of capitals and of all other relations of production and intercourse determined by capital. Hence, on the other side, the insipidity of the view that free competition is the ultimate development of human freedom; and that the negation of free competition = negation of individual freedom and of social production founded on individual freedom. It is nothing more than free development on a limited basis—the basis of the rule of capital. This kind of individual freedom is therefore at the same time the most complete suspension of all individual freedom, and the most complete subjugation of individuality under social conditions which assume the form of objective powers, even of overpowering objects—of things independent of the relations among individuals themselves. The analysis of what free competition really is, is the only rational reply to the middle-class prophets who laud it to the skies or to the socialists who damn it to hell. The statement that, within free competition, the individuals, in following purely their private interest, realize the communal or rather the *general* interest means nothing other than that they collide with one another under the conditions of capitalist production, and hence that the impact between them is itself nothing more than the recreation of the conditions under which this interaction takes place. By the way, when the illusion about competition as the so-called absolute form of free individuality vanishes, this is evidence that the conditions of competition, i.e. of production founded on capital, are already felt and thought of as *barriers,* and hence already *are* such, and more and more become such. The assertion that free competition = the ultimate form of the development of the forces of production and hence of human freedom means nothing other than that middle-class rule is the culmination of world history—certainly an agreeable thought for the parvenus of the day before yesterday.

Marx, *GRUNDRISSE* (1857–58), pp. 649–52.

2.A.3 WAGE LABOR AND THE LABOR MARKET

If we consider the original relation, before the entry of money into the self-realization process, then various conditions appear which have to have arisen, or been given historically, for money to become capital and labour to become capital-positing, capital-creating labour, wage labour. . . . The essential conditions are themselves posited in the relation as it appears originally: (1) on the one side the presence of living labour capacity as a merely *subjective* existence, separated from the *conditions* of living labour as well as from the *means of existence, the necessary goods,* the means of self-preservation of living *labour capacity;* the living possibility of labour, on the one side, in this complete abstraction; (2) the value, or objectified labour, found on the other side, must be an accumulation of use values sufficiently large to furnish the objective conditions not only for the production of the products or values required to reproduce or maintain living labour capacity, but also for the absorption of surplus labour—to supply the objective material for the latter; (3) a free exchange relation—money circulation—between both sides; between the extremes a relation founded on exchange values — not on the master-servant relation—i.e., hence, production which does not directly furnish the producer with his necessaries, but which is mediated through exchange, and which cannot therefore usurp alien labour directly, but must buy it, exchange it, from the worker himself; finally (4) one side—the side representing the objective conditions of labour in the form of independent values for-themselves—must present itself as *value,* and must regard the positing of value, self-realization, money-making, as the ultimate purpose—not direct consumption or the creation of use value.

So long as *both* sides exchange their labour with one another in the form of *objectified* labour, the relation is impossible; it is likewise impossible if *living labour capacity* itself appears as the property of the other side, hence as not engaged in exchange. (The fact that slavery is possible at individual points within the bourgeois system of production does not contradict this. However, slavery is then possible there only because it does not exist at other points; and appears as an anomaly opposite the bourgeois system itself.)

The conditions under which the relation appears at the origin, or which appear as the historic presuppositions of its becoming, reveal at first glance a two-sided character—on one side, dissolution of lower forms of living labour; on the other, dissolution of happier forms of the same.

The first presupposition, to begin with, is that the relation of slavery or serfdom has been suspended. Living labour capacity belongs to itself, and has disposition over the expenditure of its forces, through exchange. Both sides confront each other as persons. *Formally,* their relation has the equality and freedom of exchange as such. As far as concerns the legal relation, the fact that this form is a mere *semblance,* and a *deceptive semblance* appears as an *external* matter. What the free worker sells is always nothing more than a specific, particular measure of force-expenditure; labour capacity as a totality is greater than every particular expenditure. He sells the particular expenditure of force to a particular capitalist, whom he confronts as an independent *individual.* It is clear that this is not his relation to the existence of capital as capital, i.e. to the capitalist class. Nevertheless, in this way everything touching on the individual, real person leaves him a wide field of choice, of arbitrary will, and hence of formal freedom. In the slave relation, he belongs to the *individual, particular* owner, and is his labouring machine. As a totality of force-expenditure, as labour capacity, he is a thing belonging to another, and hence does not relate as subject to his particular expenditure of force, nor to the act of living labour. In the serf relation he appears as a moment of property in land itself, is an appendage of the soil, exactly like draught-cattle. In the slave relation the worker is nothing but a living labour machine, which therefore has a value for others, or rather is a value. The totality of the free worker's labour capacity appears to him as his property, as one of his moments, over which he, as subject, exercises domination, and which he maintains by expending it. . . .

The exchange of objectified labour for living labour does not yet constitute either capital on one side or wage labour on the other. The entire class of so-called *services* from the bootblack up to the king falls into this category. Likewise the free day-labourer, whom we encounter sporadically in all places where either the oriental community or the western commune consisting of free landowners dissolves into individual elements—as a consequence of increase of population, release of prisoners of war, accidents by which the individual is impoverished and loses the objective conditions of his self-sustaining labour, owing to division of labour etc. If A exchanges a value or money, i.e. objectified labour, in order to obtain a service from B, i.e. living labour, then this can belong. . . *within the relation of simple circulation.* Both in fact exchange only use values with one another; one exchanges necessaries, the other labour, a service which the other wants to consume, either directly—personal service—or he furnishes him the material etc. from which, with his labour, with the objectification of his labour, he makes a use value, a use value designed for A's consumption. For example, when the peasant takes a wandering tailor, of the kind that existed in times past, into his house, and gives him the material to make clothes with. Or if I give money to a doctor to patch up my health. What is important in these cases is the service which both do for one another. . . . *Value* generally, *value* as such,. . . does not exist for A, since he consumes the article, and is not a clothes-dealer. He has therefore bought the labour not as *value-positing* labour, but as an activity which creates utility, use value. This act is for that reason not an act which produces wealth, but the opposite, one which consumes wealth. The point for A is not the objectification in the cloth of labour as such, of a certain amount of labour time, hence *value,* but rather the satisfaction of a certain need. Here A sees his money not *realized* but *devalued* in its transposition from the form of value into that of use value. Labour is here exchanged not as use value for value, but as itself a particular use value, as value for use. The more frequently A repeats the exchange, the poorer does he become. This exchange is not an *act of wealth-getting* for him, not an act of *value creation,* but of *devaluation* of the values he has in hand, in his possession. The money which A here exchanges for living labour—service in kind, or service objectified in a thing—is not *capital* but revenue, money as a medium of circulation in order to obtain use value, money in which the form of value is posited as merely vanishing, not money which will preserve and realize itself as such through the acquisition of labour. Exchange of *money as revenue,* as a mere medium of circulation, for living labour, can never posit money as capital, nor, therefore, labour as wage labour in the economic sense. A lengthy disquisition is not required to show that to consume (spend) money is not the same as to produce money. In situations in which the greatest part of surplus labour appears as agricultural labour, and where the owner of the land therefore appears as owner both of surplus labour and of the surplus product, it is the revenue of the owner of the land which forms the labour fund for the free worker, for the worker in manufactures (here, hand crafts) as opposed to the agricultural labourers. The exchange with them[1] is a form of the consumption of the owner of the land—he divides another part of his revenue directly—for personal services, often only the illusion of services, with a heap of retainers. In Asiatic societies, where the monarch appears as the exclusive proprietor of the agricultural surplus product, whole cities arise, which are at bottom nothing more than wandering encampments, from the exchange of his revenue with the 'free hands,' as Steuart calls them. There is nothing of wage labour in this relation, but it *can* stand in opposition to slavery and serfdom, though *need* not do so, for it always repeats itself under various forms of the overall organization of labour. To the extent that *money* mediates this exchange the determination of prices will become important on both sides, but it will do so for A only in so far as he does not want to pay too much for the *use value* of the labour; not in so far as he is concerned with its *value.* The essence of the relation remains unchanged even if this price, which begins as conventional and traditional, is thereafter increasingly determined economically, first by the relation of demand and supply, finally by the production costs at which the vendors themselves of these living services can be produced; nothing is essentially changed thereby, because the determination of prices remains a merely formal moment for the exchange of mere use values, as before. This determination itself, however, is created by other relations, by the general laws and the self-determination of the ruling mode of production, acting, as it were, behind the back of this particular act of exchange. . . .

In bourgeois society itself, all exchange of personal services for revenue—including labour for personal consumption, cooking, sewing etc., garden work etc., up to and including all of the unproductive classes, civil servants, physicians, lawyers, scholars etc.—belongs under this rubric, within this category. All menial servants etc. By means of their services— often coerced —all these workers, from the least to the highest, obtain for themselves a share of the surplus product, of the capitalist's *revenue.* But it does not occur to anyone to think that by means of the exchange of his revenue for such services, i.e. through private consumption, the capitalist posits himself as a capitalist. Rather, he thereby spends the fruits of his capital. It does not change the

[1]That is, with the free workers in manufactures (hand crafts).

nature of the relation that the proportions in which revenue is exchanged for this kind of living labour are themselves determined by the general laws of production. . . .

It is here rather the performer of the service who actually posits *value;* who transposes a use value—a certain kind of labour, service etc.—into *value, money.* Hence in the Middle Ages, those who are oriented towards the production and accumulation of money proceed partly not from the side of the consuming landed nobility, but quite the opposite, from the side of living labour; they accumulate and thus become capitalists . . . for a later period. The emancipated serf becomes, in part, the capitalist.

It thus does not depend on the general relation, but rather on the natural, particular quality of the service performed, whether the recipient of payment receives it as day-wages, or as an honorarium, or as a sinecure—and whether he appears as superior or inferior in rank to the person paying for the service. However, with the presupposition of capital as the dominant power, all these relations become more or less *dishonoured.* But this does not belong here yet —this *demystification* of personal services, regardless of the lofty character with which tradition may have poetically endowed them.

It is not, then, simply the exchange of *objectified labour* for *living* labour —which appear, from this standpoint, as two different aspects, as use values in different forms, the one objective, the other subjective—which constitutes capital and hence wage labour, but rather, the exchange of objectified labour as *value,* as self-sufficient value, for living labour as *its* use value, as use value not for a specific, particular use or consumption, but as use value not for a specific, particular use or consumption, but as use value for *value.*

In the exchange of money for labour or service, with the aim of direct consumption, a real exchange always takes place; the fact that *amounts of labour* are exchanged on both sides is of merely *formal* interest for measuring the *particular* forms of the utility of labour by comparing them with each other. This concerns only the *form* of the exchange; but does not form its *content.* In the exchange of capital for labour, *value* is not a measure for the exchange of two use values, but is rather the *content of the exchange* itself.

Marx, *Grundrisse* (1857–58), pp. 463–69.

2.A.4 MONEY AND CAPITAL

The circulation of commodities is the starting point of capital. The production of commodities, their circulation, and that more developed form of their circulation called commerce, these form the historical groundwork from which it rises. The modern history of capital dates from the creation in the sixteenth century of a world-embracing commerce and a world-embracing market.

If we abstract from the material substance of the circulation of commodities, that is, from the exchange of the various use-values, and consider only the economic forms produced by this process of circulation, we find its final result to be money: this final product of the circulation of commodities is the first form in which capital appears.

As a matter of history, capital, as opposed to landed property, invariably takes the form at first of money; it appears as moneyed wealth, as the capital of the merchant and of the usurer. But we have no need to refer to the origin of capital in order to discover that the first form of appearance of capital is money. We can see it daily under our very eyes. All new capital, to commence with, comes on the stage, that is, on the market, whether of commodities, labour, or money, even in our days, in the shape of money that by a definite process has to be transformed into capital.

The first distinction we notice between money that is money only, and money that is capital, is nothing more than a difference in their form of circulation.

The simplest form of the circulation of commodities is C–M–C, the transformation of commodities into money, and the change of the money back again into commodities; or selling in order to buy. But alongside of this form we find another specifically different form: M–C–M, the transformation of money into commodities, and the change of commodities back again into money; or buying in order to sell. Money that circulates in the latter manner is thereby transformed into, becomes capital, and is already potentially capital.

Now let us examine the circuit M–C–M a little closer. It consists, like the other, of two antithetical phases. In the first phase, M–C, or the purchase, the money is changed into a commodity. In the second phase, C–M, or the sale, the commodity is changed back again into money. The combination of these two phases constitutes the single movement whereby money is exchanged for a commodity and the same commodity is again exchanged for money; whereby a commodity is bought in order to be sold, or, neglecting the distinction in form between buying and selling, whereby a commodity is bought with money, and then money is bought with a commodity. The result, in which the phases of the process vanish, is the exchange of money for money, M–M. If I purchase 2000 lbs. of cotton for £100, and resell the 2000 lbs. of cotton for £110, I have, in fact, exchanged £100 for £110, money for money.

Now it is evident that the circuit M–C–M would be absurd and without meaning if the intention were to exchange by this means two equal sums of money, £100 for £100. The miser's plan would be far simpler and surer; he sticks to his £100 instead of exposing it to the dangers of circulation. And yet, whether the merchant who has paid £100 for his cotton sells it for £110, or lets it go for £100, or even £50, his money has, at all events, gone through a characteristic and original movement, quite different in kind from that which it goes through in the hands of the peasant who sells corn, and with the money thus set free buys clothes. We have therefore to examine first the distinguishing characteristics of the forms of the circuits M–C–M and C–M–C, and in doing this the real difference that underlies the mere difference of form will reveal itself.

Let us see, in the first place, what the two forms have in common.

Both circuits are resolvable into the same two antithetical phases, C–M, a sale, and M–C, a purchase. In each of these phases the same material elements—a commodity, and money, and the same economical dramatis personae, a buyer and a seller—confront one another. Each circuit is the unity of the same two antithetical phases, and in each case this unity is brought about by the intervention of three contracting parties, of whom one only sells, another only buys, while the third both buys and sells.

What, however, first and foremost distinguishes the ciruit C–M–C from the circuit M–C–M, is the inverted order of succession of the two phases. The simple circulation of commodities begins with a sale and ends with a purchase, while the circulation of money as capital begins with a purchase and ends with a sale. In the one case both the starting point and the goal are commodities, in the other they are money. In the first form the movement is brought about by the intervention of money, in the second by that of a commodity.

In the circulation C–M–C, the money is in the end converted into a commodity, that serves as a use-value; it is spent once for all. In the inverted form, M–C–M, on the contrary, the buyer lays out money in order that, as a seller, he may recover money. By the purchase of his commodity he throws money into circulation, in order to withdraw it again by the sale of the same commodity. He lets the money go, but only with the sly intention of getting it back again. The money, therefore, is not spent, it is merely advanced.

In the circuit C–M–C, the same piece of money changes its place twice. The seller gets it from the buyer and pays it away to another seller. The complete circulation, which begins with the receipt, concludes with the payment, of money for commodities. It is the very contrary in the circuit M–C–M. Here it is not the piece of money that changes its place twice, but the commodity. The buyer takes it from the hands of the seller and passes it into the hands of another buyer. Just as in the simple circulation of commodities the double change of place of the same piece of money effects its passage from one hand into another, so here the double change of place of the same commodity brings about the reflux of the money to its point of departure.

Such reflux is not dependent on the commodity being sold for more than was paid for it. This circumstance influences only the amount of the money that comes back. The reflux itself takes place, so soon as the purchased commodity is resold, in other words, so soon as the circuit M–C–M is completed. We have here, therefore, a palpable difference between the circulation of money as capital, and its circulation as mere money.

The circuit C–M–C comes completely to an end, so soon as the money brought in by the sale of one commodity is abstracted again by the purchase of another.

If, nevertheless, there follows a reflux of money to its starting point, this can only happen through a renewal or repetition of the operation. If I sell a quarter of corn for £3, and with this £3 buy clothes, the money, so far as I am concerned, is spent and done with. It belongs to the clothes merchant. If I now sell a second quarter of corn, money indeed flows back to me, not however as a sequel to the first transaction, but in consequence of its repetition. The money again leaves me, so soon as I complete this second transaction by a fresh purchase. Therefore, in the circuit C–M–C, the expenditure of money has nothing to do with its reflux. On the other hand, in M–C–M, the reflux of the money is conditioned by the very mode of its expenditure. Without this reflux, the operation fails, or the process is interrupted and incomplete, owing to the absence of its complementary and final phase, the sale.

The circuit C–M–C starts with one commodity, and finishes with another, which falls out of circulation and into consumption. Consumption, the satisfaction of wants, in one word, use-value, is its end and aim. The circuit M–C–M, on the contrary, commences with money and ends with money. Its leading motive, and the goal that attracts it, is therefore mere exchange value.

In the simple circulation of commodities, the two extremes of the ciruit have the same economic form. They are both commodities, and commodities of equal value. But they are also use-values differing in their qualities, as, for example, corn and clothes. The exchange of products, of the different materials in which the labour of society is embodied, forms here the basis of the movement. It is otherwise in the circulation M–C–M, which at first sight appears purposeless, because tautological. Both extremes have the same economic form. They are both money, and therefore are not qualitatively different use-values; for money is but the converted form of commodities, in which their particular use-values vanish. To exchange £100 for cotton, and then this same cotton again for £100, is merely a roundabout way of exchanging money for money, the same for the same, and appears to be an operation just as purposeless as it is absurd. One sum of money is distinguishable from another only by its amount. The character and tendency of the process M–C–M, is therefore not due to any qualitative difference between its extremes, both being money, but solely to their quantitative difference. More money is withdrawn from circulation at the finish than was thrown into it at the start. The cotton that was bought for £100 is perhaps resold for £100+£10 or £110. The exact form of this process is therefore M–C–M′, where $M' = M + \triangle M$ = the original sum advanced, plus an increment. This increment or excess over the original value I call "surplus-value." The value originally advanced, therefore, not only remains intact while in circulation, but adds to itself a surplus-value or expands itself. It is this movement that converts it into capital.

Of course it is also possible, that in C–M–C, the two extremes C–C, say corn and clothes, may represent different quantities of value. The farmer may sell his corn above its value, or may buy the clothes at less than their value. He may, on the other hand, "be done" by the clothes merchant. Yet, in the form of circulation now under consideration, such differences in value are purely accidental. The fact that the corn and the clothes are equivalents, does not deprive the process of all meaning, as it does in M–C–M. The equivalence of their values is rather a necessary condition to its normal course.

The repetition or renewal of the act of selling in order to buy, is kept within bounds by the very object it aims at, namely, consumption or the satisfaction of definite wants, an aim that lies altogether outside the sphere of circulation. But when we buy in order to sell, we, on the contrary, begin and end with the same thing, money, exchange-value; and thereby the movement become interminable. No doubt, M becomes $M + \triangle M$, £100 become £110. But when viewed in their qualitative aspect alone, £110 are the same as £100, namely money; and considered quantitatively, £110 is, like £100, a sum of definite and limited value. If now, the £110 be spent as money, they cease to play their part. They are no longer capital. Withdrawn from circulation, they become petrified into a hoard, and though they remained in that state till doomsday, not a single farthing would accrue to them. If, then, the expansion of value is once aimed at, there is just the same inducement to augment the value of the £110 as that of the £100; for both are but limited expressions for exchange-value, and therefore both have the same vocation to approach, by quantitative increase, as near as possible to absolute wealth. Momentarily, indeed, the value originally advanced, the £100 is distinguishable from the surplus value of £10 that is annexed to it during circulation; but the distinction vanishes immediately. At the end of the process we do not receive with one hand the original £100, and with the other, the surplus-value of £10. We simply get a value of £110, which is in exactly the same condition and fitness for commencing the expanding process, as the original £100 was. Money ends the movement only to begin it again. Therefore, the final result of every separate circuit, in which a purchase and consequent sale are completed, forms of itself the starting point of a new circuit. The simple circulation of commodities—selling in order to buy—is a means of carrying out a purpose unconnected with circulation, namely, the appropriation of use-values, the satisfaction of wants. The circulation of money as capital is, on the contrary, an end in itself, for the expansion of value takes place only within this constantly renewed movement. The circulation of capital has therefore no limits. Thus the conscious representative of this movement, the possessor of money becomes a capitalist. His person, or rather his pocket, is the point from which the money starts and to which it returns. The expansion of value, which is the objective basis or main-spring of the circulation M–C–M, becomes his subjective aim, and it is only in so far as the appropriation of ever more and more wealth in the abstract becomes the sole motive of his operations, that he functions as a capitalist, that is, as capital personified and endowed with consciousness and a will. Use-values must therefore never be looked upon as the real aim of the capitalist; neither must the profit on any single transaction. The restless never-ending process of profit-making alone is what he aims at. This boundless greed after riches, this passionate chase after exchange-value, is common to the capitalist and the miser; but while the miser is merely a capitalist gone mad, the capitalist is a rational miser. The never-ending augmentation of exchange-value, which the miser strives after, by seeking to save his money from circulation, is attained by the more acute capitalist, by constantly throwing it afresh into circulation.

The independent form, i.e., the money-form, which the value of commodities assumes in the case of simple circulation, serves only one purpose, namely, their exchange, and vanishes in the final result of the movement. On the other hand, in the circulation M–C–M, both the money and the commodity represent only different modes of existence of value itself, the money its general mode, and the commodity its particular, or, so to say, disguised mode. It is constantly changing from one form to the other without thereby becoming lost, and thus assumes an automatically active character. If now we take in turn each of the two different forms which self-expanding value successively assumes in the course of its life, we then arrive at these two propositions: Capital is money: Capital is commodities. In truth, however, value is here the active factor in a process, in which, while constantly assuming the form in turn of money and commodities, it at the same time changes in magnitude, differentiates itself by throwing off surplus-value from itself; the original value, in other words, expands spontaneously. For the movement, in the course of which it adds surplus value, is its own movement, its expansion, therefore, is automatic expansion. Because it is value, it has acquired the occult quality of being able to add value to itself. It brings forth living offspring, or, at the least, lays golden eggs. . . .

In simple circulation, C–M–C, the value of commodities attained at the most a form independent of their use-values, i.e., the form of money; but that same value now in the circulation, M–C–M, or the circulation of capital, suddenly presents itself as an independent substance, endowed with a motion of its own, passing through a life-process of its own, in which money and commodities are mere forms which it assumes and casts off in turn. Nay, more: instead of simply representing the relations of commodities, it enters now, so to say, into private relations with itself. It differentiates itself as original value from itself as surplus-value; as the father differentiates himself from himself qua the son, yet both are one and of one age: for only by the surplus value of £10 does the £100 originally advanced become capital, and so soon as this takes place, so soon as the son, and by the son, the father, is begotten, so soon does their difference vanish, and they again become one, £110.

Value therefore now becomes value in process, money in process, and, as such, capital. It comes out of circulation, enters into it again, preserves and multiplies itself within its circuit, comes back out of it with expanded bulk, and begins the same round ever afresh. M–M, money which begets money, such is the description of Capital from the mouths of its first interpreters, the Mercantilists.

Buying in order to sell, or, more accurately, buying in order to sell dearer, M–C–M, appears certainly to be a form peculiar to one kind of capital alone, namely, merchants' capital. But industrial capital too is money, that is changed into commodities, and by the sale of these commodities, is reconverted into more money. The events that take place outside the sphere of circulation, in the interval between the buying and selling, do not affect the form of this movement. Lastly, in the case of interest-bearing capital, the circulation M–C–M appears abridged. We have its result without the intermediate stage, in the form, M–M′, "en style lapidaire" so to say, money that is worth more money, value that is greater than itself.

M–C–M is therefore in reality the general formula of capital as it appears prima facie within the sphere of circulation.

Marx, *Capital,* I (1867), pp. 163–73.

2.A.5 COMMODITIES, VALUE, AND EXCHANGE

The Two Factors of a Commodity: Use-Value And Value (The Substance of Value and the Magnitude of Value)

The wealth of those societies in which the capitalist mode of production prevails, presents itself as "an immense accumulation of commodities,"[1] its

[1]Karl Marx "A Contribution to the Critique of Political Economy," 1859, London, p. 19.

unit being a single commodity. Our investigation must therefore begin with the analysis of a commodity.

A commodity is, in the first place, an object outside us, a thing that by its properties satisfies human wants of some sort or another. The nature of such wants, whether, for instance, they spring from the stomach or from fancy, makes no difference. Neither are we here concerned to know how the object satisfies these wants, whether directly as means of subsistence, or indirectly as means of production.

Every useful thing, as iron, paper, etc., may be looked at from the two points of view of quality and quantity. It is an assemblage of many properties, and may therefore be of use in various ways. . . .

The utility of a thing makes it a use-value. But this utility is not a thing of air. Being limited by the physical properties of the commodity, it has no existence apart from that commodity. A commodity, such as iron, corn, or a diamond, is therefore, so far as it is a material thing, a use-value, something useful. This property of a commodity is independent of the amount of labour required to appropriate its useful qualities. . . . Use-values become a reality only by use or consumption: they also constitute the substance of all wealth, whatever may be the social form of that wealth. In the form of society we are about to consider, they are, in addition, the material depositories of exchange value.

Exchange value, at first sight, presents itself as a quantitative relation, as the proportion in which values in use of one sort are exchanged for those of another sort, a relation constantly changing with time and place. Hence exchange value appears to be something accidental and purely relative, and consequently an intrinsic value, for i.e., an exchange value that is inseparably connected with, inherent in commodities, seems a contradiction in terms. Let us consider the matter a little more closely.

A given commodity, e.g., a quarter of wheat is exchanged for x blacking, y silk, or z gold, etc.—in short, for other commodities in the most different proportions. Instead of one exchange value, the wheat has, therefore, a great many. But since x blacking, y silk, or z gold, etc., each represent the exchange value of one quarter of wheat, x blacking, y silk, z gold, etc., must as exchange values be replaceable by each other, or equal to each other. Therefore, first: the valid exchange values of a given commodity express something equal; secondly, exchange value, generally, is only the mode of expression, the phenomenal form, of something contained in it, yet distinguishable from it.

Let us take two commodities, for e.g., corn and iron. The proportions in which they are exchangeable, whatever those proportions may be, can always be represented by an equation in which a given quantity of corn is equated to some quantity of iron: i.e., 1 quarter corn = x cwt. iron. What does this equation tell us? It tells us that in two different things—in 1 quarter of corn and x cwt. of iron, there exists in equal quantities something common to both. The two things must therefore be equal to a third, which in itself is neither the one nor the other. Each of them, so far as it is exchange value, must therefore be reducible to this third. . . .

This common "something" cannot be [a] natural property of commodities. Such properties claim our attention only in so far as they affect the utility of those commodities, make them use-values. But the exchange of commodities is evidently an act characterised by a total abstraction from use-value. Then one use-value is just as good as another, provided only it be present in sufficient quantity. . . . As use-values, commodities are, above all, of different qualities, but as exchange values they are merely different quantities, and consequently do not contain an atom of use-value.

If then we leave out of consideration the use-value of commodities, they have only one common property left, that of being products of labour. But even the product of labour itself has undergone a change in our hands. If we make abstraction from its use-value, we make abstraction at the same time from the material elements and shapes that make the product a use-value; we see in it no longer a table, a house, yarn, or any other useful thing. Its existence as a material thing is put out of sight. Neither can it any longer be regarded as the product of the labour of the joiner, the mason, the spinner, or of any other definite kind of productive labour. Along with the useful qualities of the products themselves, we put out of sight both the useful character of the various kinds of labour embodied in them, and the concrete forms of that labour; there is nothing left but what is common to them all; all are reduced to one and the same sort of labour, human labour in the abstract.

Let us now consider the residue of each of these products; it consists of the same unsubstantial reality in each, a mere congelation of homogeneous human labour, of labour-power expended without regard to the mode of its expenditure. All that these things now tell us is, that human labour-power has been expended in their production, that human labor is embodied in them. When looked at as crystals of this social substance, common to them all, they are—Values.

We have seen that when commodities are exchanged, their exchange value manifests itself as something totally independent of their use-value. But if we abstract from their use-value there remains their Value as defined above. Therefore, the common substance that manifests itself in the exchange value of commodities, whenever they are exchanged, is their value. . . .

A use-value, or useful article, therefore, has value only because human labour in the abstract has been embodied or materialised in it. How, then, is the magnitude of this value to be measured? Plainly, by the quantity of the value-creating substance, the labour, contained in the article. The quantity of labour, however, is measured by its duration, and labour time in its turn finds its standard in weeks, days, and hours.

Some people might think that if the value of a commodity is determined by the quantity of labour spent on it, the more idle and unskillful the labourer, the more valuable would his commodity be, because more time would be required in its production. The labour, however, that forms the substance of value, is homogeneous human labour, expenditure of one uniform labour-power. The total labour-power of society, which is embodied in the sum total of the values of all commodities produced by that society, counts here as one homogeneous mass of human labour-power, composed though it be of innumerable individual units. Each of these units is the same as any other, so far as it has the character of the average labour-power of society, and takes effect as such; that is, so far as it requires for producing a commodity, no more time than is needed on an average, no more than is socially necessary. The labour-time socially necessary is that required to produced an article under the normal conditions of production, and with the average degree of skill and intensity prevalent at the time. The introduction of power looms into England probably reduced by one half the labour required to weave a given quantity of yarn into cloth. The hand-loom weavers, as a matter of fact, continued to require the same time as before; but for all that, the product of one hour of their labour represented after the change only half an hour's social labour, and consequently fell to one-half its former value.

We see then that that which determines the magnitude of the value of any article is the amount of labour socially necessary, or the labour-time socially necessary for its production. Each individual commodity, in this connexion, is to be considered as an average sample of its class. Commodities, therefore, in which equal quantities of labour are embodied, or which can be produced in the same time, have the same value. The value of one commodity is to the value of any other, as the labour-time necessary for the production of the one is to that necessary for the production of the other. . . .

The value of a commodity would therefore remain constant, if the labour-time required for its production also remained constant. But the latter changes with every variation in the productiveness of labour. This productiveness is determined by various circumstances, amongst others, by the average amount of skill of the workmen, the state of science, and the degree of its practical application, the social organization of production, the extent and capabilities of the means of production, and by physical conditions. For example, the same amount of labour in favourable seasons is embodied in eight bushels of corn, and in unfavourable, only in four. The same labour extracts from rich mines more metal than from poor mines. Diamonds are of very rare occurrence on the earth's surface, and hence their discovery costs, on an average, a great deal of labour-time. Consequently much labour is represented in a small compass. . . . If we could succeed at a small expenditure of labour, in converting carbon into diamonds, their value might fall below that of bricks. In general, the greater the productiveness of labour, the less is the labour-time required for the production of an article, the less is the amount of labour crystallised in that article, and the less is its value; and vice versa, the less the productiveness of labour, the greater is the labour-time required for the production of an article, and the greater is its value. The value of a commodity, therefore, varies directly as the quantity, and inversely as the productiveness, of the labour incorporated in it.

A thing can be a use-value, without having value. This is the case whenever its utility to man is not due to labour. Such are air, virgin soil, natural meadows, etc. A thing can be useful, and the product of human labour, without being a commodity. Whoever directly satisfies his wants with the produce of his own labour, creates, indeed, use-values, but not commodities. In order to produce the latter, he must not only produce use-values, but use-values for others, social use-values. Lastly, nothing can have value, without being an object of utility. If the thing is useless, so is the labour contained in it; the labour does not count as labour, and therefore creates no value.

The Twofold Character of the Labour Embodied In Commodities

To all different varieties of values in use there correspond as many different kinds of useful labour, classified according to the order, genus, species, and variety to which they belong in the social division of labour. . . .

In the use-value of each commodity there is contained useful labour, i.e., productive activity of a definite kind and exercised with a definite aim. Use-values cannot confront each other as commodities, unless the useful labour embodied in them is qualitatively different in each of them. In a community, the produce of which in general takes the form of commodities, i.e., in a community of commodity producers, this qualitative difference between the useful forms of labour that are carried on independently by individual producers, each on their own account, develops into a complex system, a social division of labour. . . .

The use-values, coat linen, etc., i.e., the bodies of commodities, are combinations of two elements—matter and labour. If we take away the useful labour expended upon them, a material substratum is always left, which is furnished by Nature without the help of man. The latter can work only as Nature does, that is by changing the form of matter. Nay more, in this work of changing the form he is constantly helped by natural forces. We see, then, that labour is not the only source of material wealth, of use-values produced by labour. As William Petty puts it, labour is its father and the earth its mother.

Let us now pass from the commodity considered as a use-value to the value of commodities. . . . In our capitalist society, a given portion of human labour is, in accordance with the varying demand, at one time supplied in the form of tailoring, at another in the form of weaving. This change may possibly not take place without friction, but take place it must.

Productive activity, if we leave out of sight its special form, viz., the useful character of the labour, is nothing but the expenditure of human labour-power. Tailoring and weaving, though qualitatively different productive activities, are each a productive expenditure of human brains, nerves, and muscles, and in this sense are human labour. They are but two different modes of expending human labour-power. Of course, this labour-power, which remains the same under all its modifications, must have attained a certain pitch of development before it can be expended in a multiplicity of modes. But the value of a commodity represents human labour in the abstract, the expenditure of human labour in general. And just as in society, a general or a banker plays a great part, but mere man, on the other hand, a very shabby part, so here with mere human labour. It is the expenditure of simple labour-power, i.e., of the labour-power which, on an average, apart from any special development, exists in the organism of every ordinary individual. Simple average labour, it is true, varies in character in different countries and at different times, but in a particular society it is given. Skilled labour counts only as simple labour intensified, or rather, as multiplied simple labour, a given quantity of skilled being considered equal to a greater quantity of simple labour. Experience shows that this reduction is constantly being made. A commodity may be the product of the most skilled labour, but its value, by equating it to the product of simple unskilled labour, represents a definite quantity of the latter labour alone. The different proportions in which different sorts of labour are reduced to unskilled labour as their standard, are established by a social process that goes on behind the backs of the producers, and, consequently, appear to be fixed by custom. For simplicity's sake we shall henceforth account every kind of labour to be unskilled, simple labour; by this we do no more than save ourselves the trouble of making the reduction.

Just as, therefore, in viewing the coat and linen as values, we abstract from their different use-values, so it is with the labour represented by those values: we disregard the difference between its useful forms, weaving and tailoring. . . . Only in so far as abstraction is made from their special qualities, only in so far as both possess the same quality of being human labour, do tailoring and weaving form the substance of the values of the same articles.

Coats and linen, however, are not merely values, but values of definite magnitude, and according to our assumption, the coat is worth twice as much as the ten yards of linen. Whence this difference in their values? It is owing to the fact that the linen contains only half as much labour as the coat, and consequently, that in the production of the latter, labour-power must have been expended during twice the time necessary for the production of the former.

While, therefore, with reference to use-value, the labour contained in a commodity counts only qualitatively, with reference to value it counts only quantitatively, and must first be reduced to human labour pure and simple. In the former case, it is a question of How and What, in the latter of How much? How long a time? Since the magnitude of the value of a commodity represents only the quantity of labour embodied in it, it follows that all commodities, when taken in certain proportions, must be equal in value. . . .

On the one hand all labour is, speaking physiologically, an expenditure of human labour-power, and in its character of identical abstract human labour, it creates and forms the value of commodities. On the other hand, all labour is the expenditure of human labour-power in a special form and with a definite aim, and in this, its character of concrete useful labour, it produces use-values.

Marx, *Capital,* I (1867), pp. 41–54.

B. THE CAPITAL-LABOR RELATION

The following selections, taken mainly from a lecture prepared by Marx for a Belgian workers' association in 1847, provide an early and spirited statement of the basic elements in the capital-labor relation. For Marx, capital is not simply things, for example, factories and machinery. If it were, a savage with a tool, Robinson Crusoe on his island, mom and pop in their grocery store, and Marx's "associated laborers" under conditions of genuine cooperative control of the means of production would all be capitalists. Capital is a rough proxy for the capital-labor relationship, that is, an entire constellation of social relations between capitalists and workers, based upon their respective ownership versus nonownership of the physical means of production. Wages, prices, profits, and exchange must all be understood in terms of these social relations.

The core of this social relationship is the dominance of the capitalist and the subservience of the worker within the process of production. In contrast to earlier forms of economy, however, the capitalist's authority rests strictly on ownership, not on politics or religion.

> The authority which the capitalist takes on as the personification of capital in the immediate production process, which he wears as the leader and controller of production, is essentially different from the authority on the basis of production with slaves, serfs, etc. On the basis of capitalists' production, the mass of the producers confront the social character of their production in the form of a strong, ruling authority and as a hierarchically ordered social mechanism of the labour process— which authority only comes to its bearer as the personification of the conditions of labour as against labour, and not, as in earlier forms of production, as political or theocratic rule.[3]

The capitalist's social position rests on economic means rather than on tradition, religious sanction, or physical coercion because the worker is free to leave the individual capitalist "whenever he likes." But the capitalist's dominance rests on the economic necessity of the worker, in turn based on the worker's propertylessness. The worker, "whose sole source of livelihood is the sale of his labour power, cannot leave the *whole class of purchasers, that is, the capitalist class,* without renouncing his existence." This is sometimes expressed by saying that although capitalists are characterized by free competition in their relations with each other, as a social group they have a "class monopoly" of the means of production. This suggests that there are barriers to entry into the capitalist class by workers, notably the large investments in machinery, tools, factory, and raw materials that a worker needs to control in order to become and function successfully as a capitalist. Of course, it is not impossible for an industrious and frugal worker to open a small shop or business and gradually become a capitalist through business expansion, just as the ranks of the working class are swelled by former, unsuccessful small businessmen. But, Marx suggests elsewhere, the process of becoming a capitalist, especially once the capitalist mode of production is established, is exceedingly difficult.

Besides, what is possible, though difficult, for an individual worker is impossible for the working class as a whole. *If* all workers, by some wave of a magic wand, *were* to acquire ownership of physical capital, the result would not be capitalism, but a reversion to simple commodity production. In any event, the economic growth that increases real wages also increases profits, and thereby capital, quite possibly more rapidly than wages. Thus, a growing economy is characterized not by the mass transformation of former workers into capitalists, but by the expansion and thereby the increased dominance of capital and the expanded employment of labor. Even under the most favorable economic conditions, the worker labors "anew at increasing bourgeois wealth, at enlarging the power of capital, content with forging for itself the golden chains by which the bourgeoisie drags it in its train." Under less favorable circumstances, for example, periods of unemployment and downward pressure on wages, capitalist dominance expands and the opportunities for individual workers to escape the capital-labor relationship diminish.

[3]Cited in Michael Harrington, *The Twilight of Capitalism* (New York: Simon and Schuster, 1976), pp. 96–97.

2.B.6 CAPITAL AS A SOCIAL RELATION

CAPITAL AND THE CAPITALIST

In the first act, in the exchange between capital and labour, labour as such, existing *for itself,* necessarily appeared as *the worker.* Similarly here in the second process: capital as such is posited as a value existing for itself, as egotistic value, so to speak (something to which money could only aspire). But capital in its being-for-itself is the *capitalist.* Of course, socialists sometimes say, we need capital, but not the capitalist. Then capital appears as a pure thing, not as a relation of production which, reflected in itself, is precisely the capitalist. I may well separate capital from a given individual capitalist, and it can be transferred to another. But, in losing capital, he loses the quality of being a capitalist. Thus capital is indeed separable from an individual capitalist, but not from *the* capitalist, who, as such, confronts *the* worker. Thus also the individual worker can cease to be the being-for-itself of labour; he may inherit or steal money etc. But then he ceases to be a *worker.* As a worker he is nothing more than labour in its being-for-itself.

Marx, *GRUNDRISSE* (1857–58), pp. 303–04.

WAGE LABOUR AND CAPITAL

The time has come to deal more closely with the economic relations themselves on which the existence of the bourgeoisie and its class rule, as well as the slavery of the workers, are founded. . . .

The capitalist, it seems,. . . *buys* [workers'] labour with money. They *sell* him their labour for money. But this is merely the appearance. In reality what they sell to the capitalist for money is their labour *power.* The capitalist buys this labour power for a day, a week, a month, etc. And after he has bought it, he uses it by having the workers work for the stipulated time. For the same sum with which the capitalist has bought their labour power, for example, two marks, he could have bought two pounds of sugar or a definite amount of any other commodity. The two marks, with which he bought two pounds of sugar, are the *price* of the two pounds of sugar. The two marks, with which he bought twelve hours' use of labour power, are the price of twelve hours' labour. Labour power, therefore, is a commodity, neither more nor less than sugar. The former is measured by the clock, the latter by the scales.

The workers exchange their commodity, labour power, for the commodity of the capitalist, for money, and this exchange takes place in a definite ratio. So much money for so long a use of labour power. For twelve hours' weaving, two marks. And do not the two marks represent all the other commodities which I can buy for two marks? In fact, therefore, the worker has exchanged his commodity, labour power, for other commodities of all kinds and that in a definite ratio. By giving him two marks, the capitalist has given him so much meat, so much clothing, so much fuel, light, etc., in exchange for his day's labour. Accordingly, the two marks express the ratio in which labour power is exchanged for other commodities, the *exchange value* of his labour power. The exchange value of a commodity, reckoned in *money,* is what is called its *price. Wages* are only a special name for the price of labour power, commonly called the *price of labour,* for the price of this peculiar commodity which has no other repository than human flesh and blood.

Let us take any worker, say, a weaver. The capitalist supplies him with the loom and yarn. The weaver sets to work and the yarn is converted into linen. The capitalist takes possession of the linen and sells it, say, for twenty marks. Now are the wages of the weaver a *share* in the linen, in the twenty marks, in the product of his labour? By no means. Long before the linen is sold, perhaps long before its weaving is finished, the weaver has received his wages. The capitalist, therefore, does not pay these wages with the money which he will obtain from the linen, but with money already in reserve. Just as the loom and the yarn are not the product of the weaver to whom they are supplied by his employer, so likewise with the commodities which the weaver receives in exchange for his commodity, labour power. It was possible that his employer found no purchaser at all for his linen. It was possible that he did not get even the amount of the wages by its sale. It is possible that he sells it very profitably in comparison with the weaver's wages. All that has nothing to do with the weaver. The capitalist buys the labour power of the weaver with a part of his available wealth, of his capital, just as he has bought the raw material—the yarn—and the instrument of labour—the loom—with another part of his wealth. After he has made these purchases, and these purchases include the labour power necessary for the production of linen, he produces only with the *raw materials and instruments of labour belonging to him.* For the latter include now, true enough, our good weaver as well, who has as little share in the product or the price of the product as the loom has.

Wages are, therefore, not the worker's share in the commodity produced by him. Wages are the part of already existing commodities with which the capitalist buys for himself a definite amount of productive labour power.

Labour power is, therefore, a commodity which its possessor, the wage-worker, sells to capital. Why does he sell it? In order to live.

But the exercise of labour power, labour, is the worker's own life-activity, the manifestation of his own life. And this *life-activity* he sells to another person in order to secure the necessary *means of subsistence.* Thus his life-activity is for him only a means to enable him to exist. He works in order to live. He does not even reckon labour as part of his life, it is rather a sacrifice of his life. It is a commodity which he has made over to another. Hence, also, the product of his activity is not the object of his activity. What he produces for himself is not the silk that he weaves, not the gold that he draws from the mine, not the palace that he builds. What he produces for himself is *wages,* and silk, gold, palace resolve themselves for him into a definite quantity of the means of subsistence, perhaps into a cotton jacket, some copper coins and a lodging in a cellar. And the worker, who for twelve hours weaves, spins, drills, turns, builds, shovels, breaks stones, carries loads, etc.—does he consider this twelve hours' weaving, spinning, drilling, turning, building, shovelling, stone breaking as a manifestation of his life, as life? On the contrary, life begins for him where this activity ceases, at table, in the public house, in bed. The twelve hours' labour, on the other hand, has no meaning for him as weaving, spinning, drilling, etc., but as *earnings,* which bring him to the table, to the public house, into bed. If the silk worm were to spin in order to continue its existence as a caterpillar, it would be a complete wage-worker. Labour power was not always a *commodity.* Labour was not always wage labour, that is, *free labour.* The *slave* did not sell his labour power to the slave owner, any more than the ox sells its services to the peasant. The slave, together with his labour power, is sold once and for all to his owner. He is a commodity which can pass from the hand of one owner to that of another. He is *himself* a commodity, but the labour power is not *his* commodity. The *serf* sells only a part of his labour power. He does not receive a wage from the owner of the land; rather the owner of the land receives a tribute from him.

The serf belongs to the land and turns over to the owner of the land the fruits thereof. The *free labourer,* on the other hand, sells himself and, indeed, sells himself piecemeal. He sells at auction eight, ten, twelve, fifteen hours of his life, day after day, to the highest bidder, to the owner of the raw materials, instruments of labour and means of subsistence, that is, to the capitalist. The worker belongs neither to an owner nor to the land, but eight, ten, twelve, fifteen hours of his daily life belong to him who buys them. The worker leaves the capitalist to whom he hires himself whenever he likes, and the capitalist discharges him whenever he thinks fit, as soon as he no longer gets any profit out of him, or not the anticipated profit. But the worker, whose sole source of livelihood is the sale of his labour power, cannot leave the *whole class of purchasers, that is, the capitalist class,* without renouncing his existence. He belongs not to this or that capitalist but to the *capitalist class,* and moreover, it is his business to dispose of himself, that is, to find a purchaser within this capitalist class. . . .

Capital consists of raw materials, instruments of labour and means of subsistence of all kinds, which are utilised in order to produce new raw materials, new instruments of labour and new means of subsistence. All these component parts of capital are creations of labour, products of labour, *accumulated labour.* Accumulated labour which serves as a means of new production is capital.

So say the economists.

What is a Negro slave? A man of the black race. The one explanation is as good as the other.

A Negro is a Negro. He only becomes a slave in certain relations. A cotton-spinning jenny is a machine for spinning cotton. It becomes *capital* only in certain relations. Torn from these relationships it is no more capital than gold in itself is *money* or sugar the price of sugar.

In production, men not only act on nature but also on one another. They produce only by cooperating in a certain way and mutually exchanging their activities. In order to produce, they enter into definite connections and relations with one another and only within these social connections and relations does their action on nature, does production, take place.

These social relations into which the producers enter with one another, the conditions under which they exchange their activities and participate in the whole act of production, will naturally vary according to the character of the means of production. With the invention of a new instrument of warfare, firearms, the whole internal organisation of the army necessarily changed; the relationships within which individuals can constitute an army and act as an army were transformed and the relations of different armies to one another also changed.

Thus the social relations within which individuals produce, *the social relations of production, change, are transformed, with the change and development of the material means of production, the productive forces. The relations of production in their totality constitute what are called the social relations, society, and, specifically, a society at a definite stage of historical development,* a society with a peculiar, distinctive character. *Ancient* society, *feudal* society, *bourgeois* society are such totalities of production relations, each of which at the same time denotes a special stage of development in the history of mankind.

Capital, also, is a social relation of production, *It is a bourgeois production relation,* a production relation of bourgeois society. Are not the means of subsistence, the instruments of labour, the raw materials of which capital consists, produced and accumulated under given social conditions, in definite social relations? Are they not utilised for new production under given social conditions, in definite social relations? And is it not just this definite social character which turns the products serving for new production into *capital?*

Capital consists not only of means of subsistence, instruments of labour and raw materials, not only of material products; it consists just as much of *exchange values.* All the products of which it consists are *commodities.* Capital is, therefore, not only a sum of material products; it is a sum of commodities, of exchange values, *of social magnitudes.*

Capital remains the same, whether we put cotton in place of wool, rice in place of wheat or steamships in place of railways, provided only that the cotton, the rice, the steamships—the body of capital—have the same exchange value, the same price as the wool, the wheat, the railways in which it was previously incorporated. The body of capital can change continually without the capital suffering the slightest alteration.

But while all capital is a sum of commodities, that is, of exchange values, not every sum of commodities, of exchange values, is capital. . . .

How, then, does any amount of commodities, of exchange value, become capital?

By maintaining and multiplying itself as an independent social *power,* that is, as the power *of a portion of society,* by means of its *exchange for direct, living labour power.* The existence of a class which possesses nothing but its capacity to labour is a necessary prerequisite of capital.

It is only the domination of accumulated, past, materialised labour over direct, living labour that turns accumulated labour into capital.

Capital does not consist in accumulated labour serving living labour as a means for new production. It consists in living labour serving accumulated labour as a means for maintaining and multiplying the exchange value of the latter.

What takes place in the exchange between capitalist and wage-worker?

The worker receives means of subsistence in exchange for his labour power, but the capitalist receives in exchange for his means of subsistence labour, the productive activity of the worker, the creative power whereby the worker not only replaces what he consumes but *gives to the accumulated labour a greater value than it previously possessed.* The worker receives a part of the available means of subsistence from the capitalist. For what purpose do these means of subsistence serve him? For immediate consumption. As soon, however, as I consume the means of subsistence, they are irretrievably lost to me unless I use the time during which I am kept alive by them in order to produce new means of subsistence, in order during consumption to create by my labour new values in place of the values which perish in being consumed. But it is just this noble reproductive power that the worker surrenders to the capitalist in exchange for means of subsistence received. He has, therefore, lost it for himself. . . .

Thus capital presupposes wage labour; wage labour presupposes capital. They reciprocally condition the existence of each other; they reciprocally bring forth each other.

Does a worker in a cotton factory produce merely cotton textiles? No, he produces capital. He produces values which serve afresh to command his labour and by means of it to create new values.

Capital can only increase by exchanging itself for labour power, by calling wage labour to life. The labour power of the wage-worker can only be exchanged for capital by increasing capital, by strengthening the power whose slave it is. *Hence, increase of capital is increase of the proletariat, that is, of the working class.*

The interests of the capitalist and those of the worker are, therefore, *one and the same,* assert the bourgeois and their economists. Indeed! The worker perishes if capital does not employ him. Capital perishes if it does not exploit labour power, and in order to exploit it, it must buy it. The faster capital intended for production, productive capital, increases, the more, therefore, industry prospers, the more the bourgeoisie enriches itself and the better business is, the more workers does the capitalist need, the more dearly does the worker sell himself.

The indispensable condition for a tolerable situation of the worker *is, therefore, the fastest possible growth of productive capital.*

But what is the growth of productive capital? Growth of the power of accumulated labour over living labour. Growth of the domination of the bourgeoisie over the working class. If wage labour produces the wealth of others that rules over it, the power that is hostile to it, capital, then the means of employment, that is, the means of subsistence, flow back to it from this hostile power, on condition that it makes itself afresh into a part of capital, into the lever which hurls capital anew into an accelerated movement of growth.

To say that the interests of capital and those of the workers are one and the same is only to say that capital and wage labour are two sides of one and the same relation. The one conditions the other, just as usurer and squanderer condition each other.

As long as the wage-worker is a wage-worker his lot depends upon capital. That is the much-vaunted community of interests between worker and capitalist.

Marx, *Wage Labour and Capital* (1847), MESW, pp. 72–76, 80–84.

2.B.7 CAPITAL GROWTH AND CAPITAL: LABOR RELATIONS

Are *growth of productive capital and rise of wages* really so inseparably connected as the bourgeois economists maintain? We must not take their word for it. We must not even believe them when they say that the fatter capital is, the better will its slave be fed. . . .

We must, therefore, examine more closely:

How does the growth of productive capital affect wages?

If, on the whole, the productive capital of bourgeois society grows, a *more manifold* accumulation of labour takes place. The capitals increase in number and extent. The *numerical increase* of the capitals increases the *competition between the capitalists.* The *increasing extent* of the capitals provides the means for *bringing more powerful labour armies with more gigantic instruments of war into the industrial battlefield.*

One capitalist can drive another from the field and capture his capital only by selling more cheaply. In order to be able to sell more cheaply without ruining himself, he must produce more cheaply, that is, raise the productive power of labour as much as possible. But the productive power of labour is raised, above all, by *a greater division of labour,* by a more universal introduction and continual improvement of *machinery.* The greater the labour army among whom labour is divided, the more gigantic the scale on which machinery is introduced, the more does the cost of production proportionately decrease, the more fruitful is labour. Hence, a general rivalry arises among the capitalists to increase the division of labour and machinery and to exploit them on the greatest possible scale.

If, now, by a greater division of labour, by the utilisation of new machines and their improvement, by more profitable and extensive exploitation of natural forces, one capitalist has found the means of producing with the same amount of labour or of accumulated labour a greater amount of products, of commodities, than his competitors, if he can, for example, produce a whole yard of linen in the same labour time in which his competitors weave half a yard, how will this capitalist operate?

He could continue to sell half a yard of linen at the old market price; this would, however, be no means of driving his opponents from the field and of enlarging his own sales. But in the same measure in which his production has expanded, his need to sell has also increased. The more powerful and costly means of production that he has called into life *enable* him, indeed, to sell his commodities more cheaply, they *compel* him, however, at the same time *to sell more commodities,* to conquer a much *larger* market for his commodities; consequently, our capitalist will sell his half yard of linen more cheaply than his competitors.

The capitalist will not, however, sell a whole yard as cheaply as his competitors sell half a yard, although the production of the whole yard does not cost him more than the half yard costs the others. Otherwise he would not gain anything extra but only get back the cost of production by the exchange. His possibly greater income would be derived from the fact of having set a larger capital into motion, but not from having made more of his capital than the others. Moreover, he attains the object he wishes to attain, if he puts the price of his goods only a small percentage lower than that of his competitors. He drives them from the field, he wrests from them at least a part of their sales, by *underselling* them. . . .

However, the *privileged position* of our capitalist is not of long duration; other competing capitalists introduce the same machines, the same division of labour, introduce them on the same or on a larger scale, and this introduction will become so general that the price of linen *is reduced* not only *below its old,* but *below its new cost of production.*

The capitalists find themselves, therefore, in the same position relative to one another as *before* the introduction of the new means of production, and if they are able to supply by these means double the production at the same price, they are *now* forced to supply the double product *below* the old price. On the basis of this new cost of production, the same game begins again. More division of labour, more machinery, enlarged scale of exploitation of machinery and division of labour. And again competition brings the same counteraction against this result.

We see how in this way the mode of production and the means of production are continually transformed, revolutionised, *how the division of labour is necessarily followed by greater division of labour, the application of machinery by still greater application of machinery, work on a large scale by work on a still larger scale.*

That is the law which again and again throws bourgeois production out of its old course and which compels capital to intensify the productive forces of labour, *because* it has intensified them, it, the law which gives capital no rest and continually whispers in its ear: "Go on! Go on!"

This law is none other than that which, within the fluctuations of trade periods, necessarily *levels out* the price of a commodity to its *cost of production.*

However powerful the means of production which a capitalist brings into the field, competition will make these means of production universal and from the moment when it has made them universal, the only result of the greater fruitfulness of his capital is that he must now supply *for the sme price* ten, twenty, a hundred times as much as before. But, as he must sell perhaps a thousand times as much as before in order to outweigh the lower selling price by the greater amount of the product sold, because a more extensive sale is now necessary, not only in order to make more profit but in order to replace the cost of production—the instrument of production itself, as we have seen, becomes more and more expensive—and because this mass sale becomes a question of life and death not only for him but also for his rivals, the old struggle begins again *all the more violently the more fruitful the already discovered means of production are. The division of labour and the application of machinery, therefore, will go on anew on an incomparably greater scale.*

Whatever the power of the means of production employed may be, competition seeks to rob capital of the golden fruits of this power by bringing the price of the commodities back to the cost of production, by thus making cheaper production—the supply of ever greater amounts of products for the same total price—an imperative law to the same extent as production can be cheapened, that is, as more can be produced with the same amount of labour. Thus the capitalist would have won nothing by his own exertions but the obligation to supply more in the same labour time, in a word, *more difficult conditions for the augmentation of the value of his capital.* While, therefore, competition continually pursues him with its law of the cost of production and every weapon that he forges against his rivals recoils against himself, the capitalist continually tries to get the better of competition by incessantly introducing new machines, more expensive, it is true, but producing more cheaply, and new division of labour in place of the old, and by not waiting until competition has rendered the new ones obsolete.

If now we picture to ourselves this feverish simultaneous agitation on the *whole world market,* it will be comprehensible how the growth, accumulation and concentration of capital results in an uninterrupted division of labour, and in the application of new and the perfecting of old machinery precipitately and on an ever more gigantic scale.

But how do these circumstances, which are inseparable from the growth of productive capital, affect the determination of wages?

The greater *division of labour* enables *one* worker to do the work of five, ten or twenty; it therefore multiplies competition among the workers fivefold, tenfold and twentyfold. The workers do not only compete by one selling himself cheaper than another; they compete by *one* doing the work of five, ten, twenty; and the *division of labour,* introduced by capital and continually increased, compels the workers to compete among themselves in this way.

Further, as the *division of labour* increases, labour *is simplified.* The special skill of the worker becomes worthless. He becomes transformed into a simple, monotonous productive force that does not have to use intense bodily or intellectual faculties. His labour becomes a labour that anyone can perform. Hence, competitors crowd upon him on all sides, and besides we remind the reader that the more simple and easily learned the labour is, the lower the cost of production needed to master it, the lower do wages sink, for, like the price of every other commodity, they are determined by the cost of production.

Therefore, as labour becomes more unsatisfying, more repulsive, competition increases and wages decrease. The worker tries to keep up the amount of his wages by working more, whether by working longer hours or by producing more in one hour. Driven by want, therefore, he still further increases the evil effects of the division of labour. The result is that *the more he works the less wages he receives,* and for the simple reason that he competes to that extent with his fellow workers, hence makes them into so many competitors who offer themselves on just the same bad terms as he does himself, and that, therefore, in the last resort he *competes with himself, with himself as a member of the working class.*

Machinery brings about the same results on a much greater scale, by replacing skilled workers by unskilled, men by women, adults by children. It brings about the same results, where it is newly introduced, by throwing the hand workers on to the streets in masses, and, where it is developed, improved and replaced by more productive machinery, by discharging workers in smaller batches. We have portrayed above, in a hasty sketch, the industrial war of the capitalists among themselves; *this war has the peculiarity that its battles are won less by recruiting than by discharging the army of labour. The generals, the capitalists, compete with one another as to who can discharge most soldiers of industry.*

The economists tell us, it is true, that the workers rendered superfluous by machinery find *new* branches of employment.

They dare not assert directly that the same workers who are discharged find places in the new branches of labour. The facts cry out too loudly against this lie. They really only assert that new means of employment will open up for *other component sections of the working class,* for instance, for the portion of the young generation of workers that was ready to enter the branch of industry which has gone under. That is, of course, a great consolation for the disinherited workers. The worshipful capitalists will never want for fresh exploitable fresh and blood, and will let the dead bury their dead. This is a consolation which the bourgeois give themselves rather than one which they give the workers. If the whole class of wage-workers were to be abolished owing to machinery, how dreadful that would be for capital which, without wage labour, ceases to be capital!

Let us suppose, however, that those directly driven out of their jobs by machinery, and the entire section of the new generation that was already on the watch for this employment, *find a new occupation.* Does any one imagine that it will be as highly paid as that which has been lost? *That would contradict all the laws of economics.* We have seen how modern industry always brings with it the substitution of a more simple, subordinate occupation for the more complex and higher one.

How, then, could a mass of workers who have been thrown out of one branch of industry owing to machinery find refuge in another, unless the latter *is lower, worse paid?*

The workers who work in the manufacture of machinery itself have been cited as an exception. As soon as more machinery is demanded and used in industry, it is said, there must necessarily be an increase of machines, consequently of the manufacture of machines, and consequently of the employment of workers in the manufacture of machines; and the workers engaged in this branch of industry are claimed to be skilled, even educated workers.

Since the year 1840 this assertion, which even before was only half true, has lost all semblance of truth because ever more versatile machines have been employed in the manufacture of machinery, no more and no less than in the manufacture of cotton yarn, and the workers employed in the machine factories, confronted by highly elaborate machines, can only play the part of highly unelaborate machines.

But in place of the man who has been discharged owing to the machine, the factory employs maybe *three* children and *one* woman. And did not the man's wages have to suffice for the three children and a woman? Did not the minimum of wages have to suffice to maintain and to propagate the race? What, then, does this favourite bourgeois phrase prove? Nothing more than that now four times as many workers' lives are used up in order to gain a livelihood for *one* worker's family.

Let us sum up: *The more productive capital grows, the more the division of labour and the application of machinery expands. The more the division of labour and the application of machinery expands, the more competition among the workers expands and the more their wages contract.*

In addition, the working class gains recruits from the *higher strata of society* also; a mass of petty industrialists and small rentiers are hurled down into its ranks and have nothing better to do than urgently stretch out their arms alongside those of the workers. Thus the forest of uplifted arms demanding work becomes ever thicker, while the arms themselves become ever thinner.

That the small industrialist cannot survive in a contest one of the first conditions of which is to produce on an ever greater scale, that is, precisely to be a large and not a small industrialist, is self-evident.

That the interest on capital decreases in the same measure as the mass and number of capitals increase, as capital grows; that, therefore, the small rentier can no longer live on his interest but must throw himself into industry, and, consequently, help to swell the ranks of the small industrialists and thereby of candidates for the proletariat—all this surely requires no further explanation.

Finally, as the capitalists are compelled, by the movement described above, to exploit the already existing gigantic means of production on a larger scale and to set in motion all the main-springs of credit to this end, there is a corresponding increase in industrial earthquakes, in which the trading world can only maintain itself by sacrificing a part of wealth, of products and even of productive forces to the gods of the nether world—in a word, *crises* increase. They become more frequent and more violent, if only because, as the mass of production, and consequently the need for extended markets, grows, the world market becomes more and more contracted, fewer and fewer new markets remain available for exploitation, since every preceding crisis has subjected to world trade a market hitherto unconquered or only superficially exploited. But capital does not *live* only on labour. A lord, at once aristocratic and barbarous, it drags with it into the grave the corpses of its slaves, whole hecatombs of workers who perish in the crises. Thus we see: *if capital grows rapidly, competition among the workers grows incomparably more rapidly, that is, the means of employment, the means of subsistence, of the working class decrease proportionately so much the more, and, nevertheless, the rapid growth of capital is the most favourable condition for wage labour.*

Marx, *Wage Labour and Capital* (1847), MESW, pp. 84–94.

C. LARGE-SCALE PRODUCTION AND DIVISION OF LABOR

Another distinguishing property of capitalism is the character of division of labor under its auspices. The spread of market exchange in modern times, especially under capitalism, has undoubtedly encouraged expansion of division of labor. Indeed, Marx agrees with Adam Smith that exchange depends upon the division of labor. However, he insists, the reverse is not true; that is, division of labor does not necessarily require a market exchange economy. Ancient Peru and India, for example, were characterized by an intricate division of labor. But market exchange was nonexistent or negligible in ancient societies, occuring at the fringes of society, in relations with other societies.

These interconnections between exchange and division of labor are clarified by distinguishing between division of labor "in society" and "in industry" (selection 2.C.8). The social division of labor (the butcher, baker, and candlestick maker) implies dispersion of economic power among many individual units, as in a simple exchange economy, and rests upon the exchanges of commodities by independent owners. The detailed division of labor within a workshop, by contrast, implies the concentration of economic power by one capitalist, and rests upon the exchange of labor power, not merely final commodities. Modern capitalism combines both forms, thus blending anarchy and competition in the social division of labor among industries with hierarchy, tight organization, and despotism within the individual capitalist enterprise.

Marx distinguishes several stages in the development of capitalist division of labor. To begin with, an individual must have a minimum capital to establish himself as a capitalist and employ others to work for him. Next is the stage of simple cooperation wherein the capitalist assembles a comparatively large number of workers and organizes their activity as a combined social labor process. On the one hand, this requires an even greater minimum amount of capital; on the other, it engenders economies which in turn encourage development of large-scale production. In the simplest case, however, it is not yet division of labor, though it is certainly the simultaneous employment of a large number of workers (selection 2.C.9).

The first division of labor within the capitalist enterprise itself occurs during "manufacture." In this stage, technology is still relatively simple and unmechanized, but division of labor is more complex. Division of labor increases productivity, but at the same time reduces the worker's overall dexterity and abilities, increases his dependency upon the capitalist, and creates a hierarchy of labor powers, including unskilled labor. As in cooperation, the capitalist is the undisputed master, in control of the division of labor. Consequently, the productivity gains from the development of "collective labor" not only accrue to the capitalist, but appear to emanate from capital rather than labor (selection 2.C.10).

The second stage of division of labor occurs under "modern industry," which focuses upon the application of machinery and new technology in the modern factory. Here, workers are distributed among the various machines and, in effect, become appendages to them. A militaristic discipline is enforced upon the workers, facilitated by their increased separation from the work process as a whole. Science becomes a force of production apart from direct labor and is pressed "into the service of capital." (selection 2.C.11).

2.C.8 DIVISION OF LABOR IN SOCIETY AND IN INDUSTRY

To all the different varieties of values in use there correspond as many different kinds of useful labour, classified according to the order, genus, species, and variety to which they belong in the social division of labour. This division of labour is a necessary condition for the production of commodities, but it does not follow conversely, that the production of commodities is a necessary condition for the division of labour. In the primitive Indian community there is social division of labour, without production of commodities. Or, to take an example nearer home, in every factory the labour is divided according to a system, but this division is not brought about by the operatives mutually exchanging their individual products. Only such products can become commodities with regard to each other, as result from different kinds of labour, each kind being carried on independently and for the account of private individuals. . . .

In a community, the produce of which in general takes the form of commodities, i.e., in a community of commodity producers, this qualitative difference between the useful forms of labour that are carried on independently by individual producers, each on their own account, develops into a complex system, a social division of labour. . . .

Division of Labour in Manufacture, and Division of Labour in Society

We shall now lightly touch upon the relation between the division of labour in manufacture, and the social division of labour, which forms the foundation of all production of commodities.

If we keep labour alone in view, we may designate the separation of social production into its main division or *genera*—viz., agriculture, industries, etc., as division of labour in general, and the splitting up of these families into species and sub-species, as division of labour in particular, and the division of labour within the workshop as division of labour in singular or in detail.

Division of labour in a society, and the corresponding tying down of individuals to a particular calling, develops itself, just as does the division of labour in manufacture, from opposite starting points. Within a family, and after further development within a tribe, there springs up naturally a division of labour, caused by differences of sex and age, a division that is consequently based on a purely physiological foundation, which division enlarges its materials by the expansion of the community, by the increase of population, and more especially, by the conflicts between different tribes, and the subjugation of one tribe by another. On the other hand, as I have before remarked, the exchange of products springs up at the points where different families, tribes, communities, come in contact; for, in the beginning of civilisation, it is not private individuals but families, tribes, etc., that meet on an independent footing. Different communities find different means of production and different means of subsistence in their natural environment. Hence, their modes of production, and of living, and their products are different. It is this spontaneously developed difference which, when different communities come in contact, calls forth the mutual exchange of products, and the consequent gradual conversion of those products into commodities. Exchange does not create the differences between the spheres of production, but brings such as are already different into relation, and thus converts them into more or less interdependent branches of the collective production of an enlarged society. In the latter case, the social division of labour arises from the exchange between spheres of production, that are originally distinct and independent of one another. In the former, where the physiological division of labour is the starting point, the particular organs of a compact whole grow loose, and break off, principally owing to the exchange of commodities with foreign communities, and then isolate themselves so far, that the sole bond, still connecting the various kinds of work, is the exchange of the products as commodities. In the one case, it is the making dependent what was before independent; in the other case, the making independent what was before dependent.

The foundation of every division of labour that is well developed, and brought about by the exchange of commodities, is the separation between town and country. . . .

Since the production and the circulation of commodities are the general prerequisites of the capitalist mode of production, division of labour in manufacture demands that division of labour in society at large should previously have attained a certain degree of development. Inversely, the former division reacts upon and develops and multiplies the latter. Simultaneously, with the differentiation of the instruments of labour, the industries that produce these instruments, become more and more differentiated. . . .

But, in spite of the numerous analogies and links connecting them, division of labour in the interior of a society, and that in the interior of a workshop, differ not only in degree, but also in kind. The analogy appears most indisputable where there is an invisible bond uniting the various branches of trade. For instance the cattle breeder produces hides, the tanner makes the hides into leather, and the shoemaker, the leather into boots. Here the thing produced by each of them is but a step towards the final form, which is the product of all their labours combined. There are, besides, all the various industries that supply the cattle-breeder, the tanner, and the shoemaker with the means of production. Now it is quite possible to imagine, with Adam Smith, that the difference between the above social division of labour, and the division in manufacture, is merely subjective, exists merely for the observer, who, in a manufacture, can see with one glance, all the numerous operations being performed on one spot, while in the instance given above, the spreading out of the work over great areas, and the great number of people employed in each branch of labour, obscure the connexion. But what is it that forms the bond between the independent labours of the cattle-breeder, the tanner, and the shoemaker? It is the fact that their respective products are commodities. What, on the other hand, characterises division of labour in manufactures? The fact that the detail labourer produces no commodities. It is only the common product of all the detail labourers that becomes a commodity. Division of labour in a society is brought about by the purchase and sale of the products of different branches of industry, while the connexion between the detail operations in a workshop, are due to the sale of the labour-power of several workmen to one capitalist, who applies it as combined labour-power. The division of labour in the workshop implies concentration of the means of production in the hands of one capitalist; the division of labour in society implies their dispersion among many independent producers of commodities. While within the workshop, the iron law of proportionality subjects definite numbers of workmen to definite functions, in the society outside the workshop, chance and caprice have full play in distributing the producers and their means of production among the various branches of industry. The different spheres of production, it is true, constantly tend to an equilibrium: for, on the one hand, while each producer of a commodity is bound to produce a use-value, to satisfy a particular social want, and while the extent of these wants differs quantitatively, still there exists an inner relation which settles their proportions into a regular system, and that system one of spontaneous growth; and, on the other hand, the law of the value of commodities ultimately determines how much of its disposable working-time society can expend on each particular class of commodities. But this constant tendency to equilibrium, of the various spheres of production, is exercised, only in the shape of a reaction against the constant upsetting of this equilibrium. The *a priori* system on which the division of labour, within the workshop, is regularly carried out, becomes in the division of labour within the society, an *a posteriori,* nature-imposed necessity, controlling the lawless caprice of the producers, and perceptible in the barometrical fluctuations of the market prices. Division of labour within the workshop implies the undisputed authority of the capitalist over men, that are but parts of a mechanism that belongs to him. The division of labour within the society brings into contact independent commodity-producers, who acknowledge no other authority but that of competition, of the coercion exerted by the pressure of their mutual interests. . . . The same bourgeois mind which praises division of labour in the workshop, life-long annexation of the labourer to a partial operation, and his complete subjection to capital, as being an organisation of labour that increases its productiveness —that same bourgeois mind denounces with equal vigour every conscious attempt to socially control and regulate the process of production, as an inroad upon such sacred things as the rights of property, freedom and unrestricted play for the bent of the individual capitalist. It is very characteristic that the enthusiastic apologists of the factory system have nothing more damning to urge against a general organization of the labour of society, than that it would turn all society into one immense factory.

If, in a society with capitalist production, anarchy in the social division of labour and despotism in that of the workshop are mutual conditions the one of the other, we find, on the contrary, in those earlier forms of society in which the separation of trades has been spontaneously developed, then, crystallized, and finally made permanent by law, on the one hand, a specimen of the organization of the labour of society, in accordance with an approved and authoritative plan, and on the other, the entire exclusion of division of labour in the workshop, or at all events a mere dwarflike or sporadic and accidental development of the same.

Marx, *Capital,* I (1867), pp. 49, 385–92.

2.C.9 LARGE-SCALE COOPERATIVE PRODUCTION

Capitalist production only then really begins . . . when each individual capital employs simultaneously a comparatively large number of labourers; when consequently the labour-process is carried on on an extensive scale and yields, relatively, large quantities of products. A greater number of labourers working together, at the same time, in one place (or, if you will, in the same field of labour), in order to produce the same sort of commodity under the mastership of one capitalist, constitutes, both historically and logically, the starting point of capitalist production. . . .

Even without an alteration in the system of working, the simultaneous employment of a large number of labourers effects a revolution in the material conditions of the labour-process. The buildings in which they work, the store-houses for the raw material, the implements and utensils used simultaneously or in turns by the workmen; in short, a portion of the means of production, are now consumed in common, . . . and therefore on a larger scale than before. A room where twenty weavers work at twenty looms must be larger than the room of a single weaver with two assistants. But it costs less labour to build one workshop for twenty persons than to build ten to accommodate two weavers each; thus the value of the means of production that are concentrated for use in common on a large scale does not increase in direct proportion to the expansion and to the increased useful effect of those means. . . . The effect is the same as if the means of production had cost less. The economy in their application is entirely owing to their being consumed in common by a large number of workmen. Moreover, this character of being necessary conditions of social labour, a character that distinguishes them from the dispersed and relatively more costly means of production of isolated, independent labourers, or small masters, is acquired even when the numerous workmen assembled together do not assist one another, but merely work side by side. A portion of the instruments of labour acquires this social character before the labour-process itself does so. . . .

When numerous labourers work together side by side, whether in one and the same process, or in different but connected processes, they are said to cooperate, or to work in cooperation. . . .

The sum total of the mechanical forces exerted by isolated workmen differs from the social force that is developed, when many hands take part simultaneously in one and the same undivided operation, such as raising a heavy weight, turning a winch, or removing an obstacle. In such cases the effect of the combined labour could either not be produced at all by isolated individual labour, or it could only be produced by a great expenditure of time, or on a very dwarfed scale. Not only have we here an increase in the productive power of the individual, by means of cooperation, but the creation of a new power, namely, the collective power of masses.

Apart from the new power that arises from the fusion of many forces into one single force, mere social contact begets in most industries an emulation and a stimulation of the animal spirits that heighten the efficiency of each individual workman. . . . The reason of this is that a man is, if not as Aristotle contends, a political, at all events a social animal. . . .

If the work be complicated, then the mere number of the men who cooperate allows of the various operations being apportioned to different hands, and, consequently, of being carried on simultaneously. The time necessary for the completion of the whole work is thereby shortened. . . .

On the one hand, cooperation allows of the work being carried on over an extended space; it is consequently imperatively called for in certain undertakings, such as draining, constructing dykes, irrigation works, and the making of canals, roads and railways. On the other hand, while extending the scale of production, it renders possible a relative contraction of the arena. This contraction of arena simultaneous with, and arising from, extension of scale, whereby a number of useless expenses are cut down, is owing to the conglomeration of labourers, to the aggregation of various processes, and to the concentration of the means of production. . . .

Whether the combined working-day, in a given case, acquires. . .increased productive power, because it heightens the mechanical force of labour or extends its sphere of action over a greater space, or contracts the field of production relatively to the scale of production, or at the critical moment sets large masses of labour to work, or excites emulation between individuals and raises their animal spirits, or impresses on the similar operations carried on by a number of men the stamp of continuity and many-sidedness, or performs simultaneously different operations, or economises the means of production by use in common, or lends to individual labour the character of average social labour—which ever of these be the cause of the increase, the special productive power of the combined working day is, under all circumstances, the social productive power of labour, or the productive power of social labour. This power is due to cooperation itself. When the labourer cooperates systematically with others, he strips off the fetters of his individuality, and develops the capabilities of his species.

As a general rule, labourers cannot cooperate without being brought together: their assemblage in one place is a necessary condition of their cooperation. Hence wage labourers cannot cooperate, unless they are employed simultaneously by the same capital, the same capitalist, and unless therefore their labour-powers are bought simultaneously by him. . . . Hence the number of the labourers that cooperate, or the scale of cooperation, depends, in the first instance, on the amount of capital that the individual capitalist can spare for the purchase of labour-power; in other words, on the extent to which a single capitalist has command over the means of subsistence of a number of labourers. . . .

Hence, concentration of large masses of the means of production in the hands of individual capitalists, is a material condition for the cooperation of wage-labourers, and the extent of the cooperation or the scale of production, depends on the extent of this concentration.

We saw in a former [selection] that a certain minimum amount of capital was necessary, in order that the number of labourers simultaneously employed, and, consequently, the amount of surplus-value produced, might suffice to liberate the employer himself from manual labour, to convert him from a small master into a capitalist, and thus formally to establish capitalist production. We now see that a certain minimum amount is a necessary condition for the conversion of numerous isolated and independent processes into one combined social process.

We also saw that at first, the subjection of labour to capital was only a formal result of the fact, that the labourer, instead of working for himself, works for and consequently under the capitalist. By the cooperation of numerous wage-labourers, the sway of capital develops into a requisite for carrying on the labour-process itself, into a real requisite of production. That a capitalist should command on the field of production, is now as indispensable as that a general should command on the field of battle.

All combined labour on a large scale requires, more or less, a directing authority, in order to secure the harmonious working of the individual activities, and to perform the general functions that have their origin in the action of the combined organism, as distinguished from the action of its separate organs. A single violin player is his own conductor; an orchestra requires a separate one. The work of directing, superintending, and adjusting, becomes one of the functions of capital, from the moment that the labour under the control of capital, becomes cooperative. Once a function of capital, it acquires special characteristics.

The directing motive, the end and aim of capitalist production, is to extract the greatest possible amount of surplus-value, and consequently to exploit labour-power to the greatest possible extent. As the number of the cooperating labourers increases, so too does their resistance to the domination of capital, and with it, the necessity for capital to overcome this resistance by counter-pressure. The control exercised by the capitalist is not only a special function, due to the nature of the social labour-process, and peculiar to that process, but it is, at the same time, a function of the exploitation of a social labour-process, and is consequently rooted in the unavoidable antagonism between the exploiter and the living and labouring raw material he exploits.

Again, in proportion to the increasing mass of the means of production, now no longer the property of the labourer, but of the capitalist, the necessity increases for some effective control over the proper application of those means. Moreover, the cooperation of wage labourers is entirely brought about by the capital that employs them. Their union into one single productive body and the establishment of a connexion between their individual functions, are matters foreign and external to them, are not their own act, but the act of the capital that brings and keeps them together. Hence the connexion existing between their various labours appears to them, ideally, in the shape of a preconceived plan of the capitalist, and practically in the shape of the authority of the same capitalist, in the shape of the powerful will of another, who subjects their activity to his aims. If, then, the control of the capitalist is in substance twofold by reason of the twofold nature of the process of production itself,—which, on the one hand, is a social process for producing use-values, on the other, a process for creating surplus-value—in form that control is despotic. As cooperation extends its scale, this despotism takes forms peculiar to itself. Just as at first the capitalist is relieved from actual labour so soon as his capital has reached that minimum amount with which capitalist production, as such begins, so now, he hands over the work of direct and constant supervision of the individual workmen, and groups of workmen, to a special kind of wage labourer. An industrial army of workmen, under the command of a capitalist, requires, like a real army, officers (managers), and sergeants (foremen, overlookers), who, while the work is being done, command in the name of the capitalist. The work of supervision becomes their established and exclusive function. When comparing the mode of production of isolated peasants and artizans with production by slave labour the political economist counts this labour of superintendence among the *faux frais* of production. But, when considering the capitalist mode of production, he, on the contrary, treats the work of control made necessary by the cooperative character of the labour process as identical with the different work of control, necessitated by the capitalist character of that process and the antagonism of interests between capitalist and labourer. It is not because he is a leader of industry that a man is a capitalist; on the contrary, he is a leader of industry because he is a capitalist. The leadership of industry is an attribute of capital, just as in feudal times the functions of general and judge were attributes of landed property.

The labourer is the owner of his labour-power until he has done bargaining for its sale with the capitalist; and he can sell no more than what he has—i.e., his individual, isolated labour-power. . . . Being independent of each other, the labourers are isolated persons, who enter into relations with the capitalist, but not with one another. This cooperation begins only with the labour process, but they have then ceased to belong to themselves. On entering that process, they become incorporated with capital. As cooperators, as members of a working organism, they are but special modes of existence of capital. Hence, the productive power developed by the labourer when working in cooperation, is the productive power of capital. This power is developed gratuitously, whenever the workmen are placed under given conditions, and it is capital that places them under such conditions. Because this power costs capital nothing, and because, on the other hand, the labourer himself does not develop it before his labour belongs to capital, it appears as a power with which capital is endowed by Nature—a productive power that is immanent in capital. . . .

Just as the social productive power of labour that is developed by cooperation, appears to be the productive power of capital, so cooperation itself, contrasted with the process of production carried on by isolated independent labourers, or even by small employers, appears to be a specific form of the capitalist process of production. It is the first change experienced by the actual labour-process, when subjected to capital. This change takes place spontaneously. The simultaneous employment of a large number of wage-labourers, in one and the same process, which is a necessary condition of this change, also forms the starting point of capitalist production. This point coincides with the birth of capital itself. If then, on the one hand, the capitalist mode of production presents itself to us historically, as a necessary condition to the transformation of the labour-process into a social process, so, on the other hand, this social form of the labour-process presents itself as a method employed by capital for the more profitable exploitation of labour, by increasing that labour's productiveness.

Marx, *Capital,* I (1867), pp. 353–68.

2.C.10 DIVISION OF LABOR IN MANUFACTURING

Twofold Origin of Manufacture

That cooperation which is based on division of labour, assumes its typical form in manufacture, and is the prevalent characteristic form of the capitalist process of production throughout the manufacturing period properly so called. That period, roughly speaking, extends from the middle of the sixteenth to the last third of the eighteenth century.

Manufacture takes its rise in two ways:

(1) By the assemblage, in one workshop under the control of a single capitalist, of labourers belonging to various independent handicrafts, but through whose hands a given article must pass on its way to completion. . . .

(2) Manufacture also arises in a way exactly the reverse of this—namely, by one capitalist employing simultaneously in one workshop a number of artificers, who all do the same, or the same kind of work, such as making paper, type, or needles. This is cooperation in its most elementary form. . . .

On the one hand, therefore, manufacture either introduces division of labour into a process of production, or further developes that division; on the other hand, it unites together handicrafts that were formerly separate. But whatever may have been its particular starting point, its final form is invariably the same—a productive mechanism whose parts are human beings. . . .

The Detail Labourer and His Implements

If we now go more into detail, it is, in the first place, clear that a labourer who all his life performs one and the same simple operation, converts his whole body into the automatic, specialised implement of that operation. Consequently, he takes less time in doing it, than the artificer who performs a whole series of operations in succession. But the collective labourer, who constitutes the living mechanism of manufacture, is made up solely of such specialised detail labourers. Hence, in comparison with the independent handicraft, more is produced in a given time, or the productive power of labour is increased. Moreover, when once this fractional work is established as the exclusive function of one person, the methods it employs become perfected. The workman's continued repetition of the same simple act, and the concentration of his attention on it, teach him by experience how to attain the desired effect with the minimum of exertion. But since there are always several generations of labourers living at one time, and working together at the manufacture of a given article, the technical skill, the tricks of the trade thus acquired, become established, and are accumulated and handed down. . . .

An artificer, who performs one after another the various fractional operations in the production of a finished article, must at one time change his place, at another his tools. The transition from one operation to another interrupts the flow of his labour, and creates, so to say, gaps in his working day. These gaps close up so soon as he is tied to one and the same operation all day long; they vanish in proportion as the changes in his work diminish. The resulting increased productive power is owing either to an increased expenditure of labour-power in a given time—i.e., to increased intensity of labour—or to a decrease in the amount of labour-power unproductively consumed. The extra expenditure of power, demanded by every transition from rest to motion, is made up for by prolonging the duration of the normal velocity when once acquired. On the other hand, constant labour of one uniform kind disturbs the intensity and flow of a man's animal spirits, which find recreation and delight in mere change of activity.

The productiveness of labour depends not only on the proficiency of the workman, but on the perfection of his tools. Tools of the same kind, such as knives, drills, gimlets, hammers, etc. may be employed in different processes; and the same tool may serve various purposes in a single process. But so soon as the different operations of a labour-process are disconnected the one from the other, and each fractional operation acquires in the hands of the detail labourer a suitable and peculiar form, alterations become necessary in the implements that previously served more than one purpose. The direction taken by this change is determined by the difficulties experienced in consequence of the unchanged form of the implement. Manufacture is characterized by the differentiation of the instruments of labour—a differentiation whereby implements of a given sort acquire fixed shapes, adapted to each particular application, and by the specialisation of those instruments, giving to each special instrument its full play only in the hands of a specific detail labourer.

The Collective Laborer

The collective laborer, formed by the combination of a number of detail labourers, is the mechanism specially characteristic of the manufacturing period. The various operations that are performed in turns by the producer of a commodity, and coalesce one with another during the progress of production, lay claim to him in various ways. In one operation he must exert more strength, in another more skill, in another more attention; and the same individual does not possess all these qualities in an equal degree. After Manufacture has once separated, made independent, and isolated the various operations, the labourers are divided, classified, and grouped according to their predominating qualities. If their natural endowments are, on the one hand, the foundation on which the division of labour is built up, on the other hand, Manufacture, once introduced, develops in them new powers that are by nature fitted only for limited and special functions. The collective labourer now possesses, in an equal degree of excellence, all the qualities requisite for production, and expends them in the most economical manner, by exclusively employing all his organs, consisting of particular labourers, or groups of labourers, in performing their special functions. The one-sidedness and the deficiencies of the detail labourer become perfections when he is a part of the collective labourer. The habit of doing only one thing converts him into a never failing instrument, while his connexion with the whole mechanism compels him to work with the regularity of the parts of a machine.

Since the collective labourer has functions, both simple and complex, both high and low, his members, the individual labour-powers, require different degrees of training, and must therefore have different values. Manufacture, therefore, develops a hierarchy of labour-powers, to which there corresponds a scale of wages. If, on the one hand, the individual labourers are appropriated and annexed for life by a limited function; on the other hand, the various operations of the hierarchy are parcelled out among the labourers according to both their natural and their acquired capabilities. Every process of production, however, requires certain simple manipulations, which every man is capable of doing. They too are now severed from their connexion with more pregnant moments of activity, and ossified into exclusive functions of specially appointed labourers. Hence, Manufacture begets, in every handicraft that it seizes upon, a class of so-called unskilled labourers, a class which handicraft industry strictly excluded. If it develops a one-sided specialty into a perfection, at the expense of the whole of a man's working capacity, it also begins to make a specialty of the absence of all development. Alongside of the hierarchic gradation there steps the simple separation of the labourers into skilled and unskilled. For the latter, the cost of apprenticeship vanishes; for the former, it diminishes, compared with that of artificers, in consequence of the functions being simplified. In both cases the value of labour-power falls. An exception to this law holds good whenever the decomposition of the labour-process begets new and comprehensive functions, that either had no place at all, or only a very modest one, in handicrafts. The fall in the value of labour-power, caused by the disappearance or diminution of the expense of apprenticeship, implies a direct increase of surplus-value for the benefit of capital; for everything that shortens the necessary labour-time required for the reproduction of labour-power, extends the domain of surplus-labour.

The Capitalistic Character of Manufacture

An increased number of labourers under the control of one capitalist is the natural starting-point, as well of cooperation generally, as of manufacture in particular. But the division of labour in the manufacture makes this increase in the number of workmen a technical necessity. The minimum number that any given capitalist is bound to employ is here prescribed by the previously established division of labour. On the other hand, the advantages of further division are obtainable only by adding to the number of workmen, and this can be done only by adding multiples of the various detail groups. But an increase in the variable component of the capital employed necessitates an increase in its constant component, too, in the workshops, implements, etc., and, in particular, in the raw material, the call for which grows quicker than the number of workmen. The quantity of it consumed in a given time, by a given amount of labour, increases in the same ratio as does the productive power of that labour in consequence of its division. Hence, it is a law, based on the very nature of manufacture, that the minimum amount of capital, which is bound to be in the hands of each capitalist, must keep increasing; in other words, that the transformation into capital of the social means of production and subsistence must keep extending.

In manufacture, as well as in simple cooperation, the collective working organism is a form of existence of capital. The mechanism that is made up of numerous individual detail labourers belongs to the capitalist. Hence, the productive power resulting from a combination of labourers appears to be the productive power of capital. Manufacture proper not only subjects the previously independent workman to the discipline and command of capital, but, in addition, creates a hierarchic gradation of the workmen themselves. While simple cooperation leaves the mode of working by the individual for the most part unchanged, manufacture thoroughly revolutionises it, and seizes labour-power by its very roots. It converts the labourer into a crippled monstrosity, by forcing his detail dexterity at the expense of a world of productive capabilities and instincts; just as in the States of La Plata they butcher a whole beast for the sake of his hide or his tallow. Not only is the detail work distributed to the different individuals, but the individual himself is made the automatic motor of a fractional operation, and the absurd fable of Menenius Agrippa, which makes man a mere fragment of his own body, becomes realised. If, at first, the workman sells his labour-power to capital, because the material means of producing a commodity fail him, now his very labour-power refuses its services unless it has been sold to capital. Its functions can be exercised only in an environment that exists in the workshop of the capitalist after the sale. By nature unfitted to make anything independently, the manufacturing labourer develops productive activity as a mere appendage of the capitalist's workshop. As the chosen people bore in their features the sign manual of Jehovah, so division of labour brands the manufacturing workman as the property of capital.

The knowledge, the judgment, and the will, which, though in ever so small a degree, are practised by the independent peasant or handicraftsman, in the same way as the savage makes the whole art of war consist in the exercise of his personal cunning—these faculties are now required only for the workshop as a whole. Intelligence in production expands in one direction, because it vanishes in many others. What is lost by the detail labourers, is concentrated in the capital that employs them. It is a result of the division of labour in manufactures, that the labourer is brought face to face with the intellectual potencies of the material process of production, as the property of another, and as a ruling power. This separation begins in simple cooperation, where the capitalist represents to the single workman, the oneness and the will of the associated labour. It is developed in manufacture which cuts down the labourer into a detail labourer. It is completed in modern industry, which makes science a productive force distinct from labour and presses it into the service of capital.

In manufacture, in order to make the collective labourer, and through him capital, rich in social productive power, each labourer must be made poor in individual productive powers. . . .

Some crippling of body and mind is inseparable even from division of labour in society as a whole. Since, however, manufacture carries this social separation of branches of labour much further, and also, by its peculiar division, attacks the individual at the very roots of his life, it is the first to afford the materials for, and to give a start to, industrial pathology.

"To subdivide a man is to execute him, if he deserves the sentence, to assassinate him if he does not. . . . The subdivision of labour is the assassination of a people."[1]

Marx, *Capital,* I (1867), pp. 368–75, 382–85, 395–99.

[1](D. Urquhart: Familiar Words. Lond., 1855, p. 119.) Hegel held very heretical views on division of labour. In his Rechtsphilosophie he says: "By well educated men we understand in the first instance, those who can do everything that others do."

2.C.11 DIVISION OF LABOR IN MODERN INDUSTRY

So far as division of labour reappears in the factory, it is primarily a distribution of the workmen among the specialised machines; and of masses of workmen, not however organised into groups, among the various departments of the factory, in each of which they work at a number of similar machines placed together. . . .

To work at a machine, the workman should be taught from childhood, in order that he may learn to adapt his own movements to the uniform and unceasing motion of an automaton. When the machinery, as a whole, forms a system of manifold machines, working simultaneously and in concert, the cooperation based upon it, requires the distribution of various groups of workmen among the different kinds of machines. But the employment of machinery does away with the necessity of crystallizing this distribution after the manner of Manufacture, by the constant annexation of a particular man to a particular function. Since the motion of the whole system does not proceed from the workman, but from the machinery, a change of persons can take place at any time without an interruption of the work. . . . Lastly, the quickness with which machine work is learnt by young people, does away with the necessity of bringing up for exclusive employment by machinery, a special class of operatives. With regard to the work of the mere attendants, it can, to some extent, be replaced in the mill by machines, and owing to its extreme simplicity, it allows of a rapid and constant change of the individuals burdened with this drudgery.

Although then, technically speaking, the old system of division of labour is thrown overboard by machinery, it hangs on in the factory, as a traditional habit handed down from Manufacture, and is afterwards systematically remoulded and established in a more hideous form by capital, as a means of exploiting labour-power. The life-long speciality of handling one and the same tool, now becomes the life-long speciality of serving one and the same machine. Machinery is put to a wrong use, with the object of transforming the workman, from his very childhood, into a part of a detail-machine. In this way, not only are the expenses of his reproduction considerably lessened, but at the same time his helpless dependence upon the factory as a whole, and therefore upon the capitalist, is rendered complete. Here as everywhere else, we must distinguish between the increased productiveness due to the development of the social process of production, and that due to the capitalist exploitation of that process. In handicrafts and manufacture, the workman makes use of a tool, in the factory, the machine makes use of him. There the movements of the instrument of labour proceed from him, here it is the movements of the machine that he must follow. In manufacture the workmen are parts of a living mechanism. In the factory we have a lifeless mechanism independent of the workman, who becomes its mere living appendage. . . . At the same time that factory work exhausts the nervous system to the uttermost, it does away with the many-sided play of the muscles, and confiscates every atom of freedom, both in bodily and intellectual activity. The lightening of the labour, even, becomes a sort of torture, since the machine does not free the labourer from work, but deprives the work of all interest. Every kind of capitalist production in so far as it is not only a labour-process, but also a process of creating surplus-value, has this in common, that it is not the workman that employs the instruments of labour, but the instruments of labour that employ the workman. But it is only in the factory system that this inversion for the first time acquires technical and palpable reality. By means of its conversion into an automaton, the instrument of labour confronts the labourer, during the labour-process, in the shape of capital, of dead labour, that dominates, and pumps dry, living labour-power. The separation of the intellectual powers of production from the manual labour, and the conversion of those powers into the might of capital over labour, is, as we have already shown, finally completed by modern industry erected on the foundation of machinery. The special skill of each individual insignificant factory operative vanishes as an infinitesimal quantity before the science, the gigantic physical forces, and the mass of labour that are embodied in the factory mechanism and, together with that mechanism, constitute the power of the "master." ... The technical subordination of the workman to the uniform motion of the instruments of labour, and the peculiar composition of the body of workpeople, consisting as it does of individuals of both sexes and of all ages, give rise to a barrack discipline, which is elaborated into a complete system in the factory, and which fully develops the before mentioned labour of overlooking, thereby dividing the workpeople into operatives and overlookers, into private soldiers and sergeants of an industrial army. ... The factory code in which capital formulates, like a private legislator, and at his own good will, his autocracy over his workpeople, unaccompanied by that division of responsibility, in other matters so much approved of by the bourgeoisie, and unaccompanied by the still more approved representative system, this code is but the capitalistic caricature of that social regulation of the labour-process which becomes requisite in cooperation on a great scale, and in the employment in common, of instruments of labour and especially of machinery. The place of the slave driver's lash is taken by the overlooker's book of penalties. All punishments naturally resolve themselves into fines and deductions from wages, and the law-giving talent of the factory Lycurgus so arranges matters, that a violation of his laws is, if possible, more profitable to him than the keeping of them.

We shall here merely allude to the material conditions under which factory labour is carried on. Every organ of sense is injured in an equal degree by artificial elevation of the temperature, by the dust-laden atmosphere, by the deafening noise, not to mention danger to life and limb among the thickly crowded machinery, which, with the regularity of the seasons, issues its list of the killed and wounded in the industrial battle. Economy of the social means of production, matured and forced as in a hothouse by the factory system, is turned, in the hands of capital into systematic robbery of what is necessary for the life of the workman while he is at work, robbery of space, light, air, and of protection to his person against the dangerous and unwholesome accompaniments of the productive process, not to mention the robbery of appliances for the comfort of the workman.

Marx, *Capital*, I (1867), pp. 459–66.

3 Capitalism's Progressive and Creative Properties

In general terms, Marx's indictment of capitalism's contradictory and destructive properties (Chapters 4, 5, and 6, below), that is, its tendencies toward alienation, exploitation, crisis and depression, and so on, is widely known. What is often not so fully appreciated, however, is Marx's clear identification, stronger even than in classical political economy, of capitalism's creative and progressive characteristics.

Marx's position may be clarified by contrasting it with that of classical political economy, notably that of English economist David Ricardo. Writing in the early nineteenth century and extending the analysis of Adam Smith and Thomas Malthus, Ricardo envisoned a process of economic growth under capitalist auspices, but one ultimately constrained by natural forces beyond capitalism's control. Economic growth, based on investment of capitalists' profits and accumulation of capital goods, stimulates an expanded population, which increases the demand for and price of food. Agricultural capitalists expand the production of food, but, because of "diminishing returns," at higher costs. Landlords, who perform no economic function, reap higher rents as agricultural land becomes increasingly scarce. Wages, in the aggregate, must rise to meet the rising population (although the individual worker is no better off, because his higher wages are offset by rising food prices). Profits fall, caught in the squeeze between diminishing returns and higher wage and rent costs, causing the national income to rise at a decreasing rate and leading eventually to a "stationary state" where economic growth ceases.[1]

Marx's perception of capitalism's future was quite different. Ricardo identified a no-growth economy without seriously examining the implications of such a prospect for the survival of capitalism. Marx, in contrast, envisioned the eventual supersession of capitalism as an economic system, but through the process of capitalist industrialization and economic development. Marx rejected the Malthusian population dilemma and the assumption of diminishing returns in agriculture by postulating a tremendous and more than compensating surge

[1]Actually, Ricardo's prognosis is not as gloomy as it is sometimes made out to be. His policy proposal to cope with the problem was to eliminate tariffs on agricultural imports, thus increasing competition and decreasing food prices (and thereby rents and wages). Resources could then be shifted out of agriculture, characterized by diminishing returns, into industry, characterized by "constant returns", where England had a "comparative advantage" in foreign trade. It is not clear, however, that this solution is either worldwide or permanent, within the logic of Ricardo's model. Eventually, the expansion of world population would presumably proceed to the point of worldwide diminishing returns in food production. This did not particularly bother Ricardo, however, whose vision was focused essentially upon the British economy of his time.

of technological improvements under modern capitalist industry. We shall return to the questions of capitalism's contradictions, transformation, and potential supersession; in this chapter, we focus upon the creative elements in capitalist development. It must be emphasized, however, that the two themes—capitalism's creative and destructive sides—are intimately connected. In *Capital,* Marx wrote of bringing development of the forces of production and the world market "to a certain degree of perfection" as capitalism's "historical mission," and as the basis for a "higher form of society."

Capitalism's creative elements may be characterized as its revolutionizing, universalizing, and industrializing propensities. These interconnected aspects of capitalist development are described in the following three selections. First, capitalism, notably in its industrial form, requires—and accomplishes—a "total revolution" in the transformation and dissolution of the old precapitalist economic and social relations. It is destructive of all traditional and complacent ways of life, and "constantly revolutionizes" society, tearing down all barriers to its economic and social development (selection 3.1).

Second, there is the "universalizing tendency" of capitalism, which "distinguishes it from all previous stages of production." Capitalism's universalizing propensities are dramatically demonstrated by its intensive and comprehensive development of technology and expansion of productivity, its geographically extensive development of the world market, its "civilizing influence" in creating modern bourgeois society and in extending bourgeois values and forms throughout the world, and its creation of new needs (selection 3.2).

Third, capitalism contains a "boundless drive" toward industrialization. This characteristic is evidenced by investment and capital accumulation, the development of science and the application of technology, the spread of automation in industry, the conquest of nature, and the expansion of "universal industriousness" and society's productive forces in general (selection 3.3).

These creative propensities of capitalist development, it should be emphasized, are no mere "accident"; they are directly derived from the institutional and behavioral properties of the capitalist economic system. The capitalist "mania" for wealth, stimulated by money and market exchange, yields a general development of society's productive forces. Capitalist property relations and division of labor give the capitalist the freedom, power, and incentive to industrialize. The low pay and long hours which capitalism imposes upon workers, combined with the benefits of science, technology, and large-scale production, under capitalist control, provide a "discipline" over labor and a basis for the creation and investment of economic surplus for growth. Competition among capitalists also contributes to propelling them on in the development of capital and more productive employment growth. Thus although capitalism ultimately leads to its own destruction, it is "essential" for the development of society's productive forces.

3.1 CAPITALISM'S REVOLUTIONIZING PROPERTIES

THE MANIFESTO

The bourgeoisie, historically, has played a most revolutionary part.

The bourgeoisie, wherever it has got the upper hand, has put an end to all feudal, patriarchal, idyllic relations. It has pitilessly torn asunder the motley feudal ties that bound man to his "natural superiors," and has left remaining no other nexus between man and man than naked self-interest, than callous "cash payment." It has drowned the most heavenly ecstasies of religious fervour, of chivalrous enthusiasm, of philistine sentimentalism, in the icy water of egotistical calculation. It has resolved personal worth into exchange value, and in place of the numberless indefeasible chartered freedoms, has set up that single, unconscionable freedom—Free Trade. In one word, for exploitation, veiled by religious and political illusions, it has substituted naked, shameless, direct, brutal exploitation.

The bourgeoisie has stripped of its halo every occupation hitherto honoured and looked up to with reverent awe. It has converted the physician, the lawyer, the priest, the poet, the man of science, into its paid wage-labourers.

The bourgeoisie has torn away from the family its sentimental veil, and has reduced the family relation to a mere money relation.

The bourgeoisie has disclosed how it came to pass that the brutal display of vigour in the Middle Ages, which Reactionists so much admire, found its fitting complement in the most slothful indolence. It has been the first to show what man's activity can bring about. It has accomplished wonders far surpassing Egyptian pyramids, Roman aqueducts, and Gothic cathedrals: it has conducted expeditions that put in the shade all former Exoduses of nations and crusades.

The bourgeoisie cannot exist without constantly revolutionising the instruments of production, and thereby the relations of production, and with them the whole relations of society. Conservation of the old modes of production in unaltered form, was, on the contrary, the first condition of existence for all earlier industrial classes. Constant revolutionising of production, uninterrupted disturbance of all social conditions, everlasting uncertainty and agitation distinguish the bourgeois epoch from all earlier ones. All fixed, fast-frozen relations, with their train of ancient and venerable prejudices and opinions, are swept away, all new-formed ones become antiquated before they can ossify. All that is solid melts into air, all that is holy is profaned, and man is at last compelled to face with sober senses, his real conditions of life, and his relations with his kind.

The need of a constantly expanding market for its products chases the bourgeoisie over the whole surface of the globe. It must nestle everywhere, settle everywhere, establish connexions everywhere.

The bourgeoisie has through its exploitation of the world-market given a cosmopolitan character to production and consumption in every country. To the great chagrin of Reactionists, it has drawn from under the feet of industry the national ground on which it stood. All old-established national industries have been destroyed or are daily being destroyed. They are dislodged by new industries, whose introduction becomes a life and death question for all civilised nations, by industries that no longer work up indigenous raw material, but raw material drawn from the remotest zones; industries whose products are consumed, not only at home, but in every quarter of the globe. In place of the old wants, satisfied by the productions of the country, we find new wants, requiring for their satisfaction the products of distant lands and climes. In place of the old local and national seclusion and self-sufficiency, we have intercourse in every direction, universal interdependence of nations. And as in material, so also in intellectual production. The intellectual creations of individual nations become common property. National one-sidedness and narrow-mindedness become more and more impossible, and from the numerous national and local literatures, there arises a world literature.

The bourgeoisie, by the rapid improvement of all instruments of production, by the immensely facilitated means of communication, draws all, even the most barbarian, nations into civilisation. The cheap prices of its commodities are the heavy artillery with which it batters down all Chinese walls, with which it forces the barbarians' intensely obstinate hatred of foreigners to capitulate. It compels all nations, on pain of extinction, to adopt the bourgeois mode of production; it compels them to introduce what it calls civilisation into their midst, i.e., to become bourgeois themselves. In one word, it creates a world after its own image.

The bourgeoisie has subjected the country to the rule of the towns. It has created enormous cities, has greatly increased the urban population as compared with the rural, and has thus rescued a considerable part of the population from the idiocy of rural life. Just as it has made the country dependent on the towns, so it has made barbarian and semi-barbarian countries dependent on the civilised ones, nations of peasants on nations of bourgeois, the East on the West.

The bourgeoisie keeps more and more doing away with the scattered state of the population, of the means of production, and of property. It has agglomerated population, centralised means of production, and has concentrated property in a few hands. The necessary consequence of this was political centralisation. Independent, or but loosely connected provinces, with separate interests, laws, governments and systems of taxation, became lumped together into one nation, with one government, one code of laws, one national class-interest, one frontier and one customs-tariff.

The bourgeoisie, during its rule of scarce one hundred years, has created more massive and more colossal productive forces than have all preceding generations together. Subjection of Nature's forces to man, machinery, application of chemistry to industry and agriculture, steam-navigation, railways, electric telegraphs, clearing of whole continents for cultivation, canalisation of rivers, whole populations conjured out of the ground—what earlier century had even a presentiment that such productive forces slumbered in the lap of social labour?

We see then: the means of production and of exchange, on whose foundation the bourgeoisie built itself up, were generated in feudal society. At a certain stage in the development of these means of production and of exchange, the conditions under which feudal society produced and exchanged, the feudal organisation of agriculture and manufacturing industry, in one word, the feudal relations of property became no longer compatible with the already developed productive forces; they became so many fetters. They had to be burst asunder; they were burst asunder.

Into their place stepped free competition, accompanied by a social and political constitution adapted to it, and by the economical and political sway of the bourgeois class.

Marx-Engels, *Communist Manifesto* (1848), excerpt from Part I.

THE GRUNDRISSE

The great historic quality of capital is to *create*. . .*surplus labour,* superfluous labour from the standpoint of mere use value, mere subsistence; and its historic destiny is fulfilled as soon as, on one side, there has been such a development of needs that surplus labour above and beyond necessity has itself become a general need arising out of individual needs themselves—and, on the other side, when the severe discipline of capital, acting on succeeding generations, has developed general industriousness as the general property of the new species—and, finally, when the development of the productive powers of labour, which capital incessantly whips onward with its unlimited mania for wealth, and of the sole conditions in which this mania can be realized, have flourished to the stage where the possession and preservation of general wealth require a lesser labour time of society as a whole, and where the labouring society relates scientifically to the process of its progressive reproduction, its reproduction in a constantly greater abundance; hence where labour in which a human being does what a thing could do has ceased. Accordingly, capital and labour relate to each other here like money and commodity; the former is the general form of wealth, the other only the substance destined for immediate consumption. Capital's ceaseless striving towards the general form of wealth drives labour beyond the limits of its natural paltriness and thus creates the material elements for the development of the rich individuality which is as all-sided in its production as in its consumption, and whose labour also therefore appears no longer as labour, but as the full development of activity itself, in which natural necessity in its direct form has disappeared; because a historically created need has taken the place of the natural one. This is why *capital is productive; i.e. an essential relation for the development of the social productive forces.* It ceases to exist as such only where the development of these productive forces themselves encounters its barrier in capital itself.

Marx, *Grundrisse* (1857–58), p. 325.

3.2 CAPITALISM'S UNIVERSALIZING PROPERTIES

The tendency to create the *world market* is directly given in the concept of capital itself. Every limit appears as a barrier to be overcome. Initially, to subjugate every moment of production itself to exchange and to suspend the production of direct use values not entering into exchange, i.e. precisely to posit production based on capital in place of earlier modes of production, which appear primitive from its standpoint. *Commerce* no longer appears here as a function taking place between independent productions for the exchange of their excess, but rather as an essentially all-embracing presupposition and moment of production itself.

On the other side, the production of *relative surplus value,* i.e. production of surplus value based on the increase and development of the productive forces, requires the production of new consumption; requires that the consuming circle within circulation expands as did the productive circle previously. Firstly quantitative expansion of existing consumption; secondly:

creation of new needs by propagating existing ones in a wide circle; *thirdly:* production of *new* needs and discovery and creation of new use values. In other words, so that the surplus labour gained does not remain a merely quantitative surplus, but rather constantly increases the circle of qualitative differences within labour (hence of surplus labour), makes it more diverse, more internally differentiated. For example, if, through a doubling of productive force, a capital of 50 can now do what a capital of 100 did before, so that a capital of 50 and the necessary labour corresponding to it become free, then, for the capital and labour which have been set free, a new, qualitatively different branch of production must be created, which satisfies and brings forth a new need. The value of the old industry is preserved by the creation of the fund for a new one in which the relation of capital and labour posits itself in a *new* form. Hence exploration of all of nature in order to discover new, useful qualities in things; universal exchange of the products of all alien climates and lands; new (artificial) preparation of natural objects, by which they are given new use values. The exploration of the earth in all directions, to discover new things of use as well as new useful qualities of the old; such as new qualities of them as raw materials etc.; the development, hence, of the natural sciences to their highest point; likewise the discovery, creation and satisfaction of new needs arising from society itself; the cultivation of all the qualities of the social human being, production of the same in a form as rich as possible in needs, because rich in qualities and relations—production of this being as the most total and universal possible social product, for, in order to take gratification in a many-sided way, he must be capable of many pleasures, hence cultured to a high degree—is likewise a condition of production founded on capital. This creation of new branches of production, i.e. of qualitatively new surplus time, is not merely the division of labour, but is rather the creation, separate from a given production, of labour with a new use value; the development of a constantly expanding and more comprehensive system of different kinds of labour, different kinds of production, to which a constantly expanding and constantly enriched system of needs corresponds.

Thus, just as production founded on capital creates universal industriousness on one side—i.e. surplus labour, value-creating labour—so does it create on the other side a system of general exploitation of the natural and human qualities, a system of general utility, utilising science itself just as much as all the physical and mental qualities, while there appears nothing *higher in itself,* nothing legitimate for itself, outside this circle of social production and exchange. Thus capital creates the bourgeois society, and the universal appropriation of nature as well as of the social bond itself by the members of society. Hence the great civilizing influence of capital; its production of a stage of society in comparison to which all earlier ones appear as mere *local developments* of humanity and as *nature-idolatry.* For the first time, nature becomes purely an object for humankind, purely a matter of utility; ceases to be recognized as a power for itself; and the theoretical discovery of its autonomous laws appears merely as a ruse so as to subjugate it under human needs, whether as an object of consumption or as a means of production. In accord with this tendency, capital drives beyond national barriers and prejudices as much as beyond nature worship, as well as all traditional, confined, complacent, encrusted satisfactions of present needs, and reproductions of old ways of life. It is destructive towards all of this, and constantly revolutionizes it, tearing down all the barriers which hem in the development of the forces of production, the expansion of needs, the all-sided development of production, and the exploitation and exchange of natural and mental forces.

But from the fact that capital posits every such limit as a barrier and hence gets *ideally* beyond it, it does not by any means follow that it has *really* overcome it, and, since every such barrier contradicts its character, its production moves in contradictions which are constantly overcome but just as constantly posited. Furthermore. The universality towards which it irresistibly strives encounters barriers in its own nature, which will, at a certain stage of its development, allow it to be recognized as being itself the greatest barrier to this tendency, and hence will drive towards its own suspension. . . .

While capital must on one side strive to tear down every spatial barrier to intercourse, i.e. to exchange, and conquer the whole earth for its market, it strives on the other side to annihilate this space with time, i.e. to reduce to a minimum the time spent in motion from one place to another. The more developed the capital, therefore, the more extensive the market over which it circulates, which forms the spatial orbit of its circulation, the more does it strive simultaneously for an even greater extension of the market and for greater annihilation of space by time. . . . There appears here the universalizing tendency of capital, which distinguishes it from all previous stages of production. Although limited by its very nature, it strives towards the universal development of the forces of production, and thus becomes the presupposition of a new mode of production, which is founded not on the development of the forces of production for the purpose of reproducing or at most expanding a given condition, but where the free, unobstructed, progressive and universal development of the forces of production is itself the presupposition of society and hence of its reproduction; where advance beyond the point of departure is the only presupposition.

Marx, *Grundrisse* (1857–58), pp. 408–10, 539–40.

3.3 CAPITALISM'S INDUSTRIALIZING PROPERTIES

Money, . . . as the individual of general wealth, as something emerging from circulation and representing a general quality, as a . . . *social result,* does not at all presuppose an individual relation to its owner; possession of it is not the development of any particular essential aspect of his individuality; but rather possession of what lacks individuality, since this social [relation] exists at the same time as a sensuous, external object which can be mechanically seized, and lost in the same manner. Its relation to the individual thus appears as a purely accidental one; while this relation to a thing having no connection with his individuality gives him, at the same time, by virtue of the thing's character, a general power over society, over the whole world of gratifications, labours, etc. . . .

Money is therefore not only *an* object, but is *the* object of greed. . . . Greed as such, as a particular form of the drive, i.e. as distinct from the craving for a particular kind of wealth, e.g. for clothes, weapons, jewels, women, wine etc., is possible only when general wealth, wealth as such, has become individualized in a particular thing, i.e. as soon as money is posited in its third quality. Money is therefore not only the object but also the fountainhead of greed. The mania for possessions is possible without money; but greed itself is the product of a definite social development, not *natural,* as opposed to *historical.* Hence the wailing of the ancients about money as the source of all evil. . . . Monetary greed, or mania for wealth, necessarily brings with it the decline and fall of the ancient communities. Hence it is the antithesis to them. It is itself the community, and can tolerate none other standing above it. . . . It is inherent in the simple character of money itself that it can exist as a developed moment of production only where and when *wage labour* exists; that in this case, far from subverting the social formation, it is rather a condition for its development and a driving-wheel for the development of all forces of production, material and mental. A particular individual may even today come into money by chance, and the possession of this money can undermine him just as it undermined the communities of antiquity. But the dissolution of this individual within modern society is in itself only the enrichment of the productive section of society. The owner of money, in the ancient sense, is dissolved by the industrial process, which he serves whether he wants and knows it or not. It is a dissolution which affects only his person. *As material representative of general wealth,* as *individualized exchange value,* money must be the *direct* object, aim and product of general labour, the labour of all individuals. Labour must directly produce exchange value, i.e. money. It must therefore be *wage labour.* Greed, as the urge of all, in so far as everyone wants to make money, is only created by general wealth. Only in this way can the general mania for money become the wellspring of general, self-reproducing wealth. When labour is wage labour, and its direct aim is money, then general wealth is *posited* as its aim and object. . . . Money as aim here becomes the means of general industriousness. General wealth is produced in order to seize hold of its representative. In this way the real sources of wealth are opened up. When the aim of labour is not a particular product standing in a particular relation to the particular needs of the individual, but money, wealth in its general form, then, firstly, the individual's industriousness knows no bounds; it is indifferent to its particularity, and takes on every form which serves the purpose; it is ingenious in the creation of new objects for a social need, etc. It is clear, therefore, that when wage labour is the foundation, money does not have a dissolving effect, but acts productively; whereas the ancient community as such is already in contradiction with wage labour as the general foundation. General industriousness is possible only where every act of labour produces general wealth, not a particular form of it; where therefore the individual's reward, too, is money. . . .

As the general representative of wealth and as individualized exchange value, it [money] was doubly a means for expanding the universality of wealth, and for drawing the dimensions of exchange over the whole world; for creating the true *generality* of exchange value in substance and in extension. But it is inherent in the attribute in which it here becomes developed that the illusion about its nature, i.e. the fixed insistence on one of its aspects, in the abstract, and the blindness towards the contradictions contained within it, gives it a really magical significance behind the backs of individuals. In fact, it is because of this self-contradictory and hence illusory aspect, because of this abstraction, that it becomes such an enormous instrument in the real development of the forces of social production. . . .

The development of fixed capital indicates. . . the degree of development of wealth generally, or of capital. The aim of production oriented directly towards use value, as well as of that directly oriented towards exchange value, is the product itself, destined for consumption. The part of production which is oriented towards the production of fixed capital does not produce direct objects of individual gratification, nor direct exchange values; at least not directly realizable exchange values. *Hence, only when a certain degree of productivity has already been reached—so that a part of production time is sufficient for immediate production—can an increasingly large part be applied to the production of the means of production.* This requires that society be able to wait; that a large part of the wealth already created can be withdrawn both from immediate consumption and from production for immediate consumption, in order to employ this part for labour which is *not immediately productive* (within the material production process itself). This requires a certain level of productivity and of relative overabundance, and, more specifically, a level directly related to the transformation of circulating capital into fixed capital. As the *magnitude of relative surplus labour depends on the productivity of necessary labour, so does the magnitude of labour time*—living as well as objectified—*employed on the production of fixed capital depend on the productivity of the labour time spent in the direct production of products. Surplus population* (from this standpoint), as well as *surplus production,* is a condition for this. That is, the output of the time employed in direct production must be larger, relatively, than is directly required for the reproduction of the capital employed in these branches of industry. The *smaller* the direct fruits borne by *fixed capital,* the less it intervenes in the *direct production process,* the greater must be this relative *surplus population and surplus production;* thus, more to build railways, canals, aqueducts, telegraphs etc. than to build the machinery directly active in the direct production process. . . .

As a rule, the maximum of industriousness, of labour, and the minimum of consumption—and this is the maximum of his self-denial and of his money-making—could lead to nothing else than that he would receive for his maximum of labour a minimum of wages. By his exertions he would only have diminished the general *level* of the production costs of his own labour and therefore its general price. Only as an exception does the worker succeed through will power, physical strength and endurance, greed etc., in transforming his coin into money, as an exception from his class and from the general conditions of his existence. If all or the majority are too industrious (to the degree that industriousness in modern industry is in fact left to their own personal choice, which is not the case in the most important and most developed branches of production), then they increase not the value of their commodity, but only its quantity; that is, the demands which would be placed on it as use value. If they all save, then a general reduction of wages will bring them back to earth again; for general savings would show the capitalist that their wages are in general too high, that they receive more than its equivalent for their commodity, the capacity of disposing of their own labour; since it is precisely the essence of simple exchange—and they stand in this relation towards him—that no one throws more into circulation than he withdraws; but also that no one can withdraw more than he has thrown in. An individual worker can be *industrious* above the average, more than he has to be in order to live as a worker, only because another lies below the average, is lazier; he can save only because and if another wastes. The most he can achieve on the average with his self-denial is to be able better to endure the fluctuations of prices—high and low, their cycle—that is, he can only distribute his consumption better, but never attain wealth. And that is actually what the capitalists demand. The workers should save enough at the times when business is good to be able more or less to live in the bad times, to endure short time or the lowering of wages. (The wage would then fall even lower.) That is, the demand that they should always hold to a minimum of life's pleasures and make crises easier to bear for the capitalists etc. Maintain themselves as pure labouring machines and as far as possible pay their own wear and tear. Quite apart from the sheer brutalization to which this would lead—and such a brutalization itself would make it impossible even to strive in general form, as money, stockpiled money—(and the worker's participation in the higher, even cultural satisfactions, the agitation for his own interests, newspaper subscriptions, attending lectures, educating his children, developing his taste etc., his only share of civilization which distinguishes him from the slave, is economically only possible by widening the sphere of his pleasures at the times when business is good, where saving is to a certain degree possible), [apart from this,] he would, if he saved his money in a properly ascetic manner and thus heaped up premiums for the lumpenproletariat, pickpockets etc., who would increase in proportion with the demand, he could conserve savings—if they surpass the piggy-bank amounts of the official savings banks, which pay him a minimum of interest, so that the capitalists can strike high interest rates out of his savings, or the state eats them up, thereby merely increasing the power of his enemies and his own dependence—conserve his savings and make them fruitful only by putting them into banks etc., so that, afterwards, in times of crisis he loses his deposits, after having in times of prosperity foregone all life's pleasures in order to increase the power of capital; thus has saved in every way *for* capital, not for himself.

Incidentally—in so far as the whole thing is not a hypocritical phrase of bourgeois 'philanthropy,' which consists in fobbing the worker off with 'pious wishes'—each capitalist does demand that his workers should save, but only *his own,* because they stand towards him as workers; but by no means the remaining *world of workers,* for these stand towards him as consumers. In spite of all 'pious' speeches he therefore searches for means to spur them on to consumption, to give his wares new charms, to inspire them with new needs by constant chatter etc. It is precisely this side of the relation of capital and labour which is an essential civilizing moment, and on which the historic justification, but also the contemporary power of capital rests. . . .

If relative surplus labour increases—and capital therefore increases absolutely—then there is necessarily also an increase within circulation also of *relative exchange value existing as exchange value,* money as such, and therefore, through the mediation of the production process, *absolute exchange value.* In other words, of this same amount of exchange value—or money—and the product of the realization process appears in this simple form—the product is surplus value only relative to capital, to value such as it existed before the production process; for itself, regarded as an independent existence, it is merely *quantitatively defined exchange value*—a part has become liberated, which does not exist as equivalent for already present exchange values or for already present labour time. If it is exchanged for those already present, it gives them not an equivalent but more than an equivalent, and thus liberates a part of the exchange value on their side. In a static state, this liberated exchange value by which society has become richer can only be money, in which case only the abstract form of wealth has increased; [if] in motion: [it] can realize itself only in *new* living labour (whether labour which had been dormant is set into motion, or *new workers* are created (population [growth] is accelerated) or again a new circle of exchange values, of exchange values in circulation, is expanded, which can occur on the production side if the liberated exchange value opens up a *new branch of production,* i.e. a new object of exchange, objectified labour in the form of a new use value; or the same is achieved when objectified labour is put in the sphere of circulation in a new country, by an expansion of trade). . . .

Just as capital on one side creates surplus labour, surplus labour is at the same time equally the presupposition of the existence of capital. The whole development of wealth rests on the creation of disposable time. The relation of *necessary* labour time to the *superfluous* (such it is, initially, from the standpoint of necessary labour) changes with the different stages in the development of the productive forces. In the less productive stages of exchange, people exchange nothing more than their *superfluous labour time;* this is the measure of their exchange, which therefore extends only to superfluous products. In production resting on capital, the existence of *necessary* labour time is conditional on the creation of *superfluous* labour time. . . .

Surplus time is the excess of the working day above that part of it which we call *necessary* labour time; it exists secondly as the multiplication of *simultaneous working days,* i.e. of the *labouring population.* (It can also be created—but this is mentioned here only in passing, belongs in the chapter on wage labour—by means of forcible prolongation of the working day beyond its natural limits; by the addition of women and children to the labouring population.) The first relation, that of the surplus time and the necessary time in the day, can be and is modified by the development of the productive forces, so that necessary labour is restricted to a constantly smaller fractional part. . . .

It is a law of capital, as we saw, to create surplus labour, disposable time; it can do this only by setting *necessary labour* in motion—i.e. entering into exchange with the worker. It is its tendency, therefore, to create as much labour as possible; just as it is equally its tendency to reduce necessary labour to a minimum. It is therefore equally a tendency of capital to increase the labouring population, as well as constantly to posit a part of it as surplus population—population which is useless until such time as capital can utilize it. . . . It is equally a tendency of capital to make human labour (relatively) superfluous, so as to drive it, as human labour, towards infinity. Value is nothing but objectified labour, and surplus value (realization of capital) is only the excess above that part of objectified labour which is necessary for the reproduction of labouring capacity. But labour as such is and remains the presupposition, and surplus labour exists only in relation with the necessary, hence only in so far as the latter exists. Capital must therefore constantly posit necessary labour in order to posit surplus labour; it has to multiply it (namely the *simultaneous* working days) in order to multiply the surplus; but at the same time it must suspend them as necessary, in order to posit them as surplus labour. As regards the single working day, the process is of course simple: (1) to lengthen it up to the limits of natural possibility; (2) to shorten the necessary part of it more and more (i.e. to increase the productive forces without limit). But the working day, regarded spatially—time itself regarded as space—is *many working days alongside one another.* The more working days capital can enter into exchange with at once, during which it exchanges *objectified for living labour,* the greater its realization *at once.* It can leap over the *natural* limit formed by one individual's living, working day, *at a given stage in the development of the forces of production*. . . only by positing *another* working day alongside the *first* at the same time—by the spatial addition *of more simultaneous working days.* . . . This is why capital solicits the increase of population; and the very process by means of which necessary labour is reduced makes it possible to put new necessary labour (and hence surplus labour) to work (i.e. the *production of workers* becomes cheaper, more workers can be produced in the same time, in proportion as *necessary labour time* becomes smaller or the time required for the *production of living labour capacity* becomes relatively smaller. These are identical statements.) (This still without regard to the fact that the increase in population increases the productive force of labour, since it makes possible a greater division and combination of labour etc. The increase of population is a *natural force* of labour, for which nothing is paid. From this standpoint, we use the term *natural force* to refer to the *social force.* All *natural forces of social labour* are themselves historical products.) It is, on the other side, a tendency of capital—just as in the case of the single working day—to reduce the many simultaneous necessary working days (which, as regards their value, can be taken as *one* working day) to the minimum, i.e. to posit as many as possible of them as *not necessary.* . . . At the same time, the newly created surplus capital can be realized as such only by being again exchanged for living labour. Hence the tendency of capital simultaneously to increase the *labouring population* as well as to reduce constantly its *necessary* part (constantly to posit a part of it as reserve). And the increase of population itself the chief means for reducing the necessary part. *At bottom this is only an application of the relation of the single working day.* Here already lie, then, all the contradictions which modern population theory expresses as such, but does not grasp. Capital, as the positing of surplus labour, is equally and in the same moment the positing and the not-positing of necessary labour; it exists only in so far as necessary labour both exists and does not exist.

Marx, *Grundrisse* (1857–58), pp. 222–25, 286–87, 347–48, 398–401, 707–08.

4 Capitalism's Contradictory and Destructive Properties: Alienation

Having examined capitalism's creative properties in Chapter 3, we now turn to its contradictory and destructive features, notably, alienation, exploitation, and cyclical crises, depressions, and unemployment. For Marx, these dysfunctional properties are systemic, that is, inherent in capitalism *even under competitive conditions.* In part, Marx's emphasis on competition is, no doubt, rhetorical. He wanted to demonstrate that capitalism, functioning at its competitive best, would still generate economic "contradictions" and socioeconomic conflicts. Classical and contemporary liberals often recognize such problems as exploitation or depression, but attribute them, in large part, to various forms of monopoly or market "imperfections." The policy corollary to the liberal view, therefore, is to curb monopoly power and reduce market imperfections. For Marx (see chapter 7), monopoly may indeed reinforce, heighten, or intensify capitalism's problems, but their fundamental origins lie deep within the capitalist structure of power, production, and market exchange. Consequently, they cannot be removed by mere tinkering with such things as monopoly or market imperfections (for example, through antitrust policy, free trade, and so forth). Only a comprehensive transformation of the existing mode of production (from capitalism to communism) will permit the transcendence of its economic problems. Let us now turn to Marx's analysis of these problems, commencing with alienation.

A. Basic Concepts

Although the term "alienation" is now frequently encountered in common speech and in pop psychology, Marx's interpretation of this important but elusive concept was essentially socioeconomic, not psychological. An exposition of Marxian alienation is facilitated by distinguishing alienation from "objectification" on the one hand, and "reification" on the other.

According to Marx, man, in cooperative association with others, engages in the conscious, purposive control of nature through productive activity or work, in the process transforming not only nature, but social relations and human nature itself. Marx calls this dialectical process of mutual interaction between man (M) and nature (N) through productive activity (P) "objectification." In short $M \rightleftarrows P \rightleftarrows N$. As thus understood, objectification is an inevitable dimension of the human condition and is common to all phases of social development and systems of economy. Consequently, it cannot be superseded, even under communism.

Marx's distinction between objectification and alienation, made pointedly in selection 4.A. 1, emanates from an early (1844) critque of the German philosopher Georg Hegel's analysis, as presented in Hegel's *Phenomenology of Mind.* Marx admired Hegel's emphasis upon labor as the central human activity, his identification of alienation as a fundamental human problem, and his dialectical conception of the historical emergence and eventual transcendence of alienation. His major criticism (for our purposes here) is that Hegel's analysis confused objectification and alienation. For Hegel, labor is inherently alienating, since it creates objects external to man and his consciousness. Thus, on the one hand, alienation is inevitable in the human condition and cannot be superseded through institutional change. On the other, alienation can be superseded, within the realm of consciousness, by recognizing or designating consciousness as real and objects produced by labor as mere manifestations of thought.

For Marx, by construct, it is the socioeconomic circumstances and institutions under which labor occurs and objects are produced, not the production of objects per se, which generate alienation. Institutional conditions, created or intensified by capitalism (C), interpose themselves between man and nature, man and his productive activity, and among men, with alienating consequences: alienated man (AM), alienated productive activity (AP), and alienated nature (AN). Schematically:

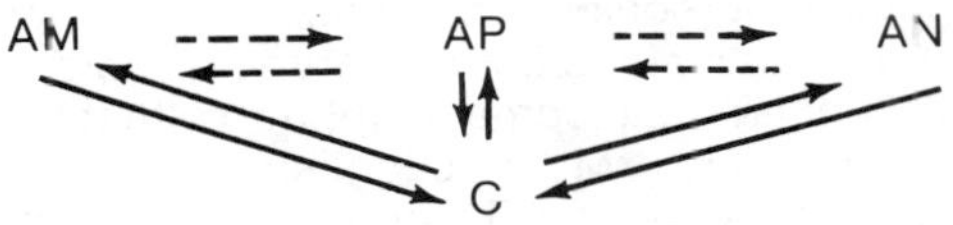

However, because alienation is rooted in socioeconomic institutions, rather than in the inevitable nature of human conditions, a process of disalienation is in principle possible, given an appropriate development of society's productive forces, in man's sociohistorical life, not merely in the realm of thought.

From the first selection, it is clear that Marx's concept of alienation has two major, interconnected aspects. One is the idea of dispossession, that is, a separation or cleavage from some person, thing, or process. Man's control over nature and productive activity is no longer, or is prevented from being, his. The second is the idea of being confronted by a strange, alien, or hostile power beyond one's control. Note the interaction of the two themes: being opposed by alien, external forces presupposes and at the same time facilitates separation or dispossession. Combining them, we may agree with David McLellan, noted biographer of Marx, that the central point of alienation is that "man has lost [or lacks] control of his own evolution and has seen this control invested in other entities. What is proper to man has become [or is] alien to him, being the attribute of something else."[1]

Growing awareness of alienation may be muted or delayed however, by capitalism's mystifying veils and illusions, notably by the process of "reification," an expression coined by Hungarian Marxist Georg Lukacs. Essentially, reification is the process whereby capitalism makes personal relations between men appear as objective relations between things. Precapitalist forms of economic organization have their mystifications and illusions, useful for concealing alienation and exploitation. For example, the *Communist Manifesto* describes how feudal exploitation is "veiled by religious

[1]David McLellan, *Marx Before Marxism* (New York: Harper, 1970), p. 169.

and political illusions." Capitalism, by contrast, has "pitilessly torn asunder" the "idyllic relations" and "sentimental veil(s)" of feudal life, leaving only the transparently clear nexus of "naked self-interest" and "callous 'cash payment."

But the commodity mode of production—money and market exchange—creates new protective veils and mystifications. Definite social relations between men (alienation, exploitation), through market exchanges, assume "the fantastic form of a relation between things" and are concealed by a veil of money. This "fetishism" or false perception of reality is "therefore inseparable from the production of commodities" (selection 4.A.2). Commodity fetishism, as thus defined, has two major consequences. First, by concealing the social relations underlying exchange, it gives workers the illusion of equality and liberty and blinds them to capitalist alienation and exploitation. Second, it encourages both workers and capitalists to accept the need to adapt to impersonal social processes which appear as alien forces beyond their control.

As capitalist industrialization spreads, Marx believes, commodity fetishism is increasingly supplemented by fetishism concerning capital. As described earlier (chapter 2), "capital" is for Marx is a social relation, not a thing. But as capitalist development proceeds, improvements in science and technology are increasingly incorporated into capital, and appear as attributes of its creative powers. These powers are then associated with the productivity or contributions of capitalists, who own the factories and machines, and employ workers. The "vulgar" apologists of capitalism simply systematize the perceptions of people "entrapped" in its alienating social conditions. The best (or worst) example of vulgar economy in the mid-nineteenth century, according to Marx, is the "trinitarian formula" concerning income distribution, that is, capital, land, labor: interest, rent, wages. Here, Marx suggests, we have the "complete mystification" of capitalist relations. Through market exchange (land for rent, money capital for interest), it appears that land and capital, and thereby landlord and capitalist, are somehow independently "productive" and are simply receiving the "share" of the national output that they have "produced" (Selection 4.A.3.). (As we shall see in chapter 5, below, Marx holds that the central distributional issue in capitalism is the division of the national income between wages and surplus. Rent and interest are then perceived as transfers of surplus from industrialists to landlords and money capitalists.)

4.A.1 ALIENATION AND OBJECTIFICATION

The fact that in the development of the productive powers of labour the objective conditions of labour, objectified labour, must grow relative to living labour—this is actually a tautological statement, for what else does growing productive power of labour mean than that less immediate labour is required to create a greater product, and that therefore social wealth expresses itself more and more in the conditions of labour created by labour itself?—this fact appears from the standpoint of capital not in such a way that one of the moments of social activity—objective labour—becomes the ever more powerful body of the other moment, of subjective, living labour, but rather—and this is important for wage labour—that the objective conditions of labour assume an ever more colossal independence, represented by its very extent, opposite living labour, and that social wealth confronts labour in more powerful portions as an alien and dominant power. The emphasis comes to be placed not on the state of being *objectified,* but on the state of being *alienated,* dispossessed, sold on the condition that the monstrous objective power which social labour itself erected opposite itself as one of its moments belongs not to the worker, but to the personified conditions of production, i.e. to capital. To the extent that, from the standpoint of capital and wage labour, the creation of the objective body of activity happens in antithesis to the immediate labour capacity— that this process of objectification in fact appears as a process of dispossession from the standpoint of labour or as appropriation of alien labour from the standpoint of capital—to that extent, this twisting and inversion is a *real [phenomenon],* not a merely *supposed one* existing merely in the imagination of the workers and the capitalists. But obviously this process of inversion is a merely *historical* necessity, a necessity for the development of the forces of production solely from a specific historic point of departure, or basis, but in no way an *absolute* necessity of production; rather, a vanishing one, and the result and the inherent purpose of this process is to suspend this basis itself, together with this form of the process. The bourgeois economists are so much cooped up within the notions belonging to a specific historic stage of social development that the necessity of the *objectification* of the powers of social labour appears to them as inseparable from the necessity of their *alienation* vis-à-vis living labour. But with the suspension of the *immediate* character of living labour, as merely *individual,* or as general merely internally or merely externally, with the positing of the activity of individuals as immediately general or *social* activity, the objective moments of production are stripped of this form of alienation; they are thereby posited as property, as the organic social body within which the individuals reproduce themselves as individuals, but as social individuals. The conditions which allow them to exist in this way in the reproduction of their life, in their productive life's process, have been posited only by the historic economic process itself; both the objective and the subjective conditions, which are only the two distinct forms of the same conditions.

The worker's propertylessness, and the ownership of living labour by objectified labour, or the appropriation of alien labour by capital—both merely expressions of the same relation from opposite poles—are fundamental conditions of the bourgeois mode of production, in no way accidents irrelevant to it. . . .

It requires no great penetration to grasp that, where, e.g., free labour or wage labour arising out of the dissolution of bondage is the point of departure, there machines can only *arise* in antithesis to living labour, as property alien to it, and as power hostile to it; i.e. that they must confront it as capital. But it is just as easy to perceive that machines will not cease to be agencies of social production when they become, e.g., property of the associated workers. In the first case, however, their distribution, i.e. that they *do not belong* to the worker, is just as much a condition of the mode of production founded on wage labour. In the second case the changed distribution would start from a *changed* foundation of production, a new foundation first created by the process of history.

Marx, *Grundrisse* (1857-58), pp. 831-33.

4.A.2 COMMODITY FETISHISM

A commodity appears, at first sight, a very trivial thing, and easily understood. Its analysis shows that it is, in reality, a very queer thing, abounding in metaphysical subtleties and theological niceties. So far as it is a value in use, there is nothing mysterious about it, whether we consider it from the point of view that by its properties it is capable of satisfying human wants, or from the point that those properties are the product of human labour. It is as clear as noon-day, that man, by his industry, changes the forms of the materials furnished by nature, in such a way as to make them useful to him. . . .

The mystical character of commodities does not originate, therefore, in their use-value. Just as little does it proceed from the nature of the determining factors of value. For, in the first place, however varied the useful kinds of labour, or productive activities, may be, it is a physiological fact, that they are functions of the human organism, and that each such function, whatever may be its nature or form, is essentially the expenditure of human brain, nerves, muscles, etc. Secondly, with regard to that which forms the ground-work for the quantitative determination of value, namely, the duration of that expenditure, or the quantity of labour, it is quite clear that there is a palpable difference between its quantity and quality. In all states of society, the labour-time that it costs to produce the means of subsistence must necessarily be an object of interest to mankind, though not of equal interest in different stages of development. And lastly, from the moment that men in any way work for one another, their labour assumes a social form.

Whence, then, arises the enigmatical character of the product of labour, so soon as it assumes the form of commodities? Clearly from this form itself. The equality of all sorts of human labour is expressed objectively by their products all being equally values; the measure of the expenditure of labour-power by the duration of that expenditure, takes the form of the quantity of value of the products of labour; and finally, the mutual relations of the producers, within which the social character of their labour affirms itself, take the form of a social relation between the products.

A commodity is therefore a mysterious thing, simply because in it the social character of men's labour appears to them as an objective character stamped upon the product of that labour; because the relation of the producers to the sum total of their own labour is presented to them as a social relation, existing not between themselves, but between the products of their labour. This is the reason why the products of labour become commodities, social things whose qualities are at the same time perceptible and imperceptible by the senses. . . . There is a physical relation between physical things. But it is different with commodities. There, the existence of the things qua commodities, and the value relation between the products of labour which stamps them as commodities, have absolutely no connection with their physical properties and with the material relations arising therefrom. There it is a definite social relation between men, that assumes, in their eyes, the fantastic form of a relation between things. . . . This I call the Fetishism which attaches itself to the products of labour, so soon as they are produced as commodities, and which is therefore inseparable from the production of commodities.

This Fetishism of commodities has its origin, as the foregoing analysis has already shown, in the peculiar social character of the labour that produces them.

As a general rule, articles of utility become commodities, only because they are products of the labour of private individuals or groups of individuals who carry on their work independently of each other. The sum total of the labour of all these private individuals form the aggregate labour of society. Since the producers do not come into social contact with each other until they exchange their products, the specific social character of each producer's labour does not show itself except in the act of exchange. In other words, the labour of the individual asserts itself as a part of the labour of society, only by means of the relations which the act of exchange establishes directly between the products, and indirectly, through them, between the producers. To the latter, therefore, the relations connecting the labour of one individual with that of the rest appear, not as direct social relations between individuals at work, but as what they really are, material relations between persons and social relations between things. . . .

Hence, when we bring the products of our labour into relation with each other as values, it is not because we see in these articles the material receptacles of homogeneous human labour. Quite the contrary; whenever, by an exchange, we equate as values our different products, by that very act, we also equate, as human labour, the different kinds of labour expended upon them. We are not aware of this, nevertheless we do it. Value, therefore, does not stalk about with a label describing what it is. It is value, rather, that converts every product into a social hieroglyphic. Later on, we try to decipher the hieroglyphic, to get behind the secret of our own social products; for to stamp an object of utility as a value, is just as much a social product as language. The recent scientific discovery, that the products of labour, so far as they are values, are but material expressions of the human labour spent in their production, marks, indeed, an epoch in the history of the development of the human race, but, by no means, dissipates the mist through which the social character of labour appears to us to be an objective character of the products themselves. The fact, that in the particular form of production with which we are dealing, viz., the production of commodities, the specific social character of private labour carried on independently, consists in the equality of every kind of that labour, by virtue of its being human labour, which character, therefore, assumes in the product the form of value—this fact appears to the producers, notwithstanding the discovery above referred to, to be just as real and final, as the fact, that, after the discovery by science of the component gases of air, the atmosphere itself remained unaltered.

What, first of all, practically concerns producers when they make an exchange, is the question, how much of some other product they get for their own in what proportions the products are exchangeable? When these proportions have, by custom, attained a certain stability, they appear to result from the nature of the products, so that, for instance, one ton of iron and two ounces of gold appear as naturally to be of equal value as a pound of gold and a pound of iron in spite of their different physical and chemical qualities appear to be of equal weight. The character of having value, when once impressed upon products, obtains fixity only by reason of their acting and reacting upon each other as quantities of value. These quantities vary continually, independently of the will, foresight and action of the producers. To them, their own social action takes the form of the action of objects, which rule the producers instead of being ruled by them. It requires a fully developed production of commodities before, from accumulated experience alone, the scientific conviction springs up, that all the different kinds of private labour, which are carried on independently of each other, and yet as spontaneously developed branches of the social division of labour, are continually being reduced to the quantitive proportions in which society requires them. And why? Because, in the midst of all the accidental and ever fluctuating exchange-relations between the products, the labour-time socially necessary for their production forcibly asserts itself like an overriding law of nature. The law of gravity thus asserts itself when a house falls about our ears. The determination of the magnitude of value by labour-time is therefore a secret, hidden under the apparent fluctuations in the relative values of commodities. Its discovery, while removing all appearance of mere accidentality from the determination of the magnitude of the values of products, yet in no way alters the mode in which that determination takes place.

Man's reflections on the forms of social life, and consequently, also, his scientific analysis of those forms, take a course directly opposite to that of their actual historical development. He begins, post festum, with the results of the process of development ready to hand before him. The characters that stamp products as commodities, and whose establishment is a necessary preliminary to the circulation of commodities, have already acquired the stability of natural, self-understood forms of social life, before man seeks to decipher, not their historical character, for in his eyes they are immutable, but their meaning. Consequently it was the analysis of the prices of commodities that alone led to the determination of the magnitude of value, and it was the common expression of all commodities in money that alone led to the establishment of their characters as values. It is, however, just this ulimate money form of the world of commodities that actually conceals, instead of disclosing, the social character of private labour, and the social relations between the individual producers. When I state that coats or boots stand in a relation to linen, because it is the universal incarnation of abstract human labour, the absurdity of the statement is self-evident. Nevertheless, when the producers of coats and boots compare those articles with linen or, what is the same thing with gold or silver, as the universal equivalent, they express the relation between their own private labour and the collective labour of society in the same absurd form.

The categories of bourgeois economy consist of such like forms. They are forms of thought expressing with social validity the conditions and relations of a definite, historically determined mode of production, viz., the production of commodities. The whole mystery of commodities, all the magic and necromancy that surrounds the products of labour as long as they take the form of commodities, vanishes therefore, so soon as we come to other forms of production.

Since Robinson Crusoe's experiences are a favorite theme with political economists, let us take a look at him on his island. Moderate though he be, yet some few wants he has to satisfy, and must therefore do a little useful work of various sorts, such as making tools and furniture, taming goats, fishing and hunting. ... In spite of the variety of his work he knows that his labour, whatever its forms, is but the activity of one and the same Robinson, and consequently, that it consists of nothing but different modes of human labour. Necessity itself compels him to apportion his time accurately between his different kinds of work. Whether one kind occupies a greater space in his general activity than another, depends on the difficulties, greater or less as the case may be, to be overcome in attaining the useful effect aimed at. This our friend Robinson soon learns by experience, and having rescued a watch, ledger, and pen and ink from the wreck, commences, like a true-born Briton, to keep a set of books. His stock-book contains a list of the objects of utility that belong to him, of the operations necessary for their production; and lastly, of the labour time that definite quantities of those objects have, on an average, cost him. All the relations between Robinson and the objects that form this wealth of his own creation, are here so simple and clear as to be intelligible without exertion. ... And yet those relations contain all that is essential to the determination of value.

Let us now transport ourselves from Robinson's island bathed in light to the European middle ages shrouded in darkness. Here, instead of the independent man, we find everyone dependent, serfs and lords, vassals and suzerains, laymen and clergy. Personal dependence here characterises the social relations of production just as much as it does the other spheres of life organized on the basis of that production. But for the very reason that personal dependence forms the groundwork of society, there is no necessity for labour and its products to assume a fantastic form different from their reality. They take shape, in the transactions of society, of services in kind and payments in kind. Here the particular and natural form of labour, and not, as in a society based on production of commodities, its general abstract form is the immedite social form of labour. Compulsory labour is just as properly measured by time, as commodity-producing labour; but every serf knows that what he expends in the service of his lord, is a definite quantity of his own personal labour-power. The tithe to be rendered to the priest is more matter of fact than his blessing. No matter, then, what we may think of the parts played by the different classes of people themselves in this society, the social relations between individuals in the performance of their labour, appear at all events as their own mutual personal relations, and are not diguised under the shape of social relations between the products of labour.

For an example of labour in common or directly associated labour, we have no occasion to go back to that spontaneously developed form which we find on the threshold of the history of all civilized races. We have one close at hand in the patriarchal industries of a peasant family, that produces corn, cattle, yarn, linen, and clothing for home use. These different articles are, as regards the family, so many products of its labour, but as between themselves, they are not commodities. The different kinds of labour, such as tillage, cattle tending, spinning, weaving and making clothes, which result in the various products, are in themselves, and such as they are, direct social functions, because functions of the family, which just as much as a society based on the production of commodities, possesses a spontaneously developed system of division of labour. The distribution of the work within the family, and the regulation of the labour-time of the several members, depend as well upon differences of age and sex as upon natural conditions varying with the seasons. The labour-power of each individual, by its very nature, operates in this case merely as a definite portion of the whole labour-power of the family, and therefore, the measure of the expenditure of individual labour-power by its duration, appears here by its very nature as a social character of their labour.

Marx, *Capital,* I (1867), pp. 81-90.

4.A.3 THE TRINITARIAN FORMULA

Capital-profit (profit of enterprise plus interest), land-ground-rent, labour-wages, this is the trinity formula which comprises all the secrets of the social production process.

Furthermore, since...interest appears as the specific characteristic product of capital, and profit of enterprise on the contrary appears as wages independent of capital, the above trinity formula reduces itself more specifically to the following:

Capital-interest, land-ground-rent, labour-wages, where profit, the specific characteristic form of surplus-value belonging to the capitalist mode of production, is fortunately eliminated.

On closer examination of this economic trinity, we find the following:

First, the alleged sources of the annually available wealth belong to widely dissimilar spheres and are not at all analogous with one another. They have about the same relation to each other as lawyer's fees, red beets and music.

Capital, land, labour! However, capital is not a thing, but rather a definite social production relation, belonging to a definite historical formation of society, which is manifested in a thing and lends this thing a specific social character. Capital is not the sum of the material and produced means of production. Capital is rather the means of production transformed into capital, which in themselves are no more capital than gold or silver in itself is money. It is the means of production monopolised by a certain section of society, confronting living labour-power as products and working conditions rendered independent of this very labour-power, which are personified through this antithesis in capital. It is not merely the products of labourers turned into independent powers, products as rulers and buyers of their producers, but rather also the social forces [of their labor and socialised] form of this labour, which confront the labourers as properties of their products. Here, then, we have a definite and, at first glance, very mystical, social form of one of the factors in a historically produced social production process.

And now alongside of this we have in the land, inorganic nature as such, . . . in all its primeval wildness. Value is labour. Therefore surplus-value cannot be earth. Absolute fertility of the soil effects nothing more than the following: a certain quantity of labour produces a certain product—in accordance with the natural fertility of the soil. The difference in soil fertility causes the same quantities of labour and capital, hence the same value, to be manifested in different quantities of agricultural products; that is, causes these products to have different individual values. The equalisation of these individual values into market-values is responsible for the fact that the "advantages of fertile over inferior soil . . . are transferred from the cultivator or consumer to the landlord." (Ricardo, *Principles,* London, 1821, p. 62.)

And finally, as third party in this union, a mere ghost—"the" Labour, which is no more than an abstraction and taken by itself does not exist at all, or, if we take [that which is behind it], the productive activity of human being in general, by which they promote the interchange with Nature, divested not only of every social form and well-defined character, but even in its bare natural existence, independent of society, removed from all societies, and as an expression and confirmation of life which the still non-social man in general has in common with the one who is in any way social. . . .

The capitalist process of production is a historically determined form of the social process of production in general. The latter is as much a production process of material conditions of human life as a process taking place under specific historical and economic production relations, producing and reproducing these production relations themselves, and thereby also the bearers of this process, their material conditions of existence and their mutual relations, i.e., their particular socioeconomic form. For the aggregate of these relations, in which the agents of this production stand with respect to Nature and to one another, and in which they produce, is precisely society, considered from the standpoint of its economic structure. Like all its predecessors, the capitalist process of production proceeds under definite material conditions, which are, however, simultaneously the bearers of definite social relations entered into by individuals in the process of reproducing their life. Those conditions, like these relations, are on the one hand prerequisites, on the other hand results and creations of the capitalist process of production; they are produced and reproduced by it. We saw also that capital—and the capitalist is merely capital personified and functions in the process of production solely as the agent of capital—in its corresponding social process of production, pumps a definite quantity of surplus-labour out of the direct producers, or labourers; capital obtains this surplus-labour without an equivalent, and in essence it always remains forced labour—no matter how much it may seem to result from free contractual agreement. This surplus-labour appears as surplus-value, and this surplus-value exists as a surplus-product. Surplus-labour in general, as labour performed over and above the given requirements, must always remain. In the capitalist as well as in the slave system, etc., it merely assumes an antagonistic form and is supplemented by complete idleness of a stratum of society. A definite quantity of surplus-labour is required as insurance against accidents, and by the necessary and progressive expansion of the process of reproduction in keeping with the development of the needs and the growth of population , which is called accumulation from the viewpoint of the capitalist. It is one of the civilising aspects of capital that it enforces this surplus-labour in a manner and under conditions which are more advantageous to the development of the productive forces, social relations, and the creation of the elements for a new and higher form than under the preceding forms of slavery, serfdom, etc. Thus it gives rise to a stage, on the hand, in which coercion and monopolisation of social development (including its material and intellectual advantages) by one portion of society at the expense of the other are eliminated; on the other hand, it creates the material means and embryonic conditions, making it possible in a higher form of society to combine this surplus-labour with a greater reduction of time devoted to material labour in general. For, depending on the development of labour productivity, surplus-labour may be large in a small total working-day, and relatively small in a large total working day. . . . The annual incomes of three classes, capitalist, landowner and labourer, [are] revenues distributed by the functioning capitalist in his capacity as direct extorter of surplus-labour and employer of labour in general. Thus, capital appears to the capitalist, land to the landlord, and labour-power, or rather labour itself, to the labourer (since he actually sells labour-power only as it is manifested, and since the price of labour-power, as previously shown, inevitably appears as the price of labour under the capitalist mode of production), as three different sources of their specific revenues, namely, profit, ground-rent and wages. They are really so in the sense that capital is a perennial pumping-machine of surplus-labour for the capitalist, land a perennial magnet for the landlord, attracting a portion of the surplus-value pumped out by capital, and finally, labour the constantly self-renewing condition and ever self-renewing means of acquiring under the title of wages a portion of the value created by the labourer and thus a part of the social product measured by this portion of value, i.e., the necessities of life. They are so, furthermore, in the sense that capital fixes a portion of the value and thereby of the product of the annual labour in the form of profit; landed property fixes another portion in the form of rent; and wage-labour fixes a third portion in the form of wages, and precisely by this transformation converts them into revenues of the capitalist, landowner, and labourer, without, however, creating the substance itself which is transformed into these various categories. The distribution rather presupposes the existence of this substance, namely, the total value of the annual product, which is nothing but materialised social labour. Nevertheless, it is not in this form that the matter appears to the agents of production, the bearers of the various functions in the production process, but rather in a distorted form. Why this takes place will be developed in the further course of our analysis. Capital, landed property and labour appear to those agents of production as three different, independent sources, from which as such there arise three different components of the annually produced value—and thereby the product in which it exists. . . .

Differential rent is bound up with the relative soil fertility, in other words, with properties arising from the soil as such. But, in the first place, in so far as it is based upon the different individual values of the products of different soil types, it is but the determination just mentioned; secondly, in so far as it is based upon the regulating general market-value, which differs from these individual values, it is a social law carried through by means of competition, which has to do neither with the soil nor the different degrees of its fertility.

It might seem as if a rational relation were expressed at least in "labour–wages." But this is no more the case than with "land–ground–rent." In so far as labour is value-creating, and is manifested in the value of commodities, it has nothing to do with the distribution of this value among various categories. In so far as it has the specifically social character of wage-labour, it is not value-creating. It has already been shown in general that wages of labour, or price of labour, is but an irrational expression for the value, or price of labour-power; and the specific social conditions, under which this labour-power is sold, have nothing to do with labour as a general agent in production. Labour is also materialised in that value component of a commodity which as wages forms the price of labour-power; it creates this portion just as much as the other portions of the product; but it is materialised in this portion no more and no differently than in the portions forming rent or profit. And, in general, when we establish labour as value-creating, we do not consider it in its concrete form as a condition of production, but in its social delimitation which differs from that of wage-labour.

Even the expression "capital–profit" is incorrect here. If capital is viewed in the only relation in which it produces surplus-value, namely, its relation to the labourer whereby it extorts surplus-labour by compulsion exerted upon labour-power, i.e., the wage-labourer, then this surplus-value comprises, outside of profit (profit of enterprise plus interest), also rent, in short, the entire undivided surplus-value. Here, on the other hand, as a source of revenue, it is placed only in relation to that portion falling to the share of the capitalist. This is not the surplus-value which it extracts generally but only that portion which it extracts for the capitalist. Still more does all connection vanish no sooner the formula is transformed into "capital–interest." . . . If wage-labour coincides with labour generally, then so do wages with the produce of labour, and the value portion representing wages with the value created by labour generally. But in this way the other portions of value, profit and rent also appear independent with respect to wages, and must arise from sources of their own, which are specifically different and independent of labour; they must arise from the participating elements of production, to the share of whose owners they fall; i.e., profit arises from the means of production, the material elements of capital, and rent arises from the land, or Nature, as represented by the landlord.

Landed property, capital and wage-labour are thus transformed from sources of revenue—in the sense that capital attracts to the capitalist, in the form of profit, a portion of the surplus-value extracted by him from labour, that monopoly in land attracts for the landlord another portion in the form of rent; and that labour grants the labourer the remaining portion of value in the form of wages—from sources by means of which one portion of value is transformed into the form of profit, another into the form of rent, and a third into the form of wages—into actual sources from which these value portions and respective portions of the product in which they exist, or for which they are exchangeable, arise themselves, and from which, therefore, in the final analysis, the value of the product itself arises.[1]

In the case of the simplest categories of the capitalist mode of production, and even of commodity-production, in the case of commodities and money, we have already pointed out the mystifying character that transforms the social relations, for which the material elements of wealth serve as bearers in production, into properties of these things themselves (commodities) and still more pronouncedly transforms the production relation itself into a thing (money). All forms of society, in so far as they reach the stage of commodity-production and money circulation, take part in this perversion. But under the capitalist mode of production and in the case of capital, which forms its dominant category, its determining production relation, this enchanted and perverted world develops still more. If one considers capital, to begin with, in the actual process of production as a means of extracting surplus-labour, then this relationship is still very simple, and the actual connection impresses itself upon the bearers of this process, the capitalists themselves, and remains in their consciousness. The violent struggle over the limits of the working-day demonstrates this strikingly. But even within this non-mediated sphere, the sphere of direct action between labour and capital, matters do not rest in this simplicity. With the development of relative surplus-value in the actual specifically capitalist mode of production, whereby the productive powers of social labour are developed, these productive powers and the social interrelations of labour in the direct labour-process seem transferred from labour to capital. Capital thus becomes a very mystic being since all of labour's social productive forces appear to be due to capital, rather than labour as such, and seem to issue from the womb of capital itself. Then the process of circulation intervenes, with its changes of substance and form, on which all parts of capital, even agricultural capital, devolve to the same degree that the specifically capitalist mode of production develops. This is a sphere where the relations under which value is originally produced are pushed completely into the background. In the direct process of production the capitalist already acts simultaneously as producer of commodities and manager of commodity-production. Hence this process of production appears to him by no means simply as a process of producing surplus-value. But whatever may be the surplus-value extorted by capital in the actual production process and appearing in commodities, the value and surplus-value contained in the commodities must first be realised in the circulation process. And both the restitution of the values advanced in production and, particularly, the surplus-value contained in the commodities seem not merely to be realised in the circulation, but actually to arise from it. . . .

In capital-profit, or still better capital-interest, land-rent, labour-wages, in this economic trinity represented as the connection between the component parts of value and wealth in general and its sources, we have the complete

[1]Wages, profit, and rent are the three original sources of all revenue, as well as of all exchangeable value (A. Smith) [*An Inquiry into the Nature and Causes of the Wealth of Nations,* Aberdeen, London, 1848, S. 43.—Ed.]

mystification of the capitalist mode of production, the conversion of social relations into things, the direct coalescence of the material production relations with their historical and social determination. It is an enchanted, perverted, topsy-turvy world, in which Monsieur le Capital and Madame la Terre do their ghost-walking as social characters and at the same time directly as mere things. It is the great merit of classical economy to have destroyed this false appearance and illusion, this mutual independence and ossification of the various social elements of wealth, this personification of things and conversion of production relations into entities, this religion of everyday life. It did so by reducing interest to a portion of profit, and rent to the surplus above average profit, so that both of them converge in surplus-value; and by representing the process of circulation as a mere metamorphosis of forms, and finally reducing value and surplus-value of commodities to labour in the direct production process. Nevertheless even the best spokesmen of classical economy remain more or less in the grip of the world of illusion which their criticism had dissolved, as cannot be otherwise from a bourgeois standpoint, and thus they all fall more or less into inconsistencies, half-truths and unsolved contradictions. On the other hand, it is just as natural for the actual agents of production to feel completely at home in these estranged and irrational forms of capital–interest, land–rent, labour–wages, since these are precisely the forms of illusion in which they move about and find their daily occupation. It is therefore just as natural that vulgar economy, which is no more than a didactic, more or less dogmatic, translation of everyday conceptions of the actual agents of production, and which arranges them in a certain rational order, should see precisely in this trinity, which is devoid of all inner connection, the natural and indubitable lofty basis for its shallow pompousness. This formula simultaneously corresponds to the interests of the ruling classes by proclaiming the physical necessity and eternal justification of their sources of revenue and elevating them to a dogma.

In our description of how production relations are converted into entities and rendered independent in relation to the agents of production, we leave aside the manner in which the interrelations, due to the world-market, its conjunctures, movements of market-prices, periods of credit, industrial and commercial cycles, alternations of prosperity and crisis, appear to them as overwhelming natural laws that irresistibly enforce their will over them, and confront them, as blind necessity. We leave this aside because the actual movement of competition belongs beyond our scope, and we need present only the inner organisation of the capitalist mode of production, in its ideal average, as it were.

In preceding forms of society this economic mystification arose principally with respect to money and interest-bearing capital. In the nature of things it is excluded, in the first place, where production for the use-value, for immediate personal requirements, predominates; and secondly, where slavery or serfdom form the broad foundation of social production, as in antiquity and during the Middle Ages. Here, the domination of the producers by the conditions of production is concealed by the relations of dominion and servitude, which appear and are evident as the direct motive power of the process of production. In early communal societies in which primitive communism prevailed, and even in the ancient communal towns, it was this communal society itself with its conditions which appeared as the basis of production, and its reproduction appeared as its ultimate purpose. Even in the medieval guild system neither capital nor labour appear untrammelled, but their relations are rather defined by the corporate rules, and by the same associated relations, and corresponding conceptions of professional duty, craftsmanship, etc. ...

Marx, *Capital,* III (1894), Chap. 48.

B. SOCIOECONOMIC FORMS OF ALIENATION

Especially in his early writings, Marx considered several forms of alienation, moving in rapid succession from alienation in the religious realm to philosophy, politics, and, finally, in the 1844 *Economic and Philosophical Manuscripts,* to the economy. Although his later works, notably the *Grundrisse (Outlines of the Critique of Political Economy)* in 1857, rival or surpass his 1844 writings both in length and in establishing connecting links with his mature economic theory, the *Manuscripts* remain Marx's most systematic and organized exposition of the socioeconomic forms of alienation. In this exposition, Marx distinguishes among four major facets of alienation: alienated labour, alienated capital, alienated needs, and alienation and money.

Alienated Labor

Marx distinguishes four major, interwoven forms of alienated labour (selection 4.B.4). First, the worker is alienated from the product of his labor. On the one hand, products have an indepenent, alien existence to workers because they do not belong to them. On the other hand, products confront workers as an autonomous power and hostile force. The worker cannot control the availability of products, even under conditions of severe economic privation or starvation. He has no role in determining the amount or composition of output except indirectly, through the expenditure of wages as a consumer. Nor does he determine the total amount of work to be done (and thereby employment).

Second, the worker is alienated from his productive activity. Work is "external" to the worker. It does not belong to him, nor is it a source of self-fulfillment. It is not voluntary, but *forced labor.* It does not satisfy a genuine human need, but serves merely as a means to obtain wages and thus satisfy other, material needs. In addition, it is work done not for himself, but for and under the direction of another person.

Next, the worker is alienated from what the German philosophers Hegel and Feuerbach had earlier called his "species life," that is, his distinctively human life as a member of the species. When alienated labor transforms "conscious life activity," which distinguishes humans from animals, into a mere means for the satisfaction of needs and the maintenance of physical existence, the worker is alienated from himself, from his own "active function," from the employment of his own creative power in conjunction with nature, and therefore from the species.

Last, workers are alienated from capital. If the worker is alienated from his product and from productive activity, then he must be under the dominion of another person, who owns the product and controls productive activity. According to Marx, this person is the capitalist. Through alienated labor, therefore, the worker not only creates his alienated relation to the product and the production process. He also creates "the domination of the non-producer. . . the capitalist (or whatever one likes to call the lord of labour). . . over production and its product."

Capital and Alienation

Thus, for Marx, capitalist property relations are "the product, the necessary result, of *alienated labour,* of the external relation of the worker to nature and to himself." Indeed, having derived capitalist property relations from alienated labor, Marx goes so far as to say that "although private property appears to be the basis and cause of alienated labour, it is rather a consequence of the latter . . ." However, once having established property as effect and alienated labour as cause, he immediately reverses direction and recognizes a reciprocal influence, demonstrating, as in many other instances, his commitment to mutual "inner-penetration" rather than linear causation as his basic methodological perspective. "At a later stage," he observes, there is a "reciprocal influence" between alienated labor and alienating capital.

> Only in the final stage of the development of private property is its secret revealed, namely, that it is on one hand the *product* of alienated labour, and on the other the *means* by which labour is alienated, *the realization of this alienation.*[2]

Having thus resolved alienated labour into "two different expressions of one and the same relation" (the capital-labor relation), Marx proceeds in selection 4.B.5, to argue that capital is *alienated* as well as alienating. True, appropriation of man's powers in the production process "appears as *alienation* [for the worker] and *alienation* as *appropriation* [for the capitalist]." But capitalists are victims as well as victimizers in the alienation process. First, although the capitalist controls the work process and the resulting product, the social network of commodity relations and competition is essentially beyond his control. "Alienation is apparent," says Marx, "and this is also the case for the capitalist," in that "*an inhuman power* rules over everything." Second, the attitude or state of mind of both capitalist and worker is alienated, the worker because his productive activity is alienated, the capitalist because he does not work. The capitalist's separation from work is his badge of freedom and power in a capitalist society. But because work, as creative productive activity, is a distinguishing property of an authentic human existence, the capitalist, like the worker, emerges from production as a "*human commodity,*" a "*mentally* and *physically* dehumanized being." Third, the capitalist's property power saves him from the direct alienation (and exploitation) on the job or out of work that the workers suffers. But the capitalist's very alienation toward workers dehumanizes himself. Compared to the worker, the capitalist is in a favored position; compared to the potentialities of communism (chapter 9), he too is alienated.[3]

As is clear from the brief excerpt from *The Holy Family* (1845) in selection 4.B.5, Marx's perception of capitalists as alienated does not lead him to lump them together with workers as responding to alienation in the same way. In 1865, the "mature Marx" returned to this theme, adding emphasis upon the potentially

[2]Marx, *Economic and Philosophical Manuscripts,* In *Karl Marx: Early Writings,* edited by T.B. Bottomore (New York: Harper, 1964), pp. 131, 133.

[3]*Ibid.*, pp. 133, 134, 138, 178.

revolutionary role of the working class, but virtually reproducing the commentary of his early writings. "The capitalist," he states,

> is rooted in his *process of alienation* and is completely content therein, whereas the worker who is its victim finds himself from the beginning in a state of rebellion against it and experiences the process as one of enslavement...[4]

Alienated Needs

Marx also comments briefly but pointedly on the alienation of human needs. Alienation does have a positive side in the development of new wants, as was seen in chapter 3. The dynamism of capitalist development "has given the people, in place of their crude wants, civilized needs and the means of satisfying them." But the main focus of the 1844 *Manuscripts* is on the negative features of alienation. Marx's comments on the creation of new, often imaginary needs, written over a century ago, have a remarkably contemporary sound, as selection 4.A.6 demonstrates. The entrepreneur, Marx holds, strives to create new needs in others, to place them in positions of dependency, and to establish an "alien power" over others for his own benefit. Of course, as depicted by classical political economy itself, the alienation of workers is most strikingly shown by the miserable and impoverished condition of their lives *relative to* "the refinement of needs and of the means to satisfy them" of the rich. Still, both capitalists and workers, Marx believed, are alienated from the "plentitude of *human* need" and from "human communal life."[5]

Money and Alienation

A final dimension of alienation emphasized in the 1844 *Manuscripts* is that of money (selection 4.B.7). As generalized purchasing power, money is the bond which binds men together in market economy. At the same time, money is the "universal agent of separation" which confuses and inverts "all human and natural qualities." Marx's early discussion of money as a constituent element in alienation should be read in conjunction with his subsequent analyses of money and market exchange as bases of alienation (selection 4.B.8). (See also selection 9.A.2 for Marx's early vision of communism as unalienated society.)

4.B.4 ALIENATED LABOUR

We have begun from the presupposition of political economy. We have accepted its terminology and its laws. We presupposed private property; the separation of labour, capital and land, as also of wages, profit and rent; the division of labour; competition; the concept of exchange value, etc. . . .

[4]Cited in TKM, p. 119.

[5]All quotations from *Karl Marx: Early Writings*, pp. 142, 164, 168–69.

Political economy begins with the fact of private property; it does not explain it. It conceives the *material* process of private property, as this occurs in reality, in general and abstract formulas which then serve it as laws. It does not *comprehend* these laws; that is, it does not show how they arise out of the nature of private property. Political economy provides no explanation of the basis for the distinction of labour from capital, of capital from land. When, for example, the relation of wages to profits is defined, this is explained in terms of the interests of capitalists; in other words, what should be explained is assumed. Similarly, competition is referred to at every point and is explained in terms of external conditions. Political economy tells us nothing about the extent to which these external and apparently accidental conditions are simply the expression of a necessary development. We have seen how exchange itself seems an accidental fact. The only motive forces which political economy recognizes are *avarice* and the *war between the avaricious, competition*. . . .

Thus we have now to grasp the real connexion between this whole system of alienation—private property, acquisitiveness, the separation of labour, capital and land, exchange and competition, value and the devaluation of man, monopoly and competition—and the system of *money*.

Let us not begin our explanation, as does the economist, from a legendary primordial condition. . . .

We shall begin from *contemporary* economic fact. The worker becomes poorer the more wealth he produces and the more his production increases in power and extent. The worker becomes an ever cheaper commodity the more goods he creates. The *devaluation* of the human world increases in direct relation with the *increase in value* of the world of things. Labour does not only create goods; it also produces itself and the worker as a *commodity,* and indeed in the same proportion as it produces goods.

This fact simply implies that the object produced by labour, its product, now stands opposed to it as an *alien being,* as a *power independent* of the producer. The product of labour is labour which has been embodied in an object and turned into a physical thing; this product is an *objectification* of labour. The performance of work is at the same time its objectification. The performance of work appears in the sphere of political economy as a *vitiation* of the worker, objectification as a *loss* and as *servitude to the object,* and appropriation as *alienation*. . . .

These consequences follow from the fact that the worker is related to the *product of his labour* as to an *alien* object. For it is clear on this presupposition that the more the worker expends himself in work the more powerful becomes the world of objects which he creates in face of himself, the poorer he becomes in his inner life, and the less he belongs to himself. . . . The worker puts his life into the object, and his life then belongs no longer to himself but to the object. The greater his activity, therefore, the less he possesses. What is embodied in the product of his labour is no longer his own. The greater this product is, therefore, the more he is diminished. The *alienation* of the worker in his product means not only that his labour becomes an object, assumes an *external* existence, but that it exists independently, *outside himself,* and alien to him, and that it stands opposed to him as an autonomous power. The life which he has given to the object sets itself against him as an alien and hostile force. . . .

Political economy conceals the alienation in the nature of labour in so far as it does not examine the direct relationship between the worker (work) and production. Labour certainly produces marvels for the rich but it produces privation for the worker. It produces palaces, but hovels for the worker. It produces beauty, but deformity for the worker. It replaces labour by machinery, but it casts some of the workers back into a barbarous kind of work and turns the others into machines. It produces intelligence, but also stupidity and cretinism for the workers.

The direct relationship of labour to its products is the relationship of the worker to the objects of his production. The relationship of property owners to the objects of production and to production itself is merely a *consequence* of this first relationship and confirms it. . . .

So far we have considered the alienation of the worker only from one aspect; namely, *his relationship with the products of his labour.* However, alienation appears not merely in the result but also in the *process* of *production,* within *productive activity* itself. How could the worker stand in an alien relationship to the product of his activity if he did not alienate himself in the act of production itself? The product is indeed only the *résumé* of activity, of production. Consequently, if the product of labour is alienation, production itself must be active alienation—the alienation of activity and the activity of aliention. The alienation of the object of labour merely summarizes the alienation in the work activity itself.

What constitutes the alienation of labour? First, that the work is *external* to the worker, that it is not part of his nature; and that, consequently, he does not fulfil himself in his work but denies himself, has a feeling of misery rather than well-being, does not develop freely his mental and physical energies but is physically exhausted and mentally debased. The worker, therefore feels himself at home only during his leisure time, whereas at work he feels homeless. His work is not voluntary but imposed, *forced labour.* It is not the satisfaction of a need, but only a *means* for satisfying other needs. Its alien character is clearly shown by the fact that as soon as there is no physical or other compulsion it is avoided like the plague. External labour, labour in which man alienates himself, is a labour of self-sacrifice, or mortification. Finally, the external character of work for the worker is shown by the fact that it is not his own work but work for someone else, that in work he does not belong to himself but to another person. . . . The activity of the worker is not his own spontaneous activity. It is another's activity and a loss of his own spontaneity.

For labour, *life activity, productive life,* now appear to man only as *means* for the satisfaction of a need, the need to maintain his physical existence. Productive life is, however, species-life. It is life creating life. In the type of life activity resides the whole character of a species, its species-character; and free, conscious activity is the species-character of human beings. Life itself appears only as a *means of life.* . . . Conscious life activity distinguishes man from the life activity of animals. Only for this reason is he a species-being. Or rather, he is only a self-conscious being, i.e. his own life is an object for him, because he is a species-being. Only for this reason is his activity free activity. Alienated labour reverses the relationship, in that man because he is a self-conscious being makes his life activity, his *being,* only a means for his *existence.* . . .

It is just in his work upon the objective world that man really proves himself as a *species-being*. This production is his active species-life. By means of it nature appears as *his* work and his reality. The object of labour is, therefore, the *objectification of man's species-life,* for he no longer reproduces himself merely intellectually, as in consciousness, but actively and in a real sense, and he sees his own reflection in a world which he has constructed. While, therefore, alienated labour takes away the object of production from man, it also takes away his *species-life,* his real objectivity as a species-being, and changes his advantage over animals into a disadvantage in so far as his inorganic body, nature, is taken from him. . . . (3) Thus alienated labour turns the *species-life of man,* and also nature as his mental species-property, into an *alien* being and into a *means* for his *individual existence.* It alienates from man his own body, external nature, his mental life and his *human* life. (4) A direct consequence of the alienation of man from the product of his labour, from his life activity and from his species-life, is that *man* is *alienated* from the *other* men. When man confronts himself he also confronts *other* men. What is true of man's relationship to his work, to the product of his work and to himself, is also true of his relationship to other men, to their labour and to the objects of their labour. . . . If the product of labour is alien to me and confronts me as an alien power, to whom does it belong? If my own activity does not belong to me but is an alien, forced activity, to whom does it belong? To a being *other* than myself. And who is this being? . . .

The *alien* being to whom labour and the product of labour belong, to whose service labour is devoted, and to whose enjoyment the product of labour goes, can only be *man* himself. If the product of labour does not belong to the worker, but confronts him as an alien power, this can only be because it belongs to a *man other than the worker.* . . . If he is related to the product of his labour, his objectified labour, as to an *alien,* hostile, powerful and independent object, he is related in such a way that another alien, hostile, powerful and independent man is the lord of this object. If he related to his own activity as to unfree activity, then he is related to it as activity in the service, and under the domination, coercion and yoke, of another man. . . .

Through alienated labour, therefore, man not only produces his relation to the object and to the process of production as to alien and hostile men; he also produces the relation of other men to his production and his product, and the relation between himself and other men. Just as he creates his own production as a vitiation, a punishment, and his own product as a loss, as a product which does not belong to him, so he creates domination of the non-producer over production and its product. As he alienates his own activity, so he bestows upon the stranger an activity which is not his own.

We have so far considered this relation only from the side of the worker, and later on we shall consider it also from the side of the non-worker.

Thus, through alienated labour the worker creates the relation of another man, who does not work and is outside the work process, to this labour. The relation of the worker to work also produces the relation of the capitalist (or whatever one likes to call the lord of labour) to work. *Private property* is, therefore, the product, the necessary result, of *alienated labour,* of the external relation of the worker to nature and to himself.

Marx, *Manuscripts* (1844), EW, pp. 120–31.

4.B.5 ALIENATION, CAPITALISTS, AND WORKERS

We have already seen that in relation to the worker, who *appropriates* nature by his labour, appropriation appears as alienation, self-activity as activity for another and of another, living as the sacrifice of life, and production of the object as loss of the object to an alien power, an alien man. Let us now consider the relation of this *alien* man to the worker, to labour, and to the object of labour.

It should be noted first that everything which appears to the worker as an *activity of alienation,* appears to the non-worker as a *condition of alienation.* Secondly, the *real, practical* attitude (as a state of mind) of the worker in production and to the product appears to the non-worker who confronts him as a *theoretical* attitude.

Thirdly, the non-worker does everything against the worker which the latter does against himself, but he does not do against himself what he does against the worker.

Marx, *Manuscripts* (1844), EW, p. 134.

Proletariat and wealth are opposites; as such they form a single whole. They are both forms of the world of private property. The question is what place each occupies in the antithesis. It is not sufficient to declare them two sides of a single whole.

Private property as private property, as wealth, is compelled to maintain *itself,* and thereby its opposite, the proletariat, in *existence.* That is the *positive* side of the contradiction, self-satisfied private property.

The proletariat, on the other hand, is compelled, as proletariat to abolish itself and thereby its opposite, the condition for its existence, what makes it the proletariat, i.e., private property. That is the *negative* side of the contradiction, its restlessness within its very self, dissolved and self-dissolving private property.

The propertied class and the class of the proletariat present the same human self-alienation. But the former class finds in this self-alienation its confirmation and its good, *its own power:* it has in it a *semblance* of human existence. The class of the proletariat feels annihilated in its self-alienation; it sees in it its own powerlessness and the reality of an inhuman existence. In the words of Hegel, the class of the proletariat is in abasement *indignation* at that abasement, an indignation to which it is necessarily driven by the contradiction between its human *nature* and its condition of life, which is the outright, decisive and comprehensive negation of that nature.

Within this antithesis the private owner is therefore the *conservative* side, the proletarian, the *destructive* side. From the former arises the action of preserving the antithesis, from the latter, that of annihilating it.

Marx, *Manuscripts* (1844), EW, pp. 120–31.

4.B.6 ALIENATED NEEDS

We have seen the importance which must be attributed, in a socialist perspective, to the *wealth* of human needs, and consequently also to a *new mode of production* and to a new *object* of production. A new manifestation of *human* powers and a new enrichment of the human being. Within the system of private property it has the opposite meaning. Every man speculates upon creating a *new* need in another in order to force him to a new sacrifice, to place him in a new dependence, and to entice him into a new kind of pleasure and thereby into economic ruin. Everyone tries to establish over others an alien power in order to find there the satisfaction of his own egoistic need. With the increasing mass of objects, therefore, the realm of alien entities to which man is subjected also increases. Every new product is a new *potentiality* of mutual deceit and robbery. Man becomes increasingly poor as a man; he has increasing need of *money* in order to take possession of the hostile being. The power of his *money* diminishes directly with the growth of the quantity of production, i.e. his need increases with the increasing *power* of money. The need for money is, therefore, the real need created by the modern economic system, and the only need which it creates. The *quantity* of money becomes increasingly its only important quality. Just as it reduces every entity to an abstraction, so it reduces itself in its own development to a *quantitative* entity. Excess and immoderation become its true standard. This is shown subjectively, partly in the fact that the expansion of production and of needs becomes an *ingenious* and always *calculating* subservience to inhuman, depraved, unnatural and *imaginary* appetites. Private property does not know how to change crude need into *human* need; its *idealism* is *fantasy, caprice* and *fancy*. No eunuch flatters his tyrant more shamefully or seeks by more infamous means to stimulate his jaded appetite, in order to gain some favour, than does the eunuch of industry, the entrepreneur, in order to acquire a few silver coins or to charm the gold from the purse of his dearly beloved neighbour. (Every product is a bait by means of which the individual tries to entice the essence of the other person, his money. Every real or potential need is a weakness which will draw the bird into the lime. Universal exploitation of human communal life.) . . . The entrepreneur accedes to the most depraved fancies of his neighbour, plays the role of pander between him and his needs, awakens unhealthy appetites in him, and watches for every weakness so that later on he may claim the remuneration for this labour of love.

This alienation is shown in part by the fact that the refinement of needs and of the means to satisfy them produces as its counterpart a bestial savagery, a complete, primitive and abstract simplicity of needs; or rather, that it simply reproduces itself in its opposite sense. For the worker even the need for fresh air ceases to be a need. Man returns to the cave dwelling again, but is now poisoned by the pestilential breath of civilization. The worker has only a *precarious* right to inhabit it, for it has become an alien dwelling which may suddenly not be available, or from which he may be evicted if he does not pay the rent. He has to *pay* for this mortuary. The dwelling full of light . . . ceases to exist for the worker. Light, air, and the simplest *animal* cleanliness cease to be human needs. *Filth,* this corruption and putrefaction which runs in the *sewers* of civilization (this is to be taken literally) becomes the *element in which man lives.* . . .

The significance which production has in relation to the wealth is *revealed* in the significance which it has for the poor. At the top its manifestation is always refined, concealed, ambiguous, an appearance; at the bottom it is rough, straightforward, candid, a reality. The *crude* need of the worker is a much greater source of profit than the *refined* need of the wealth. The cellar dwellings in London bring their landlords more than do the palaces; i.e. they constitute *greater wealth* so far as the landlord is concerned and thus, in economic terms, greater *social* wealth.

Marx, *Manuscripts* (1844), EW, pp. 168–70, 174.

4.B.7 MONEY AND ALIENATION

Money, since it has the *property* of purchasing everything, of appropriating objects to itself, is, therefore, the *object par excellence.* The universal character of this *property* corresponds to the omnipotence of money, which is regarded as an omnipotent being . . . money is the *pander* between need and object, between human life and the means of subsistence. But *that which* mediates *my* life mediates also the existence of other men for me. It is for me the *other* person. . . .

That which exists for me through the medium of *money,* that which I can pay for (i.e. which money can buy), that I *am,* the possessor of the money. My own power is as great as the power of money. The properties of money are my own (the possessor's) properties and faculties. What I *am* and *can do* is, therefore, not at all determined by my individuality. I *am* ugly, but I can buy the most beautiful woman for myself. Consequently, I am not *ugly,* for the effect of ugliness, its power to repel, is annulled by money. As an individual I am *lame,* but money provides me with twenty-four legs. Therefore, I am not lame. I am a detestable, dishonourable, unscrupulous and stupid man, but money is honoured and also is its possessor. Money is the highest good, and so its possessor is good. . . . Does not my money, therefore, transform all my incapacities into their opposites.

If *money* is the bond which binds me to *human* life, and society to me, and which links me with nature and man, is it not the bond of all *bonds.* Is it not, therefore, also the universal agent of separation? It is the real means of both *separation* and *union,* the galvano-*chemical* power of society. . . .

The power to confuse and invert all human and natural qualities, to bring about fraternization of incompatibles, the *divine* power of money, resides in its *character* as the alienated and self-alienating species-life of man. It is the alienated *power* of *humanity.*

What I as a *man* am unable to do, and thus what all my individual faculties are unable to do, is made possible for me by *money.* Money, therefore, turns each of these faculties into something which it is not, into its *opposite.* . . .

The difference between effective demand, supported by money, and ineffective demand, based upon my need, my passion, my desire, etc. is the difference between *being* and *thought,* between the merely inner representation and the representation which exists outside myself as a *real object.*

If I have no money for travel I have no *need*—no real and self-realizing need—for travel. If I have a *vocation* for study but no money for it, then I have *no* vocation, i.e. no *effective,* genuine vocation. Conversely, if I really have *no* vocation for study, but have money and the urge for it, then I have an *effective* vocation. *Money* is the external, universal means and power (not derived from man as man nor from human society as society) to change *representation* into *reality* and *reality* into *mere representation.* It transforms *real human and natural faculties* into mere abstract representations, i.e. *imperfections* and tormenting chimeras; and on the other hand, it transforms *real imperfections and fancies,* faculties which are really impotent and which exist only in the individual's imagination, into *real faculties and powers.* In this respect, therefore, money is the general inversion of *individualities,* turning them into their opposites and associating contradictory qualities with their qualities.

Money, then, appears as a *disruptive* power for the individual and for the social bonds, which claim to be self-subsistent *entities.* . . .

Since money, as the existing and active concept of value, confounds and exchanges everything, it is the universal *confusion and transposition* of all things, the inverted world, the confusion and transposition of all natural and human qualities.

Marx, *Manuscripts* (1844), EW, pp. 189–93.

C. SOCIOECONOMIC SOURCES OF ALIENATION

Although the 1844 *Manuscripts,* drawn on heavily in the preceding section, give Marx's most organized exposition of the forms of alienation, they are extremely sketchy on the subject of the sources of alienation. That workers (and capitalists, in their own way) are alienated is definitely clear; exactly why and how they have become so is left in an embryonic and underdeveloped form. One key point, however, is clear. Although alienation is not unique to capitalism, it is "universalized" and brought to its highest point under capitalist auspices. In effect, capitalist alienation is the "other side" of the coin from capitalist progressivity and industrialization. Why is this? What are the socioeconomic bases of alienation under capitalism?

Marx's answer, as it emerges more fully in subsequent works, notably the 1857–1858 *Grundrisse,* is simple but powerful. Alienation has its roots deep in the underlying institutions of capitalism itself, notably capitalist exchange relations, property relations, and combination and division of labor. Thus, alienation is neither a fluke nor simply a residual carryover from a precapitalist past (although certain parellels may be drawn between capitalist and precapitalist alienation), but is instead a fundamental constituent of the modern capitalist economy. As capitalism spreads geographically and develops technologically, its very progress carries with it the spread and intensification of alienation.

First, then, among alienation's sources are money and market exchange relations (selection 4.C.8). In the classical view of Adam Smith, competitive market exchange constitutes a system or process whereby individuals, seeking their private self-interests, are led as if "by an invisible hand, to serve an end which was no part of their intention," i.e., to produce what consumers want at low costs and prices. Marx and Engels do not deny that something like this occurs. Competitive markets do serve as social processes for the allocation of resources. At the same time, this process *at its best* is separated or alienated from human, social control. Thus, in a market economy, "an *inhuman power* rules over everything" *(Manuscripts).* Market exchange relations appear as "collisions between mutually indifferent individuals." Their mutual interconnections appear as something "alien to them, autonomous, as a thing" *(Grundrisse).* Quantities and values in the exchange process vary "independently of the will, foresight and action of the producers. To them their own social action takes the form of objects, which rule the producers instead of being ruled by them" *(Capital). At its worst,* the anarchic process of market exchange breaks down in recurrent crises and succeeding depressions (see chapter 6). Although market exchange, and thus alienation, precedes capitalism, it is universalized in the capitalist development process, both in the form of the growing world market and in the extension of money exchange relations to labor power, machinery, and land as well as commodities in general. Thus, according to Marx, the realm of alienation expands under capitalist auspices.

Second is capitalist property relations (selection 4.C.9). In his early writings, Marx perceives *private* property itself to conduce to alienation, notably by stimulating egoism and a sense of separateness and loss of community among individuals. Capitalist property relations are perceived to extend and intensify alienation's domain. As described in chapter 2, Marx's capitalism is characterized not merely by private property and market exchange, but by a capitalist class monopoly of the means of production, and thus by a propertyless proletariat, alienated from its tools or means of livelihood and subject to the control of capitalist employers. This dimension of alienation is both presupposition and result of the capitalist process. " The capitalist system presupposes the complete separation of the labourers from all property in the means by which they can realize their labour. As soon as capitalist production is once on its own legs, it not only maintains this separation, but produces it on a continually extending scale."[6]

Next is combination and division of labor (selection 4.C.10). We have already described the various stages in the development of the division of labor which Marx identifies in *Capital* (chapter 2C). The division of labor in society in general, at least when carried out to the degree in which people have one exclusive occupation or sphere of activity for all of their lives, alienates individuals both from others and from their own human potentials. Under capitalism, division of labor is extended to the organization of production within the factory. Here, as noted earlier (selection 2.C.10), the worker is converted into a "crippled monstrosity" by forcibly developing his "detail dexterity" and alienating him from a "world of productive capabilities and instincts." However, even if the more extreme (and dysfunctional) forms of division of labor within the factory were avoided, alienation would still emerge from the confrontation of the worker in the production process with "the property of another . . . as a ruling power." Combination and division of labor appears to the worker in "the shape of the authority of the . . . capitalist, in the shape of the powerful will of another, who subjects their activity to his aim."[7] Thus, the worker relates to the combination of labor "as an alien combination, as well as to his own labour as expression of his life, which, although it belongs to him, is alien to him and coerced from him."[8]

[6]Marx, *Capital,* (New York: Modern Library, n.d.), p. 785.

[7]*Ibid.*, p. 364.

[8]Marx, *Grundrisse* (New York: Vintage, 1973) p. 470.

Finally (selection 4.C.11), as capitalist industrialization proceeds, workers are increasingly alienated from machinery, science, and technology—the very bases of rapid growth and development. Instead of the machinery serving as the worker's tool, the worker becomes an "appendage" or "accessory" to the machine. Under automated systems of machinery, science and technology appear as "alien, external" to workers. This dimension of alienation is not merely a function of "modern technology," however, as some contemporary non-Marxian writers assert. Although new technologies, notably automation, stimulate radical changes in the character of work and the composition of labor (see selection 8.B.11, below), the central point of Marx is that these revolutionary forces are under capitalists' control and are thus alienated from collective, working class decision.

4.C.8 MONEY, MARKET EXCHANGE, AND DIVISION OF LABOR

THE GRUNDRISSE

To the degree that production is shaped in such a way that every producer becomes dependent on the exchange value of his commodity, i.e. as the product increasingly becomes an exchange value in reality, and exchange value becomes the immediate object of production—to the same degree must *money relations* develop, together with the contradictions immanent in the *money relation,* in the relation of the product to itself as money. The need for exchange and for the transformation of the product into a pure exchange value progresses in step with the division of labour, i.e. with the increasingly social character of production. But as the latter grows, so grows the power of *money,* i.e. the exchange relation establishes itself as a power external to and independent of the producers. What originally appeared as a means to promote production becomes a relation alien to the producers. As the producers become more dependent on exchange, exchange appears to become more independent of them, and the gap between the product as product and the product as exchange value appears to widen. Money does not create these antitheses and contradictions; it is, rather, the development of these contradictions and antitheses which creates the seemingly transcendental power of money. . . .

As soon as money has become an external thing alongside the commodity, the exchangeability of the commodity for money becomes bound up with external conditions which may or may not be present; it is abandoned to the mercy of external conditions. The commodity is demanded in exchange because of its natural properties, because of the needs for which it is the desired object. Money, by contrast, is demanded only because of its exchange value, as exchange value. Hence, whether or not the commodity is transposable into money, whether or not it can be exchanged for money, whether its exchange value can be posited for it—this depends on circumstances which initially have nothing to do with it as exchange value and are independent of that. The transposability of the commodity depends on the natural properties of the product; that of money coincides with its existence as symbolized exchange value. There thus arises the possibility that the commodity, in its specific form as product, can no longer be exchanged for, equated with, its general form as money.

By existing outside the commodity as money, the exchangeability of the commodity has become something different from and alien to the commodity, with which it first has to be brought into equation, to which it is therefore at the beginning unequal; while the equation itself becomes dependent on external conditions, hence a matter of chance. . . .

Just as the exchange value of commodity leads a double existence, as the particular commodity and as money, so does the act of exchange split into two mutually independent acts: exchange of commodities for money, exchange of money for commodities; purchase and sale. Since these have now achieved a spatially and temporally separate and mutually indifferent form of existence, their immediate identity ceases. They may correspond or not; they may balance or not; they may enter into disproportion with one another. They will of course always attempt to equalize one another; but in the place of the earlier immediate equality there now stands the constant movement of equalization, which evidently presupposes constant non-equivalence. It is now entirely possible that consonance may be reached only by passing through the most extreme dissonance. . . .

With the separation of purchase and sale, with the splitting of exchange into spatially and temporally independent acts, there further emerges another, new relation.

Just as exchange itself splits apart into two mutually independent acts, so does the overall movement of exchange itself become separate from the exchangers, the producers of commodities. Exchange for the sake of exchange separates off from exchange for the sake of commodities. . . . The rise of exchange (commerce) as an independent function torn away from the exchangers corresponds to the rise of exchange value as an independent entity, as money, torn away from products. . . . The purpose of commerce is not consumption, directly, but the gaining of money, of exchange values. This doubling of exchange—exchange for the sake of consumption and exchange for exchange—gives rise to a new disproportion. In his exchange, the merchant is guided merely by the difference between the purchase and sale of commodities; but the consumer who buys a commodity must replace its exchange value once and for all. Circulation, i.e. exchange within the mercantile estate, and the point at which circulation ends, i.e. exchange between the mercantile estate and the consumers—as much as they must ultimately condition one another—are determined by quite different laws and motives, and can enter into most acute contradiction with one another. The possibility of commercial crises is already contained in this separation. . . .

The dissolution of all products and activities into exchange values presupposes the dissolution of all fixed personal (historic) relations of dependence in production, as well as the all-sided dependence of the producers on one another. Each individual's production is dependent on the production of all others; and the transformation of his product into the necessaries of his own life is [similarly] dependent on the consumption of all others. Prices are old; exchange also; but the increasing determination of the former by costs of production, as well as the increasing dominance of the latter over all relations of production, only develop fully, and continue to develop even more completely, in bourgeois society, the society of free competition. What Adam Smith, in the true eighteenth-century manner, puts in the prehistoric period, the period preceding history, is rather a product of history.

This reciprocal dependence is expressed in the constant necessity for exchange, and in exchange value as the all-wided mediation. The economists express this as follows: Each pursues his private interest and only his private interest; and thereby serves the private interests of all, the general interest, without willing or knowing it. The real point is not that each individual's pursuit of his private interest promotes the totality of private interests, the general interest. One could just as well deduce from this abstract phrase that each individual reciprocally blocks the assertion of the others' interests, so that, instead of a general affirmation, this war of all against all produces a general negation. The point is rather that private interest is itself already a socially determined interest, which can be achieved only within the conditions laid down by society and with the means provided by society; hence it is bound to the reproduction of these conditions and means. It is the interest of private persons; but its content, as well as the form and means of its realization, is given by social conditions independent of all.

The reciprocal and all-sided dependence of individuals who are indifferent to one another forms their social connection. This social bond is expressed in *exchange value,* by means of which alone each individual's own activity or his product becomes an activity and a product for him; he must produce a general product—*exchange value,* or, the latter isolated for itself and individualized, *money.* On the other side, the power which each individual exercises over the activity of others or over social wealth exists in him as the owner of *exchange values,* of *money.* The individual carries his social power, as well as his bond with society, in his pocket. Activity, regardless of its individual manifestation, and the product of activity, regardless of its particular make-up, are always *exchange value,* and exchange value is a generality, in which all individuality and peculiarity are negated and extinguished. This indeed is a condition very different from that in which the individual or the individual member of a family or clan (later, community) directly and naturally reproduces himself, or in which his productive activity and his share in production are bound to a specific form of labour and of product, which determine his relation to others in just that specific way.

The social character of activity, as well as the social form of the product, and the share of individuals in production here appear as something alien and objective, confronting the individuals, not as their relation to one another, but as their subordination to relations which subsist independently of them and which arise out of collisions between mutually indifferent individuals. The general exchange of activities and products, which has become a vital condition for each individual—their mutual interconnection—here appears as something alien to them, autonomous, as a thing. In exchange value, the social connection between persons is transformed into a social relation between things; personal capacity into objective wealth. The less social power the medium of exchange possesses (and at this stage it is still closely bound to the nature of the direct product of labour and the direct needs of the partners in exchange) the greater must be the power of the community which binds the individuals together, the patriarchal relation, the community of antiquity, feudalism and the guild system. . . . Each individual possesses social power in the form of a thing. Rob the thing of this social power and you must give it to persons to exercise over persons. Relations of personal dependence (entirely spontaneous at the outset) are the first social forms, in which human productive capacity develops only to a slight extent and at isolated points. Personal independence founded on *objective* dependence is the second great form, in which a system of general social metabolism, of universal relations, of all-round needs and universal capacities is formed for the first time. Free individuality, based on the universal development of individuals and on their subordination of their communal, social productivity as their social wealth, is the third stage. The second stage creates the conditions for the third. Patriarchal as well as ancient conditions (feudal, also) thus disintegrate with the development of commerce, of luxury, of *money,* of *exchange value,* while modern society arises and grows in the same measure.

Exchange and division of labour reciprocally condition one another. Since everyone works for himself but his product is nothing for him, each must of course exchange, not only in order to take part in the general productive capacity but also in order to transform his own product into his own subsistence. . . . Exchange when mediated by exchange value and money, presupposes the all-round dependence of the producers on one another, together with the total isolation of their private interests from one another, as well as a division of social labour whose unity and mutual complementarity exist in the form of a natural relation, as it were, external to the individuals and independent of them. The pressure of general demand and supply on one another mediates the connection of mutually indifferent persons.

The very necessity of first transforming individual products or activities into *exchange value,* into *money,* so that they obtain and demonstrate their social *power* in this *objective* form, proves two things: (1) That individuals now produce only for society and in society; (2) that production is not *directly* social, is not 'the offspring of association,' which distributes labour internally. Individuals are subsumed under social production; social production exists outside them as their fate; but social production is not subsumed under individuals, manageable by them as their common wealth. . . . The *private exchange* of all products of labour, all activities and all wealth stands in antithesis not only to a distribution based on a natural or political super- and subordination of individuals to one another. . . but also to free exchange among individuals who are associated on the basis of common appropriation and control of the means of production. (The latter form of association is not arbitrary; it presupposes the development of material and cultural conditions which are not to be examined any further at this point.) Just as the division of labour creates agglomeration, combination, cooperation, the antithesis of private interests, class interests, competition, concentration of capital, monopoly, stock companies—so many antithetical forms of the unity which itself brings the antithesis to the fore—so does private exchange create world trade, private independence creates complete dependence on the so-called world market, and the fragmented acts of exchange create a banking and credit system whose books, as least keep a record of the balance between debit and credit in private exchange. Although the private interests within each nation divide it into as many nations at it has 'full-grown individuals,' and although the interests of exporters and of importers are antithetical here, etc. etc., national trade does obtain the *semblance* of existence in the form of the rate of exchange. Nobody will take this as a ground for believing that a *reform of the money market* can abolish the *foundations* of internal or external private trade. But within bourgeois society, the society that rests on *exchange value,* there arise relations of circulation as well as of production which are so many mines to explode it. (A mass of antithetical forms of the social unity, whose antithetical character can never be abolished through quiet metamorphosis. On the other hand, if we did not find concealed in society as it is the material conditions of production and the corresponding relations of exchange prerequisite for a classless society, then all attempts to explode it would be quixotic.) . . .

A comprehensive view over the whole of commerce and production in so far as lists of current prices in fact provide it, furnishes indeed the best proof of the way in which their own exchange and their own production confront individuals as an *obejctive* relation which is *independent* of them. In the case of the *world market,* the *connection of the individual* with all, but at the same time also the *independence of this connection from the individual,* have developed to such a high level that the formation of the world market already at the same time contains the conditions for going beyond it). . . .

(It has been said and may be said that this is precisely the beauty and the greatness of it: this spontaneous interconnection, this material and mental metabolism which is independent of the knowing and willing of individuals, and which presupposes their reciprocal independence and indifference. And, certainly, this objective connection is preferable to the lack of any connection, or to a merely local connection resting on blood ties, or on primeval, natural or master-servant relations. Equally certain is it that individuals cannot gain mastery over their own social interconnections before they have created them. But it is an insipid notion to conceive of this merely *objective bond* as a spontaneous, natural attribute inherent in individuals and inseparable from their nature (in antithesis to their conscious knowing and willing). This bond is their product. It is a historic product. It belongs to a specific phase of their development. The alien and independent character in which it presently exists vis-a-vis individuals proves only that the latter are still engaged in the creation of the conditions of their social life, and that they have not yet begun, on the basis of these conditions, to live it. It is the bond natural to individuals within specific and limited relations of production. Universally developed individuals, whose social relations, as their own communal relations, are hence also subordinated to their own communal control, are no product of nature, but of history. The degree and the universality of the development of wealth where *this* individuality becomes possible supposes production on the basis of exchange values as a prior condition, whose universality produces not only the alienation of the individual from himself and from others, but also the universality and the comprehensiveness of his relations and capacities. In earlier stages of development the single individual seems to be developed more fully, because he has not yet worked out his relationships in their fullness, or erected them as independent social powers and relations opposite himself. It is as ridiculous to yearn for a return to that original fullness as it is to believe that with this complete emptiness history has come to a standstill. The bourgeois viewpoint has never advanced beyond this antithesis between itself and this romantic viewpoint, and therefore the latter will accompany it as legitimate antithesis up to its blessed end.)

Marx, *Grundrisse* (1857-58), pp. 146–49, 156–59, 161–62.

THE MANUSCRIPTS

Alienation is apparent not only in the fact that *my* means of life belong to *someone else,* that *my* desires are the unattainable possession of *someone else,* but that everything is *something different* from itself, that my activity is *something else,* and finally (and this is also the case for the capitalist) that *an inhuman power* rules over everything. . . .

The *division of labour* is the economic expression of the *social character of labour* within alienation. Or, since *labour* is only an expression of human activity within alienation, of life activity as alienation of life, the *division of labour* is nothing but the *alienated* establishment of human activity as a *real species-activity* or *the activity of man as a species-being.* . . .

The consideration of *division of labour* and *exchange* is of the greatest interest, since they are the *perceptible, alienated* expression of human *activity* and *capacities* as the activity and capacities *proper to a species.*

To state that *private property* is the basis of the *division of labour* and *exchange* is simply to assert that *labour* is the essence of private property; an assertion which the economist cannot prove and which we wish to prove for him. It is precisely in the fact that the *division of labour* and *exchange* are manifestations of private property that we find the proof, first that *human* life needed *private property* for its realization, and secondly, that it now requires the supersession of private property.

The *division of labour* and *exchange* are the two phenomena which lead the economist to vaunt the social character of his science, while in the same breath he unconsciously expresses the contradictory nature of his science—the establishment of society through unsocial, particular interests.

Marx, *Manuscripts* (1844), EW, pp. 177–78, 181, 187.

4.C.9 CAPITALIST PROPERTY RELATIONS

THE GRUNDRISSE

Within the production process itself, surplus value, the surplus value procured through compulsion by capital, appeared as *surplus labour,* itself in the form of living labour, which, however, since it cannot create something out of nothing, finds its objective conditions laid out before it. Now this *surplus labour* appears in objectified form as *surplus product,* and, in order to realize itself as capital, this surplus product divides into a double form: as *objective condition of labour*—material and instrument; as subjective—consumption goods for the living labour now to be put to work. The general form as value—objectified labour—and objectified labour coming out of circulation—is of course the general, self-evident presupposition. Further: the surplus product in its totality—which objectifies surplus labour in its totality—now appears as *surplus capital* (in contrast to the original capital, before it had undertaken this cycle), i.e. as independent exchange value, in which living labour capacity encounters its *specific use value.* All moments which confronted living labour capacity, and employed it as *alien, external* powers, and which consumed it under *certain conditions independent of itself,* are now posited as *its own product and result.*

Firstly: surplus value or the surplus product are nothing but a specific sum of objectified living labour—the sum of surplus labour. This new *value* which confronts living labour as independent, as engaged in exchange with it, as capital is the *product of labour.* It is itself nothing other than the *excess of labour as such above necesssary labour*—in objective form and hence as *value.*

Secondly: the particular forms which this value must adopt in order to realize itself anew, i.e. to posit itself as capital—on one side as raw material and instrument, on the other as subsistence goods for labour during the act of production—are likewise, therefore, only *particular* forms of surplus labour itself. . . . The objective conditions of *surplus labour*—which are restricted to the proportion of raw material and instrument beyond the requirements of necessary labour, whereas the objective conditions of necessary labour divide within their objectivity into objective and subjective, into objective moments of labour as well as subjective (consumption goods for living labour)—therefore now appear, are therefore now posited, as the product, result, objective form, external existence of surplus labour itself. Originally, by contrast, the fact that instrument and necessaries were on hand in the amounts which made it possible for living labour to realize itself not only as *necessary,* but also as *surplus* labour—this appeared alien to living labour itself, appeared as an act of capital.

Thirdly: The independent, for-itself existence of value vis-a-vis living labour capacity—hence its existence as capital—the objective, self-sufficient indifference, the *alien quality* of the objective conditions of labour vis-a-vis living labour capacity, which goes so far that these conditions confront the person of the worker in the person of the capitalist—as personification with its own will and interest—this absolute *divorce, separation* of property, i.e. of the objective conditions of labour from living labour capacity—that they confront him as *alien property,* as the reality of other juridical persons, as the absolute realm of *their* will—and that labour therefore, on the other side, appears as *alien labour* opposed to the value personified in the capitalist, or the conditions of labour—this absolute separation between property and labour, between living labour capacity and the conditions of its realization, between objectified and living labour, between value and value-creating activity—hence also the alien quality of the content of labour for the worker himself—this divorce now likewise appears as a product of labour itself, as objectification of its own moments. For, in the new act of production itself—which merely confirmed the exchange between capital and living labour which preceded it—surplus labour, and hence the surplus product, the total product of labour in general (of surplus labour as well as necessary labour), has now been posited as capital, as independent and indifferent towards living labour capacity, or as exchange value which confronts its mere use value. Labour capacity has appropriated for itself only the subjective conditions of necessary labour—the means of subsistence for actively producing labour capacity, i.e. for its reproduction as mere labour capacity separated from the conditions of its realization—and it has posited these conditions themselves as *things, values,* which confront it in an alien, commanding personification. The worker emerges not only not richer, but emerges rather poorer from the process than he entered. For not only has he produced the conditions of necessary labour as conditions belonging to capital; but also the value-creating possibility, the realization which lies as a possibility within him, now likewise exists as surplus value, surplus product, in a word as capital, as master over living labour capacity, as value endowed with its own might and will, confronting him in his abstract, objectless, purely subjective poverty. He has produced not only the alien wealth and his own poverty, but also the relation of this wealth as independent, self-sufficient wealth, relative to himself as the poverty which this wealth consumes, and from which wealth thereby draws new vital spirits into itself, and realizes itself anew. All this arose from the act of exchange, in which he exchanged his living labour capacity for an amount of objectified labour, except that this objectified labour—these external conditions of his being, and the independent externality (to him) of these objective conditions—now appear as posited by himself, as *his own product,* as his own self-objectification as well as the objectification of himself as a power independent of himself, which moreover rules over him, rules over him through his own actions.

In *surplus capital,* all moments are products of *alien labour—alien surplus labour* transformed into capital; means of subsistence for necessary labour; the objective conditions—material and instrument—whereby necessary labour can reproduce the value exchanged for it in means of subsistence; finally the amount of material and instrument required so that new surplus labour can realize itself in them, or a new surplus value can be created.

It no longer seems here, as it still did in the first examination of the production process, as if capital, for its part, brought with it any value whatever from circulation. Rather, the objective conditions of labour now appear as labour's product—both to the extent that they are value in general, and as use values for production. But while capital thus appears as the product of labour, so does the product of labour likewise appear as capital—no longer as a simple product, nor as an exchangeable commodity, but as *capital;* objectified labour as mastery, command over living labour. The product of labour appears as *alien property,* as a mode of existence confronting living labour as independent, as *value* in its being for itself; the product of labour, objectified labour, has been endowed by living labour with a soul of its own, and establishes itself opposite living labour as an *alien power:* both these situations are themselves the product of labour. Living labour therefore now appears from its own standpoint as acting within the production process in such a way that, as it realizes itself in the objective conditions, it simultaneously repulses this realization from itself as an alien reality, and hence posits itself as insubstantial, as mere penurious labour capacity in face of this reality alienated from it, belonging not to it but to others; that it posits its own reality not as a being for it, but merely as a being for others, and hence also as mere other-being or being of another opposite itself. This realization process is at the same time the de-realization process of labour. It posits itself objectively, but it posits this, its objectivity, as its own not-being or as the being of its not-being—of capital. It returns back into itself as the mere possibility of value-creation or realization; because the whole of real wealth, the world of real value and likewise the real conditions of its own realization are posited opposite it as independent existences. As a consequence of the production process, the possibilities resting in living labour's own womb exist outside it as realities—but as *realities alien* to it, which form wealth in opposition to it. . . .

It here becomes evident that labour itself progressively extends and gives an ever wider and fuller existence to the objective world of wealth as a power alien to labour, so that, relative to values created or to the real conditions of value-creation, the penurious subjectivity of living labour capacity forms an ever more glaring contrast. The greater the extent to which labour objectifies itself, the greater becomes the objective world of values, which stands opposite it as alien—alien property. With the creation of surplus capital, labour places itself under the compulsion to create yet further surplus capital etc. etc. . . .

As regards the *surplus capital,* . . . every moment of material, instrument, necessaries, resolves into *alien labour,* which the capitalist does not appropriate by means of *exchange* for existing values, but has appropriated *without exchange.* True, the exchange of a part of *values belonging to him,* or of *objectified labour* possessed by him, for alien living labour capacity, appears as the *original precondition* for this *surplus capital.* For the formation of *surplus capital I,* if we give that name to the surplus capital emerging from the original production process, i.e. for the *appropriation of alien labour,* of *objectified alien labour,* it appears as a condition that the capitalist should possess *values,* of which he *formally* exchanges one part for living labour capacity. We say formally, because living labour must replace and return to him these *exchanged* values as well. But be this as it may. In any case, it appears as a condition for the formation of surplus capital I, i.e. for the appropriation of alien labour or of the values in which it is objectified, that there must be an exchange of values belonging to the capitalist, thrown into circulation by him, and supplied to living labour capacity by him—of values which do *not* arise from his *exchange* with living labour, or not from his relation as *capital* to *labour.*

But now let us think of this surplus capital as having been thrown back into the production process, as realizing its surplus value anew in exchange, and as appearing anew as new surplus capital at the beginning of a third production process. This, *surplus capital II,* has different presuppositions from surplus capital I. The presupposition of surplus capital I was the existence of values belonging to the capitalist and thrown by him into circulation, or, more exactly, into the exchange with living labour capacity. The presupposition of surplus capital II is nothing more than the existence of surplus capital I; i.e. in other words, the presupposition that the capitalist has already appropriated alien labour without exchange. This puts him into a position where he is able to begin the process again and again. True, in order to create surplus capital II, he had to exchange a part of the value of surplus capital I in the form of means of subsistence for living labour capacity, but the values he gave in that exchange were not values which he originally put into circulation out of his own funds; they were, rather, objectified alien labour which he appropriated without giving any equivalent whatever, and which he now re-exchanges for alien living labour;

in the same way, moreover, as the material etc. in which this new labour realizes itself and in which it creates surplus value have come into his hands without exchange, by mere appropriation. *The previous appropriation of alien labour now appears as the simple precondition for the new appropriation of alien labour;* or, his ownership of alien labour in objective (material) form, in the form of existing values, appears as the condition of his ability to appropriate new alien *living* labour capacity, hence surplus labour, labour without equivalent. The fact that he has previously confronted living labour as capital appears as the only condition required in order that he may not only maintain himself as capital, but also, as a growing capital, increasingly *appropriate* alien labour without equivalent; or, that he may extend his power, his existence as capital opposite living labour capacity, and on the other side constantly posit living labour capacity anew in its subjective, insubstantial penury as living labour capacity. Property—previous, or objectified, alien labour—appears as the only condition for further appropriation of present or living alien labour. In so far as surplus capital I was created by means of a simple exchange between objectified labour and living labour capacity—an exchange entirely based on the laws of the exchange of equivalents as measured by the quantity of labour or labour time contained in them—and *in so far as* the legal expression of this exchange presupposed nothing other than everyone's right of property over his own products, and of free disposition over them—but in so far as the relation of surplus capital II to I is therefore a consequence of this first relation—we see that, by a peculiar logic, the right of property undergoes a dialectical inversion, so that on the side of capital it becomes the right to an alien product, or the right of property over alien labour, the right to appropriate alien labour without an equivalent, and, on the side of labour capacity, it becomes the duty to relate to one's own labour or to one's own product as to *alien property.* The right of property is inverted, to become, on the one side, the right to appropriate alien labour, and, on the other, the duty of respecting the product of one's own labour, and one's own labour itself, as values belonging to others. The exchange of equivalents, however, which appeared as the original operation, an operation to which the right of property gave legal expression, has become turned round in such a way that the exchange by one side is now only illusory, since the part of capital which is exchanged for living labour capacity, firstly, is itself *alien labour,* appropriated without equivalent, and, secondly, *has to be replaced with a surplus by living labour capacity,* is thus in fact not consigned away, but merely changed from one form into another. The relation of exchange has thus dropped away entirely, or is a *mere semblance.* Furthermore, the right of property originally appeared to be based on one's own labour. Property now appears as the right to alien labour, and as the impossibility of labour appropriating its own product. The complete separation between property, and, even more so, wealth, and labour, now appears as a consequence of the law which began with their identity.

Finally, the result of the process of production and realization is, above all, the reproduction and new production of the *relation of capital and labour itself, of capitalist and worker.* This social relation, production relation, appears in fact as an even more important result of the process than its material results. And more particularly, within this process the worker produces himself as labour capacity, as well as the capital confronting him, while at the same time the capitalist produces himself as capital as well as the living labour capacity confronting him. Each reproduces itself, by reproducing its other, its negation. The capitalist produces labour as alien; labour produces the product as alien. The capitalist produces the worker, and the worker the capitalist etc. . . .

Once production founded on capital is presupposed [then] the condition that the capitalist, in order to posit himself as capital, must bring values into circulation which he created with his own labour—or by some other means, excepting only already available, previous wage labour—belongs among the antediluvian conditions of capital, belongs to its *historic presuppositions,* which, precisely as such *historic* presuppositions, are past and gone, and hence belong to the *history of its formation,* but in no way to its *contemporary* history, i.e. not to the real system of the mode of production ruled by it. While e.g. the flight of serfs to the cities is one of the *historic* conditions and presuppositions of urbanism, it is not a *condition,* not a moment of the reality of developed cities, but belongs rather to their *past* presuppositions, to the presuppositions of their becoming which are suspended in their being. The conditions and presuppositions of the *becoming,* of the *arising,* of capital presuppose precisely that it is not yet in being but merely in *becoming;* they therefore disappear as real capital arises, capital which itself, on the basis of its own reality, posits the conditions for its realization. Thus e.g. while the process in which money or value for-itself originally becomes capital presupposes on the part of the capitalist an accumulation—perhaps by means of savings garnered from products and values created by his own labour etc., which he has undertaken as a *not-capitalist,* i.e. while the presuppositions under which money becomes capital appear as given, external *presuppositions* for the arising of capital—[nevertheless,] as soon as capital has become capital as such, it creates its own presuppositions, i.e. the possession of the real conditions of the creation of new values *without exchange* —by means of its own production process. These presuppositions, which originally appeared as conditions of its becoming—and hence could not spring from its *action as capital*—now appear as results of its own realization, reality, as *posited by it—not as conditions of its arising, but as results of its presence.* It no longer proceeds from presuppositions in order to become, but rather it is itself presupposed, and proceeds from itself to create the conditions of its maintenance and growth. Therefore, the conditions which preceded the creation of surplus capital I, or which express the becoming of capital, do not fall into the sphere of that mode of production for which capital serves as the presupposition; as the historic preludes of its becoming, they lie behind it. . . . That is, individual capitals can continue to arise e.g. by means of hoarding. But the hoard is transformed into capital only by means of the exploitation of labour. The bourgeois economists who regard capital as an eternal and *natural* (not historical) form of production then attempt at the same time to legitimize it again by formulating the conditions of its becoming as the conditions of its contemporary realization; i.e. presenting the moments in which the capitalist still appropriates as not-capitalist—because he is still becoming—as the very conditions in which he appropriates *as capitalist.* These attempts at apologetics demonstrate a guilty conscience, as well as the inability to bring the mode of appropriation of capital as capital into harmony with the *general laws of property* proclaimed by capitalist society itself. ... Production based on exchange value and the community based on the exchange of these exchange values—even though they seem ... to posit property as the outcome of *labour* alone, and to posit private property over the product of one's own labour as condition—and labour as general condition of wealth, all presuppose and produce the separation of labour from its objective conditions. This exchange of equivalents proceeds; it is only the surface layer of a production which rests on the appropriation of alien labour *without exchange,* but with the *semblance of exchange.* This system of exchange rests on *capital* as its foundation, and, when it is regarded in isolation from capital, as it appears on the surface, as an *independent* system, then it is a mere *illusion,* but a *necessary illusion.* Thus there is no longer any ground for astonishment that the system of exchange values—exchange of equivalents measured through labour—turns into, or rather reveals as its hidden background, the *appropriation of alien labour without exchange,* complete separation of labour and property. For the domination of exchange value itself, and of exchange-value-producing production, *presupposes* alien labour capacity itself as an exchange value—i.e. the separation of living labour capacity from its objective conditions; a relation to them—or to its own objectivity—as alien property; a relation to them, in a word, as *capital.* Only in the period of the decline and fall of the feudal system, but where it still struggles internally—as in England in the fourteenth and first half of the fifteenth centuries—is there a golden age for labour in the process of becoming emancipated. In order for labour to relate to its objective conditions as its property again, another system must take the place of the system of private exchange, which, as we saw, posits the exchange of objectified labour for labour capacity, and therefore the appropriation of living labour without exchange. ... It is clear...that the worker cannot become *rich* in...exchange, since, in exchange for his labour capacity as a fixed, available magnitude, he surrenders its *creative power,* like Esau his birthright for a mess of pottage. Rather, he necessarily impoverishes himself, ... because the creative power of his labour establishes itself as the power of capital, as an *alien power* confronting him. He *divests* himself of labour as the force productive of wealth; capital appropriates it, as such. The separation between labour and property in the product of labour, between labour and wealth, is thus posited in this act of exchange itself. What appears paradoxical as *result* is already contained in the presupposition. The economists have expressed this more or less empirically. Thus the productivity of his labour, his labour in general, in so far as it is not a *capacity* but a motion, *real* labour, *comes* to confront the worker as an *alien power;* capital, inversely, realizes itself through the *appropriation of alien labour.*

Marx, *Grundrisse* (1857-58), pp. 450–60, 509–10, 307.

THE MANUSCRIPTS

Private property...is derived from the analysis of the concept of *alienated labour;* that is, alienated man, alienated labour, alienated life, and estranged man.

We have, of course, derived the concept of *alienated labour (alienated life)* from political economy, from an analysis of the *movement of private property.*

But the analysis of this concept shows that although private property appears to be the basis and cause of alienated labour, it is rather a consequence of the latter, just as the gods are *fundamentally* not the cause but the product of confusions of human reason. At a later stage, however, there is a reciprocal influence.

Only in the final stage of the development of private property is its secret revealed, namely, that it is on one hand the *product* of alienated labour, and on the other hand the *means* by which labour is alienated, *the realization of this alienation.*

Marx, *Manuscripts* (1844), EW, p. 131.

4.C.10 COMBINATION AND DIVISION OF LABOUR

By selling his labour to the capitalist, the worker obtains a right only to the *price of labour,* not to the *product of this labour,* nor to the value which *his labour has added to it.* ... Thus all the progress of civilization, or in other words every increase in the *powers of social production* ... in the *productive powers of labour itself*—such as results from science, inventions, division and combination of labour, improved means of communication, creation of the world market, machinery etc.—enriches not the worker but rather *capital;* hence it only magnifies again the power dominating over labour; increases only the productive power of capital. Since capital is the antithesis of the worker, this merely increases the *objective power* standing over labour. The *transformation of labour* (as living, purposive activity) into *capital* is, *in itself,* the result of the exchange between capital and labour, in so far as it gives the capitalist the title of ownership to the product of labour (and command over the same). *This transformation is posited* only in the *production process* itself. Thus, the question whether capital is productive or not is absurd. Labour itself is *productive only* if absorbed into capital, where capital forms the basis of production, and where the capitalist is therefore in command of production. The productivity of labour becomes the productive force of capital just as the general exchange value of commodities fixes itself in money. Labour, such as it exists *for itself* in the worker in opposition to capital, that is, labour in its *immediate being,* separated from capital, is *not productive.* Nor does it ever become *productive* as an activity of the worker so long as it merely enters the simple, only formally transforming process of circulation. Therefore, those who demonstrate that the productive force ascribed to capital is a *displacement, a transposition of the productive force* of labour, forget precisely that capital itself is essentially this *displacement, this transposition,* and that wage labour as such presupposes capital, so that, from its standpoint as well, capital is this *transubstantiation;* the necessary process of positing its own powers as *alien* to the worker. Therefore, the demand that wage labour be continued but capital suspended is self-contradictory, self-dissolving. ...

In order to express the relations into which capital and wage labour enter as *property relation* or *laws,* we need do no more than express the conduct of both sides in the *realization process* as an *appropriation process.* For example, the fact that surplus labour is posited as surplus value of capital means that the worker does not appropriate the product of his own labour; that it appears to him as *alien property;* inversely, that *alien labour* appears as the property of capital. This second law of bourgeois property, the inversion of the first—which, through laws of inheritance etc., attains an existence independent of the accidental transitoriness of individual capitalist—becomes just as established in law as the first. The first is the identity of labour with property; the second, labour as negated property, or property as negation of the alien quality of alien labour. In fact, in the production process of capital, as will be seen more closely in its futher development, labour is a totality—a combination of labours—whose individual component parts are alien to one another, so that the overall process as a totality is *not* the *work* of the individual worker, and is furthermore the work of the different workers together only to the extent that they are [forcibly] combined, and do not [voluntarily] enter into combination with one another. The combination of this labour appears just as subservient to and led by an alien will and an alien intelligence—having its *animating unity* elsewhere—as its material unity appears subordinate to the *objective unity* of the *machinery,* of fixed capital, which, as *animated monster,* objectifies the scientific idea, and is in fact the coordinator, does not in any way relate to the individual worker as his instrument; but rather he himself exists as an animated individual punctuation mark, as its living isolated accessory. Thus, combined labour is combination *in-itself* in a double way; not combination as a mutual relation among the individuals working together, nor as their predominance either over their particular or individual function or over the instrument of labour. Hence, just as the worker relates to the product of his labour as an alien thing, so does he relate to the combination of labour as an alien combination, as well as to his own labour as an expression of his life, which, although it belongs to him, is alien to him and coerced from him, and which A. Smith etc. therefore conceives as a *burden, sacrifice* etc. Labour itself, like its product, is *negated as the labour of the particular, isolated worker.* This isolated labour, negated, is now indeed communal or combined labour, posited. The *communal or combined labour* posited in this way—as activity and in the passive, objective form—is however at the same time posited as an other towards the really existing individual labour—as an *alien objectivity* (alien property) as well as an *alien subjectivity* (of capital). Capital thus represents both labour and its product as negated individualized labour and hence as the negated property of the individualized worker. Capital therefore is the existence of social labour—the combination of labour as subject as well as object—but this existence as itself existing independently opposite its real moments—hence itself a *particular* existence apart from them. For its part, capital therefore appears as the predominant subject and owner of *alien labour,* and its relation is itself as complete a contradiction as is that of wage labour. . . . Like all productive powers of labour, i.e. those which determine the degree of its intensity and hence of its extensive realization, the association of the workers—the cooperation and division of labour as fundamental conditions of the productivity of labour—appears as the *productive power of capital.* The collective power of labour, its character as social labour, is therefore the *collective power* of capital. Likewise *science.* Likewise the division of labour, as it appears as division of the occupations and of exchange corresponding to them. All social powers of production are productive powers of capital, and it appears as itself their subject. The association of the workers, as it appears in the factory, is therefore not posited by them but by capital. Their combination is not *their* being, but the *being* of capital. Vis-a-vis the individual worker, the combination appears accidental. He relates to his own combination and cooperation with other workers as *alien,* as modes of capital's effectiveness. Unless it appears in an inadequate form—e.g. small, self-employed capital—capital already, at a certain greater or lesser stage, presupposes concentration both in objective form, i.e. as concentration in one hand, which here still coincides with accumulation, of the necessaries of life, of raw material and instruments, or, in a word, of money as the general form of wealth; and on the other side, in subjective form, the accumulation of labour powers and their concentration at a single point under the command of the capitalist. There cannot be one capitalist for every worker, but rather there has to be a certain quantity of workers per capitalist, not like one or two journeymen per master. Productive capital, or the mode of production corresponding to capital, can be present in only two forms: manufacture and large-scale industry. In the former, the division of labour is predominant; in the second, the combination of labour powers (with a regular mode of work) and the employment of scientific power, where the combination and, so to speak, the communal spirit of labour is transferred to the machine etc. In the first situation the mass of (accumulated) workers must be large in relation to the amount of capital; in the second the fixed capital must be large in relation to the number of the many cooperating workers. But the concentration of many, and their distribution among the machinery as so many cogs . . . is however, already presupposed here.

Marx, *Grundrisse* (1857-58), pp. 308, 469–71, 585–86.

4.C.11 MACHINERY, SCIENCE, AND TECHNOLOGY

As long as the means of labour remains a means of labour in the proper sense of the term, such as it is directly, historically, adopted by capital and included in its realization process, it undergoes a merely formal modification, by appearing now as a means of labour not only in regard to its material side, but also at the same time as a particular mode of the presence of capital, determined by its total process—as *fixed capital.* But, once adopted into the production process of capital, the means of labour passes through different metamorphoses, whose culmination is the *machine,* or rather, an *automatic system of machinery* (system of machinery: the *automatic* one is merely its most complete, most adequate form, and alone transforms machinery into a system), set in motion by an automaton, a moving power that moves itself; this automaton consisting of numerous mechanical and intellectual organs, so that the workers themselves are cast merely as its conscious linkages. In the machine, and even more in machinery as an automatic system, the use value, i.e. the material quality of the means of labour, is transformed into an existence adequate to fixed capital and to capital as such; and the form in which it was adopted into the production process of capital, the direct means of labour, is superseded by a form posited by capital itself and corresponding to it. In no way does the machine appear as the individual worker's means of labour. Its distinguishing characteristic is not in the least, as with the means of labour, to transmit the worker's activity to the object; this activity, rather, is posited in such a way that it merely transmits the machine's work, the machine's action, on to the raw material—supervises it and guards against interruptions. Not as with the instrument, which the worker animates and makes into his organ with his skill and strength, and whose handling therefore depends on his virtuosity. Rather, it is the machine which possesses skill and strength in place of the worker, is itself the virtuoso, with a soul of its own in the mechanical laws acting through it; and it consumes coal, oil etc., just as the worker consumes food, to keep up its perpetual motion. The worker's activity, reduced to a mere abstraction of activity, is determined and regulated on all sides by the movement of the machinery, and not the opposite. The science which compels the inanimate limbs of the machinery, by their construction, to act purposefully, as an automaton, does not exist in the worker's consciousness, but rather acts upon him through the machine as an alien power, as the power of the machine itself. The appropriation of living labour by objectified labour—of the power or activity which creates value by value existing for-itself—which lies in the concept of capital, is posited, in production resting on machinery, as the character of the production process itself, including its material elements and its material motion. The production process has ceased to be a labour process dominated by labour as its governing unity. Labour appears, rather, merely as a conscious organ, scattered among the individual living workers at numerous points of the mechanical system; subsumed under the total process of the machinery itself, as itself only a link of the system, whose unity exists not in the living workers, but rather in the living (active) machinery, which confronts his individual, insignificant doings as a mighty organism. In machinery, objectified labour confronts living labour within the labour process itself as the power which rules it; a power which, as the appropriation of living labour, is the form of capital. The transformation of the means of labour into machinery, and of living labour into a mere living accessory of this machinery, as the means of its action, also posits the absorption of the labour process in its material character as a mere moment of the realization process of capital. The increase of the productive force of labour and the greatest possible negation of necessary labour is the necessary tendency of capital, as we have seen. The transformation of the means of labour into machinery is the realization of this tendency. In machinery, objectified labour materially confronts living labour as a ruling power and as an active subsumption of the latter under itself, not only by appropriating it, but in the real production process itself; the relation of capital as value which appropriates value-creating activity is, in fixed capital existing as machinery, posited at the same time as the relation of the use value of capital to the use value of labour capacity; further, the value objectified in machinery appears as a presupposition against which the value-creating power of the individual labour capacity is an infinitesimal, vanishing magnitude; the production in enormous mass quantities which is posited with machinery destroys every connection of the product with the direct need of the producer, and hence with direct use value; it is already posited in the form of the product's production and in the relations in which it is produced that it is produced only as a conveyor of value, and its use value only as condition to that end. In machinery, objectified labour itself appears not only in the form of product or of the product employed as means of labour, but in the form of the force of production itself. The development of the means of labour into machinery is not an accidental moment of capital, but is rather the historical reshaping of the traditional, inherited means of labour into a form adequate to capital. The accumulation of knowledge and of skill, of the general productive forces of the social brain, is thus absorbed into capital, as opposed to labour, and hence appears as an attribute of capital, and more specifically of *fixed capital,* in so far as it enters into the production process as a means of production proper. . . .

Further, in so far as machinery develops with the accumulation of society's science, of productive force generally, general social labour presents itself not in labour but in capital. The productive force of society is measured in *fixed capital,* exists there in its objective form; and, inversely, the productive force of capital grows with this general progress, which capital appropriates free of charge. This is not the place to go into the development of machinery in detail; rather only in its general apsect; in so far as the *means of labour,* as a physical thing, loses its direct form, becomes *fixed capital,* and confronts the worker physically as *capital.* In machinery, knowledge appears as alien, external to him; and living labour [as] subsumed under self-activating objectified labour. The worker appears superflous to the extent that his action is not determined by [capital's] requirements.

Marx, *Grundrisse* (1857-58), pp. 692–95.

5 Capitalism's Contradictory and Destructive Properties: Exploitation

A. BASIC CONCEPTS

As we have seen, alienation is the central theme in Marx's early writings, notably the 1844 *Manuscripts.* In Marx's mature writings, for example, *Capital* (Volume 1, 1867), alienation continues, but is vigorously supplemented by a major analysis of capitalism's second prominent contradictory property, *exploitation.*

In the dominant neoclassicist orthodoxy, "exploitation" refers to the payment to a resource owner, in exchange for a certain quantity of a resource, of an income less than the contribution to production by that resource, as measured by the "value of the marginal product." Although, the concept of exploitation is not unique to Marxian analysis, Marx's concept of exploitation differs from the perhaps more familiar neoclassical one. For Marx, exploitation arises in production, not exchange, and is based on property power, not monopoly power on the marketplace. According to Marx, the central socioeconomic issue in any society concerns the economic surplus. As Marx perceived it, the working class members of society, using but lacking ownership or control over the physical means of production, create a surplus of output or income above basic consumption. This surplus is distributed to a nonworking, owning class on the basis of property power, reinforced by the legal and political rules of society. Because the propertied class, by virtue of its ownership, has not created the surplus, but because it is in a position to control and direct its use as well as use of the labor power of the producing members of society, the surplus output or income is unearned, and the process of its creation and distribution constitutes "exploitation."

A necessary condition for exploitation is thus the creation of a surplus output, that is, an excess of total production above that necessary for subsistence of workers. In a slave or feudal economy, the surplus takes the direct form of surplus physical output. In capitalism, where both labor power and physical products enter the process of exchange as commodities, the surplus appears indirectly, as "surplus values," and essentially takes the form of profits, interest, and rents. In the absence of surplus values, depreciating machinery and factories could not be replaced, much less augmented through capital accumulation. Eventually, capital, and thus capitalists and capitalism, would disappear, and society would presumably revert to a simple exchange economy with no separation of work and ownership.

How do surplus values arise? Marx's first candidate is the exchange of commodities (selection 5.A.1). As for *use* values, it is certainly possible for buyers and sellers to mutually benefit or gain from trade. First, each participant in an exchange transaction can trade a commodity of lower utility for one with higher utility. Second, if A is more effective in the production of wine and B in corn, A may be able to obtain more corn, and B more wine, through exchange than by producing it himself. But what of *exchange* values? Might it not be possible to obtain surplus values by "buying cheap and selling dear"? Marx's answer is a clear no, at least for the economic system as a whole. On the one hand, exchangers who gain by clever dealings with others do not create surplus values, but merely transfer them. What is a "plus" for one is a "minus" for another. On the other hand, exchangers who gain surplus values as sellers (buyers) lose them as buyers (sellers), because in the absence of a class which only buys or sells, all must participate as both demanders and suppliers.

Marx's second candidate is the buying and selling of labour power (selection 5.A.2). Under normal (competitive) conditions, he contends, wage levels must be sufficient to enable workers to subsist, acquire needed skills and education, and rear their children (to serve as future workers). If wages are at this level (which includes a "historical and moral element" varying with time and place), they equal what Marx called the "value of labour power." Such wage levels, in effect, are *necessary* for the sustenance of the working class and thereby for the capital-labor relation itself. Wages lower than the value of labor power leave workers in a "crippled" state. In the extreme case, "death is the ultimate retort" of the worker paid less than the value of his labor power.[1]

Thus, although wages may well be low under capitalism, it is not low wages per se which constitute exploitation or which enable the creation of surplus values. Under competitive conditions, capitalists must pay workers competitive market wages; the capitalist who does not do so will lose his workers to his competitors. Under competitive conditions, the wage will be sufficient to equal the value of labor power. According to the rules of capitalist exchange, no one has been cheated, since the price of labor power equals its value. Special circumstances, for example, deep depression or monopsony, may cause wages temporarily to fall or be pushed below the value of labor power. However, this is not the normal situation for capitalist economy and, in any event, cannot be sustained permanently. Under normal competitive circumstances, exploitation and surplus values do not originate in the exchange process on the labor market. Indeed, the labor market is the arena of "freedom, equality, property, and Bentham," and is a "very Eden of the innate rights of man."

Although an economic surplus is a necessary condition for the demonstration of (successful) exploitation, it is not sufficient. Despite his occasionally flamboyant language, for example, that the exploitative extraction of surplus values constitutes a "theft of alien labor time" and a "miserable foundation" for the development of wealth,[2] Marx's theory of surplus value is not a natural rights doctrine comparable to that of the early nineteenth century "Ricardian socialists." Marx's point is not that because labor has created a valuable output, it has a just claim to the entirety of that output. Under socialism, where machinery and factories are owned and controlled by the "associated workers," there still must be an economic surplus above consumption for the maintenance and expansion of capital, to say nothing of collective goods such as roads (see selection 9.B.12). But if the creation and disposition of the surplus is controlled by an association of the workers, in the Marxian view, it does not constitute

[1]Robert L. Heilbroner, *The Worldly Philosophers* (New York: Simon and Schuster, 1967), chapter 6.

[2]Karl Marx, The *Grundrisse* (Outlines of the Critique of Political Economy), translated by Martin Nicolaus (New York: Harper & Row, 1973), p. 705.

exploitation. In short, for Marx, exploitation is a sociopolitico, not merely an economic, phenomenon, and is rooted in class relations of dominance and subservience in society. Under capitalism, laborers work under the direction of capitalists. Products, and surplus values, created by labor are the property of capitalists by virtue of capitalism's institutional structure (selection 5.A.3).

Consequently, just as low wages do not constitute exploitation in themselves, high and rising wages, as during a period of vigorous economic expansion, do not demonstrate the absence or supersession of exploitation. As long as workers are impelled by economic necessity to submit to the wage system and are under the direction and control of capitalists, the institutional power basis for exploitation exists. And as long as the exercise of property power by capitalists results in their ownership and control of economic surpluses created by workers, exploitation is successfully accomplished, regardless of the workers' material well-being (see also selection 7.A.3).

5.A.1 EXCHANGE AS A SOURCE OF SURPLUS?

Let us take the process of circulation in a form under which it presents itself as a simple and direct exchange of commodities. . . . So far as regards use-values, it is clear that both parties may gain some advantage. Both part with goods that, as use-values, are of no service to them, and receive others that they can make use of. And there may also be a further gain. A, who sells wine and buys corn, possibly produces more wine, with given labour time, than farmer B could, and B, on the other hand, more corn than wine-grower A could. A, therefore, may get, for the same exchange value, more corn, and B more wine, than each would respectively get without any exchange by producing his own corn and wine. With reference, therefore, to use-value, there is good ground for saying that "exchange is a transaction by which both sides gain." It is otherwise with exchange value. . . . The value of a commodity is expressed in its price before it goes into circulation, and is therefore a precedent condition of circulation, not its result.

Abstractedly considered, that is, apart from circumstances not immediately flowing from the laws of the simple circulation of commodities, there is in an exchange nothing (if we except the replacing of one use-value by another) but a metamorphosis, a mere change in the form of the commodity. The same exchange value, i.e., the same quantity of incorporated social labour, remains throughout in the hands of the owner of the commodity first in the shape of his own commodity, then in the form of the money for which he exchanged it, and lastly, in the shape of the commodity he buys with that money. This change of form does not imply a change in the magnitude of the value. . . . It is true, commodities may be sold at prices deviating from their values, but these deviations are to be considered as infractions of the laws of the exchange of commodities, which in its normal state is an exchange of equivalents, consequently, no method for increasing values.

Hence, we see that behind all attempts to represent the circulation of commodities as a source of surplus-value, there lurks a quid pro quo, a mixing up of use-value and exchange value. . . .

If commodities, or commodities and money, of equal exchange-value, and consequently equivalents, are exchanged, it is plain that no one abstracts more value from, than he throws into, circulation. There is no creation of surplus-value. And, in its normal form, the circulation of commodities demands the exchange of equivalents. But in actual practice, the process does not retain its normal form. Let us, therefore, assume an exchange of non-equivalents. . . .

Suppose then, that by some inexplicable privilege, the seller is enabled to sell his commodities above their value, what is worth 100 for 110, in which case the price is nominally raised 10 percent. The seller therefore pockets a surplus value of 10. But after he has sold he becomes a buyer. A third owner of commodities comes to him now as seller, who in this capacity also enjoys the privilege of selling his commodities 10 percent too dear. Our friend gained 10 as a seller only to lose it again as a buyer. The net result is, that all owners of commodities sell their goods to one another at 10 percent above their value, which comes precisely to the same as if they sold them at their true value. . . .

Let us make the opposite assumption, that the buyer has the privilege of purchasing commodities under their value. In this case it is no longer necessary to bear in mind that he in his turn will become a seller. He was so before he became buyer; he had already lost 10 percent in selling before he gained 10 percent as buyer. Everything is just as it was.

The creation of surplus-value, and therefore the conversion of money into capital, can consequently be explained neither on the assumption that commodities are sold above their value, nor that they are bought below their value. . . . In relation to circulation, producers and consumers meet only as buyers and sellers. To assert that the surplus-value acquired by the producer has its origin in the fact that consumers pay for commodities more than their value, is only to say in other words: The owner of commodities possesses, as a seller, the privilege of selling too dear. The seller has himself produced the commodities or represents their producer, but the buyer has to no less extent produced the commodities represented by his money, or represents their producer. The distinction between them is, that one buys and the other sells. The fact that the owner of the commodities, under the designation of producer, sells them over their value, and under the designation of consumer, pays too much for them, does not carry us a single step further.

To be consistent therefore, the upholders of the delusion that surplus-value has its origin in a nominal rise of prices or in the privilege which the seller has of selling too dear, must assume the existence of a class that only buys and does not sell, i.e., only consumes and does not produce. The existence of such a class is inexplicable from the standpoint we have so far reached, viz., that of simple circulation. But let us anticipate. The money with which such a class is constantly making purchases, must constantly flow into their pockets, without any exchange, gratis, by might or right, from the pockets of the commodity-owners themselves. To sell commodities above their value to such a class, is only to crib back again a part of the money previously given to it. . . .

A may be clever enough to get the advantage of B or C without their being able to retaliate. A sells wine worth £40 to B, and obtains from him in exchange corn to the value of £50. . . . What is a loss of value to B is surplus-value to A; what is "minus" to one is "plus" to the other. The same change would have taken place, if A, without the formality of an exchange, had directly stolen the

£10 from B. The sum of the values in circulation can clearly not be augmented by any change in their distribution. ... The capitalist class, as a whole, in any country, cannot overreach themselves.

Turn and twist then as we may, the fact remains unaltered. If equivalents are exchanged, no surplus-value results, and if non-equivalents are exchanged, still no surplus-value. Circulation, or the exchange of commodities, begets no value.

The reason is now therefore plain why, in analysing the standard form of capital, the form under which it determines the economical organisation of modern society, we entirely left out of consideration its most popular, and, so to say, antediluvian forms, merchants' capital and money-lenders' capital.

The circuit M–C–M, buying in order to sell dearer, is seen most clearly in genuine merchants' capital. But the movement takes place entirely within the sphere of circulation. Since, however, it is impossible, by circulation alone, to account for the conversion of money into capital, for the formation of surplus-value, it would appear, that merchants' capital is an impossibility, so long as equivalents are exchanged; that, therefore, it can only have its origin in the twofold advantage gained, over both the selling and the buying producers, by the merchant who parasitically shoves himself in between them. ... If the transformation of merchants' money into capital is to be explained otherwise than by the producers being simply cheated, a long series of intermediate steps would be necessary, which, as present, when the simple circulation of commodities forms our only assumption, are entirely wanting.

What we have said with reference to merchants' capital, applies still more to money-lenders' capital. In merchants' capital, the two extremes, the money that is thrown upon the market, and the augmented money that is withdrawn from the market, are at least connected by a purchase and a sale, in other words by the movement of the circulation. In money-lenders' capital the form M–C–M is reduced to the two extremes without a mean, M–M, money exchanged for more money, a form that is incompatible with the nature of money, and therefore remains inexplicable from the standpoint of the circulation of commodities. ...

In the course of our investigation, we shall find that both merchants' capital and interest-bearing capital are derivative forms, and at the same time it will become clear, why these two forms appear in the course of history before the modern standard form of capital.

We have shown that surplus-value cannot be created by circulation, and, therefore, that in its formation, something must take place in the background, which is not apparent in the circulation itself. But can surplus-value possibly originate anywhere else than in circulation, which is the sum total of all the mutual relations of commodity-owners, as far as they are determined by their commodities?. ... It is...impossible that outside the sphere of circulation, a producer of commodities can, without coming into contact with other commodity owners, expand value, and consequently convert money or commodities into capital.

It is therefore impossible for capital to be produced by circulation, and it is equally impossible for it to originate apart from circulation. It must have its origin both in circulation and yet not in circulation.

We have, therefore, got a double result.

The conversion of money into capital has to be explained on the basis of the laws that regulate the exchange of commodities, in such a way that the starting point is the exchange of equivalents. Our friend, Moneybags, who as yet is only an embryo capitalist, must buy his commodities at their value, must sell them at their value, and yet at the end of the process must withdraw more value from circulation than he threw into it at starting. His development into a full-grown capitalist must take place, both within the sphere of circulation and without it. These are the conditions of the problem.

Marx, *Capital*, I (1867), pp. 175–85.

5.A.2 THE BUYING AND SELLING OF LABOUR-POWER

The change of value that occurs in the case of money intended to be converted into capital, cannot take place in the money itself, since in its function of means of purchase and of payment, it does no more than realise the price of the commodity it buys or pays for; and, as hard cash, it is value petrified, never varying. Just as little can it originate in the second act of circulation, the resale of the commodity, which does no more than transform the article from its bodily form back again into its money-form. The change must, therefore, take place in the commodity bought by the first act, M–C, but not in its value, for equivalents are exchanged, and the commodity is paid for at its full value. We are, therefore, forced to the conclusion that the change originates in the use-value, as such, of the commodity, i.e., in its consumption. In order to be able to extract value from the consumption of a commodity, our friend, Moneybags, must be so lucky as to find, within the sphere of circulation, in the market, a commodity, whose use-value possesses the peculiar property of being a source of value, whose actual consumption, therefore, is itself an embodiment of labour, and, consequently, a creation of value. The possessor of money does find on the market such a special commodity in capacity for labour or labour-power.

By labour-power or capacity for labour is to be understood the aggregate of those mental and physical capabilities existing in a human being, which he exercises whenever he produces a use-value of any description.

But in order that our owner of money may be able to find labour-power offered for sale as a commodity, various conditions must first be fulfilled. The exchange of commodities of itself implies no other relations of dependence than those which result from its own nature. On this assumption, labour-power can appear upon the market as a commodity only if, and so far as, its possessor, the individual whose labour-power it is, offers it for sale, or sells it, as a commodity. In order that he may be able to do this, he must have it at his disposal, must be the untrammelled owner of his capacity for labour, i.e., of his person. He and the owner of money meet in the market, and deal with each other as on the basis of equal rights, with this difference alone, that one is buyer, the other seller; both, therefore, equal in the eyes of the law. The continuance of this relation demands that the owner of the labour-power should sell it only for a definite period, for if he were to sell it rump and stump, once for all, he would be selling himself, converting himself from a free man into a slave, from an owner of a commodity into a commodity. He must constantly look upon his labour-power as his own property, his own commodity, and this he can only do by placing it at the disposal of the buyer temporarily, for a definite period of time. By this means alone can he avoid renouncing his rights of ownership over it.

The second essential condition to the owner of money finding labour-power in the market as a commodity is this—that the labourer instead of being in the position to sell commodities in which his labour is incorporated, must be obliged to offer for sale as a commodity, that very labour-power, which exists only in his living self.

In order that a man may be able to sell commodities other than labour-power, he must of course have the means of production, as raw material, implements, etc. No boots can be made without leather. He requires also the means of subsistence. Nobody—not even "a musician of the future" can live upon future products, or upon use-values in an unfinished state; and ever since the first moment of his appearance on the world's stage, man always has been, and must still be a consumer, both before and while he is producing. In a society where all products assume the form of commodities, these commodities must be sold after they have been produced; it is only after their sale that they can serve in satisfying the requirements of their producer. The time necessary for their sale is superadded to that necessary for their production.

For the conversion of his money into capital; therefore, the owner of money must meet in the market with the free labourer, free in the double sense, that as a free man he can dispose of his labour-power as his own commodity, and that on the other hand he has no other commodity for sale, is short of everything necessary for the realisation of his labour-power.

The question why this free labourer confronts him in the market, has no interest for the owner of money, who regards the labour market as a branch of the general market for commodities. And for the present it interests us just as little. We cling to the fact theoretically, as he does practically. One thing, however, is clear—nature does not produce on the one side owners of money or commodities, and on the other men possessing nothing but their own labour-power. This relation has no natural basis, neither is its social basis one that is common to all historical periods. It is clearly the result of a past historical development, the product of many economical revolutions, of the extinction of a whole series of older forms of social production. . . .

The historical conditions of its capital's existence are by no means given with the mere circulation of money and commodities. It can spring into life, only when the owner of the means of production and subsistence meets in the market with the free labourer selling his labour-power. And this one historical condition comprises a world's history. Capital therefore, announces from its first appearance a new epoch in the process of social production.[1]

We must now examine more closely this peculiar commodity, labour-power. Like all others it has a value. How is that value determined?

[1]The capitalist epoch is therefore characterised by this, that labour-power takes in the eyes of the labourer himself the form of a commodity which is his property; his labour consequently becomes wage labour. On the other hand, it is only from this moment that the produce of labour universally becomes a commodity.

The value of labour-power is determined, as in the case of every other commodity, by the labour-time necessary for the production, and consequently also the reproduction, of this special article. So far as it has value, it represents no more than a definite quantity of the average labour of society incorporated in it. Labour-power exists only as a capacity, or power of the living individual. Its production consequently presupposes his existence. Given the individual, the production of labour-power consists in his reproduction of himself or his maintenance. For his maintenance he requires a given quantity of the means of subsistence. Therefore the labour-time requisite for the production of labour-power reduces itself to that necessary for the production of those means of subsistence; in other words, the value of labour-power is the value of the means of subsistence necessary for the maintenance of the labourer. Labour-power, however, becomes a reality only by its exercise; it sets itself in action only by working. But thereby a definite quantity of human muscle, nerve, brain, etc., is wasted, and these require to be restored. This increased expenditure demands a larger income. If the owner of labour-power works today, tomorrow he must again be able to repeat the same process in the same conditions as regards health and strength. His means of subsistence must therefore be sufficient to maintain him in his normal state as a labouring individual. His natural wants, such as food, clothing, fuel, and housing, vary according to the climatic and other physical conditions of his country. On the other hand, the number and extent of his so-called necessary wants, as also the modes of satisfying them, are themselves the product of historical development, and depend therefore to a great extent on the degree of civilisation of a country, more particularly on the conditions under which, and consequently on the habits and degree of comfort in which, the class of free labourers has been formed. In contradistinction therefore to the case of other commodities, there enters into the determination of the value of labour-power a historical and moral element. Nevertheless, in a given country, at a given period, the average quantity of the means of subsistence necessary for the labourer is practically known.

The owner of labour-power is mortal. If then his appearance in the market is to be continuous, and the continuous conversion of money into capital assumes this, the seller of labour-power must perpetuate himself. . . . The labour-power withdrawn from the market by wear and tear and death, must be continually replaced by, at the very least, an equal amount of fresh labour-power. Hence the sum of the means of subsistence necessary for the production of labour-power must include the means necessary for the labourer's substitutes, i.e., his children, in order that this race of peculiar commodity-owners may perpetuate its appearance in the market.

In order to modify the human organism, so that it may acquire skill and handiness in a given branch of industry, and become labour-power of a special kind, a special education or training is requisite, and this, on its part, costs an equivalent in commodities of a greater or less amount. This amount varies according to the more or less complicated character of the labour-power. The expenses of this education (excessively small in the case of ordinary labour-power), enter pro tanto into the total value spent in its production.

The value of labour-power resolves itself into the value of a definite quantity of the means of subsistence. It therefore varies with the value of these means or with the quantity of labour requisite for their production. . . .

The minimum limit of the value of labour-power is determined, by the value of the commodities, without the daily supply of which the labourer cannot renew his vital energy, consequently by the value of those means of subsistence that are physically indispensable. If the price of labour-power fall to this minimum, it falls below its value, since under such circumstances it can be maintained and developed only in a crippled state. But the value of every commodity is determined by the labour-time requisite to turn it out so as to be of normal quality. . . .

We now know how the value paid by the purchaser to the possessor of this peculiar commodity, labour-power, is determined. The use-value which the former gets in exchange, manifests itself only in the actual usufruct, in the consumption of the labour-power. The money owner buys everything necessary for this purpose, such as raw material, in the market, and pays for it at its full value. The consumption of labour-power is at one and the same time the production of commodities and of surplus value. The consumption of labour-power is completed, as in the case of every other commodity, outside the limits of the market or of the sphere of circulation. Accompanied by Mr. Moneybags and by the possessor of labour-power, we therefore take leave for a time of this noisy sphere, where everything takes place on the surface and in view of all men, and follow them both into the hidden abode of production, on whose threshold there stares us in the face "No admittance except on business." Here we shall see, not only how capital produces, but how capital is produced. We shall at last force the secret of profit making.

This sphere that we are deserting, within whose boundaries, the sale and purchase of labour-power goes on, is in fact a very Eden of the innate rights of man. There alone rule Freedom, Equality, Property and Bentham. Freedom, because both buyer and seller of a commodity, say of labour-power, are constrained only by their own free will. They contract as free agents, and the agreement they come to, is but the form in which they give legal expression to their common will. Equality, because each enters into relation with the other, as with a simple owner of commodities, and they exchange equivalent for equivalent. Property, because each disposes only of what is his own. And Bentham, because each looks only to himself. The only force that brings them together and put them in relation with each other, is the selfishness, the gain and the private interests of each. Each looks to himself only, and no one troubles himself about the rest, and just because they do so, do they all, in accordance with the pre-established harmony of things, or under the auspices of an all-shrewd providence, work together to their mutual advantage, for the common weal and in the interest of all.

On leaving this sphere of simple circulation or of exchange of commodities, which furnishes the "Free-trader Vulgaris" with his views and ideas, and with the standard by which he judges a society based on capital and wages, we think we can perceive a change in the physiognomy of our dramatis personae. He, who before was the money owner, now strides, in front as capitalist; the possessor of labour-power follows as his labourer. The one with an air of importance, smirking, intent on business; the other, timid and holding back, like one who is bringing his own hide to market and has nothing to expect but—a hiding.

Marx, *Capital,* I (1867), pp. 185–96.

5.A.3 CONDITIONS OF THE LABOR PROCESS

The labour-process, turned into the process by which the capitalist consumes labour-power, exhibits two characteristic phenomena. First, the labourer works under the control of the capitalist to whom his labour belongs; the capitalist taking good care that the work is done in a proper manner, and that the means of production are used with intelligence, so that there is no unnecessary waste of raw material, and no wear and tear of the implements beyond what is necessarily caused by the work.

Secondly, the product is the property of the capitalist and not that of the labourer, its immediate producer. Suppose that a capitalist pays for a day's labour-power at its value; then the right to use that power for a day belongs to him, just as much as the right to use any other commodity, such as a horse that he has hired for the day. To the purchaser of a commodity belongs its use, and the seller of labour-power, by giving his labour, does no more, in reality, than part with the use-value that he has sold. From the instant he steps into the workshop, the use-value of his labour-power, and therefore also its use, which is labour, belongs to the capitalist. By the purchase of labour-power, the capitalist incorporates labour, as a living ferment, with the lifeless constituents of the product. From his point of view, the labour-process is nothing more than the consumption of the commodity purchased, i.e., of labour-power; but this consumption cannot be effected except by supplying the labour-power with the means of production. The labour-process is a process between things that the capitalist has purchased, things that have become his property. The product of this process also belongs, therefore, to him, just as much as does the wine which is the product of a process of fermentation completed in his cellar. . . . The sphere of capital's exploitation and rule merely extends with its own dimensions and the number of its subjects. A larger part of their own surplus-product, always increasing and continually transformed into additional capital, comes back to them in the shape of means of payment, so that they can extend the circle of their enjoyments; can make some additions to their consumption-fund of clothes, furniture, etc., and can lay by small reserve-funds of money. But just as little as better clothing, food, and treatment, and a larger peculium, do away with the exploitation of the slave, so little do they set aside that of the wage-worker. A rise in the price of labour, as a consequence of accumulation of capital, only means, in fact, that the length and weight of the golden chain the wage-worker has already forged for himself, allow of a relaxation of the tension of it. In the controversies on this subject the chief fact has generally been overlooked, viz., the *differentia specifica* of capitalistic production. Labour-power is sold today, not with a view of satisfying, by its service or by its product, the personal needs of the buyer. His aim is augmentation of his capital, production of commodities containing more labour than he pays for, containing therefore a portion of value that costs him nothing, and that is nevertheless realised when the commodities are sold. Production of surplus-value is the absolute law of this mode of production. Labour-power is only salable so far as it preserves the means of production in their capacity of capital, reproduces its own value as capital, and yields in unpaid labour a source of additional capital. The conditions of its sale, whether more or less favourable to the labourer, include therefore the necessity of its constant reselling, and the constantly extended reproduction of all wealth in the shape of capital. Wages, as we have seen, by their very nature, always imply the performance of a certain quantity of unpaid labour on the part of the labourer. Altogether, irrespective of the case of a rise of wages with a falling price of labour, etc., such an increase only means at best quantitative diminution of the unpaid labour that the worker has to supply. This diminution can never reach the point at which it would threaten the system itself. Apart from violent conflicts as to the rate of wages (and Adam Smith has already shown that in such a conflict, taken on the whole, the master is always master), a rise in the price of labour resulting from accumulation of capital implies the following alternative:

Either the price of labour keeps on rising, because its rise does not interfere with the progress of accumulation. . . . In this case it is evident that a diminution in the unpaid labour in no way interferes with the extension of the domain of capital. Or, on the other hand, accumulation slackens in consequence of the rise in the price of labour, because the stimulus of gain is blunted. The rate of accumulation lessens; but with its lessening, the primary cause of that lessening vanishes, i.e., the disproportion between capital and exploitable labour-power. The mechanism of the process of capitalist production removes the very obstacles that it temporarily creates. The price of labour falls again to a level corresponding with the needs of the self-expansion of capital, whether the level be below, the same as, or above the one which was normal before the rise of wages took place.

Marx, *Capital,* I (1867), pp. 206, 677–79.

B. SOURCES AND DIMENSIONS OF SURPLUS VALUE

Marx's own explanation derives surplus value from the control of surplus labor *time.* Workers sell their labor power for a given sum of money—an exchange value. Capitalists obtain control over the use of labor power for the length of the working day—a use value. But capitalism contains no mechanism to guarantee that use value will coalesce with exchange value. Hence, the total working time may and usually does exceed the labor time necessary to provide sufficient recompense to permit the workers' subsistence, that is, payment in accord with the value of labor power. The excess or surplus labor time thus constitutes the basis for producing output which, if sold, "realizes" the surplus values generated in production. (selection 5.B.4).

This is not to deny a role for raw materials, machinery, or factories in the production of output, or indeed as components of value. However, competition among capitalists would plausibly push prices of these commodities toward their values. Competition among sellers would prevent divergences of prices above values, while competition among buyers would prevent divergences of prices below values. Thus, if a capitalist buys a machine for $100,000 with an expected life of ten years, its annual average contribution to the value of commodities would be $10,000. Although the machine, through wear and tear over a ten-year period, would transfer its value (ultimately reflecting the labor time, together with other associated resources, required to produce it) to commodities, it would not create surplus values. Consequently, Marx uses the expression "constant capital" to describe physical means of production, in contrast to "variable capital," or labor power, which has the unique quality of creating surplus values (selection 5.B.5).

Thus, the value of any commodity incorporates three component parts, the monies expended (or, in the case of depreciation, estimated) for constant capital and for variable capital or wages, and the surplus value: c + v + s. Subtracting c, we have, in contemporary terms, the net income of an enterprise or, in the aggregate, an economy. The ratio of s to v, or s/v, thus constitutes a rate of surplus value or "rate of exploitation." It summarizes the proportions of income going to these two major income categories. For example, if s/v = 1, then income is divided evenly between capitalists and workers. Alternatively, the working day may be divided into "necessary labor time" required to reproduce the workers' subsistence and "surplus labor time" available for production of surplus values. Supposing wages are equal to the value of labor power, s/v therefore also constitutes the ratio of surplus labor time to necessary labor time (selection 5.B.6).

In Marx's perspective, maximizing a gap between the exchange value and use value of labor power (or, alternatively expressed, between the value of labor power and that of the commodity) thus depends on minimizing the value of labor power in exchange and maximizing workers' use values in production. Under freely competitive markets, one might wonder why an expanding capitalist economy would not increase the demand for labor and, under full employment conditions, raise wages and thereby squeeze profits and surplus values. Alternatively, one might wonder whether economic expansion would not be expected to heighten the intensity of the class struggle, notably working class endeavors to push wages up, with similar results. Marx's answer, which will be described more fully in another connection later (selection 6.B.3), is that cyclical unemployment in the short run and a trend toward rising technological unemployment in the long run, because of secular increases in the ratio of constant capital to variable capital, create a surplus labor population or "reserve army of the unemployed," which tempers the tendency for wages to rise.

Given wages, the dominant means of increasing surplus values is to expand production and income by expanding the use value of labor power. This can be accomplished in two major ways. First, "absolute" surplus values may be expanded by lengthening the working day, thereby increasing surplus labor time, given necessary labor time. Second, "relative" surplus values may be expanded, notably by technological revolutions which reduce necessary labor time (selection 5.B.7). In practice, the two tend to be connected because new machinery and technologies facilitate both longer working hours (together with increased employment of women and children and intensification of labor) and increased productivity of labor (selection 5.B.8).

As capitalism progresses, relative surplus values come to predominate. The shift toward greater emphasis on relative surplus values is linked with growing constraints on expansion of absolute surplus values through lengthening the working day. One constraint is simply physical limits: there are only so many hours in a day, and continued employment of labor power requires at least some minimum period for rest and recuperation of physical powers. Another is the class struggle. For example, one factor contributing to factory legislation in England limiting the length of the working day was the political struggles of the working class (selection 7.B.9). The capitalist response was to turn to other strategies to extract surplus value—speeding up machinery, introducing new machinery, and increasing the scale of enterprise.[3] In any event, science, technology, combination and division of labor, new modes of transportation and communication, and the development of new markets—all basically

[3]Marx, *Capital,* Vol. I (New York: Modern Library, n.d.), Chap. 15, pp. 514 ff., Chap. 16.

manipulated by capitalists and relatively immune from control or eradication by even the most beneficently competitive market—create a "monstrous disproportion" between the direct application of labor time and the vast outpouring of products in an advanced and developing capitalist economy (selection 7.B.11 below). Because of property power, surplus values from these sources, at least directly and initially, go to capitalists. In short capitalism is an economic system not merely for the production of commodities, but for the production of surplus values and thereby, for Marx, for the recreation of the capital-labor relation on an expanded scale (selection 5.B.9).

5.B.4 CREATION OF SURPLUS-VALUE

We [assume], on the occasion of its sale, that the value of a day's labour-power is three shillings, and that six hours' labour are incorporated in that sum; and consequently that this amount of labour is requisite to produce the necessaries of life daily required on an average by the labourer. If now our spinner by working for one hour, can convert 1⅔ lbs. of cotton into 1⅔ lbs. of yarn,[1] it follows that in six hours he will convert 10 lbs. of cotton into 10 lbs. of yarn. Hence, during the spinning process, the cotton absorbs six hours' labour. The same quantity of labour is also embodied in a piece of gold of the value of three shillings. Consequently by the mere labour of spinning, a value of three shillings is added to the cotton.

Let us now consider the total value of the product, the 10 lbs. of yarn. Two and a half days' labour have been embodied in it, of which two days were contained in the cotton and in the substance of the spindle worn away, and half a day was absorbed during the process of spinning. The two and a half days' labour is also represented by a piece of gold of the value of fifteen shillings. Hence, fifteen shillings is an adequate price for the 10 lbs. of yarn, or the price of one pound is eighteen-pence.

Our capitalist stares in astonishment. The value of the product is exactly equal to the value of the capital advanced. The value so advanced has not expanded, no surplus-value has been created, and consequently money has not been converted into capital. The price of the yarn is fifteen shillings, and fifteen shillings were spent in the open market upon the constituent elements of the product, or, what amounts to the same thing, upon the factors of the labour-process; ten shillings were paid for the cotton, two shillings for the substance of the spindle worn away, and three shillings for the labour-power. The swollen value of the yarn is of no avail, for it is merely the sum of the values formerly existing in the cotton, the spindle, and the labour-power; out of such a simple addition of existing values, no surplus-value can possibly arise.[2] These separate values are now all concentrated in one thing; but so they were also in the sum of

[1]These figures are quite arbitrary.

[2]This is the fundamental proposition on which is based the doctrine of the Physiocrats as to the unproductiveness of all labour that is not agriculture: it is irrefutable for the orthodox economist.

fifteen shillings, before it was split up into three parts, by the purchase of the commodities.

There is in reality nothing very strange in this result. The value of one pound of yarn being eighteen-pence, if our capitalist buys 10 lbs. of yarn in the market, he must pay fifteen shillings for them. It is clear that, whether a man buys his house ready built, or gets it built for him, in neither case will the mode of acquisition increase the amount of money laid out on the house.

Our capitalist, who is at home in his vulgar economy, exclaims: "Oh! but I advanced my money for the express purpose of making more money." The way to Hell is paved with good intentions, and he might just as easily have intended to make money, without producing at all. He threatens all sorts of things. He won't be caught napping again. In future he will buy the commodities in the market, instead of manufacturing them himself. But if all his brother capitalists were to do the same, where would he find his commodities in the market? And his money he cannot eat. He tries persuasion. "Consider my abstinence; I might have played ducks and drakes with the 15 shillings; but instead of that I consumed it productively, and made yarn with it." Very well, and by way of reward he is now in possession of good yarn instead of a bad conscience; and as for playing the part of a miser, it would never do for him to relapse into such bad ways as that; we have seen before to what results such asceticism leads. Besides, where nothing is, the king has lost his rights: whatever may be the merit of his abstinence, there is nothing wherewith specially to remunerate it, because the value of the product is merely the sum of the values of the commodities that were thrown into the process of production. Let him therefore console himself with the reflection that virtue is its own reward. But no, he becomes importunate. He says: "The yarn is of no use to me: I produced it for sale." In that case let him sell it, or, still better, let him for the future produce only things for satisfying his personal wants. ... He now gets obstinate. "Can the labourer," he asks, "merely with his arms and legs, produce commodities out of nothing? Did I not supply him with the materials, by means of which, and in which alone, his labour could be embodied? And as the greater part of society consists of such ne'er-do-wells, have I not rendered society incalculable service by my instruments of production, my cotton and my spindle, and not only society, but the labourer also, whom in addition I have provided with the necessaries of life? And am I to be allowed nothing in return for all this service?" Well, but has not the labourer rendered him the equivalent service of changing his cotton and spindle into yarn? Moreover, there is here no question of service. A service is nothing more than the useful effect of a use-value, be it of a commodity, or be it of labour. But here we are dealing with exchange-value. The capitalist paid to the labourer a value of 3 shillings, and the labourer gave him back an exact equivalent in the value of 3 shillings, added by him to the cotton: he gave him value for value. Our friend, up to this time so purse-proud, suddenly assumes the modest demeanour of his own workman, and exclaims: "Have I myself not worked? Have I not performed the labour of superintendence and of overlooking the spinner? And does not this labour, too, create value?" His overlooker and his manager try to hide their smiles. Meanwhile, after a hearty laugh, he reassumes his usual mien. Though he chanted to us the whole creed of the economists, in reality, he says, he would not give a brass farthing for it. He leaves this and all such like subterfuges and juggling tricks to the professors of political economy, who are paid for it. He himself is a practical man; and though he does not always consider what he says outside his business, yet in his business he knows what he is about.

Let us examine the matter more closely. The value of a day's labour-power amounts to 3 shillings, because on our assumption half a day's labour is embodied in that quantity of labour-power, i.e., because the means of subsistence that are daily required for the production of labour-power, cost half a day's labour. But the past labour that is embodied in the labour-power, and the living labour that it can call into action; the daily cost of maintaining it, and its daily expenditure in work, are two totally different things. The former determines the exchange-value of the labour-power, the latter is its use-value. The fact that half a day's labour is necessary to keep the labourer alive during 24 hours, does not in any way prevent him from working a whole day. Therefore, the value of labour-power, and the value which that labour-power creates in the labour process, are two entirely different magnitudes; and this difference of the two values was what the capitalist had in view, when he was purchasing the labour-power. The useful qualities that labour-power possesses, and by virtue of which it makes yarn or boots, were to him nothing more than a *conditio sine qua non;* for in order to create value, labour must be expended in a useful manner. What really influenced him was the specific use-value which this commodity possesses of being *a source not only of value, but of more value than it has itself.* This is the special service that the capitalist expects from labour-power, and in this transaction he acts in accordance with the "eternal laws" of the exchange of commodities. The seller of labour-power, like the seller of any other commodity, realises its exchange-value, and parts with its use-value. He cannot take the one without giving the other. The use-value of labour-power, or in other words, labour, belongs just as little to its seller, as the use-value of oil after it has been sold belongs to the dealer who has sold it. The owner of the money has paid the value of a day's labour-power; his, therefore, is the use of it for a day; a day's labour belongs to him. The circumstance, that on the one hand the daily sustenance of labour-power costs only half a day's labour, while on the other hand the very same labour-power can work during a whole day, that consequently the value which its use during one day creates, is double what he pays for that use, this circumstance is, without doubt, a piece of good luck for the buyer, but by no means an injury to the seller.

Our capitalist foresaw this state of things, and that was the cause of his laughter. The labourer therefore finds, in the workshop, the means of production necessary for working, not only during six, but during twelve hours. Just as during the six hours' process our 10 lbs. of cotton absorbed six hours' labour, and became 10 lbs. of yarn, so now, 20 lbs. of cotton will absorb 12 hours' labour and be changed into 20 lbs. of yarn. Let us now examine the product of this prolonged process. There is now materialised in this 20 lbs. of yarn the labour of five days, of which four days are due to the cotton and the lost steel of the spindle, the remaining day having been absorbed by the cotton during the spinning process. Expressed in gold, the labour of five days is 30 shillings. This is therefore the price of the 20 lbs. of yarn, giving, as before, eighteen-pence as the price of a pound. But the sum of the values of the commodities that entered into the process amounts to 27 shillings. The value of yarn is 30 shillings. Therefore the value of the product is 1/9 greater than the value advanced for its production; 27 shillings have been transformed into 30 shillings; a surplus-value of 3 shillings has been created. The trick has at last succeeded; money has been converted into capital.

Every condition of the problem is satisfied, while the laws that regulate the exchange of commodities, have been in no way violated. Equivalent has been exchanged for equivalent. For the capitalist as buyer paid for each commodity, for the cotton, the spindle and the labour-power, its full value. He then did what is done by every purchaser of commodities; he consumed their use-value. The consumption of the labour-power, which was also the process of producing commodities, resulted in 20 lbs. of yarn, having a value of 30 shillings. The capitalist, formerly a buyer, now returns to market as a seller, of commodities. He sells his yarn at eighteen-pence a pound, which is its exact value. Yet for all that he withdraws 3 shillings more from circulation than he originally threw into it. This metamorphosis, this conversion of money into capital, takes place both within the sphere of circulation and also outside it; within the circulation, because conditioned by the purchase of the labour-power in the market; outside the circulation, because what is done within it is only a stepping-stone to the production of surplus-value, a process which is entirely confined to the sphere of production. . . .

By turning his money into commodities that serve as the material elements of a new product, and as factors in the labour-process, by incorporating living labour with their dead substance, the capitalist at the same time converts value, i.e., past, materialised, and dead labour into capital, into value big with value, a live monster that is fruitful and multiplies.

If we now compare the two processes of producing value and of creating surplus-value, we see that the latter is nothing but the continuation of the former beyond a definite point. If on the one hand the process be not carried beyond the point, where the value paid by the capitalist for the labour-power is replaced by an exact equivalent, it is simply a process of producing value; if, on the other hand, it be continued beyond that point, it becomes a process of creating surplus-value.

If we proceed further, and compare the process of producing value with the labour-process, pure and simple, we find that the latter consists of the useful labour, the work, that produces use-values. Here we contemplate the labour as producing a particular article; we view it under its qualitative aspect alone, with regard to its end and aim. But viewed as a value-creating process, the same labour-process presents itself under its quantitative aspect alone. Here it is a question merely of the time occupied by the labourer in doing the work; of the period during which the labour-power is usefully expended. Here, the commodities that take part in the process, do not count any longer as necessary adjuncts of labour-power in the production of a definite, useful object. They count merely as depositaries of so much absorbed or materialised labour; that labour, whether previously embodied in the means of production, or incorporated in them for the first time during the process by the action of labour-power, counts in either case only according to its duration; it amounts to so many hours or days as the case may be.

Moreover, only so much of the time spent in the production of any article is counted, as, under the given social conditions, is necessary. The consequences of this are various. In the first place, it becomes necessary that the labour should be carried on under normal conditions. If a self-acting mule is the implement in general use for spinning, it would be absurd to supply the spinner with a distaff and spinning wheel. The cotton too must not be such rubbish as to cause extra waste in being worked, but must be of suitable quality. Otherwise the spinner would be found to spend more time in producing a pound of yarn than is socially necessary, in which case the excess of time would create neither value nor money. But whether the material factors of the process are of normal quality or not, depends not upon the labourer, but entirely upon the capitalist. Then again, the labour-power itself must be of average efficacy. In the trade in which it is being employed, it must possess the average skill, handiness and quickness prevalent in that trade, and our capitalist took good care to buy labour-power of such normal goodness. This power must be applied with the average amount of exertion and with the usual degree of intensity; and the capitalist is as careful to see that this is done, as that his workmen are not idle for a single moment. He has bought the use of the labour-power for a definite period, and he insists upon his rights. He has no intention of being robbed. Lastly, and for this purpose our friend has a penal code of his own, all wasteful consumption of raw material or instruments of labour is strictly forbidden, because what is so wasted, represents labour superfluously expended, labour that does not count in the product or enter into its value.

Marx, *Capital,* I (1867), pp. 212–19.

5.B.5 CONSTANT CAPITAL AND VARIABLE CAPITAL

The various factors of the labour-process play different parts in forming the value of the product.

The labourer adds fresh value to the subject of his labour by expending upon it a given amount of additional labour, no matter what the specific character and utility of that labour may be. On the other hand, the values of the means of production used up in the process are preserved, and present themselves afresh as constituent parts of the value of the product; the values of the cotton and the spindle, for instance, reappear again in the value of the yarn. The value of the means of production is therefore preserved, by being transferred to the product. This transfer takes place during the conversion of those means into a product, or in other words, during the labour-process. It is brought about by labour; but how?

The labourer does not perform two operations at once, one in order to add value to the cotton, the other in order to preserve the value of the means of production. . . .

The labourer preserves the values of the consumed means of production, or transfers them as portions of its value to the product, not by virtue of his additional labour, abstractedly considered, but by virtue of the particular useful character of that labour, by virtue of its special productive form. In so far then as labour is such specific productive activity, in so far as it is spinning, weaving, or forging, it raises, by mere contact, the means of production from the dead, makes them living factors of the labour-process, and combines with them to form the new products. . . .

By the simple addition of a certain quantity of labour, new value is added, and by the quality of this added labour, the original values of the means of production are preserved in the product. . . . In the labour-process the means of production transfer their value to the product only so far as along with their use-value they lose also their exchange value. They give up to the product that value alone which they themselves lose as means of production. But in this respect the material factors of the labour-process do not all behave alike. . . .

Raw material forms the substance of the product, but only after it has changed its form. Hence raw material and auxiliary substances lost the characteristic form with which they are clothed on entering the labour-process. It is otherwise with the instruments of labour. Tools, machines, workshops, and vessels, are of use in the labour-process, only so long as they retain their original shape, and are ready each morning to renew the process with their shape unchanged. . . . If we now consider the case of any instrument of labour during the whole period of its service, from the day of its entry into the workshop, till the day of its banishment into the lumber room, we find that during this period its use-value has been completely consumed, and therefore its exchange value completely transferred to the product. For instance, if a spinning machine lasts for 10 years, it is plain that during that working period its total value is gradually transferred to the product of the 10 years. . . . It is known by experience how long on the average a machine of a particular kind will last. Suppose its use-value in the labour-process to last only six days. Then, on the average, it loses each day one-sixth of its use-value, and therefore parts with one-sixth of its value to the daily product. The wear and tear of all instruments, their daily loss of use-value, and the corresponding quantity of value they part with to the product, are accordingly calculated upon this basis.

It is thus strikingly clear, that means of production never transfer more value to the product than they themselves lose during the labour-process by the destruction of their own use-value. If such an instrument has no value to lose, if, in other words, it is not the product of human labour, it transfers no value to the product. It helps to create use-value without contributing to the formation of exchange value. In this class are included all means of production supplied by Nature without human assistance, such as land, wind, water, metals in situ, and timber in virgin forests. . . .

We have seen that the means of production transfer value to the new product, so far only as during the labour-process they lose value in the shape of their old use-value. The maximum loss of value that they can suffer in the process, is plainly limited by the amount of the original value with which they came into the process, or in other words, by the labour-time necessary for their production. Therefore the means of production can never add more value to the product than they themselves possess independently of the process in which they assist. However useful a given kind of raw material, or a machine, or other means of production may be, though it may cost £150, or, say, 500 days' labour, yet it cannot, under any circumstances, add to the value of the product more than £150. Its value is determined not by the labour-process into which it enters as a means of production, but by that out of which it has issued as a product. In the labour-process it only serves as a mere use-value, a thing with useful properties, and could not, therefore, transfer any value to the product, unless it possessed such value previously. . . .

It is otherwise with the subjective factor of the labour-process, with labour-power in action. While the labourer, by virtue of his labour being of a specialised kind that has a special object, preserves and transfers to the product the value of the means of production, he at the same time, by the mere act of working, creates each instant an additional or new value. Suppose the process of production to be stopped just when the workman has produced an equivalent for the value of his own labour-power, when, for example, by six hours' labour, he has added a value of three shillings. This value is the surplus, of the total value of the product, over the portion of its value that is due to the means of production. It is the only original bit of value formed during this process, the only portion of the value of the product created by this process. Of course, we do not forget that this new value only replaces the money advanced by the capitalist in the purchase of the labour-power, and spent by the labourer on the necessaries of life. . . .

We know, however, from what has gone before, that the labour-process may continue beyond the time necessary to reproduce and incorporate in the product a mere equivalent for the value of the labour-power. Instead of the six hours that are sufficient for the latter purpose, the process may continue for twelve hours. The action of labour-power, therefore, not only reproduces its own value, but produces value over and above it. This surplus-value is the difference between the value of the product and the value of the elements consumed in the formation of that product, in other words, of the means of production and the labour-power. . . .

That part of capital then, which is represented by the means of production, by the raw material, auxiliary material and the instruments of labour, does not, in the process of production, undergo any quantitative alteration of value. I therefore call it the constant part of capital, or, more shortly, *constant capital.*

On the other hand, that part of capital, represented by labour-power, does, in the process of production, undergo an alteration of value. It both reproduces the equivalent of its own value, and also produces an excess, a surplus-value, which may itself vary, may be more or less according to circumstances. This part of capital is continually being transformed from a constant into a variable magnitude. I therefore call it the variable part of capital, or, shortly, *variable capital.* The same elements of capital which, from the point of view of the labour-process, present themselves respectively as the objective and subjective factors, as means of production and labour-power, present themselves, from the point of view of the process of creating surplus-value, as constant and variable capital.

Marx, *Capital,* I (1867), pp. 221–33.

5.B.6 RATE OF SURPLUS-VALUE

The surplus-value generated in the process of production by C, the capital advanced, or in other words, the self-expansion of the value of the capital C, presents itself for our consideration, in the first place, as a surplus, as the amount by which the value of the product exceeds the value of its constituent element.

The capital C is made up of two components, one, the sum of money c laid out upon the means of production, and the other, the sum of money v expended upon the labour-power; c represents the portion that has become constant capital, and v the portion that has become variable capital. At first then, $C = c + v$. . . . When the process of production is finished, we get a commodity whose value $= (c + v) + s$, where s is the surplus value. . . .

From what has gone before, we know that surplus-value is purely the result of a variation in the value of v, of that portion of the capital which is transformed into labour-power; consequently, $v + s = v + v'$ or v plus an increment of v. . . .

In the first place then we equate the constant capital to zero. The capital advanced is consequently reduced from $c + v$ to v, and instead of the value of the product $(c + v) + s$ we have now the value produced $(v + s)$. Given the new value produced = £180, which sum consequently represents the whole labour expended during the process, then subtracting from it £90 the value of the variable capital, we have remaining £90, the amount of the surplus-value. This sum of £90 or s expresses the absolute quantity of surplus-value produced. The relative quantity produced, or the increase per cent of the variable capital, is determined, it is plain, by the ratio of the surplus-value to the variable capital, or is expressed by s/v. In our example this ratio is 90/90, which gives an increase of 100 per cent. This relative increase in the value of the variable capital, or the relative magnitude of the surplus-value, I call, "The rate of surplus-value."[1]

We have seen that the labourer, during one portion of the labour-process, produces only the value of his labour-power, that is, the value of his means of subsistence. Now since his work forms part of a system, based on the social division of labour, he does not directly produce the actual necessaries which he himself consumes; he produces instead a particular commodity, yarn for example, whose value is equal to the value of those necessaries or of the money with which they can be bought. The portion of his day's labour devoted to this purpose, will be greater or less, in proportion to the value of the necessaries that he daily requires on an average, or, what amounts to the same thing, in proportion to the labour-time required on an average to produce them. If the value of those necessaries represents on an average the expenditure of six hours' labour, the workman must on an average work for six hours to produce that value. If instead of working for the capitalist, he worked independently on his own account, he would, other things being equal, still be obliged to

[1]In the same way that the English use the terms "rate of profit," "rate of interest." The rate of profit is no mystery, so soon as we know the laws of surplus-value. If we reverse the process, we cannot comprehend either the one or the other.

labour for the same number of hours, in order to produce the value of his labour-power, and thereby to gain the means of subsistence necessary for his conservation or continued reproduction. But as we have seen, during that portion of his day's labour in which he produces the value of his labour-power, say three shillings, he produces only an equivalent for the value of his labour-power already advanced by the capitalist; the new value created only replaces the variable capital advanced. It is owing to this fact, that the production of the new value of three shillings takes the semblance of a mere reproduction. That portion of the working day, then, during which this reproduction takes place, I call *"necessary"* labour-time, and the labour expended during that time I call *"necessary"* labour. Necessary, as regards the labourer, because independent of the particular social form of his labour; necessary, as regards capital, and the world of capitalists, because on the continued existence of the labourer depends their existence also.

During the second period of the labour-process, that in which his labour is no longer necessary labour, the workman, it is true, labours, expends labour-power; but his labour, being no longer necessary labour, he creates no value for himself. He creates surplus-value which, for the capitalist, has all the charms of a creation out of nothing. This portion of the working day, I name surplus labour-time, and to the labour expended during that time, I give the name of surplus-labour. It is every bit as important, for a correct understanding of surplus-value, to conceive it as a mere congelation of surplus-labour-time, as nothing but materialised surplus-labour, as it is, for a proper comprehension of value, to conceive it as a mere congelation of so many hours of labour, as nothing but materialised labour. The essential difference between the various economic forms of society, between, for instance, a society based on slave labour, and one based on wage labour, lies only in the mode in which this surplus-labour is in each case extracted from the actual producer, the labourer.

Since, on the one hand, the values of the variable capital and of the labour-power purchased by that capital are equal, and the value of this labour-power determines the necessary portion of the working day; and since, on the other hand, the surplus-value is determined by the surplus portion of the working day, it follows that surplus-value bears the same ratio to variable capital, that surplus-labour does to necessary labour, or in other words, the rate of surplus-values/v = surplus labor/necessary labor. Both ratios, s/v and surplus labor/necessary labor express the same thing in different ways; in the one case by reference to materialised, incorporated labour, in the other by reference to living, fluent labour.

The rate of surplus-value is therefore an exact expression for the degree of exploitation of labour-power by capital, or of the labourer by the capitalist.[2]

Marx, *Capital,* I (1867), pp. 254–59, 345.

[2]Although the rate of surplus-value is an exact expression for the degree of exploitation of labour-power, it is, in no sense, an expression for the absolute amount of exploitation. For example, if the necessary labour = 5 hours and the surplus-labour = 5 hours, the degree of exploitation is 100%. The amount of exploitation is here measured by 5 hours. If, on the other hand, the necessary labour = 6 hours and the surplus-labour = 6 hours, the degree of exploitation remains, as before, 100% while the actual amount of exploitation has increased 20%, namely from five hours to six.

5.B.7 ABSOLUTE VERSUS RELATIVE SURPLUS-VALUE

The portion of the product that represents the surplus-value, . . . we call "surplus-produce." Just as the rate of surplus-value is determined by its relation, not to the sum total of the capital, but to its variable part; in like manner, the relative quantity of surplus-produce is determined by the ratio that this produce bears, not to the remaining part of the total product, but to that part of it in which is incorporated the necessary labour. . . .

The sum of the necessary labour and the surplus-labour, i.e., of the periods of time during which the workman replaces the value of his labour-power, and produces the surplus-value, this sum constitutes the actual time during which he works, i.e., the working day.

The rate of surplus-value alone would not give us the extent of the working day. If this rate e.g., were 100 percent, the working day might be of 8, 10, 12, or more hours. It would indicate that the 2 constituent parts of the working day, necessary-labour and surplus-labour time, were equal in extent, but not how long each of these two constituent parts was.

The working day is thus not a constant, but a variable quantity. One of its parts, certainly, is determined by the working time required for the reproduction of the labour-power of the labourer himself. But its total amount varies with the duration of the surplus-labour. The working day is, therefore, determinable, but is, per se, indeterminate.

Although the working day is not a fixed, but a fluent quantity, it can, on the other hand, only vary within certain limits. The minimum limit is, however, not determinable; of course, if we make the surplus-labour = 0, we have a minimum limit, i.e., the part of the day which the labourer must necessarily work for his own maintenance. On the basis of capitalist production, however, this necessary labour can form a part only of the working day; the working day itself can never be reduced to this minimum. On the other hand, the working day has a maximum limit. It cannot be prolonged beyond a certain point. This maximum limit is conditioned by two things. First, by the physical bounds of labour-power. Within the 24 hours of the natural day a man can expend only a definite quantity of his vital force, A horse, in like manner, can only work from day to day, 8 hours. During part of the day this force must rest, sleep; during another part the man has to satisfy other physical needs, to feed, wash, and clothe himself. Besides these purely physical limitations, the extension of the working day encounters moral ones. The labourer needs time for satisfying his intellectual and social wants, the extent and number of which are conditioned by the general state of social advancement. The variation of the working day fluctuates, therefore, within physical and social bounds. But both these limiting conditions are of a very elastic nature, and allow the greatest latitude. So we find working days of 8, 10, 12, 14, 16, 18 hours, i.e., of the most different lengths.

The capitalist has bought the labour-power at its day-rate. To him its use-value belongs during one working day. He has thus acquired the right to make the labourer work for him during one day. But what is a working day.?

At all events, less than a natural day. By how much? The capitalist has his own views of this *ultima Thule,* the necessary limit of the working day. As capitalist, he is only capital personified. His soul is the soul of capital. But capital has one single life impulse, the tendency to create value and surplus-value, to make its constant factor, the means of production, absorb the greatest possible amount of surplus-labour.

Capital is dead labour, that vampire-like, only lives by sucking living labour, and lives the more, the more labour it sucks. The time during which the labourer works, is the time during which the capitalist consumes the labour-power he has purchased of him.

If the labourer consumes his disposable time for himself, he robs the capitalist.

The capitalist then takes his stand on the law of the exchange of commodities. He, like all other buyers, seeks to get the greatest possible benefit out of the use-value of his commodity.

We see then, that, apart from extremely elastic bounds, the nature of the exchange of commodities itself imposes no limit to the working day, no limit to surplus-labour. The capitalist maintains his rights as a purchaser when he tries to make the working day as long as possible, and to make, whenever possible, two working days out of one. On the other hand, the peculiar nature of the commodity sold implies a limit to its consumption by the purchaser, and the labourer maintains his right as seller when he wishes to reduce the working day to one of definite normal duration. There is here, therefore, an antinomy, right against right, both equally bearing the seal of the law of exchanges. Between equal rights force decides. Hence is it that in the history of capitalist production, the determination of what is a working day, presents itself as the result of a struggle, a struggle between collective capital, i.e., the class of capitalists, and collective labour, i.e., the working class. . . .

Hitherto in treating of surplus-value, arising from a simple prolongation of the working day, we have assumed the mode of production to be given and invariable. But when surplus-value has to be produced by the conversion of necessary labour into surplus-labour, it by no means suffices for capital to take over the labour-process in the form under which it has been historically handed down, and then simply to prolong the duration of that process. The technical and social conditions of the process, and consequently the very mode of production must be revolutionised, before the productiveness of labour can be increased. By that means alone can the value of labour-power be made to sink, and the portion of the working day necessary for the reproduction of that value, be shortened.

The surplus-value produced by prolongation of the working day, I call *absolute surplus-value.* On the other hand, the surplus-value arising from the curtailment of the necessary labour-time, and from the corresponding alteration in the respective lengths of the two components of the working day, I call *relative surplus-value.*

Marx, *Capital,* I (1867), pp. 235–42.

5.B.8 MACHINERY AND RAISING SURPLUS VALUES

John Stuart Mill says in his Principles of Political Economy: "It is questionable if all the mechanical inventions yet made have lightened the day's toil of any human being." That is, however, by no means the aim of the capitalistic application of machinery. Like every other increase in the productiveness of labour, machinery is intended to cheapen commodities, and, by shortening that portion of the working day, in which the labourer works for himself, to lengthen the other portion that he gives, without an equivalent, to the capitalist. In short, it is a means for producing surplus-value. . . .

The starting point of Modern Industry is the revolution in the instruments of labour, and this revolution attains its most highly developed form in the organised system of machinery in a factory. . . . Let us consider some general effects of this revolution on the labourer himself.

Appropriation of Supplementary Labour-Power by Capital. The Employment of Women and Children.

In so far as machinery dispenses with muscular power, it becomes a means of employing labourers of slight muscular strength, and those whose bodily development is incomplete, but whose limbs are all the more supple. The labour of women and children was, therefore, the first thing sought for by capitalists who used machinery. That mighty substitute for labour and labourers was forthwith changed into a means for increasing the number of wage-labourers by enrolling, under the direct sway of capital, every member of the workman's family, without distinction of age or sex. Compulsory work for the capitalist usurped the place, not only of the children's play, but also of free labour at home within moderate limits for the support of the family.

The value of labour-power was determined, not only by the labour-time necessary to maintain the individual adult laborer, but also by that necessary to maintain his family. Machinery, by throwing every member of that family on to the labour market, spreads the value of the man's labour-power over his whole family. It thus depreciates his labour-power. To purchase the labour-power of a family of four workers may, perhaps, cost more than it formerly did to purchase the labour-power of the head of the family, but, in return, four days' labour takes the place of one, and their price falls in proportion to the excess of the surplus-labour of four over the surplus-labour of one. In order that the family may live, four people must now, not only labour, but expend surplus-labor for the capitalist. Thus we see, that machinery, while augmenting the human material that forms the principal object of capital's exploiting power, at the same time raises the degree of exploitation.

Machinery also revolutionises out and out the contract between the labourer and the capitalist, which formally fixes their mutual relations. Taking the exchange of commodities as our basis, our first assumption was that capitalist and labourer met as free persons, as independent owners of commodities; the one possessing money and means of production, the other labour-power. But now the capitalist buys children and young persons under age. Previously, the workman sold his own labour power, which he disposed of nominally as a free agent. Now he sells wife and child. He has become a slave dealer. . . .

By the excessive addition of women and children to the ranks of the workers, machinery at last breaks down the resistance which the male operatives in the manufacturing period continued to oppose to the despotism of capital.

Prolongation of the Working-Day.

If machinery be the most powerful means for increasing the productiveness of labour—i.e., for shortening the working time required in the production of a commodity, it becomes in the hands of capital the most powerful means, in those industries first invaded by it, for lengthening the working day beyond all bounds set by human nature. It creates, on the one hand, new conditions by which capital is enabled to give free scope to this its constant tendency, and on the other hand, new motives with which to whet capital's appetite for the labour of others.

In the first place, in form of machinery, the implements of labour become automatic, things moving and working independent of the workman. They are thenceforth an industrial *perpetuum mobile,* that would go on producing forever, did it not meet with certain natural obstructions in the weak bodies and the strong wills of its human attendants. The automaton, as capital, and because it is capital, is endowed, in the person of the capitalist, with intelligence and will; it is therefore animated by the longing to reduce to a minimum the resistance offered by that repellant yet elastic natural barrier, man. This resistance is moreover lessened by the apparent lightness of machine work, and by the more pliant and docile character of the women and children employed on it.

The productiveness of machinery is, as we saw, inversely proportional to the value transferred by it to the product. The longer the life of the machine, the greater is the mass of the products over which the value transmitted by the machine is spread, and the less is the portion of that value added to each single commodity. The active lifetime of a machine is, however, clearly dependent on the length of the working day, or on the duration of the daily labour-process multiplied by the number of days for which the process is carried on.

The wear and tear of a machine is not exactly proportional to its working time. And even if it were so, a machine working 16 hours daily for 7½ years, covers as long a working period as, and transmits to the total product no more value than, the same machine would if it worked only 8 hours daily for 15 years. But in the first case the value of the machine would be reproduced twice as quickly as in the latter, and the capitalist would, by this use of the machine, absorb in 7½ years as much surplus-value as in the second case he would in 15.

The material wear and tear of a machine is of two kinds. The one arises from use, as coins wear away by circulating, the other from non-use, as a sword rusts when left in its scabbard. The latter kind is due to the elements. The former is more or less directly proportional, the latter to a certain extent inversely proportional, to the use of the machine.

But in addition to the material wear and tear, a machine also undergoes what we may call a moral depreciation. It loses exchange-value, either by machines of the same sort being produced cheaper than it, or by better machines entering into competition with it. In both cases, be the machine ever so young and full of life, its value is no longer determined by the labour actually materialised in it, but by the labour-time requisite to reproduce either it or the better machine. It has, therefore, lost value more or less. The shorter the period taken to reproduce its total value, the less is the danger of moral depreciation; and the longer the working day, the shorter is that period. When machinery is first introduced into an industry, new methods of reproducing it more cheaply follow blow upon blow, and so do improvements, that not only affect individual parts and details of the machine, but its entire build. It is, therefore, in the early days of the life of machinery that this special incentive to the prolongation of the working day makes itself felt most acutely. . . .

Machinery produces relative surplus-value; not only by directly depreciating the value of labour-power, and by indirectly cheapening the same through cheapening the commodities that enter into its reproduction, but also, when it is first introduced sporadically into an industry, by converting the labour employed by the owner of that machinery, into labour of a higher degree and greater efficacy, by raising the social value of the article produced above its individual value, and thus enabling the capitalist to replace the value of a day's labour-power by a smaller portion of the value of the day's product. During this transition period, when the use of machinery is a sort of monopoly, the profits are therefore exceptional, and the capitalist endeavours to exploit thoroughly "the sunny time of this his first love," by prolonging the working day as much as possible. The magnitude of the profit whets his appetite for more profit.

As the use of machinery becomes more general in a particular industry, the social value of the product sinks down to its individual value, and the law that surplus-value does not arise from the labour-power that has been replaced by the machinery, but from the labour-power actually employed in working with the machinery, asserts itself. Surplus-value arises from the variable capital alone, and we saw that the amount of surplus-value depends on two factors, vis., the rate of surplus-value and the number of the workmen simultaneously employed. Given the length of the working day, the rate of surplus-value is determined by the relative duration of the necessary labour and of the surplus-labour in a day. The number of the labourers simultaneously employed depends, on its side, on the ratio of the variable to the constant capital. Now, however much the use of machinery may increase the surplus-labour at the expense of the necessary labour by heightening the productiveness of labour, it is clear that it attains this result, only by diminishing the number of workmen employed by a given amount of capital. It converts what was formerly variable capital, invested in labour-power, into machinery, which, being constant capital, does not produce surplus-value. It is impossible, for instance, to squeeze as much surplus-value out of 2 as out of 24 labourers. If each of these 24 men gives only one hour of surplus-labour in 12, the 24 men give together 24 hours of surplus-labour, while 24 hours is the total labour of the two men. Hence, the application of machinery to the production of surplus-value implies a contradiction which is immanent in it, since, of the two factors of the surplus-value created by a given amount of capital, one, the rate of surplus-value cannot be increased, except by diminishing the other, the number of workmen. This contradiction comes to light, as soon as by the general employment of machinery in a given industry, the value of the machine-produced commodity regulates the value of all commodities of the same sort; and it is this contradiction, that in its turn, drives the capitalist, without his being conscious of the fact, to excessive lengthening of the working day, in order that he may compensate the decrease in the relative number of labourers exploited, by an increase not only of the relative, but of the absolute surplus-labour.

If, then, the capitalistic employment of machinery, on the one hand, supplies new and powerful motives to an excessive lengthening of the working day, and radically changes as well the methods of labour, as also the character of the social working organism, in such a manner as to break down all opposition to this tendency, on the other hand it produces, partly by opening out to the capitalist new strata of the working class, previously inaccessible to him, partly by setting free the labourers it supplants, a surplus working population, which is compelled to submit to the dictation of capital. Hence that remarkable phenomenon in the history of Modern Industry, that machinery sweeps away every moral and natural restriction on the length of the working day. Hence, too, the economical paradox, that the most powerful instrument for shortening labour-time, becomes the most unfailing means for placing every moment of the labourer's time and that of his family, at the disposal of the capitalist for the purpose of expanding the value of his capital. . . .

Intensification of Labour

The immediate lengthening of the working day, produced by machinery in the hands of capital, leads to a reaction on the part of society, the very sources of whose life are menaced; and, thence, to a normal working day whose length is fixed by law. Thenceforth a phenomenon that we have already met with, namely, the intensification of labour, develops into great importance. Our analysis of absolute surplus-value had reference primarily to the extension or duration of the labour, its intensity being assumed as given. We now proceed to consider the substitution of a more intensified labour for labour of more extensive duration, and the degree of the former.

It is self-evident, that in proportion as the use of machinery spreads, and the experience of a special class of workmen habituated to machinery accumulates, the rapidity and intensity of labour increase as a natural consequence. Thus in England, during half a century, lengthening of the working day went hand in hand with increasing intensity of factory labour. Nevertheless the reader will clearly see, that where we have labour, not carried on by fits and starts, but repeated day after day with unvarying uniformity, a point must inevitably be reached, where extension of the working day and intensity of the labour mutually exclude one another, in such a way that lengthening of the working day becomes compatible only with a lower degree of intensity, and, a higher degree of intensity, only with a shortening of the working day. So soon as the gradually surging revolt of the working class compelled Parliament to shorten compulsorily the hours of labour, and to begin by imposing a normal working day on factories proper, so soon consequently as an increased production of surplus value by the prolongation of the working day was once for all put a stop to, from that moment capital threw itself with all its might into the production of relative surplus-value, by hastening on the further improvement of machinery. At the same time a change took place in the nature of relative surplus-value. Generally speaking, the mode of producing relative surplus-value consists in raising the productive power of the workman, so as to enable him to produce more in a given time with the same expenditure of labour. Labour-time continues to transmit as before the same value to the total product, but this unchanged amount of exchange value is spread over more use-values; hence the value of each single commodity sinks. Otherwise, however, so soon as the compulsory shortening of the hours of labour takes place. The immense impetus it gives to the development of productive power, and to economy in the means of production, imposes on the workman increased expenditure of labour in a given time, heightened tension of labour-power, and closer filling up of the pores of the working day, or condensation of labour to a degree that is attainable only within the limits of the shortened working day. This condensation of a greater mass of labour into a given period thenceforward counts for what it really is, a greater quantity of labour. In addition to a measure of its extension, i.e., duration, labour now acquires a measure of its intensity or of the degree of its condensation or density. . . .

We now come to the question: How is the labour intensified?

The first effect of shortening the working day results from the self-evident law, that the efficiency of labour-power is in an inverse ratio to the duration of its expenditure. Hence, within certain limits what is lost by shortening the duration is gained by the increasing tension of labour-power. That the workman moreover really does expend more labour-power, is ensured by the mode in which the capitalist pays him. In those industries, such as potteries, where machinery plays little or no part, the introduction of the Factory Acts has strikingly shown that the mere shortening of the working-day increases to a wonderful degree the regularity, uniformity, order, continuity, and energy of the labour.

Marx, *Capital,* I (1867), pp. 405, 430–32, 440–45, 447–49.

5.B.9 SUMMARY

Capitalist production is not merely the production of commodities, it is essentially the production of surplus-value. The labourer produces, not for himself, but for capital. It no longer suffices, therefore, that he should simply produce. He must produce surplus-value. That labourer alone is productive, who produces surplus-value for the capitalist, and thus works for the self-expansion of capital. . . . Hence the notion of a productive labourer implies not merely a relation between work and useful effect, between labourer and product of labour, but also a specific, social relation of production, a relation that has sprung up historically and stamps the labourer as the direct means of creating surplus-value. To be a productive labourer is, therefore, not a piece of luck, but a misfortune. . . .

The prolongation of the working day beyond the point at which the labourer would have produced just an equivalent for the value of his labour-power, and the appropriation of that surplus-labour by capital, this is production of absolute surplus-value. It forms the general groundwork of the capitalist system, and the starting point for the production of relative surplus-value. The latter presupposes that the working day is already divided into two parts, necessary labour, and surplus-labour. In order to prolong the surplus-labour, the necessary labour is shortened by methods whereby the equivalent for the wages is produced in less time. The production of absolute surplus-value turns exclusively upon the length of the working day; the production of relative surplus-value, revolutionises out and out the technical processes of labour, and the composition of society. It therefore presupposes a specific mode, the capitalist mode of production, a mode which, along with its methods, means, and conditions, arises and develops itself spontaneously on the foundation afforded by the formal subjection of labour to capital. In the course of this development, the formal subjection is replaced by the real subjection of labour to capital.

Marx, *Capital,* I (1867), pp. 558–59.

C. SURPLUS-VALUE, COMPETITION, AND PROFITS, AND PRICES

As we saw in chapter 2 (selection 2.A.5, above), Marx's analysis of capitalism's social relations was developed in terms of a theory of value which focused on labor. In qualitative terms, labor is represented by the "value" of its products. Conversely, values reflect the employment of labor power. Quantitatively, Marx believed that relative exchange values (e.g., P_1/P_2), under competitive equilibrium conditions, correspond to the relative amounts of labor time (e.g., L_1/L_2) required to produce commodities (under given conditions of labour quality, skill, technology, etc.). Thus: $L_1/L_2 = P_1/P_2$.

The question of the relationship between Marx's value theory and his analysis of exploitation and surplus value is very controversial. A traditional view is that Marx's "labor theory of value" is essential for demonstration of both the existence and the magnitude of surplus value. In brief, the traditional interpretation asserts that Marx's theory of exploitation stands or falls on his theory of value. An alternative view is that although it is possible to utilize (as Marx did) the labour theory of value to highlight the exposition of surplus value, and although the labor theory of value can also be used to elucidate some of Marx's key ideas concerning economic power and social relations among classes, his value theory is not a necessary foundation for his analysis of surplus value. As we have already seen, Marx's theory of surplus value may be described directly in terms of capitalist property and power relations without invoking the intricacies of the labor theory of value. Marx's value theory, however, is important for other aspects of analysis, for example, the falling rate of profit (see chapter 6 below).

In any event, the labor theory of value requires further consideration, both in its own right and in its connection with surplus value. We may distinguish two stages in the application of Marx's labor theory of value to capitalism. First is manufacturing capitalism, characterized by competitive mobility of capital (and thus equalization of profit rates) *within* industries, where firms have essentially similar technologies and hence similar ratios of constant capital to variable capital, that is, "organic compositions of capital" or c/v, in Marx's language. Second is industrial capitalism, characterized by competitive mobility of capital resources *among* as well as within industries (and thus equalization of profit rates throughout the economy), where different industries have different technologies and hence different organic compositions of capital.

The labor theory of value, as expressed above, requires an equalization of price ratios and labor time ratios. Alternatively expressed, the rates of surplus value, s/v, or profits per workers, must be equal in different enterprises. If the rate of profit on total capital invested, expressed as s/(c + v), is equal among different enterprises, then s/v will be equalized only if the organic composition of capital, c/v, is equalized. In the first stage of manufacturing capitalism, this is essentially true within any given industry. In the second stage, industrial capitalism, a complication emerges. The organic composition of capital is generally different in different sectors of the economy (e.g., high in the steel industry, low in the garment industry). But competition leads to an equalization in profit rates. Therefore, the ratios of s to v will diverge among enterprises, and price ratios will not equal labor time ratios, at least not precisely.

Marx's response to this complication (sel. 5.C.10) is to contend that although prices do not equal labor time values, they are related in a systematic way. The *overall* level of surplus value in the economy is determined by the class relations between capitalists and workers. Given the total surplus, the competitive reallocations of resources which lead to equalization of profit rates create a result wherein prices (what Marx calls "prices of production") exceed (lie below) labor time values (i.e., c + v + s) in instances where c/v is below (above) average. In the final table in selection 5.C.10, note that the sum of values equals the sum of prices, and the sum of surplus values equals the sum of profits. Thus, although individual prices and labor time values diverge, the labor theory of value still explains, for Marx, the overall workings of the price system and the overall rate of profit. In effect, competition redistributes surplus values among capitalists, but does not determine its overall level.

Although economists have continued to debate Marx's analysis of the "transformation" of values into prices down to the present, our interest here is in the broader issues of the implications of this second stage of his value theory for exploitation. Although surplus values are created in production, Marx held, they can be realized only in market exchange. What is to prevent capitalists under freely competitive conditions from expanding investment and production to such levels as to push profit rates and aggregate levels of surplus value down to zero? Marx's answer is, in effect, threefold. First, competition among capitalists, as we have seen, does plausibly result in the movement of resources from areas of low profit to high profit and thereby to an equalization of profit rates. But this redistribution of surplus values through the competitive market process, he contended, "obviously has nothing to do with the absolute amount of surplus value. . . does of course not alter in the least the total sum of the surplus value which they have to distribute among themselves."[4] In effect, Marx is here implicitly making the rough and ready assumption of free competition rather than the more exacting, but, one is tempted to say, imaginary assumption of "perfect" competition, which is supposed to eradicate all "pure economic profits" according to orthodox neoclassical economic theory.

Second, surplus values and profit rates might be pushed down closer to zero if workers were free to withdraw from the working class and themselves become capitalists. *Some* individual workers, through ability, industry, and sacrifice, do

[4]Marx, The *Grundrisse,* (New York: Random House, 1973), p. 547.

occasionally start little businesses, survive, and help push profit rates down. But because technology, credit availability, and survival during depressions increasingly favors large, established capitalists, this escape route from the capitalist system and its propensity to create and sustain surplus values is not feasible for any substantial number of workers. On the other hand, small capitalists, artisans, and peasants are propelled into the working class through bankruptcy, notably during depressions. In short, competitive equalization of profit rates, for Marx, is no guarantee of the elimination of surplus values or the reduction of profit rates to zero, even in long-run, freely competitive equilibrium.

Third, however, whatever might conceivably be true, according to orthodox, non-Marxian economics, under static and stationary conditions, Marx's methodology was dynamic. His "ultimate aim" was to "lay bare the law of motion of modern society,"[5] not to speculate about hypothetical long-run "equilibrium" circumstances under given resource, technological, and institutional conditions. Whatever the hypothetical tendency to eliminate surplus values through competitive exchange may be, it seems reasonable to conclude that a resurrected Marx would hold that through the lure of greater profit, wealth, and power, and the goad of competition and the class struggle, *this* tendency is normally overpowered in practice by the re-creation of absolute and, especially, relative surplus values in production. Thus, we return to the point that, for Marx, the exploitation of surplus values does not rest on imperfections of the capitalist exchange process per se, but on social relations within production. Because labor power has the unique capacity of creating surplus values, under the direction and control of capitalists, the nominally free exchange of labor power in the labor market conceals a deeper form of social coercion based on property power.

5.C.10 TRANSFORMATION OF SURPLUS-VALUES INTO PROFITS AND VALUES INTO PRICES

We have demonstrated that different lines of industry may have different rates of profit, corresponding to differences in the organic composition of capitals, and, within the limits indicated, also corresponding to different times of turnover; the law (as a general tendency) that profits are proportioned as the magnitudes of the capitals, or that capitals of equal magnitude yield equal profits in equal times, applies only to capitals of the same organic composition, with the same rate of surplus-value, and the same time of turnover. And these statements hold good on the assumption, which has been the basis of all our analyses so far, namely that the commodities are sold at their values. On the other hand there is no doubt that, aside from unessential, accidental, and mutually compensating distinctions, a difference in the average rate of profit of the various lines of industry does not exist in reality, and could not exist without abolishing the entire system of capitalist production. It would seem, then, as though the theory of value were irreconcilable at this point with the

[5] Marx, *Capital,* (New York: Modern Library, n.d.), Vol. I, p. 14.

actual process, irreconcilable with the real phenomena of production, so that we should have to give up the attempt to understand these phenomena.

It follows from the first part of this volume that the cost-prices are the same for the products of different spheres of production, in which equal portions of capital have been invested for purposes of production, regardless of the organic composition of such capitals. The cost-price does not show the distinction between variable and constant capital to the capitalist. A commodity for which he must advance 100 p.st. in production cost him the same amount, whether he invests 90 c + 10 v, or 10 c + 90 v. He always spends 100 p.st. for it, no more, no less. The cost-prices are the same for investments of the same amounts of capital in different spheres, no matter how much the produced values and surplus-values may differ. The equality of cost-prices is the basis for the competition of the invested capitals, by which an average rate of profit is brought about.

The organic composition of capital depends at each stage on two circumstances: First, on the technical relation of the employed labor-power to the mass of the employed means of production; secondly, on the price of these means of production. We have seen that this composition must be considered according to its percentages. We express the organic composition of a certain capital, consisting of four-fifths of constant, and one-fifth of variable capital, by the formula 80 c + 20 v. We furthermore assume in this comparison that the rate of surplus-value is unchangeable. Let it be, for instance, 100 percent. The capital of 80 c + 20 v then produces a surplus-value of 20 s, and this is equal to a rate of profit of 20 percent on the total capital. The magnitude of the actual value of the product of this capital depends on the magnitude of the fixed part of the constant capital, and on the amount of it passing by wear and tear over to the product. But as this circumstance is immaterial so far as the rate of profit and the present analysis are concerned, we assume for the sake of simplicity that the constant capital is transferred everywhere uniformly and entirely to the annual product of the capitals named. It is further assumed that these capitals realise equal quantities of surplus-value in the different spheres of production, proportional to the magnitude of their variable parts. In other words, we disregard for the present the difference which may be produced in this respect by the different lengths of the periods of turnover. This point will be discussed later.

Let us compare five different spheres of production, and let the capital in each one have a different organic composition, as follows:

CAPITALS			RATE OF SURPLUS VALUE	SURPLUS VALUE	VALUE OF PRODUCT	RATE OF PROFIT
I.	80 c	20 v	100%	20	120	20%
II.	70 c	30 v	100%	30	130	30%
III.	60 c	40 v	100%	40	140	40%
IV.	85 c	15 v	100%	15	115	15%
V.	95 c	5 v	100%	5	150	5%

Here we have considerably different rates of profit in different spheres of production with the same degree of exploitation, corresponding to the different organic composition of these capitals.

The grand total of the capitals invested in these five spheres of production is 500; the grand total of the surplus-values produced by them is 110; the total value of all commodities produced by them is 610. If we consider the amount of 500 as one single capital, and capitals I to V as its component parts (about analogous to the different departments of a cotton mill which has different proportions of constant and variable capital in its carding, preparatory spinning, spinning, and weaving rooms, on the basis of which the average proportion for the whole factory is calculated), then we should put down the average composition of this capital of 500 as 390 c + 110 v, or, in percentages, as 78 c + 22 v. In other words, if we regard each one of the capitals of 100 as one-fifth of the total capital, its average composition would be 78 c + 22 v; and every 100 would make an average surplus-value of 22. The average rate of profit would, therefore, be 22%, and, finally, the price of every fifth of the total product produced by the capital of 500 would be 122. The product of each 100 of the advanced total capital would have to be sold, then, at 122.

But in order not to arrive at entirely wrong conclusions, it is necessary to assume that not all cost-prices are equal to 100.

With a composition of 80 c + 20 v, and a rate of surplus-value of 100, the total value of the commodities produced by the first capital of 100 would be 80 c + 20 v + 20 s, or 120, provided that the whole constant capital is tranferred to the product of the year. Now, this may happen under certain circumstances in some spheres of production. But it will hardly be the case where the proportion of c to v is that of four to one. We must, therefore, remember in comparing the values produced by each 100 of the different capitals, that they will differ according to the different composition of c as to fixed and circulating parts, and that the fixed portions of different capitals will wear out more or less rapidly, thus transferring unequal quantities of value to the product in equal periods of time. But this is immaterial so far as the rate of profit is concerned. Whether the 80 c transfer the value of 80, or 50, or 5, to

CAPITALS	RATE OF SURPLUS VALUE	SURPLUS VALUE	RATE OF PROFIT	USED UP C	VALUE OF COMMODITIES	COST PRICE	
I. 80 c + 20 v	100%	20	20%	50	90	70	
II. 70 c + 30 v	100%	30	30%	51	111	81	
III. 60 c + 40 v	100%	40	40%	51	131	91	
IV. 85 c + 15 v	100%	15	15%	40	70	55	
V. 95 c + 5 v	100%	5	5%	10	20	15	
390 c + 110 v		110	100%				Total
78 c + 22 v		22	22%				Average

the annual product, whether the annual product is consequently 80 c + 20 v + 20 s = 120, or 50 c + 20 v + 20 s = 90, or 5 c + 20 v + 20 s = 45, in all of these cases the excess of the value of the product over its cost-price is 20, and in every case these 20 are calculated on a capital of 100 in ascertaining the rate of profit. The rate of profit of capital I is, therefore, in every case 20 percent. In order to make this still plainer, we transfer in the following table different portions of the constant capital of the same five capitals to the value of their product.

Now, if we consider capitals I to V once more as one single total capital, it will be seen that also in this case the composition of the sums of these five capitals amounts to 500, being 390c + 110 v, so that the average composition is once more 78 c + 22 v. The average surplus-value also remains 22 percent. If we allot this surplus-value uniformly to capitals I to V, we arrive at the following prices of the commodities:

CAPITALS	SURPLUS VALUE	VALUE	COST PRICE OF COMMODITIES	PRICE OF COMMODITIES	RATE OF PROFIT	DEVIATION OF PRICE FROM VALUE
I. 80 c + 20 v	20	90	70	92	22%	+ 2
II. 70 c + 30 v	30	111	81	103	22%	- 8
III. 60 c + 40 v	40	131	91	113	22%	-18
IV. 85 c + 15 v	15	70	55	77	22%	+ 7
V. 95 c + 5 v	5	20	15	37	22%	+17

Summing up, we find that the commodities are sold at 2 + 7 + 17 = 26 above, and 8 + 18 = 26 below their value, so that the deviations of prices from values mutually balance one another by the uniform distribution of the surplus-value, or by the addition of the average profit of 22 per 100 of advanced capital to the respective cost-prices of the commodities of I to V. One portion of the commodities is sold in the same proportion above in which the other is sold below their values. And it is only their sale at such prices which makes it possible that the rate of profit for all five capitals is uniformly 22 percent, without regard to the organic composition of these capitals. The prices which arise by drawing the average of the various rates of profit in the different spheres of production and adding this average to the cost-prices of the different spheres of production, are the *prices of production.* They are conditioned on the existence of an average rate of profit, and this, again, rests on the premise that the rates of profit in every sphere of production, considered by itself, have previously been reduced to so many average rates of profit. These special rates of profit are equal to s/C in every sphere of production, and they must be deduced out of the values of the commodities, as shown in volume I. Without such a deduction an average rate of profit (and consequently a price of production of commodities), remains a vague and senseless conception. The price of production of a commodity, then, is equal to its cost-price plus a percentage of profit apportioned according to the average rate of profit, or in other words, equal to its cost-price plus the average profit.

Since the capitals invested in the various lines of production are of a different organic composition, and since the different percentages of the variable portions of these total capitals set in motion very different quantities of labor, it follows that these capitals appropriate very different quantities of surplus-labor, or produce very different quantities of surplus-value. Consequently the rates of profit prevailing in the various lines of production are originally very different. These different rates of profit are equalised by means of competition into a general rate of profit, which is the average of all these special rates of profit. The profit allotted according to this average rate of profit to any capital, whatever may be its organic composition, is called the average profit. That price of any commodity which is equal to its cost-price plus that share of average profit on the total capital invested (not merely consumed) in its production which is allotted to it in proportion to its conditions of turnover, is called its price of production. Take, for instance, a capital of 500, of which 100 are fixed capital, and let 10 percent of this wear out during one turnover of the circulating capital of 400. Let the average profit for the time of this turnover be 10 percent. In that case the cost-price of the product created during this turnover will be 10 c (wear) + 400 (c + v), circulating capital, or a total of 410, and its price of production will be 410 (cost-price) plus 10 percent of average profit on 500, or a total of 460.

While the capitalists in the various spheres of production recover the value of the capital consumed in the production of their commodities through the sale of these, they do not secure the surplus-value, and consequently the profit, created in their own sphere by the production of these commodities, but only as much surplus-value, and profit, as falls to the share of every aliquot part of the total social capital out of the total social surplus-value, or social profit produced by the total capital of society in all spheres of production. Every 100 of any invested capital, whatever may be its organic composition, draws as much profit during one year, or any other period of time, as falls to the share of every 100 of the total social capital during the same period. The various capitalists, so far as profits are concerned, are so many stockholders in a stock company in which the shares of profit are uniformly divided for every 100 shares of capital, so that profits differ in the case of the individual capitalists only according to the amount of capital invested by each one of them in the social enterprise, according to his investment in social production as a whole, according to his shares. That portion of the price of commodities which buys back the elements of capital consumed in the production of these commodities, in other words, their cost-price, depends on the investment of capital required in each particular sphere of production. But the other element of the price of commodities, the percentage of profit added to this cost-price, does not depend on the mass of profit produced by a certain capital during a definite time in its own sphere of production, but on the mass of profit allotted for any period to each individual capital in its capacity as an aliquot part of the total social capital invested in social production. . . .

This always amounts in the end to saying that one commodity receives too little of the surplus-value while another receives too much, so that the deviations from the value shown by the prices of production mutually compensate one another. In short, under capitalist production, the general law of value enforces itself merely as the prevailing tendency, in a very complicated and approximate manner, as a never ascertainable average of ceaseless fluctuations. . . .

If the commodities are sold at their values, then, as we have shown, considerably different rates of profit arise in the various spheres of production, according to the different organic composition of the masses of capital invested in them. But capital withdraws from spheres with low rates of profit and invades others which yield a higher rate. By means of this incessant emigration and immigration, in one word, by its distribution among the various spheres in accord with a rise of the rate of profit here, and its fall there, it brings about such a proportion of supply to demand that the average profit in the various spheres of production becomes the same, so that values are converted into prices of production.

Marx, *Capital,* III (1894), pp. 181–87, 190, 230.

6 Capitalism's Contradictory and Destructive Properties: Accumulation, Crisis, Depression, and Unemployment

A. CAPITALIST REPRODUCTION AND GROWTH

Marx's theory of exploitation explains how "surplus-value emanates from capital." His theory of capitalist reproduction and growth explains how "capital emanates from surplus-value."[1] To continue, capitalist production requires what Marx calls "reproduction." Money must be transformed into physical means of production and labor power which, in turn, must be transformed into commodities. Commodities must be sold and the monies obtained again transformed into (constant and variable) capital. This process not only reproduces output and income, as Marx pointedly observes (selection 6.A.1), but it re-creates the social relations of the capitalist economy itself and thereby the conditions for the continuity of capitalist alienation and exploitation.

Alienation and exploitation, however, are not merely systemic and dysfunctional features of the capitalist mode of production in Marx's analysis, for Marx was not primarily a moralist or muckraker. Instead, they are bases for capitalism's growth, development, and eventual demise. Alienation provides the discipline and control for the "potentially general development of the forces of production" and the universality of the world market.[2] Exploitation is capitalism's means for creating, distributing to a propertied class, and investing an economic surplus, thereby generating economic growth and, as will be described more fully in chapter 7, stimulating and reinforcing tendencies toward capitalism's self-destruction.

Marx describes capitalism's processes of reproduction in terms of two stages or schemas (selection 6.A.2). First, he presents a model of capitalist economy with no capital accumulation. In this first, purposefully unrealistic scheme, depreciating machinery and factories are replaced as they wear out, but all surpluses go to capitalists' consumption (and workers are also presumed to consume all their income), so that net investment is zero. The economy is divided into two major sectors or "departments," namely, (1) those industries producing "means of production" and (2) those producing "means of consump-

[1]Marx, *Capital,* Vol. I (New York: International Publishers, 1967), p. 579.

[2]Marx, The *Grundrisse* (Outlines of the Critique of Political Economy) (New York: Random House, 1973), pp. 541–42.

tion." In each, the total value of output is composed of c + v + s. Thus, using a_1 and a_2 to denote the total value of output in the two sectors, we have:

$$\text{I} \quad a_1 = c_1 + v_1 + s_1$$
$$\text{II} \quad a_2 = c_2 + v_2 + s_2$$

If the economy is to reproduce itself at a constant level with no accumulation or retrogression, then the output of department I ($c_1 - v_1 + s_1$) must be used up as constant capital in departments I and II *and* the output of department II ($c_2 + v_2 + s_2$) must be purchased with the incomes of capitalists and workers in both departments. In brief, the following conditions must hold:

$$c_1 + v_1 + s_1 = c_1 + c_2$$
$$c_2 + v_2 + s_2 = v_1 + s_1 + v_2 + s_2$$

To some degree, these conditions are met, *by hypothesis,* within the respective departments. Thus, a portion of the income in department I becomes a demand for constant capital in that department ($c_1 = c_1$). Similarly, a portion of the income in department II becomes demand for consumption goods by workers and capitalists in that department ($v_2 + s_2 = v_2 + s_2$). Subtracting these components from the above two equations, we have the following intersectoral condition for equilibrium:

$$c_2 = v_1 + s_1$$

In effect, the supply of means of production and demand for means of consumption by workers and capitalists in sector I must equal the supply of means of consumption and demand for means of production by sector II.

Marx's second model, "reproduction on an extended scale," presumes that workers from both departments spend all their income on consumption goods, as before, but that capitalists devote some portion of their surpluses to net investment, thus engaging in positive "capital accumulation." Capitalists also enjoy consuming, and with rising surpluses, are able to indulge themselves in an increasingly luxurious style; their primary orientation, however, is toward investment. First, capital accumulation is the road to profits and wealth in a capitalist society. Second, capitalists are enticed to invest by the goad of competition as well as by the lure of profits. Indeed, ultimate bankruptcy and descent into the working class is the stern penalty facing the excessively prodigal capitalist. Third, the class struggle also stimulates a capitalist investment orientation. Rising wages in a growing economy can be tempered by the process of labor-saving technical inventions. Fourth, for Marx, capitalists are not mere pleasure seekers or utility maximizers in an ordinary sense. They seek power and dominance in their relations with workers, not merely use values in consumption, and they derive pleasure from the power and control emanating from capital accumulation.

However, a strong urge to accumulate is not sufficient. As in the first reproduction model, equilibrium in the second model rests on a very delicate intersectoral balance. Department I must provide the increased means of production for expansion ($\Delta c_1 + \Delta c_2$), not merely replacement for depreciation ($c_1 + c_2$). Given the organic composition of capital, c/v, a growth in machinery and factories requires a corollary expansion in labor power. Department II must provide the means of consumption to sustain the additional workers ($\Delta v_1 + \Delta v_2$), not merely to maintain old levels of consumption by workers ($v_1 + v_2$) and to provide consumption goods to capitalists. Consequently, the equilibrium condition stated earlier ($c_2 = v_1 + s_1$) must be amended as follows:

$$c_2 + \Delta c_2 = v_1 + s_1 + \Delta v_1$$

The first reproduction scheme is (purposefully) unrealistic because it abstracts from capital accumulation. The second reproduction scheme is (purposefully) unrealistic because its continuity depends on intersectoral balances between supplies and demands which may very well fail to occur. The moral is that capitalism is characterized by capital accumulation and growth, but steady expansion along an "equilibrium growth curve," although logically conceivable, seems highly doubtful in practice.

6.A.1 CAPITALIST REPRODUCTION

Whatever the form of the process of production in a society, it must be a continuous process, must continue to go periodically through the same phases. A society can no more cease to produce than it can cease to consume. When viewed, therefore, as a connected whole, and as flowing on with incessant renewal, every social process of production is, at the same time, a process of reproduction.

The conditions of production are also those of reproduction. No society can go on producing, in other words, no society can reproduce, unless it constantly reconverts a part of its products into means of production, or elements of fresh products. All other circumstances remaining the same, the only mode by which it can reproduce its wealth, and maintain it at one level, is by replacing the means of production—i.e., the instruments of labour, the raw material, and the auxiliary substances consumed in the course of the year—by an equal quantity of the same kind of articles; these must be separated from the mass of the yearly products, and thrown afresh into the process of production. Hence, a definite portion of each year's product belongs to the domain of production. Destined for productive consumption from the very first, this portion exists, for the most part, in the shape of articles totally unfitted for individual consumption.

If production be capitalistic in form, so, too, will be reproduction. Just as in the former the labour-process figures but as a means towards the self-expansion of capital, so in the latter it figures but as a means of reproducing as capital—i.e., as self-expanding value,—the value advanced. It is only because his money constantly functions as capital that the economical guise of a capitalist attaches to a man. If, for instance, a sum of £100 has this year been converted into capital, and produced a surplus-value of £20, it must continue during next year, and subsequent years, to repeat the same operation. As a periodic increment of the capital advanced, or periodic fruit of capital in process, surplus-value acquires the form of a revenue flowing out of capital.

If this revenue serve the capitalist only as a fund to provide for his consumption, and be spent as periodically as it is gained, then, caeteris paribus, simple reproduction will take place. And although this reproduction is a mere repetition of the process of production on the old scale, yet this mere repetition, or continuity, gives a new character to the process, or, rather, causes the disappearance of some apparent characteristics which it possessed as an isolated discontinuous process. . . .

Apart then from all accumulation, the mere continuity of the process of production, in other words simple reproduction, sooner or later, and of necessity, converts every capital into accumulated capital, or capitalised surplus-value. Even if that capital was originally acquired by the personal labour of its employer, it sooner or later becomes value appropriated without an equivalent, the unpaid labour of others materialised either in money or in some other object. We saw in [selection 2.A.4] that in order to convert money into capital something more is required than the production and circulation of commodities. We saw that on the one side the possessor of value or money, on the other, the possessor of the value-creating substance; on the one side, the possessor of the means of production and subsistence, on the other, the possessor of nothing but labour-power, must confront one another as buyer and seller. The separation of labour from its product, of subjective labour-power from the objective conditions of labour, was therefore the real foundation in fact, and the starting point of capitalist production.

But that which at first was but a starting point, becomes, by the mere continuity of the process, by simple reproduction, the peculiar result, constantly renewed and perpetuated, of capitalist production. On the one hand, the process of production incessantly converts material wealth into capital, into means of creating more wealth and means of enjoyment for the capitalist. On the other hand the labourer, on quitting the process, is what he was on entering it, a source of wealth, but devoid of all means of making that wealth his own. Since, before entering on the process, his own labour has already been alienated from himself by the sale of his labour-power, has been appropriated by the capitalist and incorporated with capital, it must, during the process, be realised in a product that does not belong to him. Since the process of production is also the process by which the capitalist consumes labour-power, the product of the labourer is incessantly converted, not only into commodities, but into capital, into value that sucks up the value-creating power, into means of subsistence that buy the person of the labourer, into means of production that command the producers. The labourer therefore constantly produces material, objective wealth, but in the form of capital, of an alien power that dominates and exploits him; and the capitalist as constantly produces labour-power, but in the form of a subjective source of wealth, separated from the objects in and by which it can alone be realised; in short he produces the labourer, but as a wage-labourer. This incessant reproduction, this perpetuation of the labourer, is the sine qua non of capitalist production. . . .

Capitalist production, therefore, of itself reproduces the separation between labour-power and the means of labour. It thereby reproduces and perpetuates the condition for exploiting the labourer. It incessantly forces him to sell his labour-power in order to live, and enables the capitalist to purchase labour-power in order that he may enrich himself. It is no longer a mere accident, that capitalist and labourer confront each other in the market as buyer and seller. It is the process itself that incessantly hurls back the labourer on to the market as a vendor of his labour-power, and that incessantly converts his own product into a means by which another man can purchase him. In reality, the labourer belongs to capital before he has sold himself to capital. His economical bondage is both brought about and concealed by the periodic sale of himself, by his change of masters, and by the oscillations in the market price of labour-power.

Capitalist production, therefore, under its aspect of a continuous connected process, of a process of reproduction, produces not only commodities, not only surplus-value, but it also produces and reproduces the capitalist relation; on the one side the capitalist, on the other the wage-labourer.

Marx, *Capital,* I (1867), pp. 619–21, 624–25, 632–33.

6.A.2 REPRODUCTION SCHEMES

The Two Departments of Social Production

The total product, and therefore the total production, of society may be divided into two major departments:

I. *Means of Production,* commodities having a form in which they must, or at least may, pass into productive consumption.

II. *Articles of Consumption,* commodities having a form in which they pass into the individual consumption of the capitalist and the working-class.

All the various branches of production pertaining to each of these two departments form one single great branch of production, that of the means of production in the one case, and that of articles of consumption in the other. The aggregate capital employed in each of these two branches of production constitutes a separate large department of the social capital.

In each department the capital consists of two parts:

1) *Variable Capital.* This capital, so far as its *value* is concerned, is equal to the value of the social labour-power employed in this branch of production; in other words, it is equal to the sum of the wages paid for this labour-power. So far as its substance is concerned, it consists of the labour-power in action, i.e., of the living labour set in motion by this capital-value.

2) *Constant Capital.* This is the value of all the means of production employed for productive purposes in this branch. These again, are divided into *fixed* capital, such as machines, instruments of labour, buildings, labouring animals, etc., and *circulating* constant capital, such as materials of production: raw and auxiliary materials, semi-finished products, etc.

The value of the total annual product created with the aid of this capital in each of the two departments consists of one portion which represents the constant capital c consumed in the process of production and only transferred to the product in accordance with its value, and of another portion added by the entire labour of the year. This latter portion is divided in turn into the replacement of the advanced variable capital v and the excess over and above it, which forms the surplus-value s. And just as the value of every individual commodity, that of the entire annual product of each department consists of c + v + s.

Portion c of the value, representing the constant capital *consumed* in production, does not coincide with the value of the constant capital *employed* in production. True, the materials of production are entirely consumed and their values completely transferred to the product. But only a portion of the employed *fixed* capital is wholly consumed and its value thus transferred to the product. Another part of the fixed capital, such as machines, buildings, etc., continues to exist and function the same as before, though depreciated to the extent of the annual wear and tear. ...

We shall base our study of simple reproduction on the following scheme, in which c stands for constant capital, v for variable capital, and s for surplus-value, assuming the rate of surplus-value s/v to be 100 percent. The figures may indicate millions of marks, francs, or pounds sterling.

I. Production of Means of Production:

$$\textit{Capital}\ldots 4{,}000_c + 1{,}000_v = 5{,}000$$
$$\textit{Commodity-Product}\ldots 4{,}000_c + 1{,}000_v + 1{,}000_s = 6{,}000,$$

existing in means of production.

II. Production of Articles of Consumption:

$$\textit{Capital}\ldots 2{,}000_c + 500_v = 2{,}500$$
$$\textit{Commodity-Product}\ldots 2{,}000_c + 500_v + 500_s = 3{,}000,$$

existing in articles of consumption.

Recapitulation: Total annual commodity-product:

$$\textit{I.}\ 4{,}000_c + 1{,}000_v + 1{,}000_s = 6{,}000 \textit{ means of production.}$$
$$\textit{II.}\ 2{,}000_c + 500_v + 500_s = 3{,}000 \textit{ articles of consumption.}$$

Total value 9,000, exclusive of the fixed capital persisting in its natural form, according to our assumption.

If we were now to examine the transformations necessary on the basis of simple reproduction, where the entire surplus-value is unproductively consumed, and leave aside for the present the money-circulation that brings them about, we should obtain at the outset three great points of support.

1) The 500_v, representing wages of the labourers, and 500_s, representing surplus-value of the capitalists, in department II, must be spent for articles of consumption. But their value exists in articles of consumption worth 1,000, held by the capitalists of department II, which replace the advanced 500_v and represent the 500_s. Consequently the wages and surplus-value of department II are exchanged within this department for products of this same department. Thereby articles of consumption to the amount of $(500_v + 500_s)$ II = 1,000, drop out of the total product.

2) The $1{,}000_v$ plus $1{,}000_s$ of department I must likewise be spent for articles of consumption; in other words, for products of department II. Hence

they must be exchanged for the remainder of this product equal to the constant capital part, $2{,}000_c$. Department II receives in return an equal quantity of means of production, the product of I, in which the value of $1{,}000_v + 1{,}000_s$ of I is incorporated. Thereby 2,000 II_c and $(1{,}000_v + 1{,}000_s)$ I, drop out of the calculation.

3) There still remain 4,000 I_c. These consist of means of production which can be used only in department I to replace its consumed constant capital, and are therefore disposed of by mutual exchange between the individual capitalists of I just as the $(500_v + 500_s)$ II by an exchange between the labourers and capitalists, or between the individual capitalists of II.

Let this serve for the moment to facilitate the understanding of what follows.

Marx, *Capital,* II (1885), excerpts from Chap. 20.

Accumulation and Reproduction On An Extended Scale

By the conversion of the commodity-capital into money the surplus-product, in which the surplus value is represented, is also turned into money. The capitalist reconverts the so metamorphosed surplus-value into additional natural elements of his productive capital. In the next cycle of production the increased capital furnishes an increased product. But what happens in the case of the individual capital must also show in the annual reproduction as a whole, just as we have seen it happen on analysing simple reproduction, namely, that the successive precipitation—in the case of individual capital—of its used-up fixed component parts in money which is being hoarded, also finds expression in the annual reproduction of society. . . .

1. First Illustration

A. Scheme of Simple Reproduction

$$\text{I. } 4{,}000_c + 1{,}000_v + 1{,}000_s = 6{,}000$$
$$\text{II. } 2{,}000_c + 500_v + 500_s = 3{,}000 \qquad \text{Total, } 9{,}000.$$

B. Initial Scheme for Accumulation on an Extended Scale

$$\text{I. } 4{,}000_c + 1{,}000_v + 1{,}000_s = 6{,}000$$
$$\text{II. } 1{,}500_c + 750_v + 750_s = 3{,}000 \qquad \text{Total, } 9{,}000.$$

Assuming that in scheme B one half of surplus-value I, i.e., 500, is accumulated, we first receive $(1{,}000_v + 500_s)$ I, or 1,500 $I_{(v+s)}$ to be replaced by 1,500 II_c. There then remains in I; $4{,}000_c$ and 500_s, the latter having to be accumulated. The replacement of $(1{,}000_v + 500_s)$ I by 1,500 II_c is a process of simple reproduction, which has been examined previously.

Let us now assume that 400 of the 500 I_s are to be converted into constant capital, and 100 into variable capital. The exchange within I of the 400_s, which are thus to be capitalised has already been discussed. They can therefore be annexed to I_c, without more ado and in that case we get for I:

$4{,}400_c + 1{,}000_v + 100_s$ (the latter to be converted into 100_v).

II in turns buys from I for the purpose of accumulation the 100 I_s (existing in means of production) which now form additional constant capital II, while the 100 in money which it pays for them are converted into the money-form of the additional variable capital of I. We then have for I a capital of $4{,}400_c + 1{,}100_v$ (the latter in money), equalling 5,500.

II has now $1{,}600_c$ for its constant capital. In order to put them to work, it must advance a further 50_v in money for the purchase of new labour-power, so that its variable capital grows from 750 to 800. This expanison of the constant and variable capital of II by a total of 150 is supplied out of its suplus-value. Hence only 600_s of the 750 II_s remain as a consumption-fund for capitalists II, whose annual product is now distributed as follows:

II. $1{,}600_c + 800_v + 600_s$ (consumption-fund), equal to 3,000.

The 150_s produced in articles of consumption, which have been converted here into $(100_s + 50_v)$ II, go entirely in their bodily form for the consumption of the labourers, 100 being consumed by labourers of I (100 I_v), and 50 by the labourers of II (50 II_v), as explained above, As a matter of fact in II, where its total product is prepared in a form suitable for accumulation, a part greater by 100 of the surplus-value in the form of *necessary* articles of consumption must be reproduced. If reproduction really starts on an extended scale, then the 100 of variable money-capital I flow back through the hands of its working-class to II, while II transfers 100_s in commodity-supply to I and at the same time 50 in commodity-supply to its own working class.

The arrangement change for the purpose of accumulation is now as follows:

I. $4{,}440_c + 1{,}100_v + 500$ consumption-fund $= 6{,}000$
II. $1{,}600_c + 800_v + 600$ consumption-fund $= 3{,}000$
Total, as before, 9,000.

Of these amounts, the following are capital:

I. $4{,}400_c + 1{,}100_v$ (money) $= 5{,}500$
II. $1{,}600_c + 800_v$ (money) $= 2{,}400$
$= 7{,}900$,

while production started out with

I. $4{,}000_c + 1{,}000_v = 5{,}000$
II. $1{,}500_c + 750_v = 2{,}250$
$= 7{,}250$.

Now, if actual accumulation takes place on this basis, that is to say, if production really goes on with this augmented capital, we obtain at the end of the following year.

$$\begin{aligned} &I.\ 4{,}400_c + 1{,}100_v + 1{,}100_s = 6{,}600 \\ &II.\ 1{,}600_c + 800_v + 800_s = 3{,}200 \end{aligned} \quad = 9{,}800.$$

Marx, *Capital,* II (1885), excerpts from Chap. 21.

B. CAPITAL ACCUMULATION, UNEMPLOYMENT AND THE FALLING RATE OF PROFIT

Leaving aside the intricacies of his reproduction schemes, Marx's basic vision of the capitalist growth process may be summarized as follows. Investment of surplus values both raises production and, by embodying new technologies, increases productivity. Given the organic composition of capital, capital accumulation stimulates an increased demand for labor, higher employment (and, as demand for labor begins to surpass its supply, increased wages), and thereby higher worker consumption. Technological improvements create new opportunities for profitable investment and bigger surpluses, while higher consumption enables capitalists to "realize" their surpluses through market exchange. For the various reasons noted earlier, capitalists generally can be relied on to reinvest most of their surpluses, thus sustaining and extending the growth process.

If something like this did not occur, the progressive properties of capitalism described in chapter 3 would have scanty foundation. But if the capitalist growth process occurred *exactly* like this, it would diverge considerably from the realities of capitalist development, which includes crises, cyclical economic fluctuations, and unemployment.

One of Marx's central hypotheses regarding the relations between capital accumulation and unemployment is presented in selection 6.B.3. According to Marx, technological improvements, accompanied by the "concentration and centralization of capital" (see selection 7.A.1, below), fosters an increase in the ratio of constant capital to labor (what Marx calls the "technical composition of capital") and thereby the organic composition of capital, c/v.[3] Consequently, the variable component in total capital (v) falls *relative* to total capital (c + v). Because the demand for labor is determined by the "variable constituent [of total capital] alone", the *relative* demand for labor falls as the accumulation process proceeds. On the side of the supply of labor, several factors combine to increase the likelihood of unemployment. First, the high productivity capitalist sector expands relative to the low productivity noncapitalist sector in the growth process, stimulating an exodus of labor, essentially from agriculture, into "modern industry," swelling the capitalist labor force. Second, increased mechanization combines with depression and tendencies toward centralization of capital to drive small businessmen into the proletariat. Third, rising wages

[3]This effect could be offset, however, if rising productivity were to reduce costs of producing constant capital and thereby prices of such capital goods as machinery. Thus, Marx did not demonstrate definitively that an increase in the "technical composition of capital" *must* be accompanied by an increase in the value of the "organic composition of capital."

during business expansion quicken the pace of the substitution of labor-saving machinery for periodically expensive labor.

The combined result of these demand and supply forces on the labor market, Marx believed, is the creation and secular enlargement of an "industrial reserve army" of the unemployed. This reserve army has important functions in Marx's analysis. It serves as a strategic "lever of capital accumulation," by providing a pool of readily available labour to facilitate capitalism's sudden expansion in one direction or another. Overall, its effect is to dampen wages. During booms, it keeps labor's "pretensions in check" by preventing wages from encroaching unduly on surpluses. Further, as will be described more fully (see chapter 7A, below), it is an important factor in the class struggle and the growing intensity of capitalism's socioeconomic conflicts and contradictions.

Paradoxically, the very process that increases surplus values and contributes to technological unemployment (a rising c/v) raises the spectre of a falling rate of profit (selection 6.B.4). In contrast to Ricardo's theory, however, (cf. chapter 3, above), Marx's vision of falling profit rates is linked to systemic forces within capitalism rather than to factors in the natural environment that would constrain any economic system.

Marx defines the rate of profit as the ratio of surplus to investment in total capital: s/(c + v). Dividing both numerator and denominator by v, this ratio may be reformulated conveniently as follows:

$$\text{Rate of Profit} \quad \frac{s}{c + v} = \frac{s/v}{c/v + 1}$$

Consequently, the rate of profit varies directly with s/v and inversely with c/v. If, for purposes of illustration, we take s/v as given, then the increase in c/v leads to a decrease in s/(c + v).

Clearly, however, this version of the falling rate of profit cannot be the end of the matter, for increases in c/v may generally be expected to stimulate (not merely to be associated with) increases in s/v. What happens to s/(c + v) in this event depends on the relative magnitudes of change in c/v and s/v. If an increase in labor productivity raises s/v sufficiently to more than offset the increase in c/v, the rate of profit, not merely its absolute level, will *rise,* not fall. Marx's more sophisticated version rests on the view that it will become increasingly difficult to expand s/v through rising labor productivity as the *relative* amount of surplus-creating labor power, or v/c, falls with the rising organic composition of capital. It is harder to extract a given amount of surplus value from two workers, even if they work twelve hours a day. Marx argues pointedly, than it is from twenty four workers, even if they work only two hours a day. The more advanced capitalism becomes, the more "terribly" it must expand productivity to add new surpluses. Surplus values rise, but "in an ever smaller relation to the development of the productive force. . . . The smaller already the fractional part falling to *necessary labour,* the greater the *surplus labour,* the less can any increase in productive force perceptibly diminish necessary labour."[4]

[4]Karl Marx, *The Grundrisse (Outlines of the Critique of Political Economy)* (New York: Random House, 1973), p. 340. If innovations embodying higher ratios of c to v do lead to lower rates of profit, one wonders why capitalists would innovate. Marx's answer, presented at the end of selection 6.B.4, emphasizes a dynamic process in which innovators, under competitive pressures, obtain special, but temporary, innovational profits, temporary because the generalization of the innovation brings a decrease in the rate of profit beyond the control of the individual capitalist.

However, even this more sophisticated version is modified by Marx in the light of "counteracting influences. . . which thwart and annul the effects of this general law, leaving it merely the character of a tendency . . . whose effects become clearly marked only under certain conditions and in the course of long periods." As identified in selection 6.B.5 these include: (1) increasing the intensity of exploitation; (2) depressing wages below the value of labor power; (3) capital-saving innovations, which reduce c/v; (4) growth of industries with a low organic composition of capital; and (5) foreign trade.

6.B.3 ACCUMULATION AND THE INDUSTRIAL RESERVE ARMY

The Increased Demand For Labour-Power That Accompanies Accumulation, The Composition Of Capital Remaining The Same.

[Now] we consider the influence of the growth of capital on the lot of the labouring class. The most important factor in this inquiry is the composition of capital and the changes it undergoes in the course of the process of accumulation.

The composition of capital is to be understood in a two-fold sense. On the side of value, it is determined by the proportion in which it is divided into constant capital or value of the means of production, and variable capital or value of labour-power, the sum total of wages. On the side of material, as it functions in the process of production, all capital is divided into means of production and living labour-power. This latter composition is determined by the relation between the mass of labour necessary for their employment on the other. I call the former the *value-composition,* the latter the *technical composition* of capital. Between the two there is a strict correlation. To express this, I call the value-composition of capital, in so far as it is determined by its technical composition and mirrors the changes of the latter, the *organic composition* of capital. Wherever I refer to the composition of capital, without further qualification, its organic composition is always understood. . . .

Growth of capital involves growth of its variable constitutent or of the part invested in labour-power. A part of the surplus-value turned into additional capital must always be re-transformed into variable capital, or additional labour-fund. If we suppose that, all other circumstances remaining the same, the composition of capital also remains constant (i.e., that a definite mass of means of production constantly needs the same mass of labour-power to set it in motion,) then the demand for labour and the subsistence-fund of the labourers clearly increase in the same proportion as the capital, and the more rapidly, the more rapidly the capital increases. Since the capital produces yearly a surplus-value, of which one part is yearly added to the original capital; since this increment itself grows yearly along with the augmentation of the capital already functioning; since lastly, under special stimulus to enrichment, such as the opening of new markets, or of new spheres for the outlay of capital in consequence of newly developed social wants, etc., the scale of accumulation may be suddenly extended, merely by a change in the division of the surplus-value or surplus-product into capital and revenue, the requirements of accumulating capital may exceed the increase of labour-power or of the number of labourers; the demand for labourers may exceed the supply, and, therefore, wages may rise. This must, indeed, ultimately be the case if the conditions supposed above continue. For since in each year more labourers are employed than in its predecessor, sooner or later a point must be reached, at which the requirements of accumulation begin to surpass the customary supply of labour, and, therefore, a rise of wages takes place. . . . The more or less favourable circumstances in which the wage-working class supports and multiplies itself, in no way alter the fundamental character of capitalist production. As simple reproduction constantly reproduces the capital-relation itself, i.e., the relation of capitalists on the one hand, and wage-workers on the other, so reproduction on a progressive scale, i.e., accumulation, reproduces the capital relation on a progressive scale, more capitalists or larger capitalists at this pole, more wage-workers at that. The reproduction of a mass of labour-power, which must incessantly reincorporate itself with capital for that capital's self-expansion; which cannot get free from capital, and whose enslavement to capital is only concealed by the variety of individual capitalists to whom it sells itself, this reproduction of labour-power forms, in fact, an essential of the reproduction of capital itself. Accumulation of capital is, therefore, increase of the proletariat. . . .

The Industrial Reserve Army

The specifically capitalist mode of production, the development of the productive power of labour corresponding to it, and the change thence resulting in the organic composition of capital, do not merely keep pace with the advance of accumulation, or with the growth of social wealth. They develop at a much quicker rate, because mere accumulation, the absolute increase of the total social capital, is accompanied by the centralisation of the individual capitals of which that total is made up; and because the change in the technological composition of the additional capital goes hand in hand with a similar change in the technological composition of the original capital. With the advance of accumulation, therefore, the proportion of constant to variable capital changes. . . . Since the demand for labour is determined not by the amount of capital as a whole, but by its variable constituent alone, that demand falls progressively with the increase of the total capital, instead of, as previously assumed, rising in proportion to it. It falls relatively to the magnitude of the total capital, and at an accelerated rate, as this magnitude increases. With the growth of the total capital, its variable constituent or the labour incorporated in it, also does increase, but in a constantly diminishing proportion. The intermediate pauses are shortened, in which accumulation works as simple extension of production, on a given technical basis. It is not merely that an accelerated accumulation of total capital, accelerated in a constantly growing progression, is needed to absorb an additional number of labourers, or even, on account of the constant metamorphosis of old capital, to keep employed those already functioning. In its turn, this increasing accumulation and centralisation becomes a source of new changes in the composition of capital, of a more accelerated diminution of its variable, as compared with its constant constituent. This accelerated relative diminution of the variable constituent, that goes along with the accelerated increase of the total capital, and moves more rapidly than this increase, takes the inverse form, at the other pole, of an apparently absolute increase of the labouring population, an increase always moving more rapidly than that of the variable capital or the means of employment. But in fact, it is capitalistic accumulation itself that constantly produces, and produces in the direct ratio of its own energy and extent, a relatively redundant population of labourers, i.e., a population of greater extent than suffices for the average needs of the self-expansion of capital, and therefore a surplus-population.

Considering the social capital in its totality, the movement of its accumulation now causes periodical changes, affecting it more or less as a whole, now distributes its various phases simultaneously over the different spheres of production. In. . . all spheres, the increase of the variable part of capital, and therefore of the number of labourers employed by it, is always connected with violent fluctuations and transitory production of surplus-population, whether this takes the more striking form of the repulsion of labourers already employed, or the less evident but not less real form of the more difficult absorption of the additional labouring population through the usual channels. With the magnitude of social capital already functioning, and the degree of its increase, with the extension of the scale of production, and the mass of the labourers set in motion, with the development of the productiveness of their labour, with the greater breadth and fulness of all sources of wealth, there is also an extension of the scale on which greater attraction of labourers by capital is accompanied by their greater repulsion; the rapidity of the change in the organic composition of capital, and in its technical form increases, and an increasing number of spheres of production becomes involved in this change, now simultaneously, now alternately. The labouring population therefore produces, along with the accumulation of capital produced by it, the means by which itself is made relatively superfluous, is turned into a relative surplus population; and it does this to an always increasing extent. This is a law of population peculiar to the capitalist mode of production. . . .

But if a surplus labouring population is a necessary product of accumulation or of the development of wealth on a capitalist basis, this surplus population becomes, conversely, the lever of capitalistic accumulation, nay, a condition of existence of the capitalist mode of production. It forms a disposable industrial reserve army, that belongs to capital quite as absolutely as if the latter had bred it at its own cost. Independently of the limits of the actual increase of population, it creates, for the changing needs of the self-expansion of capital, a mass of human material always ready for exploitation. With accumulation, and the development of the productiveness of labour that accompanies it, the power of sudden expansion of capital grows also; it grows, not merely because the elasticity of the capital already functioning increases, not merely because the absolute wealth of society expands, of which capital only forms an elastic part, not merely because credit, under every special stimulus, at once places an unusual part of this wealth at the disposal of production in the form of additional capital; it grows, also, because the technical conditions of the process of production themselves—machinery, means of transport, etc.—now admit of the rapidest transformation of masses of surplus product into additional means of production. The mass of social wealth, overflowing with the advance of accumulation, and transformable into additional capital, thrusts itself frantically into old branches of production, whose market suddenly expands, or into newly formed branches, such as railways, etc., the need for which grows out of the development of the old ones. In all such cases, there must be the possibility of throwing great masses of men suddenly on the decisive points without injury to the scale of production in other spheres. Overpopulation supplies these masses. The course characteristic of modern industry, viz., a decennial cycle (interrupted by smaller oscillations), of periods of average activity, production at high pressure, crisis and stagnation, depends on the constant formation, the greater or less absorption, and the reformation of the industrial reserve army of surplus population. In their turn, the varying phases of the industrial cycle recruit the surplus population, and become one of the most energetic agents of its reproduction. This peculiar course of modern industry, which occurs in no earlier period of human history, was also impossible in the childhood of capitalist production. The composition of capital changed but very slowly. With its accumulation, therefore, there kept pace, on the whole, a corresponding growth in the demand for labour. . . . The expansion by fits and starts of the scale of production is the preliminary to its equally sudden contraction; the latter again evokes the former, but the former is impossible without disposable human material, without an increase in the number of labourers independently of the absolute growth of the population. This increase is effected by the simple process that constantly "sets free" a part of the labourers; by methods which lessen the number of labourers employed in proportion to the increased production. The whole form of the movement of modern industry depends, therefore, upon the constant transformation of a part of the labouring population into unemployed or half-employed hands. The superficiality of Political Economy shows itself in the fact that it looks upon the expansion and contraction of credit, which is a mere symptom of the periodic changes of the industrial cycle, as their cause. As the heavenly bodies, once thrown into a certain definite motion, always repeat this, so is it with social production as soon as it is once thrown into this movement of alternate expansion and contraction. Effects, in their turn, become causes, and the varying accidents of the whole process, which always reproduces its own conditions, take on the form of periodicity. . . .

We have seen that the development of the capitalist mode of production and of the productive power of labour—at once the cause and effect of accumulation—enables the capitalist, with the same outlay of variable capital, to set in action more labour by greater exploitation (extensive or intensive) of each individual labour-power. We have further seen that the capitalist buys with the same capital a greater mass of labour-power, as he progressively replaces skilled labourers by less skilled, mature labour-power by immature, male by female, that of adults by that of young persons or children.

On the one hand, therefore, with the progress of accumulation, a larger variable capital sets more labour in action without enlisting more labourers; on the other, a variable capital of the same magnitude sets in action more labour with the same mass of labour-power; and, finally, a greater number of inferior labour-power by displacement of higher.

The production of a relative surplus-population, or the setting free of labourers, goes on therefore yet more rapidly than the technical revolution of the process of production that accompanies, and is accelerated by, the advances of accumulation; and more rapidly than the corresponding diminution of the variable part of capital as compared with the constant. If the means of production, as they increase in extent and effective power, become to a less extent means of employment of labourers, this state of things is again modified by the fact that in proportion as the productiveness of labour increases, capital increases its supply of labour more quickly than its demand for labourers. The over-work of the employed part of the working class swells the ranks of the reserve, whilst conversely the greater pressure that the latter by its competition exerts on the former, forces these to submit to overwork and to subjugation under the dictates of capital. The condemnation of one part of the working-class to enforced idleness by the over-work of the other part, and the converse, becomes a means of enriching the individual capitalists, and accelerates at the same time the production of the industrial reserve army on a scale corresponding with the advance of social accumulation. How important is this element in the formation of the relative surplus-population, is shown by the example of England. Her technical means for saving labour are colossal. Nevertheless, if tomorrow morning labour generally were reduced to a rational amount, and proportioned to the different sections of the working-class according to age and sex, the working population to hand would be absolutely insufficient for the carrying on of national production on its present scale. The great majority of the labourers now "unproductive" would have to be turned into "productive" ones.

Taking them as a whole, the general movements of wages are exclusively regulated by the expansion and contraction of the industrial reserve army, and these again correspond to the periodic changes of the industrial cycle. They are, therefore, not determined by the variations of the absolute number of the working population, but by the varying proportions in which the working class is divided into active and reserve army, by the increase or diminution in the relative amount of the surplus-population, by the extent to which it is now absorbed, now set free. . . .

The industrial reserve army, during the periods of stagnation and average prosperity, weighs down the active labour-army; during the periods of over-production and paroxysm, it holds its pretensions in check. Relative surplus-population is therefore the pivot upon which the law of demand and supply of labour works. It confines the field of action of this law within the limits absolutely convenient to the activity of exploitation and to the domination of capital.

Different Forms of the Relative Surplus-Population. The General Law of Capitalistic Accumulation.

The relative surplus population exists in every possible form. Every labourer belongs to it during the time when he is only partially employed or wholly unemployed. Not taking into account the great periodically recurring forms that the changing phases of the industrial cycle impress on it, now an acute form during the crisis, then again a chronic form during dull times—it has always three forms, the floating, the latent, the stagnant.

In the centres of modern industry—factories, manufacturers, iron-workers, mines, etc.—the labourers are sometimes repelled, sometimes attracted again in greater masses, the number of those employed increasing on the whole, although in a constantly decreasing proportion to the scale of production. Here the surplus population exists in the floating form.

In the automatic factories, as in all the great workshops, where machinery enters as a factor, or where only the modern divisions of labour is carried out, large numbers of boys are employed up to the age of maturity. When this term is once reached, only a very small number continue to find employment in the same branches of industry, whilst the majority are regularly discharged. This majority forms an element of the floating surplus-population, growing with the extension of those branches of industry. . . . That the natural increase of the number of labourers does not satisfy the requirements of the accumulation of capital, and yet all the time is in excess of them, is a contradiction inherent to the movement of capital itself. It wants larger numbers of youthful labourers, a smaller number of adults. The contradiction is not more glaring than that other one that there is a complaint of the want of hands, while at the same time many thousands are out of work, because the division of labour chains them to a particular branch of industry. . . .

As soon as capitalist production takes possession of agriculture, and in proportion to the extent to which it does so, the demand for an agricultural labouring population falls absolutely, while the accumulation of the capital employed in agriculture advances, without this repulsion being, as in non-agricultural industries, compensated by a greater attraction. Part of the agricultural population is therefore constantly on the point of passing over into an urban or manufacturing proletariat, and on the look-out for circumstances favourable to this transformation. . . . This source of relative surplus-population is thus constantly flowing. But the constant flow towards the towns presupposes, in the country itself, a constant latent surplus-population, the extent of which becomes evident only when its channels of outlet open to exceptional width. The agricultural labourer is therefore reduced to the minimum of wages, and always stands with one foot already in the swamp of pauperism.

The third category of the relative surplus-population, the stagnant, forms a part of the active labour army, but with extremely irregular employment. Hence it furnishes to capital an inexhaustible reservoir of disposable labour-power. Its conditions of life sink below the average normal level of the working class; this makes it at once the broad basis of special branches of capitalist exploitation. It is characterized by maximum of working time, and minimum of wages. . . . It recruits itself constantly from the supernumerary forces of modern industry and agriculture, and specially from those decaying branches of industry where handicraft is yielding to manufacture, manufacture to machinery. Its extent grows, as with the extent and energy of accumulation, the creation of a surplus population advances. . . .

The lowest sediment of the relative surplus-population finally dwells in the sphere of pauperism. Exclusive of vagabonds, criminals, prostitutes, in a word, the "dangerous" classes, this layer of society consists of three categories. First, those able to work. One need only glance superfically at the statistics of English pauperism to find that the quantity of paupers increases with every crisis, and diminishes with every revival of trade. Second, orphans and pauper children. These are candidates for the industrial reserve-army, and are, in times of great prosperity, as 1860, e.g., speedily and in large numbers enrolled in the active army of labourers. Third, the demoralized and ragged, and those unable to work, chiefly people who succumb to their incapacity for adaptation, due to the division of labour; people who have passed the normal age of the labourer; the victims of industry, whose number increases with the increase of dangerous machinery, of mines, chemical works, etc., the mutilated, the sickly, the widows, etc. Pauperism is the hospital of the active labour-army and the dead weight of the industrial reserve-army. Its production is included in that of the relative surplus-population, its necessity in theirs; along with the surplus-population, pauperism forms a conditon of capitalist production, and of the capitalist development of wealth. . . .

The greater the social wealth, the functioning capital, the extent and energy of its growth, and, therefore, also the absolute mass of the proletariat and the productiveness of its labour, the greater is the industrial reserve-army. The same causes which develop the expansive power of capital, develops also the labour-power at its disposal. The relative mass of the industrial reserve-army increases therefore with the potential energy of wealth. But the greater this reserve-army in proportion to the active labour-army, the greater is the mass of a consolidated surplus-population, whose misery is in inverse ratio to its torment of labour. The more extensive, finally, the lazurus-layers of the working-class, and the industrial reserve-army, the greater is official pauperism. *This is the absolute general law of capitalist accumulation.*

Marx, *Capital,* I (1867), Chap. 25.

6.B.4 THE FALLING RATE OF PROFIT

THE BASIC THEORY

With a given wage and working day, a certain variable capital, for instance of 100, represents a certain number of employed laborers. It is the index of this number. For instance, let 100 p.st. be the wages of 100 labourers for one week. If these labourers perform the same amount of necessary as of surplus-labour, in other words, if they work daily as much time for themselves as they do for the capitalist, or, in still other words, if they require as much time for the reproduction of their wages as they do for the production of surplus-value for the capitalist, then they would produce a total value of 200 p.st., and the surplus value would amount to 100 p.st. The rate of surplus-value, s/v, would be 100%. But . . . this rate of surplus-value would express itself in considerably different rates of profit, according to the different volumes of constant capitals c and consequently of total capitals C. For the rate of profit is calculated by the formula s/C.

Take it that the rate of surplus-value is 100%. Now, if

c = 50, and v = 100,	then p′ = 100/150,	or 66⅓%.
c = 100, and v = 100,	then p′ = 100/200,	or 50 %.
c = 200, and v = 100,	then p′ = 100/300,	or 33⅓%.
c = 300, and v = 100,	then p′ = 100/400,	or 25 %.
c = 400, and v = 100,	then p′ = 100/500,	or 20 %.

In this way, the same rate of surplus-value, with the same degree of labour exploitation, would express itself in a falling rate of profit, because the material growth of the constant capital, and consequently of the total capital, implies their growth in value, although not in the same proportion.

If it is furthermore assumed that this gradual change in the composition of capital is not confined to some individual spheres of production, but occurs more or less in all, or at least in the most important ones, so that they imply changes in the organic average composition of the total capital of a certain society, then the gradual and relative growth of the constant over the variable capital must necessarily lead to *a gradual fall of the average rate of profit,* so long as the rate of surplus-value, or the intensity of exploitation of labour by capital, remain the same. Now we have seen that it is one of the laws of capitalist production that its development carries with it a relative decrease of variable as compared with constant capital, and consequently as compared to the total capital, which it sets in motion. This is only another way of saying that the same number of labourers, the same quantity of labour-power set in motion by a variable capital of a given value consume in production an ever increasing quantity of means of production, such as machinery and all sorts of fixed capital raw and auxiliary materials, and consequently a constant capital of ever increasing value and volume, during the same period of time, owing to the peculiar methods of production developing within the capitalist system. This progressive relative decrease of the variable capital as compared to the constant, and consequently to the total, capital is identical with the progressive higher organic composition of the average social capital. It is, in another way, but an expression of the progressive development of the productive powers of society, which is manifested by the fact that the same number of labourers, in the same time, convert an ever growing quantity of raw and auxiliary materials into products, thanks to the growing application of machinery and fixed capital in general, so that less labour is needed for the production of the same, or of more, commodities. This growing value and volume of constant capital corresponds to a progressive cheapening of products, although the increase in the value of the constant capital indicates but imperfectly the growth in the actual mass of use-values represented by the material of the constant capital. Every individual product, taken by itself, contains a smaller quantity of labour than the same product did on a lower scale of production, in which the capital invested in wages occupies a far greater space compared to the capital invested in means of production. The hypothetical series placed at the beginning of this [reading] expresses, therefore, the actual tendency of capitalist production.

This mode of production produces a progressive decrease of the variable capital as compared to the constant capital, and consequently a continuously rising organic composition of the total capital. The immediate result of this is that the rate of surplus-value, at the same degree of labour-exploitation, expresses itself in a continually falling average rate of profit. (We shall see later why this fall does not manifest itself in an absolute form, but rather as a tendency toward a progressive fall.) This progressive tendency of the average rate of profit to fall is, therefore, but a peculiar expression of capitalist production for the fact that the social productivity of labour is progressively increasing. This is not saying that the rate of profit may not fall temporarily for other reasons. But it demonstrates at least that it is the nature of the capitalist mode of production, and a logical necessity of its development, to give expression to the average rate of surplus-value by a falling rate of average profit. Since the mass of the employed living labour is continually on the decline compared to the mass of materialised labour incorporated in productively consumed means of production, it follows that that portion of living labour, which is unpaid and represents surplus-value, must also be continually on the decrease compared to the volume and value of the invested total capital. Seeing that the proportion of the mass of surplus-value to the value of the invested total capital forms the rate of profit, this rate must fall continuously. . . .

The law of the falling tendency of the rate of profit, or of the relative decline of the appropriated surplus-labour compared to the mass of materialised labor set in motion by living labour does not argue in any way against the fact that the absolute mass of the employed and exploited labour set in motion by the social capital, and consequently the absolute mass of the surplus-labour appropriated by it, may grow. Nor does it argue against the fact that the capitals controlled by individual capitalists may dispose of a growing mass of labour and surplus-labour, even though the number of the labourers employed by them may not grow.

Take for illustration's sake a certain population of working people, for instance, two millions. Assume, furthermore, that the length and intensity of the average working day, and the level of wages, and thereby the proportion between necessary and surplus-labour, are given. In that case the aggregate labour of these two millions, and their surplus-labour expressed in surplus-value, represent always the same magnitude of values. But with the growth of the mass of the constant (fixed and circulating) capital, which this labour manipulates, the proportion of this produced quantity of values declines as compared to the value of this total capital. And the value of this capital grows with its mass, although not in the same proportion. This proportion, and consequently the rate of profit, falls in spite of the fact that the same mass of living labour is controlled as before, and the same amount of surplus-labour absorbed by the capital. This proportion changes, not because the mass of living labour decreases, but because the mass of the materialised labour set in motion by living labour increases. It is a relative decrease, not an absolute one, and has really nothing to do with the absolute magnitude of the labour and surplus-labour set in motion. The fall of the rate of profit is not due to an absolute, but only to a relative decrease of the variable part of the total capital, that is, its decrease as compared with the constant part.

The same thing which applies to any given mass of labour and surplus-labour, applies also to a growing number of labourers, and thus under the above assumptions, to any growing mass of the controlled labour in general and to its unpaid part, the surplus-labour, in particular. If the labouring population increases from two million to three million, if, furthermore, the variable capital invested in wages also rises to three million from its former amount of two million, while the constant capital rises from four million to fifteen million, then the mass of surplus-labour, and of surplus-value, under the above assumption of a constant working day and a constant rate of surplus-value, rises by 50%, that is, from two million to three million. Nevertheless, in spite of this growth in the absolute mass of surplus-labour and surplus-value by 50%, the proportion of the variable to the constant capital would fall from 2:4 to 3:15, and the proportion of the surplus-value to the total capital, expressed in millions, would be

$$\text{I. } 4c + 2v + 2s;\ C = 6,\ p' = 33\tfrac{1}{3}\%.$$
$$\text{II. } 15c + 3v + 3s;\ C = 18,\ p' = 16\tfrac{2}{3}\%.$$

While the mass of surplus-value has increased by one-half, the rate of profit has fallen by one-half. However, the profit is only the surplus-value calculated on the total social capital, so that its absolute magnitude, socially considered, is the same as the absolute magnitude of the surplus-value. In this case, the absolute magnitude of the profit would have grown by 50%, in spite of its enormous relative decrease compared to the advanced total capital, or in spite of the enormous fall of the average rate of profit. We see, then, that in spite of the progressive fall of the rate of profit, there may be an absolute increase of the number of labourers employed by capital, an absolute increase of the labor set in motion by it, an absolute increase of the mass of surplus-labor absorbed, a resulting absolute increase of the produced surplus-value, and consequently an absolute increase in the mass of the produced profit. And this increase may be progressive. And it *may* not only be so. On the basis of capitalist production, *it must* be so, aside from temporary fluctuations.

The capitalist process of production is essentially a process of accumulation. We have shown that the mass of values, which must be simply reproduced and maintained, increases progressively with the development of capitalist production to the extent that the productivity of labour grows, even if the employed labour-power should remain constant. But the development of social productivity carries with it a still greater increase of the produced use-values, of which the means of production form a part. And the additional labour, whose appropriation reconverts this additional value into capital, does not depend on the value, but on the mass of these means of production (including the means of subsistence), because the labourer in the productive process is not operating with the exchange-value, but with the use-value of the means of production. Accumulation itself, however, and the concentration of capital that goes with it, is a material means of increasing the productive power. Now, this growth of the means of production includes the increase of the labouring population, the creation of a labouring population which corresponds to the surplus-capital or even exceeds its general requirements, leading to an overpopulation of working people. A momentary excess of the surplus-capital over the labouring population controlled by it would have a twofold effect. It would, on the one hand, mitigate the conditons, which decimate the offspring of the labouring class and would facilitate marriages among them, by raising wages. This would tend to increase the labouring population. On the other hand, it would employ the methods by which relative surplus-value is created (introduction and improvement of machinery) and thereby create still more rapidly an artificial relative overpopulation, which in its turn would be a hothouse for the actual propagation of its numbers, since under capitalist production poverty propagates its kind. The nature of the capitalist process of accumulation, which process is but an element in the capitalist process of production, implies as a matter of course that the increased mass of means of production, which is to be converted into capital, must always find on hand a corresponding increase, or even an excess, of labouring people for exploitation. The progress of the process of production and accumulation *must,* therefore, be accompanied by a growth of the mass of available and appropriated surplus-labor, and consequently by a growth of the absolute mass of profit appropriated by the social capital. But the same laws of production and accumulation increase the volume and value of the constant capital in a more rapid progression than those of the variable capital invested in living labour. The same laws, then, produce for the social capital an increase in the absolute mass of profit and a falling rate of profit. . . .

The development of capitalist production and accumulation lifts the processes of labour to a higher scale and gives them greater dimensions, which imply larger investments of capital for each individual establishment. A growing concentration of capitals (accompanied by a growing number of capitalists, though not to the same extent) is therefore one of the material requirements of capitalist production as well as one of the results produced by it. Hand in hand with it, and mutually interacting, goes a progressive expropriation of the more or less direct producers. It is, then, a matter of course for the capitalists that they should control increasing armies of labourers (no matter how much the variable capital may relatively decrease in comparison to the constant capital), and that the mass of surplus-value, and of profit, appropriated by them, should grow simultaneously with the fall of the rate of profit, and in spite of it. The same causes which concentrate masses of labourers under the control of capitalists, are precisely those which also swell the mass of fixed capital, auxiliary and raw materials in a growing proportion as compared to the mass of the employed living labor.

It requires but a passing notice at this point, that, given a certain laboring population, the mass of surplus-value, and therefore the absolute mass of profit, must grow if the rate of surplus-value increases by a prolongation or intensification of the working day, or by a lowering of the value of wages through a development of the productive power of labour, and must do so in spite of the relative decrease of the variable capital compared to the constant.

The same development of the productive power of social labour, the same laws, which express themselves in a relative fall of the variable as compared to the total capital and in a correspondingly hastened accumulation, while this accumulation in its turn becomes the starting point of a further development of the productive power and of a further relative fall of the variable capital, this same development manifests itself, aside from temporary fluctuations, by a growing increase of the employed total labour-power, a growing increase of the absolute mass of surplus-value, and consequently of profits.

Now, in what form must this two-faced law with the same causes for a decrease of the *rate* of profits and a simultaneous increase of the absolute mass of profits show itself? . . .

If the variable capital decreases as compared to the constant, or to the total capital, then the rate of profit, or the relative magnitude of surplus-value calculated on the total capital, falls even though the intensity of exploitation were to remain the same, or even to increase. But it is not this relative magnitude alone which falls. The magnitude of the surplus-value or profit absorbed by the total capital of 100 also falls absolutely. At a rate of surplus-value of 100%, a capital of 60 + 40 produces a mass of surplus-value and profit amounting to 40; a capital of 70 c + 30 v a mass of profit of 30; a capital of 80 c + 20 v produces only 20 of profit. This fall refers to the mass of surplus-value, and thus of profit, and is due to the fact that the total capital of 100, with the same intensity of labour exploitation, employs less living labour, sets in motion less labour-power, and therefore produces less surplus-value. Taking any aliquot part of the social capital, that is, of capital of average composition, as a standard by which to measure surplus-value—and this is done in all calculations of profit—a relative fall of surplus-value is identical with its absolute fall. The rate of profit sinks in the above cases from 40% to 30% and 20%, because the mass of surplus-value, and of profit, produced by the same capital falls absolutely from 40 to 30 and 20. Since the magnitude of the value of capital, by which the surplus-value is measured, is given as 100, a fall in the proportion of surplus-value to this given magnitude can be only another expression for the fact that surplus-value and profit decrease absolutely. This is, of course, a tautology. But we have demonstrated that the nature of the capitalist process of production brings about this decrease.

On the other hand, the same causes which bring about an absolute decrease of surplus-value and profit on a given capital, and consequently in the percentage of the rate of profit, produce an increase of the absolute mass of surplus-value and profit appropriated by the total capital (that is, by the capitalists as a whole). How can this be explained, and what is the only way in which this can be explained, or what are the conditions on which this apparent contradiction is based?

While any aliquot part, any 100 of the social capital, any 100 of average social composition, is a given magnitude, for which a fall in the rate of profit implies a fall in the absolute magnitude of profit, just because the capital which serves as a standard of measurement is a constant magnitude, the magnitude of the social capital, on the other hand, as well as that of the capital in the hands of individual capitalists, is variable, and in keeping with our assumptions it must vary inversely to the decrease of its variable portion. . . .

We meet here once more the previously analysed law, that the relative decrease of the variable capital, or the development of the productive power of labour, requires an increasing mass of total capital for the purpose of setting in motion the same quantity of labour-power and absorbing the same quantity of surplus-labour. Consequently the possibility of a relative surplus of labouring people develops to the extent that capitalist production advances, not because the productive power of social labour *decreases,* but because it *increases.* Relative overpopulation does not arise out of an absolute disproportion between labour and means of subsistence, or of means for the production of these means of existence, but out of a disproportion due to the capitalist exploitation of labour, a disproportion between the growing increase of capital and its relatively decreasing demand for an increase of population.

A fall in the rate of profit by 50% means its fall by one-half. If the mass of profit is to remain the same, the capital must be doubled. In order that the mass of profit made at a declining rate of profit may remain the same as before, the multiplier indicating the growth of the total capital must be equal to the divisor indicating the fall of the rate of profit. . . . A capital of 1,000,000 at a rate of 40% produces 400,000, and a capital of 5,000,000 at a rate of 8% likewise produces 400,000. This applies, so long as the result is to remain the same. But if the result is to be higher, then the capital must grow at a faster rate than the rate of profit falls. In other words, in order that the variable portion of the total capital may not only remain the same, but may also increase absolutely, although its percentage in the total capital falls, the total capital must grow at a higher rate than the percentage of the variable capital falls. It must grow at such a rate that it requires in its new composition not merely the same old variable capital, but more than it for the purchase of labour-power. . . .

The law that the fall in the rate of profit due to the development of the productive powers is accompanied by an increase in the mass of profit expresses itself furthermore in the fact that a fall in the price of commodities produced by capital is accompanied by a relative increase of the masses of profit contained in them and realised by their sale.

Since the development of the productive powers and the higher composition of capital corresponding to it set in motion an ever increasing quantity of means of production with an ever decreasing quantity of labour, every aliquot part of the total product, every single commodity, or every particular quantity of commodities in the total mass of products absorbs less living labour, and also contains less materialised labour, both as to the wear and tear of fixed capital and to the raw and auxiliary materials consumed. Every single commodity, then, contains a smaller amount of labour materialised in means of production and of labour newly added during production. Hence the price of the individual commodity falls. The mass of profits contained in the individual commodities may nevertheless increase, if the rate of the absolute or relative surplus-value grows. The commodity then contains less newly added labour, but its unpaid portion grows over its paid portion. However, this is the case only within certain limits. In the course of the development of production, with the enormously growing absolute decrease of the amount of living labor newly embodied in the individual commodities, the mass of unpaid labour contained in them will likewise decrease absolutely, however much it may have grown as compared to their paid portion. The mass of profit on each individual commodity will decrease considerably with the development of the productive power of labour, in spite of the increase of the rate of surplus-value. And this reduction, the same as the fall in the rate of profits, is only delayed by the cheapening of the elements of constant capital and the other circumstances mentioned in the first part of this volume, which increase the rate of profit at a stable, or even falling, rate of surplus-value.

To say that the price of the individual commodities falls, which together make up the total product of the capital, is simply to say that a certain quantity of labour is realised in a larger quantity of commodities, so that each individual commodity contains less labour than before. This is the case even if the price of one of the parts of constant capital, such as raw material, etc., should rise. With the exception of a few cases (for instance, if the productive power of labour cheapens all the elements of constant and variable capital uniformly) the rate of profit will fall in spite of the increased rate of surplus-value, (1), because even a larger unpaid portion of the smaller total amount of newly added labour is smaller than a smaller aliquot portion of unpaid labour was in the former large amount of total labour, and (2), because the higher composition of the capital is expressed through the individual commodity by the fact that that portion of its value, in which newly added labour is materialised, decreases as compared to that portion of its value, which represents raw material, auxiliary material, and wear and tear of fixed capital. This change in the proportions of the various component parts of the price of the individual commodities, the decrease of that portion of their price, in which newly added labour is materialised, and the increase of that portion, in which formerly materialised labor is represented, is that form which expresses through the price of the individual commodities the decrease of the variable capital as compared to the constant capital. . . .

Although the *rate* of profit must be calculated by measuring the mass of the produced and realised surplus-value by the consumed portion of capital reappearing in the commodities as well as by the sum of this portion plus that portion of capital which, though not consumed, is employed and continues to serve in production, the *mass* of profit cannot be equal to anything but the mass of profit, or surplus-value, contained in the commodities themselves and to be realised by their sale.

If the productivity of industry increases, the prices of the individual commodities fall. There is less paid and unpaid labour contained in them. Let the same labour produce, say, thrice its former product. Then the individual product requires two-thirds less labour. And since the profit can constitute but a portion of the amount of labour congealed in the individual commodities, the mass of profit in the individual commodities must decrease. And this must hold good, within certain limits, even if the rate of surplus-value should rise. In any case, the mass of profits on the total product does not fall below the original mass of profits so long as the capital employs the same number of labourers at the same degree of exploitation. (This may also take place, if fewer labourers are employed at a higher rate of exploitation.) For to the same extent that the mass of profit on the individual product decreases does the number of products increase. The mass of profits remains the same, only it is distributed differently over the total amount of commodities. Nor does this alter the division of the amount of value created by newly added labour between the labourers and capitalists. The mass of profit cannot increase, so long as the same amount of labour is employed, unless the unpaid surplus-labor increases, or, supposing the intensity of exploitation to remain the same, unless the number of labourers grows. Or, both of these causes may, of course, combine to produce this result. In all these cases, which, however, according to our assumption, presuppose an increase of the constant capital as compared to the variable and an increase in the magnitude of the total capital, the individual commodity contains a smaller mass of profit and the rate of profit falls even if it is calculated on the individual commodity. A given quantity of additional labour is materialised in a larger quantity of commodities. The price of the individual commodities falls. Abstractly speaking, the rate of profit may remain the same, even though the price of the individual commodity may fall as a result of an increase in the productivity of labour and a simultaneous increase in the number of these cheaper commodities, for instance, if the increase in the productivity of labour extended its effects uniformly and simultaneously to all the elements of the commodities, so that the total price of the commodities would fall in the same proportion in which the productivity of labour would increase, while on the other hand the mutual relations of the different elements of the price of commodities would remain the same. The rate of profit might even rise, if a rise in the rate of surplus-value were accompanied by a considerable reduction in the value of the elements of constant, and particularly of fixed, capital. But in reality, as we have seen, the rate of profit will fall in the long run. In any case, a fall in the price of any individual commodity does not by itself give a clue to the rate of profit. Everything depends on the magnitude of the total capital invested in its production.

Marx, *Capital,* III (1894), pp. 347–69.

Innovation, Competition, And Falling Profit Rates

No capitalist voluntarily introduces a new method of production, no matter how much more productive it may be, and how much it may increase the rate of surplus-value, so long as it reduces the rate of profit. But every new method of production of this sort cheapens the commodities. Hence the capitalist sells them originally above their prices of production, or, perhaps, above their value. He pockets the difference, which exists between these prices of production and the market-prices of the other commodities produced at higher prices of production. He can do this, because the average labour time required socially for the production of these other commodities is higher than the labour time required under the new methods of production. His method of production is above the social average. But competition generalises it and subjects it to the general law. Then follows a fall in the rate of profit—perhaps first in this sphere of production, which gradually brings the others to its level—which is, therefore, wholly independent of the will of the capitalist.

It must be noted here, that this same law rules also those spheres of production, whose product passes neither directly nor indirectly into the consumption of the labourers or into the conditions under which their necessities are produced; it applies, therefore, also to those spheres of production, in which no cheapening of commodities can increase the relative surplus-value or cheapen labour-power. (It is true that a cheapening of constant capital may increase the rate of profit in all these lines while the exploitation of the labourer remains the same.) As soon as the new mode of production begins to expand, and thereby to furnish the tangible proof that these commodities can actually be produced more cheaply, the capitalists working under the old methods of production must sell their product below their full prices of production, because the value of these commodities has fallen, because the labour time required by these capitalists for the production of these commodities is longer than the social average. In one word—this appears as the effect of competition—these capitalists are compelled to introduce the new method of production, under which the proportion of the variable to the constant capital has been reduced.

Marx, *Capital,* III (1894), pp. 310–11.

6.B.5 COUNTERACTING FACTORS

If we consider the enormous development of the productive powers of labour, even comparing but the last thirty years with all former periods; if we consider in particular the enormous mass of fixed capital, aside from machinery in the strict meaning of the term, passing into the process of social production as a whole, then the difficulty, which has hitherto troubled the vulgar economists, namely that of finding an explanation for the falling rate of profit, gives way to its opposite, namely to the question; How is it that this fall is not greater and more rapid? There must be some counteracting influences at work, which thwart and annul the effects of this general law, leaving to it merely the character of a tendency. For this reason we have referred to the fall of the average rate of profit as a tendency to fall.

The following are the general counterbalancing causes:

Raising the Intensity of Exploitation

The rate at which labor is exploited, the appropriation of surplus-labour and surplus-value, is raised by a prolongation of the working day and an intensification of labor. These two points have been fully discussed . . . as incidents to the production of absolute and relative surplus-value. There are many ways of intensifying labour, which imply an increase of the constant capital as compared to the variable, and consequently a fall in the rate of profit, for instance setting a labourer to watch a larger number of machines. In such cases—and in the majority of manipulations serving to produce relative surplus-value—the same causes, which bring about an increase in the rate of surplus-value, may also imply a fall in the mass of surplus-value, looking upon the matter from the point of view of the total quantities of invested capital. But there are other means of intensification, such as increasing the speed of machinery, which although consuming more raw material, and, so far as the fixed capital is concerned, wearing out the machinery so much faster, nevertheless do not affect the relation of its value to the price of labour set in motion by it. It is particularly the prolongation of the working day, this invention of modern industry, which increases the mass of appropriated surplus-labour without essentially altering the proportion of the employed labour-power to the constant capital set in motion by it, and which tends to reduce this capital relatively, if anything. For the rest, we have already demonstrated—what constitutes the real secret of the tendency of the rate of profit to fall—that the manipulations made for the purpose of producing relative surplus-value amount on the whole to this: That on one side as much as possible of a certain quantity of labour is transformed into surplus-value, and that on the other hand as little labour as possible is employed in proportion to the invested capital, so that the same causes, which permit the raising of the intensity of exploitation, forbid the exploitation of the same quantity of labour by the same capital as before. These are the warring tendencies, which, while aiming at a raise in the rate of surplus-value, have at the same time a tendency to bring about a fall in the mass of surplus-value, and therefore of the rate of surplus-value produced by a certain capital. It is furthermore appropriate to mention at this point the extensive introduction of female and child labour, in so far as the whole family must produce a larger quantity of surplus-value for a certain capital than before, even in case the total amount of their wages should increase, which is by no means general.

Whatever tends to promote the production of relative surplus-value by mere improvements in methods, for instance in agriculture, without altering the magnitude of the invested capital, has the same effect. While the constant capital does not increase relatively to the variable in such cases, taking the variable capital as an index of the amount of labour-power employed, the mass of the product *does* increase in proportion to the labour-power employed. The same takes place, when the productive power of labour (whether its product passes into the consumption of the labourer or into the elements of constant capital) is freed from obstacles of circulation, of arbitrary or other restrictions which become obstacles in course of time, in short, of fetters of all kinds, without touching directly the proportion between the variable and the constant capital. . . .

The rise in the rate of surplus-value is a factor, which determines also the mass of surplus-value and thereby the rate of profit, for it takes place especially under conditions, in which, as we have seen, the constant capital is either not increased at all relatively to the variable capital, or not increased in proportion. This factor does not suspend the general law. But it causes that law to become more of a tendency, that is, a law whose absolute enforcement is checked, retarded, weakened, by counteracting influences. Since the same causes, which raise the rate of surplus-value (even a prolongation of the working time is a result of large scale industry), also tend to decrease the labour-power employed by a certain capital, it follows that these same causes also tend to reduce the rate of profit and to check the speed of this fall. If one labourer is compelled to perform as much labour as would be rationally performed by two, and if this is done under circumstances in which this one labourer can replace three, then this one will produce as much surplus-labour as was formerly produced by two, and to that extent the rate of surplus-value will have risen. But this one will not produce as much as formerly three, and to that extent the mass of surplus-value will have decreased. But this reduction in mass will be compensated, or limited, by the rise in the rate of surplus-value. If the entire population is employed at a higher rate of surplus-value, the mass of surplus-value will increase, although the population may remain the same. It will increase still more, if the population increases at the same time. And although this goes hand in hand with a relative reduction of the number of labourers employed in proportion to the magnitude of the total capital, yet this reduction is checked or moderated by the rise in the rate of surplus-value.

Before leaving this point, we wish to emphasize once more that, with a capital of a certain magnitude, the *rate* of surplus-value may rise, while its *mass* is decreasing, and vice versa. The mass of surplus-value is equal to the rate multiplied by the number of labourers; however, this rate is never calculated on the total, but only on the variable capital, actually only for a day at a time. On the other hand, with a given magnitude of a certain capital, the *rate of profit* can never fall or rise, without a simultaneous fall or rise in the *mass of surplus-value.*

Depression of Wages Below their Value

This is mentioned only empirically at this place, since it, like many other things, which might be enumerated here, has nothing to do with the general analysis of capital, but belongs in a presentation of competition, which is not given in this work. However, it is one of the most important causes checking the tendency of the rate of profit to fall.

Cheapening of the Elements of Constant Capital.

Everything that has been said. . . about the causes, which raise the rate of profit while the rate of surplus-value remains the same, or independently of the rate of surplus-value, belongs here. This applies particularly to the fact that, from the point of view of the total capital, the value of the constant capital does not increase in the same proportion as its material volume. For instance, the quantity of cotton, which a single European spinning operator works up in a modern factory, has grown in a colossal degree compared to the quantity formerly worked up by a European operator with a spinning wheel. But the value of the worked-up cotton has not grown in proportion to its mass. The same holds good of machinery and other fixed capital. In short, the same development, which increases the mass of the constant capital relatively over that of the variable, reduces the value of its elements as a result of the increased productivity of labour. In this way the value of the constant capital although continually increasing, is prevented from increasing at the same rate as its material volume, that is, the material volume of the means of production set in motion by the same amount of labour-power. In exceptional cases the mass of the elements of constant capital may even increase, while its value remains the same or even falls.

Relative Overpopulation

The production of a relative surplus-population is inseparable from the development of the productivity of labour expressed by a fall in the rate of profit, and the two go hand in hand. The relative overpopulation becomes so much more apparent in a certain country, the more the capitalist mode of production is developed in it. This, again, is on the one hand a reason, which explains why the imperfect subordination of labor to capital continues in many lines of production, and continues longer than seems at first glance compatible with the general stage of development. This is due to the cheapness and mass of the disposable or unemployed wage labourers, and to the greater resistance, which some lines of production, by their nature, oppose to a transformation of manufacture into machine production. On the other hand, new lines of production are opened up, especially for the production of luxuries, and these lines take for their basis this relative overpopulation set free in other lines of production by the increase of their constant capital. The new lines start out with living labour as their predominating element, and go by degrees through the same evolution as the other lines of production. In either case the variable capital constitutes a considerable proportion of the total capital and wages are below the average, so that both the rate and mass of surplus-value are exceptionally high. Since the average rate of profit is formed by leveling the rates of profit in the individual lines of production, the same cause, which brings about a falling tendency of the rate of profit, once more produces a counterbalance to this tendency and paralyses its effects more or less.

Foreign Trade

To the extent that foreign trade cheapens partly the elements of constant capital, partly the necessities of life for which the variable capital is exchanged, it tends to raise the rate of profit by raising the rate of surplus-value and lowering the value of the constant capital. It exerts itself generally in this direction by permitting an expansion of the scale of production. But by this means it hastens on one hand the process of accumulation, on the other the reduction of the variable as compared to the constant capital, and thus a fall in the rate of profit. In the same way the expansion of foreign trade, which is the basis of the capitalist mode of production in its stages of infancy, has become its own product in the further progress of capitalist development through its innate necessities, through its need of an ever expanding market. Here we see once more the dual nature of these effects. . . .

Another question, which by its special nature is really beyond the scope of our analysis, is the following: Is the average rate of profit raised by the higher rate of profit, which capital invested in foreign, and particularly in colonial trade realises?

Capitals invested in foreign trade are in a position to yield a higher rate of profit, because, in the first place, they come in competition with commodities produced in other countries with lesser facilities of production, so that an advanced country is enabled to sell its goods above their value even when it sells them cheaper than the competing countries. To the extent that the labour of the advanced countries is here exploited as a labour of a higher specific weight, the rate of profit rises, because labour which has not been paid as being of a higher quality is sold as such. The same condition may obtain in the relations with a certain country, into which commodities are exported and from which commodities are imported. This country may offer more materialised labor in goods than it receives, and yet it may receive in return commodities cheaper than it could produce them. In the same way a manufacturer, who exploits a new invention before it has become general, undersells his competitors and yet sells his commodities above their individual values, that is to say, he exploits the specifically higher productive power of the labour employed by him as surplus-value. By this means he secures a surplus-profit. On the other hand, capitals invested in colonies, etc., may yield a higher rate of profit for the simple reason that the rate of profit is higher there on account of the backward development, and for the added reason, that slaves, coolies, etc., permit a better exploitation of labour. We see no reason, why these higher rates of profit realised by capitals invested in certain lines and sent home by them should not enter as elements into the average rate of profit and tend to keep it up to that extent. . . .

And so we have seen in a general way, that the same causes, which produce a falling tendency in the rate of profit, also call forth counter-effects, which check and partly paralyse this fall. This law is not suspended, but its effect is weakened. Otherwise it would not be the fall of the average rate of profit, which would be unintelligible, but rather the relative slowness of this fall. The law therefore shows itself only as a tendency, whose effects become clearly marked only under certain conditions and in the course of long periods.

Before passing on to something new, we will, for the sake of preventing misunderstanding, repeat two statements, which we have substantiated at different times.

1) The same process, which brings about a cheapening of commodities in the course of development of the capitalist mode of production, also causes a change in the organic composition of the social capital invested in the production of commodities, and thereby lowers the rate of profit. We must be careful, then, not to confound the reduction in the relative cost of an individual commodity, including that portion of its cost which represents wear and tear of machinery, with the relative rise in the value of the constant as compared to the variable capital, although vice versa every reduction in the relative cost of the constant capital, whose material elements retain the same volume or increase in volume, tends to raise the rate of profit, in other words, tends to reduce the value of the constant capital to that extent as compared with the shrinking proportions of the employed variable capital.

2) The fact that the additional living labour contained in the individual commodities, which together make up the product of capital, stands in a decreasing proportion to the materials and instruments of labour consumed by them; the fact that an ever decreasing quantity of additional living labour is materialised in them, because their production requires less labour to the extent that the productive power of society is developed—this fact does not touch the proportion, according to which the living labour contained in the commodities is divided into paid and unpaid labour. On the other hand, although the total quantity of additional living labour contained in them decreases, the unpaid portion increases over the paid portion, either by an absolute, or by a proportional reduction of the paid portion; for the same mode of production, which reduces the total quantity of the additional living labour in the commodities, is accompanied by a rise of the absolute and relative surplus-value. The falling tendency of the rate of profit is accompa-

nied by a rising tendency of the rate of surplus-value, that is, in the rate of exploitation. Nothing is more absurd, for this reason, than to explain a fall in the rate of profit by a rise in the rate of wages, although there may be exceptional cases where this may apply. Statistics do not become available for actual analyses of the rates of wages in different epochs and countries, until the conditions, which shape the rate of profit, are thoroughly understood. The rate of profit does not fall, because labour becomes less productive, but because it becomes more productive. Both phenomena, the rise in the rate of surplus-value and the fall in the rate of profit, are but specific forms through which the productivity of labor seeks a capitalistic expression.

Marx, *Capital,* III (1894), pp. 272–81.

C. Crises and Cycles

According to Marx, the characteristic course of modern industry is a "decennial cycle (interrupted by smaller oscillations)" divided into phases or "periods of average activity, production at high pressure, crises and stagnation."[5] The cycle is the "characteristic reference" of Marx's analysis, as distinguished from the long-run equilibrium perspective of classical economics.[6] Capitalist crises—defined roughly as the moments of imbalance or disequilbrium between aggregate demand and supply at the peak of the cyclical expansion and thus the beginning of downward departures from the process of economic growth—and their succeeding cyclical depressions and recoveries serve several functions in Marx's analysis. First, they demonstrate a fundamental "contradiction" which arises "endogenously," from within the capitalist process itself. Second, ironically, they indirectly contribute to economic growth, both by pressuring capitalists to reduce cost and raise productivity and by stimulating sales promotion efforts to give "wares new charms, to inspire [consumers] with new needs by constant chatter, etc."[7] Third, though interrupting the growth process, they prepare the way for renewal of expansion on an enlarged scale, thus leading capitalism back to the point where it is able to go on "fully employing its productive powers without committing suicide."[8] Fourth, because they are the "most striking form in which advice is given [capitalism] to be gone and to give room to a higher state of social production,"[9] they constitute one of the most compelling reasons for capitalism's impending demise.

In his preface to Marx's *Capital,* Engels stated that the cyclical pattern of 1825 to 1867 had been replaced by a "permanent and chronic depression"[10] or at least, as noted elsewhere, "a more chronic alteration between a relatively short and slight business improvement and a relatively long, undecided depression."[11] Although there is some evidence that Marx supported this view (e.g., according to Marx, cyclical expansion reduces but does not necessarily eliminate labor

[5]Marx, *Capital,* Vol. I (New York: Modern Library, n.d.), p. 694.

[6]Leo Rogin, *The Meaning and Validity of Economic Theory* (New York: Harper, 1956), p. 376.

[7]Marx, *The Grundrisse* (New York: Random House, 1973), p. 287.

[8]*Ibid.,* p. 750.

[9]*Ibid.*

[10]Engels, in Marx, *Capital,* Vol. I, *op. cit.,* p. 31.

[11]Engels, in Marx, *Capital,* Vol. III (Chicago: Kerr, 1909), p. 574n.

unemployment—recall selection 6.A.1), his general focus was on the cycle rather than chronic depression. "There are no permanent crises," he observed pointedly.[12]

Although Marx never transformed this strong interest in cyclical fluctuations into a fully integrated "model," his commentary may be organized readily around several major questions. Why is there a cyclical expansion rather than simply steady growth? Why are there crises and downturns from the growth process? Why do cyclical downturns spread throughout the economy, thereby turning into depressions? Why does the capitalistic economy recover from depression rather than stagnating in chronic depression?

Marx's answer to the first question has already been presented briefly (selection 6.B.3), in the context of capital accumulation in general, There, we find Marx postulating periods of vigorous and "sudden expansion" in capital accumulation, based on capitalism's growing wealth, expansion of credit, and rapid exploitation of new technological and market opportunities. Expansion proceeds by "fits and starts" also because of competition and the absence, under capitalism, of an overall social plan coordinating investment activities of different enterprises.

Marx explores the second question, from various perspectives, in each of the following three selections. The ever present *possibility* of a crisis arises from two sources: "(1) the separation of purchase and sale, inevitable in any money economy, and (2) the fact that money, the universal store of value, is used as a means of payment to bridge this separation."[13] On these grounds, Marx roundly rejects "Say's Law," at least in the form of the "dogma" which "necessarily implies an equilibrium of sales and purchase" (selections 6.C.6, 6.C.7).

However, although the characteristic form of the crisis is one of macroeconomic disequilibrium (excess demand for money, excess supply of goods), the underlying causes are deeper than monetary imbalance, which could occur under any exchange economy, including simple commodity production. Under capitalism, crises are not merely possible, but highly probable. "That which appears as a crisis on the money market is in reality an expression of abnormal conditions in the process of production and reproduction."[14] Major candidates (selections 6.C.7, 6.C.8) include periodic (not merely secular or long-run) tendencies for profit rates to fall, partly because irregular accelerated bursts of capital accumulation raise the demand for labor and increase wages, which thereby may threaten to encroach on profits and momentarily check the pace of accumulation ("production crises"), partly because capitalism's proclivities to invest are made independent of and may well periodically prove to be out of balance with working class capacity to consume ("realization crises").

In explaining why the crisis becomes generalized and why the downturn instead of moving quickly back to stable equilibrium, disequilibrates further in a widening and deepening process of cyclical contraction and depression, "Marx reveals himself at his best. Here we have an explicit and quite well developed theory"[15] (see selections 6.C.7, 6.C.8). Falling profit rates stimulate increased hoarding and an excess demand for money. This causes reductions in the demand for goods, with resulting disruptions in price-profit relations. This in turn "paralyses the function of money as a medium of payment [and] is

[12]Marx, *Theories of Surplus Value* (New York: International Publishers, 1952), p. 373n.

[13]Bernice Shoul, "Karl Marx and Say's Law," *Quarterly Journal of Economics,* November 1957, pp. 620–21.

[14]Marx, *Capital,* Vol. II (Chicago: Kerr, 1909), p. 365.

[15]M.C. Howard and J.E. King. *The Political Economy of Marx* (New York: Longman, 1975), p. 218.

intensified by the collapse of the credit system." This then stimulates an even greater urge for liquidity, further reductions in demand for goods, and so on, in a mutually reinforcing, cumulative downward process, spreading throughout the economy. Actually, Marx adds, it is unnecessary for the contraction to be comprehensive; it is sufficient for it to characterize some major branch or branches of production.

Finally, Marx explains the process of eventual emergence of forces stimulating cyclical upturn and recovery (selection 6.C.8). First, machinery and buildings eventually depreciate, creating replacement demands. Second, capital values are destroyed by falling prices during depressions. Small, bankrupt capitalists sell their capital equipment to larger enterprises at subvalue prices, thus raising the rate of profits for those who remain. Third, expansion in the industrial reserve army during depressions pushes real wages down to very low levels, creating special depressionary surpluses for capitalists.[16]

6.C.6 CRITIQUE OF SAY'S LAW

Nothing can be more childish than the dogma, that because every sale is a purchase, and every purchase a sale, therefore the circulation of commodities necessarily implies an equilibrium of sales and purchases. If this means that the number of actual sales is equal to the number of purchases, it is mere tautology. But its real purport is to prove that every seller brings his buyer to market with him. Nothing of the kind. The sale and the purchase constitute one identical act, an exchange between a commodity-owner and an owner of money, between two persons as opposed to each other as the two poles of a magnet. They form two distinct acts, of polar and opposite characters, when performed by one single person. Hence the identity of sale and purchase implies that the commodity is useless, if, on being thrown into the alchemistical retort of circulation, it does not come out again in the shape of money; if, in other words, it cannot be sold by its owner, and therefore be bought by the owner of the money. That identity further implies that the exchange, if it does take place, constitutes a period of rest, an interval, long or short, in the life of the commodity. Since the first metamorphosis of a commodity is at once a sale and a purchase, it is also an independent process in itself. The purchaser has the commodity, the seller has the money, i.e., a commodity ready to go into circulation at any time. No one can sell unless some one else purchases. But no one is forthwith bound to purchase, because he has just sold. Circulation bursts through all restrictions as to time, place, and individuals, imposed by direct barter, and this it effects by splitting up, into the antithesis of a sale and a purchase, the direct identity that in barter does exist between the alienation of one's own and the acquisition of some other man's product. To say that these two independent and antithetical acts have an intrinsic unity, are essentially one, is the same as to say that this intrinsic oneness expresses itself in an external antithesis. If the interval in time between the two complemen-

[16] Marx's third factor raises the question, not clearly answered, of whether low real wages might not cause further reductions in worker consumption and, thus, greater difficulties in "realizing" surpluses.

tary phases of the complete metamorphosis of a commodity becomes too great, if the split between the sale and the purchase becomes too pronounced, the intimate connexion between them, their oneness, asserts itself by producing—a crisis. The antithesis, use-value and value; the contradictions that private labour is bound to manifest itself as direct social labour, that a particularized concrete kind of labour has to pass for abstract human labour; the contradiction between the personification of objects and the representation of persons by things; all these antitheses and contradictions, which are immanent in commodities, assert themselves, and develop their modes of motion in the antithetical phases of the metamorphosis of a commodity. These modes therefore imply the possibility, and no more than the possibility, of crisis. The conversion of this mere possibility into a reality is the result of a long series of relations, that, from our present standpoint of simple circulation, have as yet no existence. . . .

The function of money as the means of payment implies a contradiction without a terminus medius. In so far as the payments balance one another, money functions only ideally as money of account, as a measure of value. In so far as actual payments have to be made, money does not serve as a circulating medium, as a mere transient agent in the interchange of products, but as the individual incarnation of social labour, as the independent form of existence of exchange value, as the universal commodity. This contradiction comes to a head in those phases of industrial and commercial crises which are known as monetary crises. Such a crisis occurs only where the ever-lengthening chain of payments, and an artificial system of settling them, has been fully developed. Whenever there is a general and extensive disturbance of this mechanism, no matter what its cause, money becomes suddenly and immediately transformed, from its merely ideal shape of money of account, into hard cash. Profane commodities can no longer replace it. The use-value of commodities becomes valueless, and their value vanishes in the presence of its own independent form. On the eve of the crisis, the bourgeois, with the self-sufficiency that springs from intoxicating prosperity, declares money to be a vain imagination. Commodities alone are money. But now the cry is everywhere: money alone is a commodity! As the hare pants after fresh water, so pants his soul after money, the only wealth. In a crisis, the antithesis between commodities and their value-form, money, becomes heightened into an absolute contradiction.

Marx, *Capital,* I (1867), pp. 127–28, 154–55.

6.C.7 CRISES AND CYCLES IN THEORIES OF SURPLUS VALUE

Causes of Crises

The whole process of accumulation resolves itself above all into *expanded production,* which on the one hand corresponds to the natural increase of the population, and on the other forms an immanent basis for the phenomena which become manifest in *crises.* The measure of this expanded production is *capital* itself—the actual level of the conditions of production and the boundless urge of the capitalists to enrich themselves and increase their capital—and not in any way *consumption.* The latter is limited from the outset, as the greater part of the population, the working population, can only increase its consumption within very narrow limits, while to the same degree as capitalism develops, the demand for labour decreases *relatively,* although it increases *absolutely.* Moreover, all equalisations are *accidental,* and although the proportionate use of capitals in the various spheres is equalised by a continuous process, nevertheless the continuity of this process itself equally presupposes the constant disproportion, which it has continuously, often violently, to even out.

Here we have only to consider the forms which capital passes through in the various stages of its development. Hence we do not go into the real relations within which the actual process of production takes place. It is throughout assumed that commodities are sold at their value. We do not consider the competition of capitals, nor the credit system, nor the actual composition of society, which certainly does not consist merely of the two classes, workers and industrial capitalists—and which therefore consumers and producers are not identical. The first category [consumers], (whose revenues are in part not primary but secondary, derived from profits and wages), is much wider than the second [producers], and hence the way in which they spend their revenues, and the size of their revenues, brings about very considerable modifications in the economic structure and particularly in the process of circulation and reproduction of capital. It may be added that, while in dealing with money—both in so far as it represents a form different from the natural form of commodities, and in its form as means of payment—we found that it contained the possibility of crises, this emerges even more clearly when we consider the general nature of capital, even without taking into account the further actual relations which constitute the total prerequisites for the real process of production.

The view adopted by Ricardo from the inane Say, but which was really Mill's (which we shall come back to when we deal with that miserable fellow Say), that no *overproduction,* or at any rate *no general glut of the market* is possible, rests on the principle that exchange is of *products against products.* Or, as [James] Mill put it, on the "metaphysical equilibrium of sellers and buyers," [which was] further developed [to the principle of] demand being determined only by production itself, or even of the identity of demand and supply. The same principle is expressed also in the form of which Ricardo was particularly fond, that any quantity of capital can be productively employed in any country. . . .

In reproduction, just as in the accumulation of capital, the point is not only the replacement of *the same* mass of use value as the capital consists of, on the old scale or (in accumulation) on an enlarged scale, but the replacement of the *value* of the capital advanced along with the usual rate of profit. If therefore through any circumstance whatever or a combination of circumstances the market price of the commodities (of all or of the majority—it makes no difference) falls far below their price of production, then, in the first place, the reproduction of the capital will be considerably curtailed. Even more, however, will accumulation be held back. The transformation into capital of surplus value piled up in the form of money (gold or notes) would only bring loss. It therefore lies idle as a hoard in the banks, or even in the form of credit money, which in essence makes no difference. This stagnation could occur as a result of the opposite causes, when the *real preconditions* for reproduction were lacking (as for example if grain became dear, or because not enough constant capital *in natura* had been accumulated). There is a check in reproduction, and therefore in the flow of circulation. Purchase and sale come into sharp conflict, and unemployed capital appears in the form of money lying idle. The same phenomenon (and this as a rule precedes crises) can occur if the production of surplus capital takes place at a very rapid rate, and its retransformation into productive capital so increases the demand for all the elements of the latter that real production cannot keep pace, and consequently there is a rise in the prices of all commodities which enter into the formation of capital. In this case the rate of interest falls sharply, however much profits may rise, and this reduction in the rate of interest leads then to the most risky speculative ventures. The check in reproduction leads to the decrease of the variable capital, to a fall in wages and a fall in the amount of labour employed. This in turn reacts anew on prices and brings about a new fall in prices.

It must never be lost sight of that in capitalist production what matters is not direct use value, but exchange value, and in particular the expansion of surplus value. This is the driving motive of capitalist production, and it is a pretty conception that—in order to reason away the contradictions of capitalist production—abstracts from the basis of the latter and presents it as production whose aim to meet the direct consumption of the producers.

Further: as the circulation process of capital is not a one-day affair, but extends over fairly long periods before the return of the capital to its original form; as these periods however coincide with the periods within which market prices equalise with prices of production; as in the course of these periods great upheavals and changes in markets take place, since great changes in the productivity of labour and therefore in the *real value* of commodities take place—it is therefore very evident that from the starting point—the advance of the capital—until its return at the end of one of these periods, great catastrophes must occur and elements of crises must accumulate and develop —and these cannot in any way be got rid of by the pitiful claptrap that products exchange against products. . . .

When we speak of the *destruction of capital* through crises, two different kinds of things must be distinguished.

In so far as the process of reproduction is checked and the labour process is restricted or here and there is altogether stopped, *real* capital is destroyed. Machinery which is not used is not capital. Labour which is not exploited is equivalent to lost production. Raw material that lies unused is not capital. Use values (also newly constructed machinery) which are either unused or remain unfinished, commodities which rot in warehouses—all this is destruction of capital. All this is nothing but a check in the process of reproduction, so that the *actually existing* means of production do not in fact serve as means of production, are not set in operation. Hence their use value, and their exchange value, go to the devil.

But in the second place the *destruction of capital* resulting from crises means the depreciation of sums of value, preventing them from later on renewing their process of reproduction as capital on the same scale. This is the ruinous effect of the fall in the price of commodities. No use value is destroyed by this. What one loses, the other gains. [But] sums of value in operation as capitals are prevented from renewing themselves as *capital* in the hands of the same persons. The old capitalists go bankrupt, . . . the buyer of . . . commodities . . . can do very well out of it and even make a profit when trade revives. A considerable part of the nominal capital of society—that is of the *exchange value* of the existing capital—is once for all destroyed, although it is precisely this destruction, since it does not affect the use value, which may very much facilitate the new reproduction. This is at the same time a period when the money capitalist enriches himself at the cost of the industrial capitalist.

Overproduction of Commodities and Overabundance of Capital[1]

The question . . . arises: what is overabundance of capital, and what distinguishes this . . . from overproduction? . . .

The transition from the phrase *"overproduction of commodities"* to the phrase *"overabundance of capital"* represents in fact a *step forward.* In what does this consist? [In the recognition] that the producers confront one another not as mere owners of commodities, but as capitalists.

Unity of Purchase and Sale, of the Process of Production and the Process of Circulation

A . . . passage[s] from Ricardo: . . .

"Productions are always bought by productions, or by services; money is only the medium by which the exchange is effected. Too much of a particular commodity may be produced, of which there may be such a glut in the market as not to repay the capital expended on it; but this cannot be the case with respect to all commodities." . . .

In relation to crises, all authors who portray the actual movement of prices, or all practical people writing at particular stages of a crisis, have correctly ignored the allegedly theoretical twaddle and have been content to take it for granted that the doctrine of the impossibility of a market plethora, though it might be true in abstract theory, is in practice false. The regular repetition of crises has in fact reduced the rigmaroles of Say and others to a phraseology which is only used in times of prosperity, but in times of crisis is discarded.

[1]Here a distinction must be made. When Adam Smith explains the fall in the rate of profit as due to the overabundance of capital, the accumulation of capital, he is speaking of a *permanent* effect, and this is wrong. On the other hand, a transitory overabundance of capital, overproduction, crisis, is something different. There are no permanent crises.

In world market crises the contradictions and antagonisms of bourgeois production break through to the surface. But instead of investigating the nature of the conflicting elements which force their way through in the catastrophe, the apologists content themselves with denying the catastrophe itself; and, faced with its regular recurrence, with insisting that production would never lead to crises if it were carried on according to the textbooks. The apologetics consist, then, in falsifying the simplest economic relations, and especially in stubbornly maintaining the unity in face of the contradiction.

If for example purchase and sale, or the movement of metamorphosis of commodities, represent the unity of two processes—or rather the course of a single process through two opposite phases, and thus in essence the unity of the two phases—this movement is nevertheless, equally in essence, the separation of the two phases, making them independent of each other. Since in fact they belong together, the independence of the two linked phases can only show itself forcibly, as a destructive process. It is precisely the *crisis* in which their unity asserts itself—the unity of different things. The independence in relation to each other, which is assumed by these mutually dependent and complementary phases, is forcibly destroyed. The crisis therefore makes manifest the unity of the phases which have become independent of each other. No crisis would take place, were it not for this inner unity of what on the surface are phases unrelated to each other. But No!—says the apologist economist. Because there is unity, there can be *no* crisis. Which in turn is nothing but to say that the unity of opposite [factors] excludes their antagonism.

In order to prove that capitalist production cannot lead to general crises, all its conditions and definite forms, all its principles and *differentiae specificae* (specific differences) are denied; in short, capitalist prodution itself is denied. And in fact what is demonstrated is that if the capitalist mode of production—instead of being a specifically developed, unique form of social production—were a mode of production dating back to the crudest beginnings of social production, the antagonisms and contradictions peculiar to it, and therefore also their explosion in crises, would not exist.

"Productions," Ricardo, following Say, observes, "are always bought by productions, or by services; money is only the medium by which the exchange is effected."

Here therefore, in the first place, the *commodity,* in which the antagonism between exchange value and use value exists, is transformed into a simple product (use value), and consequently the exchange of commodities is transformed into a mere bartering of products, of simple use values. This is to go back not only to before capitalist production, but to before simple commodity production; and the most developed phenomenon of capitalist production—world market crisis—is flatly denied by the flat denial of the first condition of capitalist production, namely, that the product is a commodity and must therefore take the form of money and pass through the process of metamorphosis. Instead of speaking of wage labour, the term used is "services," a word in which the specific characteristic of wage labour and of its use—namely, that it increases the value of the commodities for which it is exchanged, that it produces surplus value—is again disregarded, and with it also the specific relation whereby money and commodities are transformed into capital. "Service" is labour considered only as *use value* (a secondary matter in capitalist production), just in the same way as in the word *"productions"* is the essence of the *commodity* and of the contradiction contained in it is suppressed. Then, quite consistently, *money* is conceived as merely the intermediary in the exchange of products, not as an essential and necessary form of existence of the commodity, which must present itself as exchange value—general social labour. Inasmuch as, through the transformation of the commodity into mere use value (product), the essence of exchange value is expunged, it is then easy to deny—or rather it is then necessary to deny—*money* as an essential and independent form of the commodity in the process of the metamorphosis from its original form. In this way, therefore, crises are reasoned out of existence through losing sight of or denying the first preconditions of capitalist production: the nature of the product as a commodity, the duplication of the commodity in commodity and money, the consequent separate phases in the exchange of commodities, and finally the relation of money or commodities to wage labour.

Those economists, however, are no better, who (like John Stuart Mill, for example) seek to explain crises by these simple *possibilities* of crisis contained in the metamorphosis of commodities—such as the separation between purchase and sale. These characteristics, which explain the possibility of crisis, are very far from explaining their actuality, and still less, *why* the phases of the process come into such conflict that their inner unity can only assert itself through a crisis, through a violent process. This *separation* appears in the crisis; it is the elementary form of crisis. To *explain* the crisis by its elementary form is to explain the existence of the crisis by expressing its presence in its abstract form, that is, to explain the crisis by the crisis.

Ricardo says:

> "No man produces but with a view to consume or sell, and he never sells but with an intention to purchase some other commodity, which may be immediately useful to him, or which may contribute to future production. By producing, then, he necessarily becomes either the consumer of his own goods, or the purchaser and consumer of the goods of some other person. It is not to be supposed that he should, for any length of time, be ill-formed of the commodities which he can most advantageously produce, to attain the object which he has in view, namely, the possession of other goods; and, therefore, it is not probable that he will continually produce a commodity for which there is no demand." . . .

This is the childish babble of a Say, but it is not worthy of Ricardo. In the first place no capitalist produces in order to consume his product. And when we are speaking of capitalist production, then it is correct to say "No man produces with a view to consume his own product," even if he uses portions of his product for industrial consumption. But here it is private consumption that is in question. In the earlier passage, it was forgotten that the product is a commodity. Now even the social division of labour is forgotten. In conditions in which men produce for themselves, there are in fact no crises, but also no capitalist production. Nor have we ever heard that the ancients, with their slave production, at any time experienced crises, although among the ancients too individual producers went bankrupt. The first part of the alternative is nonsense. So is the second. A man who has produced has not the choice whether he will sell or not. He *must* sell. And in crises appears precisely the circumstance that he cannot sell, or only below the price of production, or even that he must sell at a positive loss. What does it avail him or us, therefore, that he has produced in order to sell? What concerns us is precisely to discover what has cut across this good intention of his.

Further: "No man sells but with a view to purchase some other commodity, which may be immediately useful to him, or which may contribute to future production." What a pleasant portrayal of bourgeois relations! Ricardo even forgets that a man may sell in order to pay, and that these compulsory sales play a very significant role in crises. The immediate purpose of the capitalist when he sells is to transform his commodities or rather his commodity capital back again into money capital, and thereby to realise his profit. Consumption—revenue—is consequently not the determining motive of his process, which it is, however, for the man who only sells commodities in order to transform them into means of subsistence. But this is not capitalist production, in which revenue appears as a result but not as the determining purpose. Everyone sells with the immediate aim of selling; that is, in order to transform commodities into money.

During the crisis the man may be very pleased when he has made a sale, without any immediate thought of a purchase. However, if the value that has been realised is now again to function as capital it must pass through the process of reproduction, that is, be exchanged once more for labour and commodities. But crisis is precisely the moment of disturbance and interruption in the process of reproduction. And this disturbance cannot be explained by the fact that it does not take place in periods when there is no crisis. There can be no doubt that nobody "will continually produce a commodity for which there is no demand," but no one is talking about such an absurd hypothesis. Also, it has nothing whatever to do with the matter. "The possession of other goods" is not the immediate aim of capitalist production, but the appropriation of value, of money, of abstract wealth. . . .

Money is not only "the medium by which the exchange is effected," but equally it is the medium through which the exchange of product for product falls into two acts which are independent of each other and separate in space and time. . . .

In the metamorphosis of commodities the possibility of crisis shows itself in this way:

First, the commodity, which exists in its real form as a use value, and in its notional form, in its price, as an exchange value, must be transformed into money: C–M. Once this difficulty, the sale, is solved, then the purchase, M–C, presents no difficulty, as money is immediately exchangeable for everything else. . . . The possibility of crisis, in so far as it shows itself in the simple form of the metamorphosis, therefore comes from the mere fact that the differences in form—the phases—which in its movement it passes through, in the first place, are necessary complementary forms and phases; and secondly, in spite of this inner necessary connection with each other, are independent parts and forms of the process, existing independently of each other, separate in time and space, cut off and divided from each other. It lies therefore in the very separation between sale and purchase. It is only in the form of commodity that the commodity has this difficulty to overcome. As soon as it has the form of money it has got over the difficulty. But moreover, this too is due to the separation between purchase and sale. If the commodity could not be withdrawn from circulation in the form of money, or its retransformation into a commodity could not be deferred; if—as in direct barter—purchase and sale were one, the *possibility* of crisis, on the assumptions made, would disappear. For it is assumed that the commodity is a *use value* for other possessors of commodities. . . . When we say that the simple form of metamorphosis contains the possibility of crisis, we are only saying that in this form lies the very possibility of the tearing apart and division of essentially complementary phases. . . . In commodity production the transformation of the product into money, its sale, is a *conditio sine qua non.* Direct production for one's own needs does not take place. In this case, if there is no sale, there is crisis. The difficulty in transforming the *commodities*—the particular product of individual labour—into *money,* their opposite, into abstract general, social labour, consists in the fact that *money* is not the particular product of individual labour; that the man who has sold, that is, holds the commodity in the form of money, is not compelled immediately to purchase again, to transform the money back again into a particular product of individual labour. In barter, this contradiction does not exist. In the barter form no one can be a seller without being a buyer, or a buyer without being a seller. The difficulty in selling—on the assumption that the commodity to be sold has use value—arises simply from the ease with which the buyer can postpone the retransformation of the money into commodity. The difficulty in transforming the commodity into money, in selling, arises simply from the fact that the commodity must be transformed into money, but there is no need for the money to be immediately transformed into commodity, and therefore sale and purchase may fall asunder. We have said that this form contains the possibility of crisis, that is to say, the possibility that phases which are linked together, which are inseparable, become separated and consequently are forcibly reunited, their intimate connection realised by violence, which overcomes their subjective independence. And crisis is nothing but the forcible assertion of the unity of phases of the production process which have become independent of each other.

The general, abstract possibility of crisis is nothing more than the *most abstract form* of crisis, without content, without its pregnant motivating factor. Sale and purchase may be sundered. They represent, therefore, crisis *in potentia,* and their coincidence always remains a critical factor for the commodity. They may, however, pass smoothly over from one to the other.

The most abstract form of crisis and consequently the formal possibility of crisis is therefore the metamorphosis of the commodity itself; in which it is only as a developed movement that the contradiction between exchange value and use value, and between money and commodity, which the unity of the commodity comprises, is involved. But this form does not in itself contain that which transforms this possibility of crisis into a crisis; all it implies is that *the* form for a crisis exists.

And in the investigation of bourgeois economy this is the important thing. World market crises must be conceived as the real gathering together and forcible smoothing out of all the contradictions of bourgeois economy. The separate factors which converge in these crises must therefore emerge and develop in each sphere of bourgeois economy, and the further we delve into it, the more there will be on the one hand the development of new definite features of this contradiction, while on the other hand its more abstract forms must prove to be recurrent and contained in more concrete forms.

We can therefore say: Crisis in its first form is the metamorphosis of the commodity itself, the falling asunder of purchase and sale.

Crisis in its second form [arises from the] function of money as means of payment, in which money figures in two different phases divided from each other in time, in two different functions. Both of these two forms are still quite abstract, although the second is more concrete than the first.

First, . . . the general possibility of crisis . . . contained in . . . the separation of purchase and sale is therefore implicit in the movement of the capital, in so far as this capital is *also* commodity and nothing but commodity. The connection between the metamorphoses of commodities with each other results moreover in one commodity transforming itself into money, because the other is retransforming itself from the form of money into commodity. . . . This mutual confluence and intertwining of the reproduction or circulation processes of different capitals is on the one hand necessitated by the division of labour, and on the other is accidental; and thus the determination of the content of crisis is already a stage further.

Secondly, however, as concerns the possibility of crisis arising from the form of money as *means of payment,* there are already in capital a number of more concrete causes for this possibility being realised. For example, the weaver has to pay for his whole constant capital, the elements of which are supplied by spinner, flax grower, machinery manufacturer, iron manufacturer, timber merchant, coal producer, and so on. . . . Let us suppose that the weaver then sells his cloth to the *merchant* for 41,000, but in return for a bill of exchange, so that money figures as *means of payment.* Similarly, the flax grower has sold to the spinner in return for a bill of exchange, and the spinner to the weaver, ditto the machinery manufacturer to the weaver, ditto the iron manufacturer and timber merchant to the machinery manufacturer, ditto the coal producer to the spinner, weaver, machinery manufacturer, and iron and timber supplies. In addition, the iron, coal, timber and flax producers have paid each other with bills of exchange. Then if the merchant does not receive money for his commodity, he cannot pay his bill of exchange to the weaver. The flax grower has drawn on the spinner, the machinery manufacturer on the weaver and the spinner. The spinner cannot pay, because the weaver cannot pay; neither of them pays the machinery manufacturer, and the latter does not pay the suppliers of iron, timber, and coal. And all of them in turn, because they do not realise the value of their commodities, cannot replace the portion of the value which is to replace their constant capital. In this way a general crisis arises. This is nothing other than the developed *possibility of crisis* arising from money as means of payment; but we see here, in capitalist production, that very connection between mutual claims and obligations, between purchases and sales, through which the possibility can develop into actuality. . . . No crisis can exist unless sale and purchase become separated from each other and come into conflict, or the contradictions inherent in money as means of payment come to the surface; unless therefore crisis at the same time emerges in the simple form—as the contradiction between purchase and sale, or the contradiction inherent in money as means of payment. But these also are mere *forms,* general possibilities of crises; and consequently also forms, abstract forms, of actual crisis. In them the nature of crisis appears in its simplest forms, and, in so far as this form is itself its simplest content, in its simplest content. But it is not as yet a content which has *a determinate cause.* The simple circulation of money and even the circulation of money as means of payment—and both make their appearance long *before* capitalist production, without crises occurring—are possible and in fact take place without crises. On the basis of these forms alone, therefore, it is not possible to explain why they show their critical side, why the contradiction contained in them as a possibility emerges as a real contradiction. . . .

Therefore:

1. The general *possibility* of crises is given in the process of *metamorphosis of capital* itself, and in fact in a twofold way: in so far as money functions as *means of circulation,* through the separation of purchase and sale; and in so far as it functions as *means of payment,* where it has two separate aspects, as *measure of value* and as *realisation of value.* These two aspects become separated. If in the interval between them the value has altered, the commodity at the moment of its sale is not worth what it was worth at the moment when money functioned as measure of value and therefore of the reciprocal obligations; then the obligation cannot be met from the proceeds of sale of the commodities, and therefore the whole series of transactions, which depend in a backward chain on this one transaction, cannot be settled. If even for a certain time the commodities cannot be sold, although their value has not changed—in such a case money cannot function as means of payment, since it has to function as such within a definite term laid down in advance. But as the same sum of money functions here for a series of mutual transactions and obligations, the inability to pay appears not at one point only but at many, and hence crisis.

These are the formal possibilities of crises. The first-mentioned forms are possible without the latter; that is to say, crises are possible without credit, without money functioning as means of payment. But the latter forms are not possible without the former, that is, without the separation between purchase and sale. But in the latter case crisis appears not only because commodities are unsalable, but also when they cannot be sold within a certain period; and in this case crisis arises and derives its character not only from the fact that commodities cannot be sold, but from the non-fulfilment of a whole series of payments which depend on the sale of these particular commodities within this particular period of time. This is the characteristic form of money crises.

Therefore if a crisis appears because purchase and sale become separated, it develops *as a money crisis* when money has developed as *means of payment,* and, this *second form* of crises follows as a matter of course when the first makes its appearance. In investigating why the general possibility of crises becomes *an actual crisis,* in investigating the conditions of crisis, it is therefore quite superfluous to concern ourselves with those crises which arise from the development of money as means of payment. Precisely for this reason the economists like to advance this self-explanatory form as the cause of crises . . .

2. In so far as crises result from changes and revolutions in prices which do not coincide with changes in the values of commodities, they naturally cannot be investigated when we are considering capital in general, when it is assumed that prices are identical with the values of commodities.

3. The general possibility of crises is the formal metamorphosis of capital itself, the separation in time and space of purchase and sale. But this is never the cause of crisis. For it is nothing but the most general form of crisis, that is, crisis itself in its most generalised expression. It cannot however be said that the abstract form of crisis is the cause of crisis. If we seek its causes, what we want to know is why its abstract form, the form of its possibility, develops from possibility into actuality.

4. The general conditions of crises, in so far as they are independent of price fluctuations (and whether these are linked with the credit system or not; price fluctuations as distinct from fluctuations of value), must be explicable from the general conditions of capitalist production.

[We find, then, as factors in a crisis:]

The reconversion of money into capital. A definite level of production or reproduction is assumed. The fixed capital can here be considered as given, remaining the same and not entering into the process of realisation. As the reproduction of the raw material is dependent not only on the labour expended on it, but on the productivity of this labour in association with natural conditions, it is possible [even with the method of production remaining the same] for the mass of the product of the same quantity of labour to fall (with bad harvests). The value of the raw material therefore rises, while its mass falls. The proportions in which money has to flow back into the various component parts of the capital, in order to continue production on the former level, are disturbed. More must be paid out for raw material, less remains for labour, and the same quantity of labour as before cannot be absorbed. In the first place, this is not physically possible, because there is a deficiency of raw material; secondly, because a greater part of the value of the product has to be transformed into raw material, and consequently a smaller part can be transformed into variable capital. Reproduction can not be repeated at the same level. A part of the fixed capital stays idle, a part of the workers is thrown out on the streets. The rate of profit falls, because the value of the constant capital compared with the variable has risen and less variable capital is employed. The fixed charges—interest, rent—which are based on the anticipation of stable rates of profit and of exploitation of labour, remain the same, and in part cannot be paid. Hence crisis. Crisis of labour and crisis of capital. This is therefore an interruption of the reproduction process resulting from an increased value of the part of the constant capital that has to be replaced out of the value of the product. In this case, although the rate of profit falls, there is a rise in the price of the product. If this product enters into other spheres of production as a means of production, the rise in its price results in the same disturbance of reproduction in these spheres. If it enters into general consumption as a means of subsistence, it either enters also into the consumption of the workers or it does not. In the first case, the effects are the same as that of a disturbance in the variable capital, which is dealt with later. But in so far as it enters generally into consumption, the result may be (unless the consumption of it falls) a fall in the demand for other products. Hence their reconversion into money at their value will be hindered to a corresponding degree, and thus the other side of their reproduction—not the reconversion of money into productive capital, but the reconversion of commodities into money—will be disturbed. In any case the mass of profit and the mass of wages in this branch of industry falls, and this means a fall in part of the necessary returns from the sale of commodities of other branches of production.

This shortage of raw material may however also make its appearance apart from the influence of harvests or of the natural productivity of the labour which supplies the raw material. If for example an undue portion of the [accumulated] surplus value, of the surplus capital, is [expended] on machinery, etc., in a particular branch of production, the raw material, although it would have been adequate for the old level of production, will be inadequate for the new. This therefore results from the disproportionate conversion of the surplus capital into its different elements. It is a case of *overproduction of fixed capital* and produces exactly the same phenomena as in the first case.

General and Partial Overproduction

Ricardo says:

> "Too much of a *particular* commodity may be produced, of which there may be such a glut in the market as not to repay the capital expended on it; but this cannot be the case with respect to *all* commodities." . . .

That only *particular* but not *all* kinds of commodities can constitute a glut in the market, and that consequently overproduction can always only be partial, is a paltry evasion. In the first place, if the mere nature of a commodity is considered, there is nothing in it which would prevent *all* commodities being in oversupply on the market and therefore all falling below their price. What is involved here is precisely the moment of crisis. In fact, all commodities [may be in oversupply] except *money.* The necessity for *the* commodity to transform itself into money means only that the necessity exists for *all* commodities. And inasmuch as there is a difficulty in a single commodity making this metamorphosis, the difficulty can exist for all commodities. The general nature of the metamorphosis of commodities—which includes the separation of purchase and sale as well as their unity—instead of excluding the *possibility* of a general glut, is rather *the* possibility of a general glut. . . . Just as Mill says that purchase is sale, etc., so is demand supply and supply demand; but they are equally separate, and can assume independence of each other. At a given moment the supply of all commodities may be greater than the demand for all commodities, because the demand for the general commodity, money, exchange value, is greater than the demand for all particular commodities; in other words, because the compulsion for the commodity to take the form of money, to realise its exchange value, is greater than the compulsion for the commodity to be reconverted into use value. . . .

As for the antithesis between partial and universal overproduction, . . . the following further points may be noted:

First: A general rise of prices in all articles of capitalist production usually precedes a crisis. Consequently they all have a share in the following crash, and all constitute an overloading of the market at the prices which they had before the crash. The market can absorb a mass of commodities at falling prices, prices that have fallen below their prices of production, which it could not absorb at their former market prices. The excess of commodities is always relative, that is, it is an excess at certain prices. The prices at which the commodities are then absorbed are ruinous for the producer or merchant.

Secondly:

For a crisis (and therefore also overproduction) to be general, it is sufficient for it to grip the principal articles of trade.

Let us examine more closely how Ricardo tries to argue away the possibility of a general glut of the market:

> "Too much of a particular commodity may be produced, of which there may be such a glut in the market as not to repay the capital expended on it; but this cannot be the case with respect to all commodities; the demand for corn is limited by the mouths which are to eat it, for shoes and coats by the persons who are to wear them; but though a community, or a part of a community, may have as much corn, and as many hats and shoes as it is able, or may wish to consume, the same cannot be said of every commodity produced by nature or by art. Some would consume more wine if they had the ability to procure it. Others, having enough wine, would wish to increase the quantity or improve the quality of their furniture. Others might wish to ornament their grounds, or to enlarge their houses. The wish to do all or some of these is implanted in every man's breast; nothing is required but the means, and nothing can afford the means but an increase of production." . . .

Can there be a more childish line of reasoning? It runs like this. More may be produced of a particular commodity than can be consumed. But that cannot be true of *all* commodities at the same time. Because the needs which are satisfied through commodities have no limits and all these needs are not satisfied at the same time. On the contrary. The satisfaction of one need makes another so to speak latent. Therefore nothing is required but the means to satisfy these needs, and these means can only be provided through an increase of production. Therefore no general overproduction is possible. . . .

The worker can only buy . . . commodities which enter into individual consumption, as he does not himself make a profit from his labour, and does not himself possess the conditions for setting it to work—the means of labour and material of labour. Where production is developed in capitalist form, this therefore already excludes the greatest part of the producers, the workers themselves, from being consumers, buyers, of means of production. They buy no raw material and no means of labour; they buy only means of subsistence, commodities which enter directly into individual consumption. Consequently there is nothing more ridiculous than to speak of the identity of producers and consumers, since for an extraordinarily great number of branches of production—all those not producing articles for direct consumption—the mass of those engaged in production are absolutely excluded from the purchase of their own products. They are never directly consumers or buyers of this great part of their own products, although they pay a part of the value of these products in the consumption articles which they buy. This also shows the ambiguity of the word consumer and the error of identifying it with the word buyer. Industrially, it is precisely the workers who consume the machinery and raw material, who use it up in the labour process. But they do not use it up for themselves, and consequently they are not buyers of it. For them they are not use values, not commodities, but objective conditions of a process of which they themselves are the subjective conditions.

It may however be said that their employer represents them in the purchase of means of labour and materials of labour. But he represents them under different conditions from those in which they would represent themselves; that is, on the market. He has to sell a mass of commodities embodying surplus value, unpaid labour. They would have to sell only a mass of commodities which reproduced the value advanced in production—the value of the means of labour, the material of labour and the wages. He therefore has need of a wider market than they would require.

They are therefore producers, without being consumers—even when there is no interruption in the process of reproduction—in respect of all the articles which have to be consumed not individually but industrially.

So nothing is more preposterous as a means of denying crises than the assertion that consumers (buyers) and producers (sellers) are identical in capitalist production. They are completely separate. In so far as the reproduction process takes place, this identity can be asserted for only one out of every three thousand producers, that is to say, for the capitalist. It is just as false the other way round—that the consumers are producers. The landowner does not produce rent, and yet he consumes. The position is the same with the whole of money capital.

The apologetic phrases used to deny crises are important from this aspect—that they always prove the opposite of what they set out to prove. In order to deny crises, they assert unity where there is opposition and contradiction. This is important in so far as it can be said: they prove that, if the contradictions which they day-dream out of existence in fact did not exist, then too no crises would exist. But in fact crisis exists, because those contradictions exist. Every reason which they advance against crisis is a contradiction day-dreamed away—therefore a real contradiction, therefore a cause of crisis. The desire to day-dream contradictions out of the way is at the same time the expression of contradictions that are really present, but which they vainly desire *should* not exist.

What the workers in fact produce is surplus value. So long as they produce it, they are able to consume. As soon as [its production] ceases, their consumption ceases, because their production ceases. But it is in no way true that they are able to consume because they produce an equivalent for their consumption. Rather is it the case that the very moment they have produced such an equivalent, their consumption ceases, they have no equivalent to consume. Either their labour is dispended with or cut down, or in any case their wages lowered. In the latter case—when the level of production remains the same—they do not consume any equivalent for their production. But then they lack the means of subsistence, not because they do not produce enough, but because they get too little of their product for themselves.

If therefore the relations are reduced to that simply of consumer and producer, the fact is lost sight of that the producing wage-labour and the producing capitalist are two producers of a very different kind, even if we leave out of account the consumers who produce nothing at all. Once again the antagonism is denied by abstracting from an antagonism that is actually present in production. The mere relationship between wage-labourer and capitalist involves:

(1) That the greatest part of the producers (the workers) are non-consumers (non-buyers) of a very considerable part of their product, namely, of the means of labour and the material of labour.

(2) That the greatest part of the producers, the workers, can only consume an equivalent for their product so long as they produce more than this equivalent—surplus value or surplus product. They must always be *overproducers,* must always produce over and above their need, in order to be able to be consumers or buyers within the limits of their needs.

With this class of producers, therefore, the unity between production and consumption is in any case *prima facie* false. . . .

In our whole enquiry it is, of course, taken for granted that it cannot be denied that in individual spheres too much may be produced, and *for that reason* too little may be produced in other spheres; that partial crises therefore may arise from *disproportionate production* (proportionate production is, however, always only the result of disproportionate production on the basis of competition). And a general form of this disproportionate production may be overproduction of fixed capital, or on the other hand overproduction of circulating capital. . . .

However, we are not dealing here with crisis in so far as it is due to disproportionate production, that is, a disproportion in the division of the social labour among the individual spheres of production. This can only be dealt with in an examination of the competition between capitals. Here it has already been said that a rise or fall in market values consequent on this disproportion results in a withdrawal of capital from one sphere of production and its transfer to another, the migration of capital from one branch of production into the other. Of course this equalisation itself presupposes the opposite of equalisation and therefore may involve crisis; and the crisis itself may be a form of equalisation. Ricardo and others admit this form of crisis.

In the analysis of the production process we saw that the whole striving of capitalist production is directed towards the appropriation of the greatest possible amount of surplus labour, that is, to materialise the greatest possible amount of immediate labour time with the given capital. This may be done through the prolongation of the labour time, or reduction of the necessary labour time, development of the productive power of labour, the use of cooperation, division of labour, machinery, etc., in short, production on a higher level, that is, mass production. Production without regard to the limits of the market is therefore in the nature of capitalist production. . . .

Now let us return to our example of cotton cloth.

The stagnation in the market, which is oversupplied with cottons, disturbs reproduction for the weaver. This disturbance first affects his workers. The latter therefore are now to a smaller extent, or not at all, consumers of his commodity—cotton—and of other commodities which enter into their consumption. They have, it is true, a need for cottons, but they cannot buy them because they have not the means to do so, and they have not the means because they cannot continue to produce, and they cannot continue to produce because too much has been produced, too many cotton goods are in store on the market. Neither Ricardo's advice "to enlarge their production," nor his alternative, "to produce something else," can help them. They now constitute a part of the temporary overproduction, overproduction of workers, in this case of cotton producers, because there is an overproduction of cotton goods on the market.

But apart from the workers employed directly by the capital invested in cotton weaving, numbers of other producers are affected by this check in the reproduction of cotton: spinners, cotton growers, producers of spindles and looms, of iron, coal, and so on. All these would be similarly checked in their reproduction, as the reproduction of cotton goods is the condition for their own reproduction. This would take place, even if they had not overproduced in their own spheres, that is, had not produced beyond the limit set by and justified by the cotton industry when it was going swimmingly. All these industries have only this in common: that they consume their revenue (wages and profit, in so far as the latter is consumed as revenue and not accumulated) not in the form of their own product, but in the product of the spheres which produce articles of consumption, of which cotton is one. So the consumption and the demand for cotton falls, precisely because there is too much of it on the market. But so also does that of all other commodities on which, as articles of consumption, the revenue of these indirect producers of cotton cloth is spent. The means with which they can buy cotton cloth and other articles of consumption become restricted and contract, because there is too much cotton on the market. This affects also other commodities (articles of consumption). They are now suddenly in *relative* overproduction, because the means to buy them, and therewith the demand for them, have contracted. Even if there has been no overproduction in these spheres, now they are overproducing.

But if it is not only cotton, but also linen, silk and woollen goods in which overproduction has taken place, it can be understood how overproduction in these few but leading articles brings about a more or less general (*relative*) overproduction over the whole market. On the one hand a superfluity of all things needed for reproduction, and a superfluity of all kinds of unsold commodities on the market. On the other hand bankrupt capitalists and hungry workers, destitute of everything.

Nevertheless, this argument has two sides to it. If it is easy to understand how overproduction in a few leading articles of consumption must bring in its train a more or less general overproduction—the manifestation of the former —this in no way explains how overproduction of those articles can arise. For the phenomenon of general overproduction is brought about by the interdependence not only of the worker directly employed in these industries, but of all branches of industry which produce the earlier elements of their products, their constant capital in different phases. For the latter branches of industry, overproduction is an effect. But whence comes it in the former? For the latter go on producing so long as the former continue to produce, and along with this continued production a general growth of revenue, and therefore of their own consumption, seems assured.

Expansion of Production and Expansion of the Market

This question may perhaps be answered by pointing to the constantly expanding production, which expands each year for two reasons: first, because the capital invested in production is constantly growing, and secondly, because it is constantly used more productively; in the course of reproduction and accumulation there is a constant aggregation of small improvements which eventually alter the whole level of production. There is a piling up of improvements, an accumulating development of productive powers. If anyone likes to reply that the constantly expanding production requires a constantly expanding market, and that production expands more rapidly than the market, this is only putting in another way the phenomenon that has to be explained—in its real form, instead of an abstract form. The market expands more slowly than production. . . . This however merely means: the market is overfilled. Overproduction is manifest. Had the extension of the market kept pace with the extension of production, there would be no glut of the market, no overproduction.

However, the mere admission that the market must expand along with production is also from another aspect one more admission of the possibility of overproduction, since the market is limited externally in the geographical sense, the internal market is limited as compared with a market that is both internal and external, the latter again as compared with the world market —which however at each moment of time is in turn limited, [even though] in itself capable of extension. Consequently the admission that the market must expand if overproduction is not to occur, is also an admission that overproduction can occur. For since market and production are two independent factors, it is therefore possible that the expansion of one may not correspond with the expansion of the other, that the limits of the market may not be extended rapidly enough for production, or that new markets—new extensions of the market—may be rapidly overtaken by production, so that the expanded market now appears just as much a barrier as the narrower one did previously. . . .

The word *overproduction* in itself leads to error. So long as the most urgent needs of a great part of society are not satisfied, or *only* its most immediate needs, there can naturally be absolutely no talk of an *overproduction of products*—in the sense that the mass of products would be excessive in relation to the need for them. What must be said is the opposite: that in this sense, on the basis of capitalistic production, there is constant under *production*. The limit of production is the *capitalists' profit* and not at all the *need of the producers*. But overproduction of *products* and overproduction of *commodities* are two completely different things. . . .

[Ricardo and others admit] that there can be overproduction in each *particular branch of production.* The one circumstance that might prevent overproduction in *all* at the same time is, so it is alleged, that commodity exchanges against commodity, that is to say, they take refuge in the conditions of barter which they assume. But this way of escape is cut off by the very fact that trade in commodities is not barter, and therefore the seller of a commodity is not necessarily at the same time the purchaser of another. This whole subterfuge therefore rests on abstracting from *money,* and abstracting from the fact that what is in question is not the exchange of products but the circulation of commodities, for which the separation of purchase and sale is essential. . . .

The overproduction of commodities is denied, though the overproduction of capital is admitted. But capital itself consists of commodities, or in so far as it consists of money it must be reconverted into commodities of one kind or another in order to be able to function as capital. What then does overproduction of capital mean? Overproduction of quantities of value destined to produce surplus value, or, if considered in their material content, overproduction of commodities destined for reproduction—that is, reproduction on too large a scale, which is the same thing as overproduction pure and simple. Defined more exactly, this in turn means nothing but that too much has been produced for the purpose of enrichment, or that too large a part of the product has been destined, not for consumption as revenue, but for making more money, for accumulation; not to satisfy the personal requirements of its possessor, but to secure for him abstract social riches, money and more power over the labour of others—capital—or to increase the power in his hands. This is what some say. Ricardo denies it. How then do the others explain the overproduction of commodities? That production is not sufficiently widely diversified, that certain articles of consumption have not been produced in sufficiently great quantities. It is clear that this cannot refer to industrial consumption; for the manufacturer who overproduces in linen thereby of necessity increases his demand for yarn, machinery, labour, etc. Therefore the reference must be to personal consumption. Too much linen has been produced, but perhaps too few oranges. Previously money was denied, for the purpose of [denying] the separation between purchase and sale. Here, capital is denied, in order to transform the capitalists into people who carry out the simple operation C–M–C, and for individual consumption, not as capitalists with the aim of getting richer, with the aim of reconverting a part of the surplus value into capital. . . .

Overproduction is specifically conditioned by the general law of the production of capital: production is in accordance with the productive forces, that is, with the possibility that the given quantity of capital has of exploiting the maximum quantity of labour, without regard to the actual limits of the market, the needs backed by the ability to pay; and this takes place through the constant expansion of reproduction and accumulation, and therefore the constant reconversion of revenue into capital; while on the other hand the mass of producers remain restricted to the average level of needs, and on the basis of capitalist production must remain so restricted.

Marx, *Surplus Value* (1861–3), pp. 368–414.

6.C.8 CRISES AND CYCLES IN THE GRUNDRISSE *AND IN* CAPITAL

GRUNDRISSE

The *realization process* of capital—and money becomes capital only through the realization process—appears at the same time as its *devaluation process* its demonetization. . . . The *devaluation* being dealt with here is this, that capital has made the transition from the form of money into the form of a *commodity,* of a product, which has a certain price, which is to be *realized.* In its money form it existed as *value.* It now *exists* as product, and only ideally as price; but not as *value as* such. In order to *realize* itself, i.e. to maintain and to multiply itself as value, it . . . now has to enter anew into circulation in order to posit this form of general wealth anew. The capitalist now enters the process of circulation not simply as one engaged in exchange, but as *producer,* and the others engaged in exchange are, relative to him, *consumers.* They must exchange money in order to obtain his commodity for their consumption, while he exchanges his product to obtain their money. Suppose that this process breaks down—and the separation by itself implies the possibility of such a miscarriage in the individual case—then the capitalist's money has been transformed into a worthless product, and has not only not gained a new value, but also lost its original value. But whether this is so or not, in any case devaluation forms one moment of the realization process; which is already simply implied in the fact that the product of the process in its immediate form is not *value,* but first has to enter anew into circulation in order to be realized as such. Therefore, while capital is reproduced as value and new value in the production process, it is at the same time posited as *not-value,* as something which first has to be *realized as value by means of exchange.* The. . . processes of which capital forms the unity are external; they are separate in time and space. As such, the transition from one into the other, i.e. their unity as regards the individual capitalists, is accidental. Despite their *inner unity,* they exist *independently* alongside one another, each as the presupposition of the other. Regarded broadly and as a whole, this inner unity must necessarily maintain itself to the extent that the whole of production rests on capital, and it must therefore realize all the necessary moments of its self-formation, and must contain the determinants necessary to make these moments real. But at the point we have reached so far, capital still does not appear as the determinant of circulation (exchange) itself but merely as one moment of the latter, and it appears to stop being capital just as the point where it enters into circulation. As a *commodity,* capital now shares the fate of commodities in general; it is a matter of accident whether or not it is exchanged for money, whether its *price* is realized or not. . . .

As a commodity, it must be (1) a use value and, as such, an object of need, object of consumption; (2) it must be exchanged for its equivalent—in money. The new value can be realized only through a sale. . . .

Inside the production process, realization appeared totally identical with the production of surplus labour (the objectification of surplus time), and hence appeared to have no *bounds* other than those partly presupposed and partly posited within this process itself, but which are always posited within it as *barriers* to be forcibly overcome. There now appear barriers to it which lie *outside* it. To begin with, even on an entirely superficial inspection, the commodity is an exchange value only in so far as it is at the same time a *use value,* i.e. an object of consumption;. . . it ceases to be an exchange value when it ceases to be a use value. Its first barrier, then, is *consumption itself*—the *need for it.* . . . Then, secondly, there has to be an equivalent for it, and, since circulation was presupposed at the outset as a constant magnitude—as having a given volume—but since, on the other hand, capital has created a new value in the production process, it seems indeed as if no equivalent were available for it. Thus, by emerging from the production process and reentering circulation, capital (a) as *production,* appears to encounter a barrier in the available magnitude of *consumption*—of *consumption capacity.* As a specific use value,. . . at a certain level—since it satisfies only a specific need—it ceases to be required for consumption. . . . Given objects can be consumed as objects of needs only up to a certain level. . . . Hence, as *use value,* the product contains a barrier—precisely the barrier consisting of the need for it—which, however, is measured not by the need of the producers but by the total need of all those engaged in exchange. Where the need for a certain use value ceases, it ceases to be a use value. It is measured as a use value by the need for it. But as soon as it ceases to be a use value, it ceases to be an object of circulation. . . . (b) As *new value* and as *value* as such, however, it seems to encounter a barrier in the magnitude of *available equivalents,* primarily money, not as medium of circulation but as money. The surplus value. . . requires a surplus equivalent. This now appears as a second barrier. . . .

Capital, as production resting on wage labour, presupposes circulation as the necessary condition and moment of the entire motion. This specific form of production presupposes this specific form of exchange which finds its expression in the circulation of money. In order to renew itself, the entire product has to be transformed into money. . . .

These are, then, the contradictions which present themselves of their own accord to a simple, objective, non-partisan view. How they are constantly suspended in the system of production resting on capital, but also constantly created again—and are suspended only by force (although this suspension appears up to a certain point merely as a quiet equilibration)—this is another question. The important thing at present is to take note of the existence of these contradictions. . . .

The main point here—where we are concerned with the general concept of capital—is that it is this *unity of production and realization,* not *immediately* but only as a *process,* which is linked to certain conditions, and, as it appeared, *external* conditions.

The creation by capital of *absolute surplus value*—more objectified labour—is conditional upon an expansion, specifically a constant expansion, of the sphere of circulation. The *surplus value* created at one point requires the creation of surplus value at *another* point, for which it may be exchanged. . . . A precondition of production based on capital is therefore *the production of a constantly widening sphere of circulation,* whether the sphere itself is directly expanded or whether *more points within it are created as points of production.* While circulation appeared at first as a constant magnitude, it here appears as a moving magnitude, being expanded by production itself. . . . Hence, just as capital has the tendency on one side to create ever more surplus labour, so it has the complementary tendency to create more points of exchange. . . . The tendency to create the *world market* is directly given in the concept of capital itself. Every limit appears as a barrier to be overcome. Initially, to subjugate every moment of production itself to exchange and to suspend the production of direct use values not entering into exchange, i.e. precisely to posit production based on capital in place of earlier modes of production, which appear primitive from its standpoint. *Commerce* no longer appears here as a function taking place between independent productions for the exchange of their excess, but rather as an essentially all-embracing presupposition and moment of production itself.

On the other side, the production of *relative surplus value,* i.e. production of surplus value based on the increase and development of the productive forces, requires the production of new consumption; requires that the consuming circle within circulation expands as did the productive circle previously. Firstly quantitative expansion of existing consumption; secondly: creation of new needs by propagating existing ones in a wide circle; *thirdly:* production of *new* needs and discovery and creation of new use values . . .

The point here. . . is not yet to develop overproduction specifically, but only the predisposition to it, such as it is posited in primitive form in the capital relation itself. . . . In production based on capital, consumption is mediated at all points by exchange, and labour never has a *direct* use value for those who are working. Its entire basis is labour as exchange value and as the creation of exchange value. . . . To each capitalist, the total mass of all workers, with the exception of his own workers, appear not as workers, but as consumers, possessors of exchange values (wages), money, which they exchange for his commodity. They are so many centres of circulation with whom the act of exchange begins and by whom the exchange value of capital is maintained. They form a proportionally very great part—although not quite so great as is generally imagined, if one focuses on the industrial worker proper—of all consumers. The greater their number—the number of the industrial population—and the mass of money at their disposal, the greater the sphere of exchange for capital. We have seen that it is the tendency of capital to increase the industrial population as much as possible.

Actually, the relation of one capitalist to the workers of *another* capitalist is none of our concern here. It only shows every capitalist's illusion, but alters nothing in the relation of capital in general to labour. Every capitalist knows this about his worker, that he does not relate to him as producer to consumer, and [he therefore] wishes to restrict his consumption, i.e. his ability to exchange, his wage, as much as possible. Of course he would like the workers of *other* capitalists to be the greatest consumers possible of *his own* commodity. But the relation of *every* capitalist to *his own* workers is the *relation as such* of *capital and labour,* the essential relation. But this is just how the illusion arises—true for the individual capitalist as distinct from all the others—that *apart from his* workers the whole remaining working class confronts him as *consumer* and *participant in exchange,* as money-spender, and not as worker. It is forgotten that, as Malthus says, 'the very existence of a profit upon any commodity pre-supposes a *demand exterior to that of the labourer who has produced it,*' and hence the *demand of that labourer himself can never be an adequate demand.* Since one production sets the other into motion and hence creates consumers for itself in the *alien* capital's workers, it *seems* to each individual capital that the demand of the working class posited by production itself is an 'adequate demand.' On one side, this demand which production itself posits drives it forward, and must drive it forward beyond the *proportion* in which it would have to produce with regard to the workers; on the other side, if the demand *exterior to the demand of the labourer himself* disappears or shrinks up, then the collapse occurs. Capital itself then regards *demand by the worker*—i.e. the payment of the wages on which this demand rests—not as a gain but as a loss, i.e. the *immanent relation between capital and labour* asserts itself. *Here again it is the competition among capitals,* their indifference to and independence of one another, which brings it about that the individual capital relates to the workers of the entire remaining capital *not as to workers:* hence is driven beyond the right proportion. What precisely distinguishes capital from the master-servant relation is that the *worker* confronts him as consumer and possessor of exchange values, and that in the form of the *possessor of money,* in the form of money he becomes a simple centre of circulation—one of its infinitely many centres, in which his specificity as worker is extinguished.[1]

To begin with: capital forces the workers beyond necessary labour to surplus labour. Only in this way does it realize itself, and create surplus value. But on the other hand, it posits necessary labour only *to the extent* and *in so far as* it is surplus labour and the latter is *realizable* as *surplus value.* It posits surplus labour, then, as the condition of the necessary, and surplus value as the limit of objectified labour, of value as such. As soon as it cannot posit value, it does not posit necessary labour; and, given its foundation, it cannot be otherwise. It therefore restricts labour and the creation of value—by an artificial check, as the English express it—and it does so on the same grounds as and to the same extent that it posits surplus labour and surplus value. By its nature, therefore, it posits a *barrier* to labour and value-creation, in contradiction to its tendency to expand them boundlessly. And in as much as it both posits a barrier *specific* to itself, and on the other side equally drives over and beyond *every* barrier, it is the living contradiction.[2]

[1]It is quite the same with the demand created by production itself for raw material, semi-finished goods, machinery, means of communication, and for the auxiliary materials consumed in production, such as dyes, coal, grease, soap, etc. This effective, exchange-value-positing demand is adequate and sufficient as long as the producers exchange among themselves. Its inadequacy shows itself as soon as the final product encounters its limit in direct and final consumption. This *semblance,* too, which drives beyond the correct proportion, is founded in the essence of capital, which, as will be developed more closely in connection with competition, *is* something which repels itself, *is* many capitals mutually quite indifferent to one another. In so far as one capitalist *buys* from others, buys commodities, or sells, they are within the simple exchange relation; and do not relate to one another as capital. The *correct* (imaginary) proportion in which they must exchange with one another in order to realize themselves at the end as capital lies *outside* their relation to one another.

[2]Since value forms the foundation of capital, and since it therefore necessarily exists only through exchange for *counter-value,* it thus necessarily repels itself from itself. A *universal capital,* one without alien capitals confronting it, with which it exchanges—and from the present standpoint, nothing confronts it but wage labourers or itself—is therefore a non-thing. The reciprocal repulsion between capitals is already contained in capital as realized exchange value.

While capital thus, on one side, makes surplus labour and its *exchange* for *surplus labour* into the precondition of necessary labour and hence of the positing of *labour capacity* as a centre of exchange—hence already narrows and attaches conditions to the sphere of exchange from this side—it is just as essential to it, on the other side, to restrict the worker's consumption to the amount necessary to reproduce his labour capacity—to make the value which expresses *necessary labour* the barrier to the realization of labour capacity and hence of the worker's *exchange capacity,* and to strive to reduce the relation of this necessary labour to surplus labour to the minimum. [Thus we have] a new barrier to the sphere of exchange, which is, however, at the same time identical, as is the first, with the tendency of capital to relate to every limit on its self-realization as to a barrier. The boundless enlargement of its value—boundless creation of value—therefore absolutely identical here with the positing of barriers to the sphere of exchange, i.e. the possibility of realization—the realization of the value posited in the production process.

The same with the *productive force.* On the one hand, the necessary tendency of capital to raise it to the utmost, in order to increase relative *surplus time.* On the other hand, thereby decreases *necessary labour time,* hence the worker's exchange capacity. . . .

Capital, then, posits *necessary labour time* as the barrier to the exchange value of living labour capacity; *surplus labour time* as the barrier to necessary labour time; and *surplus value* as the barrier to surplus labour time; while at the same time it drives over and beyond all these barriers, to the extent that it posits *labour capacity* opposite itself as something simply engaged in exchange, as money, and surplus labour time as the only barrier, because creatrix of surplus value. (Or, from the first aspect, it posits the exchange of surplus values as the barrier to the exchange of the necessary values.)

In one and the same moment, it posits the *values on hand* in circulation—or, what is the same, the proportion of values posited by it to the values contained in it and *presupposed* in circulation—as the barrier, the necessary barrier to its value-creation; on the other hand, its productivity as the only barrier and creatrix of values. It therefore drives constantly on one side towards its own devaluation, on the other side towards the obstruction of the productive forces, and of labour which objectifies itself in values.

Marx, *Grundrisse* (1857–58), pp. 402–08, 419–23.

CAPITAL

The creation of. . .surplus-value is the object of the direct process of production. . . . As soon as the available quantity of surplus-value has been materialised in commodities, surplus-value has been produced. But this production of surplus-value is but the first act of the capitalist process of production, it merely terminates the act of direct production. . . . Now comes the second act of the process. The entire mass of commodities, the total product, which contains a portion which is to reproduce the constant and variable capital as well as a portion representing surplus-value, must be sold. If this is not done, or only partly accomplished, or only at prices which are below the prices of production, the labourer has been none the less exploited, but his exploitation does not realise as much for the capitalist. It may yield no surplus-value at all for him, or only realise a portion of the produced surplus-value, or it may even mean a partial or complete loss of his capital. The conditions of direct exploitation and those of the realisation of surplus-value are not identical. They are separated logically as well as by time and space. The first are only limited by the productive power of society, the last by the proportional relations of the various lines of production and by the consuming power of society. This last-named power is not determined either by the absolute productive power nor by the absolute consuming power, but by the consuming power based on antagonistic conditions of distribution, which reduces the consumption of the great mass of the population to a variable minimum within more or less narrow limits. The consuming power is furthermore restricted by the tendency to accumulate, the greed for an expansion of capital and a production of surplus-value on an enlarged scale. This is a law of capitalist production imposed by incessant revolutions in the methods of production themselves, the resulting depreciation of existing capital, the general competitive struggle and the necessity of improving the product and expanding the scale of production, for the sake of self-preservation and on penalty of failure. The market must, therefore, be continually extended, so that its interrelations and the conditions regulating them assume more and more the form of a natural law independent of the producers and become ever more uncontrollable. This internal contradiction seeks to balance itself by an expansion of the outlying fields of production. But to the extent that the productive power develops, it finds itself at variance with the narrow basis on which the condition of consumption rest. On this self-contradictory basis it is no contradiction at all that there should be an excess of capital simultaneously with an excess of population. For while a combination of these two would indeed increase the mass of the produced surplus-value, it would at the same time intensify the contradiction between the conditions under which this surplus-value is produced and those under which it is realised. . . .

Periodically the conflict of antagonistic agencies seeks vent in crises. The crises are always but momentary and forcible solutions of the existing contradictions, violent eruptions, which restore the disturbed equilibrium for a while.

The contradiction, generally speaking, consists in this that the capitalist mode of production has a tendency to develop the productive forces absolutely, regardless of value and of the surplus-value contained in it and regardless of the social conditions under which capitalist production takes place; while it has on the other hand for its aim the preservation of the value of the existing capital and its self-expansion to the highest limit (that is, an ever accelerated growth of this value). Its specific character is directed at the existing value of capital as a means of increasing this value to the utmost. The methods by which it aims to accomplish this comprise a fall of the rate of profit, a depreciation of the existing capital, and a development of the productive forces of labor at the expense of the already created productive forces.

The periodical depreciation of the existing capital, which is one of the immanent means of capitalist production by which the fall in the rate of profit is checked and the accumulation of capital-value through the formation of new capital promoted, disturbs the existing conditions, within which the process of circulation and reproduction of capital takes place, and is therefore accompanied by sudden stagnations and crises in the process of production.

The relative decrease of variable capital as compared to the constant, which goes hand in hand with the development of the productive forces, gives an impulse to the growth of the laboring population, while it continually creates an artificial overpopulation. The accumulation of capital, so far as its value is concerned, is checked by the falling rate of profit, in order to hasten still more the accumulation of its use-value, and this, in its turn, adds new speed to the accumulation of its value.

Capitalist production is continually engaged in the attempt to overcome these immanent barriers, but it overcomes them only by means which again place the same barriers in its way in a more formidable size.

The real barrier of capitalist production is capital itself. It is the fact that capital and its self-expansion appear as the starting and closing point, as the motive and aim of production; that production is merely production for *capital,* and not vice versa, the means of production mere means for an ever expanding system of the life process for the benefit of the *society* of producers. The barriers, within which the preservation and self-expansion of the value of capital resting on the expropriation and pauperisation of the great mass of producers can alone move, these barriers come continually in collision with the methods of production, which capital must employ for its purposes, and which steer straight toward an unrestricted extension of production, toward production for its own self, toward an unconditional development of the productive forces of society. The means, this unconditional development of the productive forces of society, comes continually into conflict with the limited end, the self-expansion of the existing capital. Thus, while the capitalist mode of production is one of the historical means by which the material forces of production are developed and the world-market required for them created, it is at the same time in continual conflict with this historical task and the conditions of social production corresponding to it. . . .

An overproduction of capital, not of individual commodities, signifies therefore simply an overaccumulation of capital—although the overproduction of capital always includes the overproduction of commodities. In order to understand what this overaccumulation is, . . . it is but necessary to assume it to be absolute. When would an overproduction of capital be absolute? When would it be an overproduction which would not affect merely a few important lines of production, but which would be so absolute as to extend to every field of production?

There would be an absolute overproduction of capital as soon as the additional capital for purposes of capitalist production would be equal to zero. The purpose of capitalist production is the self-expansion of capital, that is, the appropriation of surplus-labour, the production of surplus-value, of profit. As soon as capital would have grown to such a proportion compared with the labouring population, that neither the absolute labour time nor the relative surplus-labour time could be extended any further (this last named extension would be out of the question even in the mere case that the demand for labour would be very strong, so that there would be a tendency for wages to rise); as soon as a point is reached where the increased capital produces no larger, or even smaller, quantities of surplus-value than it did before its increase, there would be an absolute overproduction of capital. . . . In both cases there would be a strong and sudden fall in the average rate of profit, but it would be due to a change in the composition of capital which would not be caused by the development of the productive forces, but by a rise in the money-value of the variable capital (on account of the increased wages) and the corresponding reduction in the proportion of surplus-labour to necessary labour.

In reality the matter would amount to this, that a portion of the capital would lie fallow completely or partially (because it would first have to crowd some of the active capital out before it could take part in the process of self-expansion), while the active portion would produce values at a lower rate of profit, owning to the pressure of the unemployed or but partly employed capital. Matters would not be altered in this respect, if a part of the additional capital were to take the place of some old capital crowding this into the position of additional capital. We should always have on one side the sum of old capitals, on the other that of the additional capitals. The fall in the rate of profit would then be accompanied by an absolute decrease in the mass of profits, since under the conditions assumed by us the mass of the employed labour-power could not be increased and the rate of surplus-value not raised, so that there could be no raising of the mass of surplus-value. And the reduced mass of profits would have to be calculated on an increased total capital. But even assuming that the employed capital were to continue producing value at the old rate, the mass of profits remaining the same, this mass would still be calculated on an increased total capital, and this would likewise imply a fall in the rate of profits. . . .

It is evident that this actual depreciation of the old capital could not take place without a struggle, that the additional capital ΔC could not assume the functions of capital without an effort. The rate of profit would not fall on account of competition due to the overproduction of capital. The competitive struggle would rather begin, because the fall of the rate of profit and the overproduction of capital are caused by the same conditions. The capitalists who are actively engaged with their old capitals would keep as much of the new additional capitals as would be in their hands in a fallow state, in order to prevent a depreciation of their original capital and a crowding of its space within the field of production. Or they would employ it for the purpose of loading, even at a momentary loss, the necessity of keeping additional capital fallow upon the shoulders of new intruders and other competitors in general.

That portion of ΔC which would be in new hands would seek to make room for itself at the expense of the old capital, and would accomplish this in part by forcing a portion of the old capital into a fallow state. The old capital would have to give up its place to the new and retire to the place of the completely or partially unemployed additional capital.

Under all circumstances, a portion of the old capital would be compelled to lie fallow, to give up its capacity of capital and stop acting and producing value as such. The competitive struggle would decide what part would have to go into this fallow state. So long as everything goes well, competition effects a practical brotherhood of the capitalist class, as we have seen in the case of the average rate of profit, so that each shares in the common loot in proportion to the magnitude of his share of investment. But as soon as it is no longer a question of sharing profits, but of sharing losses, every one tries to reduce his own share to a minimum and load as much as possible upon the shoulders of some other competitor. However, the class must inevitably lose. . . .

How would this confict be settled and the "healthy" movement of capitalist production resumed under normal conditions? The mode of settlement. . .implies the necessity of making unproductive, or even partially destroying, some capital, amounting either to the complete value of the additional capital ΔC, or to a part of it. . . .

But under all circumstances the equilibrium is restored by making more or less capital unproductive or destroying it. This would affect to some extent the material substance of capital, that is, a part of the means of production, fixed and circulating capital, would not perform any service as capital; a portion of the running establishments would then close down. Of course, time would corrode and depreciate all means of production (except land), but this particular stagnation would cause a far more serious destruction of means of production. However, the main effect in this case would be to suspend the functions of some means of production and prevent them for a shorter or longer time from serving as means of production.

The principal work of destruction would show its most dire effects in a slaughtering of the *values* of capitals. That portion of the value of capital which exists only in the form of claims on future shares of surplus-value of profit, which consists in fact of creditor's notes on production in its various forms, would be immediately depreciated by the reduction of the receipts on which it is calculated. . . . One portion of the commodities on the market can complete its process of circulation and reproduction only by means of an immense contraction of its prices, which means a depreciation of the capital represented by it. In the same way the elements of fixed capital are more or less depreciated. Then there is the added complication that the process of reproduction is based on definite assumptions as to prices, so that a general fall in prices checks and disturbs the process of reproduction. This interference and stagnation paralyses the function of money as a medium of payment, which is conditioned on the development of capital and the resulting price relations. The chain of payments due at certain times is broken in a hundred places, and the disaster is intensified by the collapse of the credit-system. Thus violent and acute crises are brought about, sudden and forcible depreciations, an actual stagnation and collapse of the process of reproduction, and finally a real falling off in reproduction.

At the same time still other agencies would have been at work. The stagnation of production would have laid off a part of the labouring class and thereby placed the employed part in a condition, in which they would have to submit to a reduction of wages, even below the average. This operation has the same effect on capital as though the relative or absolute surplus-value had been increased at average wages. The time of prosperity would have promoted marriages among the labourers and reduced the decimation of the offspring. These circumstances, while implying a real increase in population, do not signify an increase in the actual working population, but they nevertheless affect the relations of the labourers to capital in the same way as though the number of the actually working labourers had increased. On the other hand, the fall in prices and the competitive struggle would have given to every capitalist an impulse to raise the individual value of his total product above its average value by means of new machines, new and improved working methods, new combinations, which means, to increase the productive power of a certain quantity of labor, to lower the proportion of the variable to the constant capital, and thereby to release some labourers, in short, to create an artificial overpopulation. The depreciation of the elements of constant capital itself would be another factor tending to raise the rate of profit. The mass of the employed constant capital, compared to the variable, would have increased, but the value of this mass might have fallen. The present stagnation of production would have prepared an expansion of production later on, within capitalistic limits.

And in this way the cycle would be run once more. One portion of the capital which had been depreciated by the stagnation of its function would recover its old value. For the rest, the same vicious circle would be described once more under expanded conditions of production, in an expanded market, and with increased productive forces.

However, even under the extreme conditions assumed by us this absolute overproduction of capital would not be an absolute overproduction in the sense that it would be an absolute overproduction of means of production. It would be an overproduction of means of production *only to the extent that they serve as capital,* so that the increased value of its increased mass would also imply a utilisation for the production of more value.

Yet it would be an overproduction, because capital would be unable to exploit labour to a degree required by the "healthy, normal" development of the process of capitalist production, a degree of exploitation, which would increase at least the mass of profit to the extent that the mass of the employed capital would grow; which would therefore exclude any possibility of the rate of profit falling to the same extent that capital grows, or of the rate of profits falling even more rapidly than capital grows.

Overproduction of capital never signifies anything else but overproduction of means of production—means of production and necessities of life—which may serve as capital, that is, serve for the exploitation of labour at a given degree of exploitation; for a fall in the intensity of exploitation below a certain point calls forth disturbances and stagnations in the process of capitalist production, crises, destruction of capital. It is no contradiction that this overproduction of capital is accompanied by a more or less considerable relative overpopulation. The same circumstances, which have increased the productive power of labour, augmented the mass of produced commodities, expanded the markets, accelerated the accumulation of capital both as concerns its mass and its value, and lowered the rate of profit, these same circumstances have also created a relative overpopulation, and continue to create it all the time, an overpopulation of labourers who are not employed by the surplus-capital on account of the low degree of exploitation at which they might be employed, or at least on account of the low rate of profit, which they would yield with the given rate of exploitation. . . .

The fall in the rate of profit connected with accumulation necessarily creates a competitive struggle. The compensation of the fall in the rate of profit by a rise in the mass of profit applies only to the total social capital and to the great capitalists who are firmly installed. The new additional capital, which enters upon its functions, does not enjoy any such compensating conditions. It must conquer them for itself, and so the fall in the rate of profit calls forth the competitive struggle among capitalists, not vice versa. This competitive struggle is indeed accompanied by a transient rise in wages and a resulting further fall of the rate of profit for a short time. The same thing is seen in the overproduction of commodities, the overstocking of markets. Since the aim of capital is not to minister to certain wants, but to produce profits, and since it accomplishes this purpose by methods which adapt the mass of production to the scale of production, not vice versa, conflict must continually ensue between the limited conditions of consumption on a capitalist basis and a production which forever tends to exceed its immanent barriers. Moreover, capital consists of commodities, and therefore the overproduction of capital implies an overproduction of commodities. Hence we meet with the peculiar phenomenon that the same economists, who deny the overproduction of commodities, admit that of capital. If it is said that there is no general overproduction, but that a disproportion grows up between various lines of production, then this is tantamount to saying that within capitalist production the proportionality of the individual lines of production is brought about through a continual process of disproportionality, that is, the interrelations of production as a whole enforce themselves as a blind law upon the agents of production instead of having brought the productive process under their common control as a law understood by the social mind. . . . If it is said that overproduction is only relative, then the statement is correct; but the entire mode of production is only a relative one, whose barriers are not absolute, but have absoluteness only in so far as it is capitalistic. Otherwise, how could there be a lack of demand for the very commodities which the mass of the people want, and how would it be possible that this demand must be sought in foreign countries, in foreign markets, in order that the labourers at home might receive in payment the average amount of necessities of life? This is possible only because in this specific capitalist interrelation the surplus-product assumes a form, in which its owner cannot offer it for consumption, unless it first reconverts itself into capital for him. . . . In short, all these objections to the obvious phenomena of overproduction (phenomena which do not pay any attention to these objections) amounts to this, that the barriers of capitalist production are not absolute barriers of production itself and therefore no barriers of this specific, capitalistic, production. But the contradiction of this capitalist mode of production consists precisely in its tendency to an absolute development of productive forces, a development, which comes continually in conflict with the specific conditions of production in which capital moves and alone can move.

It is not a fact that too many necessities of life are produced in proportion to the existing population. The reverse is true. Not enough is produced to satisfy the wants of the great mass decently and humanely.

It is not a fact that too many means of production are produced to employ the able-bodied portion of the population. The reverse is the case. In the first place, too large a portion of the population is produced consisting of people who are really not capable of working, who are dependent through force of circumstances on the exploitation of the labour of others, or compelled to perform certain kinds of labour which can be dignified with this name only under a miserable mode of production. In the second place, not enough means of production are produced to permit the employment of the entire able-bodied population under the most productive conditions, so that their absolute labour time would be shortened by the mass and effectiveness of the constant capital employed during working hours.

On the other hand, there is periodically a production of too many means of production and necessities of life to permit of their serving as means for the exploitation of the labourers at a certain rate of profit. Too many commodities are produced to permit of a realisation of the value and surplus-value contained in them under the conditions of distribution and consumption peculiar to capitalist production, that is, too many to permit of the continuation of this process without ever recurring explosions.

It is not a fact that too much wealth is produced. But it is true that there is periodical overproduction of wealth in its capitalistic and self-contradictory form.

The barrier of the capitalist mode of production becomes apparent:

1) In the fact that the development of the productive power of labour creates in the falling rate of profit a law which turns into an antagonism of this mode of production at a certain point and requires for its defeat periodical crises.

2) In the fact that the expansion or contraction of production is determined by the appropriation of unpaid labour, and by the proportion of this unpaid labour to materialised labour in general, or, to speak the language of the capitalists, is determined by profit and by the proportion of this profit to the employed capital, by a definite rate of profit, instead of being determined by the relations of production to social wants to the wants of socially developed human beings. The capitalist mode of production, for this reason, meets with barriers at a certain scale of production which would be inadequate under different conditions. It comes to a standstill at a point determined by the production and realisation of profit, not by the satisfaction of social needs. . . .

The following three principal facts of capitalist production must be kept in mind:

1) Concentration of means of production in a few hands, whereby they cease to appear as the property of the immediate labourers and transform themselves into social powers of production. It is true, they first become the private property of capitalists. These are the trustees of bourgeois society, but they pocket the proceeds of their trusteeship.

2) Organisation of labour itself into social labour, by social cooperation, division of labour, and combination of labour with natural sciences.

In both directions, the capitalist mode of production abolishes private property and private labour, even though it does so in contradictory forms.

3) Creation of the world market.

The stupendous productive power developing under the capitalist mode of production relatively to population, and the increase, though not in the same proportion, of capital values (not their material substance), which grow much more rapidly than the population, contradict the basis, which, compared to the expanding wealth, is ever narrowing and for which this immense productive power works, and the conditions, under which capital augments its value. This is the cause of crises. ...

It is purely a tautology to say that crises are caused by the scarcity of solvent consumers, of of a paying consumption. The capitalist system does not know any other modes of consumption but a paying one, except that of the pauper or of the "thief." If any commodities are unsalable, it means that no solvent purchasers have been found for them, in other words, consumers (whether commodities are bought in the last instance for productive or individual consumption). But if one were to attempt to clothe this tautology with a semblance of a profounder justification by saying that the working class receive too small a portion of their own product, and the evil would be remedied by giving them a larger share of it, or raising their wages, we should reply that crises are precisely always preceded by a period in which wages rise generally and the working class actually get a larger share of the annual product intended for consumption. From the point of view of the advocates of "simple" (!) common sense, such a period should rather remove a crisis. It seems, then, that capitalist production comprises certain conditions which are independent of good or bad will and permit the working class to enjoy that relative prosperity only momentarily, and at that always as a harbinger of a coming crisis. ...

Let us suppose that the whole society is composed only of industrial capitalists and wage workers. Let us furthermore make exceptions of fluctuations of prices, which prevent large portions of the total capital from reproducing themselves under average conditions and which, owing to the general interrelations of the entire process of reproduction, such as are developed particularly by credit, must always call forth general stoppages of a transient nature. Let us also make abstraction of the bogus transactions and speculations, which the credit system favors. In that case, a crisis could be explained only by a disproportion of production in various branches, and by a disproportion of the consumption of the capitalists and the accumulation of their capitals. But as matters stand, the reproduction of the capitals invested in production depends largely upon the consuming power of the non-producing classes; while the consuming power of the labourers is handicapped partly by the laws of wages, partly by the fact that it can be exerted only so long as the labourers can be employed at a profit for the capitalist class. The last cause of all real crises always remains the poverty and restricted consumption of the masses as compared to the tendency of capitalist production to develop the productive forces in such a way, that only the absolute power of consumption of the entire society would be their limit.

Marx, *Capital,* (1894), pp. 286-87, 242-303, 312-13, 568; II (1885), pp. 475-76.

7 Capitalism's Development, Transformation, and Demise

A. GROWING INTENSITY OF CAPITALISM'S ECONOMIC AND SOCIAL PROBLEMS

In addition to his analysis of capitalism's origins, social relations, and progressive and contradictory properties, Marx (and here we should add Engels) also formulated a broad theoretical vision of capitalism's prospective development, transformation, and demise. This vision had two main parts. One was an expectation of a growing intensity of capitalism's economic and social problems, illustrated by several prominent "laws of motion," and associated with an evolutionary transformation from competitive capitalism to a big business oligopoly or monopoly capitalism. The second was a qualitative process of transformation and socialization, whereby capitalism, through its own internal dialectic, was perceived as both laying the foundations for and also giving hints and suggestions of the socialist future to come.

Other than the "falling rate of profit" (selection 6.B.4), the classical Marxian vision of developmental trends and tendencies under mature capitalism contains five major themes. First is a tendency toward big business and monopoly power (selection 7.A.1). Economies of large-scale production (which Marx assumed would increase with expanded technology) increase the minimum size of business necessary for efficiency and thereby encourage "concentration" of capital, i.e., an increased absolute size or scale of enterprise. These same economies of scale, supplemented by that "new formidable weapon in the competitive struggle—the credit system" encourage, by merger and the exit of small firms from the market, a "centralization" of capital or concentration of capital and production in the hands of a smaller number of capitalists, i.e., an increased relative size of enterprise or monopolization.

The resulting monopoly power supplements the basic property power in capitalist economy, enabling enterprises to charge above-competitive prices and to pay below-competitive wages, and thereby extend the range of exploitation.[1] Monopoly is also interwoven with cycles. On the one hand, during depressions, small, bankrupt businesses sell out at subvalue prices to larger capitalists. On the other, by restricting entry, forcing small capitalists out of business, generating monopoly profits, and extending the scope of labor-saving invention, monopoly increases cyclical severity. However, monopoly for Marx is not simply an intensification of capitalism's dysfunctional properties. Its extra surpluses and large-scale operations facilitate large-scale investment projects (such as railroads) and technological changes which would occur more slowly, if at all, under more competitive conditions. Further, monopoly socializes work and production, thereby radically reducing the technological, economic, and social "distance" between mature capitalism and socialism.[2]

Second, cyclical crises are expected to become more widespread and the amplitude of accompanying depressions more severe. (This, in turn, is expected to contribute to working class discontent and prospective socialist revolution.) The major contributive factors, several of which are sketched in selection 7.A.2, are as follows. Growing wealth increases the absolute magnitude of cyclical fluctuations. The growth of the world market makes cycles more widespread. Increased durability of fixed capital lengthens the depression adjustment period during which equipment is depreciated. Expansion of credit stimulates overinvestment and speculative ventures in the boom, adding to the liquidity crisis after the ensuing downturn. As noted earlier (selection 6.B.3), the rising organic composition of capital (c/v) stimulates a relative decline in the demand for labor and, together with other factors, thereby causes an increase in the "reserve army of the unemployed," which becomes especially intense during succeeding depressions.

Third, from the perspective of the middle decades of the nineteenth century, Marx regarded the economic lot and social position of workers under capitalism as miserable. Further, the "immiserization" (to use Schumpeter's translation of the German word *Verelendung)* of workers was expected, if anything, to increase in several ways with the further development of capitalism. No doubt Marx associated a large part of the immiserization of labor with capitalism's general dysfunctional properties, i.e., alienation, exploitation, and cyclical crises and depressions, all of which were expected to become more widespread and to increase in magnitude and severity. However, some part at least of working class misery was expected to emanate from reduction in workers' real income, generally expressed in Marx's and Engels' mature writings in relative terms, i.e., *relative to* the expanding wealth, power, and luxury consumption of the capitalist and propertied rich. This prognostication is consistent, however, with (a) an increase in the percent of national income going to all workers as a class, as the size of the labor force increases and the number of capitalists diminishes; (b) a decrease in profit rates, for it is quite possible for the rate of profit to fall as the absolute "mass" of profit rises; and (c) an increase in the absolute level of real

[1]As Joan Robinson aptly phrased it in her study of Marx, "the share of labor in total output is ground between the upper and the nether millstones of monopoly and monopsony." *An Essay on Marxian Economics* (London: Macmillan, 1957), p. 76.

[2]Put succinctly, "there is less difference between large-scale capitalist enterprise and large-scale socialized enterprise on the one hand than between small-scale capitalist enterprise and large-scale capitalist enterprise on the other." William Ebenstein, *Today's isms* (Englewood Cliffs: Prentice-Hall, 1967), p. 185.

wages and/or real wages per worker.[3] The important point is that "the abyss between the labourer's position and that of the capitalist would keep widening" (selection 7.A.3).

Next, for Marx, if the historical mission of the capitalist class is the creation of the preconditions for a new, communist mode of production, the mission of the working class (notably industrial workers and the intelligentsia) is the building of a new society. The connecting linkage is that the working class, with its capacity and resolve to make the transition to and to build the new society, is itself a product of the capitalist developmental process. All of these factors—capitalism's general contradictory properties as well as its developmental trends and tendencies as it moves into maturity—stimulate a "consciousness' by workers of their class identity and social position, contribute to their association and organization, and encourge economic and political action on their collective behalf (selections 7.A.4 and 7.A.5). Labor-saving inventions, depressions, and growing capitalist monopsony power all conspire to push wages down. But labor unions provide a practical vehicle to constrain these forces and, perhaps to some degree, to raise wages. The major benefits from working class association and organization, however, are more long-run and sociopolitical in character. The universality towards which capitalism "irresistibly strives" will, at a "certain stage of its development, allow itself to be recognized as being itself the greatest barrier to this tendency, and hence will drive towards its own suspension." Increasing recognition by the working class of the product of capitalist industry "as its own and the judgment that its separation from the conditions of its realization is improper—forcibly imposed—is an enormous [advance in] awareness, and as much the knell to its doom" as the slave's growing consciousness of himself as a person and growing awareness that a person *"cannot be the property of another"* was a contributor to the earlier supersession of slavery.[4]

Last, all these trends and tendencies (together with capitalism's creative destructiveness and qualitative transformation described in Chapter 7B, below) are indicators of a society which is either in decay and disintegration or is inviting its revolutionary overthrow. Selection 7.A.6, drawn from the writings of both Marx and Engels, summarizes the system-decline of capitalism and presents Marx's brief but pointed apocalyptic vision of capitalism's final death knell.

7.A.1 CONCENTRATION AND CENTRALIZATION OF CAPITAL

It was shown how the development of the productiveness of social labour presupposes cooperation on a large scale; how it is only upon this supposition that division and combination of labour can be organised, and the means of production economised by concentration on a vast scale; how instruments of labour which, from their very nature, are only fit for use in common, such as a system of machinery, can be called into being; how huge natural forces can be

[3] John E. Elliott, *Comparative Economic Systems* (Englewood Cliffs: Prentice-Hall, 1973), pp. 145–46.

[4] Marx, *Grundrisse* (New York: Random House, 1973), pp. 410, 463.

pressed into the service of production; and how the transformation can be effected of the process of production into a technological application of science. On the basis of the production of commodities, where the means of production are the property of private persons, and where the artisan therefore either produces commodities, isolated from and independent of others, or sells his labour-power as a commodity, because he lacks the means for independent industry, cooperation on a large scale can realise itself only in the increase of individual capitals, only in proportion as the means of social production and the means of subsistence are transformed into the private property of capitalists. The basis of the production of commodities can admit of production on a large scale in the capitalistic form alone. A certain accumulation of capital, in the hands of individual producers of commodities, forms therefore the necessary preliminary of the specifically capitalistic mode of production. We had, therefore, to assume that this occurs during the transition from handicraft to capitalistic industry. It may be called primitive accumulation, because it is the historic basis, instead of the historic result of specifically capitalist production. How it itself originates, we need not here inquire as yet. It is enough that it forms the starting-point. But all methods for raising the social productive power of labour that are developed on this basis, are at the same time methods for the increased production of surplus-value or surplus-product, which in its turn is the formative element of accumulation. They are, therefore, at the same time methods of the production of capital by capital, or methods of its accelerated accumulation. The continual retransformation of surplus-value into capital now appears in the shape of the increasing magnitude of the capital that enters into the process of production. This in turn is the basis of an extended scale of production, of the methods for raising the productive power of labour that accompany it, and of accelerated production of surplus-value. If, therefore, a certain degree of accumulation of capital appears as a condition of the specifically capitalist mode of production, the latter causes conversely an accelerated accumulation of capital. With the accumulation of capital, therefore, the specifically capitalistic mode of production develops, and with the capitalist mode of production the accumulation of capital. Both these economic factors bring about, in the compound ratio of the impulses they reciprocally give one another, that change in the technical composition of capital by which the variable constituent becomes always smaller and smaller as compared with the constant.

Every individual capital is a larger or smaller concentration of means of production, with a corresponding command over a larger or smaller labour-army. Every accumulation becomes the means of new accumulation. With the increasing mass of wealth which functions as capital, accumulation increases the concentration of that wealth in the hands of individual capitalists, and thereby widens the basis of production on a large scale and of the specific methods of capitalist production. The growth of social capital is effected by the growth of many individual capitals. All other circumstances remaining the same, individual capitals, and with them the concentration of the means of production, increases in such proportion as they form aliquot parts of the total social capital. At the same time portions of the original capitals disengage themselves and function as new independent capitals. Besides other causes, the division of property, within capitalist families, plays a great part in this. With the accumulation of capital, therefore, the number of capitalists grows to a greater or less extent. Two points characterise this kind of concentration which grows directly out of, or rather is identical with, accumulation. First: The increasing concentration of the social means of production in the hands of individual capitalists is, other things remaining equal, limited by the degree of increase of social wealth. Second: The part of social capital domiciled in each particular sphere of production is divided among many capitalists who face one another as independent commodity-producers competing with each other. Accumulation and the concentration accompanying it are, therefore, not only scattered over many points, but the increase of each functioning capital is thwarted by the formation of new and the subdivision of old capitals. Accumulation, therefore, presents itself on the one hand as increasing concentration of the means of production, and of the command over labour; on the other, as repulsion of many individual capitals one from another.

This splitting-up of the total social capital into many individual capitals or the repulsion of its fractions one from another, is counteracted by their attraction. This last does not mean that simple concentration of the means of production and of the command over labour, which is identical with accumulation. It is concentration of capitals already formed, destruction of their individual independence, expropriation of capitalist by capitalist, transformation of many small into few large capitals. This process differs from the former in this, that it only presupposes a change in the distribution of capital already to hand, and functioning; its field of action is therefore not limited by the absolute growth of social wealth, by the absolute limits of accumulation. Capital grows in one place to a huge mass in a single hand, because it has in another place been lost by many. This is centralisation proper, as distinct from accumulation and concentration.

The laws of this centralisation of capitals, or of the attraction of capital by capital, cannot be developed here. A brief hint at a few facts must suffice. The battle of competition is fought by cheapening of commodities. The cheapness of commodities depends, *caeteris paribus,* on the productiveness of labour, and this again on the scale of production. Therefore, the larger capitals beat the smaller. It will further be remembered that, with the development of the capitalist mode of production, there is an increase in the minimum amount of individual capital necessary to carry on a business under its normal conditions. The smaller capitals, therefore, crowd into spheres of production which Modern Industry has only sporadically or incompletely got hold of. Here competition rages in direct proportion to the number, and in inverse proportion to the magnitudes, of the antagonistic capitals. It always ends in the ruin of many small capitalists, whose capitals partly pass into the hand of their conquerors, partly vanish. Apart from this, with capitalist production an altogether new force comes into play—the credit system.

In its beginnings, the credit system sneaks in as a modest helper of accumulation and draws by invisible threads the money resources scattered all over the surface of society into the hands of individual or associated capitalists. But soon it becomes a new and formidable weapon in the competitive struggle, and finally it transforms itself into an immense social mechanism for the centralisation of capitals.

Competition and credit, the two most powerful levers of centralization, develop in proportion as capitalist production and accumulation do. At the same time the progress of accumulation increases the matter subject to centralisation, that is, the individual capitals, while the expansion of capitalist production creates the social demand here, the technical requirements there, for those gigantic industrial enterprises, which depend for their realisation on a previous centralisation of capitals. Nowadays, then, the mutual attraction of individual capitals and the tendency to centralisation are stronger than ever before. However, while the relative expansion and energy of the centralisation movement is determined to a certain degree by the superiority of the economic mechanism, yet the progress of centralisation is by no means dependent upon the positive growth of the volume of social capital. This is the particular distinction between centralisation and concentration, the latter being but another expression for reproduction on an enlarged scale. Centralisation may take place by a mere change in the distribution of already existing capitals, a simple change in the quantitative arrangements of the components of social capital. Capital may in that case accumulate in one hand in large masses by withdrawing it from many individual hands. Centralisation in a certain line of industry would have reached its extreme limit, if all the individual capitals invested in it would have been amalgamated into one single capital.

This limit would not be reached in any particular society until the entire social capital would be united, either in the hands of one single capitalist, or in those of one single corporation.

Centralisation supplements the work of accumulation, by enabling the industrial capitalists to expand the scale of their operations. The economic result remains the same, whether this consummation is brought about by accumulation or centralisation, whether centralisation is accomplished by the violent means of annexation, by which some capitals become such overwhelming centers of gravitation for others as to break their individual cohesion and attracting the scattered fragments, or whether the amalgamation of a number of capitals, which already exist or are in process of formation, proceeds by the smoother road of forming stock companies. The increased volume of industrial establishments forms everywhere the point of departure for a more comprehensive organisation of the cooperative labor of many, for a wider development of their material powers, that is, for the progressive transformation of isolated processes of production carried on in accustomed ways into socially combined and scientifically managed processes of production.

It is evident, however, that accumulation, the gradual propagation of capital by a reproduction passing from a circular into a spiral form, is a very slow process as compared with centralisation, which needs but to alter the quantitative grouping of the integral parts of social capital. The world would still be without railroads, if it had been obliged to wait until accumulation should have enabled a few individual capitals to undertake the construction of a railroad. Centralisation, on the other hand, accomplished this by a turn of the hand through stock companies. Centralisation, by thus accelerating and intensifying the effects of accumulation, extends and hastens at the same time the revolutions in the technical composition of capital, which increase its constant part at the expense of its variable part and thereby reduce the relative demand for labor.

The masses of capital amalgamated over night by centralisation reproduce and augment themselves like the others, only faster, and thus become new and powerful levers of social accumulation. Hence, if the progress of social accumulation is mentioned nowadays, it comprizes as a matter of course the effects of centralisation. The additional capitals formed in the course of normal accumulation. . . serve mainly as vehicles for the exploitation of new inventions and discoveries, or of industrial improvements in general. However, the old capital likewise arrives in due time at the moment when it must renew its head and limbs, when it casts off its old skin and is likewise born again in its perfected industrial form, in which a smaller quantity of labor suffices to set in motion a larger quantity of machinery and raw materials. The absolute decrease of the demand for labor necessarily following therefrom will naturally be so much greater, the more these capitals going through the process of rejuvenation have become accumulated in masses by means of the movement of centralisation.

On the one hand, therefore, the additional capital formed in the course of accumulation attracts fewer and fewer labourers in proportion to its magnitude. On the other hand, the old capital periodically reproduced with change of composition, repels more and more of the labourers formerly employed by it. . . .

A fall in the rate of profit and a hastening of accumulation are in so far only different expressions of the same process as both of them indicate the development of the productive power. Accumulation in its turn hastens the fall of the rate of profit, inasmuch as it implies the concentration of labor on a large scale and thereby a higher composition of capital. On the other hand, a fall in the rate of profit hastens the concentration of capital and its centralisation through the expropriation of the smaller capitalists, the expropriation of the last survivors of the direct producers who still have anything to give up. This accelerates on one hand the accumulation, so far as mass is concerned, although the rate of accumulation falls with the rate of profit. . . .

Under competition, the increase in the minimum of capital required for the successful operation of an independent industrial establishment in keeping with the increase in productivity assumes the following aspect: As soon as the new and more expensive equipment has become universally established, smaller capitals are henceforth excluded from these enterprises. Smaller capitals can carry on an independent activity in such lines only during the incipient stage of mechanical inventioms. On the other hand, very large enterprises, such as railroads, with an extraordinarily high relative proportion of constant capital, do not yield any average rate of profit, but only a portion of it, interest. Otherwise the rate of profit would fall still lower. At the same time, this offers direct employment to large aggregations of capital in the form of stocks. . . .

We have seen that the growing accumulation of capital implies its growing concentration. Thus the power of capital, the personification of the conditions of social production in the capitalist, grows over the heads of the real producers. Capital shows itself more and more as a social power, whose agent the capitalist is, and which stands no longer in any possible relation to the things which the labor of any single individual can create. Capital becomes a strange, independent, social power, which stands opposed to society as a thing, and as the power of capitalists by means of this thing. The contradiction between capital as a general social power and as a power of private capitalists over the social conditions of production develops into an ever more irreconcilable clash, which implies the dissolution of these relations and the elaboration of the conditions of production into universal, common, social conditions. This elaboration is performed by the development of the productive powers under capitalist production, and by the course which this development pursues.

Marx, *Capital,* I (1867), pp. 684–89; III (1894), pp. 283, 308, 310.

7.A.2 CAPITALIST CRISES

CRISIS AND REVOLUTION

While the continent in the past two years was occupied with revolutions, counterrevolutions, and the torrent of speeches inseparable from them, industrial England produced a completely different article: prosperity. Here, in due course, the commercial crisis which broke out in the fall of 1845 was twice interrupted—early in 1846 by Parliament's free-trade decisions, and early in 1848 by the February Revolution. A mass of commodities in the depressed overseas markets gradually found other outlets in the meantime. The February Revolution eliminated the competition of European industry even in the overseas markets, while English industry did not lose much more in the disrupted market of the Continent than it would have lost anyhow had the crisis continued. The February Revolution, which brought continental industry momentarily almost to a standstill, thus helped the English to weather a year of crisis quite well, contributed to the liquidation of piled-up stock in the overseas markets, and substantially made possible the new industrial upswing in the spring of 1849. This upswing, which for that matter also extended to a large part of continental industry, has reached such a degree in the past three months that manufacturers claim they have never had such a prosperous time—a claim that is always made on the eve of a crisis. The factories are overloaded with orders and operate expeditiously; they try everything to elude the ten-hour law so as to gain more working hours; masses of new factories are being built in all industrial areas and old ones are being enlarged. Cash is pouring into the market, hitherto unused capital wanting to take advantage of general profits; speculation fills the discount rate, throws itself into production or on the raw materials market; and practically all articles are increasing in price, absolutely and relatively.

In short, England is blessed with "prosperity" in full bloom, and one can only inquire how long the delirium will last. Not very long, in any case. Many of the biggest markets, especially the East Indies, are already glutted; export now favors the really great markets less than the entrepôts of world commerce, whence commodities can be directed to favorable markets. Soon the colossal productive forces which English industry added to itself between 1843 and

1845, in 1846 and 1847 and especially 1849, and keeps on adding daily, will lead to a glut in the remaining markets, especially the Australian and American ones—and with the first news of this glut will come a simultaneous "panic" in speculation and production, perhaps as early as the end of the spring, or at the latest in July or August. This crisis, however, because it has to coincide with great collisions on the Continent, will have entirely different consequences from the previous ones. Hitherto every crisis has been the signal for a new advance, a new victory of the industrial bourgeoisie over landed property and over the financial bourgeoisie, but this coming one will mark the beginning of the modern English revolution.

Marx-Engels, "Revue," (1850), MR, pp. 51–52.

With...general prosperity, in which the productive forces of bourgeois society develop as luxuriantly as is at all possible within bourgeois relationships, there can be no talk of a real revolution. Such a revolution is only possible in the periods when *both* these *factors,* the *modern* productive *forces* and the *bourgeois production forms,* come in *collision* with one another. The various quarrels in which the representatives of the individual factions of the Continental Party of Order now indulge and mutually compromise themselves, far from providing the occasion for new revolutions, are, on the contrary, only possible because the basis of the relationships is momentarily so secure and (what the reaction does not know) *so bourgeois.* From it all attempts of the reaction to hold up bourgeois development will rebound just as certainly as all moral indignation and all enthusiastic proclamations of the democrats. *A new revolution is only possible in consequence of a new crisis. It is, however, also just as certain as this.*

Marx, *Class Struggles* (1850), MESW, II, p. 299.

The contradictions inherent in the movement of capitalist society impress themselves upon the practical bourgeois most strikingly in the changes of the periodic cycle, through which modern industry runs, and whose crowning point is the universal crisis. That crisis is once again approaching, although as yet but in its preliminary stage; and by the universality of its theatre and the intensity of its action it will drum dialectics even into the heads of the mushroom-upstarts of the new, holy Prusso-German empire.

Marx, *Capital,* I (1867), p. 26.

CRISES AND THE WORKING CLASS

All political economists of any standing admit that the introduction of new machinery has a baneful effect on the workmen in the old handicrafts and manufacturers with which this machinery at first competes. Almost all of them bemoan the slavery of the factory operative. And what is the great trump-card that they play? That machinery, after the horrors of the period of introduction and development have subsided, instead of diminishing, in the long run increases the number of the slaves of labour! Yes, political economy revels in the hideous theory, hideous to every "philanthropist" who believes in the eternal nature-ordained necessity for capitalist production, that after a period of growth and transition, even its crowning success, the factory system based on machinery, grinds down more workpeople than on its first introduction it throws on the streets. . . .

Nevertheless, in spite of the mass of hands actually displaced and virtually replaced by machinery, we can understand how the factory operatives, through the building of more mills and the extension of old ones in a given industry, may become more numerous than the manufacturing workmen and handicraftsmen that have been displaced. . . . Hence, a relative decrease in the number of hands is consistent with an actual increase. We assumed above that while the total capital increases, its composition remains the same, because the conditions of production remain constant. But we have already seen that, with every advance in the use of machinery, the constant component of capital, that part which consists of machinery, raw material, etc., increases, while the variable component, the part laid out in labour-power, decreases. We also know that in no other system of production is improvement so continuous, and the composition of the capital employed so constantly changing as in the factory system. These changes are, however, continually interrupted by periods of rest, during which there is a mere quantitative extension of the factories on the existing technical basis. During such periods the operatives increase in number. . . .

So long as in a given branch of industry, the factory system extends itself at the expense of the old handicrafts or of manufacture, the result is as sure as is the result of an encounter between any army furnished with breach-loaders, and one armed with bows and arrows. This first period, during which machinery conquers its field of action, is of decisive importance owing to the extraordinary profits that it helps to produce. These profits not only form a source of accelerated accumulation, but also attract into the favoured sphere of production a large part of the additional social capital that is being constantly created, and is ever on the look-out for new investments. The special advantages of this first period of fast and furious activity are felt in every branch of production that machinery invades. So soon, however, as the factory system has gained a certain breadth of footing and a definite degree of maturity, and, especially, so soon as its technical basis, machinery, is itself produced by machinery; so soon as coal mining and iron mining, the metal industries, and the means of transport have been revolutionised; so soon, in short, as the general conditions requisite for production by the modern industrial system have been established, this mode of production acquires an elasticity, a capacity for sudden extension by leaps and bounds that finds no hindrance except in the supply of raw material and in the disposal of the produce. On the one hand, the immediate effect of machinery is to increase the supply of raw material in the same way, for example, as the cotton gin augmented the production of cotton. On the other hand, the cheapness of the articles produced by machinery, and the improved means of transport and communication furnish the weapons for conquering foreign markets. By ruining handicraft production in other countries, machinery forcibly converts them into fields for the supply of its raw material. In this way East India was compelled to produce cotton, wool, hemp, jute, and indigo for Great Britain.

By constantly making a part of the hands "supernumerary," modern industry, in all countries where it has taken root, gives a spur to emigration and to the colonization of foreign lands, which are thereby converted into settlements for growing the raw material of the mother country; just as Australia, for example, was converted into a colony for growing wool. A new and international division of labour, a division suited to the requirements of the chief centres of modern industry springs up, and converts one part of the globe into a chiefly agricultural field of production, for supplying the other part which remains a chiefly industrial field. This evolution hangs together with radical changes in agriculture which we need not here further inquire into. . . .

The enormous power, inherent in the factory system, of expanding by jumps, and the dependence of that system on the markets of the world, necessarily beget feverish production, followed by over-filling of the markets, whereupon contraction of the markets brings on crippling of production. The life of modern industry becomes a series of periods of moderate activity, prosperity, overproduction, crisis and stagnation. The uncertainty and instability to which machinery subjects the employment, and consequently the conditions of existence, of the operatives become normal, owing to these periodic changes of the industrial cycle. Except in the periods of prosperity, there rages between the capitalists the most furious combat for the share of each in the markets. This share is directly proportional to the cheapness of the product. Besides the rivalry that this struggle begets in the application of improved machinery for replacing labour-power, and of new methods of production, there also comes a time in every industrial cycle, when a forcible reduction of wages beneath the value of labour-power, is attempted for the purpose of cheapening commodities.

A necessary condition, therefore, to the growth of the number of factory hands, is a proportionally much more rapid growth of the amount of capital invested in mills. This growth, however, is conditioned by the ebb and flow of the industrial cycle. It is, besides, constantly interrupted by the technical progress that at one time virtually supplies the place of new workmen, at another, actually displaces old ones. This qualitative change in mechanical industry continually discharges hands from the factory, or shuts its doors against the fresh stream of recruits, while the purely quantitative extension of the factories absorbs not only the men thrown out of work, but also fresh contingents. The workpeople are thus continually both repelled and attracted, hustled from pillar to post, while, at the same time, constant changes take place in the sex, age, and skill of the levies.

Marx, *Capital,* I (1867), pp. 488–96.

INCREASING CYCLICAL SEVERITY

Modern bourgeois society with its relations of production, of exchange and of property, a society that has conjured up such gigantic means of production and of exchange, is like the sorcerer, who is no longer able to control the powers of the nether world whom he has called up by his spells. For many a decade past the history of industry and commerce is but the history of the revolt of modern productive forces against modern conditions of production, against the property relations that are the conditions for the existence of the bourgeoisie and of its rule. It is enough to mention the commercial crises that by their periodical return put on its trial, each time more threateningly, the existence of the entire bourgeois society. In these crises a great part not only of the existing products, but also of the previously created productive forces, are periodically destroyed. In these crises there breaks out an epidemic that, in all earlier epochs, would have seemed an absurdity—the epidemic of overproduction. Society suddenly finds itself put back into a state of momentary barbarism; it appears as if a famine, a universal war of devastation had cut off the supply of every means of subsistence; industry and commerce seem to be destroyed; and why? Because there is too much civilisation, too much means of subsistence, too much industry, too much commerce. The productive forces at the disposal of society no longer tend to further the development of the conditions of bourgeois property; on the contrary, they have become too powerful for these conditions, by which they are fettered, and so soon as they overcome these fetters, they bring disorder into the whole of bourgeois society, endanger the existence of bourgeois property. The conditions of bourgeois society are too narrow to comprise the wealth created by them. And how does the bourgeoisie get over these crises? On the one hand by enforced destruction of a mass of productive forces; on the other, by the conquest of new markets, and by the more thorough exploitation of the old ones. That is to say, by paving the way for more extensive and more destructive crises, and by diminishing the means whereby crises are prevented.

Marx-Engels, *Communist Manifesto* (1848), excerpt from Part I.

The growing incompatibility between the productive development of society and its hitherto existing relations of production expresses itself in bitter contradictions, crises, spasms. The violent destruction of capital not by relations external to it, but rather as a condition of its self-preservation, is the most striking form in which advice is given it to be gone and to give room to a higher state of social production. It is not only the growth of scientific power, but the measure in which it is already posited as fixed capital, the scope and width in which it is realized and has conquered the totality of production. It is, likewise, the development of the population etc., in short, of all moments of production; in that the productive power of labour, like the application of machinery, is related to the population; whose growth in and for itself already is the presupposition as well as the result of the growth of the use values to be reproduced and hence also to be consumed. Since this decline of profit signifies the same as the decrease of immediate labour relative to the size of the objectified labour which it reproduces and newly posits, capital will atempt every means of checking the smallness of the relation of living labour to the size of the capital generally, hence also of the surplus value, if expressed as profit, relative to the presupposed capital, by reducing the allotment made to necessary labour and by still more expanding the quantity of surplus labour with regard to the whole labour employed. Hence the highest development of productive power together with the greatest expansion of existing wealth will coincide with depreciation of capital, degradation of the labourer, and a most straitened exhaustion of his vital powers. These contradictions lead to explosions, cataclysms, crises, in which by momentaneous suspension of labour and annihilation of a great portion of capital the latter is violently reduced to the point where it can go on. These contradictions, of course, lead to explosions, crises, in which momentary suspension of all labour and annihilation of a great part of the capital violently lead it back to the point where it is enabled [to go on] fully employing its productive powers without committing suicide. Yet, these regularly recurring catastrophes lead to their repetition on a higher scale, and finally to its violent overthrow.

Marx, *Grundrisse* (1857–58), pp. 749–50.

7.A.3 WORKER IMMISERIZATION

IMMISERIZATION: RELATIVE VS. ABSOLUTE

The value of wages has to be reckoned not on the basis of the quantity of necessaries which the worker receives, but on the basis of the quantity of labour which these necessaries cost—actually the proportion of the working day which he appropriates for himself; the proportionate share of the total product, or rather of the total value of this product, which the worker receives. It is possible that, reckoned in use values (quantity of commodities or money), his wages may rise as productivity increases, and yet reckoned in value they may fall, and *vice versa.* It is one of Ricardo's greatest merits that he made an examination of relative wages and established them as a definite category. Previously wages had always been looked upon as a simple element, and consequently the worker had been regarded as an animal. In Ricardo, however, he is considered in his social relationship. The position of the classes in relation to each other depends to a greater extent on the proportion which the wage forms than on the absolute amount of the wage.

Marx, *Theories of Surplus Value* (1861–3), p. 320.

The value of labour-power is determined by the value of a given quantity of necessaries. It is the value and not the mass of these necessaries that varies with the productiveness of labour. It is, however, possible that, owing to an increase of productiveness, both the labourer, and the capitalist may simultaneously be able to appropriate a greater quantity of these necessaries, without any change in the price of labour-power or in surplus-value. If the value of labour-power be three shillings, and the necessary labour-time amount to six hours, if the surplus-value likewise be three shillings, and the surplus-labour six hours, then if the productiveness of labour were doubled without altering the ratio of necessary labour to surplus-labour, there would be no change of magnitude in surplus-value and price of labour-power. The only result would be that each of them would represent twice as many use-values as before; these use-values being twice as cheap as before. Although labour-power would be unchanged in price, it would be above its value. If, however, the prices of labour-power had fallen, not to 1s. 6d., the lowest possible point consistent with its new value, but to 2s. 10d. or 2s. 6d., still this lower price would represent an increased mass of necessaries. In this way it is possible with an increasing productiveness of labour, for the price of labour-power to keep on falling, and yet this fall to be accompanied by a constant growth in the mass of the labourer's means of subsistence. But even in such case, the fall in the value of labour-power would cause a corresponding rise of surplus-value, and thus the abyss between the labourer's position and that of the capitalist would keep widening.

Marx, *Capital,* II (1885), p. 573.

If capital grows, the mass of wage labour grows, the number of wage-workers grows; in a word, the domination of capital extends over a greater number of individuals. Let us assume the most favourable case: when productive capital grows, the demand for labour grows; consequently, the price of labour, wages, goes up.

A house may be large or small; as long as the surrounding houses are equally small it satisfies all the social demands for a dwelling. But let a palace arise beside the little house, and it shrinks from a little house to a hut. The little house shows now that its owner has only very slight or no demands to make; and however high it may shoot up in the course of civilisation, if the neighbouring palace grows to an equal or even greater extent, the occupant of the relatively small house will feel more and more uncomfortable, dissatisfied and cramped within its four walls.

A noticeable increase in wages presupposes a rapid growth of productive capital. The rapid growth of productive capital brings about on equally rapid growth of wealth, luxury, social wants, social enjoyments. Thus, although the enjoyments of the worker have risen, the social satisfaction that they give has fallen in comparison with the increased enjoyments of the capitalist, which are inaccessible to the worker, in comparison with the state of development of society in general. Our desires and pleasures spring from society; we measure them, therefore, by society and not by the objects which serve for their satisfaction. Because they are of a social nature, they are of a relative nature. . . .

We see, therefore, that even if we remain *within the relation of capital and wage labour, the interests of capital and the interests of wage labour are diametrically opposed.*

A rapid increase of capital is equivalent to a rapid increase of profit. Profit can only increase rapidly if the price of labour, if relative wages, decrease just as rapidly. Relative wages can fall although real wages rise simultaneously with nominal wages, with the money value of labour, if they do not rise, however, in the same proportion as profit. If, for instance, in times when business is good, wages rise by five percent, profit on the other hand by thirty percent, then the comparative, the relative wages, have not *increased* but *decreased.*

Thus if the income of the worker increases with the rapid growth of capital, the social gulf that separates the worker from the capitalist increases at the same time, and the power of capital over labour, the dependence of labour on capital, likewise increases at the same time.

To say that the worker has an interest in the rapid growth of capital is only to say that the more rapidly the worker increases the wealth of others, the richer will be the crumbs that fall to him, the greater is the number of workers that can be employed and called into existence, the more can the mass of slaves dependent on capital be increased.

We have thus seen that:

Even the *most favourable stiuation* for the working class, the *most rapid possible growth of capital,* however much it may improve the material existence of the worker, does not remove the antagonism between his interests and the interests of the bourgeoisie, the interests of the capitalists. *Profit and wages* remain as before in *inverse proportion.*

If capital is growing rapidly, wages may rise; the profit of capital rises incomparably more rapidly. The material position of the worker has improved, but at the cost of his social position. The social gulf that divides him from the capitalist has widened.

Finally:

To say that the most favourable condition for wage labour is the most rapid possible growth of productive capital is only to say that the more rapidly the working class increases and enlarges the power that is hostile to it, the wealth that does not belong to it and that rules over it, the more favourable will be the conditions under which it is allowed to labour anew at increasing bourgeois wealth, at enlarging the power of capital, content with forging for itself the golden chains by which the bourgeoisie drags it in its train.

Marx, *Wage Labour and Capital* (1847), MESW, pp. 84–85, 88.

BE HIS PAYMENT HIGH OR LOW

The law by which a constantly increasing quantity of means of production, thanks to the advance in the productiveness of social labour, may be set in movement by a progressively diminishing expenditure of human power; this law, in a capitalist society—where the labourer does not employ the means of production, but the means of production employ the labourer—undergoes a complete inversion and is expressed thus: the higher the productiveness of labour, the greater is the pressure of the labourers on the means of employment, the more precarious, therefore, becomes their condition of existence, viz., the sale of their own labour-power for the increasing of another's wealth, or for the self-expansion of capital. The fact that the means of production, and the productiveness of labour, increase more rapidly than the productive population, expresses itself, therefore, capitalistically in the inverse form that the labouring population always increases more rapidly than the conditions under which capital can employ this increase for its own self-expansion. . . .

When analysing the production of relative surplus-value: within the capitalist system all methods for raising the social productiveness of labour are brought about at the cost of the individual labourer; all means for the development of production transform themselves into means of domination over, and exploitation of, the producers; they mutilate the labourer into a fragment of a man, degrade him to the level of an appendage of a machine, destroy every remnant of charm in his work and turn it into a hated toil; they estrange from him the intellectual potentialities of the labour-process in the same proportion as science is incorporated in it as an independent power; they distort the conditions under which he works, subject him during the labour-process to a despotism the more hateful for its meanness; they transform his life-time into working-time, and drag his wife and child beneath the wheels of the Juggernaut of capital. But all methods for the production of surplus value are at the same time methods of accumulation; and every extension of accumulation becomes again a means for the development of those methods. It follows therefore that in proportion as capital accumulates, the lot of the labourer, be his payment high or low, must grow worse. The law, finally, that always equilibrates the relative surplus-population, or industrial reserve army, to the extent and energy of accumulation, this law rivets the labourer to capital more firmly than the wedges of Vulcan did Prometheus to the rock. It establishes an accumulation of misery, corresponding with accumulation of capital. Accumulation of wealth at one pole is, therefore, at the same time accumulation of misery, agony of toil, slavery, ignorance, brutality, mental degradation, at the opposite pole, i.e., on the side of the class that produces its own product in the form of capital.

Marx, *Capital,* I (1867), pp. 708–09.

Since Lassalle's death there has asserted itself in *our* Party the scientific understanding that wages are not what they *appear* to be, namely, the *value* or *price, of labour,* but only a masked form for the *value,* or *price of labour power.* Thereby the whole bourgeois conception of wages hitherto, as well as all the criticism hitherto directed against this conception, was thrown overboard once for all and it was made clear that the wage-worker has permission to work for his own subsistence, that is, *to live,* only in so far as he works for a certain time gratis for the capitalist (and hence also for the latter's co-consumers of surplus value); that the whole capitalist system of production turns on the increase of this gratis labour by extending the working day or by developing the productivity, that is, increasing the intensity of labour power, etc.; that, consequently, the system of wage labour is a system of slavery, and indeed of a slavery which becomes more severe in proportion as the social productive forces of labour develop, whether the worker receives better or worse payment. . . .

Instead of the indefinite . . . phrase . . . "the elimination of all social and political inequality," it ought to have been said that with the abolition of class distinctions all social and political inequality arising from them would disappear of itself.

Marx, *Gotha Programme* (1875), MESW, pp. 328–29.

THE STRIFE BETWEEN WORKMAN AND MACHINE

The contest between the capitalist and the wage-labourer dates back to the very origin of capital. It raged on throughout the whole manufacturing period. But only since the introduction of machinery has the workman fought against the instrument of labour itself, the material embodiment of capital. He revolts against this particular form of the means of production, as being the material basis of the capitalist mode of production. . . .

It took both time and experience before the workpeople learnt to distinguish between machinery and its employment by capital, and to direct their attacks, not against the material instruments of production, but against the mode in which they are used. . . .

The instrument of labour, when it takes the form of a machine, immediately becomes a competitor of the workman himself. The self-expansion of capital by means of machinery is thenceforward directly proportional to the number of the workpeople whose means of livelihood have been destroyed by that machinery. The whole system of capitalist production is based on the fact that the workman sells his labour-power as a commodity. Division of labour specialises this labour-power, by reducing it to skill in handling a particular tool. So soon as the handling of this tool becomes the work of a machine, then, with the use-value, the exchange-value, too, of the workman's labour-power vanishes; the workman becomes unsalable, like paper money thrown out of currency by legal enactment. That portion of the working class, thus by machinery rendered superfluous, i.e., no longer immediately necessary for the self-expansion of capital, either goes to the wall in the unequal contest of the old handicrafts and manufactures with machinery, or else floods all the more easily accessible branches of industry, swamps the labour market, and sinks the price of labour-power below its value. It is impressed upon the workpeople, as a great consolation, first, that their sufferings are only temporary ("a temporary inconvenience"), secondly, that machinery acquires the mastery over the whole of a given field of production only by degrees, so that the extent and intensity of its destructive effect is diminished. The first consolation neutralizes the second. When machinery seizes on an industry by degrees, it produces chronic misery among the operatives who compete with it. Where the transition is rapid, the effect is acute and felt by great masses. History discloses no tragedy more horrible than the gradual extinction of the English handloom weavers, an extinction that was spread over several decades, and finally sealed in 1838. Many of them died of starvation, many with families vegetated for a long time on 2½ d. a day. On the other hand, the English cotton machinery produced an acute effect in India. The Governor General reported 1834–1835: "The misery hardly finds a parallel in the history of commerce. The bones of the cotton-weavers are bleaching the plains of India." No doubt, in turning them out of this "temporal" world, the machinery caused them no more than "a temporary inconvenience." For the rest, since machinery is continually seizing upon new fields of production, its temporary effect is really permanent. Hence, the character of independance and estrangement which the capitalist mode of production as a whole gives to the instruments of labour and to the product, as against the workman, is developed by means of machinery into a thorough antagonism. Therefore, it is with the advent of machinery, that the workman for the first time brutally revolts against the instruments of labour.

The instrument of labour strikes down the labourer. This direct antagonism between the two comes out most strongly, whenever newly introduced machinery competes with handicrafts or manufactures, handed down from former times. But even in Modern Industry the continual improvement of machinery, and the development of the automatic system, has an analogous effect. . . .

Between 1861 and 1868, 338 cotton factories disappeared, in other words more productive machinery on a larger scale was concentrated in the hands of a smaller number of capitalists. The number of power-looms decreased by 20,663; but since their product increased in the same period, an improved loom must have yielded more than an old one. Lastly the number of spindles increased by 1,612,541, while the number of operatives decreased by 50,505. The "temporary" misery, inflicted on the workpeople by the cotton-crisis, was heightened, and from being temporary made permanent, by the rapid and persistent progress of machinery.

But machinery not only acts as a competitor who gets the better of the workman, and is constantly on the point of making him superfluous. It is also a power inimical to him, and as such capital proclaims it from the roof tops and as such makes use of it. It is the most powerful weapon for repressing strikes, those periodical revolts of the working class against the autocracy of capital. According to Gaskell, the steam engine was from the very first an antagonist of human power, an antagonist that enabled the capitalist to tread under foot the growing claims of the workmen, who threatened the newly born factory system with a crisis. It would be possible to write quite a history of the inventions, made since 1830, for the sole purpose of supplying capital with weapons against the revolts of the working class. At the head of these in importance, stands the self-acting mule, because it opened up a new epoch in the automatic system.

Marx, *Capital,* I (1867), pp. 466–76.

ALIENATION AND "ECONOMIES" IN PRODUCTION

The conditions of capitalist production conceal the internal connection of things by the utter indifference, alienation, and expropriation practiced against the laborer in the matter of the material means in which his labour must be incorporated.

In the first place, the means of production constituting the constant capital represent only the money of the capitalist. . . . The labourer comes in contact with them only in the direct process of production, in which he handles them as use-values of production, as instruments of labour and materials of production. The increase or decrease of the value of these things are matters which affect his relation to the capitalist no more than the fact that he may be working up either copper or iron. . . .

In the second place, so far as these means of production in the capitalist process of labour are at the same time means of exploiting labour, the labourer is no more concerned in the relative dearness or cheapness of these means of exploitation than a horse is concerned in the dearness or cheapness of the bit and bridle by which it is steered.

In the third place, we have seen previously that the social nature of labour, the combination of the labour of a certain individual labourer with that of other labourers for a common purpose, stands opposed to that labourer and his comrades as a foreign power, as the property of a stranger which he would not care particularly to save if he were not compelled to economize with it. It is entirely different in the factories owned by the labourers themselves, for instance, in Rochdale. . . .

These economies in the employment of constant capital assume the guise of being due to the peculiar nature of the capitalist mode of production, and to the special function of the capitalist in particular. The thirst for profits and the demands of competition tend toward the greatest possible cheapening of the production of commodities, just as production on a large scale first develops in its capitalistic form.

Capitalist production promotes on the one hand the development of the productive powers of social labour, and on the other it enforces economies in the employment of constant capital.

However, capitalist production does not stop at the alienation and expropriation of the labourer, the bearer of living labour, from his interest in the economical, that is to say, rational and thrifty, use of the material requirements of his labour. In conformity with its contradictory and antagonistic nature, capitalist production proceeds to add to the economies in the use of constant capital, and thus to the means of increasing the rate of profit, a prodigality in the use of the life and health of the labourer himself.

Since the labourer passes the greater portion of his life in the process of production, the conditions of this productive process constitute the greater part of the fundamental conditions of his vital activity, his requirements of life. Economies in these requirements constitute a method of raising the rate of profit, just as we observed on previous occasions that overwork, the transformation of the labourers into laboring cattle, constitutes a means of self-expanding capital, of speeding up the production of surplus-value. Such economies are: The overcrowding of narrow and unsanitary rooms with labourers, or, in the language of the capitalist, a saving in buildings; a crowding of dangerous machinery into one and the same room without means of protection against this danger; a neglect of precautions in productive processes which are dangerous to health or life, such as mining, etc.; not to mention the absence of all provisions to render the process of production human, agreeable, or even bearable, for the labourer. From the capitalist point of view, such measures would be quite useless and senseless. No matter how economical capitalist production may be in other respects, it is utterly prodigal with human life. And its saving in one direction is offset by a waste in another, owing to the distribution of its products through trade and the competitive method. Capitalism loses on one side for society what it gains on another for the individual capitalist.

Marx, *Capital,* III (1894), pp. 102–04.

7.A.4 GROWING CLASS STRUGGLES

Not only has the bourgeoisie forged the weapons that bring death to itself; it has also called into existence the men who are to wield those weapons—the modern working class—the proletarians.

In proportion as the bourgeoisie, i.e., capital, is developed, in the same proportion is the proletariat, the modern working class, developed, a class of labourers who live only so long as they find work, and who find work only so long as their labour increases capital. These labourers, who must sell themselves piecemeal, are a commodity, like every other article of commerce, and are consequently exposed to all the vicissitudes of competition, to all the fluctuations of the market.

Owing to the extensive use of machinery and to division of labor, the work of the proletarians has lost all individual character, and consequently all charm for the workman. He becomes an appendage of the machine, and it is only the most simple, most monotonous, and most easily acquired knack that is required of him. Hence the cost of production of a workman is restricted almost entirely to the means of subsistence that he requires for his maintenance, and for the propagation of his race. But the price of a commodity, and also of labour, is equal to its cost of production. In proportion, therefore, as the repulsiveness of the work increases, the wage decreases. Nay, more—in proportion as the use of machinery and division of labor increases, in the same proportion the burden of toil also increases, whether by prolongation of the working hours, by increase of the work done in a given time, or by increased speed of the machinery, etc.

Modern industry has converted the little workshop of the patriarchal master into the great factory of the industrial capitalist. Masses of labourers, crowded into the factory, are organized like soldiers. As privates of the industrial army they are placed under the command of a perfect hierarchy of officers and sergeants. Not only are they the slaves of the bourgeois class, and of the bourgeois state, they are daily and hourly enslaved by the machine, by the overlooker, and above all by the individual bourgeois manufacturer himself. The more openly this despotism proclaims gain to be its end and aim, the more petty, the more hateful, and the more embittering it is.

The less the skill and exertion or strength implied in manual labor—in other words, the more modern industry becomes developed—the more is the labour of men superseded by that of women. Differences of age and sex have no longer any distinctive social validity for the working class. All are instruments of labour, more or less expensive to use according to their age and sex.

No sooner is the exploitation of the labourer by the manufacturer so far at an end that he receives his wages in cash, than he is set upon by the other portions of the bourgeoisie, the landlord, the shopkeeper, the pawnbroker, etc.

The low strata of the middle class—the small tradespeople, shopkeepers, and retired tradesmen generally, the handicraftsmen and peasants—all these sink gradually into the proletariat, partly because their diminutive capital does not suffice for the scale on which Modern Industry is carried on and is swamped in the competition with the large capitalists, partly because their specialized skill is rendered worthless by new methods of production. Thus the proletariat is recruited from all classes of the population.

The proletariat goes through various stages of development. With its birth begins its struggle with the bourgeoisie. At first the contest is carried on by individual labourers, then by the workpeople of a factory, then by the operatives of one trade, in one locality, against the individual bourgeois who directly exploits them. They direct their attacks not against the bourgeois conditions of production, but against the instruments of production themselves; they destroy imported wares that compete with their labour, they smash machinery to pieces, they set factories ablaze, they seek to restore by force the vanished status of the workman of the Middle Ages.

At this stage the labourers still form an incoherent mass scattered over the whole country and broken up by their mutual competition. If anywhere they unite to form more compact bodies, this is not yet the consequence of their own active union, but of the union of the bourgeoisie, which class, in order to attain its own political ends, is compelled to set the whole proletariat in motion, and is moreover yet, for a time, able to do so. At this stage, therefore, the proletarians do not fight their enemies, but the enemies of their enemies, the remnants of absolute monarchy, the landowners, the nonindustrial bourgeoisie, the petty bourgeoisie. Thus the whole historical movement is concentrated in the hands of the bourgeoisie; every victory so obtained is a victory for the bourgeoisie.

But with the development of industry the proletariat not only increases in number, it becomes concentrated in great masses, its strength grows, and it feels that strength more. The various interests and conditions of life within the ranks of the proletariat are more and more equalized, in proportion as machinery obliterates all distinction of labor and nearly everywhere reduces wages to the same low level. The growing competition among the bourgeoisie, and the resulting commercial crises, make the wages of the worker ever more fluctuating. The unceasing improvement of machinery, ever more rapidly developing, makes their livelihood more and more precarious, the collisions between individual workmen and individual bourgeois take more and more the character of collision between two classes. Thereupon the workers begin to form combinations (trade unions) against the bourgeoisie; they club together in order to keep up the rate of wages; they found permanent associations in order to make provision beforehand for these occasional revolts. Here and there the contest breaks out into riots.

Now and then the workers are victorious, but only for a time. The real fruits of their battles lie, not in the immediate result, but in the ever expanding union of the workers. This union is helped on by the improved means of communication that are created by modern industry and that place the workers of different localities in contact with one another. It was just this contact that was needed to centralize the numerous local struggles, all of the same character, into one national struggle between classes. But every class struggle is a political struggle. And that union, to attain which the burghers of the Middle Ages, with their miserable highways, required centuries, the modern proletarians, thanks to railways, achieve in a few years.

This organization of the proletarians into a class, and consequently into a political party, is continually being upset again by the competition between the workers themselves. But it ever rises up again, stronger, firmer, mightier. It compels legislative recognition of particular interests of the workers by taking advantage of the divisions among the bourgeoisie itself. Thus the ten-hour bill in England was carried.

Altogether, collisions between the classes of the old society further in many ways the course of development of the proletariat. The bourgeoisie finds itself involved in a constant battle. At first with the aristocracy, later on with those portions of the bourgeoisie itself whose interests have become antagonistic to the progress of industry, at all times with the bourgeoisie of foreign countries. In all these battles it sees itself compelled to appeal to the proletariat, to ask for its help, and thus to drag it into the political arena. The bourgeoisie itself, therefore, supplies the proletariat with its own elements of political and general education; in other words, it furnishes the proletariat with weapons for fighting the bourgeoisie.

Further, as we have already seen, entire sections of the ruling classes are, by the advance of industry, precipitated into the proletariat, or are at least threatened in their conditions of existence. These also supply the proletariat with fresh elements of enlightenment and progress.

Finally, in times when the class struggle nears the decisive hour, the process of dissolution going on within the ruling class—in fact, within the whole range of old society—assumes such a violent, glaring character that a small section of the ruling class cuts itself adrift and joins the revolutionary class, the class that holds the future in its hands. Just as, therefore, at an earlier period, a section of the nobility went over to the bourgeoisie, so now a portion of the bourgeoisie goes over to the proletariat, and in particular, a portion of the bourgeois ideologists, who have raised themselves to the level of comprehending theoretically the historical movements as a whole.

Of all the classes that stand face to face with the bourgeoisie today, the proletariat alone is a really revolutionary class. The other classes decay and finally disappear in the face of modern industry; the proletariat is its special and essential product.

The lower middle class, the small manufacturer, the shopkeeper, the artisan, the peasant, all these fight against the bourgeoisie, to save from extinction their existence as fractions of the middle class. They are therefore not revolutionary, but conservative. Nay, more—they are reactionary, for they try to roll back the wheel of history. If by chance they are revolutionary, they are so only in view of the impending transfer into the proletariat; they thus defend not their present, but their future interests, they desert their own standpoint to place themselves at that of the proletariat.

The "dangerous class," the social scum, that passively rotting mass thrown off by the lowest layers of old society, may, here and there, be swept into the movement by a proletarian revolution; its conditions of life, however, prepare it far more for the part of a bribed tool of reactionary intrigue.

In the conditions of the proletariat, those of old society at large are already virtually swamped. The proletarian is without property; his relation to his wife and children has no longer anything in common with the bourgeois family relations; modern industrial labor, modern subjugation to capital, the same in England as in France, in America as in Germany, has stripped him of every trace of national character. Law, morality, religion are to him so many bourgeois prejudices, behind which lurk in ambush just as many bourgeois interests.

All the preceding classes that got the upper hand sought to fortify their already acquired status by subjecting society at large to their conditions of appropriation. The proletarians cannot become masters of the productive forces of society except by abolishing their own previous mode of appropriation, and thereby also every other previous mode of appropriation. They have nothing of their own to secure and to fortify; their mission is to destroy all previous securities for, and insurances of, individual property.

All previous historical movements were movements of minorities, or in the interests of minorities. The proletarian movement is the self-conscious, independent movement of the immense majority, in the interest of the immense majority. The proletariat, the lowest stratum of our present society, cannot stir, cannot raise itself up, without the whole superincumbent strata of official society being sprung into the air.

Though not in substance, yet in form, the struggle of the proletariat with the bourgeoisie is at first a national struggle. The proletariat of each country must, of course, first of all settle matters with its own bourgeoisie.

In depicting the most general phases of the development of the proletariat, we traced the more or less veiled civil war raging within existing society up to the point where that war breaks out into open revolution, and where the violent overthrow of the bourgeoisie lays the foundation for the sway of the proletariat.

Hitherto every form of society has been based, as we have already seen, on the antagonism of oppressing and oppressed classes. But in order to oppress a class, certain conditions must be assured to it under which it can at least continue its slavish existence. The serf, in the period of serfdom, raised himself to membership in the commune, just as the petty bourgeois, under the yoke of feudal absolutism, managed to develop into a bourgeois.

The modern labourer, on the contrary, instead of rising with the progress of industry, sinks deeper and deeper below the conditions of existence of his own class. He becomes a pauper, and pauperism develops more rapidly than population and wealth. And here it becomes evident that the bourgeoisie is unfit any longer to be the ruling class in society, and to impose its conditions of existence upon society as an overriding law. It is unfit to rule because it is incompetent to assure an existence to its slave within his slavery, because it cannot help letting him sink into such a state that it has to feed him, instead of being fed by him. Society can no longer live under this bourgeoisie; in other words, its existence is no longer compatible with society.

The essential condition for the existence and for the sway of the bourgeois class is the formation and augmentation of capital; the condition for capital is wage labor. Wage labor rests exclusively on competition between the labourers. The advance of industry, whose involuntary promoter is the bourgeoisie, replaces the isolation of the labourers, due to competition, by their revolutionary combination, due to association. The development of Modern Industry, therefore, cuts from under its feet the very foundation on which the bourgeoisie produces and appropriates products. What the bourgeoisie therefore produces, above all, is its own gravediggers. Its fall and the victory of the proletariat are equally inevitable.

Marx-Engels, *Manifesto* (1848), excerpt from Part I.

7.A.5 LABOR UNIONS AND WAGES

Main Cases of Attempts at Raising Wages or Resisting Their Fall

Let us now seriously consider the main cases in which a rise of wages is attempted or a reduction of wages resisted.

1) We have seen that the *value of the labouring power,* or in more popular parlance, the *value of labour,* is determined by the value of necessaries, or the quantity of labour required to produce them. If, then, in a given country the value of the daily average necessaries of the labourer represented six hours of labour expressed in three shillings, the labourer would have to work six hours daily to produce an equivalent for his daily maintenance. If the whole working day was twelve hours, the capitalist would pay him the value of his labour by paying him three shillings. Half the working day would be unpaid labour, and the rate of profit would amount to 100 percent. But now suppose that, consequent upon a decrease of productivity, more labour should be wanted to produce, say, the same amount of agricultural produce, so that the price of the average daily necessaries should rise from three to four shillings. In that case the *value of labour* would rise by one third, or 33⅓ percent. Eight hours of the working day would be required to produce an equivalent for the daily maintenance of the labourer, according to his old standard of living. The surplus labour would therefore sink from six hours to four, and the rate of profit from 100 to 50 percent. But in insisting upon a rise of wages, the labourer would only insist upon getting the *increased value of his labour,* like every other seller of a commodity, who, the costs of his commodities having increased, tries to get its increased value paid. If wages did not rise, or not sufficiently rise, to compensate for the increased values of necessaries, the *price* of labour would sink below the *value of labour,* and the labourer's standard of life would deteriorate.

But a change might also take place in an opposite direction. By virtue of the increased productivity of labour, the same amount of the average daily necessaries might sink from three to two shillings, or only four hours out of the working day, instead of six, be wanted to reproduce an equivalent for the value of the daily necessaries. The working man would now be able to buy with two shillings as many necessaries as he did before with three shillings. Indeed, the *value of labour* would have sunk, but that diminished value would command the same amount of commodities as before. Then profits would rise from three to four shillings, and the rate of profit from 100 to 200 percent. Although the labourer's absolute standard of life would have remained the same, his *relative* wages, and therewith his *relative social position,* as compared with that of the capitalist, would have been lowered. If the working man should resist that reduction of relative wages, he would only try to get some share in the increased productive powers of his own labour, and to maintain his former relative position in the social scale. . . .

2) The *values* of necessaries, and consequently the *value of labour,* might remain the same, but a change might occur in their *money prices,* consequent upon a previous change in the *value of money.*

By the discovery of more fertile mines and so forth, two ounces of gold might, for example, cost no more labour to produce than one ounce did before. The *value* of gold would then be depreciated by one half, or fifty percent. As the *values* of all other commodities would then be expressed in twice their former *money prices,* so also the same with the *value of labour.* Twelve hours of labour, formerly expressed in six shillings, would now be expressed in twelve shillings. If the working man's wages should remain three shillings, instead of rising to six shillings, the *money price of his labour* would only be equal to *half the value of his labour,* and his standard of life would fearfully deteriorate. This would also happen in a greater or lesser degree if his wages should rise, but not proportionately to the fall in the value of gold. In such a case nothing would have been changed, either in the productive powers of labour, or in supply and demand, or in values. Nothing could have changed except the money *names* of those values. To say that in such a case the workman ought not to insist upon a proportionate rise of wages, is to say that he must be content to be paid with names, instead of with things. All past history proves that whenever such a depreciation of money occurs the capitalists are on the alert to seize this opportunity for defrauding the workman. A very large school of political economists assert that, consequent upon the new discoveries of gold lands, the better working of silver mines, and the cheaper supply of quicksilver, the value of precious metals has been again depreciated. This would explain the general and simultaneous attempts on the Continent at a rise of wages.

3) We have till now supposed that the *working day* has given limits. The working day, however, has, by itself, no constant limits. It is the constant tendency of capital to stretch it to its utmost physically possible length, because in the same degree surplus labour, and consequently the profit resulting therefrom, will be increased. The more capital succeeds in prolonging the working day, the greater the amount of other people's labour it will appropriate. During the seventeenth and even the first two-thirds of the eighteenth century a ten hours' working day was the normal working day all over England. During the anti-Jacobin war, which was in fact a war waged by the British barons against the British working masses, capital celebrated its bacchanalia, and prolonged the working day from ten to twelve, fourteen, eighteen hours. . . .

In prolonging the working day the capitalist may pay *higher wages* and still lower the *value of labour,* if the rise of wages does not correspond to the greater amount of labour extracted, and the quicker decay of the labouring power thus caused. This may be done in another way. Your middle-class statisticians will tell you, for instance, that the average wages of factory families in Lancashire have risen. They forget that instead of the labour of the man, the head of the family, his wife and perhaps three or four children are now thrown under the Juggernaut wheels of capital, and that the rise of the aggregate wages does not correspond to the aggregate surplus labour extracted from the family.

Even with given limits of the working day, such as now exist in all branches of industry subjected to the factory laws, a rise of wages may become necessary, if only to keep up the old standard *value of labour.* By increasing the *intensity* of labour, a man may be made to expend as much vital force in one hour as he formerly did in two. This has, to a certain degree, been effected in the trades, placed under the Factory Acts, by the acceleration of machinery, and the greater number of working machines which a single individual has now to superintend. If the increase in the intensity of labour or the mass of labour spent in an hour keeps some fair proportion to the decrease in the extent of the working day, the working man will still be the winner. If this limit is overshot, he loses in one form what he has gained in another, and ten hours of labour may then become as ruinous as twelve hours were before. In checking this tendency of capital, by struggling for a rise of wages corresponding to the rising intensity of labour, the working man only resists the depreciation of his labour and the deterioration of his race. ...

4) Capitalistic production moves through certain periodical cycles. It moves through a state of quiescence, growing animation, prosperity, over-trade, crisis, and stagnation. The market prices of commodities, and the market rates of profit, follow these phases, now sinking below their averages, now rising above them. Considering the whole cycle, you will find that one deviation of the market price is being compensated by the other, and that, taking the average of the cycle, the market prices of commodities are regulated by their values. Well! During the phase of sinking market prices and the phases of crisis and stagnation, the working man, if not thrown out of employment altogether, is sure to have his wages lowered. Not to be defrauded, he must, even with such a fall of market prices, debate with the capitalist in what proportional degree a fall of wages has become necessary. If, during the phases of prosperity, when extra profits are made, he did not battle for a rise of wages, he would, taking the average of one industrial cycle, not even receive his *average wage,* or the *value* of his labour. It is the utmost height of folly to demand that while his wages are necessarily affected by the adverse phases of the cycle, he should exclude himself from compensation during the prosperous phases of the cycle. Generally, the *values* of all commodities are only realised by the compensation of the continuously changing market prices, springing from the continuous fluctuations of demand and supply. On the basis of the present system labour is only a commodity like others. It must, therefore, pass through the same fluctuations to fetch an average price corresponding to its value. It would be absurd to treat it on the one hand as a commodity, and to want on the other hand to exempt it from the laws which regulate the prices of commodities. The slave receives a permanent and fixed amount of maintenance; the wages labourer does not. He must try to get a rise of wages in the one instance, if only to compensate for a fall of wages in the other. If he resigned himself to accept the will, the dictates of the capitalist as a permanent economical law, he would share in all the miseries of the slave, without the security of the slave.

5) In all the cases I have considered, and they form ninety-nine out of a hundred, you have seen that a struggle for a rise of wages follows only in the track of *previous* changes, and is the necessary offspring of previous changes in the amount of production, the productive powers of labour, the value of labour, the value of money, the extent or the intensity of labour extracted, the fluctuations of market prices, dependent upon the fluctuations of demand and supply, and consistent with the different phases of the industrial cycle; in one word, as reactions of labour against the previous action of capital. By treating

the struggle for a rise of wages independently of all these circumstances, by looking only upon the change of wages, and overlooking all the other changes from which they emanate, you proceed from a false premise in order to arrive at false conclusions.

The Struggle Between Capital and Labour and its Results

1) Having shown that the periodical resistance on the part of the working men against a reduction of wages, and their periodical attempts at getting a rise of wages, are inseparable from the wages system, and dictated by the very fact of labour being assimilated to commodities, and therefore subject to the laws regulating the general movement of prices; having, furthermore, shown that a general rise of wages would result in a fall in the general rate of profit, but not affect the average prices of commodities, or their values, the question now ultimately arises, how far, in this incessant struggle between capital and labour, the latter is likely to prove successful.

I might answer by a generalisation, and say that, as with all other commodities, so with labour, its *market price* will, in the long run, adapt itself to its *value;* that, therefore, despite all the ups and downs, and do what he may, the working man will, on an average, only receive the value of his labour, which resolves into the value of his labouring power, which is determined by the value of the necessaries required for its maintenance and reproduction, which value of necessaries finally is regulated by the quantity of labour wanted to produce them.

But there are some peculiar features which distinguish the *value of the labouring power, or the value of labour,* from the values of all other commodities. The value of the labouring power is formed by two elements—the one merely physical, the other historical or social. Its *ultimate limit* is determined by the *physical* element, that is to say, to maintain and reproduce itself, to perpetuate its physical existence, the working class must receive the necessaries absolutely indispensable for living and multiplying. The *value* of those indispensable necessaries forms, therefore, the ultimate limit of the *value of labour.* On the other hand, the length of the working day is also limited by ultimate, although very elastic boundaries. Its ultimate limit is given by the physical force of the labouring man. If the daily exhaustion of his vital forces exceeds a certain degree, it cannot be exerted anew, day by day. However, as I said, this limit is very elastic. A quick succession of unhealthy and short-lived generations will keep the labour market as well supplied as a series of vigorous and long-lived generations.

Besides this mere physical element, the value of labour is in every country determined by a *traditional standard of life.* It is not mere physical life, but it is the satisfaction of certain wants springing from the social conditions in which people are placed and reared up. The English standard of life may be reduced to the Irish standard; the standard of life of a German peasant to that of a Livonian peasant. The important part which historical tradition and social habitude play in this respect, you may learn from Mr. Thornton's work on *Over-population,* where he shows that the average wages in different agricultural districts of England still nowadays differ more or less according to the more or less favourable circumstances under which the districts have emerged from the state of serfdom.

This historical or social element, entering into the value of labour, may be expanded, or contracted, or altogether extinguished, so that nothing remains but the *physical limit.* During the time of the anti-Jacobin war,...the honest English farmers...depressed the wages of the agricultural labourers even beneath that *mere physical minimum,* but made up by Poor Laws the remainder necessary for the physical perpetuation of the race. This was a glorious way to convert the wages labourer into a slave, and Shakespeare's proud yeoman into a pauper.

By comparing the standard wages or values of labour in different countries, and by comparing them in different historical epochs of the same country, you will find that the *value of labour* itself is not a fixed but a variable magnitude, even supposing the values of all other commodities to remain constant.

A similar comparison would prove that not only the *market rates* of profit change but its *average* rates.

But as to *profits,* there exists no law which determines their *minimum.* We cannot say what is the ultimate limit of their decrease. And why cannot we fix that limit? Because, although we can fix the *minimum of* wages, we cannot fix their *maximum.* We can only say that, the limits of the working day being given, the *maximum* of profit corresponds to the *physical minimum of wages;* and that wages being given, the *maximum of profit* corresponds to such a prolongation of the working day as is compatible with the physical forces of the labourer. The maximum of profit is, therefore, limited by the physical minimum of wages and the physical maximum of the working day. It is evident that between the two limits of this *maximum rate of profit* an immense scale of variations is possible. The fixation of its actual degree is only settled by the continuous struggle between capital and labour, the capitalist constantly tending to reduce wages to their physical minimum, and to extend the working day to its physical maximum, while the working man constantly presses in the opposite direction.

The matter resolves itself into a question of the respective powers of the combatants.

2) As to the *limitation of the working day* in England, as in all other countries, it has never been settled except by *legislative interference.* Without the working men's continuous pressure from without that interference would never have taken place. But at all events, the result was not to be attained by private settlement between the working men and the capitalists. This very necessity of *general political action* affords the proof that in its merely economic action capital is the stronger side.

As to the *limits* of the *value of labour,* its actual settlement always depends upon supply and demand, I mean the demand for labour on the part of capital, and the supply of labour by the working men. In colonial countries the law of supply and demand favours the working man. Hence the relatively high standard of wages in the United States. Capital may there try its utmost. It cannot prevent the labour market from being continuously emptied by the continuous conversion of wages labourers into independent, self-sustaining peasants. The position of wages labourers is for a very large part of the American people but a probational state, which they are sure to leave within a longer or shorter term. To mend this colonial state of things, the paternal British Government accepted for some time what is called the modern colonisation theory, which consists in putting an artifical high price upon colonial land, in order to prevent the too quick conversion of the wages labourer into the independent peasant.

But let us now come to old civilised countries, in which capital domineers over the whole process of production. Take for example, the rise in England of agricultural wages from 1849 to 1859. What was its consequence? The farmers could not. . . raise the value of wheat, nor even its market prices. They had, on the contrary, to submit to their fall. But during these eleven years they introduced machinery of all sorts, adopted more scientific methods, converted part of arable land into pasture, increased the size of farms, and with this the scale of production, and by these and other processes diminishing the demand for labour by increasing its productive power, made the agricultural population again relatively redundant. This is the general method in which a reaction, quicker or slower, of capital against a rise of wages takes place in old, settled countries. Ricardo has justly remarked that machinery is in constant competition with labour, and can often be only introduced when the price of labour has reached a certain height, but the appliance of machinery is but one of the many methods for increasing the productive powers of labour. This very same development which makes common labour relatively redundant simplifies on the other hand skilled labour, and thus depreciates it.

The same law obtains in another form. With the development of the productive powers of labour the accumulation of capital will be accelerated, even despite a relatively high rate of wages. Hence, one might infer, as Adam Smith, in whose days modern industry was still in its infancy, did infer, that the accelerated accumulation of capital must turn the balance in favour of the working man, by securing a growing demand for his labour. From this same standpoint many contemporary writers have wondered that English capital having grown in the last twenty years so much quicker than English population, wages should not have been more enhanced. But simultaneously with the progress of accumulation there takes place a *progressive change* in the *composition of capital.* That part of the aggregate capital which consists of fixed capital, machinery, raw materials, means of production in all possible forms, progressively increases as compared with the other part of capital, which is laid out in wages or in the purchase of labour. This law has been stated in a more or less accurate manner by Mr. Barton, Ricardo, Sismondi, Professor Richard Jones, Professor Ramsay, Cherbuliez, and others. . . .

In the progress of industry the demand for labour keeps, therefore, no pace with accumulation of capital. It will still increase, but increase in a constantly diminishing ratio as compared with the increase of capital.

These few hints will suffice to show that the very development of modern industry must progressively turn the scale in favour of the capitalist against the working man, and that consequently the general tendency of capitalistic production is not to raise, but to sink the average standard of wages, or to push the *value of labour* more or less to its *minimum limit.* Such being the tendency of *things* in this system, is this saying that the working class ought to renounce their resistance against the encroachments of capital, and abandon their attempts at making the best of the occasional chances for their temporary improvement? If they did, they would be degraded to one level mass of broken wretches past salvation. I think I have shown that their struggles for the standard of wages are incidents inseparable from the whole wages system, that in 99 cases out of 100 their efforts at raising wages are only efforts at maintaining the given value of labour, and that the necessity of debating their price with the capitalist is inherent in their condition of having to sell themselves as commodities. By cowardly giving way in their everyday conflict with capital, they would certainly disqualify themselves for the initiating of any larger movement.

At the same time, and quite apart from the general servitude involved in the wages system, the working class ought not to exaggerate to themselves the ultimate working of these everyday struggles. They ought not to forget that they are fighting with effects, but not with the causes of those effects; that they are retarding the downward movement, but not changing its direction; that they are applying palliatives, not curing the malady. They ought, therefore, not to be exclusively absorbed in these unavoidable guerilla fights incessantly springing up from the never-ceasing encroachments of capital or changes of the market. They ought to understand that, with all the miseries it imposes upon them, the present system simultaneously engenders the *material conditions* and the *social forms* necessary for an economical reconstruction of society. Instead of the *conservative* motto, *"A fair day's wage for a fair day's work!"* they ought to inscribe on their banner the *revolutionary* watchword, *"Abolition of the wages system!"*

After this very long and, I fear, tedious exposition which I was obliged to enter into to do some justice to the subject-matter, I shall conclude by proposing the following resolutions:

Firstly. A general rise in the rate of wages would result in a fall of the general rate of profit, but, broadly speaking, not affect the prices of commodities.

Secondly. The general tendency of capitalist production is not to raise, but to sink the average standard of wages.

Thirdly. Trades Unions work well as centres of resistance against the encroachments of capital. They fail partially from an injudicious use of their power. They fail generally from limiting themselves to a guerilla war against the effects of the existing system, instead of simultaneously trying to change it, instead of using their organised forces as a lever for the final emancipation of the working class, that is to say, the ultimate abolition of the wages system.

Marx, *Wages, Prices, and Profits* (1865), MESW, pp. 214–29.

7.A.6 CAPITALIST DECLINE AND DEMISE

ENGELS

The contradiction between socialised production and capitalistic appropriation now presents itself as *an antagonism between the organisation of production in the individual workshop and the anarchy of production in society generally.*

The capitalistic mode of production moves in these two forms of the antagonism immanent to it from its very origin. It is never able to get out of that "vicious circle" which Fourier had already discovered. What Fourier could not, indeed, see in his time is that this circle is gradually narrowing; that the movement becomes more and more a spiral, and must come to an end, like the movement of the planets, by collision with the centre. It is the compelling force of anarchy in the production of society at large that more and more completely turns the great majority of men into proletarians; and it is the masses of the proletariat again who will finally put an end to anarchy in production. It is the compelling force of anarchy in social production that turns the limitless perfectibility of machinery under modern industry into a compulsory law by which every individual industrial capitalist must perfect his machinery more and more, under penalty of ruin.

But the perfecting of machinery is making human labour superflous. If the introduction and increase of machinery means the displacement of millions of manual by a few machine-workers, improvement in machinery means the displacement of more and more of the machine-workers themselves. It means, in the last instance, the production of a number of available wage-workers in excess of the average needs of capital, the formation of a complete industrial reserve army, as I called it in 1845,* available at the times when industry is working at high pressure, to be cast out upon the street when the inevitable crash comes, a constant dead weight upon the limbs of the working class in its struggle for existence with capital, a regulator for the keeping of wages down to the low level that suit the interests of capital. Thus it comes about, to quote Marx, that machinery becomes the most powerful weapon in the war of capital against the working class; that the instruments of labour constantly tear the means of subsistence out of the hands of the labourer; that the very product of the worker is turned into an instrument for his subjugation. Thus it comes about that the economising of the instruments of labour becomes at the same time, from the outset the most reckless waste of labour power, and robbery based upon the normal conditions under which labour functions; that machinery, the most powerful instrument for shortening labour time, becomes the most unfailing means for placing every moment of the labourer's time and that of his family at the disposal of the capitalist for the purpose of expanding the value of his capitalist. Thus it comes about that the overwork of some, becomes the preliminary condition for the idleness of others, and that modern industry, which hunts after new consumers over the whole world, forces the consumption of the masses at home down to a starvation minimum, and in

**The Condition of the Working Class in England,* p. 109. *[Note by Engels.]*

doing thus destroys its own home market. "The law that always equilibrates the relative surplus population, or industrial reserve army, to the extent and energy of accumulation, this law rivets the labourers to capital more firmly than the wedges of Vulcan did Prometheus to the rock. It establishes an accumulation of misery, corresponding with accumulation of capital. Accumulation of wealth at one pole is, therefore, at the same time, accumulation of misery, agony of toil, slavery, ignorance, brutality, mental degradation, at the opposite pole, i.e., on the side of the class that produces *its own product in the form of capital,"* (Marx's *Capital*.) And to expect any other division of the products from the capitalistic mode of production is the same as expecting the electrodes of a battery not to decompose acidulated water, not to liberate oxygen at the positive, hydrogen at the negative pole, so long as they are connected with the battery.

We have seen that the ever-increasing perfectibility of modern machinery is, by the anarchy of social production, turned into a compulsory law that forces the individual industrial capitalist always to improve his machinery, always to increase its productive force. The bare possibility of extending the field of production is transformed for him into a similar compulsory law. The enormous expansive force of modern industry, compared with which that of gases is mere child's play, appears to us now a *necessity* for expansion, both qualitative and quantitative, that laughs at all resistance. Such resistance is offered by consumption, by sales, by the markets for the products of modern industry. But the capacity for extension, extensive and intensive, of the markets is primarily governed by quite different laws that work much less energetically. The extension of the markets cannot keep pace with the extension of production. The collision becomes inevitable, and as this cannot produce any real solution so long as it does not break in pieces the capitalist mode of production, the collisions become periodic. Capitalist production has begotten another "vicious circle."

As a matter of fact, since 1825, when the first general crisis broke out, the whole industrial and commercial world, production and exchange among all civilised peoples and their more or less barbaric hangers-on, are thrown out of joint about once every ten years. Commerce is at a standstill, the markets are glutted, products accumulate, as multitudinous as they are unsalable, hard cash disappears, credit vanishes, factories are closed, the mass of the workers are in want of the means of subsistence, because they have produced too much of the means of subsistence; bankruptcy follows upon bankruptcy, execution upon execution. The stagnation lasts for years; productive forces and products are wasted and destroyed wholesale, until the accumulated mass of commodities finally filters off, more or less depreciated in value, until production and exchange gradually begin to move again. Little by little the pace quickens. It becomes a trot. The industrial trot breaks into a canter, the canter in turn grows into the headlong gallop of a perfect steeplechase of industry, commercial credit, and speculation which finally, after breakneck leaps, ends where it began—in the ditch of a crisis. And so over and over again. We have now, since the year 1825, gone through this five times, and at the present moment (1877) we are going through it for the sixth time. And the character of these crises is so clearly defined that Fourier hit all of them off when he described the first as *"crise pléthorique,"* a crisis from plethora.

In these crises, the contradiction between socialised production and capitalist appropriation ends in a violent explosion. The circulation of commodities is, for the time being, stopped. Money, the means of circulation, becomes a hindrance to circulation. All the laws of production and circulation of commodities are turned upside down. The economic collision has reached its apogee. *The mode of production is in rebellion against the mode of exchange.*

The fact that the socialised organisation of production within the factory has developed so far that it has become incompatible with the anarchy of production in society, which exists side by side with and dominates it, is brought home to the capitalists themselves by the violent concentration of capital that occurs during crises, through the ruin of large, and a still greater number of small, capitalists. The whole mechanism of the capitalist mode of production breaks down under the pressure of the productive forces, its own creations. It is no longer able to turn all this mass of means of production into capital. They lie fallow, and for that very reason the industrial reserve army must also lie fallow. Means of production, means of subsistence, available labourers, all the elements of production and of general wealth, are present in abundance. But "abundance becomes the source of distress and want" (Fourier), because it is the very thing that prevents the transformation of the means of production and subsistence into capital. For in capitalistic society the means of production can only function when they have undergone a preliminary transformation into capital, into the means of exploiting human labour power. The necessity of this transformation into capital of the means of production and subsistence stands like a ghost between these and the workers. It alone prevents the coming together of the material and personal levers of production; it alone forbids the means of production to function, the workers to work and live. On the one hand, therefore, the capitalistic mode of production stands convicted of its own incapacity to further direct these productive forces. On the other, these productive forces themselves, with increasing energy, press forward to the removal of the existing contradiction, to the abolition of their quality as capital, to the *practical recognition of their character as social productive forces.*

This rebellion of the productive forces, as they grow more and more powerful, against their quality as capital, this stronger and stronger command that their social character shall be recognised, forces the capitalist class itself to treat them more and more as social productive forces, so far as this is possible under capitalist conditions. The period of industrial high pressure, with its unbounded inflation of credit, not less than the crash itself, by the collapse of great capitalist establishments, tends to bring about that form of the socialisation of great masses of means of production which we meet with in the different kinds of joint-stock companies. Many of these means of production and of distribution are, from the outset, so colossal that, like the railways, they exclude all other forms of capitalistic exploitation. At a further stage of evolution this form also becomes insufficient. The producers on a large scale in a particular branch of industry in a particular country unite in a trust, a union for the purpose of regulating production. They determine the total amount to be produced, parcel it out among themselves, and thus enforce the selling price fixed beforehand. But trusts of this kind, as soon as business becomes bad, are generally liable to break up, and on this very account compel a yet greater concentration of association. The whole of the particular industry is turned into one gigantic joint-stock company; internal competition gives place to the internal monopoly of this one company. This has happened in 1890 with the English alkali production, which is now, after the fusion of 48 large works, in the hands of one company, conducted upon a single plan, and with a capital of £6,000,000.

In the trusts, freedom of competition changes into its very opposite—into monopoly; and the production without any definite plan of capitalistic society capitulates to the production upon a definite plan of the invading socialistic society. Certainly this is so far still to the benefit and advantage of the capitalist. But in this case the exploitation is so palpable that it must break down. No nation will put up with the production conducted by trusts, with so barefaced an exploitation of the community by a small band of dividend-mongers.

In any case, with trusts or without, the official representative of capitalist society—the state—will ultimately have to undertake the direction of production.* This necessity for conversion into state property is felt first in the great institutions for intercourse and communication—the post office, the telegraphs, the railways.

If the crises demonstrate the incapacity of the bourgeoisie for managing any longer modern productive force, the transformation of the great establishments for production and distribution into joint-stock companies, trusts and state property shows how unnecessry the bourgeoisie are for that purpose. All the social functions of the capitalist are now performed by salaried employees. The capitalist has no further social function than that of pocketing dividends, tearing off coupons, and gambling on the Stock Exchange, where the different capitalists despoil one another of their capital. At first the capitalistic mode of production forces out the workers. Now it forces out the capitalists, and reduces them, just as it reduced the workers, to the ranks of the surplus population, although not immediately into those of the industrial reserve army.

But the transformation, either into joint-stock companies and trusts, or into state ownership, does not do away with the capitalistic nature of the productive forces. In the joint-stock companies and trusts this is obvious. And

*I say "have to." For only when the means of production and distribution have *actually* outgrown the form of management by joint-stock companies, and when, therefore, the taking them over by the state has become *economically* inevitable, only then—even if it is the state of today that effects this—is there an economic advance, the attainment of another step preliminary to the taking over of all productive forces by society itself. But of late, since Bismarck went in for state ownership of industrial establishments, a kind of spurious socialism has arisen, degenerating, now and again, into something of flunkeyism, that without more ado declares *all* state ownership, even of the Bismarckian sort, to be socialistic. Certainly, if the taking over by the state of the tobacco industry is socialistic, then Napoleon and Metternich must be numbered among the founders of socialism. If the Belgian state, for quite ordinary political and financial reasons, itself constructed its chief railway lines; if Bismarck, not under any economic compulsion, took over for the state the chief Prussian lines, simply to be the better able to have them in hand in case of war, to bring up the railway employees as voting cattle for the government, and especially to create for himself a new source of income independent of parliamentary votes—this was, in no sense, a socialistic measure, directly or indirectly, consciously or unconsciously. Otherwise, the Royal Maritime Company, the Royal porcelain manufacture, and even the regimental tailor shops of the Army would also be socialistic institutions, or even, as was seriously proposed by a sly dog in Frederick William III's reign, the taking over by the state of the brothels. *[Note by Engels.]*

the modern state, again, is only the organisation that bourgeois society takes on in order to support the external conditions of the capitalist mode of production against the encroachments as well of the workers as of individual capitalists. The modern state, no matter what its form, is essentially a capitalist machine, the state of the capitalists, the ideal personification of the total national capital. The more it proceeds to the taking over of productive forces, the more does it actually become the national capitalist, the more citizens does it exploit. The workers remain wage-workers—proletarians. The capitalist relation is not done away with. It is rather brought to a head. But, brought to a head, it topples over. State ownership of the productive forces is not the solution of the conflict, but concealed within are the technical conditions that form the elements of that solution.

This solution can only consist in the practical recognition of the social nature of the modern forces of production, and therefore in the harmonising of the modes of production, appropriation, and exchange with the socialised character of the means of production. And this can only come about by society openly and directly taking possession of the productive forces which have outgrown all control except that of society as a whole. The social character of the means of production and of the products today reacts against the producers, periodically disrupts all production and exchange, acts only like a law of Nature working blindly, forcibly, destructively. But with the taking over by society of the productive forces, the social character of the means of production and of the products will be utilised by the producers with a perfect understanding of its nature, and instead of being a source of disturbance and periodical collapse, will become the most powerful lever of production itself.

Engels, *Socialism: Utopian and Socialism* (1880), MESW, pp. 422–28.

And this is the economic constitution of the whole of our present-day society: it is the working class alone which produces all values. For value is only another expression for labour, that expression whereby in our present-day capitalist society is designated the amount of socially necessary labour contained in a particular commodity. These values produced by the workers do not, however, belong to the workers. They belong to the owners of the raw materials, machines, tools and the reserve funds which allow these owners to buy the labour power of the working class. From the whole mass of products produced by it, the working class, therefore, only receives a part for itself. And, as we have just seen, the other part, which the capitalist class keeps for itself and at most has to divide with the class of landowners, becomes larger with every new discovery and invention, while the part falling to the working class (reckoned per head) either increases only very slowly and inconsiderably or not at all, and under certain circumstances may even fall.

But these discoveries and inventions which supersede each other at an ever-increasing rate, this productivity of human labour which rises day by day to an extent previously unheard of, finally gives rise to a conflict in which the present-day capitalist economy must perish. On the one hand are immeasureable riches and a superfluity of products which the purchasers cannot cope with; on the other hand, the great mass of society proletarianised, turned into wage workers, and precisely for that reason made incapable of appropriating for themselves this superfluity of products. The division of society into a small, excessively rich class and a large, propertyless class of wage workers results in the society suffocating from its own superfluity, while the great majority of its members is scarcely, or even not at all, protected from extreme want. This state of affairs becomes daily more absurd and—unnecessary. It *must* be put an end to, it *can* be put an end to. A new social order is possible in which the present class differences will have disappeared and in which—perhaps after a short transitional period of privation, but of great value morally—through the planned utilisation and extension of the already existing enormous productive forces of all members of society, and with uniform obligation to work, the means for existence, for enjoying life, for the development and employment of all bodily and mental faculties will also be available for all in an equal measure in ever-increasing fullness.

Engels, "Introduction" to *Wage Labour and Capital* (1891), MESW, I, pp. 250–51.

MARX

The most favorable condition for the workingman is the growth of capital. This must be admitted: when capital remains stationary, commerce and manufacture are not merely stationary but decline, and in this case the workman is the first victim. He will suffer before the capitalist. And in the case of the growth of capital, under the circumstances, which, as we have said, are the best for the workingman, what will be his lot? He will suffer just the same. The growth of capital implies the accumulation and the concentration of capital. This centralisation involves a greater division of labor and a greater use of machinery. The greater division of labor destroys the especial skill of the laborer; and by putting in the place of this skilled work labor which anyone can perform it increases competition among the workers.

This competition becomes more fierce as the division of labor enables a single man to do the work of three. Machinery accomplishes the same result on a much larger scale. The accumulation of productive capital forces the industrial capitalist to work with constantly increasing means of production, ruins the small manufacturer, and throws him into the ranks of the proletariat. Then, the rate of interest falling in proportion as capital accumulates, the people of small means and retired tradespeople, who can no longer live upon their small incomes, will be forced to look out for some business again and ultimately to swell the number of proletarians. Finally, the more productive capital grows, the more it is compelled to produce for a market whose requirements it does not know,—the more supply tries to force demand, and consequently crises increase in frequency and in intensity. But every crisis in turn hastens the concentration of capital, adds to the proletariat. Thus, as productive capital grows, competition among the workers grows too, and grows in a far greater proportion. The reward of labor is less for all, and the burden of labor is increased for at least some of them.

—Marx, *The Poverty of Philosophy* (1847), pp. 218–19

A fall in the rate of profit and a hastening of accumulation are in so far only different expressions of the same process as both of them indicate the development of the productive power. Accumulation in its turn hastens the fall of the rate of profit, inasmuch as it implies the concentration of labor on a large scale and thereby a higher composition of capital. On the other hand, a fall in the rate of profit hastens the concentration of capital and its centralisation through the expropriation of the smaller capitalists, the expropriation of the last survivors of the direct producers who still have anything to give up. This accelerates on one hand the accumulation, so far as mass is concerned, although the rate of accumulation falls with the rate of profit.

On the other hand, so far as the rate of self-expansion of the total capital, the rate of profit, is the incentive of capitalist production (just as this self-expansion of capital is its only purpose), its fall checks the formation of new independent capitals and thus seems to threaten the development of the process of capitalist production. It promotes overproduction, speculation, crises, surplus-capital along with surplus-population. Those economists who, like Ricardo, regard the capitalist mode of production as absolute, feel nevertheless that this mode of production creates its own limits, and therefore they attribute this limit, not to production, but to nature (in their theory of rent). But the main point in their horror over the falling rate of profit is the feeling that capitalist production meets in the development of productive forces a barrier, which has nothing to do with the production of wealth as such; and this peculiar barrier testifies to the finiteness and the historical, merely transitory character of capitalist production. It demonstrates that this is not an absolute mode for the production of wealth, but rather comes in conflict with the further development of wealth at a certain stage.

The rate of profit, that is, the relative increment of capital, is above all important for all new offshoots of capital seeking an independent location. And as soon as the formation of capital were to fall into the hands of a few established great capitals, which are compensated by the mass of profits for the loss through a fall in the rate of profits, the vital fire of production would be extinguished. It would fall into a dormant state. The rate of profit is the compelling power of capitalist production, and only such things are produced as yield a profit. Hence the fright of the English economists over the decline of the rate of profit. That the bare possibility of such a thing should worry Ricardo, shows his profound understanding of the conditions of capitalist production. The reproach moved against him, that he has an eye only to the development of the productive forces regardless of "human beings," regardless of the sacrifices in human beings and capital *values* incurred, strikes precisely his strong point. The development of the productive forces of social labor is the historical task and privilege of capital. It is precisely in this way that it unconsciously creates the material requirements of a higher mode of production. What worries Ricardo is the fact that the rate of profit, the stimulating principle of capitalist production, the fundamental premise and driving force of accumulation, should be endangered by the development of production itself. And the quantitative proportion means everything here. There is indeed something deeper than this hidden at this point, which he vaguely feels. It is here demonstrated in a purely economic way, that is, from a bourgeois point of view, within the confines of capitalist understanding, from the standpoint of capitalist production itself, that it has a barrier, that it is relative, that it is not an absolute, but only a historical mode of production corresponding to a definite and limited epoch in the development of the material conditions of production.

—Marx *Capital:* III (1894), pp. 283, 304–305.

What does the primitive accumulation of capital, i.e., its historical genesis, resolve itself into? In so far as it is not immediate transformation of slaves and serfs into wage-labourers, and therefore a mere change of form, it only means the expropriation of the immediate producers, i.e., the dissolution of private property based on the labour of its owner. Private property, as the antithesis to social, collective property, exists only where the means of labour and the external conditions of labour belong to private individuals. But according as these private individuals are labourers or not labourers, private property has a different character. The numberless shades, that it at first sight presents, correspond to the intermediate stages lying between these two extremes. The private property of the labourer in his means of production is the foundation of petty industry, whether agricultural, manufacturing or both; petty industry, again, is an essential condition for the development of social production and of the free individuality of the labourer himself. Of course, this petty mode of production exists also under slavery, serfdom, and other states of dependence. But it flourishes, it lets loose its whole energy, it attains its adequate classical form, only where the labourer is the private owner of his own means of labour set in action by himself: the peasant of the land which he cultivates, the artisan of the tool which he handles as a virtuoso. This mode of production presupposes parcelling of the soil, and scattering of the other means of production. As it excludes the concentration of these means of production, so also it excludes cooperation, division of labour within each separate process of production, the control over, and the productive application of the forces of Nature by society, and the free development of the social productive powers. It is compatible only with a system of production, and a society, moving within narrow and more or less primitive bounds. To perpetuate it would be, as Pecqueur rightly says, "to decree universal mediocrity." At a certain stage of development it brings forth the material agencies for its own dissolution. From that moment new forces and new passions spring up in the bosom of society; but the old social organization fetters them and keeps them down. It must be annihilated; it is annihilated. Its annihilation, the transformation of the individualised and scattered means of production into socially concentrated ones, of the pigmy property of the many into the huge property of the few, the expropriation of the great mass of the people from the soil, from the means of subsistence, and from the means of labour, this fearful and painful expropriation of the mass of the people forms the prelude to the history of capital. It comprises a series of forcible methods, of which we have passed in review only those that have been epoch-making as methods of the primitive accumulation of capital. The expropriation of the immediate producers was accomplished with merciless Vandalism, and under the stimulus of passions the most infamous, the most sordid, the pettiest, the most meanly odious. Self-earned private property, that is based, so to say, on the fusing together of the isolated, independent labouring-individual with the conditions of his labour, is supplanted by capitalistic private property, which rests on exploitation of the nominally free labour of others, i.e., on wages-labour.

As soon as this process of transformation has sufficiently decomposed the old society from top to bottom, as soon as the labourers are turned into proletarians, their means of labour into capital, as soon as the capitalist mode of production stands on its own feet, then the further socialisation of labour and further transformation of the land and other means of production into socially exploited and, therefore, common means of production, as well as the further expropriation of private proprietors, takes a new form. That which is now to be expropriated is no longer the labourer working for himself, but the capitalist exploiting many labourers. This expropriation is accomplished by the action of the immanent laws of capitalistic production itself, by the centralisation of capital. One capitalist always kills many. Hand in hand with this centralisation, or this expropriation of many capitalists by few, develop, on an ever extending scale, the cooperative form of the labour-process, the conscious technical application of science, the methodical cultivation of the soil, the transformation of the instruments of labour into instruments of labour only usable in common, the economising of all means of production by their use as the means of production of combined, socialised labour, the entanglement of all peoples in the net of the world-market, and this, the international character of the capitalistic regime. Along with the constantly diminishing number of the magnates of capital, who usurp and monopolise all advantages of this process of transformation, grows the mass of misery, oppression, slavery, degradation, exploitation; but with this too grows the revolt of the working-class, a class always increasing in numbers, and disciplined, united, organised by the very mechanism of the process of capitalist production itself. The monopoly of capital becomes a fetter upon the mode of production, which has sprung up and flourished along with, and under it. Centralisation of the means of production and socialisation of labour at last reach a point where they become incompatible with their capitalist integument. This integument is burst asunder. The knell of capitalist private property sounds. The expropriators are expropriated.

The capitalist mode of appropriation, the result of the capitalist mode of production, produces capitalist private property. This is the first negation of individual private property, as founded on the labour of the proprietor. But capitalist production begets, with the inexorability of a law of Nature, its own negation. It is the negation of negation. This does not re-establish private property for the producer, but gives him individual property based on the acquisitions of the capitalist era: i.e., on cooperation and the possession in common of the land and of the means of production.

The transformation of scattered private property, arising from individual labour, into capitalist private property is, naturally, a process, incomparably more protracted, violent, and difficult, than the transformation of capitalistic private property, already practically resting on socialised production, into socialised property. In the former case, we had the expropriation of the mass of the people by a few usurpers; in the latter, we have the expropriation of a few usurpers by the mass of the people.

Marx, *Capital,* I (1867), pp. 834–37.

B. CAPITALISM'S SOCIALIZATION AND TRANSFORMATION

In addition to the role of economic contradictions and class conflicts in capitalism's prospective demise, as summarized in the first section of this chapter, Marx's vision of the impending transformation from capitalism into socialism also incorporates a process of creative destruction and supersession. Socialism is conceived and nurtured in capitalism's womb, and is its product, not merely its heir apparent. It emerges on the basis of capitalism's development and creativity as well as emanates from its conflicts and contradictions. Capitalism's very success stimulates changes which both portend and facilitate the process of movement toward socialism. A general statement of these elements of capitalism's creative destruction is found in section 7.B.7.

Paralleling this general theme are specific examples of the qualitative transformation and, in effect, socialization of capitalism's institutions in the process of its evolution. A prominent illustration is the credit system, itself effect as well as cause of capital accumulation, which by encouraging the development of corporations and worker cooperatives, transforms and socializes capitalist property relations, eventually "turning over into communism."[5] The corporation, which emerges from capitalism's enlarging appetite for investment funds, profoundly transforms capitalism's structure and behavior, leading to "abolition of the capitalist mode of production within capitalist production itself." Worker cooperatives similarly evolve out of capitalist industrialization and are facilitated by the development of the credit system; constitute a new form of social property nurtured in the womb of capitalism itself; are harbingers of things to come; and both demonstrate the need for and facilitate the transition to a socialist form of worker ownership and control of the means of production (selection 7.B.8).

According to Paul Sweezy, prominent contemporary Marxist, Marx did not support the "view that socialism can be achieved through a series of piecemeal reforms." To the contrary, the "first duty" of the capitalist state, even in the modern democratic republic, "is the defense of private property."[6] Still, the political component of the class struggle, emanating from economic conflicts and contradictions generated by capitalist development, does yield important legislative reforms. Examples, in selection 7.B.9, include restriction of working hours, sanitation regulation, child labor laws, and education. These reforms, as much the product of capitalist development as its technology and industry, contribute to the departure from a laissez-faire, market-oriented economy and to the movement toward a socialist one. First, they stimulate modern industry, the factory system, and industrial concentration. Second, they bring benefits to workers and show that the class struggle can successfully yield significant social reform. Third, they constitute victory for a principle, namely triumph of the "political economy of the working class" over the "political economy of the middle class." Fourth, they provide a practical school for the political education of the working class. Last, they incorporate elements that would presumably emerge more fully in a socialist economy, thus constituting a partial socialization of capitalism and a further intimation of the socialist future.

As with corporations, worker cooperatives, and factory legislation, so too with imperialism. Marx perceived imperialism, itself a product of capitalist development, as instrumental in the movement of world economy toward social-

[5]Marx's letter to Engels, April 2, 1858. Cited in Martin Nicolaus, ed. Foreword to Marx, *Grundrisse* (New York: Random House, 1973), p. 55.

[6]Paul Sweezy, *The Theory of Capitalist Development* (New York: Monthly Review, 1956), pp. 249, 246.

ism. This theme is illustrated pointedly by Marx's discussion of British rule in India, in selection 7.B.10. The British imperial purpose focused on extraction of Indian cotton and other raw materials. But this requires "transformation of India into a reproductive country." Economic modernization, Marx continues, has consequences extending far beyond natural resource extraction per se. These include internal and external communication, political unity, a free press, private property in land, and the creation of a native entrepreneurial and bureaucratic class. The development of a railroad system is especially noteworthy, Marx argues, because railways cannot be maintained over an immense subcontinent like India without simultaneously introducing industrial products, processes, and technologies serving as inputs both to railroads and to other branches of industry, as well as stimulating the creation of native technical and managerial labor. Of course, in Marx's view, the fruits of modernization will not be fully reaped by India until either a proletarian revolution occurs in Great Britain or India itself throws off "the English yoke altogether." But capitalism, through imperialism, lays the foundations for worldwide transition to socialism.

In *Grundrisse,* excerpts from which appear in selection 7.B.11, Marx examines the creatively destructive effects of science, technology, and automated machinery in late-stage capitalism. Output comes to depend less on the amount of labor employed and more on labor productivity. Production becomes automated and labor becomes essentially a supervisory and regulatory activity. These radical and creative developments ultimately destroy capitalism's foundations and serve as preconditions for a socialist future. Production based on exchange value "breaks down," and capitalism "thus works towards its own dissolution as the form dominating production."

7.B.7 CAPITALIST DEVELOPMENT AND CREATIVE DESTRUCTION

For the first time, nature becomes purely an object for humankind, purely a matter of utility; ceases to be recognized as a power for itself; and the theoretical discovery of its autonomous laws appears merely as a ruse so as to subjugate it under human needs, whether as an object of consumption or as a means of production. In accord with this tendency, capital drives beyond national barriers and prejudices as much as beyond nature worship, as well as all traditional, confined, complacent, encrusted satisfactions of present needs, and reproductions of old ways of life. It is destructive towards all of this, and constantly revolutionizes it, tearing down all the barriers which hem in the development of the forces of production, the expansion of needs, the all-sided development of production, and the exploitation and exchange of natural and mental forces.

But from the fact that capital posits every such limit as a barrier and hence gets *ideally* beyond it, it does not by any means follow that it has *really* overcome it, and, since every such barrier contradicts its character, its production moves in contradictions which are constantly overcome but just as constantly posited. Furthermore. The universality towards which it irresistibly strives encounters barriers in its own nature, which will, at a certain stage of its development, allow it to be recognized as being itself the greatest barrier to this tendency, and hence will drive towards its own suspension. . . .

To begin with: capital forces the workers beyond necessary labour to surplus labour. Only in this way does it realize itself, and create surplus value. But on the other hand, it posits necessary labour only *to the extent* and *in so far as* it is surplus labour and the latter is *realizable* as *surplus value.* It posits surplus labour, then, as the condition of the necessary, and surplus value as the limit of objectified labour, of value as such. As soon as it cannot posit value, it does not posit necessary labour; and, given its foundation, it cannot be otherwise. It therefore restricts labour and the creation of value—by an artificial check, as the English express it—and it does so on the same grounds as and to the same extent that it posits surplus labour and surplus value. By its nature, therefore, it posits a *barrier* to labour and value-creation, in contradiction to its tendency to expand them boundlessly. And in as much as it both posits a barrier *specific* to itself, and on the other side equally drives over and beyond *every* barrier, it is the living contradiction. . . .

When the limited bourgeois form is stripped away, what is wealth other than the universality of individual needs, capacities, pleasures, productive forces etc., created through universal exchange? The full development of human mastery over the forces of nature, those of so-called nature as well as of humanity's own nature? The absolute working-out of his creative potentialities, with no presupposition other than the previous historic development, which makes this totality of development, i.e. the development of all human powers as such the end in itself, not as measured on a *predetermined* yardstick? Where he does not reproduce himself in one specificity, but produces his totality? Strives not to remain something he has become, but is in the absolute movement of becoming? In bourgeois economics—and in the epoch of production to which it corresponds—this complete working-out of the human content appears as a complete emptying-out, this universal objectification as total alienation, and the tearing-down of all limited, one-sided aims as sacrifice of the human end-in-itself to an entirely external end. This is why the childish world of antiquity appears on one side as loftier. On the other side, it really is loftier in all matters where closed shapes, forms and given limits are sought for. It is satisfaction from a limited standpoint; while the modern gives no satisfaction; or, where it appears satisfied with itself, it is *vulgar.* . . .

There appears here the universalizing tendency of capital, which distinguishes it from all previous stages of production. Although limited by its very nature, it strives towards the universal development of the forces of production, and thus becomes the presupposition of a new mode of production, which is founded not on the development of the forces of production for the purpose of reproducing or at most expanding a given condition, but where the free, unobstructed, progressive and universal development of the forces of production is itself the presupposition of society and hence of its reproduction; where advance beyond the point of departure is the only presupposition. This tendency—which capital possesses, but which at the same time, since capital is a limited form of production, contradicts it and hence drives it towards dissolution—distinguishes capital from all earlier modes of production, and at the same time contains this element, that capital is posited as a mere point of transition. All previous forms of society—or, what is the same, of the forces of social production—foundered on the development of wealth. Those thinkers of antiquity who were possessed of consciousness therefore directly denounced wealth as the dissolution of the community. The feudal system, for its part, foundered on urban industry, trade, modern agriculture (even as a result of individual inventions like gunpowder and the printing press). With the development of wealth—and hence also new powers and expanded intercourse on the part of individuals—the economic conditions on which the community rested were dissolved, along with the political relations of the various constituents of the community which corresponded to those conditions: religion, in which it was viewed in idealized form (and both [religion and political relations] rested in turn on a given relation to nature, into which all productive force resolves itself); the character, outlook etc. of the individuals. The *development of science alone*—i.e. the most solid form of wealth, both its product and its producer—was sufficient to dissolve these communities. But the *development of science,* this ideal and at the same time practical wealth, is only one aspect, one form in which the *development of the human productive forces,* i.e. of wealth, appears. Considered *ideally,* the dissolution of a given form of consciousness sufficed to kill a whole epoch. In reality, this barrier to consciousness corresponds to a *definite degree of development of the forces of material production* and hence of wealth. True, there was not only a development on the old basis, but also a *development of this basis itself.* The highest development of this *basis* itself (the flower into which it transforms itself; but it is always *this* basis, *this* plant as flower; hence wilting *after* the flowering and as consequence of the flowering) is the point at which it is itself worked out, developed, into the form in which it is compatible with the *highest development of the forces of production,* hence also the richest development of the individuals. As soon as this point is reached, the further development appears as decay, and the new development begins from a new basis. We saw earlier that property in the conditions of production was posited as identical with a limited, definite form of the community; hence of the individual with the characteristics—limited characteristics and limited development of his productive forces—required to form such a community. This presupposition was itself in turn the result of a limited historic stage of the development of the productive forces; of wealth as well as of the mode of creating it. The purpose of the community, of the individual—as well as the condition of production—[is] *the reproduction of these specific conditions of production* and of the individuals, both singly and in their social groupings and relations—as living carriers of these conditions. Capital posits the *production of wealth* itself and hence the universal development of the productive forces, the constant overthrow of its prevailing presuppositions, as the presupposition of its reproduction. Value excludes no use value; i.e. includes no particular kind of consumption etc., of intercourse, of knowledge etc. appears to it only as a barrier which it strives to overpower. Its own presupposition—value—is posited as product, not as a loftier presupposition hovering over production. The barrier to *capital* is that this entire development proceeds in a contradictory way, and that the working-out of the productive forces, of general wealth etc., knowledge etc., appears in such a way that the working individual *alienates* himself; relates to the conditions brought out of him by his labour as those not of his *own* but of an *alien wealth* and of his own poverty. But this antithetical form is itself fleeting, and produces the real conditions of its own suspension. The result is: the tendentially and potentially general development of the forces of production—of wealth as such—as a basis; likewise, the universality of intercourse, hence the world market as a basis. The basis as the possibility of the universal development of the individual, and the real development of the individuals from this basis as a constant suspension of its *barrier,* which is recognized as a barrier, not take for a *sacred limit.* Not an ideal or imagined universality of the individual, but the universality of his real and ideal relations. Hence also the grasping of his own history as a *process,* and the recognition of nature (equally present as practical power over nature) as his real body. The process of development itself posited and known as the presupposition of the same. For this, however, necessary above all that the full development of the forces of production has become the *condition of production* and not that specific *conditions of production* are posited as a limit to the development of the productive forces. . . .

The creation of a large quantity of disposable time apart from necessary labour time for society generally and each of its members (i.e. room for the development of the individuals' full productive forces, hence those of society also), this creation of not-labour time appears in the stage of capital, as of all earlier ones, as not-labour time, free time, for a few. What capital adds is that it increases the surplus labour time of the mass by all the means of art and science, because its wealth consists directly in the appropriation of surplus labour time; since *value directly its purpose,* not use value. It is thus, despite itself, instrumental in creating the means of social disposable time, in order to reduce labour time for the whole society to a diminishing minimum, and thus to free everyone's time for their own development. But its tendency always, on the one side, *to create disposable time, on the other, to convert it into surplus labour.* If it succeeds too well at the first, then it suffers from surplus production, and then necessary labour is interrupted, because *no surplus labour can be realized by capital.* The more this contradiction develops, the more does it become evident that the growth of the forces of production can no longer be bound up with the appropriation of alien labour, but that the mass of workers must themselves appropriate their own surplus labour. Once they have done so—and *disposable time* thereby ceases to have an *antithetical* existence—then, on one side, necessary labour time will be measured by the needs of the social individual, and, on the other, the development of the power of social production will grow so rapidly that, even though production is now calculated for the wealth of all, *disposable time* will grow for all. For real wealth is the developed productive power of all individuals. The measure of wealth is then not any longer, in any way, labour time, but rather disposable time. *Labour time as the measure of value* posits wealth itself as founded on poverty, and disposable time as existing *in and because of the antithesis to surplus labour time*; or, the positing of an individual's entire time as labour time, and his degradation therefore to mere worker, subsumption under labour. *The most developed machinery thus forces the worker to work longer than the savage does, or than he himself did with the simplest, crudest tools.* . . .

As the basis on which large industry rests, the appropriation of alien labour time, ceases, with its development, to make up or to create wealth, so does *direct labour* as such cease to be the basis of production, since, in one respect, it is transformed more into a supervisory and regulatory activity; but then also because the product ceases to be the product of isolated direct labour, and the *combination* of social activity appears, rather, as the producer. . . . In direct exchange, individual direct labour appears as realized in a particular product or part of the product, and its communal, social character—its character as objectification of general labour and satisfaction of the general need—as posited through exchange alone. In the production process of large-scale industry, by contrast, just as the conquest of the forces of nature by the social intellect is the precondition of the productive power of the means of labour as developed into the automatic process, on one side, so, on the other, is *the labour of the individual in its direct presence posited as suspended individual, i.e. as social, labour. Thus the other basis of this mode of production falls away.* . . .

As the system of bourgeois economy has developed for us only by degrees, so too its negation, which is its ultimate result. . . . It is evident that the material productive power already present, already worked out, existing in the form of fixed capital, together with the population etc., in short all conditions of wealth, that the greatest conditions for the reproduction of wealth, i.e. the abundant development of the social individual—that the development of the productive forces brought about by the historical development of capital itself, when it reaches a certain point, suspends the self-realization of capital, instead of positing it. Beyond a certain point, the development of the powers of production becomes a barrier for capital; hence the capital relation a barrier for the development of the productive powers of labour. When it has reached this point, capital, i.e. wage labour, enters into the same relation towards the development of social wealth and of the forces of production as the guild system, serfdom, slavery, and is necessarily stripped off as a fetter. The last form of servitude assumed by human activity, that of wage labour on one side, capital on the other, is thereby cast off like a skin, and this casting-off itself is the result of the mode of production corresponding to capital; the material and mental conditions of the negation of wage labour and of capital, themselves already the negation of earlier forms of unfree social production, are themselves results of its production process.

Marx, *Grundrisse* (1857–58), pp. 410, 421, 488, 540–42, 708–09, 712, 749.

7.B.8 CREDIT, CORPORATIONS, AND WORKER COOPERATIVES

CORPORATIONS

The general remarks, which the credit system so far elicited from us, were the following:

Formation of stock companies. By means of these:

1) An enormous expansion of the scale of production and enterprises, which were impossible for individual capitals. At the same time such enterprises as were formerly carried on by governments are socialised.

2) Capital, which rests on a socialised mode of production and presupposes a social concentration of means of production and labour-powers, is here directly endowed with the form of social capital (a capital of directly associated individuals) as distinguished from private capital, and its enterprises assume the form of social enterprises as distinguished from individual enterprises. It is the abolition of capital as private property within the boundaries of capitalist production itself.

3) Transformation of the actually functioning capitalist into a mere manager, an administrator of other people's capital, and of the owners of capital into mere owners, mere money-capitalists. Even if the dividends, which they receive, include the interest and profits of enterprise, that is, the total profit (for the salary of the manager is, or is supposed to be, a mere wage of a certain kind of skilled labor, the price of which is regulated in the labourmarket, like that of any other labour), this total profit is henceforth received only in the form of interest, that is, in the form of a mere compensation of the ownership of capital, which is now separated from its function in the actual process of reproduction in the same way, in which this function, in the person of the manager, is separated from the ownership of capital. The profit now presents itself (and not merely that portion of it, which derives its justification as interest from the profit of the borrower) as a mere appropriation of the surplus-labour of others, arising from the transformation of means of production into capital, that is, from its alienation from its actual producer, from its antagonism as another's property opposed to the individuals actually at work in production, from the manager down to the last day labourer.

In the stock companies the function is separated from the ownership of capital, and labour, of course, is entirely separated from the ownership of means of production and of surplus-labour. This result of the highest development of capitalist production is a necessary transition to the reconversion of capital into the property of the producers, no longer as the private property of individual producers, but as the common property of associates, as social property outright. On the other hand it is a transition to the conversion of all functions in the process of reproduction, which still remain connected with capitalist private property, into mere functions of the associated producers, into social functions. . . .

This is the abolition of the capitalist mode of production within capitalist production itself, a self-destructive contradiction, which represents on its face a mere phase of transition to a new form of production. It manifests its contradictory nature by its effects. It establishes a monopoly in certain spheres and thereby challenges the interference of the state. It reproduces a new aristocracy of finance, a new sort of parasites in the shape of promoters, speculators and merely nominal directors; a whole system of swindling and cheating by means of corporation juggling, stock jobbing, and stock speculation. It is private production without the control of private property.

Aside from the stock company business, which represents an abolition of capitalist private industry on the basis of the capitalist system itself and destroys private industry in proportion as it expands and seizes new spheres of production, credit offers to the individual capitalist, or to him who is regarded as a capitalist, absolute command of the capital of others and the property of others, within certain limits, and thereby of the labor of others. A command of social capital, not individual capital of his own gives him command of social labor. The capital itself, which a man really owns, or is supposed to own by public opinion, becomes purely a basis for the superstructure of credit. This is true particularly of wholesale commerce, through whose hands the greatest portion of the social product passes. All standards of measurement, all excuses which are more or less justified under capitalist production, disappear here. What the speculating wholesale merchant risks is social property, not his own. Equally stale becomes the phrase concerning the origin of capital from saving, for what he demands is precisely that others shall save for him. . . . The other phrase of the abstention is slapped in the face by his luxury, which now becomes a means of credit by itself. Conceptions, which still have some meaning in a less developed stage of capitalist production, become quite meaningless here. Both success and failure lead now simultaneously to a centralisation of capital, and thus to an expropriation on the most enormous scale. This expropriation extends here from the direct producers to the smaller and smallest capitalists themselves. It is first the point of departure of the capitalist mode of production; its complete accomplishment is the aim of this production. In the last instance it aims at the expropriation of all individuals from the means of production, which cease with the development of social production to be means of private production and products of private production, and which can henceforth be only means of production in the hands of associated producers, their social property, just as they are social products. However, this expropriation appears under the capitalist system in a contradictory form, as an appropriation of social property by a few; and credit gives to these few more and more the character of pure adventurers. Since property here exists in the form of shares of stock, its movements and transfer become purely a result of gambling at the stock exchange, where the little fish are swallowed by the sharks and the lambs by the wolves. In the stock companies the antagonism against the old form becomes apparent, in which social means of production are private property; but the conversion to the form of shares of stock still remains ensnared in the boundaries of capitalism; hence, instead of overcoming the antagonism between the character of wealth as a social one and as private wealth, the stock companies merely develop it in a new form.

The cooperative factories of the laborers themselves represent within the old form the first beginnings of the new, although they naturally reproduce, and must reproduce, everywhere in their actual organisation all the shortcomings of the prevailing system. But the antagonism between capital and labor is overcome within them, although only in the form of making the associated laborers their own capitalists, that is, enabling them to use the means of production for the employment of their own labor. They show the way, in which a new mode of production may naturally grow out of an old one, when the development of the material forces of production and of the corresponding forms of social production has reached a certain stage. Without the factory system arising out of the capitalist mode of production the cooperative factory could not develop, nor without the credit system arising out of the same mode of production. The credit system is not only the principal basis for the gradual transformation of capitalist private enterprises into capitalist stock companies, but also a means for the gradual extension of cooperative enterprises on a more or less natural scale. The capitalist stock companies as well as the cooperative factories may be considered as forms of transition from the capitalist mode of production to the associated one, with this distinction, that the antagonism is met negatively in the one, positively in the other. . . .

The credit system appears as the main lever of overproduction and overspeculation in commerce solely because the process of reproduction, which is elastic in its nature, is here forced to its extreme limits, and is so forced for the reason that a large part of the social capital is employed by people who do not own it and who push things with far less caution than the owner, who carefully weighs the possibilities of his private capital, which he handles himself. This simply demonstrates the fact that the production of values by capital based on the antagonistic nature of the capitalist system permits an actual, free, development only up to a certain point, so that it constitutes an immanent fetter and barrier of production, which are continually overstepped by the credit system. Hence the credit system accelerates the material development of the forces of production and the establishment of the world market. To bring these material foundations of the new mode of production to a certain degree of perfection, is the historical mission of the capitalist system of production. At the same time credit accelerates the violent eruptions of this antagonism, the crises and thereby the development of the elements of distintegration of the old mode of production.

Two natures, then, are immanent in the credit system. On one side, it develops the incentive of capitalist production, the accumulation of wealth by the appropriation and exploitation of the labor of others, to the purest and most colossal form of gambling and swindling, and reduces more and more the number of those, who exploit the social wealth. On the other side, it constitutes a transition to a new mode of production.

Marx, *Capital,* III (1894), pp. 515–22.

WORKER COOPERATIVES

The period passed since the Revolutions of 1848 has not been without its compensating features. We shall here only point to two great facts.

After a thirty years' struggle, fought with most admirable perseverance, the English working classes, improving a momentaneous split between the landlords and money lords, succeeded in carrying the Ten Hours' Bill. The immense physical, moral and intellectual benefits hence accruing to the factory operatives, half-yearly chronicled in the reports of the inspectors of factories, are now acknowledged on all sides. Most of the continental governments had to accept the English Factory Act in more or less modified forms, and the English parliament itself is every year compelled to enlarge its sphere of action.

But besides its practical import, there was something else to exalt the marvellous success of this working men's measure. Through their most notorious organs of science, such as Dr. Ure, Professor Senior, and other sages of that stamp, the middle class had predicted, and to their heart's content proved, that any legal restriction of the hours of labour must sound the death knell of British industry, which, vampire-like, could but live by sucking blood, and children's blood, too. In olden times, child murder was a mysterious rite of the religion of Moloch, but it was practiced on some very solemn occasions only, once a year perhaps, and then Moloch had no exclusive bias for the children of the poor. This struggle about the legal restriction of the hours of labour raged the more fiercely since, apart from frightened avarice, it told indeed upon the great contest between the blind rule of the supply and demand laws which form the political economy of the middle class, and social production controlled by social foresight, which forms the political economy of the working class. Hence the Ten Hours' Bill was not only a great practical success; it was the victory of a principle; it was the first time that in broad daylight the political economy of the middle class succumbed to the political economy of the working class.

But there was in store a still greater victory of the political economy of labour over the political economy of property. We speak of the cooperative movement, especially the cooperative factories raised by the unassisted efforts of a few bold "hands." The value of these great social experiments cannot be over-rated. By deed, instead of by argument, they have shown that production on a large scale, and in accord with the behests of modern science, may be carried on without the existence of a class of masters employing a class of hands; that to bear fruit, the means of labour need not be monopolised as a means of dominion over, and of extortion against, the labouring man himself; and that, like slave labour, like serf labour, hired labour is but a transitory and inferior form, destined to disappear before associated labour plying its toil with a willing hand, a ready mind and a joyous heart. In England, the seeds of the cooperative system were sown by Robert Owen; the working men's experiments, tried on the Continent, were, in fact, the practical upshot of the theories, not invented, but loudly proclaimed, in 1848.

At the same time, the experience of the period from 1848 to 1864 has proved beyond doubt that, however excellent in principle and however useful in practice, cooperative labour, if kept within the narrow circle of the casual efforts of private workmen, will never be able to arrest the growth in geometrical progression of monopoly, to free the masses, nor even to perceptibly lighten the burden of their miseries. It is perhaps for this very reason that plausible noblemen, philanthropic middle class spouters, and even keen political economists, have all at once turned nauseously complimentary to the very cooperative labour system they had vainly tried to nip in the bud by deriding it as the utopia of the dreamer, or stigmatising it as the sacrilege of the socialist. To save the industrious masses, cooperative labour ought to be developed to national dimensions, and, consequently, to be fostered by national means. Yet, the lords of land and the lords of capital will always use their political privileges for the defence and perpetuation of their economical monopolies. So far from promoting, they will continue to lay every possible impediment in the way of the emancipation of labour. Remember the sneer with which, last session, Lord Palmerston put down the advocates of the Irish Tenants' Right Bill. The House of Commons, cried he, is a house of landed proprietors. To conquer political power has therefore become the great duty of the working classes. They seem to have comprehended this, for in England, Germany, Italy and France there have taken place simultaneous revivals, and simultaneous efforts are being made at the political reorganisation of the working men's party.

One element of success they possess—numbers; but numbers weigh only in the balance, if united by combination and led by knowledge. Past experience has shown how disregard of that bond of brotherhood which ought to exist between the workmen of different countries, and incite them to stand firmly by each other in all their struggles for emancipation, will be chastised by the common discomfiture of their incoherent efforts. This thought prompted the working men of different countries assembled on September 28, 1864, in public meeting at St. Martin's Hall, to found the International Association.

Marx, *Address* (1864), MESW, II, pp. 438–41.

7.B.9 FACTORY LEGISLATION AND EDUCATION

The English Factory Acts are the negative expression of the greed for surplus-labour. These acts curb the passion of capital for a limitless draining of labour-power, by forcibly limiting the working day by state regulations, made by a state that is ruled by capitalist and landlord. Apart from the working-class movement that daily grew more threatening, the limiting of factory labour was dictated by the same necessity which spread guano over the English fields. The same blind eagerness for plunder that in the one case exhausted the soil, had, in the other, torn up by the roots the living force of the nation. Periodical epidemics speak on this point as clearly as the diminishing military standard in Germany and France. . . .

The Struggle for the Normal Working Day. Compulsory Limitation By Law of the Working Time. The English Factory Acts, 1833 to 1864

After capital had taken centuries in extending the working-day to its normal maximum limit, and then beyond this to the limit of the natural day of 12 hours, there followed on the birth of machinism and modern industry in the last third of the eighteenth century, a violent encroachment like that of an avalanche in its intensity and extent. All bounds of morals and nature, age and sex, day and night, were broken down. Even the ideas of day and night, of rustic simplicity in the old statutes, became so confused that an English judge, as late as 1860, needed a quite Talmudic sagacity to explain "judicially" what was day and what was night. Capital celebrated its orgies.

As soon as the working class, stunned at first by the noise and turmoil of the new system of production, recovered, in some measure, its senses, its resistance began, and first in the native land of machinism, in England. For 30 years, however, the concessions conquered by the workpeople were purely nominal. Parliament passed 5 Labour Laws between 1802 and 1833, but was shrewd enough not to vote a penny for their carrying out, for the requisite officials, etc.

They remained a dead letter. "The fact is, that prior to the Act of 1833, young persons and children were worked all night, all day, or both *ad libitum.*"

A normal working day for modern industry only dates from the Factory Act of 1833, which included cotton, wool, flax, and silk factories. Nothing is more characteristic of the spirit of capital than the history of the English Factory Acts from 1833 to 1864.

The Act of 1833 declares the ordinary factory working day to be from half-past five in the morning to half-past eight in the evening, and within these limits, a period of 15 hours, it is lawful to employ young persons (i.e., persons between 13 and 18 years of age), at any time of the day, provided no one individual young person should work more than 12 hours in any one day, except in certain cases especially provided for. . . .

But in no wise conciliated capital now began a noisy agitation that went on for several years. It turned chiefly on the age of those who, under the name of children, were limited to 8 hours work, and were subject to a certain amount of compulsory education. According to capitalistic anthropology, the age of childhood ended at 10, or at the outside, at 11. The more nearly the time approached for the coming into full force of the Factory Act, the fatal year 1836, the more wildly raged the mob of manufacturers. They managed, in fact, to intimidate the government to such an extent that in 1835 it proposed to lower the limit of the age of childhood from 13 to 12. In the meantime the pressure from without grew more threatening. Courage failed the House of Commons. It refused to throw children of 13 under the Juggernaut Car of capital for more than 8 hours a day, and the Act of 1833 came into full operation. It remained unaltered until June, 1844.

In the ten years during which it regulated factory work, first in part, and then entirely, the official reports of the factory inspectors teem with complaints as to the impossibility of putting the Act into force. As the law of 1833 left it optional with the lords of capital during the 15 hours, from 5:30 a.m. to 8:30 p.m., to make every "young person," and "every child" begin, break off, resume, or end his 12 or 8 hours at any moment they liked, and also permitted them to assign to different persons different times for meals, these gentlemen soon discovered a new "system of relays," by which the labour-horses were not changed at fixed stations, but were constantly re-harnessed at changing stations. We do not pause longer on the beauty of this system, as we shall have to return to it later. But this much is clear at the first glance: that this system annulled the whole Factory Act, not only in the spirit, but in the letter. How could factory inspectors, with this complex book-keeping in respect to each individual child or young person, enforce the legally determined work time and the granting of the legal meal-times? In a great many of the factories, the old brutalities soon blossomed out again unpunished. In an interview with the Home Secretary (1844), the factory inspectors demonstrated the impossibility of any control under the newly invented relay system. In the meantime, however, circumstances had greatly changed. The factory hands, especially since 1838, had made the Ten Hours' Bill their economical, as they had made the Charter their political, election-cry. Some of the manufacturers, even, who had managed their factories in conformity with the Act of 1833, overwhelmed Parliament with memorials on the immoral competition of their false brethren whom greater impudence, or more fortunate local circumstances, enabled to break the law. Moreover, however much the individual manufacturer might give the rein to his old lust for gain, the spokesmen and political leaders of the manufacturing class ordered a change of front and of speech towards the workpeople. They had entered upon the contest for the repeal of the Corn Laws, and needed the workers to help them to victory. They promised, therefore, not only a double-sized loaf of bread, but the enactment of the Ten Hours' Bill in the Free Trade millenium. Thus they still less dared to oppose a measure intended only to make the law of 1833 a reality. Threatened in their holiest interest, the rent of land, the Tories thundered with philanthropic indignation against the "nefarious practices" of their foes.

This was the origin of the additional Factory Act of June 7th, 1844. It came into effect on September 10th, 1844. It places under protection a new category of workers, viz., the women over 18. They were placed in every respect on the same footing as the young persons, their work time limited to twelve hours, their night-labour forbidden, etc. For the first time, legislation saw itself compelled to control directly and officially the labour of adults. . . .

To get rid of the abuses of the "spurious relay-system," the law established besides others the following important regulations: "That the hours of work of children and young persons shall be reckoned from the time when any child or young person shall begin to work in the morning." So that if A, e.g., begins work at 8 in the morning, and B at 10, B's work-day must nevertheless end at the same hour as A's. "The time shall be regulated by a public clock," for example, the nearest railway clock, by which the factory clock is to be set. The occupier is to hang up a "legible" printed notice stating the hours for the beginning and ending of work and the times allowed for the several meals. Children beginning work before 12 noon may not be again employed after 1 p.m. . . .

It has been seen that these minutiae, which, with military uniformity, regulate by stroke of the clock the times, limits, pauses of the work, were not at all the products of Parliamentary fancy. They developed gradually out of circumstances as natural laws of the modern mode of production. Their formulation, official recognition, and proclamation by the State, were the result of a long struggle of classes. One of their first consequences was that in practice the working day of the adult males in factories became subject to the same limitations, since in most processes of production the cooperation of the children, young persons, and women is indispensable. On the whole, therefore, during the period from 1844 to 1847, the 12 hours' working day became general and uniform in all branches of industry under the Factory Act. . . .

The years 1846–47 are epoch-making in the economic history of England. The Repeal of the Corn Laws, and of the duties on cotton and other raw material; free trade proclaimed as the guiding star of legislation; in a word, the arrival of the millenium. On the other hand, in the same years, the Chartist movement and the 10 hours' agitation reached their highest point. They found allies in the Tories panting for revenge. Despite the fanatical opposition of the army of perjured Free-traders, with Bright and Cobden at their head, the Ten Hours' Bill, struggled for so long, went through Parliament. . . .

Capital now entered upon a preliminary campaign in order to hinder the Act from coming into full force. [This] campaign. . .came to grief, and the Ten Hours' Act came into force May 1st, 1848. But meanwhile the fiasco of the Chartist party whose leaders were imprisoned, and whose organisation was dismembered, had shaken the confidence of the English working class in its own strength. Soon after this the June insurrections in Paris and its bloody suppression united, in England as on the Continent, all fractions of the ruling classes, landlords and capitalists, stock-exchange wolves and shop-keepers. Protectionists and Freetraders, government and opposition, priests and free-thinkers, young whores and old nuns, under the common cry for the salvation of Property, Religion, the Family and Society. The working class was everywhere proclaimed, placed under a ban, under a virtual law of suspects. The manufacturers had no need any longer to restrain themselves. They broke out in open revolt not only against the Ten Hours' Act, but against the whole of the legislation that since 1833 had aimed at restricting in some measure the "free" exploitation of labour-power. It was a pro-slavery rebellion in miniature, carried on for over two years with a cynical recklessness, a terrorist energy all the cheaper because the rebel capitalist risked nothing except the skin of his "hands." . . .

But on this apparently decisive victory of capital, followed at once a revulsion. The workpeople had hitherto offered a passive, although inflexible and unremitting resistance. They now protested in Lancashire and Yorkshire in threatening meetings. The pretended Ten Hours' Act, was thus simple humbug, parliamentary cheating, had never existed! The Factory Inspectors urgently warned the Government that the antagonism of classes had arrived at an incredible tension. Some of the masters themselves murmured: "On account of the contradictory decisions of the magistrates, a condition of things altogether abnormal and anarchial obtains. One law holds in Yorkshire, another in Lancashire; one law in one parish of Lancashire, another in its immediate neighborhood. The manufacturer in large towns could evade the law, the manufacturer in country districts could not find the people necessary for the relay-system, still less for the shifting of hands from one factory to another," etc. And the first birth-right of capital is equal exploitation of labour-power by all capitalists.

Under these circumstances a compromise between masters and men was effected that received the seal of Parliament in the additional Factory Act of August 5th, 1850. The working day for "young persons and women," was raised from 10 to 10½ hours for the first five days of the week, and was shortened to 7½ on Saturday. The work was to go on between 6 a.m. and 6 p.m. with pauses of not less than 1½ hours for meal-times, these meal-times to be allowed at one and the same time for all, and conformably to the conditions of 1844. By this an end was put to the relay-system once for all. For children's labour, the Act of 1844 remained in force. . . .

The Act of 1850 was... finally completed in 1853 by forbidding the "employment of children in the morning before and in the evening after young persons and women." Henceforth with a few exceptions the Factory Act of 1850 regulated the working day of all workers in the branches of industry that come under it. Since the passing of the first Factory Act half a century had elapsed. ...

The principle had triumphed with its victory in those great branches of industry which form the most characteristic creation of the modern mode of production. Their wonderful development from 1853 to 1860, hand-in-hand with the physical and moral regeneration of the factory workers, struck the most purblind. The masters from whom the legal limitation and regulation had been wrung step by step after a civil war of half a century, themselves referred ostentatiously to the contrast with the branches of exploitation still "free." The Pharisees of "political economy" now proclaimed the discernment of the necessity of a legally fixed working day as a characteristic new discovery of their "science." It will be easily understood that after the factory magnates had resigned themselves and become reconciled to the inevitable, the power of resistance of capital gradually weakened, whilst at the same time the power of attack of the working class grew with the number of its allies in the classes of society not immediately interested in the question. Hence the comparatively rapid advance since 1860. ...

The Struggle for the Normal Working-Day. Reaction of the English Acts on Other Countries

The reader will bear in mind that the production of surplus-value, or the extraction of surplus-labour, is the specific end and aim, the sum and substance, of capitalist production quite apart from any changes in the mode of production, which may arise from the subordination of labour to capital. He will remember that as far as we have at present gone, only the independent labourer, and therefore only the labourer legally qualified to act for himself, enters as a vendor of a commodity into a contract with the capitalist. If, therefore, in our historical sketch, modern industry, on the one hand; the labour of those who are physically and legally minors, on the other, play important parts, the former was to us only a special department, and the latter only a specially striking example of labour exploitation. Without, however, anticipating the subsequent development of our inquiry, from the mere connexion of the historic facts before us, it follows:

First. The passion of capital for an unlimited and reckless extension of the working day, is first gratified in the industries earliest revolutionised by water-power, steam, and machinery, in those first creations of the modern mode of production, cotton, wool, flax, and silk spinning, and weaving. The changes in the material mode of production, and the corresponding changes in the social relations of the producers gave rise first to an extravagance beyond all bounds, and then in opposition to this, called forth a control on the part of Society which legally limits, regulates, and makes uniform the working day and its pauses. This control appears, therefore, during the first half of the nineteenth century simply as exceptional legislation. As soon as this primitive dominion of the new mode of production was conquered, it was found that, in the meantime, not only had many other branches of production been made to adopt the same factory system, but that manufacturers with more or less obsolete methods, such as potteries, glass-making, etc., that old-fashioned handicrafts, like baking, and, finally, even that the so-called domestic industries such as nail-making had long since fallen as completely under capitalist exploitation as the factories themselves. Legislation was, therefore, compelled to gradually get rid of its exceptional character, or where, as in England, it proceeds after the manner of the Roman Casuists, to declare any house in which work was done to be a factory.

Second. The history of the regulation of the working day in certain branches of production, and the struggle still going on in others in regard to this regulation, prove conclusively that the isolated labourer, the labourer as "free" vendor of his labour-power, when capitalist production has once attained a certain stage, succumbs without any power of resistance. The creation of a normal working day is, therefore, the product of a protracted civil war, more or less dissembled, between the capitalist class and the working class. As the contest takes place in the arena of modern industry, it first breaks out in the home of that industry—England. The English factory workers were the champions, not only of the English, but of the modern working-class generally, as their theorists were the first to throw down the gauntlet to the theory of capital.[1] . . .

France limps slowly behind England. The February revolution was necessary to bring into the world the 12 hours' law, which is much more deficient than its English original. For all that, the French evolutionary method has its special advantages. It once for all commands the same limit to the working-day in all shops and factories without distinction, whilst English legislation reluctantly yields to the pressure of circumstances, now on this point now on that, and is getting lost in a hopelessly bewildering tangle of contradictory enactments. On the other hand, the French law proclaims as a principle that which in England was only won in the name of children, minors, and women, and has been only recently for the first time claimed as a general right.

In the United States of North America, every independent movement of the workers was paralysed so long as slavery disfigured a part of the Republic. Labour cannot emancipate itself in the white skin where in the black it is branded. But out of the death of slavery a new life at once arose. The first fruit of the Civil War was the eight hours' agitation, that ran with the seven-leagued boots of the locomotive from the Atlantic to the Pacific, from New England to California. The General Congress of Labour at Baltimore (August 16th, 1866) declared: "The first and great necessity of the present, to free the labour of

[1]Robert Owen, soon after 1810, not only maintained the necessity of a limitation of the working day in theory, but actually introduced the 10 hours' day into his factory at New Lanark. This was laughed at as a communistic Utopia; so were his "Combination of children's education with productive labour," and the Cooperative Societies of working-men, first called into being by him. Today, the first Utopia is a Factory Act, the second figures as an official phrase in all Factory Acts, the third is already being used as a cloak for reactionary humbug.

this country from capitalistic slavery, is the passing of a law by which eight hours shall be the normal working-day in all States of the American Union. We are resolved to put forth all our strength until this glorious result is attained." . . .

Thus the movement of the working-class on both sides of the Atlantic, that had grown instinctively out of the conditions of production themselves, endorsed the words of the English Factory Inspector, R. J. Saunders: "Further steps towards a reformation of society can never be carried out with any hope of success, unless the hours of labour be limited, and the prescribed limit strictly enforced.". . .

For "protection" against "the serpent of their agonies," the labourers must put their heads together, and, as a class, compel the passing of a law, an all-powerful social barrier that shall prevent the very workers from selling, by voluntary contract with capital, themselves and their families into slavery and death. In place of the pompous catalogue of the "inalienable rights of man" comes the modest Magna Charta of a legally limited working-day, which shall make clear "when the time which the worker sells is ended, and when his own begins.". . .

Passage of Modern Manufacture, and Domestic Industry into Modern Mechanical Industry. The Hastening of this Revolution by the Application of the Factory Acts to those Industries.

The cheapening of labour-power, by sheer abuse of the labour of women and children, by sheer robbery of every normal condition requisite for working and living, and by the sheer brutality of over-work and night-work, meets at last with natural obstacles that cannot be overstepped. So also, when based on these methods, do the cheapening of commodities and capitalist exploitation in general. So soon as this point is at last reached—and it takes many years—the hour has struck for the introduction of machinery, and for the thenceforth rapid conversion of the scattered domestic industries and also of manufactures into factory industries. . . .

England is at present experiencing. . .the conversion of manufacture, of handicrafts, and of domestic work into the factory system. . . .

This industrial revolution which takes place spontaneously, is artificially helped on by the extension of the Factory Acts to all industries in which women, young persons and children are employed. The compulsory regulation of the working day as regards its length, pauses, beginning and end, the system of relays of children, the exclusion of all children under a certain age, etc., necessitates on the one hand more machinery and the substitution of steam as a motive power in the place of muscles. On the other hand, in order to make up for the loss of time, an expansion occurs of the means of production used in common, of the furnaces, buildings, etc.; in one word, greater concentration of the means of production and a correspondingly greater concourse of workpeople. . . .

But though the Factory Acts thus artificially ripen the material elements necessary for the conversion of the manufacturing system into the factory system, yet at the same time, owing to the necessity they impose for greater outlay of capital, they hasten on the decline of the small masters, and the concentration of capital. . . .

The thoroughly conscientious investigations of the Children's Employment Commission prove that the effect of the regulation of the hours of work, in some industries, was to spread the mass of labour previously employed more evenly over the whole year; that this regulation was the first rational bridle on the murderous, meaningless caprices of fashion, caprices that consort so badly with the system of modern industry; that the development of ocean navigation and of the means of communication generally, has swept away the technical basis on which season-work was really supported, and that all other so-called unconquerable difficulties vanish before larger buildings, additional machinery, increase in the number of workpeople employed, and the alterations caused by all these in the mode of conducting the wholesale trade. But for all that, capital never becomes reconciled to such changes–and this is admitted over and over again by its own representatives–except "under the pressure of a General Act of Parliament" for the compulsory regulation of the hours of labour.

The Factory Acts. Sanitary and Education Clauses of the Same. Their General Extension in England

Factory legislation, that first conscious and methodical reaction of society against the spontaneously developed form of the process of production, is, as we have seen, just as much the necessary product of modern industry as cotton yarn, self-actors, and the electric telegraph. Before passing to the consideration of the extension of that legislation in England, we shall shortly notice certain clauses contained in the Factory Acts, and not relating to the hours of work.

Apart from their wording, which makes it easy for the capitalist to evade them, the sanitary clauses are extremely meagre, and, in fact, limited to provisions for whitewashing the walls, for insuring cleanliness in some other matters, for ventilation, and for protection against dangerous machinery. . . .

What could possibly show better the character of the capitalist mode of production, than the necessity that exists for forcing upon it, by Acts of Parliament, the simplest appliances for maintaining cleanliness and health? . . . [These Acts strikingly show] that the capitalist mode of production, owing to its very nature, excludes all rational improvement beyond a certain point. It has been stated over and over again that the English doctors are unanimous in declaring that where the work is continuous, 500 cubic feet is the very least space that should be allowed for each person. Now, if the Factory Acts, owing to their compulsory provisions, indirectly hasten on the conversion of small workshops into factories, thus indirectly attacking the proprietary rights of the smaller capitalists, and assuring a monopoly to the great ones, so, if it were made obligatory to provide the proper space for each workman in every workshop, thousands of small employers would, at one full swoop, be expropriated directly! The very root of the capitalist mode of production, i.e., the self-expansion of all capital, large or small, by means of the "free" purchase and consumption of labour-power, would be attacked. Factory legislation is therefore brought to a dead-lock before these 500 cubic feet of breathing space. The sanitary officers, the industrial inquiry commissioners, the factory inspectors, all harp, over and over again, upon the necessity for those 500 cubic feet, and upon the impossibility of wringing them out of capital. They thus, in fact, declare that consumption and other lung diseases among the workpeople are necessary conditions to the existence of capital.

Paltry as the education clauses of the Act appear on the whole, yet they proclaim elementary education to be an indispensable condition to the employment of children. The success of those clauses proved for the first time the possibility of combining education and gymnastics with manual labour, and, consequently, of combining manual labour with education and gymnastics. The factory inspectors soon found out by questioning the schoolmasters, that the factory children, although receiving only one half the education of the regular day scholars, yet learnt quite as much and often more. . . . From the Factory system budded, as Robert Owen has shown us in detail, the germ of the education of the future, an education that will, in the case of every child over a given age, combine productive labour with instruction and gymnastics, not only as one of the methods of adding to the efficiency of production, but as the only method of producing fully developed human beings.

Modern Industry, as we have seen, sweeps away by technical means the manufacturing division of labour, under which each man is bound hand and foot for life to a single detail-operation. At the same time, the capitalistic form of that industry reproduces this same division of labour in a still more monstrous shape; in the factory proper, by converting the workman into a living appendage of the machine; and everywhere outside the Factory, partly by the sporadic use of machinery and machine workers, partly by re-establishing the divisions of labour on a fresh basis by the general introduction of the labour of women and children, and of cheap unskilled labour.

The antagonism between the manufacturing division of labour and the methods of Modern Industry makes itself forcibly felt. It manifests itself, amongst other ways, in the frightful fact that a great part of the children employed in modern factories and manufactures, are from their earliest years riveted to the most simple manipulations, and exploited for years, without being taught a single sort of work that would afterwards make them of use, even in the same manufactory or factory. . . .

Modern Industry never looks upon and treats the existing form of a process as final. The technical basis of that industry is therefore revolutionary, while all earlier modes of production were essentially conservative. By means of machinery, chemical processes and other methods, it is continually causing changes not only in the technical basis of production, but also in the functions of the labourer, and in the social combinations of the labour-process. At the same time, it thereby also revolutionizes the division of labour within the society, and incessantly launches masses of capital and of workpeople from one branch of production to another. But if Modern Industry, by its very nature, therefore necessitates variation of labour, fluency of function, universal mobility of the labourer, on the other hand, in its capitalistic form, it reproduces the old division of labour with its ossified particularisations. We have seen how this absolute contradiction between the technical necessities of Modern Industry, and the social character inherent in its capitalistic form, dispels all fixity and security in the situation of the labourer; how it constantly threatens, by taking away the instruments of labour, to snatch from his hands his means of subsistence, and, by suppressing his detail-function, to make him superfluous. We have seen, too, how this antagonism vents its rage in the creation of that monstrosity, an industrial reserve army, kept in misery in order to be always at the disposal of capital; in the incessant human sacrifices from among the working class, in the most reckless squandering of labour-power, and in the devastation caused by a social anarchy which turns every economical progress into a social calamity. This is the negative side. But if, on the one hand, variation of work at present imposes itself after the manner of an overpowering natural law, and with the blindly destructive action of a natural law that meets with resistance, at all points, Modern Industry, on the other hand, through its catastrophes imposes the necessity of recognising, as a fundamental law of production, variation of work, consequently fitness of the labourer for varied work, consequently the greatest possible development of his varied aptitudes. It becomes a question of life and death for society to adapt the mode of production to the normal functioning of this law, Modern Industry, indeed, compels society, under penalty of death, to replace the detail-worker of today, crippled by life-long repetition of one and the same trivial operation, and thus reduced to the mere fragment of a man, by the fully developed individual, fit for a variety of labours, ready to face any change of production, and to whom the different social functions he performs, are but so many modes of giving free scope to his own natural and acquired powers.

One step already spontaneously taken towards effecting this revolution is the establishment of technical and agricultural schools, and of "écoles d'enseignement professionnel," in which the children of the working-men receive some little instruction in technology and in the practical handling of the various implements of labour. Though the Factory Act, that first and meagre concession wrung from capital, is limited to combining elementary education with work in the factory, there can be no doubt that when the working class comes into power, as inevitably it must, technical instruction, both theoretical and practical, will take its proper place in the working-class schools. There is also no doubt that such revolutionary ferments, the final result of which is the abolition of the old division of labour, are diametrically opposed to the capitalistic form of production, and to the economic status of the labourer corresponding to that form. But the historical development of the antagonisms, immanent in a given form of production, is the only way in which that form of production can be dissolved and a new form established. . . .

The necessity for a generalization of the Factory Acts, for transforming them from an exceptional law relating to mechanical spinning and weaving—those first creations of machinery—into a law affecting social production as a whole, arose, as we have seen, from the mode in which Modern Industry was historically developed. In the rear of that industry, the traditional form of manufacture, of handicraft, and of domestic industry, is entirely revolutionised; manufactures are constantly passing into the factory system, and handicrafts into manufactures; and lastly, the spheres of handicraft and of the domestic industries become, in a, comparatively speaking, wonderfully short time, dens of misery in which capitalistic exploitation obtains free play for the wildest excesses. There are two circumstances that finally turn the scale: first, the constantly recurring experience that capital, so soon as it finds itself subject to legal control at one point, compensates itself all the more recklessly at other points; secondly, the cry of the capitalists for equality in the conditions of competition, i.e., for equal restraint on all exploitation of labour. . . .

If the general extension of factory legislation to all trades for the purpose of protecting the working class both in mind and body has become inevitable, on the other hand, as we have already pointed out, that extension hastens on the general conversion of numerous isolated small industries into a few combined industries carried on upon a large scale; it therefore accelerates the concentration of capital and the exclusive predominance of the factory system. It destroys both the ancient and the transitional forms, behind which the dominion of capital is still in part concealed, and replaces them by the direct and open sway of capital; but thereby it also generalises the direct opposition to this sway. While in each individual workshop it enforces uniformity, regularity, order, and economy, it increases by the immense spur which the limitation and regulation of the working day give to technical improvement, the anarchy and the catastrophes of capitalist production as a whole, the intensity of labour, and the competition of machinery with the labourer. By the destruction of petty and domestic industries it destroys the last resort of the "redundant population," and with it the sole remaining safety-valve of the whole social mechanism. By maturing the material conditions, and the combination on a social scale of the processes of production, it matures the contradictions and antagonisms of the capitalist form of production, and thereby provides, along with the elements for the formation of a new society, the forces for exploding the old one.

Modern Industry and Agriculture

If the use of machinery in agriculture is for the most part free from the injurious physical effect it has on the factory operative, its action in superseding the labourers is more intense, and finds less resistance. . . .

In the sphere of agriculture, modern industry has a more revolutionary effect than elsewhere, for this reason, that it annihilates the peasant, that bulwark of the old society, and replaces him by the wage labourer. Thus the desire for social changes, and the class antagonisms are brought to the same level in the country as in the towns. The irrational, old fashioned methods of agriculture are replaced by scientific ones. Capitalist production completely tears asunder the old bond of union which held together agriculture and manufacture in their infancy. But at the same time it creates the material conditions for a higher synthesis in the future, viz., the union of agriculture and industry on the basis of the more perfected forms they have each acquired during their temporary separation. Capitalist production, by collecting the population in great centres, and causing an ever increasing preponderance of town population, on the one hand concentrates the historical motive-power of society; on the other hand, it disturbs the circulation of matter between man and the soil, i.e., prevents the return to the soil of its elements consumed by man in the form of food and clothing; it therefore violates the conditions necessary to lasting fertility of the soil. By this action it destroys at the same time the health of the town labourer and the intellectual life of the rural labourer. But while upsetting the naturally grown conditions for the maintenance of that circulation of matter, it imperiously calls for its restoration as a system, as a regulating law of social production, and under a form appropriate to the full development of the human race. In agriculture as in manufacture, the transformation of production under the sway of capital, means, at the same time, the martyrdom of the producer; the instrument of labour becomes the means of enslaving, exploiting, and impoverishing the labourer; the social combination and organization of labour-processes is turned into an organised mode of crushing out the workman's individual vitality, freedom, and independence. The dispersion of the rural labourers over larger areas breaks their power of resistance while concentration increases that of the town operatives. In modern agriculture, as in the urban industries, the increased productiveness and quantity of the labour set in motion are bought at the cost of laying waste and consuming by disease labour-power itself. Moreover, all progress in capitalistic agriculture is a progress in the art, not only of robbing the labourer, but of robbing the soil; all progress in increasing the fertility of the soil for a given time, is a progress towards ruining the lasting sources of that fertility. The more a country starts its development on the foundation of modern industry, like the United States, for example, the more rapid is this process of destruction. Capitalist production, therefore, develops technology, and the combining together of various processes into a social whole, only by sapping the original sources of all wealth—the soil and the labourer.

Marx, *Capital,* I (1867), pp. 263 ff. 514 ff.

7.B.10 IMPERIALISM

THE BRITISH RULE IN INDIA

I share not the opinion of those who believe in a golden age of Hindustan. . . .

There cannot, however, remain any doubt but that the misery inflicted by the British on Hindustan is of an essentially different and infinitely more intensive kind than all Hindustan had to suffer before. . . . This is no distinctive feature of British colonial rule, but only an imitation of the Dutch. . . .

All the civil wars, invasions, revolutions, conquests, famines, strangely complex, rapid and destructive as the successive action in Hindustan may appear, did not go deeper than its surface. England has broken down the entire framework of Indian society, without any symptoms of reconstitution yet appearing. This loss of his old world, with no gain of a new one, imparts a particular kind of melancholy to the present misery of the Hindu, and separates Hindustan, ruled by Britain, from all its ancient traditions, and from the whole of its past history.

There have been in Asia, generally, from immemorial times, but three departments of Government: that of Finance, or the plunder of the interior; that of War, or the plunder of the exterior; and finally, the department of Public Works. Climate and territorial conditions, especially the vast tracts of desert, extending from the Sahara, through Arabia, Persia, India and Tartary, to the most elevated Asiatic highlands, constituted artificial irrigation by canals and waterworks the basis of Oriental agriculture. As in Egypt and India, inundations are used for fertilizing the soil of Mesopotamia, Persia, etc.; advantage is taken of a high level for feeding irrigative canals. This prime necessity of an economical and common use of water, which, in the Occident, drove private enterprise to voluntary association, as in Flanders and Italy, necessitated, in the Orient where civilization was too low and the territorial extent too vast to call into life voluntary association, the interference of the centralizing power of Government. Hence an economical function devolved upon all Asiatic Governments, the function of providing public works. This artificial fertilization of the soil, dependent on a Central Government, and immediately decaying with the neglect of irrigation and drainage, explains the otherwise strange fact that we now find whole territories barren and desert that were once brilliantly cultivated, as Palmyra, Petra, the ruins in Yemen, and large provinces of Egypt, Persia and Hindustan; it also explains how a single war of devastation has been able to depopulate a country for centuries, and to strip it of all its civilization.

Now, the British in East India accepted from their predecessors the departments of finance and of war, but they have neglected entirely that of public works. Hence the deterioration of an agriculture which is not capable of being conducted on the British principle of free competition, of *laissez-faire* and *laissez-aller.* But in Asiatic empires we are quite accustomed to see agriculture deteriorating under one government and reviving again under some other government. There the harvests correspond to good or bad governments, as they change in Europe with good or bad seasons. Thus the oppression and neglect of agriculture, bad as it is, could not be looked upon as the final blow dealt to Indian society by the British intruder, had it not been attended by a circumstance of quite different importance, a novelty in the annals of the whole Asiatic world. However changing the political aspect of India's past must appear, its social condition has remained unaltered since its remotest antiquity, until the first decennium of the nineteenth century. The hand-loom and the spinning-wheel, producing their regular myriads of spinners and weavers, were the pivots of the structure of that society. . . . It was the British intruder who broke up the Indian hand-loom and destroyed the spinning-wheel. England began with driving the Indian cottons from the European market; it then introduced twist into Hindustan and in the end inundated the very mother country of cotton with cottons. From 1818 to 1836 the export of twist from Great Britain to India rose in the proportion of 1 to 5,200. In 1824 the export of British Muslins to India hardly amounted to 1,000,000 yards, while in 1837 it surpassed 64,000,000 yards. But at the same time the population of Dacca decreased from 150,000 inhabitants to 20,000. This decline of Indian towns celebrated for their fabrics was by no means the worst consequence. British steam and science uprooted, over the whole surface of Hindustan, the union between agriculture and manufacturing industry.

These two circumstances—the Hindu, on the one hand, leaving, like all Oriental peoples, to the Central Government the care of the great public works, the prime condition of his agriculture and commerce, dispersed, on the other hand, over the surface of the country, and agglomerated in small centres by the domestic union of agricultural and manufacturing pursuits—these two circumstances had brought about, since the remotest times, a social system of particular features—the so-called *village system,* which gave to each of these small unions their independent organization and distinct life. . . .

These small stereotype forms of social organism have been to the greater part dissolved, and are disappearing, not so much through the brutal interference of the British tax-gatherer and the British soldier, as to the working of English steam and English free trade. Those family-communities were based on domestic industry, in that peculiar combination of hand-weaving, hand-spinning and hand-tilling agriculture which gave them self-supporting power. English interference having placed the spinner in Lancashire and the weaver in Bengal, or sweeping away both Hindu spinner and weaver, dissolved these small semi-barbarian, semi-civilized communities, by blowing up their economical basis, and thus produced the greatest, and, to speak the truth, the only *social* revolution ever heard of in Asia.

Now, sickening as it must be to human feeling to witness those myriads of industrious patriarchal and inoffensive social organizations disorganized and dissolved into their units, thrown into a sea of woes, and their individual members losing at the same time their ancient form of civilization and their hereditary means of subsistence, we must not forget that these idyllic village communities, inoffensive though they may appear, had always been the solid foundation of Oriental despotism, that they restrained the human mind within the smallest possible compass, making it the unresisting tool of superstition, enslaving it beneath traditional rules, depriving it of all grandeur and historical energies. We must not forget the barbarian egotism which, concentrating on some miserable patch of land, had quietly witnessed the ruin of empires, the perpetration of unspeakable cruelties, the massacre of the population of large towns, with no other consideration bestowed upon them than on natural events, itself the helpless prey of any aggressor who deigned to notice it at all. We must not forget that this undignified, stagnatory, and vegetative life, that this passive sort of existence evoked on the other part, in contradistinction, wild, aimless, unbounded forces of destruction, and rendered murder itself a religious rite in Hindustan. We must not forget that these little communities were contaminated by distinctions of caste and by slavery, that they subjugated man to external circumstances instead of elevating man to be the sovereign of circumstances, that they transformed a self-developing social state into never changing natural destiny, and thus brought about a brutalizing worship of nature, exhibiting its degradation in the fact that man, the sovereign of nature, fell down on his knees in adoration of Hanuman, the monkey, and Sabbala, the cow.

England, it is true, in causing a social revolution in Hindustan, was actuated only by the vilest interests, and was stupid in her manner of enforcing them. But that is not the question. The question is, can mankind fulfil its destiny without a fundamental revolution in the social state of Asia? If not, whatever may have been the crimes of England she was the unconscious tool of history in bringing about that revolution.

Marx, Articles on *India* (1853), MESW, II, pp. 649-64.

THE FUTURE RESULTS OF THE BRITISH RULE IN INDIA

England has to fulfil a double mission in India: one destructive, the other regenerating—the annihilation of old Asiatic society, and the laying of the material foundations of Western society in Asia.

Arabs, Turks, Tartars, Moguls, who had successively overrun India, soon became *Hinduized,* the barbarian conquerors being, by an eternal law of history, conquered themselves by the superior civilization of their subjects. The British were the first conquerors superior, and, therefore, inaccessible to Hindu civilization. They destroyed it by breaking up the native communities, by uprooting the native industry, and by levelling all that was great and elevated in the native society. The historic pages of their rule in India report hardly anything beyond that destruction. The work of regeneration hardly transpires through a heap of ruins. Nevertheless it has begun.

The political unity of India, more consolidated, and extending farther than it ever did under the Great Moguls, was the first condition of its regeneration. That unity, imposed by the British sword, will now be strengthened and perpetuated by the electric telegraph. The native army, organized and trained by the British drill-sergeant, was the sine qua non of Indian self-emancipation, and of India ceasing to be the prey of the first foreign intruder. The free press, introduced for the first time into Asiatic society, and managed principally by the common offspring of Hindus and Europeans, is a new and powerful agent of reconstruction. The *zemindari* and *ryotwari* themselves, abominable as they are, involve two distinct forms of private property in land—the great desideratum of Asiatic society. From the Indian natives, reluctantly and sparingly educated at Calcutta, under English superintendence, a fresh class is springing up, endowed with the requirements for government and imbued with European science. Steam has brought India into regular and rapid communication with Europe, has connected its chief ports with those of the whole southeastern ocean, and has revindicated it from the isolated position which was the prime law of its stagnation. The day is not far distant when, by a combination of railways and steam vessels, the distance between England and India, measured by time, will be shortened to eight days, and when that once fabulous country will thus be actually annexed to the Western world.

The ruling classes of Great Britain have had, till now, but an accidental, transitory and exceptional interest in the progress of India. The aristocracy wanted to conquer it, the moneyocracy to plunder it, and the millocracy to undersell it. But now the tables are turned. The millocracy have discovered that the transformation of India into a reproductive country had become of vital importance to them, and that, to that end, it is necessary, above all, to gift her with means of irrigation and of internal communication. They intend now drawing a net of railways over India. And they will do it. The results must be appreciable.

It is notorious that the productive powers of India are paralyzed by the utter want of means for conveying and exchanging its various produce. Nowhere, more than in India, do we meet with social destitution in the midst of natural plenty, for want of the means of exchange. . . .

The introduction of railways may be easily made to subserve agricultural purposes by the formation of tanks, where ground is required for embankment, and by the conveyance of water along the different lines. Thus irrigation, the sine qua non of farming in the East, might be greatly extended, and the frequently recurring local famines, arising from the want of water, would be averted. The general importance of railways, viewed under this head, must become evident, when we remember that irrigated lands, even in the districts near Ghauts, pay three times as much in taxes, afford ten or twelve times as much employment, and yield twelve or fifteen times as much profit, as the same area without irrigation. . . .

We know that the municipal organization and the economical basis of the village communities have been broken up, but their worst feature, the dissolution of society into stereotype and disconnected atoms, has survived their vitality. The village isolation produced the absence of roads in India, and the absence of roads perpetuated the village isolation. On this plan a community existed with a given scale of low conveniences, almost without intercourse with other villages, without the desires and efforts indispensable to social advance. The British having broken up this self-sufficient *inertia* of the villages, railways will provide the new want of communication and intercourse. Besides,

> "one of the effects of the railway system will be to bring into every village affected by it such knowledge of the contrivances and appliances of other countries, and such means of obtaining them, as will first put the hereditary and stipendiary village artisanship of India to full proof of its capabilities, and then supply its defects." (Chapman, *The Cotton and Commerce of India.)*

I know that the English millocracy intend to endow India with railways with the exclusive view of extracting at diminished expenses the cotton and other raw materials for their manufacturers. But when you have once introduced machinery into the locomotion of a country, which possesses iron and coals, you are unable to withhold it from its fabrication. You cannot maintain a net of railways over an immense country without introducing all those industrial processes necessary to meet the immediate and current wants of railway locomotion, and out of which there must grow the application of machinery to those branches of industry not immediately connected with railways. The railway system will therefore become, in India, truly the forerunner of modern industry. This is the more certain as the Hindus are allowed by British authorities themselves to possess particular aptitude for accommodating themselves to entirely new labour, and acquiring the requisite knowledge of machine. Ample proof of this fact is afforded by the capacities and expertness of the native engineers in the Calcutta mint, where they have been for years employed in working the steam machinery, by the natives attached to the several steam-engines in the Hardwar coal districts, and by other instances. . . .

Modern industry, resulting from the railway system, will dissolve the hereditary divisions of labour, upon which rest the Indian castes, those decisive impediments to Indian progress and Indian power.

All the English bourgeoisie may be forced to do will neither emancipate nor materially mend the social condition of the mass of the people, depending not only on the development of the productive powers, but on their appropriation by the people. But what they will not fail to do is to lay down the material premises for both. Has the bourgeoisie ever done more? Has it ever effected a progress without dragging individuals and peoples through blood and dirt, through misery and degradation?

The Indians will not reap the fruits of the new elements of society scattered among them by the British bourgeoisie, till in Great Britain itself the now ruling classes shall have been supplanted by the industrial proletariat, or till the Hindus themselves shall have grown strong enough to throw off the English yoke altogether. At all events, we may safely expect to see, at a more or less remote period, the regeneration of that great and interesting country. . . .

The devastating effects of English industry, when contemplated with regard to India, a country as vast as Europe, and containing 150 millions of acres, are palpable and confounding. But we must not forget that they are only the organic results of the whole system of production as it is now constituted. That production rests on the supreme rule of capital. The centralisation of capital is essential to the existence of capital as an independent power. The destructive influence of that centralisation upon the markets of the world but reveal, in the most gigantic dimensions, the inherent organic laws of political economy now at work in every civilised town. The bourgeois period of history has to create the material basis of the new world—on the one hand universal intercourse founded upon the mutual dependency of mankind, and the means of that intercourse; on the other hand the development of the productive powers of man and the transformation of material production into a scientific domination of natural agencies. Bourgeois industry and commerce create these material conditions of a new world in the same way as geological revolutions have created the surface of the earth. When a great social revolution shall have mastered the results of the bourgeois epoch, the market of the world and the modern powers of production, and subjected them to the common control of the most advanced peoples, then only will human progress cease to resemble that hideous pagan idol, who would not drink the nectar but from the skulls of the slain.

Marx, Articles on *India* (1853), MESW, II, pp. 649-64.

7.B.11 SCIENCE, TECHNOLOGY, AND LABOR

The full development of capital, therefore, takes place—or capital has posited the mode of production corresponding to it—only when the means of labour has not only taken the economic form of *fixed capital,* but has also been suspended in its immediate form, and when *fixed capital* appears as a machine within the production process, opposite labour; and the entire production process appears as not subsumed under the direct skilfulness of the worker, but rather as the technological application of science. [It is,] hence, the tendency of capital to give production a scientific character; direct labour [is] reduced to a mere moment of this process. As with the transformation of value into capital, so does it appear in the further development of capital, that it presupposes a certain given historical development of the productive forces on one side—science too [is] among these productive forces—and, on the other, drives and forces them further onwards.

Thus the quantitative extent and the effectiveness (intensity) to which capital is developed as fixed capital indicate the general degree to which capital is developed as capital, as power over living labour, and to which it has conquered the production process as such. Also, in the sense that it expresses the accumulation of objectified productive forces, and likewise of objectified labour. However, while capital gives itself its adequate form as use value within the production process only in the form of machinery and other material manifestations of fixed capital, such as railways etc. . . . this in no way means that this use value—machinery as such—is capital, or that its existence as machinery is identical with its existence as capital; any more than gold would cease to have use value as gold if it were no longer *money.* Machinery does not lose its use value as soon as it ceases to be capital. While machinery is the most appropriate form of the use value of fixed capital, it does not at all follow that therefore subsumption under the social relation of capital is the most appropriate and ultimate social relation of production for the application of machinery.

To the degree that labour time—the mere quantity of labour—is posited by capital as the sole determinant element, to that degree does direct labour and its quantity disappear as the determinant principle of production—of the creation of use values—and is reduced both quantitatively, to a smaller proportion, and qualitatively, as an, of course, indispensable but subordinate moment, compared to general scientific labour, technological application of natural sciences, on one side, and to the general productive force arising from social combination in total production on the other side—a combination which appears as a natural fruit of social labour (although it is a historic product). Capital thus works towards its own dissolution as the form dominating production. . . .

In one respect the transformation of the production process from the simple labour process into a scientific process, which subjugates the forces of nature and compels them to work in the service of human needs, appears as a quality of *fixed capital* in contrast to living labour; . . . individual labour as such has ceased altogether to appear as productive, is productive, rather, only in these common labours which subordinate the forces of nature to themselves, and. . . this elevation of direct labour into social labour appears as a reduction of individual labour to the level of helplessness in face of the communality represented by and concentrated in capital. . . .

Fixed capital, in its character as means of production, whose most adequate form [is] machinery, produces value, i.e. increases the value of the product, in only two respects: (1) in so far as it *has* value; i.e. is itself the product of labour, a certain quantity of labour in objectified form; (2) in so far as it increases the relation of surplus labour to necessary labour, by enabling labour, through an increase of its productive power, to create a greater mass of the products required for the maintenance of living labour capacity in a shorter time. It is therefore a highly absurd bourgeois assertion that the worker shares with the capitalist, because the latter, with fixed capital (which is, as far as that goes, itself a product of labour, and of *alien labour* merely appropriated by capital) makes labour easier for him (rather, he robs it of all independence and attractive character, by means of the machine), or makes his labour shorter. Capital employs machinery, rather, only to the extent that it enables the worker to work a larger part of his time for capital, to relate to a larger part of his time as time which does not belong to him, to work longer for another. Through this process, the amount of labour necessary for the production of a given object is indeed reduced to a minimum, but only in order to realize a maximum of labour in the maximum number of such objects. The first aspect is important, because capital here—quite unintentionally—reduces human labour, expenditure of energy, to a minimum. This will redound to the benefit of emancipated labour, and is the condition of its emancipation. . . .

In machinery, the appropriation of living labour by capital achieves a direct reality in this respect as well: It is, firstly, the analysis and application of mechanical and chemical laws, arising directly out of science, which enables the machine to perform the same labour as that previously performed by the worker. However, the development of machinery along this path occurs only when large industry has already reached a higher stage, and all the sciences have been pressed into the service of capital; and when, secondly, the available machinery itself already provides great capabilities. Invention then becomes a business, and the application of science to direct production itself becomes a prospect which determines and solicits it. But this is not the road along which machinery, by and large, arose, and even less the road on which it progresses in detail. This road is, rather, dissection—through the division of labour, which gradually transforms the workers' operations into more and more mechanical ones, so that at a certain point a mechanism can step into their places. . . . Thus, the specific mode of working here appears directly as becoming transferred from the worker to capital in the form of the machine, and his own labour capacity devalued thereby. Hence the workers' struggle against machinery. What was the living worker's activity becomes the activity of the machine. Thus the appropriation of labour by capital confronts the worker in a coarsely sensuous form; capital absorbs labour into itself—'as though its body were by love possessed.'

The exchange of living labour for objectified labour—i.e. the positing of social labour in the form of the contradiction of capital and wage labour—is the ultimate development of the *value-relation* and of production resting on value. Its presupposition is—and remains—the mass of direct labour time, the quantity of labour employed, as the determinant factor in the production of wealth. But to the degree that large industry develops, the creation of real wealth comes to depend less on labour time and on the amount of labour employed than on the power of the agencies set in motion during labour time, whose 'powerful effectiveness' is itself in turn out of all proportion to the direct labour time spent on their production, but depends rather on the general state of science and on the progress of technology, or the application of this science to production. (The development of this science, especially natural science, and all others with the latter, is itself in turn related to the development of material production.) Agriculture, e.g., becomes merely the application of the science of material metabolism, its regulation for the greatest advantage of the entire body of society. Real wealth manifests itself, rather—and large industry reveals this—in the monstrous disproportion between the labour time applied, and its product, as well as in the qualitative imbalance between labour, reduced to a pure abstraction, and the power of the production process it superintends. Labour no longer appears so much to be included within the production process; rather, the human being comes to relate more as watchman and regulator to the production process itself. (What holds for machinery holds likewise for the combination of human activities and the development of human intercourse.) No longer does the worker insert a modified natural thing as middle link between the object and himself; rather, he inserts the process of nature, transformed into an industrial process, as a means between himself and inorganic nature, mastering it. He steps to the side of the production process instead of being its chief actor. In this transformation, it is neither the direct human labour he himself performs, nor the time during which he works, but rather the appropriation of his own general productive power, his understanding of nature and his mastery over it by virtue of his presence as a social body—it is, in a word, the development of the social individual which appears as the great foundation-stone of production and of wealth. The *theft of alien labour time, on which the present wealth is based,* appears a miserable foundation in face of this new one, created by large-scale industry itself. As soon as labour in the direct form has ceased to be the great well-spring of wealth, labour time ceases and must cease to be its measure, and hence exchange value [must cease to be the measure] of use value. The *surplus labour of the mass* has ceased to be the condition for the development of general wealth, just as the *non-labour of the few,* for the development of the general powers of the human head. With that, production based on exchange value breaks down, and the direct, material production process is stripped of the form of penury and antitheses. The free development of individualities, and hence not the reduction of necessary labour time so as to posit surplus labour, but rather the general reduction of the necessary labour of society to a minimum, which then corresponds to the artistic, scientific etc. development of the individuals in the time set free, and with the means created, for all of them. Capital itself is the moving contradiction, [in] that it presses to reduce labour time to a minimum, while it posits labour time, on the other side, as sole measure and source of wealth. Hence it diminishes labour time in the necessary form so as to increase it in the superfluous form; hence posits the superfluous in growing measure as a condition—question of life or death—for the necessary. On the one side, then, it calls to life all the powers of science and of nature, as of social combination and of social intercourse, in order to make the creation of wealth independent (relatively) of the labour time employed on it. On the other side, it wants to use labour time as the measuring rod for the giant social forces thereby created, and to confine them within the limits required to maintain the already created value as value. Forces of production and social relations—two different sides of the development of the social individual—appear to capital as mere means, and are merely means for it to produce on its limited foundation. In fact, however, they are the material conditions to blow this foundation sky-high. 'Truly wealthy a nation, when the working day is 6 rather than 12 hours. *Wealth* is not command over surplus labour time' (real wealth), 'but rather, *disposable time* outside that needed in direct production, for *every individual* and the whole society.' . . .

Nature builds no machines, no locomotives, railways, electric telegraphs, self-acting mules etc. These are products of human industry; natural material transformed into organs of the human will over nature, or of human participation in nature. They are *organs of the human brain, created by the human hand;* the power of knowledge, objectified. The development of fixed capital indicates to what degree general social knowledge has become a *direct force of production,* and to what degree, hence, the conditions of the process of social life itself have come under the control of the general intellect and been transformed in accordance with it. To what degree the powers of social production have been produced, not only in the form of knowledge, but also as immediate organs of social practice, of the real life process.

Marx, *Grundrisse* (1857-58), pp. 699-706.

8 Capitalism's Transition to Socialism

A. REVOLUTION, REFORM, AND THE STATE

Marx was a revolutionary as well as a scientist (selection 8.A.1). On the one hand, Marx and Engels believed that the prospective revolutionary transition to socialism would emanate from the contradictions, conflicts, creative destruction, and qualitative changes of capitalism itself as described in Chapter 7. On the other, Marx became a socialist *before, not after,* the rigorous development of his socioeconomic theories of capitalism. As a young man in the early and mid-1840s, he formulated "an intellectual and practical programme, from which he never afterwards deviated. His aim was to transform speculative philosophy into a critical social theory which would be of use to men overcome by misery."[1] This original, youthful vision, however, was both supplemented by and interwoven with the scientific study of economic and social processes perceived as "independent of human volition" and as demonstrating a strategic element of "historical necessity." Marx's solution to the "tension" between the scientific and the revolutionary dimensions of his thought consisted "in treating the socialist labour movement (whose guide and *spiritus rector* he had become in his closing years) as the prime agent of history" and of revolutionary change. He believed the coming socialist revolution to be "determinedly propelled by causal circumstances," which circumstances could be understood and guided, first by the socialist "theorist who has perceived the meaning of events, and at a second remove by the socialist movement itself; hence theory and practice can be unified, on condition that the former is permitted to guide the latter.[2]"

This blend of scientific and revolutionary elements pervades the various selections in this section. Excerpts from Marx's writings on the dimensions of revolution (selection 8.A.2) clearly show that for Marx, "revolution" constitutes a comprehensive as well as rapid transformation from one form of economy, society, and polity to another. By this definition, radical political change, although necessary, is insufficient for a genuine (Marxian) revolution. Thus, the political overthrow of the "existing ruling power," without the economic foundation of industrial revolution or the genuine reconstruction of society and social classes, is a mere coup d'etat, not a true or complete revolution.

[1]T. B. Bottomore, *Karl Marx: Selected Writings in Sociology & Social Philosophy* (New York: McGraw-Hill, 1964), p. 27.

[2]Quotations from George Lichtheim, *Marxism, An Historical and Critical Study* (New York: Praeger, 1963), pp. 236–37.

By a "bold stroke of analytic strategy,"[3] Marx analyzes capitalism economically, but defines it *sociologically,* in terms of class division and capitalist control over workers. Thus, socialist revolution is the means of emancipation for workers from class oppression and, conversely, the working class is perceived as the historic agent of the coming socialist revolution.[4] In fulfilling its own "historic destiny," however, the proletariat emancipates not only itself but humanity as a whole from "*all* the inhuman life conditions of modern society which are comprehended in its situation" (selection 8.A.3).

Although (as described earlier, selection 7.B.9) the class struggle, especially in the context of evolving democratic politics, may yield significant social reforms, political revolution remains a necessary condition in the Marxian view for the genuine emancipation of the working class and transition to a socialist economy. It would be unrealistic to expect the capitalist state, even a democratic one, to accept, much less to lead, a social revolution which would transfer economic power from capitalists to workers and establish a radically altered socialist economic structure (selection 8.A.4).

Given these views on revolution and the class struggle, it is not surprising that Marx and Engels sharply reject the various proposals for social reform and reconstruction by their contemporaries, including socialists (selection 8.A.5). Mere social reformers of one variety or another, for example, are criticized for their limited vision and unambitious aspirations. Even the socialist and communist systems of St. Simon, Fourier, and Robert Owen, "revolutionary" though they were "in many respects," are rejected as hopelessly unrealistic or "utopian." For Marx and Engels, genuine socialist revolution is expected to occur in the ripeness and "fullness of time,"[5] after decades of evolutionary development of preconditions for revolution. The so-called utopian socialists are "utopian" precisely because they (1) formulated their visions of ideal socialist or communist societies in the early nineteenth century, when capitalism was immature, and the preconditions for socialism had not been laid; and (2) failed to accompany their often detailed visions and proposals for a new form of society by effective contact with or understanding of the prospective revolutionary role of the industrial proletariat. Consequently, they were compelled to appeal to "the ruling class. . . to the feeling and purses of the bourgeois" and to attempt to demonstrate the validity of their ideas and ideals through voluntary experiments and cooperative associations. These attempts, formulated at a time when the class struggle as well as the economy was relatively underdeveloped, were of a "purely utopian character" and therefore "necessarily doomed to failure."

At the same time, Marx explicitly rejects the "revolutionary" activity of socialist "conspirators" (selection 8.A.6). These "democratic bohemians," he argues, are not genuine socialist revolutionaries, dedicated to working class organization or to "theoretical elucidation of the working class and its interest." Instead, they are "alchemists of revolution" who, through their violent acts and "daring coups," endeavor to make a revolution "extempore, without a condition for revolution." These types of "revolutionary" activity, in Marx's view, are as out of touch with the realities and laws of motion of modern industrial capitalism or the real aspirations and potentials for the working class as those of the social

[3]Joseph A. Schumpeter, *Capitalism Socialism and Democracy* (New York: Harper, 1950), p. 19.

[4]Two other possibilities, noted by later writers, both Marxist and non-Marxist, should at least be mentioned here. One is that the working class, tamed by rising living standards and social reform, fails to acquire the necessary revolutionary elan or ardor. The other is that the political overthrow of the "existing ruling power" is accomplished by professional socialist revolutionaries, with a very low level of coparticipation by the working class itself.

[5]Schumpeter, *op. cit.,* p. 58.

reformers and utopian socialists. Of course, in a repressive political environment which forbids working class organization, communist and worker associations may well have to function secretly. But the historic task of such associations is still to create an *"opposition party of the future"* and thereby an effective basis for a genuine social revolution, not merely the "narrow ambitions" of cloak and dagger activity leading to a mere coup d'etat or "overthrow" of an existing *government.*

8.A.1 MARX AS SCIENTIST AND REVOLUTIONARY

Just as Darwin discovered the law of development of organic nature, so Marx discovered the law of development of human history: the simple fact, hitherto concealed by an overgrowth of ideology, that mankind must first of all eat, drink, have shelter and clothing, before it can pursue politics, science, art, religion, etc.; that therefore the production of the immediate material means of subsistence and consequently the degree of economic development attained by a given people or during a given epoch form the foundation upon which the state institutions, the legal conceptions, art, and even the ideas on religion, of the people concerned have been evolved, and in the light of which they must, therefore, be explained, instead of vice versa, as had hitherto been the case.

But that is not all. Marx also discovered the special law of motion governing the present-day capitalist mode of production and the bourgeois society that this mode of production has created. The discovery of surplus value suddenly threw light on the problem, in trying to solve which all previous investigations, of both bourgeois economists and socialist critics, had been groping in the dark.

Two such discoveries would be enough for one lifetime. Happy the man to whom it is granted to make even one such discovery. But in every single field which Marx investigated—and he investigated very many fields, none of them superficially—in every field, even in that of mathematics, he made independent discoveries.

Such was the man of science. But this was not even half the man. Science was for Marx a historically dynamic, revolutionary force. However great the joy with which he welcomed a new discovery in some theoretical science whose practical application perhaps it was as yet quite impossible to envisage, he experienced quite another kind of joy when the discovery involved immediate revolutionary changes in industry, and in historical development in general. For example, he followed closely the development of the discoveries made in the field of electricity and recently those of Marcel Deprez.

For Marx was before all else a revolutionist. His real mission in life was to contribute, in one way or another, to the overthrow of capitalist society and of the state institutions which it had brought into being, to contribute to the liberation of the modern proletariat, which *he* was the first to make conscious of its own position and its needs, conscious of the conditions of its emancipation. Fighting was his element. And he fought with a passion, a tenacity and a success such as few could rival. His work on the first *Rheinische Zeitung* (1842), the Paris *Vorwärts* (1844), the *Deutsche Brüsseler Zeitung,*

(1847), the *Neue Rheinische Zeitung* (1848-49), the *New York Tribune* (1852-61), and in addition to these a host of militant pamphlets, work in organisations in Paris, Brussels and London, and finally, crowning all, the formation of the great International Working Men's Association—this was indeed an achievement of which its founder might well have been proud even if he had done nothing else.

Engels, Speech at the Graveside of Karl Marx (1883), MESW, 435-36.

8.A.2 DIMENSIONS OF REVOLUTION

The so-called Revolutions of 1848 were but poor incidents—small fractures and fissures in the dry crust of European society. However, they denounced the abyss. Beneath the apparently solid surface, they betrayed oceans of liquid matter, only needing expansion to rend into fragments continents of hard rock. Noisily and confusedly they proclaimed the emancipation of the Proletarian, i.e., the secret of the nineteenth century, and of the revolution of that century. That social revolution, it is true, was no novelty invented in 1848. Steam, electricity, and the self-acting mule were revolutionists of a rather more dangerous character than even citizens Barbès, Raspail and Blanqui. But, although the atmosphere in which we live, weighs upon every one with a 20,000 lb. force, do you feel it? No more than European society before 1848 felt the revolutionary atmosphere enveloping and pressing it from all sides. There is one great fact, characteristic of this our nineteenth century, a fact which no party dares deny. On the one hand, there have started into life industrial and scientific forces, which no epoch of the former human history had ever suspected. On the other hand, there exist symptoms of decay, far surpassing the horrors recorded of the latter times of the Roman empire. In our days everything seems pregnant with its contrary. Machinery, gifted with the wonderful power of shortening and fructifying human labour, we behold starving and overworking it. The new-fangled sources of wealth, by some strange weird spell, are turned into sources of want. The victories of art seem bought by the loss of character. At the same pace that mankind masters nature, man seems to become enslaved to other men or to his own infamy. Even the pure light of science seems unable to shine but on the dark background of ignorance. All our invention and progress seem to result in endowing material forces with intellectual life, and in stultifying human life into a material force. This antagonism between modern industry and science on the one hand, modern misery and dissolution on the other hand; this antagonism between the productive powers, and the social relations of our epoch is a fact, palpable, overwhelming, and not to be controverted. Some parties may wail over it; others may wish to get rid of modern arts, in order to get rid of modern conflicts. Or they may imagine that so signal a progress in industry wants to be completed by as signal a regress in politics. On our part, we do not mistake the shape of the shrewd spirit that continues to mark all these contradictions. We know that to work well the new-fangled forces of society, they only want to be mastered by new-fangled men—and such are the working men. They are as much the invention of modern time as machinery itself. In the signs that bewilder the middle class, the aristocracy and the poor prophets of regression, we do recognise...the Revolution. The English working men are the first born sons of modern industry. They will then, certainly, not be the last in aiding the social revolution produced by that industry, a revolution which means the emancipation of their own class all over the world, which is as universal as capital-rule and wages-slavery. I know the heroic struggles the English working class have gone through since the middle of the last century—struggles no less glorious, because they are shrouded in obscurity, and buried by the middle class historian. To revenge the misdeeds of the ruling class, there existed in the middle ages, in Germany, a secret tribunal, called the *"Vehmgericht."* If a red cross was seen marked on a house, people knew that its owner was doomed by the *"Vehm."* All the houses of Europe are now marked with the mysterious red cross. History is the judge—its executioner, the proletarian.

Marx, speech for the *People's Paper* (1856), MESW, II, pp. 427–29.

The more powerful the State, and therefore the more *political* a country is, the less likely it is to seek the basis of *social* evils and to grasp the *general* explanation of them, in the *principle of the State* itself, that is in the *structure of society,* of which the State is the active, conscious and official expression. *Political* thought is really *political* thought in the sense that the thinking takes place within the framework of politics. The clearer and more vigorous political thought is, the *less* it is able to grasp the nature of social evils. The *classical* period of political thought is the *French Revolution.* Far from recognizing the source of social defects in the principle of the State, the heroes of the French Revolution looked for the sources of political evils in the defective social organization. Thus, for example, Robespierre saw in the coexistence of great poverty and great wealth only an obstacle to *genuine democracy.* He wished, therefore, to establish a universal *Spartan* austerity. The principle of politics is the will. The more partial, and the more perfected, *political* thought becomes, the more it believes in the *omnipotence* of the will, the less able it is to see the *natural* and mental *limitations* on the will, the less capable it is of discovering the source of social evils. . . .

The more developed and universal is the *political* thought of a people, the more the *proletariat*—at least at the beginning of the movement—wastes its forces on foolish and futile uprisings which are drowned in blood. Because the proletariat thinks politically it sees the source of bad social conditions in *will,* and all the means of improvement in *force* and the *overthrow* of a particular form of State. Consider, for example, the first outbreaks of the *French* proletariat. The workers of Lyons believed that they were pursuing only political aims, that they were only soldiers of the Republic, when in reality they were the soldiers of socialism. In this way their *political* understanding obscured from them the roots of their social misery, it distorted their insight into their real aims and *eclipsed* their *social instinct.* . . .

The *social life* from which the worker is *shut out* is a social life very different in kind and extent from that of the *political* sphere. This social life, from which *his own labour* excludes him, is *life* itself, physical and cultural life, human morality, human activity, human enjoyment, real *human* existence. Human life is the *true social life* of man. As the irremediable exclusion from this life is much more complete, more unbearable, dreadful and contradictory, than the exclusion from political life, so is the ending of this exclusion, and even a limited reaction, a *revolt* against it, more fundamental, as *man* is more fundamental than the *citizen, human life* more than *political life.* The *industrial* revolt may thus be *limited* but it has a *universal* significance; the *political* revolt may be universal, but it conceals under a *gigantic* form a *narrow* spirit. . . .

A *social* revolution has thus a *universal* aspect, because, though it may occur in only *one* manufacturing district, it is a human protest against an inhuman life, because it begins from the *single real individual,* and because the *social life,* against his exclusion from which the individual reacts, is the *real* social life of man, a really *human* life. The *political aspect* of a revolution consists in the movement of the politically uninfluential classes to end their *exclusion* from *political life and power.* Its standpoint is that of the State, an *abstract* whole, which *only* exists by virtue of its separation from real life, and which is *unthinkable* without the *organized* opposition between the universal idea and the individual existence of man. A revolution of a *political* kind also organizes, therefore, in accordance with this *narrow* and *discordant* outlook, a ruling group in society at the expense of society. . . .

A *"social"* revolution with a *political* aspect is either a contradiction in terms, if "A Prussian" means by social revolution a social revolution *as distinct from* a political one, and yet attributes to this social revolution a political rather than a social aspect. Or else a *"social revolution with a political aspect"* is simply a *paraphrase* of what used to be called simply a *"political revolution"* or *"revolution" tout court.* Every revolution breaks up the *old society*; to this extent it is *social.* Every revolution overthrows *the existing ruling power*; to this extent it is *political*. . . .

Revolution in general—the *overthrow* of the existing ruling power and the *dissolution* of existing social relationships—is a *political act.* Without *revolution socialism* cannot develop. It requires this *political act* as it needs the *overthrow* and the *dissolution.* But as soon as its *organizing activity* begins, as soon as its *own purpose* and *spirit* come to the fore, socialism sheds this *political* covering.

Marx, "Critical Marginal Notes on the Article 'The King of Prussia and Social Reform. By a Prussian' " (1844), SSP, pp. 217–18, 236–38.

If the proletariat destroys the political rule of the bourgeoisie, that will only be a temporary victory, only an element in the sevice of the *bourgeois revolution* itself, as in 1794, so long as in the course of history, in its "movement," the material conditions are not yet created which make necessary the abolition of the bourgeois mode of production and thus the definitive overthrow of bourgeois political rule. The reign of terror in France could only serve, therefore, to clear away from the soil of France through its powerful blows, the remnants of feudalism. The anxious and considerate bourgeoisie would never have completed this task in decades. The bloody action of the people thus only prepared the way for it. Similarly, the collapse of the absolute monarchy would have been temporary, had not the economic conditions for the rule of the bourgeois class already ripened. Men do not build themselves a new world out of the fruits of the earth, as *vulgar* superstition believes, but out of the historical accomplishments of their declining civilization. They must, in the course of their development, begin by themselves *producing* the *material* conditions of a new society, and no effort of mind or will can free them from this destiny.

Marx, "Moral Critique and the Criticism of Morality" (1847), SSP, p. 240.

The most comprehensive contradiction of this constitution, however, consisted in the following: The classes whose social slavery the constitution is to perpetuate, proletariat, peasantry, petty bourgeois, it puts in possession of political power through universal suffrage. And from the class whose old social power it sanctions, the bourgeoisie, it withdraws the political guarantees of this power. It forces its political rule into democratic conditions, which at every moment help the hostile classes to victory and jeopardise the very foundations of bourgeois society. From the former classes it demands that they should not go forward from political to social emancipation; from the others that they should not go back from social to political restoration.

Marx, *Class Struggles,* (1850), MESW, II, pp. 214–15, 232.

8.A.3 REVOLUTION AND CLASS STRUGGLE

From the relation of alienated labour to private property it also follows that the emancipation of society from private property, from servitude, takes the political form of the *emancipation of the workers;* not in the sense that only the latter's emancipation is involved, but because this emancipation includes the emancipation of humanity as a whole. For all human servitude is involved in the relation of the worker to production, and all the types of servitude are only modifications or consequences of this relation.

Marx, *Manuscripts* (1844), EW, pp. 132–33.

Private property drives itself in its economic movement towards its own dissolution, only, however, through a development which does not depend on it, of which it is unconscious and which takes place against its will, through the very nature of things; only inasmuch as it produces the proletariat *as* proletariat, that misery conscious of its spiritual and physical misery, that dehumanization conscious of its dehumanization and therefore self-abolishing. The proletariat executes the sentence that private property pronounced on itself by begetting the proletariat, just as it carries out the sentence that wage-labour pronounced on itself by bringing forth wealth for others and misery for itself. When the proletariat is victorious, it by no means becomes the absolute side of society, for it is victorious only by abolishing itself and its opposite. Then the proletariat disappears as well as the opposite which determines it, private property.

When socialist writers ascribe this historic role to the proletariat, it is not, as Critical Criticism pretends to think, because they consider the proletarians as *gods.* Rather the contrary. Since the abstraction of all humanity, even of the *semblence* of humanity, is practically complete in the full-grown proletariat; since the conditions of life of the proletariat sum up all the conditions of life of society today in all their inhuman acuity; since man has lost himself in the proletariat, yet at the same time has not only gained theoretical consciousness of that loss, but through urgent, no longer disguisable, absolutely imperative *need*—that practical expression of *necessity*—is driven directly to revolt against that inhumanity; it follows that the proletariat can and must free itself. But it cannot free itself without abolishing the conditions of its own life. It cannot abolish the conditions of its own life without abolishing *all* the inhuman conditions of life of society today which are summed up in its own situation. Not in vain does it go through the stern but steeling school of *labour*. The question is not what this or that proletarian, or even the whole of the proletariat at the moment *considers* as its aim. The question is *what the proletariat is,* and what, consequent on that *being,* it will be compelled to do. Its aim and historical action is irrevocably and obviously demonstrated in its own life situation as well as in the whole organization of bourgeois society today. There is no need to dwell here upon the fact that a large part of the English and French proletariat is already *conscious* of its historic task and is constantly working to develop that consciousness into complete clarity.

Marx-Engels, *The Holy Family* (1845), FLP, pp. 52–53.

I regret deeply to be unable, for the moment at least, to leave London, and thus to be prevented from expressing verbally my feelings of pride and gratitude on receiving the invitation to sit as Honorary Delegate at the Labour Parliament. The mere assembling of such a Parliament marks a new epoch in the history of the world. The news of this great fact will arouse the hopes of the working classes throughout Europe and America.

Great Britain, of all other countries, has seen developed on the greatest scale the despotism of capital and the slavery of labour. In no other country have the intermediate stations between the millionaire commanding whole industrial armies and the wage slave living only from hand to mouth so gradually been swept away from the soil. There exist here no longer, as in continental countries, large classes of peasants and artisans almost equally dependent on their own property and their own labour. A complete divorce of property from labour has been effected in Great Britain. In no other country, therefore, the war between the two classes that constitute modern society has assumed so colossal dimensions and features so distinct and palpable.

But it is precisely from these facts that the working classes of Great Britain, before all others, are competent and called for to act as leaders in the great movement that must finally result in the absolute emancipation of labour. Such they are from the conscious clearness of their position, the vast superiority of their numbers, the disastrous struggles of their past, and the moral strength of their present.

It is the working millions of Great Britain who first have laid down the real basis of a new society—modern industry, which transformed the destructive agencies of nature into the productive power of man. The English working classes, with invincible energies, by the sweat of their brows and brains, have called into life the material means of ennobling labour itself, and of multiplying its fruits to such a degree as to make general abundance possible.

By creating the inexhaustible productive powers of modern industry they have fulfilled the first condition of the emancipation of labour. They have now to realize its other condition. They have to free those wealth-producing powers from the infamous shackles of monopoly, and subject them to the joint control of the producers, who, till now, allowed the very products of their hands to turn against them and be transformed into as many instruments of their own subjugation.

The labouring classes have conquered nature; they have now to conquer man. To succeed in this attempt they do not want strength, but the organization of their common strength, organization of the labouring classes on a national scale—such, I suppose, is the great and glorious end aimed at by the Labour Parliament.

Marx, *Letter to the Labour Parliament* (1854), AB, pp. 216–17.

The unification and fraternization of nations is a phrase used today by all parties, particularly the bourgeois free-trade men. Of course there does exist a certain kind of fraternization among the bourgeois classes of all nations. It is the fraternization of the oppressors against the oppressed, the exploiters against the exploited. Just as the bourgeois class of any one country unites and fraternizes against the proletarians of that country, despite competition and conflict among the members of the bourgeoisie themselves, so also the bourgeoisie of all countries fraternize and unite against the proletarians of all countries, despite their mutual conflict and competition in the world market. For nations really to unite, they must have a mutual interest. For their interest to become mutual, the present property relationships must be abolished, for they condition the exploitation of nations among themselves. To abolish the present property relationships is the interest of the working class. It alone, moreover, possesses the means to do it. The victory of the proletariat over the bourgeoisie is at the same time a victory over the national and industrial conflicts with which the various nations nowadays confront each other inimically. The victory of the proletariat over the bourgeoisie is therefore at the same time the liberation signal of all oppressed nations.

The old Poland is indeed lost, and we would be the last to wish its restoration. But not only is the old Poland lost. The old Germany, the old France, the old England, the whole old social system is lost. The loss of the old social system, however, is no loss for those who have nothing to lose by it, and in all contemporary countries this is the case with the great majority. They have, rather, everything to gain through the ruin of the old system, which will lead to the creation of a new one that is no longer based on class conflicts.

Of all countries, England is the one where the conflict between proletariat and bourgeoisie is most developed. Hence the victory of the English proletarians over the English bourgeoisie is decisive for the victory of all the oppressed over their oppressors. Hence Poland is not to be freed in Poland, but in England. You Chartists therefore do not have to express pious wishes for the liberation of nations. Defeat your own internal enemies and you will have the proud awareness of having defeated the entire old social system.

Marx, Speech on Poland (1847), MR, pp. 35–36.

N.B. as to political movement: The political movement of the working class has as its object, of course, the conquest of political power for the working class, and for this it is naturally necessary that a previous organisation of the working class, itself arising from their economic struggles, should have been developed up to a certain point.

On the other hand, however, every movement in which the working class comes out *as a class* against the ruling classes and attempts to force them by pressure from without is a political movement. For instance, the attempt in a particular factory or even a particular industry to force a shorter working day out of the capitalists by strikes, etc., is a purely economic movement. On the other hand the movement to force an eight-hour day, etc., *law* is a *political* movement. And in this way, out of the separate economic movements of the workers there grows up everywhere a *political* movement, that is to say a movement of the *class,* with the object of achieving its interests in a general form, in a form possessing a general social force of compulsion. If these movements presuppose a certain degree of previous organisation, they are themselves equally a means of the development of this organisation.

Where the working class is not yet far enough advanced in its organisation to undertake a decisive campaign against the collective power, i.e., the political power of the ruling classes, it must at any rate be trained for this by continual agitation against and a hostile attitude towards the policy of the ruling classes. Otherwise it will remain a plaything in their hands, as the September revolution in France showed, and as is also proved up to a certain point by the game Messrs. Gladstone & Co. are bringing off in England even up to the present time.

Marx, Letter to Bolte (1871), SC, pp. 318–19.

In England combination is authorised by an Act of Parliament, and it is the economic system which has forced Parliament to grant this legal authorisation. In 1825, when, under the Minister Huskisson, Parliament had to modify the law in order to bring it more and more into line with the conditions resulting from free competition, it had of necessity to abolish all laws forbidding combinations of workers. The more modern industry and competition develop, the more there are elements which call forth and strengthen combination, and as soon as combination becomes an economic fact, daily gaining in solidity, it is bound before long to become a legal fact.

Thus the article of the Penal Code proves at the most that modern industry and competition were not yet well developed under the Constituent Assembly and under the Empire.

Economists and Socialists* are in agreement on one point: the condemnation of *combinations*. Only they attribute different motives to their act of condemnation.

The economists say to the workers: Do not combine. By combination you hinder the regular progress of industry, you prevent manufacturers from carrying out their orders, you disturb trade and you precipitate the invasion of machines which, by rendering your labour in part useless, force you to accept a still lower wage. Besides, whatever you do, your wages will always be determined by the relation of hands demanded to hands supplied, and it is an effort as ridiculous as it is dangerous for you to revolt against the eternal laws of political economy.

The Socialists say to the worker: Do not combine, because what will you gain by it anyway? A rise in wages? The economists will prove to you quite clearly that the few ha' pence you may gain by it for a few moments if you succeed, will be followed by a permanent fall. Skilled calculators will prove to you that it would take you years merely to recover, through the increase in your wages, the expenses incurred for the organisation and upkeep of the combinations.

And we, as Socialists, tell you that, apart from the money question, you will continue none the less to be workers, and the masters will still continue to be the masters, just as before. So no combination! No politics! For is not entering into combination engaging in politics?

The economists want the workers to remain in society as it is constituted and as it has been signed and sealed by them in their manuals.

The Socialists want the workers to leave the old society alone, the better to be able to enter the new society which they have prepared for them with so much foresight.

In spite of both of them, in spite of manuals and utopias, combination has not ceased for an instant to go forward and grow with the development and growth of modern industry. It has now reached such a stage, that the degree to which combination has developed in any country clearly marks the rank it occupies in the hierarchy of the world market. England, whose industry has attained the highest degree of development, has the biggest and best organised combinations.

In England they have not stopped at partial combinations which have no other objective than a passing strike, and which disappear with it. Permanent combinations have been formed, *trades unions,* which serve as ramparts for the workers in their struggles with the owners. And at the present time all these local *trades unions* find a rallying point in the *National Association of United Trades,* the central committee of which is in London, and which already numbers 80,000 members. The organisation of these strikes, combinations, *trades unions* went on simultaneously with the political struggles of the workers who now constitute a large political party, under the name of Chartists.

*On the word "Socialists" Engels added the following note in the German edition of 1885: "That is, the Socialists of that time: the Fourierists in France, the Owenites in England." — Ed.

The first attempts of workers to *associate* among themselves always take place in the form of combinations.

Large-scale industry concentrates in one place a crowd of people unknown to one another. Competition divides their interests. But the maintenance of wages, this common interest which they have against their boss, unites them in a common thought of resistance—*combination.* Thus combination always has a double aim, that of stopping the competition among themselves, in order to bring about a general competition with the capitalist. If the first aim of resistance was merely the maintenance of wages, combinations, at first isolated, constitute themselves into groups as the capitalists in their turn unite in the idea of repression, and in face of always united capital, the maintenance of the association becomes more necessary to them than that of wages. This is so true that English economists are amazed to see the workers sacrifice a good part of their wages in favour of associations, which, in the eyes of these economists, are established solely in favour of wages. In this struggle—a veritable civil war—are united and developed all the elements necessary for a coming battle. Once it has reached this point, association takes on a political character.

Economic conditions had first transformed the mass of the people of the country into workers. The domination of capital has created for this mass a common situation, common interests. This mass is thus already a class as against capital, but not yet for itself. In the struggle, of which we have noted only a few phases, this mass becomes united, and constitutes itself as a class for itself. The interests it defends become class interests. But the struggle of class against class is a political struggle.

In the bourgeoisie we have two phases to distinguish: that in which it constituted itself as a class under the regime of feudalism and absolute monarchy, and that in which, already constituted as a class, it overthrew feudalism and monarchy to make society into a bourgeois society. The first of these phases was the longer and necessitated the greater efforts. This too began by partial combinations against the feudal lords.

Marx, *Poverty of Philosophy* (1847), IP, pp. 143–46.

8.A.4 THE CLASS BASIS OF THE STATE

It is always the direct relation of the owners of the conditions of production to the direct producers, which reveals the innermost secret, the hidden foundation of the entire social construction, and with it of the political form of the relations between sovereignty and dependence, in short, of the corresponding form of the state.

Marx, *Capital,* III (1894), p. 919.

Civil society embraces the whole material intercourse of individuals within a definite stage of the development of productive forces. It embraces the whole commercial and industrial life of a given stage and, insofar, transcends the State and the nation, though, on the other hand again, it must assert itself in its foreign relations as nationality, and inwardly must organise itself as State. The word "civil" society emerged in the eighteenth century, when property relationships had already extricated themselves from the ancient and medieval communal sociaty. Civil society as such only develops with the bourgeoisie; the social organisation evolving directly out of production and commerce, which in all ages forms the basis of the State and of the rest of the idealistic superstructure, has, however, always been designated by the same name. . . .

The first form of property, in the ancient world as in the Middle Ages, is tribal property, determined with the Romans chiefly by war, with the Germans by the rearing of cattle. In the case of the ancient peoples, since several tribes live together in one town, the tribal property appears as State property, and the right of the individual to it as mere "possession" which, however, like tribal property as a whole, is confined to landed property only. Real private property began with the ancients, as with modern nations, with movable property. . . . In the case of the nations which grew out of the Middle Ages, tribal property evolved through various stages—feudal landed property, corporative movable property, capital invested in manufacture—to modern capital, determined by big industry and universal competition, i.e. pure private property, which has cast off all semblance of a communal institution and has shut out the State from any influence on the development of property. To this modern private property corresponds the modern State, which, purchased gradually by the owners of property by means of taxation, has fallen entirely into their hands through the national debt, and its existence has become wholly dependent on the commercial credit which the owners of property, the bourgeois, extend to it, as reflected in the rise and fall of State funds on the stock exchange. By the mere fact that it is a *class* and no longer an *estate,* the bourgoisie is forced to organize itself no longer locally, but nationally, and to give a general form to its mean average interest. Through the emancipation of private property from the community, the State has become a separate entity, beside and outside civil society; but it is nothing more than the form of organisation which the bourgeois necessarily adopt both for internal and external purposes, for the mutual guarantee of their property and interests. The independence of the State is only found nowadays in those countries where the estates have not yet completely developed into classes, where the estates, done away with in more advanced countries, still have a part to play, and where there exists a mixture; countries, that is to say, in which no one section of the population can achieve dominance over the others. This is the case particularly in Germany. The most perfect example of the modern State is North America. The modern French, English and American writers all express the opinion that the State exists only for the sake of private property, so that this fact has penetrated into the consciousness of the normal man.

Since the State is the form in which the individuals of a ruling class assert their common interests, and in which the whole civil society of an epoch is epitomised, it follows that the State mediates in the formation of all common institutions and that the institutions receive a political form. Hence the illusion that law is based on the will, and indeed on the will divorced from its real basis —on *free* will. Similarly, justice is in its turn reduced to the actual laws. . . .

Out of the contradictions between the interest of the individual and that of the community the latter takes an independent form as the *State,* divorced from the real interests of individual and community, and at the same time as an illusory communal life, always based, however, on the real ties existing in every family and tribal conglomeration—such as flesh and blood, language, division of labour on a larger scale, and other interests—and especially, . . . on the classes, already determined by the division of labour, which in every such mass of men separate out, and of which one dominates all the others. It follows from this that all struggles within the State, the struggle between democracy, aristocracy, and monarchy, the struggle for the franchise, etc. etc. are merely the illusory forms in which the real struggles of the different classes are fought out among one another. . . . Further, it follows that every class which is struggling for mastery, even when its domination, as in the case with the proletariat, postulates the abolition of the old form of society in its entirety and of domination itself, must first conquer for itself political power in order to represent its interest in turn as the general interest, which immediately it is forced to do. Just because individuals seek *only* their particular interest, which for them does not coincide with their communal interest, the latter will be imposed on them as an interest "alien" to them, and "independent" of them, as in its turn a particular, peculiar "general" interest; or they themselves must remain within this discord, as in democracy. On the other hand, too, the *practical* struggle of these particular interests, which constantly *really* run counter to the communal and illusory communal interests, makes *practical* intervention and control necessary through the illusory "general" interest in the form of the State.

Marx-Engels, *The German Ideology* (1845–46), excerpts from Part I.

In modern history at least it is, therefore, proved that all political struggles are class struggles, and all class struggles for emancipation, despite their necessarily political form—for every class struggle is a political struggle—turn ultimately on the question of *economic* emancipation. Therefore, here at least, the state—the political order—is the subordinate, and civil society—the realm of economic relations—the decisive element. The traditional conception, to which Hegel, too, pays homage, saw in the state the determining element, and in civil society the element determined by it. Appearances correspond to this. As all the driving forces of the actions of any individual person must pass through his brain, and transform themselves into motives of his will in order to set him into action, so also all the needs of civil society—no matter which class happens to be the ruling one—must pass through the will of the state in order to secure general validity in the form of laws. That is the formal aspect of the matter—the one which is self-evident. The question arises, however, what is the content of this merely formal will—of the individual as well as of the state—and whence is this content derived? Why is just this willed and not something else? If we enquire into this we discover that in modern history the will of the state is, on the whole, determined by the changing needs of civil society, by the supremacy of this or that class, in the last resort, by the development of the productive forces and relations of exchange.

But if even in our modern era, with its gigantic means of production and communication, the state is not an independent domain with an independent development, but one whose existence as well as development is to be explained in the last resort by the economic conditions of life of society, then this must be still more true of all earlier times when the production of the material life of man was not yet carried on with these abundant auxiliary means, and when, therefore, the necessity of such production must have exercised a still greater mastery over men. If the state even today, in the era of big industry and of railways, is on the whole only a reflection, in concentrated form, of the economic needs of the class controlling production, then this must have been much more so in an epoch when each generation of men was forced to spend a far greater part of its aggregate lifetime in satisfying material needs, and was therefore much more dependent on them than we are today. An examination of the history of earlier periods, as soon as it is seriously undertaken from this angle, most abundantly confirms this. But, of course, this cannot be gone into here.

If the state and public law are determined by economic relations, so, too, of course is private law, which indeed in essence only sanctions the existing economic relations between individuals which are normal in the given circumstances. The form in which this happens can, however, vary considerably. It is possible, as happened in England, in harmony with the whole national development, to retain in the main the forms of the old feudal laws while giving them a bourgeois content; in fact, directly reading a bourgeois meaning into the feudal name. But, also, as happened in western continental Europe, Roman Law, the first world law of a commodity-producing society, with its unsurpassably fine elaboration of all the essential legal relations of simple commodity owners (of buyers and sellers, debtors and creditors, contracts, obligations, etc.) can be taken as the foundation. . . . If, therefore, bourgeois legal rules merely express the economic life conditions of society in legal form, then they can do so well or ill according to circumstances.

The state presents itself to us as the first ideological power over man. Society creates for itself an organ for the safeguarding of its common interests against internal and external attacks. This organ is the state power. Hardly come into being, this organ makes itself independent vis-a-vis society; and, indeed, the more so, the more it becomes the organ of a particular class, the more it directly enforces the supremacy of that class. The fight of the oppressed class against the ruling class becomes necessarily a political fight, a fight first of all against the political dominance of this class. The consciousness of the interconnection between this political struggle and its economic basis becomes dulled and can be lost altogether. While this is not wholly the case with the participants, it almost always happens with the historians. Of the ancient sources on the struggles within the Roman Republic only Appian tells us clearly and distinctly what was at issue in the last resort—namely, landed property.

But once the state has become an independent power vis-a-vis society, it produces forthwith a further ideology. It is indeed among professional politicians, theorists of public law and jurists of private law that the connection with economic facts gets lost for fair. Since in each particular case the economic facts must assume the form of juristic motives in order to receive legal sanction; and since, in so doing, consideration of course has to be given to the whole legal system already in operation, the juristic form is, in consequence, made everything and the economic content nothing. Public law and private law are treated as independent spheres, each having its own independent historical development, each being capable of and needing a systematic presentation by the consistent elimination of all inner contradictions.

Engels, *Ludwig Feuerbach* (1888), MESW, pp. 626–28.

The state is. . . by no means a power forced on society from without; just as little is it "the reality of the ethical idea," "the image and reality of reason," as Hegel maintains. Rather, it is a product of society at a certain stage of development; it is the admission that this society has become entangled in an insoluble contradiction with itself, that it has split into irreconcilable antagonisms which it is powerless to dispel. But in order that these antagonisms and classes with conflicting economic interests might not consume themselves and society in fruitless struggle, it became necessary to have a power seemingly standing above society that would alleviate the conflict, and keep it within the bounds of "order"; and this power, arisen out of society but placing itself above it, and alienating itself more and more from it, is the state.

As distinct from the old gentile order, the state, first, divides its subjects *according to territory.* As we have seen, the old gentile associations, built upon and held together by ties of blood, became inadequate, largely because they presupposed that the members were bound to a given territory, a bond which had long ceased to exist. The territory remained, but the people had become mobile. Hence, division according to territory was taken as the point of departure, and citizens were allowed to exercise their public rights and duties wherever they settled, irrespective of gens and tribe. This organisation of citizens according to locality is a feature common to all states. That is why it seems natural to us; but we have seen what long and arduous struggles were needed before it could replace, in Athens and Rome, the old organisation according to gentes.

The second distinguishing feature is the establishment of a *public power* which no longer directly coincides with the population organising itself as an armed force. This special public power is necessary because a self-acting armed organisation of the population has become impossible since the split into classes. The slaves also belonged to the population; the 90,000 citizens of Athens formed only a privileged class as against the 365,000 slaves. The people's army of the Athenian democracy was an aristocratic public power against the slaves, whom it kept in check; however, a gendarmerie also became necessary to keep the citizens in check, as we related above. This public power exists in every state; it consists not merely of armed men but also of material adjuncts, prisons and institutions of coercion of all kinds, of which gentile [clan] society knew nothing. It may be very insignificant, almost infinitesimal, in societies where class antagonisms are still undeveloped and in out-of-the-way places as was the case at certain times and in certain regions in the United

States of America. It [the public power] grows stronger, however, in proportion as class antagonisms within the state become more acute, and as adjacent states become larger and more populous. We have only to look at our present-day Europe, where class struggle and rivalry in conquest have tuned up the public power to such a pitch that it threatens to swallow the whole of society and even the state.

In order to maintain this public power, contributions from the citizens become necessary—*taxes.* These were absolutely unknown in gentile society; but we know enough about them today. As civilisation advances, these taxes become inadequate; the state makes drafts on the future, contracts loans, *public debts.* Old Europe can tell a tale about these, too.

Having public power and the right to levy taxes, the officials now stand, as organs of society, *above* society. The free, voluntary respect that was accorded to the organs of the gentile [clan] constitution does not satisfy them, even if they could gain it; being the vehicles of a power that is becoming alien to society, respect for them must be enforced by means of exceptional laws by virtue of which they enjoy special sanctity and inviolability. The shabbiest police servant in the civilised state has more "authority" than all the organs of gentile society put together; but the most powerful prince and the greatest statesman, or general, of civilisation may well envy the humblest gentile chief for the unstrained and undisputed respect that is paid to him. The one stands in the midst of society, the other is forced to attempt to represent something outside and above it.

Because the state arose from the need to hold class antagonisms in check, but because it arose, at the same time, in the midst of the conflict of these classes, it is, as a rule, the state of the most powerful, economically dominant class, which, through the medium of the state, becomes also the politically dominant class, and thus acquires new means of holding down and exploiting the oppressed class. Thus, the state of antiquity was above all the state of the slave owners for the purpose of holding down the slaves, as the feudal state was the organ of the nobility for holding down the peasant serfs and bondsmen, and the modern representative state is an instrument of exploitation of wage labour by capital. By way of exception, however, periods occur in which the warring classes balance each other so nearly that the state power, as ostensible mediator, acquires, for the moment, a certain degree of independence of both. Such was the absolute monarchy of the seventeenth and eighteenth centuries, which held the balance between the nobility and the class of burghers; such was the Bonapartism of the First, and still more of the Second French Empire, which played off the proletariat against the bourgeoisie and the bourgeoisie against the proletariat. The latest performance of this kind, in which ruler and ruled appear equally ridiculous, is the new German Empire of the Bismarck nation: here capitalists and workers are balanced against each other and equally cheated for the benefit of the impoverished Prussian cabbage junkers.

In most of the historical states, the rights of citizens are, besides, apportioned according to their wealth, thus directly expressing the fact that the state is an organisation of the possessing class for its protection against the non-possessing class. It was so already in the Athenian and Roman classification according to property. It was so in the medieval feudal state, in which the alignment of political power was in conformity with the amount of land owned. It is seen in the electoral qualifications of the modern representative states. Yet this political recognition of property distinctions is by no means essential. On the contrary, it marks a low stage of state development. The highest form of the state, the democratic republic, which under our modern conditions of society is more and more becoming an inevitable necessity, and is the form of state in which alone the last decisive struggle between proletariat and bourgeoisie can be fought out—the democratic republic officially knows nothing any more of property distinctions. In it wealth exercises its power indirectly, but all the more surely. On the one hand, in the form of the direct corruption of officials, of which America provides the classical example; on the other hand, in the form of an alliance between government and Stock Exchange, which become the easier to achieve the more the public debt increases and the more joint-stock companies concentrate in their hands not only transport but also production itself, using the Stock Exchange as their centre. The latest French republic as well as the United States is a striking example of this; and good old Switzerland has contributed its share in this field. But that a democratic republic is not essential for this fraternal alliance between government and Stock Exchange is proved by England and also by the new German Empire, where one cannot tell who was elevated more by universal suffrage, Bismarck or Bleichröder. And lastly, the possessing class rules directly through the medium of universal suffrage. As long as the oppressed class, in our case, therefore, the proletariat, is not yet ripe to emancipate itself, it will in its majority regard the existing order of society as the only one possible and, politically, will form the tail of the capitalist class, its extreme Left wing. To the extent, however, that this class matures for its self-emancipation, it constitutes itself as its own party and elects its own representatives, and not those of the capitalists. Thus, universal suffrage is the gauge of the maturity of the working class. It cannot and never will be anything more in the present-day state; but that is sufficient. On the day the thermometer of universal suffrage registers boiling point among the workers, both they and the capitalists will know what to do.

The state, then, has not existed from all eternity. There have been societies that did without it, that had no idea of the state and state power. At a certain stage of economic development, which was necessarily bound up with the split of society into classes, the state became a necessity owing to this split. We are now rapidly approaching a stage in the development of production at which the existence of these classes not only will have ceased to be a necessity, but will become a positive hindrance to production. They will fall as inevitably as they arose at an earlier stage. Along with them the state will inevitably fall. Society, which will reorganise production on the basis of a free and equal association of the producers, will put the whole machinery of state where it will then belong: into the museum of antiquities, by the side of the spinning-wheel and the bronze axe.

Engels, *Origin of the Family, Private Property and the State* (1884), MESW, pp. 586–89.

Economic, political and other reflections are just like those in the human eye, they pass through a condensing lens and therefore appear upside down, standing on their heads. . . .

On the whole, the economic movement gets its way, but it has also to suffer reactions from the political movement which it established and endowed with relative independence itself, from the movement of the state power on the one hand and of the opposition simultaneously engendered on the other. Just as the movement of the industrial market is, in the main and with the reservations already indicated, reflected in the money market and, of course, in inverted form, so the struggle between the classes already existing and already in conflict with one another is reflected in the struggle between government and opposition, but also in inverted form, no longer directly but indirectly, not as a class struggle but as a fight for political principles, and so distorted that it has taken us thousands of years to get behind it again.

The reaction of the state power upon economic development can be one of three kinds: it can run in the same direction, and then development is more rapid; it can oppose the line of development, in which case nowadays state power in every great nation will go to pieces in the long run; or it can cut off the economic development from certain paths, and impose on it certain others. This case ultimately reduces itself to one of the two previous ones. But it is obvious that in cases two and three the political power can do great damage to the economic development and result in the squandering of great masses of energy and material.

Then there is also the case of the conquest and brutal destruction of economic resources, by which, in certain circumstances, a whole local or national economic development could formerly be ruined. Nowadays such a case usually has the opposite effect, at least among great nations: in the long run the defeated power often gains more economically, politically and morally than the victor.

It is similar with law. As soon as the new division of labour which creates professional lawyers becomes necessary, another new and independent sphere is opened up which, for all its general dependence on production and trade, still has its own capacity for reacting upon these spheres as well. In a modern state, law must not only correspond to the general economic position and be its expression, but must also be an expression which is *consistent in itself,* and which does not, owing to inner contradictions, look glaringly inconsistent. And in order to achieve this, the faithful reflection of economic conditions is more and more infringed upon. . . .

The reflection of economic relations as legal principles is necessarily also a topsy turvy one: it happens without the person who is acting being conscious of it; the jurist imagines he is operating with *a priori* principles, whereas they are really only economic reflexes; so everything is upside down. And it seems to me obvious that this inversion, which, so long as it remains unrecognised, forms what we call *ideological conception,* reacts in its turn upon the economic basis and may, within certain limits, modify it. The basis of the law of inheritance—assuming that the stages reached in the development of the family are equal—is an economic one. But it would be difficult to prove, for instance, that the absolute liberty of the testator in England and the severe restrictions imposed upon him in France are only due in every detail to economic causes.

Both react back, however, on the economic sphere to a very considerable extent, because they influence the division of property.

Engels, letter to Schmidt (1890), SC, pp. 478, 480–82.

8.A.5 CRITIQUE OF SOCIAL REFORM AND NON-MARXIAN SOCIALISM

SOCIALIST AND COMMUNIST LITERATURE

Reactionary Socialism and Feudal Socialism

Owing to their historical position, it became the vocation of the aristocracies of France and England to write pamphlets against modern bourgeois society. In the French revolution of July, 1830, and in the English reform agitation, these aristocracies again succumbed to the hateful upstart. Thenceforth a serious political contest was altogether out of the question. A literary battle alone remained possible. But even in the domain of literature the old cries of the Restoration period had become impossible.

In order to arouse sympathy, the aristocracy were obliged to lose sight, apparently, of their own interests, and to formulate their indictment against the bourgeoisie in the interest of the exploited working class alone. Thus the aristocracy took their revenge by singing lampoons on their new master, and whispering in his ears sinister prophecies of coming catastrophe.

In this way arose feudal socialism; half lamentation, half lampoon; half echo of the past, half menace of the future; at times, by its bitter, witty, and incisive criticism, striking the bourgeoisie to the very heart's core, but always ludicrous in its effect, through total incapacity to comprehend the march of modern history.

The aristocracy, in order to rally the people to them, waved the proletarian alms bag in front for a banner. But the people, so often as it joined them, saw on their hindquarters the old feudal coats of arms, and deserted with loud and irreverent laughter.

One section of the French Legitimists, and "Young England," exhibited this spectacle.

In pointing out that their mode of exploitation was different from that of the bourgeosie, the feudalists forgot that they exploited under circumstances and conditions that were quite different, and that are now antiquated. In showing that under their rule the modern proletariat never existed, they forget that the modern bourgeoisie is the necessary offspring of their own form of society.

For the rest, so little do they conceal the reactionary character of their criticism that their chief accusation against the bourgeoisie amounts to this, that under the bourgeois regime a class is being developed which is destined to cut up root and branch the old order of society.

What they upbraid the bourgeoisie with is not so much that it creates a proletariat, as that it creates a revolutionary proletariat.

In political practice, therefore, they join in all coercive measures against the working class; and in ordinary life, despite their high-falutin phrases, they stoop to pick up the golden apples dropped from the tree of industry, and to barter truth, love, and honor for traffic in wool, beetroot sugar, and potato spirits.

As the parson has ever gone hand in hand with the landlord, so has clerical socialism with feudal socialism.

Nothing is easier than to give Christian asceticism a socialist tinge. Has not Christianity declaimed against private property, against marriage, against the state? Has it not preached, in the place of these, charity and poverty, celibacy and mortification of the flesh, monastic life and Mother Church? Christian Socialism is but the holy water with which the priest consecrates the heart-burnings of the aristocrat.

Petty-Bourgeois Socialism

The feudal aristocracy was not the only class that was ruined by the bourgeoisie, not the only class whose conditions of existence pined and perished in the atmosphere of modern bourgeois society. The medieval burgesses and the small peasant bourgeoisie were the precursors of the modern bourgeoisie. In those countries which are but little developed, industrially and commercially, these two classes still vegetate side by side with the rising bourgeoisie.

In countries where modern civilization has become fully developed, a new class of petty bourgeois has been formed, fluctuating between proletariat and bourgeoisie, and ever renewing itself as a supplementary part of bourgeois society. The individual members of this class, however, are being constantly hurled down into the proletariat by the action of competition, and as modern industry develops, they can see the moment approaching when they will completely disappear as an independent section of modern society, to be replaced, in manufacture, agriculture and commerce, by overlookers, bailiffs and shopmen.

In countries like France, where the peasants constitute far more than half of the population, it was natural that writers who sided with the proletariat against the bourgeoisie should use, in their criticism of the bourgeois regime, the standard of the peasant and petty bourgeois, and from the standpoint of these intermediate classes should take up the cudgels for the working class. Thus arose petty-bourgeois socialism. Sismondi was the head of this school, not only in France but also in England.

This school of socialism dissected with great acuteness the contradictions in the conditions of modern production. It laid bare the hypocritical apologies of economists. It proved, incontrovertibly, the disastrous effects of machinery and division of labor; the concentration of capital and land in a few hands; overproduction and crises; it pointed out the inevitable ruin of the petty bourgeois and peasant, the misery of the proletariat, the anarchy in production, the crying inequalities in the distribution of wealth, the industrial war of extermination between nations, the dissolution of old moral bonds, of the old family relations, of the old nationalities.

In its positive aims, however, this form of socialism aspires either to restore the old means of production and of exchange, and with them the old property relations and the old society, or to cramp the modern means of production and of exchange within the framework of the old property relations that have been, and were bound to be exploded by those means. In either case, it is both reactionary and utopian.

Its last words are: corporate guilds for manufacture; patriarchal relations in agriculture.

Ultimately, when stubborn historical facts had dispersed all intoxicating effects of self-deception, this form of socialism ended in a miserable fit of the blues.

German or "True" Socialism

The socialist and communist literature of France, a literature that originated under the pressure of a bourgeoisie in power, and that was the expression of the struggle against this power, was introduced into Germany at a time when the bourgeoisie, in that country, had just begun its contest with feudal absolutism.

German philosophers, would-be philosophers, and *beaux esprits* eagerly seized on this literature, only forgetting that when these writings immigrated from France into Germany, French social conditions had not immigrated along with them. In contact with German social conditions, this French literature lost all its immediate practical significance and assumed a purely literary aspect. Thus to the German philosophers of the eighteenth century the demands of the first French Revolution were nothing more than the demands of "practical reason" in general, and the utterance of the will of the revolutionary French bourgeoisie signified in their eyes the laws of pure Will, of Will as it was bound to be, of true human Will generally.

The work of the German literati consisted solely in bringing the new French ideas into harmony with their ancient philosophical conscience, or rather, in annexing the French ideas without deserting their own philosophical point of view.

This annexation took place in the same way in which a foreign language is appropriated, namely by translation.

It is well known how the monks wrote silly lives of Catholic saints over the manuscripts on which the classical works of ancient heathendom had been written. The German literati reversed this process with the profane French literature. They wrote their philosophical nonsense beneath the French original. For instance, beneath the French criticism of the economic functions of money, they wrote "Alienation of Humanity," and beneath the French criticism of the bourgeois state they wrote, "Dethronement of the Category of the General," and so forth.

The introduction of these philosophical phrases at the back of the French historical criticisms they dubbed "Philosophy of Action," "True Socialism,"

"German Science of Socialism," "Philosophical Foundation of Socialism," and so on.

The French socialist and communist literature was thus completely emasculated. And since it ceased in the hands of the German to express the struggle of one class with the other, he felt conscious of having overcome "French one-sidedness" and of representing, not true requirements, but the requirements of Truth, not the interests of the proletariat, but the interests of Human Nature, of Man in general, who belongs to no class, has no reality, who exists only in the misty realm of philosophical fantasy.

This German socialism which took its schoolboy task so seriously and solemnly, and extolled its poor stock in trade in such mountebank fashion, meanwhile gradually lost its pedantic innocence.

The fight of the German, and especially of the Prussian, bourgeoisie against feudal aristocracy and absolute monarchy—in other words, the liberal movement—became more earnest.

By this the long-wished-for opportunity was offered to "True Socialism" of confronting the political movement with the socialist demands, of hurling the traditional anathemas against liberalism, against representative government, against bourgeois competition, bourgeois freedom of the press, bourgeois legislation, bourgeois liberty and equality, and of preaching to the masses that they had nothing to gain, and everything to lose, by this bourgeois movement. German socialism forgot, in the nick of time, that the French criticism whose silly echo it was presupposed the existence of modern bourgeois society, with its corresponding economic conditions, and the political constitution adapted thereto, the very things whose attainment was the object of the pending struggle in Germany.

To the absolute governments, with their following of parsons, professors, country squires, and officials, it served as a welcome scarecrow against the threatening bourgeoisie.

It was a sweet finish after the bitter pills of floggings and bullets with which these same governments, just at that time, dosed the German working-class risings.

While this "True Socialism" thus served the government as a weapon for fighting the German bourgeoisie, it, at the same time, directly represented a reactionary interest, the interest of the German philistines. In Germany the petty-bourgeois class, a relic of the sixteenth century, and since then constantly cropping up again under various forms, is the real social basis of the existing state of things.

To preserve this class is to preserve the existing state of things in Germany. The industrial and political supremacy of the bourgeoisie threatens it with certain destruction; on the one hand, from the concentration of capital, on the other, from the rise of a revolutionary proletariat. "True Socialism" appeared to kill these two birds with one stone. It spread like an epidemic.

The robe of speculative cobwebs, embroidered with flowers of rhetoric, steeped in the dew of sickly sentiment, this transcendental robe in which the German socialists wrapped their sorry "eternal truths," all skin and bones, served to wonderfully increase the sale of their goods among such a public.

And on its part German socialism recognized, more and more, its own calling as the bombastic representative of the petty-bourgeois philistine.

It proclaimed the German nation to be the model nation, and the German petty philistine to be the typical man. To every villainous meanness of this model man it gave a hidden, higher socialistic interpretation, the exact contrary of its true character. It went to the extreme length of directly opposing the "brutally destructive" tendency of communism, and of proclaiming its supreme and impartial contempt of all class struggles. With very few exceptions, all the so-called socialist and communist publications that now (1847) circulate in Germany belong to the domain of this foul and enervating literature.

Conservative or Bourgeois Socialism

A part of the bourgeoisie is desirous of redressing social grievances, in order to secure the continued existence of bourgeois society.

To this section belong economists, philanthropists, humanitarians, improvers of the condition of the working class, organizers of charity, members of societies for the prevention of cruelty to animals, temperance fanatics, hole-and-corner reformers of every imaginable kind. This form of socialism has, moreover, been worked out into complete systems.

We may cite Proudhon's *Philosophie de la Misere* as an example of this form.

The socialistic bourgeois want all the advantages of modern social conditions without the struggles and dangers necessarily resulting therefrom. They desire the existing state of society minus its revolutionary and disintegrating elements. They wish for a bourgeoisie without a proletariat. The bourgeoisie naturally conceives the world in which it is supreme to be the best; and bourgeois socialism develops this comfortable conception into various more or less complete systems. In requiring the proletariat to carry out such a system, and thereby to march straightway into the social New Jerusalem, it but requires, in reality, that the proletariat should remain within the bounds of existing society, but should cast away all its hateful ideas concerning the bourgeoisie.

A second and more practical, but less systematic, form of this socialism sought to depreciate every revolutionary movement in the eyes of the working class by showing that no mere political reform, but only a change in the material conditions of existence, in economical relations, could be of any advantage to them. By changes in the material conditions of existence, this form of socialism, however, by no means understands abolition of the bourgeois relations of production, an abolition that can be effected only by a revolution, but administrative reforms, based on the continued existence of these relations; reforms, therefore, that in no respect affect the relations between capital and labor, but, at the best, lessen the cost, and simplify the administrative work, of bourgeois government.

Bourgeois socialism attains adequate expression when, and only when, it becomes a mere figure of speech.

Free trade: for the benefit of the working class. Protective duties: for the benefit of the working class. Prison reform: for the benefit of the working class. This is the last word and the only seriously meant word of bourgeois socialism.

It is summed up in the phrase: the bourgeois is a bourgeois—for the benefit of the working class.

Critical-Utopian Socialism and Communism

We do not here refer to that literature which, in every great modern revolution, has always given voice to the demands of the proletariat: such as the writings of Babeuf and others.

The first direct attempts of the proletariat to attain its own ends were made in times of universal excitement, when feudal society was being overthrown. These attempts necessarily failed, owing to the then undeveloped state of the proletariat, as well as to the absence of the economic conditions for its emancipation, conditions that had yet to be produced, and could be produced by the impending bourgeois epoch alone. The revolutionary literature that accompanied these first movements of the proletariat had necessarily a reactionary character. It inculcated universal asceticism and social leveling in its crudest form.

The socialist and communist systems properly so called, those of St. Simon, Fourier, Owen, and others, spring into existence in the early undeveloped period. . . of the struggle between proletariat and bourgeoisie. . . .

The founders of these systems see, indeed, the class antagonisms, as well as the action of the decomposing elements in the prevailing form of society. But the proletariat, as yet in its infancy, offers to them the spectacle of a class without any historical initiative or any independent political movement.

Since the development of class antagonism keeps even pace with the development of industry, the economic situation, as they find it, does not as yet offer to them the material conditions for the emancipation of the proletariat. They therefore search after a new social science, after new social laws that are to create these conditions.

Historical action is to yield to their personal inventive action, historically created conditions of emancipation to fantastic ones, and the gradual, spontaneous class organization of the proletariat to an organization of society specially contrived by these inventors. Future history resolves itself, in their eyes, into the propaganda and the practical carrying out of their social plans.

In the formation of their plans they are conscious of caring chiefly for the interests of the working class, as being the most suffering class. Only from the point of view of being the most suffering class does the proletariat exist for them.

The undeveloped state of the class struggle, as well as their own surroundings, causes socialists of this kind to consider themselves far superior to all class antagonisms. They want to improve the condition of every member of society, even that of the most favored. Hence they habitually appeal to society at large, without distinction of class; nay, by preference to the ruling class. For how can people, when once they understand their system, fail to see in it the best possible plan of the best possible state of society?

Hence they reject all political, and especially all revolutionary action; they wish to attain their ends by peaceful means, and endeavor, by small experiments, necessarily doomed to failure, and by the force of example, to pave the way for the new social Gospel.

Such fantastic pictures of future society, painted at a time when the proletariat is still in a very undeveloped state, and has but a fantastic conception of its own position, correspond with the first instinctive yearnings of that class for a general reconstruction of society.

But these socialist and communist publications contain a critical element. They attack every principle of existing society. Hence they are full of the most valuable materials for the enlightenment of the working class. The practical measures proposed in them, such as the abolition of the distinction between town and country, of the family, of the carrying on of industries for the account of private individuals, and of the wage system, the proclamation of social harmony, the conversion of the functions of the state into a mere superintendence of production, all these proposals point solely to the disappearance of class antagonisms which were at that time only just cropping up, and which in these publications are recognized under their earliest, indistinct and undefined forms only. These proposals, therefore, are of a purely utopian character. . . .

Marx-Engels, *Communist Manifesto,* excerpts from Part III.

8.A.6 CRITIQUE OF CONSPIRATORIAL REVOLUTION

We know the tendency of Romance people toward conspiracies, and the role they have played in modern Spanish, Italian, and French history. After the defeat of the Spanish and Italian conspirators in the early 1820s, Lyon and especially Paris became the centers of revolutionary associations. It is known how up to 1830 the liberal bourgeois stood at the head of the conspiracies against the Restoration. . . .

With the formation of proletarian conspiracies there came the need for a division of labor among them; the members divided themselves into occasional conspirators—*conspirateurs d'occasion*—workers who practiced conspiracy as a side issue, merely attended meetings and held themselves in readiness for the order of the chiefs to assemble at an appointed place—and the professional conspirators, who devoted full time to conspiracy and lived off it. The professionals formed the middle layer between workers and chiefs, and often smuggled themselves into the two other layers.

The life style of this class of people conditions their whole character from the first. Proletarian conspiracy offers them only a limited and uncertain existence, of course. Hence they are constantly forced to resort to the money chests of the conspiracies. . . . These democratic bohemians of proletarian origin. . . are either workers who have given up their work and thus became dissolute, or characters who come out of the lumpen proletariat and carry into their new existence all the dissolute habits of that class. . . .

The whole life of these professional conspirators bears the characteristic stamp of the bohemian. Recruiting officers of conspiracy, they move from bistro to bistro, feel the pulse of the workers, seek out their people, cajole them into conspiracy. . . .

It is they who throw up and command the barricades, organize the resistance, plunder the arsenals, lead in the seizure of arms and munitions in homes, and in the midst of the insurrection carry out those daring coups which so often cause disarray in government ranks. In a word, they are the officers of insurrection.

It goes without saying that these conspirators do not at all confine themselves to organizing the revolutionary proletariat. Their business consists precisely in forestalling the revolutionary process, in driving it artifically toward crisis, in making a revolution extempore, without a condition for revolution. For them the only condition for revolution is the sufficient organization of their conspiracy. They are the alchemists of revolution; as we see in their rigid conceptions, they share entirely the intellectual confusion and the ignorance of the old alchemists. They seize on new discoveries which are supposed to achieve revolutionary miracles: incendiary bombs, demolition machines of magical effectiveness, riots that are to be the more miraculous and surprising the less rational ground they have. Occupied with such projects, they have no other aim than to overthrow the next government, and have the deepest contempt for theoretical elucidation of the working class and its interests. . . .

Marx-Engels, article in *Neue Rheinische Zeitung* (1850), MR, pp. 53–55.

THE SECRET PROLETARIAN SOCIETIES

After the defeat of the Revolution of 1848–49, the proletarian party on the Continent lost what it had, by way of exception, possessed in that short period: freedom of the press, of speech, and the right of association, that is, the legal means for party organization. Despite the Reaction, both the bourgeois-liberal and the petty bourgeois-democratic parties found in the social position of the classes they represented the conditions which enabled them to keep more or less together and represent their common interests. For the proletarian party after 1849, as before 1848, there was only one way open —the way of *secret association*. Hence after 1849 there arose on the Continent a whole series of secret proletarian associations, exposed by the police, condemned by the courts, broken by imprisonment, but always rebuilt anew by conditions.

One segment of these secret societies aimed directly at the overthrow of the existing political system. This was justified in France, where the proletariat was defeated by the bourgeoisie and where an attack on the existing government coincided with an attack on the bourgeoisie. Another segment aimed at the creation of a proletarian party, without troubling itself about the existing governments. This was necessary in countries like Germany, where the bourgeoisie and the proletariat were equally subordinate to the semifeudal governments; hence a victorious assault on the existing governments could only help the bourgeoisie or the so-called middle classes to achieve supremacy, rather than break their power. No doubt here, too, the members of the proletarian party would have to participate anew in a revolution against the status quo, but it was not their task to prepare that revolution, to agitate or conspire or plot for it. They could leave this preparation of revolution to general conditions and to the directly participating classes. The proletarian party had to leave it to them if it were not to renounce its own party position and the historic tasks which emerge from the general conditions of existence of the proletariat. For the proletariat, the existing governments were merely ephemeral phenomena and the status quo only a short stopping point which a petty and narrow democracy was left to work itself off.

The "Communist League" was therefore not a conspiratorial society, but a society which was secretly to accomplish the organization of the proletarian party, because the German proletariat was officially denied. . .the right of publishing, speech, and association. When such a society conspires, it is only in the same sense that steam and electricity conspire against the status quo.

It goes without saying that such a secret society, which aims to construct, not a *government,* but an *opposition party of the future,* could offer little attraction for individuals who on the one hand feel their personal insignificance sprout under the theatrical cloak of conspiracy, and on the other satisfy their narrow ambitions on the day of the next revolution, but above all appear to themselves momentarily important, share in the spoils of demagogy, and want to be welcomed by the democratic charlatans.

Marx, *Revelations* (1852), MR, pp. 57–58.

B. REVOLUTIONARY STRATEGY AND THE TRANSITION

Given the overall view of revolution discussed in the first section of this chapter, a number of practical questions arise, namely, where, when, and how will the revolution occur? In the 1840s, Marx occasionally envisioned the possibility of a fairly early socialist revolution. The typical model, as exemplified by Germany, was one of a prospective bourgeois revolution (in which the proletariat would not only participate, but play a major role), followed, at some unspecified time, by a more thorough proletarian, socialist revolution. Usually, though, especially after the failures of the 1848 Revolutions to bring continuing or major social change, and after the economic development of the 1850s and 1860s and his own socioeconomic studies, Marx's response to questions of where and when were in terms of "when the time is ripe," i.e., in highly industrialized countries which have fulfilled the various preconditions discussed in Chapter 7. From this perspective, it is not surprising to find Marx issuing warnings against the ineffectuality of "premature" revolution, as illustrated in selection 8.B.7.

Suppose that a genuine working class revolution occurs in an industrially developed capitalist economy, when the time is "ripe," and the various preconditions for transition to socialism have been laid. In this context, would a social revolution in Marx's sense also require revolution in the *popular* sense, i.e., "overthrow of the government by force and violence?" Clearly, this would depend on the specific conditions and history of the particular country involved. In their early writings, Marx and Engels emphasized that an economically and politically dominant capitalist class would not voluntarily and peacefully abdicate its positions of wealth and power, and that its dislodgement probably would require a violent overthrow of capitalist state power. "Force," Marx observed in his discussion of primitive capitalist accumulation (selection 1.4), "is the midwife of every old society pregnant with a new one." In their mature works, by contrast, Marx and especially Engels emphasized the distinct possibility of a peaceful transition to socialism under democratic auspices. Because of the high level of class consciousness in England, for example, universal suffrage there would be "a far more socialistic measure than anything which has been honoured with that name on the Continent." Alternative views on the issue of revolutionary violence are presented in selection 8.B.8.

The *Communist Manifesto,* although most widely known for its overall vision of capitalist development, also provides a discussion of the strategy of transition to socialism, involving three steps (selection 8.B.9). The first step is for the proletariat to "win the battle of democracy" and achieve political supremacy. The second step is to engage in several measures which in themselves appear "economically insufficient and untenable" (most of which, indeed, have been implemented in modern industrial societies) but which make "despotic inroads on the rights of property." The third is to transfer the physical means of production, by degrees, to worker-state control. Although very brief, the strategy is rather sophisticated, and certainly departs substantially from notions that the "day of the revolution dawned bright and clear."

The strategy outlined in the *Manifesto* implies a reasonably nonhostile environment, as, for example, in England. What if the political environment is inhospitable, as in Germany during the 1850s? Then, Marx suggests, an alternative strategy is necessary. The socialist labor movement is advised to support the petty-bourgeois democrats when they are "likewise oppressed," but prudently to prepare for additional class struggles when, after the democrats have won their revolution, they turn against the working class to prevent further social change (selection 8.B.10).

We must briefly note that although Marx's concept of "dictatorship of the proletariat" is usually reproduced in discussions of classical Marxism, it actually plays a very small role in the writings of Marx and Engels, typically appearing in letters or unpublished papers (selection 8.B.11). Because Marx's comments are highly abbreviated, almost cryptic, we must rely on Engels, who is a reasonable proxy in this instance. The concept has two major propositions. (1) The political form of the "dictatorship of the proletariat" is the modern democratic republic. As far as the *working class* is concerned, the worker-state during the transitional period is subject to greater working class control and thereby is *more* sensitive and responsive to the interest of the overwhelming majority of the population, i.e., is more democratic than capitalist democracy which, despite its democratic political form, constitutes a "dictatorship of the bourgeoisie" in socioeconomic terms. (2) Granted its democratic political form, the socioeconomic content of working class rule, as far as the *capitalist class* is concerned, would presumably be perceived as dictatorial. In effect, the "dictatorship of the proletariat" is somewhat analogous to the Roman "dictura," i.e., an institution established by and within a democracy which is given special temporary powers within a certain domain to accomplish particular purposes. In

Marx's concept, the particular purpose is the transfer of power to the worker-state and the transition to socialist institutions.[6]

8.B.7 WARNINGS AGAINST PREMATURITY

The "question" of the forthcoming Zurich Congress about which you inform me seems to me—a mistake. The thing to be done at any definite given moment of the future, the thing *immediately* to be done, depends of course entirely on the given historical conditions in which one has to act. But this question is in the *clouds* and therefore is really the statement of a phantom problem to which the only answer can be—the *criticism of the question* itself. No equation can be solved unless the elements of its solution are involved in its terms. Moreover the embarrassments of a government which has suddenly come into being through a people's victory have nothing specifically "socialist" about them. On the contrary. The victorious bourgeois politicians at once feel themselves embarrassed by their "victory" while the socialist can at least take action without any embarrassment. One thing you can at any rate be sure of: a socialist government does not come into power in a country unless conditions are so developed that it can above all take the necessary measures for intimidating the mass of the boureoisie sufficiently to gain time—the first *desideratum [requisite]*—for lasting action.

Perhaps you will point to the Paris Commune; but apart from the fact that this was merely the rising of a town under exceptional conditions, the majority of the Commune was in no sense socialist, nor could it be. With a small amount of sound common sense, however, they could have reached a compromise with Versailles useful to the whole mass of the people—the only thing that could be reached at the time. The appropriation of the Bank of France alone would have been enough to dissolve all the pretensions of the Versailles people in terror, etc., etc.

The general demands of the French bourgeoisie laid down before 1789 were roughly just the same, *mutatis mutandis* [with corresponding alterations] as the first immediate demands of the proletariat are pretty uniformly today in all countries with capitalist production. But had any eighteenth-century Frenchman the faintest idea *a priori* beforehand of the way in which the demands of the French bourgeoisie would be accomplished? The doctrinaire and necessarily fantastic anticipations of the programme of action for a revolution of the future only divert us from the struggle of the present. The dream that the end of the world was at hand inspired the early Christians in

[6]The concept of the "dictatorship of the proletariat" as a dictatorship *by* a centralized politicoeconomic elite *over* a working class which lacks any effective means to hold the leadership accountable or responsive to workers' interests is a twentieth century invention. Whether the one might lead to the other and, if so, how that might be prevented remains a controversy to this day. Projection of twentieth century experiences onto Marx and Engels, however, seems misplaced criticism.

their struggle with the Roman Empire and gave them confidence in victory. Scientific insight into the inevitable disintegration of the dominant order of society continually proceeding before our eyes, and the ever-growing passion into which the masses are scourged by the old ghosts of government—while at the same time the positive development of the means of production advances with gigantic strides—all this is a sufficient guarantee that with the moment of the outbreak of a real proletarian revolution there will also be given the conditions (though these are certain not to be idyllic) of its next immediate *modus operandi* [form of action].

It is my conviction that the critical juncture for a new International Workingmen's Association has not yet arrived and for this reason I regard all workers' congresses, particularly socialist congresses, in so far as they are not related to the immediate given conditions in this or that particular nation, as not merely useless but harmful. They will always fade away in innumerable stale generalised banalities.

Marx, *Letter to Nieuwenhuis* (1881), SC, pp. 386–87.

8.B.8 REVOLUTION AND VIOLENCE

CLASS ANTAGONISM AND REVOLUTIONARY VIOLENCE

An oppressed class in the vital condition of every society based on antagonism of classes. . . .

The antagonism between the proletariat and the bourgeoisie is a struggle of class against class, a struggle which carried to its highest expression is a total revolution. Indeed, is it at all surprising that a society founded on the opposition of classes should culminate in brutal *contradiction,* the shock of body against body, as its final *dénouement*?

Do not say that social movement excludes political movement. There is never a political movement which is not at the same time social.

It is only in an order of things in which there are no more classes and class antagonisms that *social evolutions* will cease to be *political revolutions.* Till then, on the eve of every general reshuffling of society, the last word of social science will always be: *"Le combat ou la mort, la lutte sanguinaire ou le néant. C'est ainsi que la question est invinciblement posée."*—George Sand.*

Marx, *Poverty of Philosophy* (1847), IP, pp. 146–47.

*"Combat or death: bloody struggle or extinction. It is thus that the question is inexorably put."—*Ed.*

THE HAGUE CONGRESS: SPEECH AT AMSTERDAM

The Hague Congress...proclaimed the necessity for the working classes to fight, in the political as well as the social sphere, against the old society, a society which is collapsing. ... A group had formed in our midst advocating the workers' abstention from politics.

We have thought it important to point out how very dangerous and baneful to our cause we considered these principles to be.

The worker will some day have to win political supremacy in order to organise labour along new lines; he will have to defeat the old policy supporting old institutions, under penalty—as in the case of the ancient Christians, who neglected and scorned it—of never seeing their kingdom on earth.

But we have by no means affirmed that this goal would be achieved by identical means.

We know of the allowances we must make for the institutions, customs and traditions of the various countries; and we do not deny that there are countries such as America, England, and I would add Holland if I knew your institutions better, where the working people may achieve their goal by peaceful means. If that is true, we must also recognise that in most of the continental countries it is force that will have to be the lever of our revolutions; it is force that we shall some day have to resort to in order to establish a reign of labour.

Marx, speech on The Hague Congress (1872), AAS, pp. 84–85.

THE ENGLISH CASE

It is possible that the struggle between the workers and the capitalists will be less terrible and less bloody than the struggle between the feudal lords and the bourgeoisie in England and France. Let us hope so.[1]

In England, for example, the way is open for the working class to develop their political power. In a place where they can achieve their goal more quickly and more securely through peaceful propaganda, insurrection would be a folly.[2]

England is the one country in which a peaceful revolution is possible; but—he added after a pause—history does not tell us so. You English like the Romans in many things are most like them in your ignorance of your own history.[3] If the unavoidable evolution turn into a revolution, it would not only be the fault of the ruling class, but also of the working class.[4]

[1]Marx, speech in the Polish emigre paper *Glos Wolny* (1867). Cited in Avineri, *KM,* p. 215.

[2]Marx, *Woodhull & Claflin's Weekly* (1871). Cited in Avineri, *KM,* p. 216.

[3]Marx, remark to Hyndman, (1870s), in H. M. Hyndman, *The Record of an Adventurous Life* (London, 1911), p. 273. Cited in Avineri, *KM,* pp. 216–17.

[4]Marx, letter to Hyndman (1880), in Hyndman, *op. cit.,* p. 283. Cited in Avineri, *KM,* p. 217.

ENGELS' REASSESSMENT

When the February Revolution broke out, all of us, as far as our conceptions of the conditions and the course of revolutionary movements were concerned, were under the spell of previous historical experience, particularly that of France. It was, indeed, the latter which had dominated the whole of European history since 1789, and from which now once again the signal had gone forth for general revolutionary change. It was, therefore, natural and unavoidable that our conceptions of the nature and the course of the "social" revolution proclaimed in Paris in February 1848, of the revolution of the proletariat, should be strongly coloured by memories of the prototypes of 1789 and 1830. Moreover, when the Paris uprising found its echo in the victorious insurrections in Vienna, Milan and Berlin; when the whole of Europe right up to the Russian frontier was swept into the movement; when thereupon in Paris, in June, the first great battle for power between the proletariat and the bourgeoisie was fought; when the very victory of its class so shook the bourgeoisie of all countries that it fled back into the arms of the monarchist-feudal reaction which had just been overthrown—there could be no doubt for us, under the circumstances then obtaining, that the great decisive combat had commenced, that it would have to be fought out in a single, long and vicissitudinous period of revolution, but that it could only end in the final victory of the proletariat. . . .

All revolutions up to the present day have resulted in the displacement of one definite class rule by another; but all ruling classes up to now have been only small minorities in relation to the ruled mass of the people. One ruling minority was thus overthrown; another minority seized the helm of state in its stead and refashioned the state institutions to suit its own interests. This was on every occasion the minority group qualified and called to rule by the given degree of economic development; and just for that reason, and only for that reason, it happened that the ruled majority either participated in the revolution for the benefit of the former or else calmly acquiesced in it. But if we disregard the concrete content in each case, the common form of all these revolutions was that they were minority revolutions. Even when the majority took part, it did so—whether wittingly or not—only in the service of a minority; but because of this, or even simply because of the passive, unresisting attitude of the majority, this minority acquired the appearance of being the representative of the whole people. . . .

When, as Marx showed in . . . the spring of 1850, the development of the bourgeois republic that arose out of the "social" Revolution of 1848 had even concentrated real power in the hands of the big bourgeoisie—monarchistically inclined as it was into the bargain—and, on the other hand, had grouped all the other social classes, peasantry as well as petty bourgeoisie, round the proletariat, so that, during and after the common victory, not they but the proletariat grown wise by experience had to become the decisive factor—was there not every prospect then of turning the revolution of the minority into a revolution of the majority?

History has proved us, and all who thought like us, wrong. It has made it clear that the state of economic development on the Continent at that time was not, by a long way, ripe for the elimination of capitalist production; it has proved this by the economic revolution which, since 1848, has seized the whole of the Continent, and has caused big industry to take real root in France, Austria, Hungary, Poland and, recently, in Russia, while it has made Germany positively an industrial country of the first rank—all on a capitalist basis, which in the year 1848, therefore, still had great capacity for expansion. But it is just this industrial revolution which has everywhere produced clarity in class relations, has removed a number of intermediate forms handed down from the period of manufacture and in Eastern Europe even from guild handicraft, has created a genuine bourgeoisie and a genuine large-scale industrial proletariat and has pushed them into the foreground of social development. However, owing to this, the struggle between these two great classes, a struggle which, apart from England, existed in 1848 only in Paris and, at the most, in a few big industrial centres, has spread over the whole of Europe and reached an intensity still inconceivable in 1848. At that time the many obscure evangels of the sects, with their panaceas; today the *one* generally recognised, crystal-clear theory of Marx, sharply formulating the ultimate aims of the struggle. At that time the masses, sundered and differing according to locality and nationality, linked only by the feeling of common suffering, undeveloped, helplessly tossed to and fro from enthusiasm to despair; today the *one* great international army of Socialists, marching irresistibly on and growing daily in number, organisation, discipline, insight and certainty of victory. If even this mighty army of the proletariat has still not reached its goal, if, far from winning victory by one mighty stroke, it has slowly to press forward from position to position in a hard, tenacious struggle, this only proves, once and for all, how impossible it was in 1848 to win social transformation by a simple surprise attack. . . .

[The reversion to the empire under] the *coup d'etat* of the. . .pseudo-democratic pretender, Louis Bonaparte. . .in 1851 gave new proof of the unripeness of the proletarian aspirations of that time. But it was itself to create the conditions under which they were bound to ripen. Internal tranquillity ensured the full development of the new industrial boom; the necessity of keeping the army occupied and of diverting the revolutionary currents outwards produced the wars in which Bonaparte, under the pretext of asserting "the principle of nationality," sought to hook annexations for France. His imitator, Bismarck, adopted the same policy for Prussia; he made his *coup d'etat,* his revolution from above, in 1866. . . . But Europe was too small for two Bonapartes and the irony of history so willed it that Bismarck overthrew Bonaparte, and King William of Prussia not only established the little German empire, but also the French republic. The general result, however, was that in Europe the independence and internal unity of the great nations, with the exception of Poland, had become a fact. Within relatively modest limits, it is true, but, for all that, on a scale large enough to allow the development of the working class to proceed without finding national complications any longer a serious obstacle. The gravediggers of the Revolution of 1848 had become the executors of its will. And alongside of them already rose threateningly the heir of 1848, the proletariat, in the shape of the *International.*

After the war of 1870–71, Bonaparte vanishes from the stage and Bismarck's mission is fulfilled, so that he can now sink back again into the ordinary *Junker.* The period, however, is brought to a close by the Paris Commune. An underhand attempt by Thiers to steal the cannon of the Paris

National Guard called forth a victorious rising. It was shown once more that in Paris none but a proletarian revolution is any longer possible. After the victory power fell, quite of itself and quite undisputed, into the hands of the working class. And once again it was proved how impossible even then, twenty years after the time described in our work, this rule of the working class still was. On the one hand, France left Paris in the lurch, looked on while it bled profusely from the bullets of MacMahon; on the other hand, the Commune was consumed in unfruitful strife between the two parties which split it, the Blanquists (the majority) and the Proudhonists (the minority), neither of which knew what was to be done. The victory which came as a gift in 1871 remained just as unfruitful as the surprise attack of 1848.

It was believed that the militant proletariat had been finally buried with the Paris Commune. But, completely to the contrary, it dates its most powerful resurgence from the Commune and the Franco-Prussian War. The recruitment of the whole of the population able to bear arms into armies that henceforth could be counted only in millions, and the introduction of firearms, projectiles and explosives of hitherto undreamt-of efficacy, created a complete revolution in all warfare. This revolution, on the one hand, put a sudden end to the Bonapartist war period and ensured peaceful industrial development by making any war other than a world war of unheard-of cruelty and absolutely incalculable outcome an impossibility. On the other hand, it caused military expenditure to rise in geometrical progression and thereby forced up taxes to exorbitant levels and so drove the poorer classes of people into the arms of socialism. The annexation of Alsace-Lorraine, the immediate cause of the mad competition in armaments, was able to set the French and German bourgeoisie chauvinistically at each other's throats; for the workers of the two countries it became a new bond of unity. And the anniversary of the Paris Commune became the first universal day of celebration of the whole proletariat.

The war of 1870–71 and the defeat of the Commune transferred the centre of gravity of the European workers' movement for the time being from France to Germany, as Marx had foretold. In France it naturally took years to recover from the blood-letting of May 1871. In Germany, on the other hand, where industry—fostered, in addition, in positively hothouse fashion by the blessing of the French milliards—developed more and more rapidly, Social-Democracy experienced a still more rapid and enduring growth. Thanks to the intelligent use which the German workers made of the universal suffrage introduced in 1866, the astonishing growth of the party is made plain to all the world by incontestable figures: 1871, 102,000; 1874, 352,000; 1877, 493,000 Social-Democratic votes. Then came recognition of this advance by high authority in the shape of the Anti-Socialist Law; the party was temporarily broken up, the number of votes dropped to 312,000 in 1881. But that was quickly overcome, and then, under the pressure of the Exceptional Law, without a press, without a legal organisation and without the right of combination and assembly, rapid expansion really began: 1884, 550,000; 1887, 763,000; 1890, 1,427,000 votes. Thereupon the hand of the state was paralysed. The Anti-Socialist Law disappeared; socialist votes rose to 1,787,000, over a quarter of all the votes cast. The government and the ruling classes had exhausted all their expedients —uselessly, purposelessly, unsuccessfully. The tangible proofs of their impotence, which the authorities, from night watchman to the imperial chancellor, had had to accept—and that from the despised workers!—these proofs were counted in millions. The state was at the end of its tether, the workers only at the beginning of theirs.

But, besides, the German workers rendered a second great service to their cause in addition to the first, a service performed by their mere existence as the strongest, best disciplined and most rapidly growing Socialist Party. They supplied their comrades in all countries with a new weapon, and one of the sharpest, when they showed them how to make use of universal suffrage.

There had long been universal suffrage in France, but it had fallen into disrepute through the misuse to which the Bonapartist government had put it. After the Commune there was no workers' party to make use of it. It also existed in Spain since the republic, but in Spain boycott of elections was ever the rule of all serious opposition parties. The experience of the Swiss with universal suffrage was also anything but encouraging for a workers' party. The revolutionary workers of the Latin countries had been wont to regard the suffrage as a snare, as an instrument of government trickery. It was otherwise in Germany. The *Communist Manifesto* had already proclaimed the winning of universal suffrage, of democracy, as one of the first and most important tasks of the militant proletariat, and Lassalle had again taken up this point. Now, when Bismarck found himself compelled to introduce this franchise as the only means of interesting the mass of the people in his plans, our workers immediately took it in earnest and sent August Bebel to the first, constituent Reichstag. And from that day on, they have used the franchise in a way which has paid them a thousandfold and has served as a model to the workers of all countries. The franchise has been...transformed by them from a means of deception, which it was before, into an instrument of emancipation. And if universal suffrage had offered no other advantage than that it allowed us to count our numbers every three years; that by the regularly established, unexpectedly rapid rise in the number of our votes it increased in equal measure the workers' certainty of victory and the dismay of their opponents, and so became our best means of propaganda; that it accurately informed us concerning our own strength and that of all hostile parties, and thereby provided us with a measure of proportion for our actions second to none, safeguarding us from untimely timidity as much as from untimely foolhardiness—if this had been the only advantage we gained from the suffrage, it would still have been much more than enough. But it did more than this by far. In election agitation it provided us with a means, second to none, of getting in touch with the mass of the people where they still stand aloof from us; of forcing all parties to defend their views and actions against our attacks before all the people; and, further, it provided our representatives in the Reichstag with a platform from which they could speak to their opponents in parliament, and to the masses without, with quite other authority and freedom than in the press or at meetings. Of what avail was their Anti-Socialist Law to the government and the bourgeoisie when election campaigning and socialist speeches in the Reichstag continually broke through it?

With this successful utilisation of universal suffrage, however, an entirely new method of proletarian struggle came into operation, and this method quickly developed further. It was found that the state institutions, in which the rule of the bourgeoisie is organised, offer the working class still further opportunities to fight these very state institutions. The workers took part in elections to particular Diets, to municipal councils and to trades courts; they contested with the bourgeoisie every post in the occupation of which a sufficient part of the proletariat had a say. And so it happened that the bourgeoisie and the government came to be much more afraid of the legal than of the illegal action of the workers' party, of the results of elections than of those of rebellion.

For here, too, the conditions of the struggle had essentially changed. Rebellion in the old style, street fighting with barricades, which decided the issue everywhere up to 1848, was to a considerable extent obsolete.

Let us have no illusions about it: a real victory of an insurrection over the military in street fighting, a victory as between two armies, is one of the rarest exceptions. And the insurgents counted on it just as rarely. . . .

Even in the classic time of street fighting. . .the barricade produced more of a moral than a material effect. It was a means of shaking the steadfastness of the military. If it held out until this was attained, victory was won; if not, there was defeat. This is the main point, which must be kept in view, likewise, when the chances of possible future street fighting are examined.*

Already in 1849, these chances were pretty poor. Everywhere the bourgeoisie had thrown in its lot with the governments, "culture and property" had hailed and feasted the military moving against insurrection. The spell of the barricade was broken; the soldier no longer saw behind it "the people," but rebels, agitators, plunderers, levellers, the scum of society; the officer had in the course of time become versed in the tactical forms of street fighting, he no longer marched straight ahead and without cover against the improvised breastwork, but went round it through gardens, yards and houses. And this was now successful, with a little skill, in nine cases out of ten.

But since then there have been very many more changes, and all in favour of the military. If the big towns have become considerably bigger, the armies have become bigger still. Paris and Berlin have, since 1848, grown less than fourfold, but their garrisons have grown more than that. By means of the railways, these garrisons can, in twenty-four hours, be more than doubled, and in forty-eight hours they can be increased to huge armies. The arming of this enormously increased number of troops has become incomparably more effective. In 1848 the smooth-bore, muzzle-loading percussion gun, today the small-calibre, breech-loading magazine rifle, which shoots four times as far, ten times as accurately and ten times as fast as the former. At that time the relatively ineffective round shot and grape-shot of the artillery; today the percussion shells, of which one is sufficient to demolish the best barricade. At that time the pick-axe of the sapper for breaking through firewalls; today the dynamite cartridge.

On the other hand, all the conditions of the insurgents' side have grown worse. An insurrection with which all sections of the people sympathise will hardly recur; in the class struggle all the middle strata will probably never group themselves round the proletariat so exclusively that in comparison the

*In *Die Neue Zeit* and in the 1895 edition of *The Class Struggles in France,* this sentence is omitted.—*Ed.*

party of reaction gathered round the bourgeoisie will well-nigh disappear. The "people," therefore, will always appear divided, and thus a most powerful lever, so extraordinarily effective in 1848, is gone. . . .

Does that mean that in the future street fighting will no longer play any role? Certainly not. It only means that the conditions since 1848 have become far more unfavourable for civilian fighters and far more favourable for the military. In future, street fighting can, therefore, be victorious only if this disadvantageous situation is compensated by other factors. . . .

The time of surprise attacks, of revolutions carried through by small conscious minorities at the head of unconscious masses, is past. Where it is a question of a complete transformation of the social organisation, the masses themselves must also be in it, must themselves already have grasped what is at stake, what they are going in for, body and soul. The history of the last fifty years has taught us that. But in order that the masses may understand what is to be done, long, persistent work is required, and it is just this work that we are now pursuing, and with a success which drives the enemy to despair. . . .

Of course, our foreign comrades do not thereby in the least renounce their right to revolution. The right to revolution is, after all, the only *really* "historical right," the only right on which all modern states without exception rest. . . .

But whatever may happen in other countries, the German Social-Democracy occupies a special position and therewith, at least in the immediate future, has a special task. The two million voters whom it sends to the ballot box, together with the young men and women who stand behind them as non-voters, form the most numerous, most compact mass, the decisive "shock force" of the international proletarian army. This mass already supplies over a fourth of the votes cast; and as the by-elections to the *Reichstag,* the Diet elections in individual states, the municipal council and trades court elections demonstrate, it increases incessantly. Its growth proceeds as spontaneously, as steadily, as irresistibly, and at the same time as tranquilly as a natural process. All government intervention has proved powerless against it. We can count even today on two and a quarter million voters. If it continues in this fashion, by the end of the century we shall conquer the greater part of the middle strata of society, petty bourgeois and small peasants, and grow into the decisive power in the land, before which all other powers will have to bow, whether they like it or not. To keep this growth going without interruption until it or itself gets beyond the control of the prevailing governmental system, not to fritter away this daily increasing shock force in vanguard skirmishes, but to keep it intact until the decisive day,* that is our main task. And there is only one means by which the steady rise of the socialist fighting forces in Germany could be temporarily halted, and even thrown back for some time: a clash on a big scale with the military, a blood-letting like that of 1871 in Paris. In the long run that would also be overcome. To shoot a party which numbers millions out of existence is too much even for all the magazine rifles of Europe and America. But the normal development would be impeded, the shock force

*In *Die Neue Zeit* and the 1895 edition of *The Class Struggles in France,* the words "not to fritter away this daily increasing shock force in vanguard skirmishes, but to keep it intact until the decisive day" are omitted.—*Ed.*

would, perhaps, not be available at the critical moment, the decisive combat* would be delayed, protracted and attended by heavier sacrifices.

The irony of world history turns everything upside down. We, the "revolutionists," the "overthrowers"—we are thriving far better on legal methods than on illegal methods and overthrow. The parties of Order, as they call themselves, are perishing under the legal conditions created by themselves. They cry despairingly with Odilon Barrot: *la légalité nous tue,* legality is the death of us; whereas we, under this legality, get firm muscles and rosy cheeks and look like life eternal. And if *we* are not so crazy as to let ourselves be driven to street fighting in order to please them, then in the end there is nothing left for them to do but themselves break through this fatal legality. . . .

Engels, "Introduction" to Marx's *Class Struggles* (1891), MESW, pp. 654–66.

8.B.9 THE **MANIFESTO** *AND THE COMMUNIST PROGRAM*

Proletarians and Communists

In what relation do the Communists stand to the proletarians as a whole?

The Communists do not form a separate party opposed to other working-class parties.

They have no interest separate and apart from those of the proletariat as a whole.

They do not set up any sectarian principles of their own, by which to shape and mold the proletarian movement.

The Communists are distinguished from the other working-class parties by this only: (1) In the national struggles of the proletarians of the different countries, they point out and bring to the front the common interests of the entire proletariat independently of all nationality. (2) In the various stages of development which the struggle of the working class against the bourgeoisie has to pass through, they always and everywhere represent the interest of the movement as a whole.

The Communists, therefore, are on the one hand, practically, the most advanced and resolute section of the working-class parties of every country, that section which pushes forward all others; on the other hand, theoretically, they have over the great mass of the proletariat the advantage of clearly understanding the line of march, the conditions, and the ultimate general results of the proletarian movement.

The immediate aim of the Communists is the same as that of all the other proletarian parties, formation of the proletariat into a class, overthrow of the bourgeois supremacy, conquest of political power by the proletariat.

*In *Die Neue Zeit* and the 1895 edition of *The Class Struggles in France,* the words "the shock force would, perhaps, not be available at the critical moment" are omitted, and the word "decision" is given instead of "the decisive combat."—*Ed.*

The theoretical conclusions of the Communists are in no way based on ideas or principles that have been invented, or discovered, by this or that would-be universal reformer.

They merely express, in general terms, actual relations springing from an existing class struggle, from a historical movement going on under our very eyes. The abolition of existing property relations is not at all a distinctive feature of communism.

All property relations in the past have continually been subject to historical changes consequent upon the change in historical conditions.

The French Revolution, for example, abolished feudal property in favor of bourgeois property.

The distinguishing feature of communism is not the abolition of property generally, but the abolition of bourgeois property. But modern bourgeois private property is the final and most complete expression of the system of producing and appropriating products that is based on class antagonism, on the exploitation of the many by the few.

In this sense, the theory of the Communists may be summed up in the single sentence: Abolition of private property.

We Communists have been reproached with the desire of abolishing the right of personally acquiring property as the fruit of a man's own labour, which property is alleged to be the groundwork of all personal freedom, activity, and independence.

Hard-won, self-acquired, self-earned property! Do you mean the property of the petty artisan and of the small peasant, a form of property that preceded the bourgeois form? There is no need to abolish that; the development of industry has to a great extent already destroyed it, and is still destroying it daily.

Or do you mean modern bourgeois private property?

But does wage labour create any property for the labourer? Not a bit. It creates capital, i.e., that kind of property which exploits wage labour, and which cannot increase except upon condition of getting a new supply of wage labour for fresh exploitation. Property, in its present form, is based on the antagonism of capital and wage labour. Let us examine both sides of this antagonism.

To be a capitalist is to have not only a purely personal but a social status in production. Capital is a collective product, and only by the united action of many members, nay, in the last resort, only by the united action of all members of society, can it be set in motion.

Capital is therefore not a personal, it is a social power.

When, therefore, capital is converted into common property, into the property of all members of society, personal property is not thereby transformed into social property. It is only the social character of the property that is changed. It loses its class character.

Let us now take wage labour.

The average price of wage labour is the minimum wage, i.e., that quantum of the means of subsistence which is absolutely requisite to keep the labourer in bare existence as a labourer. What, therefore, the wage labourer appropriates by means of his labor merely suffices to prolong and reproduce a bare existence. We by no means intend to abolish this personal appropriation of the products of labour, an appropriation that is made for the maintenance and reproduction of human life, and that leaves no surplus wherewith to command the labour of others. All that we want to do away with is the miserable character of this appropriation, under which the labourer lives merely to increase capital, and is allowed to live only insofar as the interest of the ruling class requires it.

In bourgeois society, living labour is but a means to increase accumulated labor. In Communist society, accumulated labour is but a means to widen, to enrich, to promote the existence of the labourer.

In bourgeois society, therefore, the past dominates the present; in Communist society, the present dominates the past. In bourgeois society capital is independent and has individuality, while the living person is dependent and has no individuality.

And the abolition of this state of things is called by the bourgeois abolition of individuality and freedom! And rightly so. The abolition of bourgeois individuality, bourgeois independence, and bourgeois freedom is undoubtedly aimed at.

By freedom is meant, under the present bourgeois conditions of production, free trade, free selling and buying.

But if selling and buying disappears, free selling and buying disappears also. This talk about free selling and buying, and all the other "brave words" of our bourgeoisie about freedom in general, have a meaning, if any, only in contrast with restricted selling and buying, with the fettered traders of the Middle Ages, but have no meaning when opposed to the communistic abolition of buying and selling, of the bourgeois conditions of production, and of the bourgeoisie itself.

You are horrified at our intending to do away with private property. But in your existing society private property is already done away with for nine-tenths of the population; its existence for the few is solely due to its non-existence in the hands of those nine-tenths. You reproach us, therefore, with intending to do away with a form of property the necessary condition for whose existence is the nonexistence of any property for the immense majority of society.

In a word, you reproach us with intending to do away with your property. Precisely so; that is just what we intend.

From the moment when labour can no longer be converted into capital, money, or rent, into a social power capable of being monopolized—i.e., from the moment when individual property can no longer be transformed into bourgeois property, into capital—from that moment, you say, individuality vanishes.

You must, therefore, confess that by "individual" you mean no other person than the bourgeois, than the middle-class owner of property. This person must indeed be swept out of the way, and made impossible.

Communism deprives no man of the power to appropriate the products of society: all that it does is to deprive him of the power to subjugate the labour of others by means of such appropriation.

It has been objected that upon the abolition of private property all work will cease, and universal laziness will overtake us.

According to this, bourgeois society ought long ago to have gone to the dogs through sheer idleness; for those of its members who work acquire nothing, and those who acquire anything do not work. The whole of this objection is but another expression of the tautology that there can no longer be any wage labour when there is no longer any capital. . . .

The Communists are further reproached with desiring to abolish countries and nationalities.

The workingmen have no country. We cannot take away from them what they have not got. Since the proletariat must first of all acquire political supremacy, must rise to be the leading class of the nation, must constitute itself the nation, it is so far itself national, though not in the bourgeois sense of the word.

National differences, and antagonisms between peoples, are daily more and more vanishing, owing to the development of the bourgeoisie, to freedom of commerce, to the world market, to uniformity in the mode of production and in the conditions of life corresponding thereto.

The supremacy of the proletariat will cause them to vanish still faster. United action, of the leading civilized countries at least, is one of the first conditions for the emancipation of the proletariat.

In proportion as the exploitation of one individual by another is put an end to, the exploitation of one nation by another will also be put an end to. In proportion as the antagonism between classes within the nation vanishes, the hostility of one nation to another will come to an end. . . .

We have seen above that the first step in the revolution by the working class is to raise the proletariat to the position of ruling class, to win the battle of democracy.

The proletariat will use its political supremacy to wrest, by degrees, all capital from the bourgeoisie, to centralize all instruments of production in the hands of the state, i.e., of the proletariat organized as the ruling class; and to increase the total of productive forces as rapidly as possible.

Of course, in the beginning this cannot be effected except by means of despotic inroads on the rights of property, and on the conditions of bourgeois production, by means of measures, therefore, which appear economically insufficient and untenable, but which, in the course of the movement, outstrip themselves, necessitate further inroads upon the old social order, and are unavoidable as a means of entirely revolutionizing the mode of production.

These measures will of course be different in different countries.

Nevertheless, in the most advanced countries the following will be pretty generally applicable:

1. Abolition of property in land and application of all rents of land to public purposes.
2. A heavy progressive or graduated income tax.
3. Abolition of all right of inheritance.
4. Confiscation of the property of all emigrants and rebels.
5. Centralization of credit in the hands of the state, by means of a national bank with state capital and an exclusive monopoly.
6. Centralization of the means of communication and transport in the hands of the state.
7. Extension of factories and instruments of production owned by the state,

the bringing into cultivation of wastelands, and the improvement of the soil generally in accordance with a common plan.

8. Equal liability of all to labour. Establishment of industrial armies, especially for agriculture.
9. Combination of agriculture with manufacturing industries; gradual abolition of the distinction between town and country, by a more equable distribution of population over the country.
10. Free education for all children in public schools. Abolition of children's factory labour in its present form. Combination of education with industrial production, etc., etc.

Position of the Communists in Relation to the Various Existing Opposition Parties

The Communists fight for the attainment of the immediate aims, for the enforcement of the momentary interests of the working class; but in the movement of the present, they also represent and take care of the future of that movement. In France the Communists ally themselves with the Social Democrats against the conservatives and radical bourgeoisie, reserving, however, the right to take up a critical position in regard to phrases and illusions traditionally handed down from the great Revolution.

In Switzerland they support the Radicals, without losing sight of the fact that this party consists of antagonistic elements, partly of democratic socialists in the French sense, partly of radical bourgeois.

In Poland they support the party that insists on an agrarian revolution as the prime condition for national emancipation, that party which fomented the insurrection of Cracow in 1846.

In Germany they fight with the bourgeoisie whenever it acts in a revolutionary way, against the absolute monarchy, the feudal squirearchy, and the petty bourgeoisie.

But they never cease, for a single instant, to instill into the working class the clearest possible recognition of the hostile antagonism between bourgeoisie and proletariat, in order that the German workers may straightway use, as so many weapons against the bourgeoisie, the social and political conditions that the bourgeoisie must necessarily introduce along with its supremacy, and in order that, after the fall of the reactionary classes in Germany, the fight against the bourgeoisie itself may immediately begin.

The Communists turn their attention chiefly to Germany because that country is on the eve of a bourgeois revolution that is bound to be carried out under more advanced conditions of European civilization, and with a more developed proletariat, than that of England was in the seventeenth, and of France in the eighteenth century, and because the bourgeois revolution in Germany will be but the prelude to an immediately following proletarian revolution.

In short, the Communists everywhere support every revolutionary movement against the existing social and political order of things.

In all these movements they bring to the front, as the leading question in each, the property question, no matter what its degree of development at the time.

Finally, they labour everywhere for the union and agreement of the democratic parties of all countries.

The Communists disdain to conceal their views and aims. They openly declare that their ends can be attained only by the forcible overthrow of all existing social conditions. Let the ruling classes tremble at a Communist revolution. The proletarians have nothing to lose but their chains. They have a world to win.

Workingmen of all countries, unite!

Marx-Engels, *Communist Manifesto,* excerpts from Parts II and IV.

8.B.10 REVOLUTIONARY STRATEGY IN AN INHOSPITABLE ENVIRONMENT

THE CENTRAL COUNCIL TO THE LEAGUE

Brothers! ... After the defeat of the revolutionary parties of Germany and France in July 1849, almost all the members of the Central Council came together again in London, supplemented their numbers with new revolutionary forces, and set about the reorganisation of the League with renewed zeal.

Reorganisation can only be carried out by an emissary and the Central Council considers it extremely important that the emissary should leave precisely at this moment when a new revolution[1] is imminent, when the Workers' Party, therefore, must act in the most organised, most united and most independent fashion if it is not to be exploited and taken in tow again by the bourgeoisie as in 1848.

Brothers! We told you as early as 1848 that the German liberal bourgeois would soon come to power and would immediately turn their newly acquired power against the workers. You have seen how this has been fulfilled. In fact, it was the bourgeois who, after the March movement of 1848, immediately took possession of the state power and used this power at once to force back the workers, their allies in the struggle, into their former oppressed position. If the bourgeoisie was not able to accomplish this without uniting with the feudal

[1]When the Address of the Central Council to the Communist League was written in March 1850, Marx still believed that a new upsurge of the revolutionary wave was imminent. However, in September 1850, after a careful analysis of the world economic situation, he had already come to the conclusion that an upward movement in the development of capitalism had set in. This upward movement is the "mother of counter-revolution" just as "the world trade crisis of 1847 has been the real mother of the February and March Revolutions."

party which had been defeated in March, without finally even surrendering power once again to this feudal absolutist party, still it has secured conditions for itself which, in the long run, owing to the financial embarrassment of the government would have placed power in its hands and would have safeguarded all its interests, if it were possible that the revolutionary movement was already passing into a so-called peaceful development. The bourgeoisie would not even have found it necessary, in order to safeguard their domination, to make themselves obnoxious to the people by violent measures since all such violent steps had already been taken by the feudal counter-revolution. Developments, however, will not take this peaceful course. On the contrary, the revolution which will accelerate this development is near at hand, whether it will be called forth by an independent upheaval of the French proletariat or by the invasion of the Holy Alliance against the revolutionary Babylon.

And the role, this so treacherous role, which the German liberal bourgeois of 1848 have played against the people, will in the coming revolution be taken over by the democratic petty bourgeois, who at present occupy the same position in the opposition as the liberal bourgeois before 1848. This party, the Democratic Party,...is far more dangerous to the workers than the previous liberal one. ...

[Its] fractions now...call themselves "republicans" or "Reds," just as the republican petty bourgeois in France now call themselves socialists. ... It is evident...that the altered name of this party does not make the slightest change in relation to the workers, but merely proves that they are now obliged to turn against the bourgeoisie, which is united with absolutism, and to support themselves on the proletariat.

The petty-bourgeois Democratic Party in Germany is very powerful; it comprises not only the great majority of the bourgeois inhabitants of the towns, the small industrial businessmen and guild masters, it numbers among its following the peasants and the rural proletariat, in so far as the latter has not yet found a support in the independent proletariat of the towns.

The relation of the revolutionary workers' party to petty-bourgeois democracy is this: it marches together with it against the section which it aims at overthrowing, it opposes the petty-bourgeois in everything by which they desire to establish themselves.

The democratic petty bourgeois, far from desiring to revolutionise all society for the revolutionary proletarians, strive for a change in social conditions by means of which existing society will be made as tolerable and comfortable as possible for them. Hence they demand above all diminution of state expenditure by restricting the bureaucracy and shifting the chief taxes on to the big landowners and bourgeois. Further, they demand the abolition of the pressure of big capital on small, through public credit institutions and laws against usury, by which means it will be possible for them and the peasants to obtain advances, on favourable conditions, from the state instead of from the capitalists; and, further, they demand the establishment of bourgeois property relations in the countryside by the complete abolition of feudalism. In order to accomplish all this, they require a democratic state constitution, whether constitutional or republican, giving a majority to them and their allies, the peasants, as well as a democratic local government which would give them control over municipal property and over a series of functions now performed by the bureaucrats.

The domination and speedy increase of capital is further to be counteracted partly by limiting the right of inheritance and party by transferring as many works as possible to the state. As far as the workers are concerned, it remains certain above all that they are to remain wage workers as before; the democratic petty bourgeois only desire better wages and a secure existence for the workers and hope to achieve this through partial employment by the state and through charity measures, in short, they hope to bribe the workers by more or less concealed alms and to break their revolutionary force by making their position tolerable for the moment. . . . But these demands can in no wise suffice for the party of the proletariat. While the democratic petty bourgeois wish to bring the revolution to a conclusion as quickly as possible and with the achievement at most of the above demands, it is our interest and our task to make the revolution permanent, until all more or less possessing classes have been displaced from domination, until the proletariat has conquered state power, and the association of proletarians, not only in one country but in all the dominant countries of the world, has advanced so far that competition among the proletarians of these countries has ceased and that at least the decisive productive forces are concentrated in the hands of the proletarians. For us the issue cannot be the alteration of private property but only its abolition, not the smoothing over of class antagonisms but the abolition of classes, not the improvement of existing society but the foundation of a new one. That, during the further development of the revolution, petty-bourgeois democracy will for a moment obtain predominating influence in Germany is not open to doubt. The question, therefore, arises as to what the attitude of the proletariat and in particular of the League will be in relation to it:

1. During the continuance of the present conditions where the petty-bourgeois democrats are likewise oppressed;
2. In the next revolutionary struggle which will give them the upper hand;
3. After this struggle, during the period of preponderance over the overthrown classes and the proletariat.

1) At the present moment, when the democratic petty bourgeois are everywhere oppressed, they preach in general unity and reconciliation to the proletariat, they offer them their hand and strive for the establishment of a large opposition party which will embrace all shades of opinion in the Democratic Party, i.e., they strive to involve the workers in a party organisation in which general Social-Democratic phrases predominate, behind which their special interests are concealed and in which the particular demands of the proletariat may not be brought forward for the sake of beloved peace. Such a union would turn out solely to their advantage and altogether to the disadvantage of the proletariat. The proletariat would lose its whole independent, laboriously obtained position and once more sink down to being an appendage of official bourgeois democracy. This union must, therefore, be most decisively rejected. Instead of once again stooping to serve as the applauding chorus of the bour-

geois democrats, the workers, and above all the League, must strive to establish an independent, secret and open, organisation of the Workers' Party alongside the official democrats and make each local section the central point and nucleus of workers' associations in which the attitude and interests of the proletariat will be discussed independently of bourgeois influences. . . . In the case of a struggle against a common opponent no special union is required. As soon as such an opponent has to be fought directly, the interests of both parties, for the moment, coincide, and, as previously, so also in the future, this union calculated only for the moment will arise of itself. It is self-evident that in the coming bloody conflicts, as in all earlier ones, it is the workers who, in the main, will have to win the victory by their courage, determination and self-sacrifice. As previously, so also in this struggle, the mass of the petty bourgeois will behave as long as possible in a hesitating, undecided and inactive manner, and then, as soon as the victory has been decided, take possession of it for themselves, call upon the workers to maintain tranquillity and return to their work, guard against so-called excesses and exclude the proletariat from the fruits of victory. It is not in the power of the workers to restrain the petty-bourgeois democrats from doing this, but it is in their power to make it difficult for them to push forward in the face of the armed proletariat and to dictate such conditions to them that the rule of the bourgeois democrats from the outset bears within it the seeds of its downfall, and their later supplanting by the rule of the proletariat will be considerably facilitated. Above all things, the workers must counteract, as much as is at all possible during the conflict and immediately after the struggle, the bourgeois endeavours to allay the storm, and must compel the democrats to carry out their present terrorist phrases. They must act so as to prevent the immediately revolutionary excitement from being suppressed again immediately after the victory. On the contrary, they must maintain it as long as possible. Far from opposing so-called excesses, instances of popular revenge against hated individuals or public buildings that are only associated with hateful recollections, such instances must not only be tolerated but the leadership of them must be taken in hand. During the struggle and after the struggle the workers must at every opportunity put forward their own demands alongside of the demands of the bourgeois democrats. They must demand guarantees for the workers as soon as the democratic bourgeois set about taking over the government. If necessary they must obtain these guarantees by force and in general they must ensure that the new rulers pledge themselves to all possible concessions and promises—the surest way to compromise them. In general, they must in every way restrain as far as possible the intoxication of victory and the enthusiasm for the new state of things, which make their appearance after every victorious street battle, by a calm and cold-blooded estimate of the conditions and by unconcealed mistrust in the new government. Alongside of the new official governments they must establish simultaneously their own revolutionary workers' governments, whether in the form of municipal committees and municipal councils or in the form of workers' clubs or workers' committees, so that the bourgeois-democratic governments not only immediately lose their backing by the workers but from the outset see themselves supervised and threatened by authorities which are backed by the whole mass of the workers. In a word, from the first moment of victory mistrust must be directed not against the conquered reactionary party, but against the workers' previous allies, against the party that wishes to exploit the common victory for itself alone.

2) But in order to be able energetically and threateningly to oppose this party whose treachery to the workers will begin from the first hour of victory, the workers must be armed and organised. . . . Destruction of the influence of the bourgeois democrats on the workers, immediate independent and armed organisation of the workers and the bringing about of conditions as difficult and compromising as possible for the immediately inevitable rule of bourgeois democracy, these are the main points which the proletariat and hence the League must keep in view during and after the coming insurrection.

3) As soon as the new governments have consolidated themselves to some extent, their struggle against the workers will immediately begin. In order here to oppose the democratic petty bourgeois by force it is above all necessary that the workers shall be independently organised and centralised through their clubs. After the overthrow of the existing governments, the Central Council will, as soon as it is at all possible, betake itself to Germany, immediately convene a congress and put before the latter the necessary provisions for the centralisation of the workers' clubs under a leadership established in the chief seat of the movement. The speedy organisation of at least a provincial union of the workers' clubs is one of the most important points for the strengthening and development of the Workers' Party; the immediate consequence of the overthrow of the existing governments will be the election of a National Assembly. Here the proletariat must see to it:

1. That under no pretext are numbers of workers excluded by any kind of trickery on the part of local authorities or government commissioners.

2) That everywhere workers' candidates are put up alongside of the bourgeois-democratic candidates, that they should consist as far as possible of members of the League, and that their election is promoted by all possible means. Even where there is no prospect whatsoever of their being elected, the workers must put up their own candidates in order to preserve their independence, to count their forces and to bring before the public their revolutionary attitude and party standpoint. In this connection they must not allow themselves to be seduced by the phrases of the democrats, such as, for example, that by this action they are splitting the Democratic Party and giving the reaction the possibility of victory. The final intention of all such phrases is that the proletariat shall be duped. The advance which the proletarian party is bound to make by such an independent action is infinitely more important than the disadvantage that might be caused by the presence of a few reactionaries in the representative body. If the democracy from the outset comes out decisively and with the use of terror against the reaction, then the influence of the latter in the elections will be destroyed in advance.

The first point on which the bourgeois democrats will come into conflict with the workers will be the abolition of feudalism. As in the first French Revolution, the petty bourgeois will give the feudal lands to the peasants as free property, that is to say, try to leave the rural proletariat in existence and form a petty-bourgeois peasant class which will go through the same cycle of impoverishment and indebtedness which the French peasant is now going through.

The workers must oppose this plan in the interests of the rural proletariat and in their own interests. They must demand that the confiscated feudal property remain state property and be converted into labour colonies cultivated by the associated rural proletariat with all the advantages of large-scale agriculture, through which the principle of common property immediately obtains a firm basis in the midst of the tottering bourgeois property relations. Just as the democrats combine with the peasants so must the workers combine with the rural proletariat. Further, the democrats will work either directly for the federated republic or, at least, if they cannot avoid the single and indivisible republic, they will attempt to cripple the central government by the utmost possible autonomy and independence on the part of the municipalities and provinces. The workers, in opposition to this plan, must not only strive for the single and indivisible German republic, but also strive in it for the most decisive centralisation of power in the hands of the state authority. They must not allow themselves to be led astray by the democratic talk of freedom for the municipalities, of self-government, etc. In a country like Germany where there are so many relics of the Middle Ages to be abolished, where there is so much local and provincial obstinacy to be broken, it must under no circumstances be permitted that every village, every town, and every province should put a new obstacle in the path of revolutionary activity, which can proceed in all its force only from the centre. It is not to be tolerated that the present state of things should be renewed, whereby Germans must fight separately for one and the same advance in every town and in every province. Least of all is it to be tolerated that there should be perpetuated by a so-called free municipal constitution a form of property, namely municipal property, which still lags behind modern private property and which everywhere is necessarily passing into the latter, together with the quarrels resulting from it between poor and rich municipalities, as well as the municipal civil law, with its trickery against the workers, that exists alongside of state civil law. As in France in 1793 so today in Germany the carrying through of the strictest centralisation is the task of the really revolutionary party.[1]

We have seen how the democrats will come to power with the next move-

[1]It must be recalled today that this passage is based on a misunderstanding. At that time it was considered—thanks to the Bonapartists and liberal falsifiers of history—as established that the French centralised machine of administration had been introduced by the Great Revolution and in particular that it had been operated by the Convention as an inevitable and decisive weapon for overcoming the royalist and federalist reaction and the external enemy. It is now, however, a well-known fact that throughout the whole revolution up to the eighteenth Brumaire the whole administration of the departments, arrondissements and municipalities consisted of authorities elected by the respective inhabitants themselves, which acted with complete freedom within the general state laws; that this provincial and local self-government, similar to the American, was precisely the most powerful lever of the revolution and indeed to such an extent that Napoleon, immediately after his *coup d'état* of the eighteenth Brumaire, hastened to replace it by the administration through prefects, which still exists and which, therefore, was a pure instrument of reaction from the beginning. But just as little as local and provincial self-government is in contradiction to political, national centralisation, so is it to an equally little extent necessarily bound up with that narrow-minded, cantonal or communal self-seeking which appears so repulsive in Switzerland, and which all the South German federal republicans wanted to make the rule in Germany in 1849. [*Note by F. Engels to the Zurich edition of 1885.*].

ment, how they will be compelled to propose more or less socialist measures. It will be asked what measures the workers ought to propose in reply. At the beginning of the movement, of course, the workers cannot yet propose any directly communist measures. But they can:

1) Compel the democrats to interfere in as many spheres as possible of the existing social order, to disturb its regular course and to compromise themselves, as well as to concentrate the utmost possible productive forces, means of transport, factories, railways, etc., in the hands of the state;

2) They must drive the proposals of the democrats, who in any case will not act in a revolutionary but in a merely reformist manner, to the extreme and transform them into direct attacks against private property; thus, for example, if the petty bourgeois propose purchase of the railways and factories, then the workers must demand that these railways and factories shall be simply confiscated by the state without compensation as being the property of reactionaries. If the democrats propose proportional taxes, the workers must demand progressive taxes; if the democrats themselves put forward a moderate progressive tax, the workers must insist on a tax with rates which rise so steeply that large-scale capital is ruined by it; if the democrats demand the regulation of state debts, the workers demand state bankruptcy. Thus, the demands of the workers must everywhere be governed by the concessions and measures of the democrats. . . .

[The German workers] will have to do the most for their final victory by becoming enlightened as to their class interests, by taking up their own independent party position as soon as possible and by not allowing themselves for a single moment to be led astray from the independent organisations of the party of the proletariat by the hypocritical phrases of the democratic petty bourgeois. Their battle-cry must be: the permanent revolution.

Marx-Engels, *Address of the Central Committee to the Communist League,* MESW, II, pp. 154–68.

8.B.11 DICTATORSHIP OF THE PROLETARIAT

And now as to myself, no credit is due to me for discovering the existence of classes in modern society or the struggle between them. Long before me bourgeois historians had described the historical development of this class struggle and bourgeois economists the economic anatomy of the classes. What I did that was new was to prove: 1) that the *existence of classes* is only bound up with *particular historical phases in the development of production,* 2) that the class struggle necessarily leads to *the dictatorship of the proletariat,* 3) that this dictatorship itself only constitutes the transition to the *abolition of all classes* and to a *classless society.* . . .

Marx, Letter to Wedemeyer (1852), MESW, p. 679.

Between capitalist and communist society lies the period of the revolutionary transformation of the one into the other. Corresponding to this is also a political transition period in which the state can be nothing but *the revolutionary dictatorship of the proletariat.*

Marx, *Gotha Programme* (1875), MESW, p. 331.

From the very outset the Commune was compelled to recognise that the working class, once come to power, could not go on managing with the old state machine; that in order not to lose again its only just conquered supremacy, this working class must, on the one hand, do away with all the old repressive machinery, previously used against it itself, and, on the other, safeguard itself against its own deputies and officials, by declaring them all, without exception, subject to recall at any moment. What had been the characteristic attribute of the former state? Society had created its own organs to look after its common interests, originally through simple division of labour. But these organs, at whose head was the state power, had in the course of time, in pursuance of their own special interests, transformed themselves from the servants of society into the masters of society. This can be seen, for example, not only in the hereditary monarchy, but equally so in the democratic republic. Nowhere do "politicians" form a more separate and powerful section of the nation than precisely in North America. There, each of the two major parties which alternately succeed each other in power is itself in turn controlled by people who make a business of politics, who speculate on seats in the legislative assemblies of the Union as well as of the separate states, or who make a living by carrying on agitation for their party and on its victory are rewarded with positions. It is well known how the Americans have been trying for thirty years to shake off this yoke, which has become intolerable, and how in spite of it all they continue to sink ever deeper in this swamp of corruption. It is precisely in America that we see best how there takes place this process of the state power making itself independent in relation to society, whose mere instrument it was originally intended to be. Here there exists no dynasty, no nobility, no standing army, beyond the few men keeping watch on the Indians, no bureaucracy with permanent posts or the right to pensions. And nevertheless we find here two great gangs of political speculators, who alternately take possession of the state power and exploit it by the most corrupt means and for the most corrupt ends—and the nation is powerless against these two great cartels of politicians, who are ostensibly its servants, but in reality dominate and plunder it.

Against this transformation of the state and the organs of the state from servants of society into masters of society—an inevitable transformation in all previous states—the Commune made use of two infallible means. In the first place, it filled all posts—administrative, judicial and educational—by election on the basis of universal suffrage of all concerned, subject to the right of recall at any time by the same electors. And, in the second place, all officials, high or low, were paid only the wages received by other workers. The highest salary paid by the Commune to anyone was 6,000 francs. In this way an effective barrier to place-hunting and careerism was set up, even apart from the binding mandates to delegates to representative bodies which were added besides.

This shattering of the former state power and its replacement by a new and truly democratic one is described in detail in the third section of *The Civil War*. But it was necessary to dwell briefly here once more on some of its features, because in Germany particularly the superstitious belief in the state has been carried over from philosophy into the general consciousness of the bourgeoisie and even of many workers. According to the philosophical conception, the state is the "realisation of the idea," or the Kingdom of God on earth, translated into philosophical terms, the sphere in which eternal truth and justice is or should be realised. And from this follows a superstitious reverence for the state and everything connected with it, which takes root the more readily since people are accustomed from childhood to imagine that the affairs and interests common to the whole of society could not be looked after otherwise than as they have been looked after in the past, that is, through the state and its lucratively positioned officials. And people think they have taken quite an extraordinarily bold step forward when they have rid themselves of belief in hereditary monarchy and swear by the democratic republic. In reality, however, the state is nothing but a machine for the oppression of one class by another, and indeed in the democratic republic no less than in the monarchy; and at best an evil inherited by the proletariat after its victorious struggle for class supremacy, whose worst sides the victorious proletariat, just like the Commune, cannot avoid having to lop off at once as much as possible until such time as a generation reared in new, free social conditions is able to throw the entire lumber of the state on the scrap heap.

Of late, the Social-Democratic philistine has once more been filled with wholesome terror at the words: Dictatorship of the Proletariat. Well and good, gentlemen, do you want to know what this dictatorship looks like? Look at the Paris Commune. That was the Dictatorship of the Proletariat.

Engels, *"Introduction" to the Civil War in France* (1891), MESW, pp. 261–62.

First. If anything at all is certain it is that our party and the working class can come to power only under the form of the democratic republic. This is even the specific form for the dictatorship of the proletariat, as the great French revolution has already demonstrated. It is certainly unthinkable that our best people should become ministers under an emperor, like Miquel.

Now it does not seem legally possible that one puts the demand for a republic directly into the program, although that was as possible even under Louis Philippe in France as it now is in Italy. But the fact that one may not even draw up an openly republican party program in Germany proves how colossal the illusion is, as if one could in a comfortable peaceful way there establish the republic, and not only the republic but the communist social order.

—Engels, "Zur Kritik des sozialdemokratischen Programmentwurfes 1891" (Toward a Critique of the Social Democratic Program Draft 1891). Cited in Freedman, MST, p. 278.

C. REVOLUTIONARY EXPERIENCE AND PROSPECTS

Selections in this concluding section focus on revolutionary experience and prospects in various countries. Selection 8.C.12 gives an overview of Marx's outlook for the future, with reference to England (the classic case), Germany, and (briefly) the United States. Selection 8.C.13 describes class struggles in France between 1848 and 1851. This selection presents a view of class relations that is much broader than the simplified two-class model of the *Manifesto;* it also introduces an interesting variation into the theory of capitalism vis-a-vis the working class and prospective revolution. Although more politically advanced than England (and more steeped in revolutionary experience), France was less economically developed; its large agricultural sector contained a politically strategic but conservative and passive class of small peasantry, whose system of small and inefficient landholdings was established by the French Revolution. Although the government, under the ineffectual though despotic Louis Napoleon, presented itself as the protector of society against the perceived excesses of prospective proletarian democracy, it was actually controlled by financial capitalists and bankers. Without modifying the legal forms of property, these people, according to Marx, were regulating the economy, holding industrial labor in check, and, through financial manipulation (public debt, government loans, subsidies), bilking the citizenry for their own private benefit.

As noted earlier, in Marx's letter of 1881 to Dutch socialist Domela-Nieuwenhuis (selection 8.B.7), Marx believed that the Paris Commune, a short-lived popular uprising of 1870–71, was "merely a revolt of a city under exceptional conditions," and that "the majority of the Commune was in no way socialistic, and could not be." At the same time, Marx found much to admire in the organization and functioning of the Commune, as a prospective model of the transition period as well as of the future society[7] (selection 8.C.14).

In the final selection of this chapter (8.C.15), Marx briefly and Engels at greater length explore the possibilities of social revolution in Russia. According to Engels, "Russia is undoubtedly on the eve of a revolution" against Czarist autocracy and reaction. What of the possibility that because of its experience with communal ownership of land, Russia might bypass western patterns of development and move directly to communist forms of ownership? Marx's brief answer: Whatever possibilities exist depend upon the Russian Revolution's becoming "the signal for a proletarian revolution in the West, so that both complement each other."[8]

8.C.12 OVERVIEW

In this work I have to examine the capitalist mode of production, and the conditions of production and exchange corresponding to that mode. Up to the present time, their classic ground is England. That is the reason why England is used as the chief illustration in the development of my theoretical ideas. If,

[7]See Shlomo Avineri, *The Social & Political Thought of Karl Marx* (New York: Cambridge, 1968), pp. 239 ff. for further discussion of this theme.

[8]This prospect figured heavily in the early twentieth century writings of Russian Marxists as well in the policy debates between Stalin and Trotsky in the 1920s.

however, the German reader shrugs his shoulders at the condition of the English industrial and agricultural laborers, or in optimist fashion comforts himself with the thought that in Germany things are not nearly so bad, I must plainly tell him, *"De te fabula narratur!"*

Intrinsically, it is not a question of the higher or lower degree of development of the social antagonisms that result from the natural laws of capitalist production. It is a question of these laws themselves, of these tendencies working with iron necessity towards inevitable results. The country that is more developed industrially only shows, to the less developed, the image of its own future.

But apart from this. Where capitalist production is fully naturalised among the Germans (for instance, in the factories proper) the condition of things is much worse than in England, because the counterpoise of the Factory Acts is wanting. In all other spheres, we, like all the rest of Continental Western Europe, suffer not only from the development of capitalist production, but also from the incompleteness of that development. Alongside of modern evils, a whole series of inherited evils oppress us, arising from the passive survival of antiquated modes of production, with their inevitable train of social and political anachronisms. We suffer not only from the living, but from the dead. *Le mort saisit le vif!*

The social statistics of Germany and the rest of Continental Western Europe are, in comparison with those of England, wretchedly compiled. But they raise the veil just enough to let us catch a glimpse of the Medusa head behind it. We should be appalled at the state of things at home, if, as in England, our governments and parliaments appointed periodically commissions of enquiry into economic conditions; if these commissions were armed with the same plenary power to get at the truth; if it was possible to find for this purpose men as competent, as free from partisanship and respect of persons as are the English factory-inspectors, her medical reporters on public health, her commissioners of enquiry into the exploitation of women and children, into housing and food. Perseus wore a magic cap that the monsters he hunted down might not see him. We draw the magic cap down over eyes and ears as a make-believe that there are no monsters. Let us not deceive ourselves on this. As in the eighteenth century, the American war of independence sounded the tocsin for the European middle-class, so in the nineteenth century, the American civil war sounded it for the European working-class. In England the progress of social disintegration is palpable. When it has reached a certain point, it must react on the continent. There it will take a form more brutal or more humane, according to the degree of development of the working-class itself. Apart from higher motives, therefore, their own most important interests dictate to the classes that are for the nonce the ruling ones, the removal of all legally removable hindrances to the free development of the working-class. For this reason, as well as others, I have given so large a space in this volume to the history, the details, and the results of English factory legislation. One nation can and should learn from others. And even when a society has got upon the right track for the discovery of the natural laws of its movement—and it is the ultimate aim of this work, to lay bare the economic law of motion of modern society—it can neither clear by bold leaps, nor remove by legal enactments, the obstacles offered by the successive phases of its normal development. But it can shorten and lessen the birth-pangs.

To prevent possible misunderstanding, a word. I paint the capitalist and the landlord in no sense *couleur de rose.* But here individuals are dealt with only in so far as they are the personifications of economic categories, embodiments of particular class-relations and class-interests. My stand-point, from which the evolution of the economic formation of society is viewed as a process of natural history, can less than any other make the individual responsible for relations whose creature he socially remains, however much he may subjectively raise himself above them.

In the domain of Political Economy, free scientific enquiry meets not merely the same enemies as in all other domains. The peculiar nature of the material it deals with, summons as foes into the field of battle the most violent, mean and malignant passions of the human breast, the Furies of private interest. The English Established Church e.g., will more readily pardon an attack on 38 of its 39 articles than on $^1/_{39}$ of its income. . . . The representatives of the English Crown in foreign countries there declare in so many words that in Germany, in France, to be brief, in all the civilised states of the European continent, a radical change in the existing relations between capital and labor is as evident and inevitable as in England. At the same time, on the other side of the Atlantic Ocean, Mr. Wade, vice-president of the United States, declared in public meetings that, after the abolition of slavery, a radical change of the relations of capital and of property in land is next upon the order of the day. These are signs of the times, not to be hidden by purple mantles or black cassocks. They do not signify that tomorrow a miracle will happen. They show that, within the ruling-classes themselves, a foreboding is dawning, that the present society is no solid crystal, but an organism capable of change, and is constantly changing.

Marx, *Capital,* I (1867), pp. 13–16.

8.C.13 FRANCE

THE CLASS STRUGGLES IN FRANCE

With the exception of a few short chapters, every important part of the annals of the revolution from 1848 to 1849 carries the heading: *Defeat of the revolution!*

But what succumbed in these defeats was not the revolution. It was the pre-revolutionary traditional appendages, results of social relationships, which had not yet come to the point of sharp class antagonisms—persons, illusions, conceptions, projects, from which the revolutionary party before the February Revolution was not free, from which it could be freed, not by the *victory of February,* but only by a series of *defeats.*

In a word: revolutionary advance made headway not by its immediate tragi-comic achievements, but on the contrary by the creation of a powerful, united counter-revolution, by the creation of an opponent, by fighting whom the party of revolt first ripened into a real revolutionary party.

To prove this is the task of the following pages.

After the July [1830] Revolution, when the Liberal banker, Laffitte, led his godfather, the Duke of Orleans, in triumph to the Hotel de Ville, he let fall the words: *"From now on the bankers will rule."* Laffitte had betrayed the secret of the revolution.

It was not the French bourgeoisie that ruled under Louis Philippe, but a *fraction* of it, bankers, stock exchange kings, railway kings, owners of coal and iron works and forests, a part of the landed proprietors that rallied round them—the so-called *finance aristocracy.* It sat on the throne, it dictated laws in the Chambers, it conferred political posts from cabinet portfolios to the tobacco bureau.

The real *industrial bourgeoisie* formed part of the official opposition, i.e., it was represented only as a minority in the Chambers. Its opposition was expressed all the more decisively, the more unalloyed the autocracy of the finance aristocracy became, and the more it itself imagined that its domination over the working class was ensured after the mutines of 1832, 1834 and 1839, which had been drowned in blood. . . .

The *petty bourgeoisie* of all degrees, and the *peasantry* also, were completely excluded from political power. Finally, in the official opposition,. . . there were the *ideological* representatives and spokesmen of the above classes, their savants, lawyers, doctors, etc., in a word: their so-called *talents.*

The July monarchy, owing to its financial need, was dependent from the beginning on the big bourgeoisie, and its dependence on the big bourgeoisie was the inexhaustible source of a growing financial need. It was impossible to subordinate state administration to the interests of national production without balancing the budget, establishing a balance between state expenses and income. And how was this balance to be established, without limiting state expenditure, i.e., without encroaching on interests which were so many supports of the ruling system, and without redistributing taxes, i.e., without putting a considerable share of the burden of taxes on the shoulders of the big bourgeoisie itself?

Moreover the fraction of the bourgeoisie that ruled and legislated through the Chambers had a *direct interest* in *state indebtedness.* The *state deficit* was even the main object of its speculation and played the chief role in its enrichment. At the end of each year a new deficit. After expiry of four or five years a new loan. And every new loan offered new opportunities to the finance aristocracy for defrauding the state which was kept artificially on the verge of bankruptcy—it had to contract with the bankers under the most unfavourable conditions. Each new loan gave a further opportunity for plundering the public, that had invested its capital in state bonds, by stock exchange manipulations into the secrets of which the government and the majority in the Chambers were admitted. In general, the fluctuation of state credits and the possession of state secrets gave the bankers and their associates in the Chambers and on the throne the possibility of evoking sudden, extraordinary fluctuations in the quotations of state bonds, the result of which was always bound to be the ruin of a mass of smaller capitalists and the fabulously rapid enrichment of the big gamblers. . . . The enormous sums which, in this way, flowed through the hands of the state facilitated, moreover, swindling contracts for deliveries, bribery, defalcations and all kinds of roguery. The defrauding of the state, just as it occurred on a large scale in connection with loans, was repeated in detail, in the state works. The relationship between Chamber and government multiplied itself as the relationship between individual departments and individual *entrepreneurs.*

In the same way as the ruling class exploited state expenditure in general and state loans, they exploited the *building of railways.* The Chambers piled the main burdens on the state, and secured the golden fruits to the speculating finance aristocracy. One recalls the scandals in the Chamber of Deputies, when by chance it came out that all the members of the majority, including a number of ministers, had taken part as shareholders in the very railway construction which as legislators they caused to be carried out afterwards at the cost of the state. . . .

The July monarchy was nothing other than a joint stock company for the exploitation of French national wealth, the dividends of which were divided among ministers, Chambers, 240,000 voters and their adherents. Louis Philippe was the director of this company. . . . Trade, industry, agriculture, shipping, the interests of the industrial bourgeoisie, were bound to be continually prejudiced and endangered under this system. The bourgeoisie in the July days had inscribed on its banner: *gouvernement à bon marché,* cheap government.

While the finance aristocracy made the laws, was at the head of the administration of the state, had command of all the organised public powers, dominated public opinion through facts and through the press, the same prostitution, the same shameless cheating, the same mania to get rich was repeated in every sphere, . . . to get rich not by production, but by pocketing the already available wealth of others. . . . The finance aristocracy, in its mode of acquisition as well as in its pleasures, is nothing but the *resurrection of the* lumpenproletariat *at the top of bourgeois society.* . . .

The eruption of the general discontent was finally accelerated and the sentiment for revolt ripened by *two economic world events.*

The *potato blight* and the *bad harvests* of 1845 and 1846 increased the general ferment among the people. The high cost of living of 1847 called forth bloody conflicts in France as well as on the rest of the Continent. As against the shameless orgies of the finance aristocracy, the struggle of the people for the first necessities of life! . . .

The second great economic event which hastened the outbreak of the revolution was a *general commercial and industrial crisis* in England. . . . The after effect of this crisis on the Continent had not yet spent itself when the February Revolution broke out.

The devastation of trade and industry caused by the economic epidemic made the autocracy of the finance aristocracy still more unbearable. Throughout the whole of France the bourgeois opposition evoked the *banquet agitation* for an *electoral reform* which should win for them the majority in the Chambers and overthrow the Ministry of the Bourse. In Paris the industrial crisis had, in particular, the result of throwing a number of manufacturers and big traders, who under the existing circumstances could no longer do any business in the foreign market, on to the home market. They set up large establishments, the competition of which ruined the *epiciers* and *boutiquiers en masse.* Hence the innumerable bankruptcies among this section of the Paris bourgeoisie, and hence their revolutionary action in February. It is known how. . . the July monarchy had to give way to a Provisional Government.

The *Provisional Government* which emerged from the February barricades necessarily mirrored in its composition the different parties which shared in the victory. It could not be anything but a *compromise between the different classes* which together had overturned the July throne, but whose interests were mutually antagonistic. The great *majority* of its members consisted of representatives of the bourgeoisie. . . . The working class had only two representatives, Louis Blanc and Albert.

If Paris, as a result of political centralisation, rules France, the workers, in moments of revolutionary earthquakes, rule Paris. The first act in the life of the Provisional Government was an attempt to escape from this overpowering influence, by an appeal from intoxicated Paris to sober France. Lamartine disputed the right of the barricade fighters to proclaim the republic, on the ground that only the majority of Frenchmen had that right; they must await their votes, the Parisian proletariat must not besmirch its victory by a usurpation. The bourgeoisie allowed the proletariat only *one* usurpation—that of fighting. . . .

Even the memory of the limited aims and motives which drove the bourgeoisie into the February Revolution was extinguished by the proclamation of the republic on the basis of universal suffrage. Instead of a few small fractions of the bourgeoisie, whole classes of French society were suddenly hurled into the circle of political power, forced to leave the boxes, the stalls and the gallery and to act in person upon the revolutionary stage! With the constitutional monarchy the semblance of a state power independently confronting bourgeois society also vanished, as well as the whole series of subordinate struggles which this semblance of power called forth!

The proletariat, by dictating the republic to the Provisional Government and through the Provisional Government to the whole of France, stepped into the foreground forthwith as an independent party, but at the same time challenged the whole of bourgeois France to enter the lists against it. What it won was the terrain for the fight for its revolutionary emancipation, but in no way this emancipation itself!

The first thing that the February republic had to do was rather to *complete the rule of the bourgeoisie* by allowing, besides the finance aristocracy, *all the propertied classes* to enter the circle of political power. The majority of the great landowners, the Legitimists, were emancipated from the political nullity to which they had been condemned by the July Monarchy. . . . The nominal proprietors, who form the great majority of the French people, the *peasants,* were put by universal suffrage in the position of arbiters of the fate of France. The February republic finally brought the rule of the bourgeoisie clearly into prominence, since it struck off the crown behind which capital kept itself concealed.

Just as the workers by fighting in the July [1830] days had won the *bourgeois monarchy,* so by fighting in the February [1848] days they won the *bour-*

geois republic. Just as the July monarchy had to proclaim itself as a monarchy *surrounded by republican institutions* so the February republic was forced to proclaim itself a republic *surrounded by social institutions.* The Parisian proletariat *compelled* this concession, too. . . .

In common with the bourgeoisie the workers had made the February Revolution, and *alongside* the bourgeoisie they sought to put through their interests, just as they had installed a worker in the Provisional Government itself alongside the bourgeois majority. *Organisation of labour!* But wage labour is the existing bourgeois organisation of labour. Without it there is no capital, no bourgeoisie, no bourgeois society. *Their own Ministry of Labour!* But the Ministries of Finance, of Trade, of Public Works—are not these the *bourgeois* Ministries of Labour? And *alongside* these a *proletarian* Ministry of Labour must be a Ministry of impotence, a Ministry of pious wishes, a commission of the Luxembourg. Just as the workers thought to emancipate themselves side by side with the bourgeoisie, so they thought they would be able to consummate a proletarian revolution within the national walls of France, side by side with the remaining bourgeois nations. But French production relations are conditioned by the foreign trade of France, by her position on the world market and the laws thereof; how should France break them without a European revolutionary war, which would strike back at the despot of the world market, England?

A class in which the revolutionary interests of society are concentrated, so soon as it has risen up, finds directly in its own situation the content and the material of its revolutionary activity: foes to be laid low, measures, dictated by the needs of the struggle, to be taken; the consequence of its own deeds drive it on. It makes no theoretical inquiries into its own task. The French working class had not attained this standpoint; it was still incapable of accomplishing its own revolution.

The development of the industrial proletariat is, in general, conditioned by the development of the industrial bourgeoisie. Only under its rule does the proletariat win the wider national existence which can raise its revolution to a national one, and itself create the modern means of production, which become just so many means of its revolutionary emancipation. Only bourgeois rule tears up the roots of feudal society and levels the ground on which a proletarian revolution is alone possible. In France industry is more developed and the bourgeoisie more revolutionary than elsewhere on the Continent. But was not the February Revolution directed immediately against the finance aristocracy? This fact proved that the industrial bourgeoisie did not rule France. The industrial bourgeoisie can only rule where modern industry shapes all property relations in conformity with itself, and industry can only win this power when it has conquered the world market, for national bounds are not wide enough for its development. But French industry, to a great extent, maintains its command even of the national market only through a more or less modified system of prohibitive duties. If, therefore, the French proletariat, at the moment of a revolution, possesses in Paris actual power and influence which spur it on to a drive beyond its means, in the rest of France it is crowded into single, scattered industrial centres, being almost lost in the superior numbers of peasants and petty bourgeois. The struggle against capital in its developed, modern form, in its culminating phase, the struggle of the industrial wage workers against the industrial bourgeois is in France a partial fact, which after the February days could so much the less supply against capital's secondary modes of exploitation, that of the peasants against the usury in mortgages, of the petty bourgeois against the wholesale dealer, banker and manufacturer, in a word, against bankruptcy, was still hidden in the general uprising against the finance aristocracy. Nothing is more understandable, then, than that the Paris proletariat sought to put through its own interests *side by side* with those of the bourgeoisie, instead of enforcing them as the revolutionary interests of society itself, and that it let the *red* flag be lowered to the tricolour. The French workers could not take a step forward, could not touch a hair of the bourgeois order before the course of the revolution had forced the mass of the nation, peasants and petty bourgeois, standing between the proletariat and the bourgeoisie to revolt against this order, against the rule of capital, to attach itself to the proletariat as its vanguard. . . .

Thus in the approaching *mêlée* between bourgeoisie and proletariat, all the advantages, all the decisive posts, all the middle sections of society were in the hands of the bourgeoisie, at the same time as the waves of the February Revolution rose high over the whole Continent, and each new post brought a new bulletin of revolution, now from Italy, now from Germany, now from the remotest parts of Southeastern Europe, and maintained the general exuberance of the people, giving it constant testimony of a victory that it had already lost. . . .

In the Constituent National Assembly, which met on May 4 [1848], the *bourgeois republicans, the republicans of the National* had the upper hand. Legitimists and even Orleanists at first only dared to show themselves under the mask of bourgeois republicanism. Only in the name of the republic could the fight against the proletariat be undertaken.

The republic dates from May 4, not from February 25, i.e., the republic recognised by the French people; it is not the republic which the Paris proletariat thrust upon the Provisional Government, not the republic with social institutions, not the dream picture which hovered before the fighters on the barricades. The republic proclaimed by the National Assembly, the sole legitimate republic, is the republic which is no revolutionary weapon against the bourgeois order, but rather its political reconstitution, the political reconsolidation of bourgeois society, in a word, *the bourgeois republic.* From the tribune of the National Assembly this contention resounded and in the entire republican and anti-republican bourgeois press it found its echo.

And we have seen how the February republic in reality was not and could not be other than a *bourgeois* republic; how the Provisional Government, nevertheless, was forced by the immediate pressure of the proletariat to announce it as a *republic with social institutions,* how the Paris proletariat was still incapable of going beyond the bourgeois republic otherwise than in *ideas,* in *imagination;* how it everywhere acted in its service when it really came to action; how the promises made to it became an unbearable danger for the new republic; how the whole life process of the Provisional Government was comprised in a continuous fight against the demands of the proletariat.

In the National Assembly all France sat in judgment on the Paris proletariat. It broke immediately with the social illusions of the February Revolution; it roundly proclaimed the *bourgeois republic,* nothing but the bourgeois republic. It at once excluded the representatives of the proletariat, Louis Blanc and Albert, from the Executive Commission appointed by it; it threw out the proposal of a special Labour Ministry, and received with stormy applause the statement of the Minister Trélat: "The question is merely one of *bringing labour back to its old conditions.*"

But all this was not enough. The February republic was won by the workers with the passive support of the bourgeoisie. The proletarians regarded themselves, and rightly, as the victors of February, and they made the proud claims of victors. They had to be vanquished on the streets, they had to be shown that they were worsted as soon as they fought, not *with* the bourgeoisie, but *against* the bourgeoisie. Just as the February republic, with its socialist concessions, required a battle of the proletariat, united with the bourgeoisie, against monarchy, so a second battle was necessary in order to sever the republic from the socialist concessions, in order to officially work out the bourgeois republic as dominant. The bourgeoisie had to refute the demands of the proletariat with arms in its hands. And the real birthplace of the bourgeois republic is not the *February victory;* it is the *June defeat.* . . .

The workers were left no choice. They had to starve or start to fight. They answered on June 22 with the tremendous insurrection in which the first great battle was fought between the two classes that split modern society. It was a fight for the preservation or annihilation of the *bourgeois order.* The veil that shrouded the republic was torn to pieces. . . .

The Paris proletariat was *forced* into the June insurrection by the bourgeoisie. In this lay its doom. Its immediate, admitted needs did not drive it to want to win the forcible overthrow of the bourgeoisie, nor was it equal to this task. The *Moniteur* had to inform it officially that the time was past when the republic saw any occasion to do honour to its illusions, and its defeat first convinced it of the truth that the slightest improvement in its position remains a *utopia within* the bourgeois republic, a utopia that becomes a crime as soon as it wants to realise it. In place of its demands, exuberant in form, but petty and even bourgeois still in content, the concession of which it wanted to wring from the February republic, there appeared the bold slogan of revolutionary struggle: *Overthrow the bourgeoisie! Dictatorship of the working class!*

By making its burial place the birth place of the bourgeois republic, the proletariat compelled the latter to come out forthwith in its pure form as the state whose admitted object is to perpetuate the rule of capital, the slavery of labour. Constantly faced by the scarred, irreconcilable, invincible enemy—invincible because its existence is the condition of the bourgeoisie's own life—bourgeois rule, freed from all fetters, was bound to turn immediately into *bourgeois terrorism.* With the proletariat removed for the time being from the stage and bourgeois dictatorship recognised officially, the middle sections, in the mass, had more and more to side with the proletariat as their position became more unbearable and their antagonism to the bourgeoisie became more acute. Just as earlier in its upsurge, so now they had to find in its defeat the cause of their misery.

If the June insurrection raised the self-reliance of the bourgeoisie all over the Continent, and caused it to league itself openly with the feudal monarchy against the people, what was the first sacrifice to this alliance? The Continental bourgeoisie itself. The June defeat prevented it from consolidating its rule and from bringing the people, half satisfied and half out of humour, to a standstill at the lowest stage of the bourgeois revolution.

Finally, the defeat of June divulged to the despotic powers of Europe the secret that France under all conditions must maintain peace abroad in order to be able to wage civil war at home. Thus the peoples who had begun the fight for their national independence were abandoned to the superior power of Russia, Austria and Prussia, but, at the same time, the fate of these national revolutions was subordinated to the fate of the proletarian revolution, robbed of its apparent independence, its independence of the great social revolution. The Hungarian shall not be free, nor the Pole, nor the Italian, as long as the worker remains a slave!

Finally, with the victory of the Holy Alliance, Europe took on a form that makes every fresh proletarian upheaval in France directly coincide with a *world war.* The new French revolution is forced to leave its national soil forthwith and *conquer the European terrain,* on which alone the revolution of the nineteenth century can be carried through.

Only through the defeat of June, therefore, were all the conditions created under which France can seize the *initiative* of the European revolution. Only after baptism in the blood of the June insurgents did the tricolour become the flag of the European revolution—*the red flag.*

And we cry: *The revolution is dead—Long live the revolution!*

February 25, 1848, had granted the *republic* to France, June 25 thrust the *revolution* on her. And revolution, after June, meant: *overthrow of bourgeois society,* whereas, before February, it had meant *overthrow of the form of state.*

The June fight had been led by the republican fraction of the bourgeoisie; with victory, the state power inevitably fell to its share. . . .

The smashing of the revolutionary force of the workers simultaneously shattered the political influence of the *democratic republicans,* i.e, of the republicans in the sense of the *petty bourgeoisie.* . . . Together with the bourgeois republicans they had conspired on April 16 against the proletariat, together with them they had warred against it in the June days. Thus they themselves blasted the background against which their party stood out as a power, for the petty bourgeoisie can only preserve a revolutionary attitude to the bourgeoisie as long as the proletariat stands behind it.

After the June days, the Constituent Assembly remained the *exclusive representative of bourgeois republicanism,* and it put this face forward all the more decidedly, the more the influence of the tricolour republicans collapsed outside the Assembly. If the question was one of maintaining the form of the bourgeois republic, then the Assembly had the votes of the democratic republicans at its disposal, if one of maintaining the *content,* then even its mode of speech no longer separated it from the royalist bourgeois factions. For it is precisely the interests of the bourgeoisie, the material conditions of its class rule and class exploitation, that form the content of the bourgeois republic. . . .

No one had fought more fanatically in the June days for the salvation of property and the restoration of credit than the Parisian petty bourgeois—keepers of cafes and restaurants, *marchands de vins,* [wine merchants] small traders, shopkeepers, handicraftsmen, etc. The shopkeeper had pulled himself together and marched against the barricades, in order to restore the traffic which leads from the streets into the shop. But behind the barricade stood the customers and the debtors; before it the creditors of the shop. And when the barricades were thrown down and the workers were crushed and the shopkeepers, drunk with victory, rushed back to their shops, they found the entrance barred by a saviour of property, an official agent of credit, who presented them with threatening letters: Overdue bill of exchange! Overdue house rent! Overdue promissory note! Ruined shop! Ruined shopkeeper! . . .

The petty bourgeois saw with horror that, by striking down the workers, they had delivered themselves up unresisting into the hands of their creditors. Their bankruptcy, which since February had been dragging on in chronic fashion and had been apparently ignored, was openly declared after June. . . .

December 10, 1848, was the day of the *peasant insurrection.* Only from this day does the February of the French peasants date. The symbol that expressed their entry into the revolutionary movement, clumsily cunning, knavishly naive, doltishly sublime, a calculated superstition, a pathetic burlesque, a cleverly stupid anachronism, a world historic piece of buffoonery and an undecipherable hieroglyphic for the understanding of the civilised—this symbol bore the unmistakable features of the class that represents barbarism within civilisation. The republic had announced itself to this class with the *tax collector* ; it announced itself to the republic with the emperor. [Louis] Napoleon was the only man who had exhaustively represented the interests and the imagination of the peasant class, newly created in 1789. By writing his name on the front page of the republic, it declared war abroad and the enforcing of its class interests at home. Napoleon, for the peasants, was not a person but a programme. With banners, with beat of drums and blare of trumpets, they marched to the polling booths shouting: *plus d'impôts, à bas les riches, à bas la république, vive l'Empereur.* No more taxes, down with the rich, down with the republic, long live the emperor! Behind the emperor was hidden the peasant war. The republic that they voted down was the *republic of the rich.*

December 10 was the *coup d'état* of the peasants, which overthrew the existing government. And from that day on, when they had taken a government from France and given one to her, their eyes were turned steadily on Paris. For a moment active heroes of the revolutionary drama, they could no longer be forced back into the passive and spineless role of the chorus.

The other classes helped to complete the election victory of the peasants. The election of Napoleon, for the *proletariat,* meant the deposition of Cavaignac, the overthrow of the Constituent Assembly, the dismissal of bourgeois republicanism, the rescinding of the June victory. For the *petty bourgeoisie,* Napoleon meant the rule of the debtors over the creditors. For the majority of the *big bourgeoisie* the election of Napoleon meant an open breach with the fraction of which it had had to make use, for a moment, against the revolution, but which became intolerable to it as soon as this fraction sought to consolidate the position of the moment into the constitutional position. Napoleon in place of Cavaignac, for the majority of the big bourgeoisie, meant the monarchy in place of the republic, the beginning of the royalist restoration, a shy hint at Orleans, the lily hidden beneath the violet. Finally, the *army* voted for Napoleon against the Mobile Guard, against the peace idyll, for war.

Thus it happened, as the *Neue Rheinische Zeitung* stated, that the most simple-minded man in France acquired the most multifarious significance. Just because he was nothing, he could signify everything save himself. . . .

Our whole exposition has shown how the republic, from the first day of its existence, did not overthrow the finance aristocracy, but consolidated it. . . .

The question will be asked how the bourgeoisie in coalition could bear and suffer the rule of finance, which under Louis Philippe depended on the exclusion or subordination of the remaining bourgeois factions.

The answer is simple.

First of all, the finance aristocracy itself forms a weighty, authoritative part of the royalist coalition, whose common governmental power is the republic. . . . In general, the combination of large landed property with this finance is a *normal fact*. Proof: *England*; proof: even *Austria*.

In a country like France, where the volume of national production stands at a disproportionately lower level than the amount of the national debt, where the state revenue forms the most important subject of speculation and the Bourse the chief market for the investment of capital that wants to turn itself to account in an unproductive way—in such a country a countless number of people of all bourgeois or semi-bourgeois classes must participate in the state debt, in the Bourse gamblings, in finance. Do not all these subaltern participants find their natural mainstays and commanders in the faction which represents this interest in its vastest outlines, which represents it as a whole?

By what is the reversion of the state property to high finance conditioned? By the constantly growing indebtedness of the state. And the indebtedness of the state? By the constant excess of its expenditure over its income, a disproportion which is simultaneously the cause and effect of the system of state loans.

In order to escape from this indebtedness, the state must either restrict its expenditure, i.e., simplify and curtail the government organism, govern as little as possible, employ as small a personnel as possible, enter as little into relations with bourgeois society as possible. This path was impossible for the Party of Order, whose means of repression, whose official interference for reasons of state and whose universal presence through organs of state were bound to increase in the same measure as its rule and the conditions for existence of its class were threatened from more numerous sides. The *gendarmerie* could not be reduced in the same measure as attacks on persons and property increase.

Or the state must seek to elude the debts and produce an immediate but transitory balance in its budget, by putting extraordinary taxes on the shoulders of the wealthiest classes. In order to withdraw the national wealth from exploitation by the Bourse, was the Party of Order to sacrifice its own wealth on the altar of the fatherland? *Pas si bête!* [Not so stupid!]

Therefore, without a complete revolution in the French state, no revolution in the French state's budget. Along with this state budget necessarily goes state indebtedness, and with state indebtedness necessarily goes the rule of the trade in state debts, of the state creditors, the bankers, the money dealers and the wolves of the Bourse. Only a fraction of the Party of Order was directly concerned in the overthrow of the finance aristocracy—the manufacturers. We are not speaking of the middle, of the smaller industrials; we are speaking of the rulers of the factory interest, who had formed the broad basis of the dynastic opposition under Louis Philippe. Their interest is indubitably reduction of the costs of production, therefore reduction of the taxes, which enter into production, therefore reduction of the state debts, the interest on which enters into the taxes, therefore the overthrow of the finance aristocracy.

In England—and the largest French manufacturers are petty bourgeois as against their English rivals—we really find the manufacturers, a Cobden, a Bright, at the head of the crusade against the bank and the stock exchange aristocracy. Why not in France? In England industry rules; in France, agriculture. In England industry requires *free trade;* in France, protection, national monopoly besides other monopolies. French industry does not dominate French production; the French industrialists, therefore, do not dominate the French bourgeoisie. In order to put through their interest against the remaining fractions of the bourgeoisie, they cannot, like the English, take the lead of the movement and simultaneously push their class interest to the fore; they must follow in the train of the revolution, and serve interests which are opposed to the collective interests of their class. In February they had misunderstood their position; February sharpened their wits. And who is more directly threatened by the workers than the employer, the industrial capitalist? The manufacturer, therefore, of necessity became in France the most fanatical member of the Party of Order. The reduction of this *profit* by finance, *what is that compared with the abolition of profit by the proletariat?*

In France, the petty bourgeois does what normally the industrial bourgeois would have to do; the worker does what normally would be the task of the petty bourgeois; and the task of the worker, who solves that? No one. It is not solved in France; it is proclaimed in France. It is not solved anywhere within the national walls; the class war within French society turns into a world war, in which the nations confront one another. The solution begins only at the moment when, through the world war, the proletariat is pushed to the head of the people that dominates the world market, to the head of England. The revolution, which finds here, not its end, but its organisational beginning, is no short-lived revolution. The present generation is like the Jews, whom Moses led through the wilderness. It has not only a new world to conquer, it must go under, in order to make room for the men who are fit for a new world. . . .

The country folk—over two-thirds of the total French population—consist for the most part of so-called free *landed proprietors.* The first generation, gratuitously freed by the revolution of 1789 from its feudal burdens, had paid no price for the soil. But the following generations paid, under the form of the *price of land,* what their semi-serf forefathers had paid in the form of rent, tithes, *corvée,* [Compulsory unpaid labour of serfs rendered to feudal lords] etc. The more, on the one hand, the population grew and the more, on the other hand, the division of the soil increased—so much the higher became the price of the holdings, for the extent of the demand for them increased with their smallness. . . . On the other hand: under the system of fragmentation of holdings the earth is purely an *instrument of production* for its proprietors. Now in the same measure as land is divided its fruitfulness diminishes. The application of machinery to the land, the division of labour, the ample means of improving the soil, such as cutting drainage and irrigation channels and the like, become more and more impossible, while the *unproductive costs* of cultivation increase in the same proportion as the division of the instrument of production itself. . . .

Thus it came about that the French peasant, in the form of interest on the mortgages encumbering the soil and in the form of interest on the *advances made by the usurer without mortgages,* cedes to the capitalist not only ground rent, not only the industrial profit, in a word, not only the *whole net profit,* but even *a part of the wages,* and that therefore he has sunk to the level of the *Irish tenant farmer.* — all under the pretence of being a *private proprietor.* . . .

The condition of the French peasants, when the republic had added new burdens to their old ones, can be understood. It can be seen that their exploitation differs only in *form* from the exploitation of the industrial proletariat. The exploiter is the same: *capital.* The individual capitalists exploit the individual peasants through *mortgages* and *usury*; the capitalist class exploits the peasant class through the state taxes. The peasant's title to property is the talisman by which capital captivated him hitherto, the pretext under which it set him against the industrial proletariat. Only the fall of capital can raise the peasant; only an anti-capitalist, a proletarian government can break his economic misery, his social degradation. The *constitutional republic,* that is the dictatorship of his united exploiters; the *Social-Democratic,* the *Red* republic, that is the dictatorship of his allies. And the scale rises or falls, according to the votes that the peasant casts into the ballot box. He himself must decide his fate—so spoke the Socialist in pamphlets, almanacs, calendars and leaflets of all kinds. . . . But most understandable was the language of the actual experiences that the peasant class had from the use of the suffrage, and of the disillusionments overwhelming him, blow upon blow, in revolutionary haste. *Revolutions are the locomotives of history.* . . .

Little by little we have seen peasants, petty bourgeois, the middle classes in general, stepping alongside the proletariat, driven into open antagonism to the official republic and treated by it as antagonists. *Revolt against bourgeois dictatorship, need of a change in society, adherence to democratic-republican institutions as organs of their movement, grouping round the proletariat as the decisive revolutionary power*—these were the common characteristics of the *so-called party of Social-Democracy, the party of the Red republic.* This *party of anarchy,* as its opponents christened it, is no less a coalition of different interests than the *Party of Order.* From the smallest reform of the old social disorder to the overthrow of the old social order, from bourgeois liberalism to revolutionary terrorism, as wide apart as this lie the extremes that form the starting and final point of the party of "anarchy."

Abolition of the protective duties—socialism! For it strikes at the monopoly of the *industrial* faction of the Party of Order. Regulation of the state budget—socialism! For it strikes at the monopoly of the *financial* faction of the Party of Order. Free admission of foreign meat and corn—socialism! For it strikes at the monopoly of the third faction of the Party of Order, *large landed property.* The demands of the free-trade party, i.e., of the most advanced English bourgeois party, appear in France as so many socialist demands. Voltairianism—socialism! For it strikes at the fourth faction of the Party of Order, the *Catholic.* Freedom of the press, right of association, universal public education—socialism, socialism! They strike at the entire monopoly of the Party of Order.

So swiftly had the march of the revolution ripened conditions, that the friends of reform of all shades, the most moderate claims of the middle classes, were compelled to group themselves around the banner of the most extreme party of revolution, round the red flag.

Yes, manifold as was the *socialism* of the different large sections of the party of anarchy, according to the economic conditions and the total revolutionary requirements of their class or fraction of a class arising out of these, in one point it is in harmony: in proclaiming itself as *the means of emancipating the proletariat* and the emancipation of the latter as its *object.* . . .

Under the somewhat similar sounding, general socialist phrases of the *"party of anarchy,"* is concealed the *socialism* of the *National,* of the *Presse* and the *Siècle,* which more or less consistently wants to overthrow the rule of the finance aristocracy and to free industry and trade from their hitherto existing fetters. This is the socialism of industry, of trade and of agriculture, whose rulers in the Party of Order deny these interests, in so far as they no longer coincide with their private monopolies. From this *bourgeois socialism,* to which, as to every variety of socialism, a section of the workers and petty bourgeois naturally rallies, specific *petty-bourgeois socialism,* socialism *par excellence,* is distinct. Capital hounds this class chiefly as its *creditors,* so it demands *credit institutions;* capital crushes it by *competition,* so it demands *associations* supported by the state; capital overwhelms it by *concentration,* so it demands *progressive taxes,* limitations on inheritance, taking over of large works by the state, and other measures that *forcibly stem the growth of capital.* Since it dreams of the peaceful achievement of its socialism—allowing perhaps, for a second February Revolution lasting a brief day—naturally the coming historical process appears to it as the *application of systems,* which the thinkers of society, whether in companies or as individual inventors, devise or have devised. Thus they become the eclectics or adepts of the existing socialist *systems,* of *doctrinaire socialism,* which was the theoretical expression of the proletariat only so long as it had not yet developed further into a free historical self-movement.

While this *utopia, doctrinaire socialism,* which subordinates the total movement to one of its moments, which puts in place of common, social production the brainwork of individual pedants and, above all, in fantasy does away with the revolutionary struggle of the classes and its requirements by small conjuring tricks or great sentimentality; while this doctrinaire socialism, which at bottom only idealises the present society, takes a picture of it without shadows and wants to achieve its ideal against the reality of society; while this socialism passes from the proletariat to the petty bourgeoisie; while the struggle of the different socialist chiefs among themselves sets forth each of the so-called systems as a pretentious adherence to one of the transit points of the social revolution as against another—the *proletariat* rallies more and more round *revolutionary socialism,* round *communism,* for which the bourgeoisie has itself found the name of *Blanqui.* This socialism is the *declaration of the permanence of the revolution, the class dictatorship* of the proletariat as the inevitable transit point to the *abolition of class differences generally,* to the abolition of all the production relations on which they rest, to the abolition of all the social relations that correspond to these relations of production, to the revolutionising of all the ideas that result from these social connections.

The scope of this exposition does not permit of developing the subject further. . . .

Marx, *Class Struggles* (1850), MESW, II, pp. 192–201, 204, 213, 215–28, 233–34, 274–83, 287–89.

THE EIGHTEENTH BRUMAIRE OF LOUIS BONAPARTE

Hegel remarks somewhere that all facts and personages of great importance in world history occur, as it were, twice. He forgot to add: the first time as tragedy, the second as farce. Caussidière for Danton, Louis Blanc for Robespierre, the *Montagne* of 1848 to 1851 for the *Montagne* of 1793 to 1795, the Nephew [Louis Bonaparte] for the Uncle [Napoleon Bonaparte]. And the same caricature occurs in the circumstances attending the second edition of the eighteenth Brumaire!

Men make their own history, but they do not make it just as they please; they do not make it under circumstances chosen by themselves, but under circumstances directly encountered, given and transmitted from the past. The tradition of all the dead generations weighs like a nightmare on the brain of the living. . . .

The February Revolution was a surprise attack, a *taking* of the old society *unawares,* and the people proclaimed this unexpected *stroke* as a deed of world importance, ushering in a new epoch. On December 2 the February Revolution is conjured away by a cardsharper's trick, and what seems overthrown is no longer the monarchy but the liberal concessions that were wrung from it by centuries of struggle. Instead of *society* having conquered a new content for itself, it seems that the *state* only returned to its oldest form, to the shamelessly simple domination of the sabre and the cowl. This is the answer to the *coup de main* [unexpected stroke] of February 1848, given by the *coup de tête* [rash act] of December 1851. Easy come, easy go. Meanwhile the interval of time has not passed by unused. During the years 1848 to 1851 French society has made up, and that by an abbreviated because revolutionary method, for the studies and experiences which, in a regular, so to speak, textbook course of development, would have had to precede the February Revolution, if it was to be more than a ruffling of the surface. Society now seems to have fallen back behind its point of departure; it has in truth first to create for itself the revolutionary point of departure, the situation, the relations, the conditions under which alone modern revolution becomes serious.

Bourgeois revolutions, like those of the eighteenth century, storm swiftly from success to success; their dramatic effects outdo each other; men and things seem set in sparkling brilliants; ecstasy in the everyday spirit; but they are short-lived; soon they have attained their zenith, and a long crapulent depression lays hold of society before it learns soberly to assimilate the results of its storm-and-stress period. On the other hand, proletarian revolutions, like those of the nineteenth century, criticise themselves constantly, interrupt themselves continually in their own course, come back to the apparently accomplished in order to begin it afresh, deride with unmerciful thoroughness the inadequacies, weaknesses and paltrinesses of their first attempts, seem to throw down their adversary only in order that he may draw new strength from the earth and rise again, more gigantic, before them, recoil ever and anon from the indefinite prodigiousness of their own aims, until a situation has been created which makes all turning back impossible, and the conditions themselves cry out:

Hic Rhodus, hic salta![1]

. . . Let us recapitulate in general outline the phases that the French Revolution went through from February 24, 1848, to December 1851.

Three main periods are unmistakable: *the February period*; May 4, 1848, to May 28, 1849: *the period of the constitution of the republic,* or *of the Constituent National Assembly*; May 28, 1849, to December 2, 1851: *the period of the constitutional republic* or *of the Legislative National Assembly.*

The *first period,* from February 24, or the overthrow of Louis Philippe, to May 4, 1848, the meeting of the Constituent Assembly, the *February period* proper, may be described as the *prologue* to the revolution. Its character was officially expressed in the fact that the government improvised by it itself declared that it was *provisional* and, like the government, everything that was mooted, attempted or enunciated during this period proclaimed itself to be only *provisional.* Nothing and nobody ventured to lay claim to the right of existence and of real action. All the elements that had prepared or determined the revolution, the dynastic opposition, the republican bourgeoisie, the democratic-republican petty bourgeoisie and the social-democratic workers, provisionally found their place in the February *government.* . . .

The *second period,* from May 4, 1848, to the end of May 1849, is the period of the *constitution,* the *foundation, of the bourgeois republic.* . . .

The *bourgeois monarchy* of Louis Philippe can be followed only by a *bourgeois republic,* that is to say, whereas a limited section of the bourgeoisie ruled in the name of the king, the whole of the bourgeoisie will now rule on behalf of the people. The demands of the Paris proletariat are utopian nonsense, to which an end must be put. To this declaration of the Constituent National Assembly the Paris proletariat replied with the *June Insurrection,* the most colossal event in the history of European civil wars. The bourgeois republic triumphed. On its side stood the aristocracy of finance, the industrial bourgeoisie, the middle class, the petty bourgeois, the army, the *lumpenproletariat* organised as the Mobile Guard, the intellectual lights, the clergy and the rural population. On the side of the Paris proletariat stood none but itself. More than three thousand insurgents were butchered after the victory, and fifteen thousand were transported without trial. With this defeat the proletariat passes into the *background* of the revolutionary stage. It attempts to press forward again on every occasion, as soon as the movement appears to make a fresh start, but with ever decreased expenditure of strength and always slighter results. As soon as one of the social strata situated above it gets into

[1]Here Rhodes, jump here!—*Ed.*

revolutionary ferment, the proletariat enters into an alliance with it and so shares all the defeats that the different parties suffer, one after another. But these subsequent blows become the weaker, the greater the surface of society over which they are distributed. The more important leaders of the proletariat in the Assembly and in the press successively fall victims to the courts, and ever more equivocal figures come to head it. In part it throws itself into *doctinaire experiments, exchange banks and workers' associations, hence into a movement in which it renounces the revolutionising of the old world by means of the latter's own great, combined resources, and seeks, rather, to achieve its salvation behind society's back, in private fashion, within its limited conditions of existence, and hence necessarily suffers shipwreck.* It seems to be unable either to rediscover revolutionary greatness in itself or to win new energy from the connections newly entered into, until *all classes* with which it contended in June themselves lie prostrate beside it. But at least it succumbs with the honours of the great, world-historic struggle; not only in France, but all Europe trembles at the June earthquake, while the ensuing defeats of the upper classes are so cheaply bought that they require bare-faced exaggeration by the victorious party to be able to pass for events at all, and become the more ignominious the further the defeated party is removed from the proletarian party.

The defeat of the June insurgents, to be sure, had now prepared, had levelled the ground on which the bourgeois republic could be founded and built up, but it had shown at the same time that in Europe the questions at issue are other than that of "republic or monarchy." It had revealed that here *bourgeois republic* signifies the unlimited despotism of one class over other classes. It had proved that in countries with an old civilisation, with a developed formation of classes, with modern conditions of production and with an intellectual consciousness in which all traditional ideas have been dissolved by the work of centuries, *the republic* signifies *in general only the political form of revolution of bourgeois society* and not its *conservative form of life,* as, for example, in the United States of North America, where, though classes already exist, they have not yet become fixed, but continually change and interchange their elements in constant flux, where the modern means of production, instead of coinciding with a stagnant surplus population, rather compensate for the relative deficiency of heads and hands, and where, finally, the feverish, youthful movement of material production, which has to make a new world its own, has left neither time nor opportunity for abolishing the old spirit world.

During the June days all classes and parties had united in the *party of Order* against the proletarian class as the *party of Anarchy,* of socialism, of communism. They had "saved" society from *"the enemies of society."* They had given out the watchwords of the old society, *"property, family, religion, order,"* to their army as passwords and had proclaimed to the counter-revolutionary crusaders: "In this sign thou shalt conquer!" From that moment, as soon as one of the numerous parties which had gathered under this sign against the June insurgents seeks to hold the revolutionary battlefield in its own class interest, it goes down before the cry: "Property, family, religion, order." Society is saved just as often as the circle of its rulers contracts, as a more exclusive interest is maintained against a wider one. Every demand of the simplest bourgeois financial reform, of the most ordinary liberalism, of the most formal republicanism, of the most shallow democracy, is simultaneously castigated as an "attempt on society" and stigmatised as "socialism."...

On the threshold of the February Revolution, the *social republic* appeared as a phrase, as a prophecy. In the June days of 1848, it was drowned in the blood of the *Paris proletariat,* but it haunts the subsequent acts of the drama like a ghost. The *democratic republic* announces its arrival. On June 13, 1849, it is dissipated together with its *petty bourgeois,* who have taken to their heels, but in its flight it blows its own trumpet with redoubled boastfulness. The *parliamentary republic,* together with the bourgeoisie, takes possession of the entire stage; it enjoys its existence to the full, but December 2, 1851 buries it to the accompaniment of the anguished cry of the royalists in coalition: "Long live the Republic!"

The French bourgeoisie balked at the domination of the working proletariat; it has brought the *lumpenproletariat* to domination, with the chief of the Society of December 10 at the head. ...

If the overthrow of the parliamentary republic contains within itself the germ of the triumph of the proletarian revolution, its immediate and palpable result was *the victory of [Louis] Bonaparte over parliament, of the executive power over the legislative power, of force without phrases over the force of phrases.* In parliament the nation made its general will the law, that is, it made the law of the ruling class its general will. Before the executive power it renounces all will of its own and submits to the superior command of an alien will, to authority. The executive power, in contrast to the legislative power, expresses the heteronomy of a nation, in contrast to its autonomy. France, therefore, seems to have escaped the despotism of a class only to fall back beneath the despotism of an individual, and, what is more, beneath the authority of an individual without authority. The struggle seems to be settled in such a way that all classes, equally impotent and equally mute, fall on their knees before the rifle butt.

But the revolution is thoroughgoing. It is still journeying through purgatory. It does its work methodically. By December 2, 1851, it had completed one half of its preparatory work; it is now completing the other half. First it perfected the parliamentary power, in order to be able to overthrow it. Now that it has attained this, it perfects the *executive power,* reduces it to its purest expression, isolates it, sets it up against itself as the sole target, in order to concentrate all its forces of destruction against it. And when it has done this second half of its preliminary work, Europe will leap from its seat and exultantly exclaim: Well grubbed, old mole!*

This executive power with its enormous bureaucratic and military organisation, with its ingenious state machinery, embracing wide strata, with a host of officials numbering half a million, besides an army of another half million, this appalling parasitic body, which enmeshes the body of French society like a net and chokes all its pores, sprang up in the days of the absolute monarchy, with the decay of the feudal system, which it helped to hasten. The seignorial privileges of the landowners and towns became transformed into so many attributes of the state power, the feudal dignitaries into paid officials

*Shakespeare, *Hamlet,* Act I, Scene V.—*Ed.*

and the motley pattern of conflicting mediaeval plenary powers into the regulated plan of a state authority whose work is divided and centralised as in a factory. The first French Revolution, with its task of breaking all separate local, territorial, urban and provincial powers in order to create the civil unit of the nation, was bound to develop what the absolute monarchy had begun: centralisation, but at the same time the extent, the attributes and the agent of governmental power. Napoleon perfected this state machinery. The Legitimist monarchy and the July monarchy added nothing but a greater division of labour, growing in the same measure as the division of labour within bourgeois society created new groups of interests, and, therefore, new material for state administration. Every *common* interest was straightway severed from society, counterposed to it as a higher, *general* interest, snatched from the activity of society's members themselves and made an object of government activity, from bridge, a schoolhouse and the communal property of a village community to the railways, the national wealth and the national university of France. Finally, in its struggle against the revolution, the parliamentary republic found itself compelled to strengthen, along with the repressive measures, the resources and centralisation of governmental power. All revolutions perfected this machine instead of smashing it. The parties that contended in turn for domination regarded the possession of this huge state edifice as the principal spoils of the victor.

But under the absolute monarchy, during the first Revolution, under Napoleon, bureaucracy was only the means of preparing the class rule of the bourgeoisie. Under the Restoration, under Louis Philippe, under the parliamentary republic, it was the instrument of the ruling class, however much it strove for power of its own.

Only under the second Bonaparte does the state seem to have made itself completely independent. As against civil society, the state machine has consolidated its position so thoroughly that the chief of the Society of December 10 suffices for its head, an adventurer blown in from abroad, raised on the shield by a drunken soldiery, which he has bought with liquor and sausages, and which he must continually ply with sausage anew. Hence the downcast despair, the feeling of most dreadful humiliation and degradation that oppresses the breast of France and makes her catch her breath. She feels dishonoured.

And yet the state power is not suspended in mid air. Bonaparte represents a class, and the most numerous class of French society at that, the *small-holding [Parzellen] peasants.*

Just as the Bourbons were the dynasty of big landed property and just as the Orleans were the dynasty of money, so the Bonapartes are the dynasty of the peasants, that is, the mass of the French people. Not the Bonaparte who submitted to the bourgeois parliament, but the Bonaparte who dispersed the bourgeois parliament is the chosen of the peasantry. For three years the towns had succeeded in falsifying the meaning of the election of December 10 and in cheating the peasants out of the restoration of the empire. The election of December 10, 1848, has been consummated only by the *coup d'état* of December 2, 1851.

The small-holding peasants form a vast mass, the members of which live in similar conditions but without entering into manifold relations with one another. Their mode of production isolates them from one another instead of bringing them into mutual intercourse. The isolation is increased by France's bad means of communication and by the poverty of the peasants. Their field of production, the small holding, admits of no division of labour in its cultivation, no application of science and, therefore, no diversity of development, no variety of talent, no wealth of social relationships. Each individual peasant family is almost self-sufficient; it itself directly produces the major part of its consumption and thus acquires its means of life more through exchange with nature than in intercourse with society. A small holding, a peasant and his family; alongside them another small holding, another small holding, another peasant and another family. A few score of these make up a village, and a few score of villages make up a Department. In this way, the great mass of the French nation is formed by simple addition of homologous magnitudes, much as potatoes in a sack form a sack of potatoes. In so far as millions of families live under economic conditions of existence that separate their mode of life, their interests and their culture from those of the other classes, and put them in hostile opposition to the latter, they form a class. In so far as there is merely a local interconnection among these small-holding peasants, and the identity of their interests begets no community, no national bond and no political organisation among them, they do not form a class. They are consequently incapable of enforcing their class interests in their own name, whether through a parliament or through a convention. They cannot represent themselves, they must be represented. Their representative must at the same time appear as their master, as an authority over them, as an unlimited governmental power that protects them against the other classes and sends them rain and sunshine from above. The political influence of the small-holding peasants, therefore, finds its final expression in the executive power subordinating society to itself.

Historical tradition gave rise to the belief of the French peasants in the miracle that a man named Napoleon would bring all the glory back to them. And an individual turned up who gives himself out as the man because he bears the name of Napoleon, in consequence of the *Code Napoléon,* which lays down the *la recherche de la paternité est interdite* [inquiry into paternity is forbidden]. After a vagabondage of twenty years and after a series of grotesque adventures, the legend finds fulfilment and the man becomes Emperor of the French. The fixed idea of the Nephew was realised, because it coincided with the fixed idea of the most numerous class of the French people.

But, it may be objected, what about the peasant risings in half of France, the raids on the peasants by the army, the mass incarceration and transportation of peasants?

Since Louis XIV, France has experienced no similar persecution of the peasants "on account of demagogic practices."

But let there be no misunderstanding. The Bonaparte dynasty represents not the revolutionary, but the conservative peasant; not the peasant that strikes out beyond the condition of his social existence, the small holding, but rather the peasant who wants to consolidate this holding, not the country folk, who linked up with the towns, want to overthrow the old order through their own energies, but on the contrary those who, in stupefied seclusion within this old order, want to see themselves and their small holdings saved and favoured by the ghost of the empire. It represents not the enlightenment, but the superstition of the peasant; not his judgment, but his prejudice; not his future, but his past; not his modern Cevennes, but his modern Vendée.

The three years' rigorous rule of the parliamentary republic had freed a part of the French peasants from the Napoleonic illusion and had revolutionised them, even if only superficially; but the bourgeoisie violently repressed them, as often as they set themselves in motion. . . . The bourgeoisie punished them with states of siege and punitive expeditions. And this same bourgeoisie now cries out about the stupidity of the masses, the vile multitude, that has betrayed it to Bonaparte. It has itself forcibly strengthened the empire sentiments [*Imperialismus*] of the peasant class, it conserved the conditions that form the birthplace of this peasant religion. The bourgeoisie, to be sure, is bound to fear the stupidity of the masses as long as they remain conservative, and the insight of the masses as soon as they become revolutionary.

In the risings after the *coup d'état*, a part of the French peasants protested, arms in hand, against their own vote of December 10, 1848. The school they had gone through since 1848 had sharpened their wits. But they had made themselves over to the underworld of history; history held them to their word, and the majority was still so prejudiced that in precisely the reddest Departments the peasant population voted openly for Bonaparte. In its view, the National Assembly had hindered his progress. He had now merely broken the fetters that the towns had imposed on the will of the countryside. In some parts the peasants even entertained the grotesque notion of a convention side by side with Napoleon.

After the first revolution had transformed the peasants from semi-villeins into freeholders, Napoleon confirmed and regulated the conditions on which they could exploit undisturbed the soil of France which had only just fallen to their lot and slake their youthful passion for property. But what is now causing the ruin of the French peasant is his small holding itself, the division of the land, the form of property which Napoleon consolidated in France. It is precisely the material conditions which made the feudal peasant a small-holding peasant and Napoleon an emperor. Two generations have sufficed to produce the inevitable result: progressive deterioration of agriculture, progressive indebtedness of the agriculturist. The "Napoleonic" form of property, which at the beginning of the nineteenth century was the condition for the liberation and enrichment of the French country folk, has developed in the course of this century into the law of their enslavement and pauperisation. And precisely this law is the first of the *"idées napoléoniennes"* which the second Bonaparte has to uphold. If he still shares with the peasants the illusion that the cause of their ruin is to be sought, not in this small-holding property itself, but outside it, in the influence of secondary circumstances, his experiments will burst like soap bubbles when they come in contact with the relations of production.

The economic development of small-holding property has radically changed the relation of the peasants to the other classes of society. Under Napoleon, the fragmentation of the land in the countryside supplemented free competition and the beginning of big industry in the towns. The peasant class was the ubiquitous protest against the landed aristocracy which had just been overthrown. The roots that small-holding property struck in French soil deprived feudalism of all nutriment. Its landmarks formed the natural fortifications of the bourgeoisie against any surprise attack on the part of its old overlords. But in the course of the nineteenth century the feudal lords were replaced by urban usurers; the feudal obligation that went with the land was replaced by the mortgage; aristocratic landed property was replaced by bourgeois capital. The small holding of the peasant is now only the pretext that allows the capitalist to draw profits, interest and rent from the soil, while leaving it to the tiller of the soil himself to see how he can extract his wages. The mortgage debt burdening the soil of France imposes on the French peasantry payment of an amount of interest equal to the annual interest on the entire British national debt. Small-holding property, in this enslavement by capital to which its development inevitably pushes forward, has transformed the mass of the French nation into troglodytes. Sixteen million peasants (including women and children) dwell in hovels, a large number of which have but one opening, others only two and the most favoured only three. And windows are to a house what the five senses are to the head. The bourgeois order, which at the beginning of the century set the state to stand guard over the newly arisen small holding and manured it with laurels, has become a vampire that sucks out its blood and brains and throws them into the alchemistic cauldron of capital. The *Code Napoleon* is now nothing but a *codex* of distraints, forced sales and compulsory auctions. To the four million (including children, etc.) officially recognised paupers, vagabonds, criminals and prostitutes in France must be added five million who hover on the margin of existence and either have their haunts in the countryside itself or, with their rags and their children, continually desert the countryside for the towns and the towns for the countryside. The interests of the peasants, therefore, are no longer, as under Napoleon, in accord with, but in opposition to the interests of the bourgeoisie, to capital. Hence the peasants find their natural ally and leader in the *urban proletariat,* whose task is the overthrow of the bourgeois order. But *strong and unlimited government*—and this is the second *"idée napoléonienne,"* which the second Napoleon has to carry out—is called upon to defend this "material" order by force. This *"ordre matériel"* also serves as the catchword in all of Bonaparte's proclamations against the rebellious peasants.

Besides the mortgage which capital imposes on it, the small holding is burdened by *taxes.* Taxes are the source of life for the bureaucracy, the army, the priests and the court, in short, for the whole apparatus of the executive power. Strong government and heavy taxes are identical. By its very nature, small-holding property forms a suitable basis for an all-powerful and innumerable bureaucracy. It creates a uniform level of relationships and persons over the whole surface of the land. Hence it also permits of uniform action from a supreme centre on all points of this uniform mass. It annihilates the aristocratic intermediate grades between the mass of the people and the state power. On all sides, therefore, it calls forth the direct interference of this state power and the interposition of its immediate organs. Finally, it produces an unemployed surplus population for which there is no place either on the land or in the towns, and which accordingly reaches out for state offices as a sort of respectable alms, and provokes the creation of state posts. By the new markets which he opened at the point of the bayonet, by the plundering of the Continent, Napoleon repaid the compulsory taxes with interest. These taxes were a spur to the industry of the peasant, whereas now they rob his industry of its last resources and complete his inability to resist pauperism. And an enormous bureaucracy, well-gallooned and well-fed, is the *"idée napoléonienne"* which is most congenial of all to the second Bonaparte. How could it be otherwise, seeing that alongside the actual classes of society he is forced to create an artificial caste, for which the maintenance of his regime becomes a bread-and-butter question? Accordingly, one of his first financial operations was the raising of officials' salaries to their old level and the creation of new sinecures.

Another *"idée napoléonnienne"* is the domination of the *priests* as an instrument of government. But while in its accord with society, in its dependence on natural forces and its submission to the authority which protected it from above, the small holding that had newly come into being was naturally religious, the small holding that is ruined by debts, at odds with society and authority, and driven beyond its own limitations naturally becomes irreligious. . . .

Lastly, the culminating point of the *"idées napoléoniennes"* is the preponderance of the *army.* The army was the *point d'honneur* [matter of honor, a point of special touch] of the small-holding peasants, it was they themselves transformed into heroes, defending their new possessions against the outer world, glorifying their recently won nationhood, plundering and revolutionising the world. The uniform was their own state dress; war was their poetry; the small holding, extended and rounded off in imagination, was their fatherland, and patriotism the ideal form of the sense of property. But the enemies against whom the French peasant has now to defend his property are not the Cossacks; they are the *huissiers* [bailiffs] and the tax collectors. The small holding lies no longer in the so-called fatherland, but in the register of mortgages. The army itself is no longer the flower of the peasant youth; it is the swamp-flower of the peasant *lumpenproletariat.* It consists in large measure of *remplaçants,* of substitutes, just as the second Bonaparte is himself only a *remplaçant,* the substitute for Napoleon. It now performs its deeds of valour by hounding the peasants in masses like chamois, by doing *gendarme* duty, and if the internal contradictions of his system chase the chief of the Society of December 10 over the French border, his army, after some acts of brigandage, will reap, not laurels, but thrashings.

One sees: *all* "idées napoléoniennes" *are ideas of the undeveloped small holding in the freshness of its youth*; for the small holding that has outlived its day they are an absurdity. They are only the hallucinations of its death struggle, words that are transformed into phrases, spirits transformed into ghosts. But the parody of the empire [*des Imperialismus*] was necessary to free the mass of the French nation from the weight of tradition and to work out in pure form the opposition between the state power and society. With the progressive undermining of small-holding property, the state structure erected upon it collapses. The centralisation of the state that modern society requires arises only on the ruins of the military-bureaucratic government machinery which was forged in opposition to feudalism.*

*In the 1852 edition this paragraph ended with the following lines, which Marx omitted in the 1869 edition: "The demolition of the state machine will not endanger centralisation. Bureaucracy is only the low and brutal form of a centralisation that is still afflicted with its opposite, with feudalism. When he is disappointed in the Napoleonic Restoration, the French peasant will part with his belief in his small holding, the entire state edifice erected on this small holding will fall to the ground and *the proletarian revolution will obtain that chorus without which its solo song becomes a swan song in all peasant countries."—Ed.*

The condition of the French peasants provides us with the answer to the riddle of the *general elections of December 20 and 21,* which bore the second Bonaparte up Mount Sinai, not to receive laws, but to give them.

Manifestly, the bourgeoisie had now no choice but to elect Bonaparte. . . . After the *coup d'état*, the French bourgeoisie cried: Only the chief of the Society of December 10 can still save bourgeois society! Only theft can still save property; only perjury, religion; bastardy, the family; disorder, order!

As the executive authority which has made itself an independent power, Bonaparte feels it to be his mission to safeguard "bourgeois order." But the strength of this bourgeois order lies in the middle class. He looks on himself, therefore, as the representative of the middle class and issues decrees in this sense. Nevertheless, he is somebody solely due to the fact that he has broken the political power of this middle class and daily breaks it anew. Consequently, he looks on himself as the adversary of the political and literary power of the middle class. But by protecting its material power, he generates its political power anew. The cause must accordingly be kept alive; but the effect, where it manifests itself, must be done away with. But this cannot pass off without slight confusions of cause and effect, since in their interaction both lose their distinguishing features. New decrees that obliterate the border line. As against the bourgeoisie, Bonaparte looks on himself, at the same time, as the representative of the peasants and of the people in general, who wants to make the lower classes of the people happy within the frame of bourgeois society. New decrees that cheat the "True Socialists" of their statecraft in advance. But, above all, Bonaparte looks on himself as the chief of the Society of December 10, as the representative of the *lumpenproletariat* to which he himself, his entourage, his government and his army belong, and whose prime consideration is to benefit itself and draw California lottery prizes from the state treasury. And he vindicates his position as chief of the Society of December 10 with decrees, without decrees and despite decrees.

This contradictory task of the man explains the contradictions of his government, the confused groping about which seeks now to win, now to humiliate first one class and then another and arrays all of them uniformly against him, whose practical uncertainty forms a highly comical contrast to the imperious, categorical style of the government decrees, a style which is faithfully copied from the Uncle.

Industry and trade, hence the business affairs of the middle class, are to prosper in hothouse fashion under the strong government. The grant of innumerable railway concessions. But the Bonapartist *lumpenproletariat* is to enrich itself. The initiated play *tripotage* [hanky-panky] on the *bourse* with the railway concessions. But no capital is forthcoming for the railways. Obligation of the Bank to make advances on railway shares. But, at the same time, the Bank is to be exploited for personal ends and therefore must be cajoled. Release of the Bank from the obligation to publish its report weekly. Leonine agreement of the Bank with the government. The people are to be given employment. Initiation of public works. But the public works increase the obligations of the people in respect of taxes. Hence reduction of the taxes by an onslaught on the *rentiers,* by conversion of the five percent bonds to four-and-a-half percent. But, once more, the middle class must receive a *douceur* [sop]. Therefore doubling of the wine tax for the people, who buy it *en détail,* and halving of the wine tax for the middle class, who drink it *en gros*. Dissolution of the actual workers' associations, but promises of miracles of association in the future. The peasants are to be helped. Mortgage banks that expedite their getting into debt and accelerate the concentration of property. But these banks are to be used to make money out of the confiscated estates of the House of Orleans. No capitalist wants to agree to this condition, which is not in the decree, and the mortgage bank remains a mere decree, etc., etc.

Bonaparte would like to appear as the patriarchal benefactor of all classes. But he cannot give to one class without taking from another. . . .

Driven by the contradictory demands of his situation and being at the same time, like a conjurer, under the necessity of keeping the public gaze fixed on himself, as Napoleon's substitute, by springing constant surprises, that is to say, under the necessity of executing a *coup d'état en miniature* every day, Bonaparte throws the entire bourgeois economy into confusion, violates everything that seemed inviolable to the Revolution of 1848, makes some tolerant of revolution, others desirous of revolution, and produces actual anarchy in the name of order, while at the same time stripping its halo from the entire state machine, profanes it and makes it at once loathsome and ridiculous. The cult of the Holy Tunic of Treves he duplicates at Paris in the cult of the Napoleonic imperial mantle. But when the imperial mantle finally falls on the shoulders of Louis Bonaparte, the bronze statue of Napoleon will crash from the top of the Vendôme Column.

Marx, *Eighteenth Brumaire,* excerpts from Parts I and VII (1851–52), MESW, pp. 97–105, 168–180.

8.C.14 THE PARIS COMMUNE

On the dawn of the 18th of March [1871], Paris arose to the thunderburst of "Vive la Commune!" What is the Commune, that sphinx so tantalising to the bourgeois mind?

> "The proletarians of Paris," said the Central Committee in its manifesto of the 18th March, "amidst the failures and treasons of the ruling classes, have understood that the hour has struck for them to save the situation by taking into their own hands the direction of public affairs. . . . They have understood that it is their imperious duty and their absolute right to render themselves masters of their own destinies, by seizing upon the governmental power."

But the working class cannot simply lay hold of the ready-made state machinery, and wield it for its own purposes.

The centralised State power, with its ubiquitous organs of standing army, police, bureaucracy, clergy, and judicature—organs wrought after the plan of a systematic and hierarchic division of labour,—originates from the days of absolute monarchy, serving nascent middle-class society as a mighty weapon in its struggles against feudalism. Still, its development remained clogged by all manner of medieval rubbish, seignorial rights, local privileges, municipal and guild monopolies and provincial constitutions. The gigantic broom of the French Revolution of the eighteenth century swept away all these relics of bygone times, thus clearing simultaneously the social soil of its last hindrances to the superstructure of the modern State edifice raised under the First Empire, itself the offspring of the coalition wars of old semi-feudal Europe against modern France. During the subsequent *régimes* the Government, placed under parliamentary control—that is, under the direct control of the propertied classes—became not only a hotbed of huge national debts and crushing taxes; with its irresistible allurements of place, pelf, and patronage, it became not only the bone of contention between the rival factions and adventurers of the ruling classes; but its political character changed simultaneously with the economic changes of society. At the same pace at which the progress of modern industry developed, widened, intensified the class antagonism between capital and labour, the State power assumed more and more the character of the national power of capital over labour, of a public force organised for social enslavement, of an engine of class despotism. After every revolution marking a progressive phase in the class struggle, the purely repressive character of the State power stands out in bolder and bolder relief. The Revolution of 1830, resulting in the transfer of Government from the landlords to the capitalists, transferred it from the more remote to the more direct antagonists of the working men. The bourgeois Republicans, who, in the name of the Revolution of February, took the State power, used it for the June massacres, in order to convince the working class that "social" republic meant the Republic ensuring their social subjection, and in order to convince the royalist bulk of the bourgeois and landlord class that they might safely leave the cares and emoluments of Government to the bourgeois "Republicans." However, after their one heroic exploit of June, the bourgeois Republicans had, from the front, to fall back to the rear of the "Party of Order"—a combination formed by all the rival fractions and factions of the appropriating class in their now openly declared antagonism to the producing classes. The proper form of their joint-stock Government was the *Parliamentary Republic,* with Louis Bonaparte for its President. Theirs was a *régime* of avowed class terrorism and deliberate insult toward the "vile multitude." If the Parliamentary Republic, as M. Thiers said, "divided them (the different fractions of the ruling class) least," it opened an abyss between that class and the whole body of society outside their spare ranks. The restraints by which their own divisions had under former *régimes* still checked the State power, were removed by their union; and in view of the threatening upheaval of the proletariat, they now used that State power mercilessly and ostentatiously as the national war-engine of capital against labour. In their uninterrupted crusade against the producing masses they were, however, bound not only to invest the executive with continually increased powers of repression, but at the same time to divest their own parliamentary strong-hold—the National Assembly—one by one, of all its own means of defence against the Executive. The Executive, in the person of Louis Bonaparte, turned them out. The natural offspring of the "Party-of-Order" Republic was the Second Empire.

The empire, with the *coup d'état* for its certificate of birth, universal suffrage for its sanction, and the sword for its sceptre, professed to rest upon the peasantry, the large mass of producers not directly involved in the struggle of capital and labour. It professed to save the working class by breaking down Parliamentarism, and, with it, the undisguised subserviency of Government to the propertied classes. It professed to save the propertied classes by upholding their economic supremacy over the working class; and, finally, it professed to unite all classes by reviving for all the chimera of national glory. In reality, it was the only form of government possible at a time when the bourgeoisie had already lost, and the working class had not yet acquired, the faculty of ruling the nation. It was acclaimed throughout the world as the saviour of society. Under its sway, bourgeois society, freed from political cares, attained a development unexpected even by itself. Its industry and commerce expanded to colossal dimensions; financial swindling celebrated cosmopolitan orgies; the misery of the masses was set off by a shameless display of gorgeous, meretricious and debased luxury. The State power, apparently soaring high above society, was at the same time itself the greatest scandal of that society and the very hotbed of all its corruptions. Its own rottenness, and the rottenness of the society it had saved, were laid bare by the bayonet of Prussia, herself eagerly bent upon transferring the supreme seat of that *régime* from Paris to Berlin. Imperialism is, at the same time, the most prostitute and the ultimate form of the State power which nascent middle-class society had commenced to elaborate as a means of its own emancipation from feudalism, and which full-grown bourgeois society had finally transformed into a means for the enslavement of labour by capital.

The direct antithesis to the empire was the Commune. The cry of "social republic," with which the revolution of February was ushered in by the Paris proletariat, did but express a vague aspiration after a Republic that was not only to supersede the monarchical form of class-rule, but class-rule itself. The Commune was the positive form of that Republic.

Paris, the central seat of the old governmental power, and, at the same time, the social stronghold of the French working class, had risen in arms against the attempt of Thiers and the Rurals to restore and perpetuate that old governmental power bequeathed to them by the empire. Paris could resist only because, in consequence of the siege, it had got rid of the army, and replaced it by a National Guard, the bulk of which consisted of working men. This fact was now to be transformed into an institution. The first decree of the Commune, therefore, was the suppression of the standing army, and the substitution for it of the armed people.

The Commune was formed of the municipal councillors, chosen by universal suffrage in the various wards of the town, responsible and revocable at short terms. The majority of its members were naturally working men, or acknowledged representatives of the working class. The Commune was to be a working, not a parliamentary, body, executive and legislative at the same time. Instead of continuing to be the agent of the Central Government, the police was at once stripped of its political attributes, and turned into the responsible and at all times revocable agent of the Commune. So were the officials of all other branches of the Administration. From the members of the Commune downwards, the public service had to be done at *workmen's wages.* The vested interests and the representation allowances of the high dignitaries of State disappeared along with the high dignitaries themselves. Public functions ceased to be the private property of the tools of the Central Government. Not only municipal administration, but the whole initiative hitherto exercised by the State was laid into the hands of the Commune.

Having once got rid of the standing army and the police, the physical force elements of the old Government, the Commune was anxious to break the spiritual force of repression, the "parson-power," by the disestablishment and disendowment of all churches as proprietary bodies. The priests were sent back to the recesses of private life, there to feed upon the alms of the faithful in imitation of their predecessors, the Apostles. The whole of the educational institutions were opened to the people gratuitously, and at the same time cleared of all interference of Church and State. Thus, not only was education made accessible to all, but science itself freed from the fetters which class prejudice and governmental force had imposed upon it.

The judicial functionaries were to be divested of that sham independence which had but served to mask their abject subserviency to all succeeding governments to which, in turn, they had taken, and broken, the oaths of allegiance. Like the rest of public servants, magistrates and judges were to be elective, responsible, and revocable.

The Paris Commune was, of course, to serve as a model to all the great industrial centres of France. The communal *régime* once established in Paris and the secondary centres, the old centralised Government would in the provinces, too, have to give way to the self-government of the producers. In a rough sketch of national organisation which the Commune had no time to develop, it states clearly that the Commune was to be the political form of even the smallest country hamlet, and that in the rural districts the standing army was to be replaced by a national militia, with an extremely short term of service. The rural communes of every district were to administer their common affairs by an assembly of delegates in the central town, and these district assemblies were again to send deputies to the National Delegation in Paris, each delegate to be at any time revocable and bound by the *mandat impératif* (formal instructions) of his constituents. The few but important functions which still would remain for a central government were not to be suppressed, as has been intentionally misstated, but were to be discharged by Communal, and therefore strictly responsible agents. The unity of the nation was not to be broken, but on the contrary, to be organised by the Communal Constitution and to become a reality by the destruction of the State power which claimed to be the embodiment of that unity independent of, and superior to, the nation itself, from which it was but a parasitic excrescence. While the merely repressive organs of the old governmental power were to be amputated, its legitimate functions were to be wrested from an authority usurping preeminence over society itself, and restored to the responsible agents of society. Instead of deciding once in three or six years which member of the ruling class was to misrepresent the people in Parliament, universal suffrage was to serve the people, constituted in Communes, as individual suffrage serves every other employer in the search for the workmen and managers in his business. And it is well known that companies, like individuals, in matters of real business generally know how to put the right man in the right place, and, if they for once make a mistake, to redress it promptly. On the other hand, nothing could be more foreign to the spirit of the Commune than to supersede universal suffrage by hierarchic investiture. . . .

The multiplicity of interpretations to which the Commune has been subjected, and the multiplicity of interests which construed it in their favour, show that it was a thoroughly expansive political form, while all previous forms of government had been emphatically repressive. Its true secret was this. It was essentially a working-class government, the produce of the struggle of the producing against the appropriating class, the political form at last discovered under which to work out the economic emancipation of labour.

Except on this last condition, the Communal Constitution would have been an impossibility and a delusion. The political rule of the producer cannot coexist with the perpetuation of his social slavery. The Commune was therefore to serve as a lever for uprooting the economical foundations upon which rests the existence of classes, and therefore of class-rule. With labour emancipated, every man becomes a working man, and productive labour ceases to be a class attribute.

It is a strange fact. In spite of all the tall talk and all the immense literature, for the last sixty years, about Emancipation of Labour, no sooner do the working men anywhere take the subject into their own hands with a will, than up rises at once all the apologetic phraseology of the mouthpieces of present society with its two poles of Capital and Wages Slavery (the landlord now is but the sleeping partner of the capitalist), as if capitalist society was still in its purest state of virgin innocence, with its antagonisms still undeveloped, with its delusions still unexploded, with its prostitute realities not yet laid bare. The Commune, they exclaim, intends to abolish property, the basis of all civilisation! Yes, gentlemen, the Commune intended to abolish that class-property which makes the labour of the many the wealth of the few. It aimed at the expropriation of the expropriators. It wanted to make individual property a truth by transforming the means of production, land and capital, now chiefly the means of enslaving and exploiting labour, into mere instruments of free and associated labour. But this is Communism, "impossible" Communism! Why, those members of the ruling classes who are intelligent enough to perceive the impossibility of continuing the present system—and they are many—have become the obtrusive and full-mouthed apostles of co-operative production. If cooperative production is not to remain a sham and a snare; if it is to supersede the Capitalist system; if united cooperative societies are to regulate national production upon a common plan, thus taking it under their own control, and putting an end to the constant anarchy and periodical convulsions which are the fatality of Capitalist production—what else, gentlemen, would it be but Communism, "possible" Communism?

The working class did not expect miracles from the Commune. They have no ready-made utopias to introduce *par décret du peuple.* They know that in order to work out their own emancipation, and along with it that higher form to which present society is irresistibly tending by its own economical agencies, they will have to pass through long struggles, through a series of historic processes, transforming circumstances and men. They have no ideals to realise, but to set free the elements of the new society with which old collapsing bourgeois society itself is pregnant. In the full consciousness of their historic mission, and with the heroic resolve to act up to it, the working class can afford to smile at the coarse invective of the gentlemen's gentlemen with the pen and inkhorn, and at the didactic patronage of well-wishing bourgeois-doctrinaires, pouring forth their ignorant platitudes and sectarian crotchets in the oracular tone of scientific infallibility.

When the Paris Commune took the management of the revolution in its own hands; when plain working men for the first time dared to infringe upon the Governmental privilege of their "natural superiors," and, under circumstances of unexampled difficulty, performed their work modestly, conscientiously, and efficiently,—performed it at salaries the highest of which barely amounted to one-fifth of what, according to high scientific authority, is the minimum required for a secretary to a certain metropolitan school board, —the old world writhed in convulsions of rage at the sight of the Red Flag, the symbol of the Republic of Labour, floating over the Hôtel de Ville.

And yet, this was the first revolution in which the working class was openly acknowledged as the only class capable of social initiative, even by the great bulk of the Paris middle class—shopkeepers, tradesmen, merchants—the wealthy capitalists alone excepted. . . .

The Commune was perfectly right in telling the peasants that "its victory was their only hope." Of all the lies hatched at Versailles and re-echoed by the glorious European penny-a-liner, one of the most tremendous was that the Rurals represented the French peasantry. Think only of the love of the French peasant for the men to whom, after 1815, he had to pay the milliard of indemnity. In the eyes of the French peasant, the very existence of a great landed proprietor is in itself an encroachment on his conquests of 1789. The bourgeois, in 1848, had burdened his plot of land with the additional tax of forty-five cents in the franc; but then he did so in the name of the revolution; while now he had fomented a civil war against the revolution, to shift on to the peasant's shoulders the chief load of the five milliards of indemnity to be paid to the Prussian. The Commune, on the other hand, in one of its first proclamations, declared that the true originators of the war would be made to pay its cost. The Commune would have delivered the peasant of the blood tax,—would have given him a cheap government,—transformed his present bloodsuckers, the notary, advocate, executor, and other judicial vampires, into salaried communal agents, elected by, and responsible to, himself. It would have freed him of the tyranny of the *garde champêtre*, the gendarme, and the prefect; would have put enlightenment by the schoolmaster in the place of stultification by the priest. And the French peasant is, above all, a man of reckoning. He would find it extremely reasonable that the pay of the priest, instead of being extorted by the taxgatherer, should only depend upon the spontaneous action of the parishioners' religious instincts. Such were the great immediate boons which the rule of the Commune—and that rule alone—held out to the French peasantry. It is, therefore, quite superfluous here to expatiate upon the more complicated but vital problems which the Commune alone was able, and at the same time compelled, to solve in favour of the peasant, viz., the hypothecary debt, lying like an incubus upon his parcel of soil, the *prolétariat foncier* (the rural proletariat), daily growing upon it, and his expropriation from it enforced, at a more and more rapid rate, by the very development of modern agriculture and the competition of capitalist farming. . . .

If the Commune was thus the true representative of all the healthy elements of French society, and therefore the truly national Government, it was, at the same time, as a working men's Government, as the bold champion of the emancipation of labour, emphatically international. Within sight of the Prussian army, that had annexed to Germany two French provinces, the Commune annexed to France the working people all over the world. . . .

The great social measure of the Commune was its own working existence. Its special measures could but betoken the tendency of a government of the people by the people. Such were the abolition of the nightwork of journeymen bakers; the prohibition, under penalty, of the employers' practice to reduce wages by levying upon their work-people fines under manifold pretexts,—a process in which the employer combines in his own person the parts of legislator, judge, and executor, and filches the money to boot. Another measure of this class was the surrender, to associations of workmen, under reserve of compensation, of all closed workshops and factories, no matter whether the respective capitalists had absconded or preferred to strike work.

The financial measures of the Commune, remarkable for their sagacity and moderation, could only be such as were compatible with the state of a besieged town. Considering the colossal robberies committed upon the city of Paris by the great financial companies and contractors, under the protection of Haussmann,* the Commune would have had an incomparably better title to confiscate their property than Louis Napoleon had against the Orleans family. The Hohenzollern and the English oligarchs, who both have derived a good deal of their estates from Church plunder, were, of course, greatly shocked at the Commune clearing but 8,000 *f.* out of secularisation. . . .

Wonderful, indeed, was the change the Commune had wrought in Paris! No longer any trace of the meretricious Paris of the Second Empire. No longer was Paris the rendezvous of British landlords, Irish absentees, American ex-slaveholders and shoddy men, Russian ex-serfowners, and Wallachian boyards. No more corpses at the morgue, no nocturnal burglaries, scarcely any robberies; in fact, for the first time since the days of February, 1848, the streets of Paris were safe, and that without any police of any kind. . . .

Opposed to this new world at Paris, behold the old world at Versailles—that assembly of the ghouls of all defunct *régimes*, Legitimists and Orleanists, eager to feed upon the carcass of the nation,—with a tail of antediluvian Republicans, sanctioning, by their presence in the Assembly, the slaveholders' rebellion. . . . There it was, this Assembly, the representative of everything

***During the Second Empire, Baron Haussmann was Prefect of the Department of the Seine, that is, of the City of Paris. He introduced a number of changes in the layout of the city for the purpose of facilitating the crushing of workers' insurrections. [Note to the Russian edition of 1905 edited by V. I. Lenin.]**

dead in France, propped up to the semblance of life by nothing but the swords of the generals of Louis Bonaparte.

Marx, *Civil War in France* (1871), MESW, pp. 288–300.

If you look at the last chapter of my *Eighteenth Brumaire* you will find that I say that the next attempt of the French revolution will be no longer, as before, to transfer the bureaucratic military machine from one hand to another, but to *smash* it, and that is essential for every real people's revolution on the Continent. And this is what our heroic Party comrades, in Paris are attempting. What elasticity, what historical initiative, what a capacity for sacrifice in these Parisians! After six months of hunger and ruin, caused rather by internal treachery than by the external enemy, they rise, beneath Prussian bayonets, as if there had never been a war between France and Germany and the enemy were not at the gates of Paris. History has no like example of a like greatness. If they are defeated only their "good nature" will be to blame. They should have marched at once on Versailles, after first Vincy and then the reactionary section of the Paris National Guard had themselves retreated. The right moment was missed because of conscientious scruples. They did not want to *start the civil war,* as if that mischievous *abortion* Thiers had not already started the civil war with his attempt to disarm Paris. Second mistake: The Central Committee surrendered its power too soon, to make way for the Commune. Again from a too "honourable" scrupulosity! However that may be, the present rising in Paris—even if it be crushed by the wolves, swine and vile curs of the old society—is the most glorious deed of our Party since the June insurrection, in Paris.

Marx, letter to Kugelmann (1871), LK, p. 123.

8.C.15 RUSSIA AND THE WEST

THE COMMUNIST MANIFESTO: PREFACE TO THE RUSSIAN EDITION OF 1882

The first Russian edition of the *Manifesto of the Communist Party,* translated by Bakunin, was published early in the 'sixties by the printing office of the *Kolokol.* Then the West could see in it (the Russian edition of the *Manifesto*) only a literary curiosity. Such a view would be impossible today.

What a limited field the proletarian movement occupied at that time (December 1847) is most clearly shown by the last section: the position of the Communists in relation of the various opposition parties in the various countries. Precisely Russia and the United States are missing here. It was the time when Russia constituted the last great reserve of all European reaction, when the United States absorbed the surplus proletarian forces of Europe through immigration. Both countries provided Europe with raw materials and were at the same time markets for the sale of its industrial products. Both were therefore, in one way or another, pillars of the existing European system.

How very different today! Precisely European immigration fitted North America for a gigantic agricultural production, whose competition is shaking the very foundations of European landed property—large and small. At the same time it enabled the United States to exploit its tremendous industrial resources with an energy and on a scale that must shortly break the industrial monopoly of Western Europe, and especially of England, existing up to now. Both circumstances react in a revolutionary manner upon America itself. Step by step the small and middle land ownership of the farmers, the basis of the whole political constitution, is succumbing to the competition of giant farms; at the same time a mass industrial proletariat and a fabulous concentration of capital funds are developing for the first time in the industrial regions.

And now Russia! During the Revolution of 1848–49 not only the European princes, but the European bourgeois as well, found their only salvation from the proletariat just beginning to awaken in Russian intervention. The tsar was proclaimed the chief of European reaction. Today he is prisoner of war of the revolution in Gatchina, and Russia forms the vanguard of revolutionary action in Europe.

The Communist Manifesto had as its object the proclamation of the inevitable impending dissolution of modern bourgeois property. But in Russia we find, face to face with the rapidly flowering capitalist swindle and bourgeois property, just beginning to develop, more than half the land owned in common by the peasants. Now the question is: can the Russian *obshchina,* though greatly undermined, yet a form of the primeval common ownership of land, pass directly to the higher form of communist common ownership? Or on the contrary, must it first pass through the same process of dissolution such as constitutes the historical evolution of the West?

The only answer to that possible today is this: If the Russian Revolution becomes the signal for a proletarian revolution in the West, so that both complement each other, the present Russian common ownership of land may serve as the starting point for a communist development.

Marx-Engels, Preface to 2nd Russian Edition of *Communist Manifesto* (1882), MESW, I, pp. 191–92.

MARX ON RUSSIA

If Russia continues to pursue the path she has followed since 1861, she will lose the finest chance* ever offered by history to a nation, in order to undergo all the fatal vicissitudes of the capitalist regime.

The chapter on primitive accumulation does not pretend to do more than trace the path by which, in Western Europe, the capitalist order of economy emerged from the womb of the feudal order of economy. It therefore describes the historic movement which by divorcing the producers from their means of production converts them into wage earners (proletarians in the modern sense of the word) while it converts into capitalists those who hold the means of production in possession. In that history, "all revolutions are epoch-making

*I.e. The finest chance of escaping capitalist development. [*Ed. Eng. ed.*]

which serve as levers for the advancement of the capitalist class in course of formation; above all those which, after stripping great masses of men of their traditional means of production and subsistence, suddenly fling them on to the labour market. But the basis of this whole development is the expropriation of the cultivators.

"This has not yet been radically accomplished except in England . . . but all the countries of Western Europe are going through the same movement," etc. (*Capital,* French Edition, 1879, p. 315). At the end of the chapter the historic tendency of production is summed up thus: That it itself begets its own negation with the inexorability which governs the metamorphoses of nature; that it has itself created the elements of a new economic order, by giving the greatest impulse at once to the productive forces of social labour and to the integral development of every individual producer; that capitalist property, resting as it actually does already on a form of collective production, cannot do other than transform itself into social property. At this point I have not furnished any proof, for the good reason that this statement is itself nothing else than the short summary of long developments previously given in the chapters on capitalist production.

Now what application to Russia can my critic make of this historical sketch? Only this: If Russia is tending to become a capitalist nation after the example of the Western European countries, and during the last years she has been taking a lot of trouble in this direction—she will not succeed without having first transformed a good part of her peasants into proletarians; and after that, once taken to the bosom of the capitalist regime, she will experience its pitiless laws like other profane peoples. That is all. But that is not enough for my critic. He feels himself obliged to metamorphose my historical sketch of the genesis of capitalism in Western Europe into an historico-philosphic theory of the *marche genérale* [general path] imposed by fate upon every people, whatever the historic circumstances in which it finds itself, in order that it may ultimately arrive at the form of economy which will ensure, together with the greatest expansion of the productive powers of social labour, the most complete development of man. But I beg his pardon. (He is both honouring and shaming me too much.) Let us take an example.

In several parts of *Capital* I allude to the fate which overtook the plebeians of ancient Rome. They were originally free peasants, each cultivating his own piece of land on his own account. In the course of Roman history they were expropriated. The same movement which divorced them from their means of production and subsistence involved the formation not only of big landed property but also of big money capital. And so one fine morning there were to be found on the one hand free men, stripped of everything except their labour power, and on the other, in order to exploit this labour, those who held all the acquired wealth in possession. What happened? The Roman proletarians became, not wage labourers but a *mob* of do-nothings more abject than the former "poor whites" in the southern country of the United States, and alongside of them there developed a mode of production which was not capitalist but dependent upon slavery. Thus events strikingly analogous but taking place in different historic surroundings led to totally different results. By studying each of these forms of evolution separately and then comparing them one can easily find the clue to this phenomenon, but one will never arrive there by the universal passport of a general historico-philosophical theory, the supreme virtue of which consists in being super-historical.

Marx, Reply To Michaelovsky (1877), SC, pp. 353–55.

If capitalist production must establish its reign in Russia, the great majority of Russian people, that is, of the Russian peasants, must be converted into wage earners, and consequently expropriated by the preliminary abolition of its communist property. But in any case the western precedent would not prove anything at all concerning the 'historical fatality' of this process.

In this western movement, we are concerned with the transformation of one form of private property into another form of private property. Whether one affirms or denies the fatality of this transformation the reasons for or against have nothing to do with my analysis of the genesis of the capitalist regime. At most one could infer that, considering the present state of the great majority of Russian peasants, their conversion into small-scale proprietors would merely be the prologue to their rapid expropriation. . . .

At the same time as the commune is being bled and tortured, its land sterilised and pauperised, the literary lacqueys of the 'new columns of society' ironically characterise the wounds inflicted on the commune as so many symptoms of its spontaneous and incontestable decrepitude, and argue that it is dying a natural death and that a good turn will be served by shortening its agony. Here there is no longer a problem to be solved; it is a question very simply of fighting an enemy. Thus it is no longer a theoretical problem. To save the Russian commune, there must be a Russian revolution. Moreover, the Russian government and the 'new columns of society' are doing their best to prepare the masses for just such a catastrophe. If the revolution occurs at an opportune moment, if it concentrates all its forces to ensure the free development of the rival commune, this commune will soon become an element that regenerates Russian society and renders it superior to the countries enslaved by the capitalist regime.

Drafts of letter to Vera Zassoulitch (1881); *Œuvres*, ed. Rubel, II 1560, 1573. Cited in McLellan, KM, p. 137.

ENGELS ON RUSSIA

The following lines were written on the occasion of a controversy into which I was drawn by Mr. Peter Nikitich Tkachov. . . .

[This] reprint. . .deals chiefly with social conditions in Russia, as they have developed since 1861, since the so-called emancipation of the peasants.

The development of things in Russia is of the greatest importance for the German working class. The present Russian empire constitutes the last great stronghold of all West European reaction. . . . No revolution in Western Europe can finally conquer as long as the present Russian state exists beside it. Germany, however, is its next-door neighbour, hence Germany is the first to receive the shock of the Russian armies of reaction. The overthrow of Russian tsardom, the dissolution of the Russian empire, is consequently one of the first conditions for the final victory of the German proletariat.

But this overthrow need by no means necessarily be brought about from without, although a foreign war might greatly hasten it. Within the Russian empire itself there are forces working strongly for its ruin.

The first of these is the *Poles.* Century-long oppression has put them in a position where they must either be revolutionary and support every really revolutionary rising of the West as the first step towards the liberation of Poland or perish. . . .

But the activity of the Poles is territorially limited. It is confined to Poland, Lithuania and Little Russia; the real heart of the Russian empire, Great Russia, remains practically excluded from its action. The forty million Great Russians are much too big a people and have had much too special a development for it to be possible that a movement could be imposed on them from without. This however is by no means necessary. It is true that the mass of the Russian people, the peasants, have for centuries past vegetated apathetically from generation to generation in a sort of stupor, outside of history, and the only variations which somewhat interrupted this desolate state consisted in isolated fruitless revolts and in renewed oppression by nobility and government. The Russian government itself put an end to this living outside of history (1861) by the abolition of serfdom, which could not be put off any longer, and the redemption of the *corvée*—a measure drafted with such excessive cunning that it spells certain ruin for the majority both of the peasants and the nobles. Hence the circumstances themselves in which the Russian peasant is now placed drive him into the movement, a movement which certainly is still only in its very earliest beginnings but which is irresistibly driven onward by the economic position of the mass of the peasants which grows worse from day to day. The resentful discontent of the peasants is already a fact with which both the government and all dissatisfied and opposition parties must reckon.

It follows from this that when Russia is spoken of in the following pages, not the whole Russian empire is meant but only Great Russia, i.e., the territory whose most western gubernias are Pskov and Smolensk, the most southern, Kursk and Voronezh.

On the subject matter, Mr. Tkachov offers the following reasons why just at the present time a social revolution could be made in Russia with the greatest of ease, much more easily than in Western Europe.

> "We have no city proletariat, that is undoubtedly true, but to balance that we have also no bourgeoisie. . . our workers will have to fight only against the *political power*—the *power of capital* is with us still only in germ. And you, sir, are well aware that the fight against the former is much easier than against the latter."

The revolution which modern socialism strives to achieve is, briefly, the victory of the proletariat over the bourgeoisie, and the organisation of a new society by the destruction of all class differences. For this, there must be not only a proletariat that carries out this revolution, but also a bourgeoisie in whose hands the social productive forces have so far developed as to allow of the final destruction of class differences. Among savages and semi-savages there often exist likewise no class differences, and every people has passed through such a state. To reestablish this state could not occur to us for the simple reason that class differences necessarily emerge out of it as the social productive forces develop. Only at a certain level of development of the social productive forces, even at a very high level for our modern conditions, will it be possible to raise production to such an extent that the abolition of class differences can be a real progress and lasting without causing stagnation or even decline in the mode of social production. But the productive forces have reached this level of development only in the hands of the bourgeoisie. The bourgeoisie, therefore, in this respect also is just as necessary a pre-condition of the socialist revolution as the proletariat itself. Hence a man who can say that this revolution can be more easily carried out in a country, because, although having no proletariat, it has no bourgeoisie either, only proves that he has still to learn the ABC of socialism.

The Russian workers—and these workers are, as Mr. Tkachov himself says, "peasants and as such not proletarians but *owners*"—have therefore an easier task because they do not have to fight with the power of capital, but "simply with the political power," with the Russian state. And this state:

> "only appears from a distance as a power...it has no roots in the economic life of the people; it does not embody the interests of any particular estate. ... In your country the state is no imaginary power. It stands four square on the basis capital; it embodies in itself (!!) certain economic interests. ... In our country this situation is just reversed—the form of our society owes its existence to the state, to a state more or less hanging in the air, one that has nothing in common with the existing social order, and that has its roots in the past, but not in the present."

We will waste no time over the confused notion that the economic interests need the state, which they themselves create, in order to acquire a *body,* or the bold contention that the Russian form of society (which must include also the communal ownership of the peasants) owes its existence to the state, or over the contradiction that this same state "has nothing in common" with the existing social order which, however, is supposed to be its very own creation. Let us rather examine at once this "state hanging in the air," which does not represent the interests of even a single estate.

In European Russia the peasants possess 105 million dessiatines, the nobility (as I here term the big landowners for brevity) 100 million dessiatines, of which about half belong to 15,000 nobles, who consequently each possess on the average 33,000 dessiatines. The land of the peasants is therefore only a trifle bigger than that of the nobles. The nobles, one sees, have not the slightest interest in the existence of the Russian state, which guards them in the possession of half the country. Let us continue. The peasants, from their half, pay

195 million rubles land tax annually, the nobles—13 million! The lands of the nobles are on the average twice as fertile as those of the peasants because during the arrangements for redemption of the *corvée* the state not only took the greater part but also the best part of the land from the peasants and gave it to the nobles, and indeed for this worst land the peasants had to pay the nobility the price of the best. And the Russian nobility has no interest in the existence of the Russian state!

The peasants—taken in the mass—have been brought by the redemption settlements into a most miserable and wholly untenable position. Not only has the greatest and best part of their land been taken from them, so that in all the fertile parts of the country the peasant land is far too small—for Russian agricultural conditions—for them to be able to live from it. Not only were they charged an excessive price for it, advanced to them by the state and for which they now have to pay interest and amortisation to the state. Not only is almost the whole burden of the land tax thrown upon them, while the nobility escapes almost scotfree—so that the land tax alone consumes the entire ground rent value of the peasant land and more, and all further payments, which the peasant has to make and which we will speak of immediately, are direct deductions from that part of his income which represents his wages. No. In addition to the land tax, to the interest and amortisation instalments on the money advanced by the state, since the recent introduction of local government there are the provincial and district taxes as well. The most essential result of this "reform" was fresh tax burdens for the peasant. The state retained its revenue as a whole, but passed on a large part of its expenditure to the provinces and districts, which imposed new taxes to meet them, and in Russia it is the rule that the higher estates of society are practically free from taxation and the peasant pays almost everything. . . .

It is clear that the position of the Russian peasants since the emancipation from serfdom has become an intolerable, and in the long run, an untenable one, and that for this reason alone a revolution in Russia is approaching. The question is only, what can be, what will be the result of this revolution. Mr. Tkachov says it will be a social one. This is pure tautology. Every real revolution is a social one, in that it brings a new class to power and allows it to remodel society in its own image. But he wishes to say it will be a socialist one, it will introduce into Russia the form of society aimed at by West European socialism, even before we in the West succeed in doing so—and that, in a condition of society in which both proletariat and bourgeoisie only appear sporadically and at a low stage of development. And this is supposed to be possible because the Russians are, so to speak, the chosen people of socialism and have artels and communal ownership of land. . . .

[Artels] are established by a contract signed by all the members. If now these members cannot bring together the necessary capital, as very often happens, for instance, in the case of cheese-dairies and fisheries (for nets, boats, etc.), the artel falls a prey to the usurer, who advances the amount lacking at high interest, and thereafter pockets the greater part of the labour proceeds. Still more shamefully exploited however are the artels which hire themselves as a whole to an employer as a wage force. They direct their industrial activity themselves and thus save the capitalist the cost of supervision. The latter lets the members huts to live in and advances them the means of subsistence, whereby again the most disgraceful truck system develops. . . . Here then the artel serves to *facilitate* considerably the exploitation of the worker by the capitalist. On the other hand again, there are also artels which themselves employ workers who are *not* members of the association.

It is clear, therefore, that the artel is a cooperative society which has arisen spontaneously and is therefore still very undeveloped, and as such neither exclusively Russian nor even Slavonic. Such societies are formed wherever the need for them exists. For instance, in Switzerland among the dairy farmers, in England among the fishermen, where they even assume very varied forms. The Silesian navvies (Germans, not Poles), who built so many German railways in the 'forties, were organised in complete artels. The predominance of this form in Russia proves, it is true, the existence of a strong impulse to association in the Russian people, but is far from proving their ability to jump without more ado, by aid of this impulse, from the artel into the socialist form of society. For that, it is necessary above all that the artel itself should be capable of development, that it shed its primitive form, in which, as we saw, it serves the workers less than it does capital, and rise *at least* to the standpoint of the West European cooperative societies. . . .

The modern cooperative society has at least proved that it can run a big industry advantageously on its own account (spinning and weaving in Lancashire). The artel is so far not only incapable of doing this, it must of necessity be destroyed by big industry if it does not develop further.

The communal ownership of the Russian peasants was discovered about the year 1845 by the Prussian *Regierungsrat* [Civil Councillor] Haxthausen and trumpeted to the world as something absolutely wonderful, although Haxthausen could still have found survivals enough of it in his Westphalian homeland, and, as a government official, it was even part of his duty to know them thoroughly. It was from Haxthausen that Herzen, himself a Russian landowner, first learned that his peasants owned the land in common, and he made use of the fact to describe the Russian peasants as the real bearers of socialism, as born communists in contrast to the workers of the ageing, decayed European West, who have had to acquire socialism artificially and painfully. From Herzen this knowledge came to Bakunin, and from Bakunin to Mr. Tkachov. . . .

In reality communal ownership of the land is an institution which is to be found on a low level of development among all Indo-Germanic races from India to Ireland and even among the Malays who have developed under Indian influence, for instance, in Java. . . . In Western Europe, including Poland and Little Russia, at a certain stage in the social development this communal ownership became a fetter, a brake on agricultural production, and was more and more eliminated. In Great Russia (i.e., Russia proper), on the other hand, it has persisted until today, thereby proving in the first place that agricultural production and the social conditions in the countryside corresponding to it are there still on a very undeveloped level, as is also actually the case. The Russian peasant only lives and has his being in his village, the rest of the world only exists for him in so far as it affects his village. This is so much the case that in Russian the same word "*mir*" means on the one hand "world" and on the other "peasant community." "*Ves mir,*" the whole world, means for the peasant the meeting of the community members. Hence, when Mr. Tkachov speaks of the "*world* outlook" of the Russian peasants, he has obviously translated the Russian *mir* incorrectly. Such a complete isolation of the individual communities from one another, which creates throughout the country, it is true, similar, but the very opposite of common, interests, is the natural basis for *oriental despotism*, and from India to Russia this form of society, wherever it prevailed, has always produced it and always found its complement in it. Not only the Russian state in general, but even its specific form, tsarist despotism, instead of hanging in the air, is the necessary and logical product of the Russian social conditions with which, according to Mr. Tkachov, it has "nothing in common"! Further development of Russia in a *bourgeois* direction would here also destroy communal ownership little by little, without its being necessary for the Russian government to intervene with "bayonet and knout." And this all the more because the communally owned land in Russia is not cultivated by the peasants collectively and only the product divided, as is still the case in some districts in India; on the contrary, from time to time the land is divided up among the various heads of families, and each cultivates his allotment for himself. Consequently, great differences in prosperity are possible, among the members of the community, and also here and there millionaires—who play the usurer and suck the blood of the mass of the peasants. No one knows this better than Mr. Tkachov. While he wishes to fool the German workers into thinking that the "idea of collective ownership" can only be driven out of the Russian peasants, these instinctive, traditional communists, by bayonet and knout he writes on page 15 of his Russian pamphlet: "Among the peasants a class of usurers (kulaks), is making its way, a class of people who *buy up* and lease the lands of farmers and nobles—a peasant aristocracy." These are the same kind of bloodsuckers as we described more fully above.

What dealt the severest blow to communal ownership was again the redemption of the *corvée*. The greater and better part of the land was allotted to the nobility; for the peasant there remained scarcely enough, often not enough, to live on. In addition the forests were given to the nobles; the wood for fuel, building and implements, which the peasant formerly could fetch there for nothing, he has now to buy. Thus the peasant has nothing now but his house and the bare land, without means to cultivate it, and on the average without land enough to support him and his family from one harvest to the next. Under such circumstances and under the pressure of taxes and usurers, communal ownership of the land is no blessing, it becomes a fetter. The peasants often run away, with or without their family, to earn their living as wandering labourers, and leave their land behind them.

It is clear that communal ownership in Russia is long past its flourishing period and to all appearances is moving towards its dissolution. Nevertheless the possibility undeniably exists of transforming this social form into a higher one, if it should last until circumstances are ripe for that, and if it shows itself capable of development in such a way that the peasants no longer cultivate the land separately, but collectively; and to transform it into this higher form, without it being necessary for the Russian peasants to go through the intermediate stage of bourgeois small ownership. This, however, can only happen if, before the complete break-up of communal ownership, a proletarian revolution is successfully carried out in Western Europe, creating for the Russian peasant the pre-conditions necessary for such a transformation, in particular, the material conditions which he needs in order to carry through the reconstruction of his whole agricultural system thereby necessarily involved. It is therefore sheer bounce for Mr. Tkachov to say that the Russian peasants, although "owners," stand "nearer to socialism" than the propertyless workers of Western Europe. Exactly the contrary is the case. If anything can still save Russian communal ownership and give it a chance of growing into a new form really capable of life, it is a proletarian revolution in Western Europe.

Mr. Tkachov treats the political revolution just as lightly as he does the economic one. "The Russian people," he relates, "protests incessantly" against its enslavement, now in the form "of religious sects. . .refusal to pay taxes. . .robber bands. . .incendiarism. . .revolts. . .and hence the Russian people may be termed instinctive revolutionaries." . . .

There is no doubt Russia is on the eve of a revolution. Her finances are in extreme disorder. Increasing taxation proves of no avail, the interest on old state loans is paid by means of new loans, and every new loan meets with greater difficulties; money can now only be raised under the pretext of building railways! The administration, as of old, corrupt from top to bottom, the officials living more from theft, bribery and extortion than from their salaries. The entire agricultural production—by far the most essential for Russia—thrown into complete disorder by the redemption settlement of 1861; the big landowners without sufficient labour, the peasants without sufficient land, oppressed by taxation and sucked dry by usurers, the yield from agriculture declining from year to year. The whole held together with great difficulty and only outwardly by an oriental despotism whose arbitrariness we in the West simply cannot imagine; a despotism which not only from day to day comes into more glaring contradiction with the views of the enlightened classes and in particular with those of the rapidly developing bourgeoisie of the capital cities, but which, under its present bearer, has lost faith in itself, one day making concessions to liberalism and the next cancelling them again in terror, and thus bringing itself more and more into disrepute. With all that, a growing recognition among the englightened strata of the nation concentrated in the capital that this position is untenable, that a revolution is imminent, and the illusion that it will be possible to guide this revolution into a smooth, constitutional channel. Here we have united all the conditions of a revolution, of a revolution which, possibly started by the upper classes of the capital, even perhaps by the government itself, must be rapidly carried further, beyond the first constitutional phase, by the peasants; of a revolution, which will be of the greatest importance for the whole of Europe if only because it will destroy at one blow the last, so far intact, reserve of the entire European reaction. This revolution is surely approaching. Only two events can delay it: a successful war against Turkey or Austria, for which money and firm alliances are necessary, or—a premature attempt at insurrection which would drive the property-owning classes back into the arms of the government.

Engels, *On Russia* (1877), MESW, II, pp. 669–85.

9 Capitalism's Supersession and Successors: Socialism and Communism

This final chapter examines Marx's unique vision of postcapitalist society, and, to some extent, the closely related though not identical views of Engels on this subject. We may grant that Marx prudently refused to write "recipes for the cookshops of the future." Still, he (and Engels) wrote far more extensively on this subject than is popularly supposed, especially on broad aspects of the character, organization, and structure of the prospective future society (in contrast to analytic models of prospective socialist behavior).

A. EVOLUTION OF THE MARXIAN VIEW OF COMMUNISM

Valuable perspective on the Marxian view of communism[1] may be obtained by a review of the evolution of the subject in the Marx-Engels writings. In his early (1843) study, *On the Jewish Question* (selection 9.A.1), Marx distinguishes between mere political emancipation, important though that was relative to earlier illiberal and despotic forms of political organization, and genuine "human emancipation," i.e., the radical reconstruction of man's socioeconomic life and the termination of alienation or separation between private and public sectors of society and among men based on egoistic pursuits of strictly individual gain.

In the 1844 *Economic and Philosophical Manuscripts* (and briefly in the earlier 1844 Notes on James Mill, selection 9.A.2), Marx identifies his view of communism as that of an authentic human community which has superseded the various forms of alienation examined earlier (selection 4.B.4). This genuine, unalienated communism is contrasted with a "crude communism" which is perceived to emerge at a low level of economic development and which has simply transferred the capitalist function to society as a "universal capitalist," thus

[1]Although Marx typically used the term "communism" to describe the future society, it was essentially interchangeable with "socialism," especially in the early writings. Subsequently (selection 9.B.12), he distinguished between a "lower phase" and a "higher phase" of communism. In the post-Marx literature, these have often been described more simply as "socialism" and (full or pure) "communism," respectively. For example, Soviet leaders from Stalin onward have identified the Soviet economic system as "socialist," although perhaps (as announced in the early 1960s), in the process of transition to (a higher stage of) "communism." West European democratic socialists occasionally refer to such societies as Sweden, for example, as partially "socialist." The word "communism" is occasionally used to refer to societies whose political structures are controlled by one communist party or another. This does not necessarily imply achievement of the classical Marx-Engels vision of "communism," in either its "lower" or "higher phase."

retaining most of the alienating (and, one would presume, exploitative) properties associated with the Marxian view of private property capitalism.

In *The German Ideology* of 1845–46, Marx and Engels put communism into historical perspective by identifying its preconditions and bases (selection 9.A.3). Communism, they state, "is for us not a *state of affairs* still to be established, not an *ideal* to which reality [will] have to adjust. We call communism the *real* movement which abolishes the present state of affairs." *The German Ideology* is also notable for its identification of the working class as the historic agent of the prospective movement toward communism, and for specification of some of communism's prominent institutional characteristics.

In all three of these early works of the 1840s, Marx and Engels clearly perceive communism as a prospective reconciliation of individual and society (selection 9.A.4). On the one hand, the individual under communism is perceived as a "social individual," not an atomistic unit of economic decision in effect isolated and separated from other individuals by capitalist institutions (e.g., private property, market exchange). On the other, "society" under communism is not a crude collectivist organism in which all individuality has been stifled. Instead, communism is perceived by the young authors to provide an environment in which the individuality of all members of society can flourish.

Especially from *The German Ideology* onward, Marx and Engels focus on capitalism as a class-structured society, characterized by deep and enlarging class struggles. Communism, by contrast, is perceived as a potential *classless* society, in the sense of termination of a division of society into those who do and those who do not own the physical means of production (selection 9.A.5). The proletariat is described as a "universal" class; its emancipation from the dominant-subservient relationship prevalent in capitalism contains the potential for the elimination of all classes.

Of the two writers, Marx was more philosophically trained and more politically attuned. Engels, by contrast, had direct business experience and was more practical-minded. In the writings of the 1840s, Engels was far more impressed than Marx with the potentialities of science and technology. In his 1847 "Principles of Communism," written as a first draft for the *Manifesto,* Engels presents a vision of the eradication of poverty and achievement of abundance for all members of society under communism, free from the disruptions of capitalist cycles and depressions (selection 9.A.6).

In the *Grundrisse* of 1857–58, Marx develops one general and two specific dimensions of the future society. The general point, as already indicated briefly in chapter 7 (especially selection 7.B.1), is that of the intimate dialectical relationship between socialism and capitalism. For Marx, socialism is an extension and universalization of the capitalist developmental process. Socialism does not merely succeed capitalism; it *supersedes* it. Although socialism goes beyond capitalism, it contains within it trends and tendencies initiated and cultivated by capitalism. In effect, socialism is (the extension of) capitalism without capitalism's alienating, exploitative, and contradictory institutions or behavior. As such, it fulfills the potentialities and promises of capitalism and is the realization of capitalism's "historic destiny." The two specific points are that the science, technology, and automation of late-stage capitalism, continued and socially directed under communist auspices, may be used both to reduce working hours and thereby expand "free time" for individual development and to radically reorganize and humanize the work process itself (selection 9.A.7).

In a famous passage in *Capital,* Marx continues the theme of the potentialities for the free and creative use of greater leisure under communism unleashed by technological improvements and rising productivity. Communist production, though eliminating the various contradictory properties of capitalism, still remains a "realm of necessity." Beyond production of material products lies the "realm of freedom," i.e., the leisure time for cultural and artistic pursuits. The foundation for the "realm of freedom" is reduction of the working day (selection 9.A.8).

9.A.1 COMMUNISM AS HUMAN EMANCIPATION

The question [is one] of the *relation between political emancipation and human emancipation.* ...

To be *politically* emancipated . . . is not to be finally and completely emancipated . . . , because political emancipation is not the final and absolute form of *human* emancipation.

The limits of political emancipation appear at once in the fact that the *state* can liberate itself from a constraint without man himself being *really* liberated; that a state may be a *free state* without man himself being a *free man.* ...

For example, the state as a state abolishes *private property* (i.e. man decrees by *political* means the *abolition* of private property) when it abolishes the *property qualification* for electors and representatives, as has been done in many of the North American States. Hamilton interprets this phenomenon quite correctly from the political standpoint: *The masses have gained a victory over property owners and financial wealth.* Is not private property ideally abolished when the non-owner comes to legislate for the owner of property? The *property qualification* is the last *political* form in which private property is recognized.

But the political suppression of private property not only does not abolish private property; it actually presupposes its existence. The state abolishes, after its fashion, the distinctions established by *birth, social rank, education, occupation,* when it decrees that birth, social rank, education, occupation are *non-political* distinctions; when it proclaims, without regard to these distinctions, that every member of society is an *equal* partner in popular sovereignty, and treats all the elements which compose the real life of the nation from the standpoint of the state. But the state, none the less, allows private property, education, occupation, to *act* after *their* own fashion, namely as private property, education, occupation, and to manifest their *particular* nature. Far from abolishing these *effective* differences, it only exists so far as they are presupposed; it is conscious of being a *political state* and manifests its *universality* only in opposition to these elements. ...

The perfected political state is, by its nature, the *species-life* of man as *opposed* to his material life. All the presuppositions of this egoistic life continue to exist in *civil society outside* the political sphere, as qualities of civil society. Where the political state has attained to its full development, man leads, not only in thought, in consciousness, but in *reality,* in *life,* a double existence—celestial and terrestrial. He lives in the *political community,* where he regards himself as a *communal being,* and in *civil society* where he acts simply as a *private individual,* treats other men as means, degrades himself to the role of a mere means, and becomes the plaything of alien powers. The political state. . . stands in the same opposition to civil society, and overcomes it in the same manner as religion overcomes the narrowness of the profane world; i.e. it has always to acknowledge it again, reestablish it, and allow itself to be dominated by it. Man, in his *most intimate* reality, in civil society, is a profane being. Here, where he appears both to himself and to others as a real individual he is an *illusory* phenomenon. In the state, on the contrary, where he is regarded as a species-being, man is the imaginary member of an imaginary sovereignty, divested of his real, individual life, and infused with an unreal universality.

Political emancipation certainly represents a great progress. It is not, indeed, the final form of human emancipation, but it is the final form of human emancipation *within* the framework of the prevailing social order. It goes without saying that we are speaking here of real, practical emancipation.

Man emancipates himself *politically* from religion by expelling it from the sphere of public law to that of private law. . . . It has been relegated among the numerous private interests and exiled from the life of the community as such. But one should have no illusions about the scope of political emancipation. The division of man into the *public person* and the *private person,* the *displacement* of religion from the state to civil society—all this is not a stage in political emancipation but its consummation. . .

What prevails in the so-called Christian state is not man but alienation. . . .

Political democracy is Christian in the sense that man, not merely one man but every man, is there considered a sovereign being, a supreme being; but it is uneducated, unsocial man, man just as he is in his fortuitous existence, man as he has been corrupted, lost to himself, alienated, subjected to the rule of inhuman conditions and elements, by the whole organization of our society—in short man who is not yet a *real* species-being. . . .

We have shown, therefore, that political emancipation from religion leaves religion in existence, although this is no longer a privileged religion. The contradiction in which the adherent of a particular religion finds himself in relation to his citizenship is only *one aspect* of the universal *secular contradiction between the political state and* civil society. . . . The emancipation of the state from religion is not the emancipation of the real man from religion.

We. . . say. . ., therefore, . . .that *political emancipation* itself is not *human* emancipation. If you want to be politically emancipated, without emancipating yourselves humanly, the inadequacy and the contradiction is not entirely in yourselves but in the *nature* and the *category* of political emancipation. . . .

Let us consider for a moment the so-called rights of man; let us examine them in their most authentic form, that which they have among those who *discovered* them, the North Americans and the French! These rights of man are, in part, *political* rights, which can only be exercised if one is a member of a community. Their content is *participation* in the *community* life, in the *political* life of the community, the life of the state. They fall in the category of *political liberty,* of *civil rights.* . . .

A distinction is made between the rights of man and the rights of the citizen. Who is this *man* distinct from the *citizen*? No one but the *member of civil society.* Why is the member of civil society called "man," simply man, and why are his rights called "rights of man"? How is this fact to be explained? By the relation between the political state and civil society, and by the nature of political emancipation.

Let us notice first of all that the so-called *rights of man,* as distinct from the *rights of the citizen,* are simply the rights of a *member of civil society,* that is, of egoistic man, of man separated from other men and from the community. The most radical constitution, that of 1793, says: *Declaration of the Rights of Man and of the Citizen:* Article 2. "These rights, etc. (the natural and imprescriptible rights) are: *equality, liberty, security, property.*

What constitutes liberty?

Article 6. "Liberty is the power which man has to do everything which does not harm the rights of others."

Liberty is, therefore, the right to do everything which does not harm others. The limits within which each individual can act without harming others are determined by law, just as the boundary between two fields is marked by a stake. It is a question of the liberty of man regarded as an isolated monad, withdrawn into himself. . . . But liberty as a right of man is not founded upon the relations between man and man, but rather upon the separation of man from man. It is the right of such separation. The right of the *circumscribed* individual, withdrawn into himself.

The practical application of the right of liberty is the right of private property. What constitutes the right of private property?

Article 16 (*Constitution* of 1793). "The right of *property* is that which belongs to every citizen of enjoying and disposing *as he will* of his goods and revenues, of the fruits of his work and industry."

The right of property is, therefore, the right to enjoy one's fortune and to dispose of it as one will; without regard for other men and independently of society. It is the right of self-interest. This individual liberty, and its application, form the basis of civil society. It leads every man to see in other men, not the *realization,* but rather the *limitation* of his own liberty. . . .

There remain the other rights of man, equality and security.

The term "equality" has here no political significance. It is only the equal right to liberty as defined above; namely that every man is equally regarded as a self-sufficient monad. The Constitution of 1795 defines the concept of liberty in this sense.

Article 5 (*Constitution* of 1795). "Equality consists in the fact that the law is the same for all, whether it protects or punishes."

And security?

Article 8 (*Constitution* of 1793). "Security consists in the protection afforded by society to each of its members for the preservation of his person, his rights, and his property."

Security is the supreme social concept of civil society; the concept of the police. The whole society exists only in order to guarantee for each of its members the preservation of his person, his rights and his property.

The concept of security is not enough to raise civil society above its egoism. Security is, rather, the *assurance* of its egoism.

None of the supposed rights of man, therefore, go beyond the egoistic man, man as he is, as a member of civil society; that is, an individual separated from the community, withdrawn into himself, wholly preoccupied with his private interest and acting in accordance with his private caprice. Man is far from being considered, in the rights of man, as a species-being; on the contrary, species-life itself—society—appears as a system which is external to the individual and as a limitation of his original independence. The only bond between men is natural necessity, need and private interest, the preservation of their property and their egoistic persons.

It is difficult enough to understand that a nation which has just begun to liberate itself, to tear down all the barriers between different sections of the people and to establish a political community, should solemnly proclaim (*Declaration* of 1791) the rights of the egoistic man, separated from his fellow men and from the community, and should renew this proclamation at a moment when only the most heroic devotion can save the nation (and is, therefore, urgently called for), and when the sacrifice of all the interests of civil society is in question and egoism should be punished as a crime. (*Declaration of the Rights of Man, etc.* 1793.) The matter becomes still more incomprehensible when we observe that the political liberators reduce citizenship, the *political community,* to a mere *means* for preserving these so-called rights of man; and consequently, that the citizen is declared to be the servant of egoistic "man," that the sphere in which man functions as a species-being is degraded to a level below the sphere where he functions as a partial being, and finally that it is man as a bourgeois and not man as a citizen who is considered the *true* and *authentic* man. . . .

Political emancipation is at the same time the *dissolution* of the old society, upon which the sovereign power, the alienated political life of the people, rests. Political revolution is a revolution of civil society. What was the nature of the old society? It can be characterized in one word: *feudalism.* The old civil society had a *directly political* character; that is, the elements of civil life such as property, the family, and types of occupation had been raised, in the form of lordship, caste and guilds, to elements of political life. They determined, in this form, the relation of the individual to the *state as a whole*; that is, his *political* situation, or in other words, his separation and exclusion from the other elements of society. For this organization of national life did not constitute property and labour as social elements; it rather succeeded in *separating* them from the body of the state, and made them *distinct* societies within society. Nevertheless, at least in the feudal sense, the vital functions and conditions of civil society remained political. They excluded the individual from the body of the state, and transformed the *particular* relation which existed between his corporation and the state into a general relation between the individual and social life, just as they transformed his specific civil activity and situation into a general activity and situation. As a result of this organization, the state as a whole and its consciousness, will and activity—the general political power—also necessarily appeared as the *private* affair of a ruler and his servants, separated from the people.

The political revolution which overthrew this power of the ruler, which made state affairs the affairs of the people, and the political state a matter of *general* concern, i.e. a real state, necessarily shattered everything—estates, corporations, guilds, privileges—which expressed the separation of the people from community life. The political revolution therefore *abolished* the *political character of civil society.* It dissolved civil society into its basic elements, on the one hand *individuals,* and on the other hand the *material and cultural elements* which formed the life experience and the civil situation of these individuals. It set free the political spirit which had, so to speak, been dissolved, fragmented and lost in the various culs-de-sac of feudal society; it reassembled these scattered fragments, liberated the political spirit from its connexion with civil life and made of it the community sphere, the *general* concern of the people, in principle independent of these particular elements of civil life. A *specific* activity and situation in life no longer had any but an individual significance. They no longer constituted the general relation between the individual and the state as a whole. Public affairs as such became the general affair of each individual, and political functions became general functions.

But the consummation of the idealism of the state was at the same time the consummation of the materialism of civil society. The bonds which had restrained the egoistic spirit of civil society were removed along with the political yoke. Political emancipation was at the same time an emancipation of civil society from politics and from even the *semblance* of a general content.

Feudal society was dissolved into its basic element, *man*; but into *egoistic* man who was its real foundation.

Man in this aspect, the member of civil society, is now the foundation and presupposition of the *political* state. He is recognized as such in the rights of man.

But the liberty of egoistic man, and the recognition of this liberty, is rather the recognition of the *frenzied* movement of the cultural and material elements which form the content of his life.

Thus man was not liberated from religion; he received religious liberty. He was not liberated from property; he received the liberty to own property. He was not liberated from the egoism of business; he received the liberty to engage in business.

The *formation of the political state,* and the dissolution of civil society into independent *individuals* whose relations are regulated by *law,* as the relations between men in the corporations and guilds were regulated by *privilege,* are accomplished by *one and the same act.* Man as a member of civil society—*non-political* man—necessarily appears as the *natural* man. The rights of man appear as natural rights because *conscious* activity is concentrated upon political *action. Egoistic* man is the *passive, given* result of the dissolution of society, an object of *direct apprehension* and consequently a *natural* object. The *political revolution* dissolves civil society into its elements without *revolutionizing* these elements themselves or subjecting them to criticism. This revolution regards civil society, the sphere of human needs, labour, private interests and civil law, as the *basis of its own existence,* as a self-subsistent *precondition,* and thus as its *natural basis.* Finally, man as a member of civil society is identified with *authentic man, man* as distinct from citizen, because he is man in his sensuous, individual and *immediate* existence, whereas *political* man is only abstract, artificial man, man as an *allegorical, moral* person. Thus man as he really is, is seen only in the form of *egoistic* man, and man in his *true* nature only in the form of the *abstract citizen.* . . .

Every emancipation is a *restoration* of the human world and of human relationships to *man himself.*

Political emancipation is a reduction of man, on the one hand to a member of civil society, an *independent* and *egoistic* individual, and on the other hand, to a *citizen,* to a moral person.

Human emancipation will only be complete when the real, individual man has absorbed into himself the abstract citizen; when as an individual man, in his everyday life, in his work, and in his relationships, he has become a *species-being*; and when he has recognized and organized his own powers (*forces propres*) as *social* powers so that he no longer separates this social power from himself as *political* power.

Marx, *The Jewish Question* (1843), EW, pp. 10–16, 19–31.

9.A.2 COMMUNISM AS THE SUPERSESSION OF ALIENATION

FREE HUMAN PRODUCTION

It is the basic presupposition of private property that man *produces* only in order to *own.* The purpose of production is to *own.* It not only has such a *useful* purpose; it also has a *selfish* purpose. Man only produces in order to *own* something for himself. The object of his production is the objectification of his *immediate*, selfish *need.* . . .

As soon as exchange occurs, there is an overproduction beyond the immediate boundary of ownership. But this overproduction does not exceed selfish need. Rather it is only an *indirect* way of satisfying a need which finds its objectification in the production of another person. Production has become a *source of income,* labour for profit. While formerly need determined the extent of production, now production, or rather the *owning of the product,* determines how far needs can be satisfied.

I have produced for myself and not for you, just as you have produced for yourself and not for me. The result of my production as such has as little direct connection with you as the result of your production has with me, that is, our production is not production of man for man as man, not *socialized* production. No one is gratified by the product of another. Our mutual production means nothing for us as human beings. Our exchange, therefore, cannot be the mediating movement in which it would be acknowledged that my product means anything for you because it is an *objectification* of your being, your need. *Human nature* is not the bond of our production for each other. Exchange can only set in *motion* and confirm the *relationship* which each of us has to his own product and to the production of the other person. Each of us sees in his product only his *own* objectified self-interest and in the product of another person, *another* self-interest which is independent, alien, and objectified.

As a human being, however, you do have a human relation to my product; you *want* my product. It is the object of your desire and your will. But your want, desire, and will for my product are impotent. In other words, your *human* nature, necessarily and intimately related to my human production, is not your *power,* not your sharing in this production, because the *power* of human nature is not acknowledged in my production. Rather it is the *bond* which makes you dependent upon me because it makes you dependent on my product. It is far from being the *means* of giving you *power* over my production; rather it is the *means* of giving me power over you.

When I produce *more* than I can consume, I subtly *reckon* with your need. I produce only the *semblance* of a surplus of the object. In truth I produce a *different* object, the object of your production which I plan to exchange for this surplus, an exchange already accomplished in thought. My *social* relationship with you and my labour for your want is just plain *deception* and our mutual redintegration is *deception* just as well. Mutual pillaging is its base. Its background is the intent to pillage, to defraud. Since our exchange is selfish on your side as well as mine and since every self-interest attempts to surpass that of another person, we necessarily attempt to defraud each other. The power I give my object over yours, however, requires your *acknowledgment* to become real. Our mutual acknowledgment of the mutual power of our objects is a battle and the one with more insight, energy, power, and cleverness is the winner. If my physical strength suffices, I pillage you directly. If there is no physical power, we mutually dissemble and the more adroit comes out on top. It makes no difference for the *entire* relationship who the winner is, for the *ideal* and *intended* victory takes place on both sides; in his own judgment each of the two has overcome the other.

On both sides exchange necessarily requires the *object* of mutual production and mutual ownership. The ideal relationship to the mutual objects of our production is our mutual need. But the *real* and *truly effective* relationship is only the mutually *exclusive ownership* of mutual production. It is your *object,* the *equivalent* of my object, that gives your want for my object *value, dignity,* and *efficacy* for me. Our mutual product, therefore, is the *means*, the *intermediary,* the *instrument,* the *acknowledged power* of our mutual needs. Your *demand* and the *equivalent of your property* are terms which for me are *synonymous* and equally valid, and your demand is effective only when it has an effect on me. Without this effect your demand is merely an unsatisfied effort on your part and without consequence for me. You have no relationship to my object as a human being because I *myself* have no human relation to it. But the *means* is the *real power* over an object, and we mutually regard our product as the *power* each one has over the other and over himself. In other words, our own product is turned against us. It appeared to be our property, but actually we are its property. We ourselves are excluded from *true* property because our *property* excludes the other human being.

Our objects in their relation to one another constitute the only intelligible language we use with one another. We would not understand a human language, and it would remain without effect. On the one hand, it would be felt and spoken as a plea, as begging, and as *humiliation* and hence uttered with shame and with a feeling of supplication; on the other hand, it would be heard and rejected as *effrontery* or *madness.* We are so much mutually alienated from human nature that the direct language of this nature is an *injury to human dignity* for us, while the alienated language of objective values appears as justified, self-confident, and self-accepted human dignity.

To be sure, from your point of view your product is an *instrument,* a *means* for the appropriation of my product and for the satisfaction of your need. But from my point of view it is the *goal* of our exchange. I regard you as a means and instrument for the production of this object, that is, my goal, and much more so than I regard you as related to my object. But (1) each of us actually *does* what the other thinks he is doing. You actually made yourself the means, the instrument, and the producer of *your* own object in order to appropriate mine; (2) for you, your own object is only the *sensuous shell* and *concealed form* of my object; its production *means* and *expressly* is the *acquisition* of my object. You indeed become the *means* and *instrument* of your object; your greed is the *slave* of this object, and you performed slavish services so that the object is never again a remission of your greed. This mutual servitude to the object is actually manifested to us at the beginning of its development as the relationship of *lordship* and *slavery,* and is only the *crude* and *frank* expression of our *essential* relationship.

Our *mutual* value is the *value* of our mutual objects for us. Man himself, therefore, is mutually *valueless* for us.

Suppose we had produced things as human beings: in his production each of us would have *twice affirmed* himself and the other. (1) In my *production* I would have objectified my *individuality* and its *particularity,* and in the course of the activity I would have enjoyed an individual *life;* in viewing the object I would have experienced the individual joy of knowing my personality as an *objective, sensuously perceptible,* and *indubitable* power. (2) In your satisfaction and your use of my product I would have had the *direct* and conscious satisfaction that my work satisfied a *human* need, that it objectified *human* nature, and that it created an object appropriate to the need of another *human* being. (3) I would have been the *mediator* between you and the species and you would have experienced me as a redintegration of your own nature and a necessary part of your self; I would have been affirmed in your thought as well as your love. (4) In my individual life I would have directly created your life; in my individual activity I would have immediately *confirmed* and *realized* my true *human* and *social* nature.

Our productions would be so many mirrors reflecting our nature.

What happens so far as I am concerned would also apply to you.

Let us summarize the various factors in the supposition above:

My labour would be a *free manifestation of life* and an *enjoyment* of *life.* Under the presupposition of private property it is an *externalization of life* because I work *in order to live* and provide for myself the *means* of living. Working *is not* living.

Furthermore, in my labour the *particularity* of my individuality would be affirmed because my *individual* life is affirmed. Labour then would be *true, active property.* Under the presupposition of private property my individuality is externalized to the point where I *hate* this *activity* and where it is a *torment* for me. Rather it is then only the *semblance* of an activity, only a *forced* activity, imposed upon me only by *external* and accidental necessity and *not* by an *internal* and *determined* necessity.

My labour can appear in my object only according to its nature; it cannot appear as something *different* from itself. My labour, therefore, is manifested as the objective, sensuous, perceptible, and indubitable expression of my *self-loss* and my *powerlessness.*

Marx, *Notes on James Mill* (1844), YM, pp. 277–82.

PRIVATE PROPERTY AND COMMUNISM

The antithesis of *propertylessness* and *property* so long as it is not comprehended as the antithesis of *labour* and *capital,* still remains an antithesis of indifference, not grasped in its *active connection,* its *internal* relation—an antithesis not yet grasped as a *contradiction.* It can find expression in this *first* form even without the advanced development of private property (as in ancient Rome, Turkey, etc.). It does not yet *appear* as having been established by private property itself. But labour, the subjective essence of private property as exclusion of property, and capital, objective labour as exclusion of labour, constitute *private property* as its developed state of contradiction—hence a dynamic relationship moving inexorably to its resolution.

The transcendence of self-estrangement follows the same course as self-estrangement. *Private property* is first considered only in its objective aspect—but nevertheless with labour as its essence. Its form of existence is therefore *capital,* which is to be annulled "as such" (Proudhon). Or a *particular form* of labour—labour levelled down, parcelled, and therefore unfree—is conceived as the source of private property's *perniciousness* and of its existence in estrangement from men; for instance, *Fourier,* who, like the physiocrats, also conceived *agricultural labour* to be at least the *exemplary* type, whilst *Saint-Simon* declares in contrast that *industrial labour* as such is the essence, and now also aspires to the *exclusive* rule of the industrialists and the improvement of the workers' condition. Finally, *communism* is the *positive* expression of annulled private property—at first as *universal* private property. By embracing this relation as a *whole,* communism is:

1) In its first form only a *generalization* and *consummation* of this relationship. It shows itself as such in a twofold form: on the one hand, the dominion of *material* property bulks so large that it wants to destroy *everything* which is not capable of being possessed by all as *private property.* It wants to abstract *by force* from talent, etc. For it the sole purpose of life and existence is direct, physical *possession.* The category of *labourer* is not done away with, but extended to all men. The relationship of private property persists as the relationship of the community to the world of things . . . [in] this as yet completely crude and thoughtless communism. Just as the woman passes from marriage to general prostitution, so the entire world of wealth (that is, of man's objective substance) passes from the relationship of exclusive marriage with the owner of private property to a state of universal prostitution with the community. In negating the *personality* of man in every sphere, this type of communism is really nothing but the logical expression of private property, which is this negation. General *envy* constituting itself as a power is the

disguise in which *avarice* re-establishes itself and satisfies itself, only in *another* way. The thoughts of every piece of private property—inherent in each piece as such—are *at least* turned against all *wealthier* private property in the form of envy and the urge to reduce to a common level, so that this envy and urge even constitute the essence of competition. The crude communism is only the consummation of this envy and of this levelling-down proceeding from the *preconceived* minimum. It has a *definite, limited* standard. How little this annulment of private property is really an appropriation is in fact proved by the abstract negation of the entire world of culture and civilization, the regression to the *unnatural* simplicity of the *poor and undemanding* man who has not only failed to go beyond private property, but has not yet even attained to it.

The community is only a community of *labour,* and an equality of *wages* paid out by the communal capital—the *community* as the universal capitalist. Both sides of the relationship are raised to an *imagined* universality—*labour* as a state in which every person is put, and *capital* as the acknowledged universality and power of the community. . . .

The first positive annulment of private property—*crude* communism—is thus merely one *form* in which the vileness of private property, which wants to set itself up as the *positive community, comes to the surface.*

2) Communism (a) of a political nature still—democratic or despotic; (b) with the annulment of the state, yet still incomplete, and being still affected by private property (i.e., by the estrangement of man). In both forms communism already knows itself to be re-integration or return of man to himself, the transcendence of human self-estrangement; but since it has not yet grasped the positive essence of private property, and just as little the *human* nature of need, it remains captive to it and infected by it. It has, indeed, grasped its concept, but not its essence.

3) *Communism* as the *positive* transcendence of *private property,* or *human self-estrangement*, and therefore as the real *appropriation of the human* essence by and for man; communism therefore as the complete return of man to himself as a *social* (i.e., human) being—a return become conscious, and accomplished within the entire wealth of previous development. This communism, as fully-developed naturalism, equals humanism, and as fully-developed humanism equals naturalism; it is the *genuine* resolution of the conflict between man and nature and between man and man—the true resolution of the strife between existence and essence, between objectification and self-confirmation, between freedom and necessity, between the individual and the species. Communism is the riddle of history solved, and it knows itself to be this solution.

The entire movement of history is, therefore, both its *actual* act of genesis (the birth act of its empirical existence) and also for its thinking consciousness the *comprehended* and *known* process of its *coming-to-be.* That other, still immature communism, meanwhile, seeks an *historical* proof for itself—a proof in the realm of the existent—amongst disconnected historical phenomena opposed to private property, tearing single phases from the historical process and focussing attention on them as proofs of its historical pedigree (a horse ridden hard especially by Cabet, Villegardelle, etc.). By so doing it simply makes clear that by far the greater part of this process contradicts its claims, and that, if it has once been, precisely its being in the *past* refutes its pretension to being *essential*.

That the entire revolutionary movement necessarily finds both its empirical and its theoretical basis in the movement of *private property*—in that of the economy, to be precise—is easy to see.

This *material*, immediately *sensuous* private property is the material sensuous expression of *estranged human* life. Its movement—production and consumption—is the *sensuous* revelation of the movement of all production hitherto—i.e., the realization or the reality of man. Religion, family, state, law, morality, science, art, etc., are only *particular* modes of production, and fall under its general law. The positive transcendence of *private property* as the appropriation of *human* life is, therefore, the positive transcendence of all estrangement—that is to say, the return of man from religion, family, state, etc., to his *human*, i.e., *social* mode of existence. Religious estrangement as such occurs only in the realm of *consciousness*, of man's inner life, but economic estrangement is that of *real life;* its transcendence therefore embraces both aspects. It is evident that the *initial* stage of the movement amongst the various peoples depends on whether the true and for them *authentic* life of the people manifests itself more in consciousness or in the external world—is more ideal or real. Communism begins from the outset (*Owen*) with atheism; but atheism is at first far from being *communism;* indeed, it is still mostly an abstraction.

The philanthropy of atheism is therefore at first only *philosophical*, abstract, philanthropy, and that of communism is at once *real* and directly bent on *action*. . . .

4) Just as *private property* is only the sensuous expression of the fact that man becomes *objective* for himself and at the same time becomes to himself a strange and inhuman object; just as it expresses the fact that the assertion of his life is the alienation of his life, that his realization is his loss of reality, is an *alien* reality: conversely, the positive transcendence of private property—i.e., the *sensuous* appropriation for and by man of the human essence and of human life, of objective man, of human *achievements*—is not to be conceived merely in the sense of *direct*, one-sided *gratification*—merely in the sense of *possessing*, of *having*. Man appropriates his total essence in a total manner, that is to say, as a whole man. Each of his *human* relations to the world—seeing, hearing, smelling, tasting, feeling, thinking, being aware, sensing, wanting, acting, loving—in short, all the organs of his individual being, like those organs which are directly social in their form, are in their *objective* orientation or in their *orientation to the object*, the appropriation of that object, the appropriation of the *human* world; their orientation to the object is the *manifestation of the human world;* it is human *efficaciousness* and human *suffering*, for suffering, apprehended humanly, is an enjoyment of self in man.

Private property has made us so stupid and one-sided that an object is only *ours* when we have it—when it exists for us as capital, or when it is directly possessed, eaten, drunk, worn, inhabited, etc.,—in short, when it is *used* by us. Although private property itself again conceives all these direct realizations of possession as *means of life*, and the life which they serve as means is the *life of private property*—labour and conversion into capital.

In place of *all* these physical and mental senses there has therefore come the sheer estrangement of *all* these senses—the sense of *having*. The human being had to be reduced to this absolute poverty in order that he might yield his inner wealth to the outer world.

The transcendence of private property is therefore the complete *emancipation* of all human senses and attributes; but it is this emancipation precisely because these senses and attributes have become, subjectively and objectively, *human*. . . . Need or enjoyment have consequently lost their *egotistical* nature. and nature has lost its mere *utility* by use becoming *human* use.

In the same way, the senses and enjoyments of other men have become my *own* appropriation. Besides these direct organs, therefore, *social* organs develop in the *form* of society; thus, for instance, activity in direct association with others, etc., has become an organ for *expressing* my own *life*, and a mode of appropriating *human life*. . . .

To recapitulate; man is not lost in his object only when the object becomes for him a *human* object or objective man. This is possible only when the object becomes for him a *social* object, he himself for himself a social being, just as society becomes a being for him in this object.

On the one hand, therefore, it is only when the objective world becomes everywhere for man in society the world of man's essential powers[1]—human reality, and for that reason the reality of his *own* essential powers—that all *objects* become for him the *objectification of himself*, become objects which confirm and realize his individuality, become *his* objects: that is, *man himself* becomes the object. The manner in which they become *his* depends on the *nature of the objects* and on the nature of the *essential power* corresponding *to it;* for it is precisely the *determinateness* of this relationship which shapes the particular, *real* mode of affirmation. . . .

On the other hand, looking at this in its subjective aspect: . . . because my object can only be the confirmation of one of my essential powers and can therefore only be so for me as my essential power is present for itself as a subjective capacity, . . . the *senses* of the social man are *other* senses than those of the non-social man. . . .

The *sense* caught up in crude practical need has only a *restricted* sense. For the starving man, it is not the human form of food that exists, but only its abstract being as food; it could just as well be there in its crudest form, and it would be impossible to say wherein this feeding-activity differs from that of *animals*. The care-burdened man in need has no sense for the finest play; the dealer in minerals sees only the mercantile value but not the beauty and the unique nature of the mineral: he has no mineralogical sense. Thus, the objectification of the human essence both in its theoretical and practical aspects is required to make man's *sense human*, as well as to create the *human sense* corresponding to the entire wealth of human and natural substance.

Just as resulting from the movement of *private property*, of its wealth as well as its poverty—or of its material and spiritual wealth and poverty—the budding society finds to hand all the material for this *development:* so

[1] "Essential powers"—*Wesenskrafte:* i.e. powers belonging to a person as part of his essential nature.

established society produces man in this entire richness of his being—produces the *rich* man *profoundly endowed with all the senses*—as its enduring reality. . . .

It will be seen how in place of the *wealth* and *poverty* of political economy come the *rich human being* and rich *human* need. The *rich* human being is simultaneously the human being *in need of* a totality of human life-activities—the man in whom his own realization exists as an inner necessity, as *need.* Not only *wealth,* but likewise the *poverty* of man—given socialism—receives in equal measure a *human* and therefore social significance. Poverty is the passive bond which causes the human being to experience the need of the greatest wealth—the *other* human being. The dominion of the objective being in me, the sensuous outburst of my essential activity, is *emotion,* which thus becomes here the *activity* of my being.

5) A *being* only considers himself independent when he stands on his own feet; and he only stands on his own feet when he owes his *existence* to himself. A man who lives by the grace of another regards himself as a dependent being. But I live completely by the grace of another if I owe him not only the sustenance of my life, but if he has, moreover, *created* my *life*—if he is the *source* of my life; and if it is not of my own creation, my life has necessarily a source of this kind outside it. . . .

Since for the socialist man the *entire so-called history of the world* is nothing but the begetting of man through human labour, nothing but the coming-to-be of nature for man, he has the visible, irrefutable proof of his *birth* through himself, of his *process* of *coming-to-be.* Since the *real existence* of man and nature has become practical, sensuous and perceptible—since man has become for man as the being of nature, and nature for man as the being of man—the question about an *alien* being, about a being above nature and man—a question which implies the admission of the inessentiality of nature and of man—has become impossible in practice. *Atheism,* as the denial of this inessentiality, has no longer any meaning, for atheism is a *negation of God,* and postulates the *existence of man* through this negation; but socialism as socialism no longer stands in any need of such a mediation. It proceeds from the *practically and theoretically sensuous consciousness* of man and of nature as the *essence.* Socialism is man's *positive self-consciousness* no longer mediated through the annulment of religion, just as *real life* is man's positive reality, no longer mediated through the annulment of private property, through *communism.* Communism is the position as the negation of the negation, and is hence the *actual* phase necessary for the next stage of historical development in the process of human emancipation and recovery. *Communism* is the necessary pattern and the dynamic principle of the immediate future, but communism as such is not the goal of human development—the structure of human society.

Marx, *Manuscripts* (1844), excerpts from the third manuscript.

9.A.3 COMMUNISM AS THE MOVEMENT OF HISTORY

Material Bases of Communism

This "alienation" (to use a term which will be comprehensible to the philosophers) can, of course, only be abolished given two *practical* premises. For it to become an "intolerable" power, i.e. a power against which men make a revolution, it must necessarily have rendered the great mass of humanity "propertyless", and produced, at the same time, the contradiction of an existing world of wealth and culture, both of which conditions presuppose a great increase in productive power, a high degree of its development. And, on the other hand, this development of productive forces (which itself implies the actual empirical existence of men in their *world-historical,* instead of local, being) is an absolutely necessary practical premise because without it *want* is merely made general, and with *destitution* the struggle for necessities and all the old filthy business would necessarily be reproduced; and furthermore, because only with this universal development of productive forces is a *universal* intercourse between men established, which produces in all nations simultaneously the phenomenon of the "propertyless" mass (universal competition), makes each nation dependent on the revolutions of the others, and finally has put *world-historical,* empirically universal individuals in place of local ones. Without this, (1) communism could only exist as a local event; (2) the *forces* of intercourse themselves could not have developed as *universal,* hence intolerable powers: they would have remained home-bred conditions surrounded by superstition; and (3) each extension of intercourse would abolish local communism. Empirically, communism is only possible as the act of the dominant peoples "all at once" and simultaneously, which presupposes the universal development of productive forces and the world intercourse bound up with communism. Moreover, the mass of *propertyless* workers—the utterly precarious position of labour-power on a mass scale cut off from capital or from even a limited satisfaction and, therefore, no longer merely temporarily deprived of work itself as a secure source of life—presupposes the *world market* through competition. The proletariat can thus only exist *world-historically*, just as communism, its activity, can only have a "world-historical" existence. World-historical existence of individuals means, existence of individuals which is directly linked up with world history.

Communism is for us not a *state of affairs* which is to be established, an *ideal* to which reality [will] have to adjust itself. We call communism the *real* movement which abolishes the present state of things. The conditions of this movement result from the premises now in existence. . . .

History is nothing but the succession of the separate generations, each of which exploits the materials, the capital funds, the productive forces handed down to it by all preceding generations, and thus, on the one hand, continues the traditional activity in completely changed circumstances and, on the other, modifies the old circumstances with a completely changed activity. . . .

The further the separate spheres, which interact on one another, extend in the course of this development, the more the original isolation of the separate nationalities is destroyed by the developed mode of production and intercourse and the division of labour between various nations naturally brought forth by these, the more history becomes world history. Thus, for instance, if in England a machine is invented, which deprives countless workers of bread in India and China, and overturns the whole form of existence of these empires, this invention becomes a world-historical fact. ... From this it follows that this transformation of history into world history is...a quite material, empirically verifiable act, an act the proof of which every individual furnishes as he comes and goes, eats, drinks and clothes himself.

This conception of history depends on our ability to expound the real process of production, starting out from the material production of life itself, and to comprehend the form of intercourse connected with this and created by this mode of production (i.e. civil society in its various stages), as the basis of all history; and to show it in its action as State, to explain all the different theoretical products and forms of consciousness, religion, philosophy, ethics, etc. etc. and trace their origins and growth from that basis; by which means, of course, the whole thing can be depicted in its totality (and therefore, too, the reciprocal action of these various sides on one another). It has not, like the idealistic view of history, in every period to look for a category, but remains constantly on the real *ground* of history; it does not explain practice from the idea but explains the formation of ideas from material practice; and accordingly it comes to the conclusion that all forms and products of consciousness cannot be dissolved by mental criticism, by resolution into "self-consciousness" or transformation into "apparitions", "spectres", "fancies", etc. but only by the practical overthrow of the actual social relations which gave rise to this idealistic humbug; that not criticism but revolution is the driving force of history, also of religion, of philosophy and all other types of theory. It shows that history does not end by being resolved into "self-consciousness" as "spirit of the spirit", but that in it at each stage there is found a material result: a sum of productive forces, an historically created relation of individuals to nature and to one another, which is handed down to each generation from its predecessor; a mass of productive forces, capital funds and conditions, which, on the one hand, is indeed modified by the new generation, but also on the other prescribes for it its conditions of life and gives it a definite development, a special character. It shows that circumstances make men just as men make circumstances.

This sum of productive forces, capital funds and social forms of intercourse, which every individual and generation finds in existence as something given, is the real basis...which...decides also whether or not the periodically recurring revolutionary convulsion will be strong enough to overthrow the basis of the entire existing system. And if these material elements of a complete revolution are not present (namely, on the one hand the existing productive forces, on the other the formation of a revolutionary mass, which revolts not only against separate conditions of society up till then, but against the very "production of life" till then, the "total activity" on which it was based), then, as far as practical development is concerned, it is absolutely immaterial whether the *idea* of this revolution has been expressed a hundred times already, as the history of communism proves. ...

Historical Contradictions and Communist Revolution

The relation of the productive forces to the form of intercourse is the relation of the form of intercourse to the occupation or activity of the individuals. (The fundamental form of this activity is, of course, material, on which depend all other forms—mental, political, religious, etc. The various shaping of material life is, of course, in every case dependent on the needs which are already developed, and the production, as well as the satisfaction, of these needs is an historical process. . . . The conditions under which individuals have intercourse with each other, . . . which appear first as conditions of self-activity, later as fetters upon it, form in the whole evolution of history a coherent series of forms of intercourse, the coherence of which consists in this: in the place of an earlier form of intercourse, which has become a fetter, a new one is put, corresponding to the more developed productive forces and, hence, to the advanced mode of the self-activity of individuals—a form which in its turn becomes a fetter and is then replaced by another. Since these conditions correspond at every stage to the simultaneous development of the productive forces, their history is at the same time the history of the evolving productive forces taken over by each new generation, and is, therefore, the history of the development of the forces of the individuals themselves.

Since this evolution takes place naturally, i.e. is not subordinated to a general plan of freely combined individuals, it proceeds from various localities, tribes, nations, branches of labour, etc. each of which to start with develops independently of the others and only gradually enters into relation with the others. Furthermore, it takes place only very slowly; the various stages and interests are never completely overcome, but only subordinated to the prevailing interest and trail along beside the latter for centuries afterwards. It follows from this that within a nation itself the individuals, even apart from their pecuniary circumstances, have quite different developments, and that an earlier interest, the peculiar form of intercourse of which has already been ousted by that belonging to a later interest, remains for a long time afterwards in possession of a traditional power in the illusory community (State, law), which has won an existence independent of the individuals; a power which in the last resort can only be broken by a revolution. This explains why, with reference to individual points which allow of a more general summing-up, consciousness can sometimes appear further advanced than the contemporary empirical relationships, so that in the struggles of a later epoch one can refer to earlier theoreticians as authorities.

On the other hand, in countries which, like North America, begin in an already advanced historical epoch, the development proceeds very rapidly. Such countries have no other natural premises than the individuals, who settled there and were led to do so because the forms of intercourse of the old countries did not correspond to their wants. Thus they begin with the most advanced individuals of the old countries, and, therefore, with the correspondingly most advanced form of intercourse, before this form of intercourse has been able to establish itself in the old countries. This is the case with all colonies, insofar as they are not mere military or trading stations. . . .

This contradiction between the productive forces and the form of intercourse, which, as we saw, has occurred several times in past history, without, however, endangering the basis, necessarily on each occasion burst out in a revolution, taking on at the same time various subsidiary forms, such as all-embracing collisions, collisions of various classes, contradiction of consciousness, battle of ideas, etc., political conflict, etc. From a narrow point of view one may isolate one of these subsidiary forms and consider it as the basis of these revolutions; and this is all the more easy as the individuals who started the revolutions had illusions about their own activity according to their degree of culture and the stage of historical development.

Thus all collisions in history have their origin, according to our view, in the contradiction between the productive forces and the form of intercourse. Incidentally, to lead to collisions in a country, this contradiction need not necessarily have reached its extreme limit in this particular country. The competition with industrially more advanced countries, brought about by the expansion of international intercourse, is sufficient to produce a similar contradiction in countries with a backward industry (e.g. the latent proletariat in Germany brought into view by the competition of English industry.) . . .

Our investigation hitherto started from the instruments of production, and it has already shown that private property was a necessity for certain industrial stages. In *industrie extractive* private property still coincides with labour; in small industry and all agriculture up till now property is the necessary consequence of the existing instruments of production; in big industry the contradiction between the instrument of production and private property appears from the first time and is the product of big industry; moreover, big industry must be highly developed to produce this contradiction. And thus only with big industry does the abolition of private property become possible.

In big industry and competition the whole mass of conditions of existence, limitations, biases of individuals, are fused together into the two simplest forms: private property and labour. With money every form of intercourse, and intercourse itself, is considered fortuitous for the individuals. Thus money implies that all previous intercourse was only intercourse of individuals under particular conditions, not of individuals as individuals. These conditions are reduced to two: accumulated labour or private property, and actual labour. If both or one of these ceases, then intercourse comes to a standstill. The modern economists themselves, e.g. Sismondi, Cherbuliez, etc., oppose "association of individuals" to "association of capital". On the other hand, the individuals themselves are entirely subordinated to the division of labour and hence are brought into the most complete dependence on one another. Private property, insofar as within labour itself it is opposed to labour, evolves out of the necessity of accumulation, and has still, to begin with, rather the form of the communality; but in its further development it approaches more and more the modern form of private property. The division of labour implies from the outset the division of the *conditions* of labour, of tools and materials, and thus the splitting-up of accumulated capital among different owners, and thus, also, the division between capital and labur, and the different forms of property itself. The more the division of labour develops and accumulation grows, the sharper are the forms that this process of differentiation assumes. Labour itself can only exist on the premise of this fragmentation.

Thus two facts are here revealed. First the productive forces appear as a world for themselves, quite independent of and divorced from the individuals, alongside the individuals: the reason for this is that the individuals, whose forces they are, exist split up and in opposition to one another, whilst, on the other hand, these forces are only real forces in the intercourse and association of these individuals. Thus, on the one hand, we have a totality of productive forces, which have, as it were, taken on a material form and are for the individuals no longer the forces of the individuals but of private property, and hence of the individuals only insofar as they are owners of private property themselves. Never, in any earlier period, have the productive forces taken on a form so indifferent to the intercourse of individuals *as* individuals, because their intercourse itself was formerly a restricted one. On the other hand, standing over against these productive forces, we have the majority of the individuals from whom these forces have been wrested away, and who, robbed thus of all real life-content, have become abstract individuals, but who are, however, only by this fact put into a position to enter into relation with one another *as individuals.*

The only connection which still links them with the productive forces and with their own existence–labour–has lost all semblance of self-activity and only sustains their life by stunting it. While in the earlier periods self-activity and the production of material life were separated, in that they devolved on different persons, and while, on account of the narrowness of the individuals themselves, the production of material life was considered as a subordinate mode of self-activity, they now diverge to such an extent that altogether material life appears as the end, and what produces this material life, labour (which is now the only possible but, as we see, negative form of self-activity), as the means.

Thus things have now come to such a pass that the individuals must appropriate the existing totality of productive forces, not only to achieve self-activity, but, also, merely to safeguard their very existence. This appropriation is first determined by the object to be appropriated, the productive forces, which have been developed to a totality and which only exist within a universal intercourse. From this aspect alone, therefore, this appropriation must have a universal character corresponding to the productive forces and the intercourse.

The appropriation of these forces is itself nothing more than the development of the individual capacities corresponding to the material instruments of production. The appropriation of a totality of instruments of production is, for this very reason, the development of a totality of capacities in the individuals themselves.

This appropriation is further determined by the persons appropriating. Only the proletarians of the present day, who are completely shut off from all self-activity, are in a position to achieve a complete and no longer restricted self-activity, which consists in the appropriation of a totality of productive forces and in the thus postulated development of a totality of capacities. All earlier revolutionary appropriations were restricted; individuals, whose self-activity was restricted by a crude instrument of production and a limited intercourse, appropriated this crude instrument of production, and hence merely achieved a new state of limitation. Their instrument of production became their property, but they themselves remained subordinate to the division of labour and their own instrument of production. In all expropriations up to now, a mass of individuals remained subservient to a single instrument of production; in the appropriation by the proletarians, a mass of instruments of production must be made subject to each individual, and property to all. Modern universal intercourse can be controlled by individuals, therefore, only when controlled by all.

This appropriation is further determined by the manner in which it must be effected. It can only be effected through a union, which by the character of the proletariat itself can again only be a universal one, and through a revolution, in which, on the one hand, the power of the earlier mode of production and intercourse and social organisation is overthrown, and, on the other hand, there develops the universal character and the energy of the proletariat, without which the revolution cannot be accomplished; and in which, further, the proletariat rids itself of everything that still clings to it from its previous position in society.

Only at this stage does self-activity coincide with material life, which corresponds to the development of individuals into complete individuals and the casting-off of all natural limitations. The transformation of labour into self-activity corresponds to the transformation of the earlier limited intercourse into the intercourse of individuals as such. With the appropriation of the total productive forces through united individuals, private property comes to an end. Whilst previously in history a particular condition always appeared as accidental, now the isolation of individuals and the particular private gain of each man have themselves become accidental. . . .

Finally, from the conception of history we have sketched we obtain these further conclusions: (1) In the development of productive forces there comes a stage when productive forces and means of intercourse are brought into being, which, under the existing relationships, only cause mischief, and are no longer productive but destructive forces (machinery and money); and connected with this a class is called forth, which has to bear all the burdens of society without enjoying its advantages, which, ousted from society, is forced into the most decided antagonism to all other classes; a class which forms the majority of all members of society, and from which emanates the consciousness of the necessity of a fundamental revolution, the communist consciousness, which may, of course, arise among the other classes too through the contemplation of the situation of this class. (2) The conditions under which definite productive forces can be applied are the conditions of the rule of a definite class of society, whose social power, deriving from its property, has its *practical*-idealistic expression in each case in the form of the State; and, therefore, every revolutionary struggle is directed against a class, which till then has been in power. (3) In all revolutions up till now the mode of activity always remained unscathed and it was only a question of a different distribution of this activity, a new distribution of labour to other persons, whilst the communist revolution is directed against the preceding *mode* of activity, does away with *labour,* and abolishes the rule of all classes with the classes themselves, because it is carried through by the class which no longer counts as a class in society, is not recognised as a class, and is in itself the expression of the dissolution of all classes, nationalities, etc. within present society; and (4) Both for the production on a mass scale of this communist consciousness, and for the success of the cause itself, the alteration of men on a mass scale is necessary, an alteration which can only take place in a practical movement, a *revolution;* this revolution is necessary, therefore, not only because the *ruling* class cannot be overthrown in any other way, but also because the class *overthrowing* it can only in a revolution succeed in ridding itself of all the muck of ages and become fitted to found society anew.

Marx-Engels, *The German Ideology* (1845–46), excerpts from Part I.

9.A.4 COMMUNISM AS RECONCILIATION OF INDIVIDUAL AND SOCIETY

MAN AS A SOCIAL BEING

When one studies the materialist theories of the original goodness of man, the equality of intellectual endowment among men, the omnipotence of education, experience and habit, the influence of external circumstances upon man, the great importance of industry, the value of pleasure, etc., there is no need for extraordinary penetration to discover what necessarily connects them with communism and socialism. If man derives all his knowledge from the sensible world and from his experience of the sensible world, then this is to say that the empirical world should be arranged in such a way that man experiences and assimilates there what is really human, that he experiences himself as man. If enlightened self-interest is the principle of all morality it is necessary for the private interest of each man to coincide with the general interest of humanity. If man is not free, in the materialist's sense, that is, if he is not negatively free to avoid this or that event, but is positively free to express his true individuality, then rather than punishing individuals for their crimes we should destroy the social conditions which engender crime, and give to each individual the scope which he needs in society in order to develop his life. If man is formed by circumstances, these circumstances must be humanly formed. If man is, by nature, a social being, he only develops his real nature in society, and the power of his nature should be measured not by the power of private individuals but by the power of society.

Marx-Engels, *Holy Family* (1845). Cited in Bottomore, SSP, p. 243.

We have seen how, on the assumption that private property has been positively superseded, man produces man, himself and then other men; how the object which is the direct activity of his personality is at the same time his existence for other men and their existence for him. Similarly, the material of labour and man himself as a subject are the starting-point as well as the result of this movement (and because there must be this starting-point private property is a historical necessity). Therefore, the *social* character is the universal character of the whole movement; *as* society itself produces *man* as *man,* so it is *produced* by him. Activity and mind are social in their content as well as in their *origin;* they are *social* activity and social mind. The *human* significance of nature only exists for *social* man, because only in this case is nature a *bond* with other *men,* the basis of his existence for others and of their existence for him. Only then is nature the *basis* of his own *human* experience and a vital element of human reality. The *natural* existence of man has here become his *human* existence and nature itself has become human for him. Thus *society* is the accomplished union of man with nature, the veritable resurrection of nature, the realized naturalism of man and the realized humanism of nature.

Social activity and social mind by no means exist *only* in the form of activity or mind which is directly communal. Nevertheless, communal activity and mind, i.e. activity and mind which express and confirm themselves directly in a *real association* with other men, occur everywhere where this direct expression of sociability arises from the content of the activity or corresponds to the nature of mind.

Even when I carry out *scientific* work, etc., an activity which I can seldom conduct in direct association with other men, I perform a *social,* because *human,* act. It is not only the material of my activity—such as the language itself which the thinker uses—which is given to me as a social product. My *own existence* is a social activity. For this reason, what I myself produce I produce for society, and with the consciousness of acting as a social being.

My universal consciousness is only the *theoretical* form of that whose *living* form is the real community, the social entity, although at the present day this universal consciousness is an abstraction from real life and is opposed to it as an enemy. That is why the *activity* of my universal consciousness as such is my *theoretical* existence as a social being.

It is above all necessary to avoid postulating "society" once again as an abstraction confronting the individual. The individual *is* the *social being.* The manifestation of his life—even when it does not appear directly in the form of a communal manifestation, accomplished in association with other men—is, therefore, a manifestation and affirmation of *social life.* Individual human life and species-life are not different things, even though the mode of existence of individual life is necessarily either a more *specific* or a more *general* mode of species-life, or that of species-life a *specific* or more *general* mode of individual life.

In his *species-consciousness* man confirms his real *social life,* and reproduces his real existence in thought; while conversely, species-life confirms itself in species-consciousness and exists for itself in its universality as a thinking being. Though man is a unique individual—and it is just his particularity which makes him an individual, a really *individual* communal being—he is equally the *whole,* the ideal whole, the subjective existence of society as thought and experienced. He exists in reality as the representation and the real mind of social existence, and as the sum of human manifestations of life.

Marx, *Manuscripts* (1844), EW, pp. 157–58.

INDIVIDUALS, CLASS, AND COMMUNITY

In the Middle Ages the citizens in each town were compelled to unite against the landed nobility to save their skins. The extension of trade, the establishment of communications, led the separate towns to get to know other towns, which had asserted the same interests in the struggle with the same antagonist. Out of the many local corporations of burghers there arose only gradually the burgher *class*. The conditions of life of the individual burghers became, on account of their contradiction to the existing relationships and of the mode of labour determined by these, conditions which were common to them all and independent of each individual. The burghers had created the conditions insofar as they had torn themselves free from feudal ties, and were created by them insofar as they were determined by their antagonism to the feudal system which they found in existence. When the individual towns began to enter into associations, these common conditions developed into class conditions. The same conditions, the same contradiction, the same interests necessarily called forth on the whole similar customs everywhere. The bourgeoisie itself, with its conditions, develops only gradually, splits according to the division of labour into various fractions and finally absorbs all propertied classes it finds in existence (while it develops the majority of the earlier propertyless and a part of the hitherto propertied classes into a new class, the proletariat) in the measure to which all property found in existence is transformed into industrial or commercial capital. The separate individuals form a class only insofar as they have to carry on a common battle against another class; otherwise they are on hostile terms with each other as competitors. On the other hand, the class in its turn achieves an independent existence over against the individuals, so that the latter find their conditions of existence predestined, and hence have their position in life and their personal development assigned to them by their class, become subsumed under it. This is the same phenomenon as the subjection of the separate individuals to the division of labour and can only be removed by the abolition of private property and of labour itself. We have already indicated several times how this subsuming of individuals under the class brings with it their subjection to all kinds of ideas, etc. . . .

This subsuming of individuals under definite classes cannot be abolished until a class has taken shape, which has no longer any particular class interest to assert against the ruling class.

The transformation, through the division of labour, of personal powers (relationships) into material powers, cannot be dispelled by dismissing the general idea of it from one's mind, but can only be abolished by the individuals again subjecting these material powers to themselves and abolishing the division of labour. This is not possible without the community. Only in community [with others has each] individual the means of cultivating his gifts in all directions; only in the community, therefore, is personal freedom possible. In the previous substitutes for the community, in the State, etc. personal freedom has existed only for the individuals who developed within the relationships of the ruling class, and only insofar as they were individuals of this class. The illusory community, in which individuals have up till now combined, always took on an independent existence in relation to them, and was at the same time, since it was the combination of one class over against another, not only a completely illusory community, but a new fetter as well. In a real community the individuals obtain their freedom in and through their association.

Individuals have always built on themselves, but naturally on themselves within their given historical conditions and relationships, not on the "pure" individual in the sense of the ideologists. But in the course of historical evolution, and precisely through the inevitable fact that within the division of labour social relationships take on an independent existence, there appears a division within the life of each individual, insofar as it is personal and insofar as it is determined by some branch of labour and the conditions pertaining to it. (We do not mean it to be understood from this that, for example, the rentier, the capitalist, etc. cease to be persons; but their personality is conditioned and determined by quite definite class relationshps, and the division appears only in their opposition to another class and, for themselves, only when they go bankrupt.) In the estate (and even more in the tribe) this is as yet concealed: for instance, a nobleman always remains a nobleman, a commoner always a commoner, apart from his other relationships, a quality inseparable from his individuality. The division between the personal and the class individual, the accidental nature of the conditions of life for the individual, appears only with the emergence of the class, which is itself a product of the bourgeoisie. This accidental character is only engendered and developed by competition and the struggle of individuals among themselves. Thus, in imagination, individuals seem freer under the dominance of the bourgeoisie than before, because their conditions of life seem accidental; in reality, of course, they are less free, because they are more subjected to the violence of things. The difference from the estate comes out particularly in the antagonism between the bourgeoisie and the proletariat. When the estate of the urban burghers, the corporations, etc. emerged in opposition to the landed nobility, their condition of existence—movable property and craft labour, which had already existed latently before their separation from the feudal ties—appeared as something positive, which was asserted against feudal landed property, and, therefore, in its own way at first took on a feudal form. Certainly the refugee serfs treated their previous servitude as something accidental to their personality. But here they only were doing what every class that is freeing itself from a fetter does; and they did not free themselves as a class but separately. Moreover, they did not rise above the system of estates, but only formed a new estate, retaining their previous mode of labour even in their new situation, and developing it further by freeing it from its earlier fetters, which no longer corresponded to the development already attained.

For the proletarians, on the other hand, the condition of their existence, labour, and with it all the conditions of existence governing modern society, have become something accidental, something over which they, as separate individuals, have no control, and over which no *social* organisation can give them control. The contradiction between the individuality of each separate proletarian and labour, the condition of life forced upon him, becomes evident to him himself, for he is sacrificed from youth upwards and, within his own class, has no chance of arriving at the conditions which would place him in the other class.

Thus, while the refugee serfs only wished to be free to develop and assert those conditions of existence which were already there, and hence, in the end, only arrived at free labour, the proletarians, if they are to assert themselves as individuals, will have to abolish the very condition of their existence hitherto (which has, moreover, been that of all society up to the present), namely, labour. Thus they find themselves directly opposed to the form in which, hitherto, the individuals, of which society consists, have given themselves collective expression, that is, the State. In order, therefore, to assert themselves as individuals, they must overthrow the State.

It follows from all we have been saying up till now that the communal relationship into which the individuals of a class entered, and which was determined by their common interests over against a third party, was always a community to which these individuals belonged only as average individuals, only insofar as they lived within the conditions of existence of their class—a relationship in which they participated not as individuals but as members of a class. With the community of revolutionary proletarians, on the other hand, who take their conditions of existence and those of all members of society under their control, it is just the reverse; it is as individuals that the individuals participate in it. It is just this combination of individuals (assuming the advanced stage of modern productive forces, of course) which puts the conditions of the free development and movement of individuals under their control —conditions which were previously abandoned to chance and had won an independent existence over against the separate individuals just because of their separation as individuals, and because of the necessity of their combination which had been determined by the division of labour, and through their separation had become a bond alien to them. Combination up till now . . . was an agreement upon these conditions, within which the individuals were free to enjoy the freaks of fortune (compare, e.g., the formation of the North American State and the Southern American republics). This right to the undisturbed enjoyment, within certain conditions, of fortuity and chance has up till now been called personal freedom. These conditions of existence are, of course, only the productive forces and forms of intercourse at any particular time.

Communism differs from all previous movements in that it overturns the basis of all earlier relations of production and intercourse, and for the first time consciously treats all natural premises as the creatures of hitherto existing men, strips them of their natural character and subjugates them to the power of the united individuals. Its organisation is, therefore, essentially economic, the material production of the conditions of this unity; it turns existing conditions into conditions of unity. The reality, which communism is creating, is precisely the true basis for rendering it impossible that anything should exist independently of individuals, insofar as reality is only a product of the preceding intercourse of individuals themselves. Thus the communists in practice treat the conditions created up to now by production and intercourse as inorganic conditions, without, however, imagining that it was the plan or the destiny of previous generations to give them material, and without believing that these conditions were inorganic for the individuals creating them.

Marx-Engels, *The German Ideology* (1845–46), excerpts from Part I.

Reconciliation of Individuals and Society

Needs and Conditions

He [Stirner] imagines that people up to now have always formed a concept of man, and then won freedom for themselves to the extent that was necessary to realise this concept; that the measure of freedom that they achieved was determined each time by their idea of the ideal of man at the time. . . .

In reality, of course, what happened was that people won freedom for themselves each time to the extent that was dictated and permitted not by their ideal of man, but by the existing productive forces. All conquests of freedom hitherto, however, have been based on restricted productive forces. The production which these productive forces could provide was insufficient for the whole of society and made development possible only if some persons satisfied their needs at the expense of others, and therefore some—the minority—obtained the monopoly of development, while others—the majority—owing to the constant struggle to satisfy their most essential needs, were for the time being (i.e. until the birth of new revolutionary productive forces) excluded from any development. Thus, society has hitherto always developed within the framework of a contradiction—in antiquity the contradiction between free men and slaves, in the Middle Ages that between nobility and serfs, in modern times that between the bourgeoisie and the proletariat. This explains, on the one hand, the abnormal, "inhuman", means with which the oppressed class satisfies its needs, and, on the other hand, the narrow limits within which intercourse, and with it the whole ruling class, develops. Hence this restricted character of development consists not only in the exclusion of one class from development, but also in the narrowmindedness of the excluding class, and the "inhuman" is to be found also within the ruling class. This so-called "inhuman" is just as much a product of present-day conditions as the "human" is; it is their negative aspect, the rebellion—which is not based on any new revolutionary productive force—against the prevailing conditions brought about by the existing productive forces, and against the way of satisfying needs that corresponds to these conditions. The positive expression "human" corresponds to the definite conditions *predominant* at a certain stage of production and to the way of satisfying needs determined by them, just as the negative expression "inhuman" corresponds to the attempt, within the existing mode of production, to negate these predominant conditions and the way of satisfying needs prevailing under them, an attempt that this stage of production daily engenders afresh. . . .

Personal Versus General Interests

How is it that personal interests always develop, against the will of individuals, into class interests, into common interests which acquire independent existence in relation to the individual persons, and in their independence assume the form of *general* interests? How is it that as such they come into contradiction with actual individuals and in this contradiction, by which they are defined as *general* interests, they can be conceived by consciousness as *ideal* and even as religious, holy interests? How is it that in this process of private interests acquiring independent existence as class interests the personal behaviour of the individual is bound to undergo substantiation, alienation, and at the same time exists as a power independent of him and without him, created by intercourse, and becomes transformed into social relations, into a series of powers which determine and subordinate the individual, and which, therefore, appear in the imagination as "holy" powers? Within the frameworks of definite *modes of production,* which, of course, are not dependent on the will, alien practical forces, which are independent not only of isolated individuals but even of all of them together, always come to stand above people. ...

Incidentally, even in the banal, petty-bourgeois German form in which [Stirner] perceives the contradiction of personal and general interests, he should have realised that individuals have always started out from themselves, and could not do otherwise, and that therefore both the aspects he noted are aspects of the personal development of individuals; both are equally engendered by the empirical conditions of life, both are only expressions of *one and the same* personal development of people and are therefore only in *seeming* contradiction to each other. ...

Communism is simply incomprehensible to [Stirner] because the communists do not put egoism against self-sacrifice or self-sacrifice against egoism, nor do they express this contradiction theoretically either in its sentimental or in its highflown ideological form; on the contrary, they demonstrate the material basis engendering it, with which it disappears of itself. The communists do not preach *morality* at all, such as Stirner preaches so extensively. They do not put to people the moral demand: love one another, do not be egoists, etc.; on the contrary, they are very well aware that egoism, just as much as self-sacrifice, *is* in definite circumstances a necessary form of the self-assertion of individuals. Hence, the communists by no means want...to do away with the "private individual" for the sake of the "general", self-sacrificing man. ...

Theoretical communists, the only ones who have time to devote to the study of history, are distinguished precisely because they alone have *discovered* that throughout history the "general interest" is created by individuals who are defined as "private persons". They know that this contradiction is only a *seeming* one because one side of it, the so-called "general", is constantly being produced by the other side, private interest, and by no means opposes the latter as an independent force with an independent history—so that this contradiction is in practice always being destroyed and reproduced. Hence it is not a question of the Hegelian "negative unity" of two sides of a contradiction, but of the materially determined destruction of the preceding materially determined mode of life of individuals, with the disappearance of which this contradiction together with its unity also disappears.

The Free Development of Individuals

The transformation of the individual relationship into its opposite, a merely material relationship, the distinction of individuality and chance by the individuals themselves, as we have already shown, is an historical process and at different stages of development assumes different, ever sharper and more universal forms. In the present epoch, the domination of material conditions over individuals, and the suppression of individuality by chance, has assumed its sharpest and most universal form, thereby setting existing individuals a very definite task. It has set them the task of replacing the domination of circumstances and of chance over individuals by the domination of individuals over chance and circumstances. It has not put forward the demand that "I should develop myself"; it has instead called for liberation from one quite definite mode of development. This task, dictated by present-day conditions, coincides with the task of the communist organisation of society.

We have already shown above that the abolition of a state of things in which relationships become independent of individuals, in which individuality is subservient to chance and the personal relationships of individuals are subordinated to general class relationships, etc.—the abolition of this state of things is determined in the final analysis by the abolition of division of labour. We have also shown that the abolition of division of labour is determined by the development of intercourse and productive forces to such a degree of universality that private property and division of labour become fetters on them. We have further shown that private property can be abolished only on condition of an all-round development of individuals, because the existing character of intercourse and productive forces is an all-round one, and only individuals that are developing in an all-round fashion can appropriate them, i.e. can turn them into free manifestations of their lives. We have shown that at the present time individuals *must* abolish private property, because the productive forces and forms of intercourse have developed so far that, under the domination of private property, they have become destructive forces, and because the contradiction between the classes has reached its extreme limit. Finally, we have shown that the abolition of private property and of the division of labour is itself the union of individuals on the basis created by modern productive forces and world intercourse.

Within communist society, the only society in which the original and free development of individuals ceases to be a mere phrase, this development is determined precisely by the connection of individuals, a connection which consists partly in the economic prerequisites and partly in the necessary solidarity of the free development of all, and, finally, in the universal character of the activity of individuals on the basis of the existing productive forces. Here, therefore, the matter concerns individuals at a definite historical stage of development and by no means merely individuals chosen at random, even disregarding the indispensable communist revolution which itself is a general condition of their free development. The individuals' consciousness of their mutual relations will, of course, likewise become something quite different, and, therefore, will no more be the "principle of love" or *dévoument*, than it will be egoism.

Marx-Engels, *German Ideology* (1845–46), excerpts from Parts 2 and 3.

9.A.5 COMMUNISM AS CLASSLESS SOCIETY

An oppressed class is the vital condition for every society founded on the antagonism of classes. The emancipation of the oppressed class thus implies necessarily the creation of a new society. For the oppressed class to be able to emancipate itself it is necessary that the productive powers already acquired and the existing social relations should no longer be capable of existing side by side. Of all the instruments of production, the greatest productive power is the revolutionary class itself. The organisation of revolutionary elements as a class supposes the existence of all the productive forces which could be engendered in the bosom of the old society.

Does this mean that after the fall of the old society there will be a new class domination culminating in a new political power? No.

The condition for the emancipation of the working class is the abolition of every class, just as the condition for the liberation of the Third Estate, of the bourgeois order, was the abolition of all estates and all orders.*

The working class, in the course of its development, will substitute for the old civil society an association which will exclude classes and their antagonism, and there will be no more political power properly so-called, since political power is precisely the official expression of antagonism in civil society.

Marx, *Poverty of Philosophy* (1847), IP, pp. 146–47.

When, in the course of development, class distinctions have disappeared, and all production has been concentrated in the hands of a vast association of the whole nation, the public power will lose its political character. Political power, properly so called, is merely the organized power of one class for suppressing another. If the proletariat during its contest with the bourgeoisie is compelled by the force of circumstances to organize itself as a class, if, by means of a revolution, it makes itself the ruling class and, as such, sweeps away by force the old conditions of production, then it will, along with these conditions, have swept away the conditions for the existence of class antagonisms, and of classes generally, and will thereby have abolished its own supremacy as a class.

In place of the old bourgeois society, with its classes and class antagonisms, we shall have an association in which the free development of each is the condition for the free development of all.

Marx-Engels, *Communist Manifesto* (1848), excerpt from Part II.

*Estates here in the historical sense of the estates of feudalism, estates with definite and limited privileges. The revolution of the bourgeoisie abolished the estates and their privileges. Bourgeois society knows only *classes*. It was, therefore, absolutely in contradiction with history to describe the proletariat as the 'Fourth Estate.' *[Note by F. Engels to the German edition, 1885.]*

9.A.6 COMMUNISM AS ABUNDANCE

QUESTION: *What are the consequences of these regularly recurring commercial crises?*

Answer: First, although in its initial stages large-scale industry itself gave birth to free competition, now it has outgrown its own creation. Competition and in general the carrying on of industry by individual capitalists has become a fetter upon production, and this fetter must be shattered. Large-scale industry, so long as it is conducted as at present, can recover its prosperity only through a seven-yearly upheaval which is a menace to civilization, not merely casting the proletariat into a well of misery but likewise causing the ruin of a great number of bourgeois. Either large-scale industry must be abolished, which is quite out of the question, or it needs a totally different social order wherein to function. The new social order would no longer be led by individual factory owners competing one against the other, but industrial production would be led by the whole of society according to a settled plan and according to the needs of all the members of society.

Secondly, large-scale industry and the resulting limitless expansion of production makes it possible to inaugurate a social order wherein so many necessities of life are produced that every member of society will be able to develop and exercise all his energies and capacities in the fullest freedom. It thus appears that precisely those qualities of large-scale industry which now produce all misery and all crises will in another social order promote the abolition of such suffering and catastrophical trade fluctuations. Thus it is obvious that:

1) All those evils are from now on to be ascribed to a social order which is no longer compatible with the actual requirements of society.

2) The means are ready to hand for putting an end to these evils through a new social order.

QUESTION: *What form will this new social order assume?*

Answer: First of all, the running of industries and all branches of production will be taken out of the hands of individuals and competing individuals. All branches of production will be operated by society as a whole, this is to say that industry will be run according to a common account, according to a common plan and by the participation of all members of society. Competition therefore will be done away with, and association will take its place. Since the running of industry by individual capitalists inevitably presupposes the existence of private property, and since free competition is the outcome of the individual ownership of industrial concerns, private ownership cannot be separated from free competition and individually owned industrial concerns. Thus private ownership will also have to be abolished, and in its stead we shall have the utilization of all the instruments of production and the distribution of the products among all members of society by common agreement. In a word, we shall have what is called community of goods. The term "abolition of private property" is indeed the most succinct and significant way of formulating the change in the total social order rendered necessary by the development of industry. The communists are right, therefore, to place this in the forefront of their demands.

QUESTION: *Was the abolition of private property not possible at an earlier date?*

Answer: No. Every change in the social order, every revolution in property relations, is the necessary outcome of the creation of new productive forces which cannot fit properly into the old system of property relations. Private property itself came to birth in this way. For private property has not always existed. When toward the close of the Middle Ages a new method of production was introduced, the manufacturing system, this new system, having outgrown the feudalist and the guild property relations, created a new form of property, private property. No other property form than that of private property was possible during the period of manufacture and in the early stages of the development of large-scale industry; no other order of society was possible than that founded upon private property. There must always be a dominant class controlling the forces of production and a poverty-stricken, oppressed class, so long as there is not enough produced to supply not only the immediate wants of all the members of society, but also a surplus of products for the increase of social capital and for the further development of the forces of production. . . . It is obvious that hitherto the productive forces had not been developed widely enough to provide enough for all members of society, and that private property had not yet become a fetter, a hindrance, to these productive forces. In our day, when the productive forces have attained so high a degree of development that, *firstly,* capitalists and productive forces are called into being on a scale hitherto unheard of and the means exist for multiplying these forces without limit; that, *secondly,* these productive forces are concentrated in the hands of a few bourgeois whilst the great mass of the people are falling into the ranks of the proletariat, the condition of the latter becoming more wretched and unendurable in proportion to the accumulation of wealth by the bourgeois; that, *thirdly,* these mighty and easily multiplied productive forces have so vastly outgrown the bourgeois and his private property that they constantly involve the social order in colossal disturbances —the abolition of private property is not only possible but even in the highest degree necessary.

QUESTION: *Will it be possible to bring about the abolition of private property by peaceful methods?*

Answer: This is greatly to be desired, and communists would be the last persons in the world to stand in the way of a peaceful solution. Communists know only too well the futility and, indeed, the harmfulness of conspiratorial methods. They know only too well that revolutions are not made deliberately and arbitrarily, but that everywhere and at all times revolutions have been the necessary outcome of circumstances quite independent of the will or the guidance of particular parties and whole classes. But they also perceive that the development of the proletariat in nearly all civilized countries is violently suppressed, and that in this way opponents of communism are working full force to promote a revolution. Should the oppressed proletariat at long last thus be driven into a revolution, then we communists will rally to the cause of the workers and be just as prompt to act as we are now to speak.

QUESTION: *Will it be possible to abolish private property all at once?*

Answer: No. This would be just as impossible as to multiply all at once the existing forces of production to the degree necessary for the inauguration of the community. The proletarian revolution, which in all probability is coming, will for this reason, only be able to transform present society gradually. Private property will be abolished only when the means of production have become available in sufficient quantities.

QUESTION: *Can such a [social] revolution take place in one country alone?*

Answer: No. Large-scale industry, by creating a world market, has so linked up the peoples of the earth, and especially the civilized peoples, that each of them is dependent on what happens in other lands. Further, the social development of all civilized countries has become so similar that everywhere the struggle between bourgeoisie and proletariat, the two classes of society upon which the issue depends, has become the dominating struggle of the day. The communist revolution will, therefore, not be a national revolution alone; it will take place in all civilized countries, or at least in England, America, France and Germany, at one and the same time. In each of these countries it will take a longer or a shorter time to develop according to whether one country or the other has a more developed industry, greater wealth, a more important quantity of productive forces at its disposal. The revolution will therefore assume its slowest pace and be most difficult of achievement in Germany; in England it will go ahead quickly and easily. It will exercise considerable influence upon all other countries of the world, totally changing and very much hastening the present process of their development. This is to be a universal revolution, and will, therefore, have a universal field for its operations.

QUESTION: *What will be the consequences of the final abolition of private ownership?*

Answer: In this case society has deprived the capitalists of their private use of the forces of production, transport, exchange and distribution, and is able to administer all these in a planned way according to the need of society as a whole and according to the means at its command. Then, most important of all, the evil consequences now associated with big industry will be eliminated. Crises will cease to be; the increase of production, which in the present order of society spells over-production and is such a great cause of suffering, will then not even suffice to meet the need and will have to be greatly stimulated. Instead of bringing wretchedness in its wake, over-production beyond the immediate wants of society will satisfy the needs of all, and create new needs, and at the same time the means for their gratification. It will cause and stimulate further progress, it will achieve this progress without, as heretofore, thereby throwing society into confusion. Once liberated from the yoke of private ownership, large-scale industry will develop on a new scale that will dwarf the present machine industry as conspicuously as this has dwarfed the manufacturing system of earlier days. The growth of industry will provide a quantity of products sufficient to gratify the needs of all. The same will be true for agricultural production, hitherto cramped and hindered by the weight of private ownership and the excessive subdivision of farming land. Here scientific methods and improvements of all sorts will soon result in a totally new leap forward, which will provide amply for society's needs. Thus society will have at its disposal such a quantity of products that distribution among its members will be equitable and satisfactory. The division of society into various antagonistic classes will then become superfluous. Nay, more; not only will such class divisions be superfluous, they will be incompatible with the new social order. Classes came into existence through the division of labor; the division of labor, as hitherto known, will disappear entirely. Mechanical and chemical auxiliaries do not alone suffice to develop industrial and agricultural production to the level we have described. The faculties of the men who set these auxiliaries in motion must undergo a corresponding development. Just as the peasant and the worker in manufacture of the last century were forced to change the whole of their habits and customs, and even had to become totally different human beings when they were swept into the current of large-scale industry, so also, communal production by the whole of society and the resulting new development of production will need entirely different men, and, indeed, will also produce them. The men of today cannot be expected to adapt themselves to the methods involved in communal production, for now each individual is engaged in one branch of production to the exclusion of all others, is shackled and exploited by it; he can cultivate only one of his faculties at the cost of all others, knows only one branch, or, indeed, only a branch of a branch of production as a whole. Even contemporary industry finds such workers less and less useful. But when the whole of society shall carry on industry in common and according to plan, then men will be needed whose faculties have been developed from every point of view, men able to comprehend the entire system of production. The division of labor already undermined by the machine system, the division of labor which compels one man to be a peasant, another a cobbler, another a factory hand, another a stock market operator, will disappear completely. Education will teach the young folk to familiarize themselves quickly with the whole system of production, they will be in a position to pass from one branch of industry to another according to the needs of society or their own inclinations. They will no longer, as today, be onesided in their development as a result of the division of labor. Thus a communistically organized society will be able to provide opportunities for the all-round cultivation of all-round faculties. Simultaneously with this development, social classes necessarily must vanish, for on the one hand classes cannot exist in a communist society, and, on the other, the very organization of this society provides the means of abolishing these class differences.

It follows from all this that the contrast between town and countryside will likewise disappear. The fact that agriculture and industrial production will be carried on by the same individuals rather than by two different classes of society, lies at the very foundation of communist association and is, if only for material reasons alone, an essential feature of such association. The dispersal of the agricultural population throughout the countryside, in contrast with the crowding of the industrial population in the towns, corresponds to the fact that both agriculture and industry have reached but a very low state of development. It constitutes an obstacle to future development, an obstacle that can be felt even now.

The general association of all members of society for the purpose of common and planned utilization of the productive forces, the expansion of production so that it suffices to provide for the needs of all, the cessation of that condition whereby the satisfaction of the needs of one is effected only at the cost of the needs of others, the complete destruction of classes and their antagonisms, the all-round development of the talents of all the members of society by means of the abolition of the hitherto prevalent division of labor by means of industrial education, the variation of activities, the participation of all in the enjoyments produced by all, the unification of town and countryside —such are the main results of the abolition of private ownership.

Engels, *Principles of Communism* (1847), pp. 177–80, 182–85.

9.A.7 WORK AND LEISURE

The labour of the individual looked at in the act of production itself, is the money with which he directly buys the product, the object of his particular activity; but it is a *particular* money, which buys precisely only this *specific* product. In order to be *general money* directly, it would have to be not a *particular,* but *general* labour from the outset; i.e. it would have to be *posited* from the outset as a link in *general production.* But on this presupposition it would not be exchange which gave labour its general character; but rather its presupposed communal character would determine the distribution of products. The communal character of production would make the product into a communal, general product from the outset. The exchange which originally takes place in production—which would not be an exchange of exchange values but of activities, determined by communal needs and communal purposes—would from the outset include the participation of the individual in the communal world of products. On the basis of exchange values, labour is *posited* as general only through *exchange.* But on this foundation it would be *posited* as such before exchange; i.e. the exchange of products would in no way be the *medium* by which the participation of the individual in general production is mediated. Mediation must, of course, take place. In the first case, which proceeds from the independent production of individuals—no matter how much these independent productions determine and modify each other *post festum* through their interrelations—mediation takes place through the exchange of commodities, through exchange value and through money; all these are expressions of one and the same relation. In the second case, the *presupposition is itself mediated;* i.e. a communal production, communality, is presupposed as the basis of production. The labour of the individual is posited from the outset as social labour. Thus, whatever the particular material form of the product he creates or helps to create, what he has bought with his labour is not a specific and particular product, but rather a specific share of the communal production. He therefore has no particular product to exchange. His product is *not an exchange value.* The product does not first have to be transposed into a particular form in order to attain a general character for the individual. Instead of a division of labour, such as is necessarily created with the exchange of exchange values, there would take place an organization of labour whose consequence would be the participation of the individual in communal consumption. In the first case the social character of production is *posited* only *post festum* with the elevation of products to exchange values and the exchange of these exchange values. In the second case *the social character of production* is presupposed, and participation in the world of products, in consumption, is not mediated by the exchange of mutually independent labours or products of labour. It is mediated, rather, by the social conditions of production within which the individual is active. . . .

On the basis of communal production, the determination of time remains, of course, essential. The less time the society requires to produce wheat, cattle etc., the more time it wins for other production, material or mental. Just as in the case of an individual, the multiplicity of its development, its enjoyment and its activity depends on economization of time. Economy of time, to this all economy ultimately reduces itself. Society likewise has to distribute its time in a purposeful way, in order to achieve a production adequate to its overall needs; just as the individual has to distribute his time correctly in order to achieve knowledge in proper proportions or in order to satisfy the various demands on his activity. Thus, economy of time, along with the planned distribution of labour time among the various branches of production, remains the first economic law on the basis of communal production. It becomes law, there, to an even higher degree. However, this is essentially different from a measurement of exchange values (labour or products) by labour time. The labour of individuals in the same *branch of work,* and the various kinds of work, are different from one another not only quantitatively but also qualitatively. What does a solely *quantitative* difference between things presuppose? The identity of their *qualities.* Hence, the quantitative measure of labours presupposes the equivalence, the identity of their quality. . . .

A. Smith's view, [is] that *labour never changes its value,* in the sense that a *definite amount of labour* is always a definite *amount of labour for the worker,* i.e., with A. Smith, a sacrifice of the *same quantitative magnitude.* Whether I obtain much or little for an hour of work—which depends on its productivity and other circumstances—I have *worked* one hour. What I have had to pay for the result of my work, my wages, is always the same *hour of work,* let the result vary as it may. 'Equal quantities of labour must at all times and in all places have the same value for the worker. In his normal state of health, strength and activity, and with the common degree of skill and facility which he may possess, he must always give up the *identical portion of his tranquility, his freedom,* and his *happiness.*" . . . In the sweat of thy brow shalt thou labour! was Jehovah's curse on Adam. And this is labour for Smith, a curse. 'Tranquility' appears as the adequate state, as identical with 'freedom' and 'happiness.' It seems quite far from Smith's mind that the individual, 'in his normal state of health, strength, activity, skill, facility,' also needs a normal portion of work, and of the suspension of tranquility. Certainly, labour obtains its measure from the outside, through the aim to be attained and the obstacles to be overcome in attaining it. But Smith has no inkling whatever that this overcoming of obstacles is in itself a liberating activity—and that, further, the external aims become stripped of the semblance of merely external natural urgencies, and become posited as aims which the individual himself posits—hence as self-realization, objectification of the subject, hence real freedom, whose action is, precisely, labour. He is right, of course, that, in its historic forms as slave-labour, serf-labour, and wage-labour, labour always appears as repulsive, always as *external forced labour;* and not-labour, by contrast, as 'freedom, and happiness.' This holds doubly: for this contradictory labour; and, relatedly, for labour which has not yet created the subjective and objective conditions for itself (or also, in contrast to the pastoral etc. state, which it has lost), in which labour becomes attractive work, the individual's self-realization, which in no way means that it becomes mere fun, mere amusement, as Fourier, with *grisette*-like naivete, conceives it. Really free working, e.g. composing, is at the same time precisely the most damned seriousness, the most intense exertion. The work of material production can achieve this character only (1) when its social character is posited, (2) when it is of a scientific and at the same time general character, not merely human exertion as a specifically harnessed natural force, but exertion as subject, which appears in the production process not in a merely natural, spontaneous form, but as an activity regulating all the forces of nature. A. Smith, by the way, has only the slaves of capital in mind. For example, even the semi-artistic worker of the Middle Ages does not fit into his definition. *But* what *we* want *here initially* is not to go into his view on labour, his philosophical view, but into the economic moment. Labour regarded merely as a *sacrifice,* and hence value-positing, as a *price* paid for things and hence giving them price depending on whether they cost more or less labour, is a purely *negative* characterization. This is why Mr. Senior, for example, was able to make capital into a source of production in the same sense as labour, a source *sui generis* of the production of *value,* because the capitalist too brings a *sacrifice,* the sacrifice of *abstinence,* in that he grows wealthy instead of eating up his product directly. Something that is merely negative creates nothing. If the worker should, e.g. enjoy his work—as the miser certainly enjoys Senior's *abstinence* —then the product does not lose any of its value. Labour *alone* produces; it is the only *substance* of products as *values.* . . . The negation of tranquility, as mere negation, ascetic sacrifice, creates nothing. *Someone may castigate and flagellate himself all day long like the monks etc., and this quantity of sacrifice he contributes will remain totally worthless.* The *natural price* of things is not the sacrifice made for them. This recalls, rather, the pre-industrial view which wants to achieve wealth by sacrificing to the gods. There has to be something besides sacrifice. The sacrifice of tranquility can also be called the sacrifice of laziness, unfreedom, unhappiness, i.e. negation of a negative state. A. Smith considers labour psychologically, as to the fun or displeasure it holds for the individual. But it is something else, too, in addition to this *emotional* relation with his activity—firstly, for others, since A's mere sacrifice would be of no use for B; secondly, a definite relation by his own self to the thing he works on, and to his own working capabilities. It is a *positive, creative activity.*

Marx, *Grundrisse* (1857–58), pp. 171–73, 610–14.

The more the productiveness of labour increases, the more can the working-day be shortened; and the more the working-day is shortened, the more can the intensity of labour increase. From a social point of view, the productiveness increases in the same ratio as the economy of labour, which, in its turn, includes not only economy of the means of production, but also the avoidance of all useless labour. The capitalist mode of production, while on the one hand, enforcing economy in each individual business, on the other hand, begets, by its anarchical system of competition, the most outrageous squandering of labour-power and of the social means of production, not to mention the creation of a vast number of employments, at present indispensable, but in themselves superfluous.

The intensity and productiveness of labour being given, the time which society is bound to devote to material production is shorter, and as a consequence, the time at its disposal for the free development, intellectual and social, of the individual is greater, in proportion as the work is more and more evenly divided among all the able-bodied members of society, and as a particular class is more and more deprived of the power to shift the natural burden of labour from its own shoulders to those of another layer of society. In this direction, the shortening of the working-day finds at last a limit in the generalisation of labour. In capitalist society spare time is acquired for one class by converting the whole life-time of the masses into labour-time.

Marx, *Capital,* I (1867), p. 581.

9.A.8 REALM OF NECESSITY AND REALM OF FREEDOM

We have seen that the capitalist process of production is a historically determined form of the social process of production in general. This process is on the one hand the process by which the material requirements of life are produced, and on the other hand a process which takes place under specific historical and economic conditions of production and which produces and reproduces these conditions of production themselves, and with them the human agents of this process, their material conditions of existence and their mutual relations, that is, their particular economic form of society. For the aggregate of these relations, in which the agents of this production live with regard to nature and to themselves, and in which they produce, is precisely their society, considered from the point of view of its economic structure. Like all its predecessors, the capitalist process of production takes place under definite material conditions, which are at the same time the bearers of definite social relations maintained towards one another by the individuals in the process of producing their life's requirements. These conditions and these relations are on the one hand prerequisites, on the other hand results and creations of the capitalist process of production. They are produced and reproduced by it. We have also seen that capital (the capitalist is merely capital personified and functions in the process of production as the agent of capital), in the social process of production corresponding to it, pumps a certain quantity of surplus labor out of the direct producer, or laborer. It extorts this surplus without returning an equivalent. This surplus labor always remains forced labor in essence, no matter how much it may seem to be the result of free contract. This surplus labor is represented by a surplus-value, and this surplus-value is materialized in a surplus product. It must always remain surplus labor in the sense that it is labor performed above the normal requirements of the producer. In the capitalist system as well as in the slave system, etc., it merely assumes an antagonistic form and is supplemented by the complete idleness of a portion of society. A certain quantity of surplus labor is required for the purpose of discounting accidents, and by the necessary and progressive expansion of the process of reproduction in keeping with the development of the needs and the advance of population, called accumulation from the point of view of the capitalist. It is one of the civilizing sides of capital that it enforces this surplus labor in a manner and under conditions which promote the development of the productive forces, of social conditions, and the creation of the elements for a new and higher formation better than did the preceding forms of slavery, serfdom, etc. Thus it leads on the one hand to a stage, in which the coercion and the monopolization of the social development (including its material and intellectual advantages) by a portion of society at the expense of the other portion are eliminated; on the other hand it creates the material requirements and the germ of conditions, which make it possible to combine this surplus labor in a higher form of society with a greater reduction of the time devoted to material labor. For, according to the development of the productive power of labor, surplus labor may be large in a small total labor day, and relatively small in a large total labor day. If the necessary labor time equals three, and the surplus labor three, then the total working day is equal to six, and the rate of surplus labor 100 percent. If the necessary labor is equal to nine, and the surplus labor three, then the total working day is twelve and the rate of surplus labor only 33⅓ percent. Furthermore, it depends upon the productivity of labor, how much use-value shall be produced in a definite time, hence also in a definite surplus labor time. The actual wealth of society, and the possibility of a continual expansion of its process of reproduction, do not depend upon the duration of the surplus labor, but upon its productivity and upon the more or less fertile conditions of production, under which it is performed. In fact, the realm of freedom does not commence until the point is passed where labor under the compulsion of necessity and of external utility is required. In the very nature of things it lies beyond the sphere of material production in the strict meaning of the term. Just as the savage must wrestle with nature, in order to satisfy his wants, in order to maintain his life and reproduce it, so civilized man has to do it, and he must do it in all forms of society and under all possible modes of production. With his development the realm of natural necessity expands, because his wants increase; but at the same time the forces of production increase, by which these wants are satisfied. The freedom in this field cannot consist of anything else but of the fact that socialized man, the associated producers, regulate their interchange with nature rationally, bring it under their common control, instead of being ruled by it as by some blind power; that they accomplish their task with the least expenditure of energy and under conditions most adequate to their human nature and most worthy of it. But it always remains a realm of necessity. Beyond it begins that development of human power, which is its own end, the true realm of freedom, which, however, can flourish only upon that realm of necessity as its basis. The shortening of the working day is its fundamental premise.

Marx, *Capital*, III (1894), pp. 952–55.

B. COMMUNISM'S ORGANIZATION AND BEHAVIOR

Marx's and Engels' commentaries on the institutional structure and functioning of postcapitalist economic society, at least from the standpoint of rigorous economic analysis, are relatively slim compared to their in-depth analysis of capitalism. This partly reflects Marx's methodological aversion to detailed utopia building and his conviction that the specific institutional and behavioral content of communist society would depend on the particular circumstances and state of mind in which the working class found itself. The general contours, however, are clear enough, and are summarized in this concluding section.

As to institutional structure, the prominent elements probably could be derived by comparison and contrast with other systems of economy even if Marx had never described his own version of socialism. First, in contrast to private enterprise economies, ownership and control of the physical means of production would be social or collective rather than private. Second, in contrast to market-directed economies, socialism would substitute overall planning for market exchange as the dominant social process for economic coordination. Third, in contrast to all forms of economy (market or planned, private or social) that separate work and ownership, Marx's socialism would reintegrate these two processes around the theme of worker control, both in production, at the level of individual enterprises, and in government, concerning policy direction for the economy as a whole. Fourth, it would place industrial division of labor under worker and social control and work to reduce, if not eliminate, its dehumanizing character and consequences.

In fact, Marx (and Engels) did describe his version of socialism essentially, though briefly, in this manner, as shown in selection 9.B.9. What Marx and Engels did not do was examine these properties of socialist economy in depth. Overall planning and collective ownership and control, by themselves, imply centralization in economic organization; worker control of industry and government policy implies decentralization and democratization. Just how and in what proportions are these possibly competing institutional criteria to be combined? Marx and Engels did not provide definitive answers, leaving ample room for debates over decentralized versus centralized versions of Marxian socialism.[2]

The prospective economic functioning of a socialist society is described in the succeeding three selections. It is clear from selection 9.B.10 that both Marx and Engels recognize the phenomenon of the allocation of scarce resources among alternative uses and the importance of maintaining the "proper proportion between the different kinds of work to be done and the various wants of the community." It is equally clear that resource allocation and what contemporary neoclassical economists call "allocative efficiency" is not preeminent among Marxian priorities. Engels, as is indicated in selection 9.B.11, placed much

[2]John E. Elliott, "Marx and Contemporary Models of Socialist Economy," *History of Political Economy*, Summer 1976, pp. 176-76; and "Marx's Socialism in the Context of his Typology of Economic Systems," *Journal of Comparative Economics*, March 1978.

greater emphasis on growth rates, dynamic efficiency, full employment and economic stability, abolition of poverty, and reduction if not elimination of income inequality. His central point was that with crises and cyclical fluctuations essentially eliminated through overall economic planning, science and technology could unleash virtually uninterrupted abundance and growth.

Marx's focus, in his 1875 *Critique of the Gotha Program* (selection 9.B.12), is on income distribution, work, and the supersession of exploitation and alienation. These topics are linked with the process of evolution from a "lower phase" of communism "as it *emerges* from capitalist society" and a "higher phase" wherein "the narrow horizon of bourgeois right can be fully left behind." This is presumably a gradual process, even in an industrialized economy. Market exchange, the quid pro quo principle of commodity economy, work, material incentives, division of labor, alienation, the state as an agency representing the interests of the dominant class in society—all these are modified in the process of moving from communism's "lower" to its "higher" phase. In short, for Marx, the first stage of communism is not the last. Early socialism "epitomizes the basic shortcomings of capitalist society only in order to radicalize and overcome them."[3]

Marx's analysis, in this selection, of the macroeconomic aspects of income distribution should be especially noted. The "total social product," he explains, is divided into three main parts. First is investment (both for replacement and expansion), to which is added reserve funds against disasters. Second is collectively provided goods. Other than provision for those unable to work, this includes the *"general costs of administration"* and such goods as education and health care, intended for the "common satisfaction of needs," the former diminishing, the latter growing "in proportion as the new society develops." Third is individual consumer goods, which are available only after these various collective needs have been attended to. Does this constitute "exploitation"? For Marx, the answer is no, on the ground that the working class, rather than capitalists, now in control of the apparatus of production and of government policy, collectively decides to allocate a portion of total resources to these nonindividual consumption purposes.

In contrast to classical liberals, Marx and Engels believed that the working class must (and can) capture control of major economic and political institutions and can construct new institutions to direct society to the pursuit of their collective interests. In contrast to anarchists, e.g., the Russian writer Bakunin (selection 9.B.13), Marx and Engels insist that it is the capitalist class and capitalist institutions (including the capitalist state) that are the barriers to working class control, not the state per se. With the transformation of the socioeconomic structure, the "state," as an alien institution separate from the rest of society, can be superseded (Marx) or at least will "wither away" (Engels). Also, in contrast to the anarchist view, Engels argues in this final selection that communism cannot eliminate the need for authority or organization in industry. What it can do is to bring organization and authority under working class control. The crucial presumption in this argument, as in the preceding selection, is that working class control over production and politics is genuine and effective.

[3]Shlomo Avineri, *The Social and Political Thought of Karl Marx* (Cambridge: Cambridge University Press, 1968), p. 227.

9.B.9 COMMUNISM'S BASIC INSTITUTIONS

COLLECTIVE OWNERSHIP AND OVERALL PLANNING

The emancipation of the class of producers involves all mankind, without distinction of sex or race; . . .

The producers can only be free when they are in possession of the means of production; . . .

There are only two forms in which the means of production can belong to them:

1. The individual form, which was never a universal phenomenon and is being ever more superseded by the progress of industry,
2. The collective form, the material and mental elements for which are created by the very development of capitalist society; . . .

Collective appropriation can only proceed from a revolutionary action of the class of producers—the proletariat—organized in an independent political party;

This *collective appropriation* must be striven for by all means that are available to the proletariat, including universal suffrage, which will thus be transformed from the instrument of fraud that it has been up till now into an instrument of emancipation.

Marx, *Introduction to the Programme of the French Workers' Party* (1880), KMPW, III, pp. 376–77.

The life-process of society, which is based on the process of material production, does not strip off its mystical veil until it is treated as production by freely association men, and is consciously regulated by them in accordance with a settled plan. This, however, demands for society a certain material groundwork or set of conditions of existence which in their turn are the spontaneous product of a long and painful process of development.

Political economy has indeed analysed, however incompletely, value and its magnitude, and has discovered what lies beneath these forms. But it has never once asked the question why labour is represented by the value of its product and labour time by the magnitude of that value. These formulae, which bear stamped upon them in unmistakable letters, that they belong to a state of society, in which the process of production has the mastery over man, instead of being controlled by him, such formulae appear to the bourgeois intellect to be as much a self-evident necessity imposed by nature as productive labour itself. Hence forms of social production that preceded the bourgeois form, are treated by the bourgeoisie in much the same way as the Fathers of the Church treated pre-Christian religions.

Marx, *Capital,* I (1867), pp. 92–93.

The nonsense about the necessity of proving the concept of value arises from complete ignorance both of the subject dealt with and of the method of science. Every child knows that a country which ceased to work, I will not say for a year, but for a few weeks, would die. Every child knows, too, that the mass of products corresponding to the different needs require different and quantitatively determined masses of the total labour of society. That this necessity of distributing social labour in definite proportions cannot be done away with by the *particular form* of social production, but can only change the *form it assumes,* is self-evident. No natural laws can be done away with. What can change, in changing historical circumstances, is the *form* in which these laws operate. And the form in which this proportional division of labour operates, in a state of society where the interconnection of social labour is manifested in the *private exchange* of the individual products of labour, is precisely the *exchange value* of these products. . . .

The vulgar economist has not the faintest idea that the actual everyday exchange relations need not be directly identical with the magnitudes of value. The point of bourgeois society consists precisely in this, that *a priori* there is no conscious social regulation of production. The reasonable and the necessary in nature asserts itself only as a blindly working average. And then the vulgar economist thinks he has made a great discovery, when, as against the disclosures of the inner connection, he proudly claims that in appearance things look different.

Marx, Letter to Kugelmann (1868), LK, pp. 73–74.

COMMUNISM AND THE DIVISION OF LABOR: AN EARLY STATEMENT

The division of labour offers us the first example of how, as long as man remains in natural society, that is, as long as a cleavage exists between the particular and the common interest, as long, therefore, as activity is not voluntarily, but naturally, divided, man's own deed becomes an alien power opposed to him, which enslaves him instead of being controlled by him. For as soon as the distribution of labour comes into being, each man has a particular, exclusive sphere of activity, which is forced upon him and from which he cannot escape. He is a hunter, a fisherman, a shepherd, or a critical critic, and must remain so if he does not want to lose his means of livelihood; while in communist society, where nobody has one exclusive sphere of activity but each can become accomplished in any branch he wishes, society regulates the general production and thus makes it possible for me to do one thing today and another tomorrow, to hunt in the morning, fish in the afternoon, rear cattle in the evening, criticise after dinner, just as I have a mind, without ever becoming hunter, fisherman, shepherd or critic. This fixation of social activity, this consolidation of what we ourselves produce into an objective power above us, growing out of our control, thwarting our expectations, bringing to naught our calculations, is one of the chief factors in historical development up till now. . . .

The social power, i.e. the multiplied productive force, which arises through the co-operation of different individuals as it is determined by the division of labour, appears to these individuals, since their co-operation is not voluntary but has come about naturally, not as their own united power, but as an alien force existing outside them, of the origin and goal of which they are ignorant, which they thus cannot control, which on the contrary passes through a peculiar series of phases and stages independent of the will and the action of man, nay even being the prime governor of these.

How otherwise could for instance property have had a history at all, have taken on different forms, and landed property, for example, according to the different premises given, have proceeded in France from parcellation to centralisation in the hands of a few, in England from centralisation in the hands of a few to parcellation, as is actually the case today? Or how does it happen that trade, which after all is nothing more than the exchange of products of various individuals and countries, rules the whole world through the relation of supply and demand—a relation which, as an English economist says, hovers over the earth like the fate of the ancients, and with invisible hand allots fortune and misfortune to men, sets up empires and overthrows empires, causes nations to rise and to disappear—while with the abolition of the basis of private property, with the communistic regulation of production (and, implicit in this, the destruction of the alien relation between men and what they themselves produce), the power of the relation of supply and demand is dissolved into nothing, and men get exchange, production, the mode of their mutual relation, under their own control again?

In history up to the present it is certainly an empirical fact that separate individuals have, with the broadening of their activity into world-historical activity, become more and more enslaved under a power alien to them (a pressure which they have conceived of as a dirty trick on the part of the so-called universal spirit, etc.), a power which has become more and more enormous and, in the last instance, turns out to be the *world market.* But it is just as empirically established that, by the overthrow of the existing state of society by the communist revolution. . . and the abolition of private property which is identical with it, this power. . . will be dissolved; and that then the liberation of each single individual will be accomplished in the measure in which history becomes transformed into world history. From the above it is clear that the real intellectual wealth of the individual depends entirely on the wealth of his real connections. Only then will the separate individuals be liberated from the various national and local barriers, be brought into practical connection with the material and intellectual production of the whole world and be put in a position to acquire the capacity to enjoy this all-sided production of the whole earth (the creations of man). *All-round* dependence, this natural form of the *world-historical* co-operation of individuals, will be transformed by this communist revolution into the control and conscious mastery of these powers, which, born of the action of men on one another, have till now overawed and governed men as powers completely alien to them. . . .

The individuals, who are no longer subject to the division of labour, have been conceived by the philosophers as an ideal, under the name "Man". They have conceived the whole process which we have outlined as the evolutionary process of "Man", so that at every historical stage "Man" was substituted for the individuals and shown as the motive force of history. The whole process was thus conceived as a process of the self-estrangement of "Man", and this was essentially due to the fact that the average individual of the later stage was always foisted on to the earlier stage, and the consciousness of a later age on to the individuals of an earlier. Through this inversion, which from the first is an abstract image of the actual conditions, it was possible to transform the whole of history into an evolutionary process of consciousness.

Marx-Engels, *The German Ideology* (1845–46), excerpts from Part I.

THE LATER ENGELS: *ANTI-DUHRING*

In every society in which production has developed spontaneously—and our present society is of this type—it is not the producers who control the means of production, but the means of production which control the producers. In such a society each new lever of production is necessarily transformed into a new means for the subjection of the producers to the means of production. This is most of all true of that lever of production which, prior to the introduction of large-scale industry, was by far the most powerful—the division of labour. The first great division of labour, the separation of town and country, condemned the rural population to thousands of years of degradation, and the people of the towns to subjection to each one's individual trade. It destroyed the basis of the intellectual development of the former and the physical development of the latter. When the peasant appropriates his land, and the citizen his trade, to just the same extent his land appropriates the peasant and his trade the citizen. In the division of labour, man is also divided. All other physical and mental faculties are sacrificed to the development of one single activity. This stunting of man's faculties grows in the same measure as the division of labour, which attains its highest development in manufacture. Manufacture splits up each trade into its separate fractional operations, allots each of these to an individual labourer as his life calling, and thus chains him for life to a particular detail function and a particular tool. "It converts the labourer into a crippled monstrosity, by forcing his detail dexterity at the expense of a world of productive capabilities and instincts. . . . The individual himself is made the automatic motor of a fractional operation" (Marx) [*Capital*, Vol. I, p. 396 (Kerr edition)]. – a motor which in many cases becomes perfect only through the literal physical and mental crippling of the labourer. The machinery of modern industry degrades the labourer from a machine to the mere appendage of a machine. "The life-long speciality of handling one and the same tool, now becomes the life-long speciality of serving one and the same machine. Machinery is put to a wrong use, with the object of transforming the workman, from his very childhood, into a part of a detail-machine" (Marx). [*Capital*, Vol. I, p. 461 (Kerr edition)]. And not only the labourers, but also the classes directly or indirectly exploiting the labourers are made subject, through the division of labour, to the tool of their function; the empty-minded bourgeois to his own capital and his own thirst for profits; the lawyer to his fossilised legal conceptions, which dominate him as a power independent of him; the "educated classes" in general to their manifold local limitations and one-sidedness, to their own physical and mental short-sightedness, to their stunted specialised education and the fact that they are chained for life to this specialised activity itself—even when this specialised activity is merely to do nothing.

In making itself the master of all the means of production, in order to use them in accordance with a social plan, society puts an end to the former subjection of men to their own means of production. It goes without saying that society cannot itself be free unless every individual is free. The old mode of production must therefore be revolutionised from top to bottom, and in particular the former division of labour must disappear. Its place must be taken by an organisation of production in which, on the one hand, no individual can put on to other persons his share in productive labour, this natural condition of human existence; and in which on the other hand, productive labour, instead of being a means to the subjection of men, will become a means to their emancipation, by giving each individual the opportunity to develop and exercise all his faculties, physical and mental, in all directions; in which, therefore, productive labour will become a pleasure instead of a burden.

Today this is no longer a phantasy, no longer a pious wish. The present development of productive forces is already adequate as the basis on which the increase in production which must follow from the very fact of the socialisation of the productive forces—the abolition of the barriers and disturbing factors and of the waste of products and means of production resulting from the capitalist mode of production—can reduce the time required for labour, with every individual taking his share, to what on our present conceptions would be a small amount.

Nor is the abolition of the former division of labour a demand which could only be carried through at the cost of the productivity of labour. On the contrary. Large-scale industry has made it a necessary condition of production itself. "The employment of machinery does away with the necessity of crystallising this distribution after the manner of manufacture by the constant annexation of a particular man to a particular function. Since the motion of the whole system does not proceed from the workman, but from the machinery, a change of persons can take place at any time without an interruption of the work. . . . Lastly, the quickness with which machine work is learnt by young people does away with the necessity of bringing up for exclusive employment by machinery, a special class of operatives." [*Capital,* Vol. I, p. 460 (Kerr edition).] But while the capitalist mode of employment of machinery necessarily perpetuates the old division of labour with its fossilized specialisation, although it has become superfluous from a technical standpoint, the machinery itself rebels against this anachronism. The technical basis of modern industry is revolutionary. "By means of machinery, chemical processes and other methods, it is continually causing changes not only in the technical basis of production, but also in the functions of the labourer, and in the social combinations of the labour process. At the same time, it thereby also revolutionises the division of labour within the society, and incessantly launches masses of capital and of workpeople from one branch of production to another. Modern industry, by its very nature, therefore necessitates variation of labour, fluency of function, universal mobility of the labourer. . . . We have seen how this absolute contradiction . . . vents its rage in the incessant human sacrifices from among the working class, in the most reckless squandering of labour power and in the devastation caused by social anarchy. This is the negative side. But if, on the one hand, variation of work imposes itself after the manner of an overpowering natural law, and with the blindly destructive action of a natural law that meets with resistance at all points, modern industry, on the other hand, through its catastrophes imposes the necessity of recognising, as a fundamental law of production, variation of work, consequently fitness of the labourer for varied work, consequently the greatest possible development of his varied aptitudes. It becomes a question of life and death for society to adapt the mode of production to the normal functioning of this law. Modern industry, indeed, compels society, under penalty of death, to replace the detail worker of today, crippled by life-long repetition of one and the same operation, and thus reduced to the mere fragment of a man, by the fully developed individual, fit for a variety of labours, ready to face any change of production, and to whom the different social functions he performs are but so many modes of giving free scope to his own natural and acquired powers." (Marx, *Capital.*) [*Capital,* Vol. I, pp. 533–4 (Kerr edition).]

Large-scale industry . . . has . . . to a considerable extent freed production from the restrictions of place. Water-power was local; steam-power is free. Though water-power was necessarily confined to the countryside, steam-power is by no means necessarily confined to the towns. It is the capitalist mode of its utilisation which concentrates it mainly in the towns and changes factory villages into factory towns. But in so doing, it at the same time undermines the conditions of its own exploitation. The first necessity for the steam engine, and a main requirement of almost all branches of production, is relatively pure water. The factory town, however, transforms all water into stinking ditch water. However much therefore concentration in the towns is a basic condition of capitalist production, each individual industrial capitalist is constantly striving to get away from the large towns necessarily created by it, and to move towards exploitation in the countryside. This process can be studied in detail in the textile industry districts of Lancashire and Yorkshire; modern capitalist industry is constantly bringing new large towns into being by constantly fleeing from the towns into the country. The position in the engineering industry areas is very similar, where, in part, other causes produce the same effects.

Once more, only the abolition of the capitalist character of modern industry can do away with this new vicious circle, this contradiction in modern industry, which is constantly reproducing itself. Only a society which makes possible the harmonious cooperation of its productive forces on the basis of one single vast plan can allow industry to settle in whatever form of distribution over the whole country is best adapted to its own development and the maintenance of development of the other elements of production.

Accordingly, abolition of the antithesis between town and country is not merely possible. It has become a direct necessity of industrial production itself, just as it has become a necessity of agricultural production and, moreover, of public health. The present poisoning of the air, water and land can only be put an end to by the fusion of town and country; and only this fusion will change the situation of the masses now languishing in the towns, and enable their excrement to be used for the production of plants instead of for the production of disease.

Capitalist industry has already made itself relatively independent of the local limitations arising from the location of sources of raw materials. The textile industry, in the main, works up imported raw materials. Spanish iron ore is worked up in England and Germany and Spanish and South American copper ores are used in England. Every coalfield now supplies fuel to an industrial area beyond its own borders, an area which is widening every year. Along the whole of the European coast steam engines are driven by English and to some extent also by German and Belgian coal. Society liberated from the barriers of capitalist production can go much further still. By producing a race of producers with an all-round training who understand the scientific basis of industrial production as a whole, and each of whom has had practical experience in a whole series of branches of production from start to finish, this society will bring into being a new productive force which will fully compensate for the labour required for the transport of raw materials of fuel from great distances.

The abolition of the separation between town and country is therefore not utopian, even in so far as it presupposes the most equal distribution possible of large-scale industry over the whole country. It is true that in the huge towns civilisation has bequeathed us a heritage to rid ourselves of which will take much time and trouble. But this heritage must and will be got rid of, however protracted the process may be. . . .

Engels, *Anti-Duhring* (1878), pp. 318–24.

9.B.10 VALUE, LABOR, MONEY, AND RESOURCE ALLOCATION

(Only when production will be under the conscious and prearranged control of society, will society establish a direct relation between the quantity of social labor time employed in the production of definite articles and the quantity of the demand of society for them.) The commodities must then be sold below their market-value, and a portion of them may even become unsalable. The opposite takes place, if the quantity of social labor employed in the production of a certain kind of commodities is too small to meet the social demand for them. But if the quantity of social labor spent in the production of a certain article corresponds to the social demand for it, so that the quantity produced is that which is the ordinary on that scale of production and for that same demand, then the article is sold at its market-value. The exchange, or sale, of commodities at their value is the rational way, the natural law of their equilibrium.

Marx, *Capital,* III (1894), p. 221.

The general rule in differential rent is that the market-value always stands above the total price of production of the mass of products. For instance, take Table I. The ten quarters of the total product are sold at 600 shillings, because the market price is determined by the price of production of A, which amounts to 60 shillings per quarter. But the actual price of production is:

A	*1 qr.*	*= 60 sh.*		*1 qr. = 60 sh.*
B	*2qrs.*	*= 60 sh.*		*1 qr. = 30 sh.*
C	*3 qrs.*	*= 60 sh.*		*1 qr. = 20 sh.*
D	*4 qrs.*	*= 60 sh.*		*1 qr. = 15 sh.*
	10 qrs.	*= 240 sh.*	*Average*	*1 qr. = 24 sh.*

The actual price of production of these 10 quarters is 240 shillings. But they are sold at 600 shillings, 250% too dear. The actual average price for 1 quarter is 24 shillings; the market price is 60 shillings, also 250% too dear.

This is a determination by the market-value, which is enforced on the basis of capitalist production by means of competition; it creates a false social value. This arises from the law of the market-value, to which the products of the soil are subject. The determination of the market-value of the products, including the products of the soil, is a social act, although performed by society unconsciously and unintentionally. It rests necessarily upon the exchange-value of the product, not upon the soil and its differences in fertility.

If we imagine that the capitalistic form of society is abolished and society is organized as a conscious and systematic association, then those 10 quarters represent a quantity of independent labor, which is equal to that contained in 240 shillings. In that case society would not buy this product of the soil at two and a half times the labour time contained in it. The basis of a class of land owners would thus be destroyed. This would have the same effect as a cheapening of the product to the same amount by foreign imports. While it is correct to say that, by retaining the present mode of production but paying the differential rent to the state, the prices of the products of the soil would remain the same, other circumstances remaining unchanged, it is wrong to say that the value of the products would remain the same, if capitalist production were superseded by association. The sameness of the market prices for commodities of the same kind is the way in which the social character of value asserts itself on the basis of capitalist production, as it does of any production resting on the exchange of commodities between individuals. What society in its capacity as a consumer pays too much for the products of the soil, what constitutes a minus for the realisation of its labour time in agricultural production, is now a plus for a portion of society, for the landlords.

Marx, *Capital,* III (1894), pp. 773–74.

In the case of socialized production, the money-capital is eliminated. Society distributes labour-power and means of production to the different lines of occupation. The producers may eventually receive paper checks, by means of which they withdraw from the social supply of means of consumption a share corresponding to their labour-time. These checks are not money. They do not circulate.

Marx, *Capital,* II (1885), p. 412.

Let us now picture to ourselves, by way of change, a community of free individuals, carrying on their work with the means of production in common, in which the labour-power of all the different individuals is consciously applied as the combined labour-power of the community. All the characteristics of Robinson's labour are here repeated, but with this difference, that they are social, instead of individual. Everything produced by him was exclusively the result of his own personal labour, and therefore simply an object of use for himself. The total product of our community is a social product. One portion serves as fresh means of production and remains social. But another portion is consumed by the members as means of subsistence. A distribution of this portion amongst them is consequently necessary. The mode of this distribution will vary with the productive organization of the community, and the degree of historical development attained by the producers. We will assume, but merely for the sake of a parallel with the production of commodities, that the share of each individual producer in the means of subsistence is determined by his labour-time. Labour-time would, in that case, play a double part. Its apportionment in accordance with a definite social plan maintains the proper portion between the different kinds of work to be done and the various wants of the community. On the other hand, it also serves as a measure of the portion of the common labour borne by each individual and of his share in the part of the total product destined for individual consumption. The social relations of the individual producers, with regard both to their labour and to its products, are in this case perfectly simple and intelligible, and that with regard not only to production but also to distribution.

Marx, *Capital,* I (1867), pp. 90–91.

There is a certain difference between the expenses incidental to bookkeeping, or the unproductive expenditure of labour-time on one side, and that of mere selling and buying time on the other. The latter arise only from the definite social form of the process of production, they are due to the fact that it is a production of commodities. Bookkeeping, for the control and ideal survey of the process, becomes necessary to the extent that the process assumes a social scale and loses its purely individual character. It is, therefore, more necessary in capitalist production than in scattered handicraft and agricultural production, and still more necessary in cooperative than in capitalist production. But the expenses of bookkeeping are reduced to the extent that production is concentrated and becomes social bookkeeping.

Marx, *Capital,* II (1885), p. 153.

For socialism, which will emancipate human labour power from its position as a *commodity,* the discovery that labour has no value and can have none is of great importance. With this discovery all attempts . . . to regular the future distribution of the necessaries of life as a kind of more exalted wages, necessarily fall to the ground. And from it too comes the further understanding that distribution, in so far as it is governed by purely economic considerations, is regulated by the interests of production, and production is most encouraged by a mode of distribution which allows *all* members of society to develop, maintain and exert their capacities in all possible directions. It is true that, to the mode of thought of the educated classes, . . . , it must seem monstrous that in time to come there will no longer be any professional porters or architects, and that the man who for half an hour gives instructions as an architect will also push a barrow for a period, until his activity as an architect is once again required. It is a fine sort of socialism which perpetuates the professional porter!

If the equality of value of labour time means that each labourer produces equal values in equal periods of time, without there being any need to take an average, then this is obviously false. If we have two workers, even in the same branch of industry, the value they produce in one hour of labour time will always vary with the intensity of their labour and their skill—and not even an economic commune, at any rate not on our globe, can remedy this inconvenience. . . .

How then are we to solve the whole important question of the higher wages paid for compound labour? In a society of private producers, private individuals or their families pay the costs of training the skilled worker; hence the higher price paid for trained labour power also comes first of all to private individuals; the clever slave is sold for a higher price, and the clever wage earner is paid higher wages. In a socialistically organised society, these costs are born by society, and to it therefore belong also the fruits, the greater values produced by skilled labour. The labourer himself has no claim to extra payment. And from this, incidentally, also follows the moral that there is frequently a drawback to the popular demand of the workers for "the full proceeds of labour."

Engels, *Anti-Duhring* (1878), pp. 221–22.

Commodity production. . .is by no means the only form of social production. In the ancient Indian communities and in the family communities of the southern Slavs, products are not transformed into commodities. The members of the community are directly associated for production; the work is distributed on the basis of tradition and requirements, and likewise the products in so far as they are destined for consumption. Direct social production and direct distribution exclude all exchange of commodities, therefore also the transformation of the products into commodities (at any rate within the community) and consequently also their transformation into *values.*

From the moment when society enters into possession of the means of production and uses them in direct association for production, the labour of each individual, however varied its specifically useful character may be, is immediately and directly social labour. The quantity of social labour contained in a product has then no need to be established in a roundabout way; daily experience shows in a direct way how much of it is required on the average. Society can calculate simply how many hours of labour are contained in a steam-engine, a bushel of wheat of the last harvest, or a hundred square yards of cloth of a certain quality. It could therefore never occur to it still to express the quantity of labour put into the products, which it will then know directly and in its absolute amount in a third product, and moreover in a measure which is only relative, fluctuating, inadequate, though formerly unavoidable for lack of a better, and not in its natural, adequate and absolute measure, *time.* Just as little as it would occur to chemical science still to express atomic weights in a roundabout way, relatively, by means of the hydrogen atom if it was once able to express them absolutely, in their adequate measure, namely in actual weight, in billionths or quadrillionths of a gram. On the assumptions we made above, therefore, society will also not assign values to products. It will not express the simple fact that the hundred square yards of cloth have required for their production, let us say, a thousand hours of labour in the oblique and meaningless way, that they have the *value* of a thousand hours of labour. It is true that even then it will still be necessary for society to know how much labour each article of consumption requires for its production. It will have to arrange its plan of production in accordance with its means of production, which include, in particular, its labour forces. The useful effects of the various articles of consumption, compared with each other and with the quantity of labour required for their production, will in the last analysis determine the plan. People will be able to manage everything very simply, without the intervention of the famous "value."*

Engels, *Anti-Duhring* (1872), pp. 337–38.

9.B.11 COMMUNISM'S PROSPECTIVE ECONOMIC PERFORMANCE: PROSPERITY AND GROWTH

State ownership of the productive forces is not the solution of [class] conflict, but concealed within it are the technical conditions that form the elements of that solution.

This solution can only consist in the practical recognition of the social nature of the modern forces of production, and therefore in the harmonising of the modes of production, appropriation, and exchange with the socialised character of the means of production. And this can only come about by society openly and directly taking possession of the productive forces which have outgrown all control except that of society as a whole. The social character of the means of production and of the products today reacts against the producers, periodically disrupts all production and exchange, acts only like a law of Nature working blindly, forcibly, destructively. But with the taking over by

*As long ago as 1844 I stated that the above-mentioned balancing of useful effects and expenditure of labour would be all that would be left, in a communist society, of the concept of value as it appears in political economy (*Deutsch-Franzosische Jahrbucher*, p. 95). The scientific justification for this statement, however, as can be seen, was only made possible by Marx's *Capital. [Note by F. Engels.]*

society of the productive forces, the social character of the means of production and of the products will be utilised by the producers with a perfect understanding of its nature, and instead of being a source of disturbance and periodical collapse, will become the most powerful lever of production itself.

Active social forces work exactly like natural forces: blindly, forcibly, destructively, so long as we do not understand, and reckon with, them. But when once we understand them, when once we grasp their action, their direction, their effects, it depends only upon ourselves to subject them more and more to our own will, and by means of them to reach our own ends. And this holds quite especially of the mighty productive forces of today. As long as we obstinately refuse to understand the nature and the character of these social means of action—and this understanding goes against the grain of the capitalist mode of production and its defenders—so long these forces are at work in spite of us, in opposition to us, so long they master us, as we have shown above in detail.

But when once their nature is understood, they can, in the hands of the producers working together, be transformed from master demons into willing servants. The difference is as that between the destructive force of electricity in the lightning of the storm, and electricity under command in the telegraph and the voltaic arc; the difference between a conflagration, and fire working in the service of man. With this recognition, at last, of the real nature of the productive forces of today, the social anarchy of production gives place to a social regulation of production upon a definite plan, according to the needs of the community and of each individual. Then the capitalist mode of appropriation, in which the product enslaves first the producer and then the appropriator, is replaced by the mode of appropriation of the products that is based upon the nature of the modern means of production; upon the one hand, direct social appropriation, as means to the maintenance and extension of production—on the other, direct individual appropriation, as means of subsistence and of enjoyment. . . .

Since the historical appearance of the capitalist mode of production, the appropriation by society of all the means of production has often been dreamed of, more or less vaguely, by individuals, as well as by sects, as the ideal of the future. But it could become possible, could become a historical necessity, only when the actual conditions for its realisation were there. Like every other social advance, it becomes practicable, not by men understanding that the existence of classes is in contradiction to justice, equality, etc., not by the mere willingness to abolish these classes, but by virtue of certain new economic conditions. The separation of society into an exploiting and an exploited class, a ruling and an oppressed class, was the necessary consequence of the deficient and restricted development of production in former times. So long as the total social labour only yields a produce which but slightly exceeds that barely necessary for the existence of all; so long, therefore, as labour engages all or almost all the times of the great majority of the members of society—so long, of necessity, this society is divided into classes. Side by side with the great majority, exclusively bond slaves to labour, arises a class freed from directly productive labour, which looks after the general affairs of society: the direction of labour, state business, law, science, art, etc. It is, therefore, the law of division of labour that lies at the basis of the division into classes. But this does not prevent this division into classes from being carried out by means of violence and robbery, trickery and fraud. It does not prevent the ruling class, once having the upper hand, from consolidating its power at the expense of the working class, from turning its social leadership into an intensified exploitation of the masses.

But if, upon this showing, division into classes has a certain historical justification, it has this only for a given period, only under given social conditions. It was based upon the insufficiency of production. It will be swept away by the complete development of modern productive forces. And, in fact, the abolition of classes in society presupposes a degree of historical evolution at which the existence, not simply of this or that particular ruling class, but of any ruling class at all, and, therefore, the existence of class distinction itself has become an obsolete anachronism. It presupposes, therefore, the development of production carried out to a degree at which appropriation of the means of production and of the products, and, with this, of political domination, of the monopoly of culture, and of intellectual leadership by a particular class of society, has become not only superfluous but economically, politically, intellectually, a hindrance to development.

This point is now reached. Their political and intellectual bankruptcy is scarcely any longer a secret to the bourgeoisie themselves. Their economic bankruptcy recurs regularly every ten years. In every crisis, society is suffocated beneath the weight of its own productive forces and products, which it cannot use, and stands helpless, face to face with the absurd contradiction that the producers have nothing to consume, because consumers are wanting. The expansive force of the means of production bursts the bonds that the capitalist mode of production had imposed upon them. Their deliverance from these bonds is the one precondition for an unbroken, constantly accelerated development of the productive forces, and therewith for a practically unlimited increase of production itself. Nor is this all. The socialised appropriation of the means of production does away, not only with the present artificial restrictions upon production, but also with the positive waste and devastation of productive forces and products that are at the present time the inevitable concomitants of production, and that reach their height in the crises. Further, it sets free for the community at large a mass of means of production and of products, by doing away with the senseless extravagance of the ruling classes of today and their political representatives. The possibility of securing for every member of society, by means of socialised production, an existence not only fully sufficient materially, and becoming day by day more full, but an existence guaranteeing to all the free development and exercise of their physical and mental faculties—this possibility is now for the first time here, but *it is here.*

With the seizing of the means of production by society, production of commodities is done away with, and, simultaneously, the mastery of the product over the producer. Anarchy in social production is replaced by systematic, definite organisation. The struggle for individual existence disappears. Then for the first time man, in a certain sense, is finally marked off from the rest of the animal kingdom, and emerges from mere animal conditions of existence into really human ones. The whole sphere of the conditions of life which environ man, and which have hitherto ruled man, now comes under the dominion and control of man, who for the first time becomes the real, conscious lord of Nature, because he has now become master of his own social organisation. The laws of his own social action, hitherto standing face to face with man as laws of Nature foreign to, and dominating him, will then be used with full understanding, and so mastered by him. Man's own social organisation, hitherto confronting him as a necessity imposed by Nature and history, now becomes the result of his own free action. The extraneous objective forces that have hitherto governed history pass under the control of man himself. Only from that time will man himself, more and more consciously, make his own history—only from that time will the social causes set in movement by him have, in the main and in a constantly growing measure, the results intended by him. It is the ascent of man from the kingdom of necessity to the kingdom of freedom. . . .

The proletariat seizes the public power, and by means of this transforms the socialised means of production, slipping from the hands of the bourgeoisie, into public property. By this act, the proletariat frees the means of production from the character of capital they have thus far borne, and gives their socialised character complete freedom to work itself out. Socialised production upon a predetermined plan becomes henceforth possible. The development of production makes the existence of different classes of society thenceforth an anachronism. In proportion as anarchy in social production vanishes, the political authority of the state dies out. Man, at last the master of his own form of social organisation, becomes at the same time the lord over Nature, his own master—free.

To accomplish this act of universal emancipation is the historical mission of the modern proletariat. To thoroughly comprehend the historical conditions and thus the very nature of this act, to impart to the now oppressed proletarian class a full knowledge of the conditions and of the meaning of the momentous act it is called upon to accomplish, this is the task of the theoretical expression of the proletarian movement, scientific socialism.

Engels, *Socialism: Utopian and Scientific,* MESW, pp. 728–32, 734.

9.B.12 COMMUNISM'S LOWER AND HIGHER PHASES AND DISTRIBUTION

Let us take first of all the words "proceeds of labour" in the sense of the product of labour; then the cooperative proceeds of labour are the *total social product.*

From this must now be deducted:

First, cover for replacement of the means of production used up.

Secondly, additional portion for expansion of production.

Thirdly, reserve or insurance funds to provide against accidents, dislocations caused by natural calamities, etc.

These deductions from the "undiminished proceeds of labour" are an economic necessity and their magnitude is to be determined according to available means and forces, and partly by computation of probabilities, but they are in no way calculable by equity.

There remains the other part of the total product, intended to serve as means of consumption.

Before this is divided among the individuals, there has to be deducted again, from it:

First, the general costs of administration not belonging to production.

This part will, from the outset, be very considerably restricted in comparison with present-day society and it diminishes in proportion as the new society develops.

Secondly, that which is intended for the common satisfaction of needs, such as schools, health services, etc.

From the outset this part grows considerably in comparison with present-day society and it grows in proportion as the new society develops.

Thirdly, funds for those unable to work, etc., in short, for what is included under so-called official poor relief today.

Only now do we come to the "distribution" which the programme, under Lessallean influence, alone has in view in its narrow fashion, namely, to that part of the means of consumption which is divided among the individual producers of the cooperative society.

The "undiminished proceeds of labour" have already unnoticeably become converted into the "diminished" proceeds, although what the producer is deprived of in his capacity as a private individual benefits him directly or indirectly in his capacity as a member of society.

Just as the phrase of the "undiminished proceeds of labour" has disappeared, so now does the phrase of the "proceeds of labour" disappear altogether.

Within the cooperative society based on common ownership of the means of production, the producers do not exchange their products; just as little does the labour employed on the products appear here *as the value* of these products, as a material quality possessed by them, since now, in contrast to capitalist society, individual labour no longer exists in an indirect fashion but directly as a component part of the total labour. The phrase "proceeds of labour," objectionable also today on account of its ambiguity, thus loses all meaning.

What we have to deal with here is a communist society, not as it was *developed* on its own foundations, but, on the contrary, just as it *emerges* from capitalist society; which is thus in every respect, economically, morally and intellectually, still stamped with the birth marks of the old society from whose womb it emerges. Accordingly, the individual producer receives back from society—after the deductions have been made—exactly what he gives to it. What he has given to it is his individual quantum of labour. For example, the social working day consists of the sum of the individual hours of work; the individual labour time of the individual producer is the part of the social working day contributed by him, his share in it. He receives a certificate from society that he has furnished such and such an amount of labour (after deducting his labour for the common funds), and with this certificate he draws from the social stock of means of consumption as much as costs the same amount of labour. The same amount of labour which he has given to society in one form he receives back in another.

Here obviously the same principle prevails as that which regulates the exchange of commodities, as far as this is exchange of equal values. Content and form are changed, because under the altered circumstances no one can give anything except his labour, and because, on the other hand, nothing can pass to the ownership of individuals except individual means of consumption. But, as far as the distribution of the latter among the individual producers is concerned, the same principle prevails as in the exchange of commodity-equivalents: a given amount of labour in one form is exchanged for an equal amount of labour in another form.

Hence, *equal right* here is still in principle—*bourgeois right,* although principle and practice are no longer at loggerheads, while the exchange of equivalents in commodity exchange only exists *on the average* and not in the individual case.

In spite of this advance, this *equal right* is still constantly stigmatised by a bourgeois limitation. The right of the producers is *proportional* to the labour they supply; the equality consists in the fact that measurement is made with an *equal standard,* labour.

But one man is superior to another physically or mentally and so supplies more labour in the same time, or can labour for a longer time; and labour, to serve as a measure, must be defined by its duration or intensity, otherwise it ceases to be a standard of measurement. This *equal* right is an unequal right for unequal labour. It recognises no class differences, because everyone is only a worker like everyone else; but it tacitly recognises unequal individual endowment and thus productive capacity as natural privileges. *It is, therefore, a right of inequality, in its content, like every right.* Right by its very nature can consist only in the application of an equal standard; but unequal individuals (and they would not be different individuals if they were not unequal) are measurable only by an equal standard in so far as they are brought under an equal point of view, are taken from one *definite* side only, for instance, in the present case, are regarded *only as workers* and nothing more is seen in them, everything else being ignored. Further, one worker is married, another not; one has more children than another, and so on and so forth. Thus, with an equal performance of labour, and hence an equal share in the social consumption fund, one will in fact receive more than another, one will be richer than another, and so on. To avoid all these defects, right instead of being equal would have to be unequal.

But these defects are inevitable in the first phase of communist society as it is when it has just emerged after prolonged birth pangs from capitalist society. Right can never be higher than the economic structure of society and its cultural development conditioned thereby.

In a higher phase of communist society, after the enslaving subordination of the individual to the division of labour, and therewith also the antithesis between mental and physical labour, has vanished; after labour has become not only a means of life but life's prime want; after the productive forces have also increased with the all-round development of the individual, and all the springs of cooperative wealth flow more abundantly—only then can the narrow horizon of bourgeois right be crossed in its entirety and society inscribe on its banners: From each according to his ability, to each according to his needs!

I have dealt more at length with the "undiminished proceeds of labour," on the one hand, and with "equal right" and "fair distribution," on the other, in order to show what a crime it is to attempt, on the one hand, to force on our Party again, as dogmas, ideas which in a certain period had some meaning but have now become obsolete verbal rubbish, while again perverting, on the other, the realistic outlook, which it cost so much effort to instil into the Party but which has now taken root in it, by means of ideological nonsense about right and other trash so common among the democrats and French Socialists.

Quite apart from the analysis so far given, it was in general a mistake to make a fuss about so-called *distribution* and put the principal stress on it.

Any distribution whatever of the means of consumption is only a consequence of the distribution of the conditions of production themselves. The latter distribution, however, is a feature of the mode of production itself. The capitalist mode of production, for example, rests on the fact that the material conditions of production are in the hands of non-workers in the form of property in capital and land, while the masses are only owners of the personal condition of production, of labour power. If the elements of production are so distributed, then the present-day distribution of the means of consumption results automatically. If the material conditions of production are the cooperative property of the workers themselves, then there likewise results a distribution of the means of consumption different from the present one. Vulgar socialism (and from it in turn a section of the democracy) has taken over from the bourgeois economists the consideration and treatment of distribution as independent of the mode of production and hence the presentation of socialism as turning principally on distribution. After the real relation has long been made clear, why retrogress again?

Marx, *Gotha Programme* (1875), MESW, pp. 322–25.

9.B.13 WORKERS AND THE STATE

THE CHARACTER OF THE PARIS COMMUNE

The centralized state machinery which, with its ubiquitous and complicated military, bureaucratic, clerical and judiciary organs, entoils (enmeshes) the living civil society like a boa constrictor, was first forged in the days of absolute monarchy as a weapon of nascent modern society in its struggle of emancipation from feudalism. The seignorial privileges of the medieval lords and cities and clergy were transformed into the attribues of a unitary state power, displacing the feudal dignitaries by salaried state functionaries, transferring the arms from medieval retainers of the landlords and the corporations of townish citizens to a standing army; substituting for the checkered (particoloured) anarchy of conflicting medieval powers the regulated plan of a state power, with a systematic and hierarchic division of labour. The first French revolution with its task to found national unity (to create a nation) had to break down all local, territorial, townish and provincial independence. It was, therefore, forced to develop what absolute monarchy had commenced, the centralization and organization of state power, and to expand the circumference and the attributes of the state power, the number of its tools, its independence, and its supernaturalist sway over real society which in fact took the place of the medieval supernaturalist heaven, with its saints. Every minor solitary interest engendered by the relations of social groups was separated from society itself, fixed and made independent of it and opposed to it in the form of state interest, administered by state priests with exactly determined hierarchical functions.

This parasitical [excrescence upon] civil society, pretending to be its ideal counterpart, grew to its full development under the sway of the first Bonaparte. The Restoration and the monarchy of July [1830] added nothing to it but a greater division of labour, growing at the same measure in which the division of labour within civil society created new groups of interests, and therefore new material for state action. In their struggle against the revolution of 1848, the parliamentary republic of France and the governments of all continental Europe were forced to strengthen, with their measures of repression against the popular movement, the means of action and the centralization of that governmental power. All revolutions thus only perfected the state machinery instead of throwing off this deadening incubus. The fractions and parties of the ruling classes which alternately struggled for supremacy, considered the occupancy (control) (seizure) and the direction of this immense machinery of government as the main booty of the victor. It centred in the creation of immense standing armies, a host of state vermin, and huge national debts. During the time of the absolute monarchy it was a means of the struggle of modern society against feudalism, crowned by the French revolution, and under the first Bonaparte it served not only to subjugate the revolution and annihilate all popular liberties, it was an instrument of the French revolution to strike abroad, to create for France on the Continent, instead of feudal monarchies, more or less states after the image of France. Under the Restoration and the monarchy of July it became not only a means of the forcible class domination of the middle class, and a means of adding to the direct economic exploitation a second exploitation of the people by assuring to their families all the rich places of the state household. During the time of the revolutionary struggle of 1848 at last it served as a means of annihilating that revolution and all aspirations at the emancipation of the popular masses. But the state parasite received only its last development during the Second Empire. The governmental power with its standing army, its all-directing bureaucracy, its stultifying clergy and its servile tribunal hierarchy had grown so independent of society itself that a grotesquely mediocre adventurer with a hungry band of desperadoes behind him sufficed to wield it. It did no longer want the pretext of an armed coalition of old Europe against the modern world founded by the revolution of 1789. It appeared no longer as a means of class domination, subordinate to its parliamentary ministry or legislature. Humbling under its sway even the interests of the ruling classes, whose parliamentary show work it supplanted by self-elected Corps Législatifs and self-paid Senates, sanctioned in its absolute sway by universal suffrage, the acknowledged necessity for keeping up 'order,' that is the rule of the landowner and the capitalist over the producer, cloaking under the tatters of a masquerade of the past, the orgies of the corruption of the present and the victory of the most parasite fraction, the financial swindler, the *debauchery* of all the reactionary influences of the past let loose—a pandemonium of infamies—the state power had received its last and supreme expression in the Second Empire. Apparently the final victory of this governmental power over society, it was in fact the orgy of all the corrupt elements of that society. To the eye of the uninitiated it appeared only as the victory of the executive over the legislative, of the final defeat of the form of class rule pretending to be the autocracy of society by its form pretending to be a superior power to society. But in fact it was only the last degraded and the only possible form of that class ruling, as humiliating to those classes themselves as to the working classes which they kept fettered by it.

4 September was only the revindication of the republic against the grotesque adventurer that had assassinated it. The true antithesis to the *Empire itself*—that is to the state power, the centralized executive, of which the Second Empire was only the exhausting formula—was *the Commune.* This state power forms in fact the creation of the middle class, first a means to break down feudalism, then a means to crush the emancipatory aspirations of the producers, of the working class. All reactions and all revolutions had only served to transfer that organized power—that organized force of the slavery of labour—from one hand to the other, from one fraction of the ruling classes to the other. It had served the ruling classes as a means of subjugation and of pelf. It had sucked new forces from every new change. It had served as the instrument of breaking down every popular rise and served it to crush the working classes after they had fought and been ordered to secure its transfer from one part of its oppressors to the others. This was, therefore, a revolution not against this or that Legitimate, Constitutional, Republican or Imperialist form of state power. It was a revolution against the *state* itself, this supernaturalist abortion of society, a resumption by the people for the people of its own social life. It was not a revolution to transfer it from one fraction of the ruling classes to the other, but a revolution to break down this horrid machinery of class domination itself. It was not one of those dwarfish struggles between the executive and the parliamentary forms of class domination, but a revolt against both these forms, integrating each other, and of which the parliamentary form was only the deceitful by-work of the executive. The Second Empire was the final form of this state usurpation. The Commune was its definite negation, and, therefore, the initiation of the social revolution of the nineteenth century. Whatever therefore its fate at Paris, it will make its way round the world. It was at once acclaimed by the working class of Europe and the United States as the magic word of delivery. The glories and the antediluvian deeds of the Prussian conqueror seemed only hallucinations of a bygone past.

It was only the working class that could formulate by the word 'Commune'—and initiate by the fighting Commune of Paris—this new aspiration. Even the last expression of that state power in the Second Empire, although humbling for the pride of the ruling classes and casting to the winds their parliamentary pretensions of self-government, had been only the last possible form of their class rule. While politically dispossessing them, it was the orgy under which all the economic and social infamies of their regime got full sway. The middling bourgeoisie and the petty middle class were by their economical conditions of life excluded from initiating a new revolution and induced to follow in the track of the ruling classes or be the followers of the working class. The peasants were the passive economical basis of the Second Empire, of that last triumph of a *state* separate of and independent from society. Only the proletarians, fired by a new social task to accomplish by them for all society, to do away with all classes and class rule, were the men to break the instrument of that class rule—the state, the centralized and organized governmental power usurping to be the master instead of the servant of society. In the active struggle against them by the ruling classes, supported by the passive adherence of the peasantry, the Second Empire, the last crowning at the same time as the most signal prostitution of the state—which had taken the place of the medieval church—had been engendered. It had sprung into life against them. By them it was broken, not as a peculiar form of governmental (centralized) power, but as its most powerful, elaborated into seeming independence from society, expression, and, therefore, also its most prostitute reality, covered by infamy from top to bottom, having centred in absolute corruption at home and absolute powerlessness abroad.

But this one form of class rule had only broken down to make the executive, the governmental state machinery, the great and single object of attack to the revolution.

Parliamentarism in France had come to an end. Its last term and fullest sway was the parliamentary republic from May 1848 to the coup d'état. The Empire that killed it was its own creation. Under the Empire with its Corps Législatif and its Senate – in this form it has been reproduced in the military monarchies of Prussia and Austria—it had been a mere farce, a mere by-word for despotism in its crudest form. Parliamentarism then was dead in France, and in workmen's revolution certainly was not to awaken it from this death.

The *Commune*—the reabsorption of the state power by society as its own living forces instead of as forces controlling and subduing it, by the popular masses themselves, forming their own force instead of the organized force of their suppression—the political form of their social emancipation, instead of the artificial force (appropriated by their oppressors) (their own force opposed to and organized against them) of society wielded for their oppression by their enemies. The form was simple, like all great things. The reaction of former revolutions—the time wanted for all historical developments, and in the past always lost in all revolutions, in the very days of popular triumph, whenever it had rendered its victorious arms, to be turned against itself—first by displacing the army by the National Guard. 'For the first time since 4 September the republic is liberated from the *government of its enemies*. . . to the city a national militia that defends the citizens against the power (the government) *instead of a permanent army that defends the government* against the citizens'. (Proclamation of Central Committee of 22 March.) (The people had only to organize this militia on a national scale, to have done away with the standing armies; the first economical condition sine qua non for all social improvements, discarding at once this source of taxes and state debt, and this constant danger to government usurpation of class rule—of the regular class rule or an adventurer pretending to save all classes); at the same time the safest guarantee against foreign aggression and making in fact the costly military apparatus impossible in all other states; the emancipation of the peasant from the blood-tax and [from being] the most fertile source of all state taxation and state debts. Here already the point in which the Commune is a *luck for the peasant,* the first word of his emancipation. With the 'independent police' abolished, and its ruffians supplanted by servants of the Commune. The general suffrage, till now abused either for the parliamentary sanction of the Holy State Power, or a play in the hands of the ruling classes, only employed by the people to sanction (choose the instruments of) parliamentary class rule once in many years, adapted to its real purposes, to choose by the communes their own functionaries of administration and initiation. The delusion as if administration and political governing were mysteries, transcendent functions only to be trusted to the hands of a trained caste—state parasites, richly paid sycophants and sinecurists, in the higher posts, absorbing the intelligence of the masses and turning them against themselves in the lower places of the hierarchy. Doing away with the state hierarchy altogether and replacing the haughty masters of the people by always removable servants, a mock responsibility by a real responsibility, as they act continuously under public supervision. Paid like skilled workmen, £12 a month, the highest salary not exceeding £240 a year, a salary somewhat more than a fifth, according to a great scientific authority, Professor Huxley, [of that needed] to satisfy a clerk for the Metropolitan School Board. The whole sham of state mysteries and state pretensions was done away with by a Commune, mostly consisting of simple working men, organizing the defence of Paris, carrying war against the praetorians of Bonaparte, securing the supplies for that immense town, filling all the posts hitherto divided between government, police, and prefecture, doing their work publicly, simply, under the most difficult and complicated circumstances, and doing it, as Milton did his *Paradise Lost,* for a few pounds, acting in bright daylight, with no pretensions to infallibility, not hiding itself behind circumlocution offices, not ashamed to confess blunders by correcting them. Making in one order the public functions—military, administrative, political—*real workmen's functions,* instead of the hidden attributes of a trained caste; (keeping order in the turbulence of civil war and revolution) (initiating measures of general regeneration). Whatever the merits of the single measures of the Commune, its greatest measure was its own organization, extemporized with the foreign enemy at one door, and the class enemy at the other, proving by its life its vitality, confirming its thesis by its action. Its appearance was a victory over the victors of France. Captive Paris resumed by one bold spring the leadership of Europe, not depending on brute force, but by taking the lead of the social movement, by giving body to the aspirations of the working class of all countries.

With all the great towns organized into communes after the model of Paris, no government could have repressed the movement by the surprise of sudden reaction. Even by this preparatory step the time of incubation, the guarantee of the movement [would have been won]. All France organized into self-working and self-governing communes, the standing army replaced by the popular militias, the army of state parasites removed, the clerical hierarchy displaced by the schoolmaster, the state judges transformed into Communal organs, the suffrage for the national representation not a matter of sleight of hand for an all-powerful government but the deliberate expression of organized communes, the state functions reduced to a few functions for general national purposes.

Such is the *Commune—the political form of the social emancipation,* of the liberation of labour from the usurpations (slave-holding) of the monopolists of the means of labour, created by the labourers themselves or forming the gift of nature. As the state machinery and parliamentarism are not the real life of the ruling classes, but only the organized general organs of their dominion, the political guarantees and forms and expressions of the old order of things, so the Commune is not the social movement of the working class and therefore of a general regeneration of mankind, but the organized means of action. The Commune does not do away with the class struggles, through which the working classes strive to the abolition of all classes and, therefore, of all [class rule] (because it does not represent a peculiar interest. It represents the liberation of 'labour,' that is the fundamental and natural condition of individual and social life which only by usurpation, fraud, and artificial contrivances can be shifted from the few upon the many), but it affords the rational medium in which that class struggle can run through its different phases in the most rational and humane way. It could start violent reactions and as violent revolutions. It begins the *emancipation of labour*—its great goal—by doing away with the unproductive and mischievous work of the state parasites, by cutting away the springs which sacrifice an immense portion of the national produce to the feeding of the state monster on the one side, by doing, on the other, the real work of administration, local and national, for workingmen's wages. It begins therefore with an immense saving, with economical reform as well as political transformation.

The Communal organization once firmly established on a national scale, the catastrophes it might still have to undergo would be sporadic slaveholders' insurrections, which, while for a moment interrupting the work of peaceful progress, would only accelerate the movement, by putting the sword into the hand of the social revolution.

The working class know that they have to pass through different phases of class struggle. They know that the superseding of the economical conditions of the slavery of labour by the conditions of free and associated labour can only be the progressive work of time (that economical transformation), that they require not only a change of distribution, but a new organization of production, or rather the delivery (setting free) of the social forms of production in present organized labour (engendered by present industry), of the trammels of slavery, of their present class character, and their harmonious national and international coordination. They know that this work of regeneration will be again and again relented and impeded by the resistance of vested interests and class egotisms. They know that the present 'spontaneous action of the natural laws of capital and landed property'—can only be superseded by 'the spontaneous action of the laws of the social economy of free and associated labour' by a long process of development of new conditions, as was the 'spontaneous action of the economic laws of slavery' and the 'spontaneous action of the economic laws of serfdom.' But they know at the same time that great strides may be [made] at once through the Communal form of political organization and that the time has come to begin that movement for themselves and mankind.

Marx, *Draft to "Civil War in France"* (1871), KMPW, III, pp. 246–54.

THE CONSPECTUS OF BAKUNIN'S STATE AND ANARCHY

> "We have already expressed our profound aversion to the theory of Lassalle and Marx which advises the workers *to establish (a people's State)* — at least as an immediate principal goal if not as an ultimate ideal — which, they explain, will be simply 'the proletariat *(transformed into the ruling class)*'. If the proletariat will be the ruling class, the question arises, whom will it rule? (This means) that another proletariat will still remain which will be subject to this new rule, this new (State)."

It means that as long as other classes, and the capitalist class in particular, still exist, and as long as the proletariat fights against them (for its enemies and the old organisation of society do not vanish as a result of its coming to power) it must employ *coercive* measures, that is, government measures; so long it is still a class itself, and the economic conditions which give rise to the class struggle and the existence of classes have not yet disappeared and must be forcibly removed or transformed, and the process of their transformation accelerated by the use of force.

> "For example, the common peasant, (the peasant rabble), who, as we know, [are not regarded] with favour by the Marxists, and are at the lowest stage of civilisation, will probably be governed by the urban and industrial proletariat."

That is to say, whatever large number of peasants exist as private proprietors, and where they even constitute a more or less considerable majority, as in all countries of the West European continent where they have not disappeared and been supplanted by agricultural day-labourers as in England, the following alternatives exist: either the peasants prevent and doom to failure every workers' revolution, as they have done in France up to now, or the proletariat (for the peasant proprietor does not belong to the proletariat; even where he does belong to it by reason of his position, he does not consider himself as belinging to it) functioning as the government must take steps that will directly improve his position and thus win him over to the revolution; these steps moreover further the transition from private to communal ownership of land in such a way, that the peasant comes to it of his own accord on economic grounds. But one must not affront the peasant, for instance by proclaiming the abolition of the right of inheritance or the abolition of his property — the latter can only be done where the peasant has been ousted by the capitalist tenant farmers, so that the real cultivator is as much a proletarian, a wage-worker, as the urban worker, and consequently shares with him, not indirectly, but *directly,* the same interests; still less should parcelled property be reinforced by enlarging the parcel simply by allowing the peasants to annex the larger estates, as Bakunin advocated in his revolutionary campaign.

> "Or if the matter is regarded from a national standpoint, one has to assume that as regards the Germans the Slavs will for that very reason be placed in the same servile subordination to the victorious German proletariat in which the latter now stands in relation to its bourgeoisie" (p. 278).

Schoolboy nonsense! A radical social revolution depends on particular historical conditions of economic development; they are its prerequisites. Thus a revolution is possible only where, together with capitalist production, the industrial proletariat occupies at least an important place within the population. And to have any chance of success it must *mutatis mutandis* be able immediately to do at least as much for the peasants as the French bourgeoisie during its revolution did for the French peasants of the time. A fine idea to assume that the rule of the workers stands for the subjugation of agricultural workers. This is where the inmost thoughts of Mr. Bakunin are revealed. He understands nothing whatever about social revolution; all he knows about it is political phrases; its economic prerequisites do not exist for him. Since all the economic forms, developed or undeveloped, that have existed till now included the enslavement of the worker (whether in the shape of the wage-worker or the peasant, etc.) he presumes that a *radical revolution* is equally possible in all of them. What is more, he wants the European social revolution, which is based on the economic foundation of capitalist production, to be carried out on the level of the Russian or Slav agricultural or pastoral nations, and not to overstep this level, although he perceives that navigation creates distinctions among brethren, but only *navigation,* since these distinctions are known to all politicians! The basis of Bakunin's social revolution is the *will,* and not the economic conditions.

> "Where there is (State) there is bound to be (domination), consequently slavery too; domination without slavery, whether upon or disguised, is inconceivable, and that is why we are enemies of the State" (p. 278).
>
> "What is meant by the proletariat transformed into the ruling class?"

It means that the proletariat, instead of fighting individually against the economically privileged classes, has gained sufficient strength and is sufficiently well organised to employ general means of compulsion in its struggle against these classes. It can, however, use only economic means designed to abolish its own distinctive trait as a wage-earner, and hence to abolish itself as a class. Its complete victory is consequently also the end of its domination, since its class character has disappeared.

> "Will perhaps the proletariat as a whole head the government?"

Does in a trade union, for instance, the whole union constitute the executive committee? Will all division of labour in a factory disappear and also the various functions arising from it? And will everybody be at the top in Bakunin's construction built from the bottom upwards? There will in fact be no below then. Will all members of the commune also administer the common affairs of the region? In that case there will be no difference between commune and region.

> "The Germans number nearly 40 million. Will, for example, all 40 million be members of the government?"

Certainly, for the thing begins with the self-government of the commune.

> "The whole people will govern and no one will be governed."

If a man has self-control, then, according to this principle, he has no self-control, for he is only himself and nobody else.

> "Then there will be no government and no state, but if there should be a state then there will also be rulers and slaves" (p. 279).

That is simply to say, when class rule has disappeared a state in the now accepted political sense of the world no longer exists.

> "This dilemma contained in the theory of the Marxists is easily solved. By people's government they" (i.e., Bakunin) "understand governing the people by means of a small number of representatives elected by the people."

This democratic drivel, political claptrap is asinine. Elections are a political form which exists in the smallest Russian commune and artel. The nature of the elections is determined not by the name, but by the economic basis, the economic interrelations of the voters, and from the moment when the functions have ceased to be political ones (1) government functions no longer exist; (2) the distribution of general functions becomes a routine matter and does not entail any domination; (3) elections completely lose their present political character.

> "The universal right of election of representatives and rulers of the state by the whole people"—

(such a thing as the whole people in the present sense of the word is a phantasm)—

> "this last word of the Marxists as well as of the democratic school—is a lie, which conceals the despotism of the *ruling minority,* and is all the more dangerous for appearing as the expression of a would-be popular will."

Under collective property the so-called popular will disappears to be replaced by the genuine will of the cooperative.

> "Hence the result is that the vast majority of the people is governed by a privileged minority. But this minority will consist of workmen, say the Marxists."

Where?

> "Yes it may perhaps consist of former workmen, but as soon as they become representatives or rulers of the people they *cease to be workmen*"

—no more than does a manufacturer today cease to be a capitalist on becoming a town-councillor—

> "and view all ordinary workers from the eminence of state; they will then no longer represent the people, but only themselves and their pretensions to govern the people. Anyone who doubts this does not understand human nature" (p. 279).

If Mr. Bakunin understood at least the position of a manager in a cooperative factory, all his illusions about domination would go to the devil. He ought to have asked himself what form the functions of management could assume in such a workers' state, if he chooses to call it thus.

> On p. 279 he writes: "But these elected men will become fervently convinced and also learned socialists. The words which the Lassalleans and Marxists constantly use in their writings and speeches—

the words *"learned socialism"* have never been used "and *scientific socialism"* used only in contradistinction to utopian socialism which seeks to foist new fantasies upon the people instead of confining its field of investigation to the social movement created by the people; see my book against Proudhon—

> "only go to prove that the so-called people's state will be nothing but a rather despotic rule over the masses of the people exercised by a very small aristocracy of genuine or spurious scholars. The people is not scientifically trained, it will accordingly be completely relieved of all the cares of government and wholly included in the herd that has to be governed. A fine liberation!" (pp. 279–80).
>
> "The Marxists are aware of this" (!) "contradiction and realising that the government of scholars" (what a fantastic notion!) "will be the world's most oppressive, resented and despicable government and that despite its democratic forms it will in fact be a dictatorship, they seek consolation in the thought that this dictatorship will be a provisional and shortlived measure."

Non, mon cher! [in the thought] that the *class rule* of the workers over the resisting strata of the old world can only continue until the economic basis that makes the existence of classes possible has been destroyed.

> "They say that their only concern and aim will be to educate and raise the people" (arm-chair politician!) "both economically and politically to such a level that any sort of government will soon become superfluous, that the state will completely lose its political, i.e., authoritarian, nature, and that it will automatically become a free organisation of economic interests and communes. This is an obvious contradiction. If their state is really a people's state, then why should it be abolished and if its abolition is essential to the real liberation of the people, how dare they call it a people's state?" (p. 280).

Leaving aside this harping on Liebknecht's *people's state,* which is nonsense directed against the Communist Manifesto, etc., this means simply that since the proletariat, during the period of struggle to overthrow the old society, still acts on the basis of the old society and consequently within political forms which more or less belong to that society, it has, during this period of struggle, not yet attained its ultimate structure, and to achieve its liberation it employs means which will be discarded after the liberation; hence Mr. B. concludes that the proletariat should rather do nothing at all and wait for the *day of universal liquidation*—the Last Judgment.

"By our polemic" (which was, of course, published before my book against Proudhon, before the Communist Manifesto, and even before Saint-Simon) "against them" (a wonderful hysteron proteron) "*we* have made them *admit* that freedom, or anarchy" (Mr. Bakunin has merely translated Proudhon's and Stirner's anarchy into the crude language of the Tartars),

> "that is, the free organisation of the working masses from below upwards" (nonsense) "is the ultimate goal of social development, and that every state, including the people's state, is a yoke that creates despotism on the one hand, and slavery on the other" (p. 280).

Marx, *On Bakunin* (1874), AAS, pp. 147–52.

ON ANARCHISM

Anarchy, then, is the great war-horse of their master Bakunin, who has taken nothing from the socialist systems except a set of slogans. What all socialists understand by anarchy is this: once the aim of the proletarian movement, the abolition of classes, has been attained, the power of the State, which serves to keep the great majority of producers under the yoke of a numerically small exploiting minority, disappears, and the functions of government are transformed into simple administrative functions. The Alliance puts matters the other way round. It proclaims anarchy in the proletarian ranks as the surest means of breaking the powerful concentration of social and political forces in the hands of the exploiters. Under this pretext it demands of the International, at the very moment when the old world is seeking to crush it, that it should replace its organisation by anarchy.

Marx-Engels, *Fictitious Splits in the International* (1872), AAS, p. 74.

ENGELS ON BAKUNIN

Bakunin, who up till 1868 had intrigued against the International, joined it after he had made a fiasco at the Berne Peace Conference and at once began to conspire *within it* against the General Council. Bakunin has a peculiar theory of his own, a medley of Proudhonism and communism, the chief point of which is in the first place that he does not regard capital, and therefore the class contradiction between capitalists and wage earners which has arisen through social development, as the main evil to be abolished—instead he regards the *state* as the main evil. While the great mass of the Social-Democratic workers hold our view that state power is nothing more than the organisation with which the ruling classes, landlords and capitalists have provided themselves in order to protect their social prerogatives, Bakunin maintains that it is the *state* which has created capital, that the capitalist has his capital *only by favour of the state.* As, therefore, the state is the chief evil, it is above all the state which must be done away with and then capitalism will go to hell of itself. We, on the contrary, say: do away with capital, the appropriation of the whole means of production in the hands of the few, and the state will fall away of itself. The difference is an essential one. Without a previous social revolution the abolition of the state is nonsense; the abolition of capital *is* in itself the social revolution and involves a change in the whole method of production. Further, however, as for Bakunin the state is the main evil, nothing must be done which can maintain the existence of any state, whether it be a republic, a monarchy or whatever it may be. Hence therefore *complete abstention from all politics.* To perpetrate a political action, and especially to take part in an election, would be a betrayal of principle. The thing to do is to conduct propaganda, abuse the state, organise, and when *all* the workers are won over, i.e., the majority, depose the authorities, abolish the state and replace it by the organisation of the International. This great act, with which the millennium begins, is called *social liquidation.*

All this sounds extremely radical, and is so simple that it can be learnt by heart in five minutes; that is why this theory of Bakunin's has also speedily found favour in Spain and Italy, among young lawyers, doctors and other doctrinaires.

But the mass of the workers will never allow themselves to be persuaded that the public affairs of their country are not also their own affairs; they are by nature *political* and whoever tries to make out to them that they should leave politics alone will in the end get left in the lurch. To preach that the workers should in all circumstances abstain from politics is to drive them into the arms of the priests or the bourgeois republicans.

Now as, according to Bakunin, the International is not to be formed for political struggle but in order that it may at once replace the old state organisation as soon as social liquidation takes place, it follows that it must come as near as possible to the Bakunist ideal of the society of the future. In this society there will above all be no *authority,* for authority = state = an absolute evil. (How these people propose to run a factory, work a railway or steer a ship without having in the last resort one deciding will, without a unified direction, they do not indeed tell us.) The authority of the majority over the minority also ceases. Every individual and every community is autonomous, but as to how a society, even of only two people, is possible unless each gives up some of his autonomy, Bakunin again remains silent.

Engels, Letter to Cuno (1872), SC, pp. 319–21.

ENGELS ON AUTHORITY

A number of Socialists have latterly launched a regular crusade against what they call the *principle of authority.* It suffices to tell them that this or that act is *authoritarian* for it to be condemned. This summary mode of procedure is being abused to such an extent that it has become necessary to look into the matter somewhat more closely. Authority, in the sense in which the word is used here, means: the imposition of the will of another upon ours; on the other hand, authority presupposes subordination. Now, since these two words sound bad and the relationship which they represent is disagreeable to the subordinated party, the question is to ascertain whether there is any way of dispensing with it, whether—given the conditions of present-day society—we could not create another social system, in which this authority would be given no scope any longer and would consequently have to disappear. On examining the economic, industrial and agricultural conditions which form the basis of present-day bourgeois society, we find that they tend more and more to replace isolated action by combined action of individuals. Modern industry with its big factories and mills, where hundreds of workers supervise complicated machines driven by steam, has superseded the small workshops of the separate producers; the carriages and wagons of the highways have been substituted by railway trains, just as the small schooners and sailing feluccas have been by steamboats. Even agriculture falls increasingly under the dominion of the machine and of steam, which slowly but relentlessly put in the place of the small proprietors big capitalists, who with the aid of hired workers cultivate vast stretches of land. Everywhere combined action, the complication of processes dependent upon each other, displaces independent action by individuals. But whoever mentions combined action speaks of organisation; now, is it possible to have organisation without authority?

Supposing a social revolution dethroned the capitalists, who now exercise their authority over the production and circulation of wealth. Supposing, to adopt entirely the point of view of the anti-authoritarians, that the land and the instruments of labour had become the collective property of the workers who use them. Will authority have disappeared or will it only have changed its form? Let us see.

Let us take by way of example a cotton spinning mill. The cotton must pass through at least six successive operations before it is reduced to the state of thread, and these operations take place for the most part in different rooms. Furthermore, keeping the machines going requires an engineer to look after the steam engine, mechanics to make the current repairs, and many other labourers, whose business it is to transfer the products from one room to another, and so forth. All these workers, men, women and children, are obliged to begin and finish their work at the hours fixed by the authority of the steam, which cares nothing for individual autonomy. The workers must, therefore, first come to an understanding on the hours of work; and these hours, once they are fixed, must be observed by all, without any exception. Thereafter particular questions arise in each room and at every moment concerning the mode of production, distribution of materials, etc., which must be settled at once on pain of seeing all production immediately stopped; whether they are settled by decision of a delegate placed at the head of each branch of labour or, if possible, by a majority vote, the will of the single individual will always have to subordinate itself, which means that questions are settled in an authoritarian way. The automatic machinery of a big factory is much more despotic than the small capitalists who employ workers ever have been. At least with regard to the hours of work one may write upon the portals of these factories: *Leave, ye that enter in, all autonomy behind!* If man, by dint of his knowledge and inventive genius, has subdued the forces of nature, the latter avenge themselves upon him by subjecting him, in so far as he employs them, to a veritable despotism independent of all social organisation. Wanting to abolish authority in large-scale industry is tantamount to wanting to abolish industry itself, to destroy the power loom in order to return to the spinning wheel.

Let us take another example—the railway. Here too the cooperation of an infinite number of individuals is absolutely necessary, and this cooperation must be practised during precisely fixed hours so that no accidents may happen. Here, too, the first condition of the job is a dominant will that settles all subordinate questions, whether this will is represented by a single delegate or a committee charged with the execution of the resolutions of the majority of persons interested. In either case there is very pronounced authority. Moreover, what would happen to the first train dispatched if the authority of the railway employees over the Hon. passengers were abolished?

But the necessity of authority, and of imperious authority at that, will nowhere be found more evident than on board a ship on the high seas. There, in time of danger, the lives of all depend on the instantaneous and absolute obedience of all to the will of one.

When I submitted arguments like these to the most rabid anti-authoritarians the only answer they were able to give me was the following: Yes, that's true, but here it is not a case of authority which we confer on our delegates, *but of a commission entrusted!* These gentlemen think that when they have changed the names of things they have changed the things themselves. This is how these profound thinkers mock at the whole world.

We have thus seen that, on the one hand, a certain authority, no matter how delegated, and, on the other hand, a certain subordination, are things which, independently of all social organisation, are imposed upon us together with the material conditions under which we produce and make products circulate.

We have seen, besides, that the material conditions of production and circulation inevitably develop with large-scale industry and large-scale agriculture, and increasingly tend to enlarge the scope of this authority. Hence it is absurd to speak of the principle of authority as being absolutely evil, and of the principle of autonomy as being absolutely good. Authority and autonomy are relative things whose spheres vary with the various phases of the development of society. If the autonomists confined themselves to saying that the social organisation of the future would restrict authority solely to the limits within which the conditions of production render it inevitable, we could understand each other; but they are blind to all facts that make the thing necessary, and they passionately fight the word.

Why do the anti-authoritarians not confine themselves to crying out against political authority, the state? All Socialists are agreed that the political state, and with it political authority, will disappear as a result of the coming social revolution, that is, that public functions will lose their political character and be transformed into the simple administrative functions of watching over the true interests of society. But the anti-authoritarians demand that the authoritarian political state be abolished at one stroke, even before the social conditions that gave birth to it have been destroyed. They demand that the first act of the social revolution shall be the abolition of authority. Have these gentlemen ever seen a revolution? A revolution is certainly the most authoritarian thing there is; it is the act whereby one part of the population imposes its will upon the other part by means of rifles, bayonets and cannon—authoritarian means, if such there be at all; and if the victorious party does not want to have fought in vain, it must maintain this rule by means of the terror which its arms inspire in the reactionaries. Would the Paris Commune have lasted a single day if it had not made use of this authority of the armed people against the bourgeois? Should we not, on the contrary, reproach it for not having used it freely enough? Therefore, either one of two things: either the anti-authoritarians don't know what they are talking about, in which case they are creating nothing but confusion; or they do know, and in that case they are betraying the movement of the proletariat. In either case they serve the reaction.

Engels, *On Authority* (1874), AAS, pp. 100–04.

THE FUTURE OF THE STATE

By more and more transforming the great majority of the population into proletarians, the capitalist mode of production brings into being the force which, under penalty of its own destruction, is compelled to carry out this [proletarian] revolution. By more and more driving towards the conversion of the vast socialised means of production into state property, it itself points the way for the carrying through of this [proletarian] revolution. *The proletariat seizes the state power, and transforms the means of production in the first instance into state property.* But in doing this, it puts an end to itself as the proletariat, it puts an end to all class differences and class antagonisms, it puts an end also to the state as the state. Former society, moving in class antagonisms, had need of the state, that is, an organisation of the exploiting class at each period for the maintenance of its external conditions of production; that is, therefore, for the forcible holding down of the exploited class in the conditions of oppression (slavery, villcinage or serfdom, wage labour) determined by the existing mode of production. The state was the official representative of society as a whole, its embodiment in a visible corporation; but it was this only in so far as it was the state of that class which itself, in its epoch, represented society as a whole; in ancient times, the state of the slave-owning citizens; in the Middle Ages, of the feudal nobility; in our epoch, of the bourgeoisie. When ultimately it becomes really representative of society as a whole, it makes itself superfluous. As soon as there is no longer any class of society to be held in subjection; as soon as, along with class domination and the struggle for individual existence based on the former anarchy of production, the collisions and excesses arising from these have also been abolished, there is nothing more to be repressed which would make a special repressive force, a state, necessary. The first act in which the state really comes forward as the representative of society as a whole—the taking possession of the means of production in the name of society—is at the same time its last independent act as a state. The interference of the state power in social relations becomes superfluous in one sphere after another, and then ceases of itself. The government of persons is replaced by the administration of things and the direction of the processes of production. The state is not "abolished," *it withers away*. It is from this standpoint that we must appraise the phrase "free people's state"—both its justification at times for agitational purposes, and its ultimate scientific inadequacy—and also the demand of the so-called anarchists that the state should be abolished overnight.

Engels, *Anti-Duhring* (1872, pp. 306–07.

Contemporary civil society is the consequently realized principle of individualism; individual existence is the ultimate aim: activity, work, content etc. are mere means. . . . The atomisation into which civil society is driven by its political act is necessarily caused by the fact that the commonwealth (*Gemeinwesen*), the communist essence (*das kommunistische Wesen*) within which the individual exists, civil society, is being divorced from the state, or because the political state is a mere abstraction of it.

Hegel starts with the state and transforms man into a subjectified state (*versubjektivierter Staat*); democracy begins with man and transforms the state into objectified man (*verobjektivierter Mensch*). Just as religion does not create man, but man creates religion, so the constitution does not create the people, but the people the constitution. In a certain respect democracy relates to all other constitutions as Christianity relates to all other forms of religion. Christianity is religion *par excellence*, the essence of religion, man who became God as a separate religion. Thus democracy also constitutes the essence of all forms of political constitution, the essence of socialised man (des sozialisierten Menschen) as a special constitution. Democracy relates to all other political constitutions as the species relates to its varieties. . . In Democracy the formal principle is also identical with the material principle. Democracy is thus the true unity of the universal and the particular. . . . Democracy is the genus Constitution. Monarchy is one species, and a poor one at that. Democracy is content and form. Monarchy is *supposed* to be only a form, but it falsifies the content.

In monarchy the whole, the people, is subsumed under one of its particular modes of being, the political constitution. In democracy the *constitution itself* appears only as *one* determination, that is, the self-determination of the people. In monarchy we have the people of the constitution; in democracy the constitution of the people. Democracy is the solved *riddle* of all constitutions.

Here, not merely *implicitly* and in essence but *existing* in reality, the constitution is constantly brought back to its actual basis, the *actual human being*, the *actual people*, and established as the people's *own* work. The constitution appears as what it is, a free product of man. . . .

Incidentally, it goes without saying that all forms of state have democracy *for* their truth and that they are therefore untrue insofar as they are not democracy.

In the states of antiquity the political state makes up the content of the state to the exclusion of the other spheres. The modern state is a compromise between the political and the unpolitical state. . . . It is obvious that the political constitution as such is brought into being only where the private spheres have won an independent existence. Where trade and landed property are not free and have not yet become independent, the political constitution too does not yet exist. The Middle Ages were the *democracy of unfreedom*. . . .

What distinguishes the modern state from these states characterised by the substantial unity between people and state is. . . that the constitution itself has been developed into a *particular* actuality alongside the actual life of the people—that the political state has become the *constitution* of the rest of the state. . . . To democracy all other forms of state stand as its Old Testament. Man does not exist for the law but the law for man—it is a *human manifestation*; whereas in the other forms of state man is a *legal manifestation*. That is the fundamental distinction of democracy.

All other *state forms* are definite, distinct, *particular forms of state*. . . . In monarchy, for example, and in the republic as a merely particular form of state, political man has his particular mode of being alongside unpolitical man, man as a private individual. Property, contract, marriage, civil society, all appear here. . . as *particular* modes of existence alongside the *political* state, as the *content* to which the *political state* is related as *organising form*: properly speaking, the relation of the political state to this content is merely that of reason, inherently without content, which defines and delimits, which now affirms and now denies. In democracy the political state, which stands alongside this content and distinguishes itself from it, is itself merely a *particular* content and particular *form of existence* of the people. In monarchy, for example, this particular, the political constitution, has the significance of the *general* that dominates and determines everything particular. In democracy the state as particular is *merely* particular; as general, it is the truly general, i.e., not something determinate in distinction from the other content. The French have recently interpreted this as meaning that in true democracy the *political state is annihilated*. This is correct insofar as the political state *qua* political state, as constitution, no longer passes for the whole. . . .

The vote is the actual relation of actual civil society to the civil society of the legislative power, to the representative element. To put it in another way: voting is the immediate, direct, not only imagined, but also active relation of civil society to the political state. It goes without saying that the right to vote is the main political interest of actual civil society. In universal suffrage, both active and passive, civil society has really raised itself for the first time to an abstraction of itself, to political being as its real universal essential being. But the perfection of this abstraction is also at the same time the abolition

(*Aufhebung*) of this abstraction. By positing its political being as its real being, civil society has also shown that its civil, non-political being is inessential... Within the abstract political state the reform of the suffrage is hence a claim for the dissolution (*Auflösung*) of the political state, as well as for the dissolution (*Auflösung*) of civil society.

Marx, *Critique of Hegel's Philosophy of Right*. Opening two paragraphs and final paragraph excerpted from Karl Marx/Frederick Engels, *Werke*, Vol. I (Berlin: 1956); translated and cited in Shlomo Avineri, *The Social and Political Thought of Karl Marx*, pp. 33–37. Remaining portions of the selection from *MECW*, 3, pp. 30–33.

Bibliography

A. A Chronology of Works by Marx and Engels Cited in this Book

Date[1]	*Author*[2]	*Title*	*English Edition*[3]	*Selections*
1843	M	Critique of Hegel's Philosophy of Right	IP 1976	9B.13
1843	M	On the Jewish Question	EW	9A.1
1844	M	Exerpts from James Mill's Elements of Political Economy	YM	9A.2
1844	M	Economic and Philosophical Manuscripts	EW	1.3, 4B.4, 4B.5, 4B.5, 4B.6, 4B.7, 4C.8, 4C.9 8A.3, 9A.2
1844	M	Critical Marginal Notes on the Article 'The King of Prussia and Social Reform. By a Prussian'	SSP	8A.2
1844	M & E	The Holy Family, or a Critique of Critical Criticism	FLP 1951	4A.5, 8A.3
1845	M	Theses on Feuerbach	MESW	1.1
1845–46	M & E	The German Ideology	IP 1947	1.1, 1.2, 8A.4, 9A.3, 9A.4, 9B.9
1846–47	M	The Poverty of Philosophy	IP N.D.	7A.6, 8A.3, 8A.8, 9A.5
1847	M	Speeches on Poland	MR	8A.3

[1]Date of composition, except for *Capital,* where the date of first publication is given.

[2]M = Marx, E = Engels.

[3]Abbreviations used are found on p. viii.

Date[1]	Author[2]	Title	English Edition[3]	
1847	M	Moral Critique and the Criticism of Morality	SSP	8A.3
1847	M	Wage-Labour and Capital	MESW I	2B.6, 2B.7, 7A.3
1847	E	Principles of Communism	IP 1971	9A.6
1847–50	M & E	Manifesto of the Communist Party	MESW I	1.3, 3.1, 7A.2, 7A.4, 8A.5, 8B.9, 9A.5
1848–50	M	Articles in the Neue Rheinische Zeitung	MR	8A.6
1850	M & E	Address of the Central Committee to the Communist League	MESW II	8B.10
1850	M	Reviews from the Neue Rheinische Zeitung. Revue	MR	7A.2
1850	M	The Class Struggles in France, 1848 to 1850	MESW II	7A.2, 8A.2, 8C.13
1852	M	The Eighteenth Brumaire of Louis Bonaparte	MESW II	8C.13
1852	M	Revelations on the Cologne Communist Trial	MR	8A.6
1852	M	Letter to Wedemeyer	MESW I	8B.11
1852–55	M	Articles on Britain	AB	1.3
1853	M	The British Rule in India	MESW II	7B.10
1854	M	Letter to the Labour Parliament	AB	8A.3
1856	M	Speech at the Anniversary of the People's Paper	MR	8A.3
1857–58	M	Grundrisse	RH 1973	2A.1, 2A.2, 2A.3, 2B.6, 3.1, 3.2, 3.3, 4A.1, 4A.8, 4A.9, 4A.10, 4A.11, 6C.8, 7A.2, 7B.7, 7B.11, 9A.4
1859	M	A Contribution to the Critique of Political Economy (Preface)	IP 1970	1.1
1861–63	M	Theories of Surplus Value	IP 1952	6C.7, 7A.3

1864	M	Inaugural Address of the International Working Men's Association	MESW II	7B.8
1865	M	Wages, Price and Profit	MESW I	7A.5
1867	M	Capital, Vol. 1	ML	1.4, 2A.4, 2A.5, 2C.8, 2C.9, 2C.10, 2C.11, 4A.2, 4A.3, 5A.1, 5A.2, 5A.3, 5B.4, 5B.5, 5B.6, 5B.7, 5B.8, 5B.9, 6A.1, 6B.3, 6C.6, 7A.1, 7A.2, 7A.3, 7A.6, 7B.9, 8C.12, 9A.7, 9B.9, 9B.10
1868	M	Letter to Kugelmann	LK	9B.9
1871	M	First Draft of the Civil War in France	KMPW III	9B.13
1871	M	The Civil War in France	MESW	8C.14
1871	M	Letter to Bolte	SC	8A.3
1871	M	Letter to Kugelmann	LK	8C.14
1872	M	Speech at the Hague Congress	AAS	8A.8
1872	M & E	Ficticious Splits in the International	AAS	9B.13
1872	E	Letter to Cuno	SC	9B.13
1874	E	On Authority	AAS	9B.13
1874–75	M	Conspectus of Bakunin's Book Statism and Anarchy	AAS	9B.13
1875	M	Critique of the Gotha Programme	MESW II	7A.3, 8B.11, 9B.12
1876–78	E	Anti-Dühring	IP 1939	9B.9, 9B.10, 9B.13
1877	M	Reply to Michaelovsky	SC	8C.15
1877	E	Social Relations in Russia	MESW II	8C.15
1880	M	Letter to Hyndman	KM	8B.8
1880	E	Socialism: Utopian and Scientific	MESW I	1.3, 7A.6, 7B.8, 9B.11

[1]Date of composition, except for *Capital,* where the date of first publication is given.

[2]M = Marx, E = Engels.

[3]Abbreviations used are found on p. viii.

Date[1]	Author[2]	Title	English Edition[3]	
1880	M	Introduction to the Programme of the French Workers' Party	KMPW III	9B.9
1881	M	Letter to Nieuwenhuis	SC	8A.7
1881	M	Letter to Zassoulitch	TKM	8C.15
1882	M & E	Preface to the 2nd Russian edition of the Manifesto of the Community Party	MESW I	8C.15
1883	E	Speech at the Graveside of Karl Marx	MESW I	8A.1
1884	E	The Origin of the Family, Private Property, and the State	MESW	8A.4
1885	M	Capital, Vol. 2	K 1909	6A.2, 6C.8, 7A.3, 9B.10
1886	E	Ludwig Feuerbach and the End of Classical German Philosophy	MESW I	8A.4
1890	E	Letter to Schmidt	SC	8A.4
1891	E	Introduction to Marx's The Class Struggles in France, 1848 to 1850	MESW II	8B.8
1891	E	Introduction to Marx's The Civil War in France	MESW	8B.11
1891	E	Introduction to Marx's Wage-Labour and Capital	MESW I	7A.6
1891	E	Toward a Critique of the Social Democratic Program, Draft	ME	8B.11
1892	E	Introduction to Socialism: Utopian and Scientific	MESW I	1.3
1894	M	Capital, Vol. 3	K 1909	5B.10, 6B.4, 6B.5, 6C.8, 7A.1, 7A.3, 7A.6, 8A.4, 9A.8, 9B.10

[1]Date of composition, except for *Capital,* where the date of first publication is given.

[2]M = Marx, E = Engels.

[3]Abbreviations used are found on p. viii.

A Supplementary Reading List

1. Capitalism's Origins and Predecessors
   In addition to Avineri and McLellan cited on p. viii:
   - Bober, M. M. *Karl Marx's Interpretation of History* (N.Y.: Norton, 1948).
   - Cohen, G. A. *Karl Marx's Theory of History* (Princeton: Princeton University Press, 1978).
   - Dupré, Louis. *The Philosophical Foundations of Marxism* (N.Y.: Harcourt Brace, 1966).
   - Plamenetz, John. *German Marxism and Russian Communism* (London: Longmans, Green, 1954).
2. Capitalism's Institutional Structure and Social Relations
   In addition to Avineri and McLellan cited on p. viii:
   - Avineri, *Marx's Socialism* (N.Y.: Lieber-Atherton, 1972).
   - Bottomore, Tom, editor. *Karl Marx* (Englewood Cliffs: Prentice-Hall, 1973).
   - Duncan, Graeme. *Mill and Marx: Two Views of Social Conflict and Social Harmony* (Cambridge: Cambridge University Press, 1973).
   - Smelser, Neil J. *Karl Marx: On Society and Social Change* (Chicago: University of Chicago Press, 1973).
   - Sweezy, Paul M. *The Theory of Capitalist Development* (N.Y.: Monthly Review Press, 1956).
3. Capitalism's Progressive and Creative Properties
   In addition to Avineri:
   - Elliott, John E. "Marx's *Grundrisse:* Vision of Capitalism's Creative Destruction." *Journal of Post Keynesian Economics,* Winter 1977–78.
   - Harris, Donald J. "On Marx's Scheme of Reproduction and Accumulation." *Journal of Political Economy,* Vol. 80, 1973.
   - Howard, M. C. and J. E. King. *The Political Economy of Marx* (London: Longman, 1975), chapter 6.
   - Mandel, Ernest. *The Formation of the Economic Thought of Karl Marx* (N.Y.: Monthly Review Press, 1971), chapters 4, 7.
   - Steindel, Joseph. "Karl Marx and the Accumulation of Capital." In David Horowitz, editor, *Marx and Modern Economics* (N.Y.: Monthly Review Press, 1968).
   - Sweezy, Paul M. "Karl Marx and the Industrial Revolution." In R. V. Eagly, editor, *Events, Ideology, and Economic Theory* (Detroit: Wayne State University Press, 1968).
4. Capitalism's Contradictory and Destructive Properties: Alienation
   In addition to Avineri and McLellan:
   - Althusser, Louis. *For Marx* (London: NLB Press, 1977), chapters 1–2, 5.

Axelos, Kostas. *Alienation, Praxis, and Techne in the Theory of Karl Marx* (Austin: University of Texas Press, 1976).
Elliott, John E. "Continuity and Change in the Evolution of Marx's Theory of Alienation." *History of Political Economy,* Fall 1979.
Mészáros, István. *Marx's Theory of Alienation* (N.Y.: Harper & Row, 1970).
Mandel, Ernest. *The Formation of the Economic Thought of Karl Marx,* chapter 10.
Ollman, Bertell. *Alienation: Marx's Conception of Man in Capitalist Society* (Cambridge: Cambridge University Press, 1976).
Tucker, Robert. *Philosophy and Myth in Karl Marx* (Cambridge: Cambridge University Press, 1972).

5. Capitalism's Contradictory and Destructive Properties: Exploitation

Dobb, Maurice. *Theories of Value and Distribution since Adam Smith* (Cambridge: Cambridge University Press, 1973).
Gamble, Andrew and Paul Walton. *From Alienation to Surplus Value.* (London: Sheed and Ward, 1976).
Howard, M. C. and J. E. King, *The Political Economy of Marx,* chapters 4-5.
Mandel, Ernest. *The Formation of the Economic Thought of Karl Marx,* chapters 3, 6, 9.
Meek, Ronald. *Studies in the Labor Theory of Value* (N.Y.: Monthly Review Press, 1956).
Morishima, Michio. *Marx's Economics: A Dual Theory of Value and Growth* (Cambridge: Cambridge University Press, 1973).
Sweezy, Paul M. *The Theory of Capitalist Development,* chapters 2-4, 7.

6. Capitalism's Contradictory and Destructive Properties

In addition to the sources cited for Topic 3:

Dobb, Maurice. "Economic Crises," *Political Economy and Capitalism* (London: Routledge and Kegan Paul, 1940), chapter 4.
Fan-Hung. "Keynes and Marx on the Theory of Capital Accumulation, Money and Interest." In David Horowitz, *Marx and Modern Economics.*
Robinson, Joan. *An Essay on Marxian Economics* (N.Y.: Macmillian, 1960).
Shoul, Bernice. "Karl Marx and Say's Law." *Quarterly Journal of Economics,* November 1957.
Sweezy, Paul M. *The Theory of Capitalist Development,* chapters 8-12.

7. Capitalism's Development, Transformation, and Demise

Avineri, Shlomo, *The Social and Political Thought of Karl Marx,* chapter 6.
Meek, Ronald. "Marx's Doctrine of Increasing Misery." In *Economics and Ideology* (London: Chapman and Hall, 1967).
Rosenberg, Nathan. "Marx as a Student of Technology." *Monthly Review,* July-August 1976.
Schumpeter, Joseph A. *Capitalism, Socialism and Democracy* (N.Y.: Harper & Row, 1950), Parts 1-2.
Sowell, Thomas. "Marx's 'Increasing Misery' Doctrine." *American Economic Review,* December 1960.
Sweezy, Paul M. *The Theory of Capitalist Development,* chapter 11.

8. Capitalism's Transition to Socialism

In addition to Avineri and McLellan:

Avineri, Shlomo, *Marx's Socialism,* chapters 1, 6-8.
Draper, Hal. *Karl Marx's Theory of Revolution,* Vol. 1, *State and Bureaucracy,* Vol. 2, *The Politics of Social Classes* (N.Y.: Monthly Review Press, 1977, 1978).
Duncan, Graeme. *Mill and Marx: Two Views of Social Conflict and Social Harmony,* chapters 3-4.
Sanderson, J. *An Interpretation of the Political Thought of Marx and Engels* (London: Longmans, 1969).
Sweezy, Paul M. *The Theory of Capitalist Development,* Part IV.
Tucker, Robert. *The Marxian Revolutionary Idea* (N.Y.: Norton, 1969), chapter 1.

9. Capitalism's Supersession and Successors: Socialism and Communism
In addition to Avineri and McLellan:

Duncan, Graeme. *Mill and Marx: Two Views of Social Conflict and Social Harmony,* chapter 5.

Elliott, John E. "Marx's Socialism in the Context of his Typology of Economic Systems." *Journal of Comparative Economics,* March 1978.

Elliott, John E. "Marx and Engels on Communism, Scarcity, and Division of Labor." *Economic Inquiry,* April 1980.

Mandel, Ernest. *The Formation of the Economic Thought of Karl Marx,* chapter 11.

Sanderson, J. *An Interpretation of the Political Ideas of Marx and Engels,* chapter 6.

Wiles, P. J. D. *The Political Economy of Communism* (Cambridge: Cambridge University Press, 1964), Part IV.